Readings for an Introduction to Philosophy

James R. Hamilton Charles E. Reagan B. R. Tilghman

READINGS
for an Introduction to
PHILOSOPHY

Macmillan Publishing Co., Inc.
New York

MACMILLAN PUBLISHING CO., INC.
866 Third Avenue, New York, New York 10022

COLLIER MACMILLAN CANADA, LTD.

Library of Congress Cataloging in Publication Data

Main entry under title:

Readings for an introduction to philosophy.

Bibliography: p.
1. Philosophy—Introductions—Collected works.
I. Hamilton, James R. II. Reagan, Charles E.
III. Tilghman, B. R.
BD21.R37 190'.8 74-33098
ISBN 0-02-349550-2

Printing: 1 2 3 4 5 6 7 8 Year: 6 7 8 9 0 1 2

ACKNOWLEDGMENTS

W. T. STACE, *The Concept of Morals.* Reprinted with permission of Macmillan Publishing Co., Inc., from *The Concept of Morals,* by W. T. Stace. Copyright 1937 by Macmillan Publishing Co., Inc., renewed 1965 by Walter T. Stace.

RUTH BENEDICT, "Anthropology and the Abnormal," *The Journal of General Psychology,* **10** (1934), 59–82. Reprinted with permission of *The Journal Press.*

A. A. KROEBER and C. KLUCKHOLN, "Culture: A Critical Review of Concepts and Definitions," reprinted with permission of the Peabody Museum of Archaeology and Ethnology from *Peabody Museum Papers,* 47, 1 (1952), 174–179.

A. J. AYER, *Language, Truth and Logic,* 1936, pp. 103–113. Reprinted with permission of Victor Gollancz, Ltd.

PHILIPPA FOOT, "Moral Beliefs." Reprinted with permission of the Editor of The Aristotelian Society from "Moral Beliefs" by Philippa Foot in *Proceedings of Aristotelian Society,* 1958–9, 83–94. © 1959 The Aristotelian Society.

SUPREME COURT OF THE UNITED STATES, "Roe v. Wade." Reprinted from *The United States Law Week,* Syllabus no. 70-18, Vol. 41, No. 28, 1973, by permission of *The United States Law Week.*

THOMAS, J. O'DONNELL, "A Traditional Catholic's View," *Abortion in a Changing World,* ed. Robert E. Hall, M.D. (Proceedings of an International Conference, Hot Springs, Va., Nov. 1968) Columbia University Press, New York, 1970, pp. 34–38. Reprinted by permission of the Association for the Study of Abortion.

PHILIPPA FOOT, "The Problem of Abortion and the Doctrine of the Double Effect," *Oxford Review,* 1967, 29–41. Reprinted with the permission of the author.

JUDITH JARVIS THOMSON, "A Defense of Abortion," by Judith Jarvis Thomson, *Philosophy and Public Affairs,* vol. 1, no. 1 (copyright © 1971 by Princeton University Press), pp. 47–66. Reprinted by permission of Princeton University Press.

JOHN HOSPERS, "Meaning and Free Will," *Philosophy and Phenomenological Research,* **10,** 3 (1950), 313–30. Reprinted with permission of the International Phenomenological Society.

ROBERT C. BOLLES, *Theory of Motivation.* From pp. 1–10 in *Theory of Motivation* by Robert C. Bolles. Copyright © 1967 by Robert C. Bolles. By permission of Harper & Row, Publishers, Inc.

R. S. PETERS, *The Concept of Motivation.* Reprinted with permission of Humanities Press, Inc., New Jersey, and Routledge & Kegan Paul Ltd.

JEAN-PAUL SARTRE, *Being and Nothingness.* Reprinted with the permission of Philosophical Library, Inc. From *Being and Nothingness* by Jean-Paul Sartre. Copyright © 1956 by Philosophical Library, Inc.

JOHN B. WATSON, *Behaviorism.* Reprinted from *Behaviorism* by John B. Watson. By permission of W. W. Norton & Company. Copyright 1924, 1925, 1930 by W. W. Norton & Company, Inc. Copyright renewed 1952, 1953, 1958 by John B. Watson.

B. F. SKINNER, *Science and Human Behavior.* Reprinted with permission of Macmillan Publishing Co., Inc. Copyright © 1953 by Macmillan Publishing Co., Inc.

J. J. C. SMART, "Sensations and Brain Processes," *Philosophical Review,* LXVIII (1959), 141–156. Reprinted by permission of the author and the editors of the *Philosophical Review.*

NORMAN MALCOLM, "Scientific Materialism and the Identity Theory," *Dialogue: Canadian Philosophical Review,* 3, 2 (1964), 115–125. Reprinted with permission of the author.

JOHN W. COOK, "Human Beings," from *Studies in the Philosophy of Wittgenstein,* Peter Winch, ed., 1969, pp. 117–128 and 149–151. Reprinted with permission of Humanities Press, Inc., New Jersey, and Routledge & Kegan Paul Ltd.

KENNETH LOVELL, *Educational Psychology and Children*, 1967. Reprinted with permission of The University of London Press.

GILBERT RYLE, "Teaching and Training," from *The Concept of Education* by R. S. Peters, ed., 1967, pp. 451–463. Reprinted with permission of Humanities Press, Inc., New Jersey, and Routledge & Kegan Paul Ltd.

WILLIAM JAMES, "Pragmatism's Conception of Truth," from *Pragmatism*, New York: David McKay, 1909, pp. 131–156. Reprinted by permission.

W. MONTAGUE, "The Method of Pragmatism," from *The Ways of Knowing*, 1925, pp. 131–133 and 156–167. Reprinted with permission of Allen & Unwin, Ltd.

O. K. BOUWSMA, "Descartes' Evil Genius," reprinted from *Philosophical Essays* by O. K. Bouwsma by permission of The University of Nebraska Press. Copyright © 1965 by The University of Nebraska Press.

A. J. AYER, *The Foundations of Empirical Knowledge*, 1955, pp. 1–11. Reprinted with permission of St. Martin's Press, Inc., Macmillan, London & Basingstoke.

M. D. VERNON, *The Psychology of Perception*, 1962, pp. 11–14. Reprinted with permission of Penguin Books, Ltd. Copyright © M. D. Vernon, 1962.

J. L. AUSTIN, *Sense and Sensibilia*, 1962, pp. 6–19. Reprinted with permission of The Clarendon Press, Oxford. © 1962 Oxford University Press.

IMMANUEL KANT, *The Philosophy of Law*, part II, W. Hastie, trans., Edinburgh: T. & T. Clark, 1887, pp. 194–198. Reprinted by permission of the publisher.

KARL MENNINGER, "The Crime of Punishment," *Saturday Review*, Sept. 7, 1968, 21–25, 55. Copyright © *Saturday Review* Sept. 7, 1968. Reprinted with permission of the author and the *Saturday Review*.

THOMAS S. SZASZ, "A Psychiatrist Dissents from Durham," *Journal of Nervous and Mental Disease*, **131**: 58–63, 1960. Copyright 1960, The Williams & Wilkins Co. Reproduced by permission.

A. M. QUINTON, "On Punishment," *Analysis*, XIV (1954), 133–142. Reprinted with permission of Basil Blackwell & Mott Ltd.

KURT BAIER, "Is Punishment Retributive?" *Analysis*, XVI (1955), 25–27. Reprinted with permission of Basil Blackwell & Mott Ltd.

JAMES Q. WILSON, MARK H. MOORE, and DAVID WHEAT, JR., "The Problem of Heroin," *The Public Interest*, No. 29 (Fall 1972), pp. 3–12, 21–23, and 25–27. Reprinted with permission of the authors.

ROBERT PAUL WOLFF, *The Poverty of Liberalism*, Copyright © 1968, by Robert Paul Wolff, reprinted by permission of Beacon Press.

JOEL FEINBERG, "Legal Paternalism." This material is here reprinted from Vol. 1, no. 1 of the Canadian Journal of Philosophy, by permission of the Canadian Association for Publishing in Philosophy.

ST. THOMAS AQUINAS, "Five Proofs of God's Existence," from *Basic Writings of Saint Thomas Aquinas*, Anton C. Pegis, ed., 1945, pp. 21–24, Copyright, 1945, by Random House, Inc.

J. J. C. SMART, "The Existence of God." *Church Quarterly Review*, 1955. Reprinted by permission of the author and the *Church Quarterly Review*.

WILLIAM JAMES, "The Will to Believe," *The New World*, June 1896. Reprinted with permission of *The New World*.

A. J. AYER, *Language, Truth and Logic*, 1936, pp. 114–120. Reprinted with permission of Victor Gollancz Ltd.

PAUL TILLICH, "Symbols of Faith," pp. 41–54, in *Dynamics of Faith* by Paul Tillich, Vol. 10 of World Perspectives, edited by Ruth Nanda Anshen. Copyright © 1957 by Paul Tillich. By permission of Harper & Row, Publishers, Inc.

RAPHAEL DEMOS, "Are Religious Dogmas Cognitive and Meaningful?" from *Academic Freedom, Logic, and Religion*, 1953. Reprinted with permission of University of Pennsylvania Press.

RUDOLF BULTMANN, "What Sense Is There to Speak of God?" *The Christian Scholar*, **43** (1960), 213–222. Reprinted with permission of the Department of Higher Education, The National Council of Churches.

PAUL F. SCHMIDT, *Religious Knowledge and Religious Claims*. Reprinted with permission of Macmillan Publishing Co., Inc., from *Religious Knowledge* by Paul F. Schmidt. Copyright © 1961 by The Free Press, A Division of Macmillan Publishing Co., Inc.

R. B. BRAITHWAITE, *An Empiricist's View of the Nature of Religious Beliefs*, New York: Cambridge University Press, 1953, pp. 11–28 and 29–35. Reprinted by permission of the publishers.

ST. AUGUSTINE, *The Confessions of St. Augustine*. From *The Confessions of St. Augustine*, trans. by F. J. Sheed, Copyright 1954, Sheed & Ward, Inc., New York.

S. I. HAYAKAWA, *Language In Thought and Action*. From *Language In Thought and Action*, by S. I. Hayakawa, copyright, 1941, 1949, 1963, 1964, by Harcourt Brace Jovanovich, Inc. Reprinted by permission of the publishers.

JONATHAN SWIFT, *Gulliver's Travels*, London: Oxford University Press, 1947. Reprinted by permission of the publisher.

WILLIAM JAMES, "What Pragmatism Means," from *Pragmatism*, New York: David McKay, 1909, pp. 43–45. Reprinted by permission.

LEWIS CARROLL, *Through the Looking Glass*. Reprinted by permission of Random House, Inc., New York.

FRIEDRICH WAISMANN, *Principles of Linguistic Philosophy*, 1965. Reprinted with permission of St. Martin's Press, Inc., Macmillan, London & Basingstoke.

JERROLD J. KATZ, "Mentalism in Linguistics," *Language*, Vol. 40, No. 2 (April-June, 1964), 124, 126–134 and 135–137. Published by the Linguistic Society of America. Reprinted with permission of the author and publisher.

B. F. SKINNER, *Verbal Behavior*. B. F. Skinner, *Verbal Behavior*, © 1957, pp. 433–452. Reprinted by permission of Prentice-Hall, Inc., Englewood Cliffs, New Jersey.

MAURICE MERLEAU-PONTY, "The Body as Expression, and Speech," from *Phenomenology of Perception*, Colin Smith, trans., 1962, pp. 174–190. Reprinted with permission of Humanities Press, Inc., New Jersey, and Routledge & Kegan Paul Ltd.

GILBERT RYLE, "A Puzzling Element in the Notion of Thinking." Reprinted with permission of the author and publisher.

Preface

At the outset we should like to answer two questions. First, since there are a great many introductory texts in philosophy already on the market, many of them quite good and most of them competently written or compiled, why then yet another? Secondly, what exactly may you expect to find in this text? It is hoped that our answer to the first of these questions will go a long way toward answering the second.

It is probably correct to say that an introductory text in the expository style—which tells the student what a certain view is, summarizes the arguments for and against the view, and offers some evaluations of those arguments—is the sort of text that makes the subject matter of philsophy most clear to students. But it is our opinion that texts in the *anthology* style, although suffering from a certain lack of clarity and precision in presentation, have some definite advantages over expository texts. The most significant advantage is that such a text affords the student more opportunity to *do* some philosophy and to catch on for himself to what doing philosophy is all about. For, with such a text, the student and the teacher must dig out the views and arguments. Not incidentally too, with such a text there are fewer preconceptions built into the text concerning what the proper construal of the views and arguments is on any particular issue; this, we believe *can* make the classroom situation more stimulating.

A second important advantage of anthology-style texts is that they afford the student the opportunity to encounter people actually practicing the craft of philosophy. This, together with suitable introductions by teachers concerning such things as the intellectual milieu in which given selections were written, often gives the student a much sounder appreciation of the views, and the arguments for them, than mere summaries of the positions can. A third advantage we think anthology-style texts have is that, if done properly, they let the student see a philosophical discussion *in progress*, as it were. Thus, the student may come to see that new evaluations of both the quality and the nature of philosophical arguments are possible—and to see this, again, from first-hand experience, working with *progressions* of selections on particular issues.

It is primarily for these reasons that we prefer to use an anthology text in our own introductory classes. But the more standard texts of this sort have, in our opinion, several specific characteristics that make them less useful in introductory classes than they might be. For example, many standard introductory anthologies group together, in *general* areas of philosophical inquiry, selections that time has proved to be classics in the area, without regard either to whether those pieces speak to the same or even similar issues or to whether those pieces can be readily understood by introductory-level students. Another common failing of anthology texts is the lack of any exhibition of the relevance of philosophical discussion to disciplines other than philosophy. Some recent texts have attempted to overcome this. But many of them, we believe, have purchased "relevance" at the price of discussing popular issues of morality and faith without addressing *any* substantive *philosophical* issues. Yet another flaw of many anthologies is the inclusion of pieces *solely* on the basis that they have had *historical* interest without regard to their *philosophical* merit, if any.

To avoid these and similar problems, we have adopted several principles that have, for the most part, been our central guides in selecting the pieces in this text. They are as follows:

1. Within each general area of philosophical inquiry we have chosen two distinct issues or positions for discussion. Each reading, then, is chosen with an eye to helping the student *work through* the particular issue or position at hand.

2. We have not always chosen the very best selection, philosophically speaking, to represent a given view or argument. So some classics are not presented here. Instead we have, within reasonable limits of competency, chosen those pieces that are comprehensible to introductory students with no previous training in philosophy.

3. We have chosen for discussion issues in the general areas of philosophy that have had, and in most cases still do have, some clear relevance to theorizing in areas outside of philosophy; for example, anthropology, law, linguistics, and psychology. We have also included selections on each issue by people whose expertise is *in those other disciplines.*

4. We have included pieces that have had historical interest whenever the pieces can make some substantial contribution to the student's understanding of the issue at hand; and in no other case.

5. Finally, we have included, as the final selection(s) in each section, at least one reading that we think represents the direction to be taken in the correct resolution or solution of the issue. We have done this because, in our opinion, far too many introductory texts leave the student with the idea that philosophical issues are eternally moot and that philosophy is but a round of endless debate. No philosopher that we know of holds that view—though one could hardly guess that from sampling the introductory texts written by many of them. So it strikes us as both philosophically deplorable and pedagogically unsound to fail at least to take a stand and a stab at resolving the issues we present to our students.

We cannot conclude without giving thanks to Debra Evans for her thoughtful and diligent labor that proved indispensible in assembling and preparing the matter of this book and also to Connie Welborn for typing the manuscript.

J. R. H.
C. E. R.
B. R. T.

Contents

PART 3 Introduction to Epistemology 215

Learning, Knowledge, and Truth 217

Scepticism and Perception 294

PART 4 Introduction to Social and Political Philosophy 327

Punishment 329

Paternalism 359

PART 5 Introduction to Philosophy of Religion 411

PART 6 Introduction to Philosophy of Language 495

What Is Philosophy?

"What is philosophy?" is probably the first and most natural question for a student to ask when beginning an introductory course. A definition of the subject seems more important for philosophy than other subjects because it is not usually taught on the high school level and so the student has had no exposure to philosophy at all. Secondly, students have come to expect all of their courses—at least on the introductory level—to begin with some definition or brief account of what the course is all about.

Frequently, the question, "What is philosophy?" is answered by one or some of the following traditional answers:

1. Aristotle, *Metaphysics*, Book IV, Chapter 1.

> Philosophy is the "science which investigates being as being and the attributes which belong to this in virtue of its own nature. . . . Now this is not the same as any of the so-called special sciences. . . . [And] since we are seeking the first principles and highest causes, clearly there must be some thing to which these belong in virtue of its own nature. . . . Therefore it is of being as being that we must also grasp the first cause."

2. Plato, *The Republic*.

> The philosopher is "the spectator of all time and all existence."

3. Ludwig Wittgenstein, *Philosophical Investigations*.

> What is your aim in philosophy?—To shew the fly the way out of the fly-bottle.

4. F. H. Bradley, *Appearance and Reality*.

> Metaphysics is giving bad reasons for what we believe on instinct.

5. Wilfrid Sellars, *Science, Perception and Reality*.

What is characteristic of philosophy is not a special subject-matter, but the aim of knowing one's way around with respect to the subject-matters of all the special disciplines.

6. Melvin Rader, *The Enduring Questions.*

Philosophy is an effort to give unity to human arts and sciences by a critical examination of the grounds of our meanings, values, and beliefs.

7. C. D. Broad, *Scientific Thought.*

It's [philosophy's] object is to take over the results of the various sciences, to add to them the results of the religious and ethical experiences of mankind, and then to reflect upon the whole. The hope is that, by this means, we may be able to reach some general conclusions as to the nature of the universe, and as to our position and prospects in it.

But we think that these are poor answers to the question because they are either so obscure that only a veteran philosopher could possibly know what they mean, or they are flippant evasions of the question, or they are literal nonsense. We suggest that it is not by accident that such is the fate of the one-line answers. Later on, we will try to give an answer to our question, but we can assure the reader that it will not be of the variety we have just criticized.

Philosophy, however, is not unique in that a one-line answer to the "What is . . . ?" question is at best a slogan and at worst a confusion. If we look at the answer given to other "What is . . . ?" questions, we see that they suffer from the same defects as do the slogans of philosophers. For example, suppose we ask, "What is psychology?" We would probably not be offered any unqualified answer, because there are so many *kinds* of psychology: clinical, behavioristic, physiological, psychoanalytic, educational, industrial, and so on, all with, perhaps, different aims and methods. But to exemplify the point we are making, we might take the popular answer to "What is psychology?" that many behaviorists offer: "Psychology is the science whose goal is to explain, predict and control behavior." (Watson et al.) But this won't do as an introductory account of psychology because it really tells us nothing. We don't know what it means until we understand the special concept of *behavior* that is the key to understanding the account. Until we do understand this concept, the definition is no more than a slogan. We think, however, that by the time one does understand *behavior,* one is beyond the introductory stage and either no longer asks the "What is psychology?" question or will accept as an answer only a very detailed, sophisticated account that will be neither one sentence nor appropriate for the novice. Our point here is that philosophy is not unique in being unable to offer a brief description for the novice that will not suffer the defects of the examples we have previously offered.

A second difficulty we will point out here is that philosophy is, in at least one respect, unique vis-à-vis other disciplines. "What is psychology?" is not a problem—or a question—for the practicing psychologist, because we presuppose some answer to it when we are doing psychology. It is a philosophical question (in a sense that will become clear as one works through the text). Unlike other disciplines in which the answer to the "What is . . . ?" question is taken for granted, it is the task of philosophy to answer these questions not only for physics, psychology, sociology, and so on, but also for itself. Only philosophy has the task of defining itself.

Now this should not be taken to mean that sociologists are not concerned with answering the question, "What is sociology?" They are. The point is that when they are attempting to answer it, they are doing philosophy and not sociology. This point should serve as a reminder that philosophical questions arise in other disciplines and frequently persons with "tags" other than *philosopher* are called upon to deal with philosophical problems.

But surely, one might object, we know what we mean by the word *philosophy*; for we use it every day. We talk about the President's philosophy on the economy, or the football coach's philosophy, or about "developing one's philosophy of life," or even about a company's philosophy. So the word is used in many ways: It may mean a person's policy or someone's strategy or practical maxims, or one's values and attitudes towards situations encountered in everyday life, or, with reference to our last example, a company's advertising slogan.

In addition to these uses, *philosophy* has been taken to include religion and the study of religious dogma, a study of witchcraft or the occult, editorializing and social commentary, political propagandizing and manifestoes, mysticism, parapsychology, astrology, and a whole host of other activities, doctrines, and practices.

But we do not mean any of these things by *philosophy*. (Here is the usual place where the temptation to offer a new slogan is the greatest.) We think that if a person is seriously asking the question "What is philosophy?" then he ought to be willing to expend the effort required to answer it. Our view is that only by carefully working through several philosophical problems, by understanding the issues, the intellectual milieu of the controversy, the arguments, rebuttals, and sometimes, solutions, will a person come to understand philosophy and philosophers.

So, we offer our readers a selection of articles on representative philosophical problems (the ones in which our students have shown the greatest interest). We try to focus the articles on particular problems rather than general areas. In addition, we have included selections by nonphilosophers (officially) to illustrate our contention that while philosophy has some indigenous problems, many philosophical problems arise in other disciplines. We have given brief introductions to each section in order to situate the problem in its intellectual perspective. At the end of each section study questions are included to serve as a partial guide to reading and as a test of understanding. Finally, we have included a brief bibliography at the end of each part to point the way for outside reading or for use as an aid in writing a paper.

What Is Philosophy?

The question, "What is philosophy?" is best left to the end of a philosophy course. At that point, however, the successful student will already know what philosophy is and lament only his inability to capture what it is in one sentence. We share our student's frustration on this point.

But we promised earlier to answer the question, "What is philosophy?" The answer begins on the next page.

PART 1

Introduction to Ethics

In this part we present two typical examples of the problems that arise in the area of philosophy called *ethics*. But before we introduce those problems, a few remarks about ethics may be helpful.

First off, it will be convenient for us to mention explicitly the fact that in this introduction we are going to restrict arbitrarily our uses of the terms *ethics* and *ethical* to refer to distinctively *philosophical* views, theories, problems, and arguments. Of course, one often hears a question such as "What is the ethical thing to do?" or such expressions as "business ethics," "professional ethics," and so on. But here we shall refer to such problems, codes of conduct, and arguments as *moral problems*, *moral beliefs*, and *moral arguments*. The distinction we are marking is fairly straightforward. People in their everyday lives follow moral codes, have genuine crises about what they ought to do, and argue about these things. However, even though philosophers are keenly interested in such matters, *their* views, problems, and arguments usually arise *about*, and *not directly within*, matters of everyday morals. So it is helpful to mark the difference between what people are concerned with in everyday life and what philosophers are concerned with *about* the everyday concerns of people. We choose to do this by the arbitrary device of using the word *morals* and its relatives to refer to the ordinary concerns of people, while restricting our use of the word *ethics* and its relatives to refer to the somewhat special concerns of the philosophers.

But so far this doesn't tell you anything about the concerns of philosophers. All you have been told is that the philosophical area called ethics is comprised of views, theories, problems, and arguments *about* matters of morals. But what is it about matters of morals that interest philosophers? The best way we know of to answer this question is to introduce you to three sorts of *problems* with which philosophers deal.

A. First there are problems that concern what moral beliefs people actually have. Here we are interested in accurately *describing* the behavior of people and what distinctively moral beliefs they have about their own behavior and the behavior of others. It is often said that philosophers are not concerned about this task—that this is really the job of the anthropologist or sociologist. And this is partly right. For if one anthropologist or sociologist describes a group as having a certain moral belief when they do not have such a belief, he may have made this mistake because his research was poorly conducted or shallow and slap-dash. It is the task of other researchers in those fields to correct him—it is not the job of philosophers to dispute about what the facts are. But there is another way in which someone may misdescribe the behavior and beliefs of a group. Such cases arise when descriptions are given that employ concepts inappropriate for an adequate description of the behavior and beliefs we want to describe. There are several ways in which such misdescriptions can occur; we shall mention two of those ways.

Suppose one wants to describe, for example, the game of football. It is clear that concepts appropriate for recording and reporting mere bodily movements will not do here. For if one describes the movements of the bodies in the immediate vicinity of the field of play, one cannot be said to have described the *game*. In this conceptual framework there is no way of telling—nor any point to telling—the differences between fans, players, coaches, cheerleaders, officials, or even mascots. In this framework of concepts there is no way of accounting for the reaction of the fans when a first down is made. Nor can an account of the intentions of the various participants be given. In terms of the concepts useful for describing mere bodily movements, there is no crucial difference between a touchdown play and any other play—indeed it is hard to see how even the concept of a *play* can occur here.

Now it is clear that just the opposite kind of mistake can occur. Suppose one uses the concepts utilized in describing a war as the framework in which now to describe football. This way of speaking must be metaphorical; for there are crucial differences between football and war. It can, of course, be a very interesting and sometimes illuminating metaphor. But it just will not do as a conceptual framework in which to *describe* the game accurately. Whereas in the first case too much of what goes on in football was left out of the "description," in this case too much would be packed in. In great part what is left out in the first "description" is the intentions of the participants; what is packed into the second "description" is intentions that the participants do not have.

Usually, of course, *actual* cases of misdescription of a group's behavior and belief are far subtler than we have just presented. Here the philosopher may be of some help in detecting, analyzing, and correcting misdescriptions of this kind. For the philosopher's stock in trade is understanding, analyzing, seeing the implications of, and (on very few occasions) recommending changes that arise in the logic of *concepts*.

B. The second sort of problem that arises in ethics has to do, not with what people actually believe or how they actually behave, but with what *reasons* they can and cannot give for their beliefs and behavior. That is, philosophers are interested here in what could or should count as a *good reason* for some moral belief and/or a *defensible justification* for some behavior. Frequently these interests are occasioned by reflection upon the writings of moralists on a particular moral issue. For when such people argue about moral problems they implicitly or explicitly appeal to principles that deserve philosophical scrutiny. Just as frequently, however, philosophers find that they are not content with examining the principles appealed to in particular moral debates. So, rightly or wrongly the challenge that philosophers have traditionally seen here is to produce or develop some fundamental principle(s) that *make* beliefs and actions *right*.

Here we encounter what philosophers call *normative theories* in ethics. They are called *normative* because, if they were true, they would tell us which of our moral beliefs are right, what our moral beliefs ought to be, and (possibly) even what we ought to do. Typically, the core of such a normative theory is the recommendation that we accept some right-making principles as true. Two examples of such principles, in simplified form, are:

1. What makes an action or moral belief morally right or wrong is whether or not it is in accordance with the will of God.
2. What makes an action or moral belief morally right or wrong is whether or not it produces the greatest possible happiness for the greatest number of people.

(It should be stressed that these are just two examples of the many competing normative views that have been developed in Western philosophy over the last 2,500 years.)

It is obvious that, as in any other discipline where theories are formed, no two genuinely competing theories can both be true. This makes it important that philosophers not only develop normative views but also develop ways of evaluating and weighing competing theories. One of the tests philosophers have devised for evaluating normative theories is the test for logical consistency. If, by adopting a normative view, we are led to even a single case where the view dictates that two or more mutually exclusive actions ought to be done or beliefs ought to be held, then the view is said to be logically inconsistent. Any inconsistent theory should be regarded with suspicion. At the least it cannot be regarded as *the* right normative theory—though it may be applicable in some cases.

Another such test is the test for adequacy. If, by adopting a normative view, we are led to endorse actions or beliefs that we would normally regard as morally outrageous (such as wanton murder of innocents), then at the very least the theory is not adequate for explaining *why* right actions *are* right and wrong actions *are* wrong. The point here is that no adequate normative moral theory should lead to results that are, to our best understanding, morally wrong.

C. It is an interesting fact about normative theories that one cannot discuss them for very long without realizing that, in the very proposing of basic right-making principles, they also are implicitly arguing for a particular view of the *meaning* and/or use of moral concepts. Take for example the principle, (2), just mentioned. It is clear that (2) is not only a proposal of right-making characteristics; for the characteristic is itself a *natural* property that actions, practices, and beliefs might have. It is merely a matter of *fact* whether an action, practice, or belief is or is not conducive to general happiness. Thus, someone who accepts (2) is actually arguing that this is what the moral concepts of *right* and *wrong* mean: that is, according to this view, *right* just *means* "whatever is conducive to general happiness." Thus, with this view, the meaning of the moral concept is given in nonmoral terms.

It is this kind of problem or issue, concerning the meaning of moral terms, that is at the core of the third set of problems that arise in ethics. Philosophers call these *metaethical* problems because they are general problems *about*, not *in*, descriptive and normative ethics.

It is our belief that it is not realistically possible for us to give you a definitive list of the many forms that problems about the meaning of moral concepts can take. Rather, we will list some questions illustrative of the sort of problems philosophers have worried about in metaethics.

1. "What does *murder* mean?"
2. "Is it part of what we mean by *adultery* that *any* action that gets correctly described as a case of adultery is *prima facie* wrong?"
3. "What is the correct *form* of reasoning to employ when disagreements arise in matters of morals?"
4. "Can one always disagree in matters of morals?"
5. "Suppose someone has proposed (as on page 7) that moral judgments are really factual and objective; can one legitimately derive a statement about what we *ought* to do from statements about what the *facts* are?"
6. "Can there be an absolute universal moral code?" "If so, why?" "If not, what is it about the meaning and/or use of moral concepts which prevents this?"
7. "Is there what might be called a 'distinctively *moral* situation'; and, if there is, what are its characteristics?"

You can see from even this brief list that questions about moral concepts may take a variety of forms. This situation, complex as it is, is further complicated by the fact that metaethical issues may very well have consequences for what we can and cannot say in descriptive and normative ethics. For, if one gives an analysis of the meaning of certain moral terms in connection with a metaethical problem, this analysis may rule out as nonsensical some otherwise attractive normative theory. Or again, such an analysis may force us to take a good hard look at some descriptions of peoples' beliefs and actions that we have accepted heretofore.

Finally, then, it will be important for you to realize—as indeed you will from the moment you begin reading the selections in this part—that all three kinds of problems are likely to be intimately interwoven in *any* single issue in ethics. The classification we have given here should not lead you to think that there are three unique and discrete disciplines (descriptive ethics, normative ethics, and metaethics). We do not have *three* disciplines, just *one*—namely, ethics. The point of this classification lies simply in its usefulness in helping us to see when one or another *aspect* of ethics is being emphasized in a particular issue and how those various aspects of ethics are interrelated in that particular issue.

Moral Relativism

The so-called *relativist thesis*, once thought to be a necessary consequence of correct anthropological descriptions of "uninfected" primitive societies, has received very little attention from philosophers and anthropologists in the last ten to fifteen years. It seems that they think that whatever can be said about the thesis has been said. Whether or not they are right about this, for most students in colleges and universities it is still an issue that is very much alive: usually, most students believe it to be true that what is right for one cultural group may differ from what is right for another cultural group. For this reason alone it is worthwhile to choose this problem as a representative example of philosophical reasoning about matters of morals. (There are many other examples one might have chosen.)

There is an equally important reason that has less to do with what you are interested in than it has to do with what we want to help get you interested in. That reason is that one cannot go very far into a discussion of relativism without considering various theories concerning the meaning of moral judgments (and/or standards); and such a consideration involves us in issues that are in the forefront of contemporary ethical theory. Indeed, anyone who wished to confront students with the sorts of problems philosophers are currently interested in could find no more natural entry into those problems than we have with the relativist thesis.

It should be obvious from what we have just said that the thesis that morality is relative is a metaethical thesis. To say that morality is relative is to say that there cannot possibly be any universally binding moral standards and/or judgments. In order to justify such a claim one would have to argue for some view concerning the *nature* of moral standards and judgments. And this just means that one will have to argue for some view about the meaning and/or use of moral standards and judgments. (This could take the form of arguing for a view about the meaning and/or use of certain very important moral *terms.*) In connection with this line of reasoning we have selected several articles we think reflect the kinds of considerations one must deal with in order to effect a serious rational evaluation of the relativist thesis.

The first of these is a selection by W. T. *Stace*, from his book, *The Concept of Morals*. We have chosen passages that deal with three aspects of the problem. The first passage focuses on trying to state exactly what the thesis claims: This is achieved by contrasting the relativist thesis with its opposite, the *absolutist thesis*. The second aspect is a general account of the historical motivations lying behind both theses. The third passage deals with an important error in one typical argument in favor of relativism. Here Stace reviews the claim that the *variability* of moral customs proves the *relativity* of morality. He then shows, in several telling paragraphs, that this is a very weak argument. In so doing, he also reveals the nonfactual character of the relativist thesis. Thus, in these passages, Stace not only gets us off on the right foot by clarifying what the relativist thesis claims, he also shows us why the truth of the claim is not a purely factual, but rather a philosophical, matter.

The next two selections are by anthropologists. We have included them not only in support of our claim that philosophical problems frequently arise outside of philosophy, but also because the views have merit on their own. In the selection by Ruth *Benedict* (from her famous article, "Anthropology and the Abnormal") there are four interesting features that the reader should look for. First of all Benedict advocates what might be called the hard relativist line. That is, she seems to think that *no* human values at all could conceivably be universally binding. Secondly, she focuses her arguments *not* on traditional *moral* values but on the psychoanalytic concepts *normal* and *abnormal* (which, incidentally, she believes are only *variants* of the moral concepts *good* and *bad*). Thus, she not only argues for moral relativism—she extends the argument to cover psychological judgments as well! The third feature is that she presents us with a real problem of exposition. For at first she *seems* to be making the simple argument that cultural variability proves moral and psychological relativity—and this Stace has shown is a very weak argument. On the other hand, in several crucial paragraphs, Benedict actually argues for a certain view of the *meaning* of moral and psychological terms. Yet again it *does* seem that she believes her review of the variability of cultures lends actual *support* to her view of the *meaning* of moral and psychological terms. The last feature is that Benedict's article is subject to criticism at several levels: (a) she gives descriptions of cultures that seem inconsistent and may be improper in other ways as well; (b) she makes, in the paragraphs just mentioned, a clear metaethical claim that deserves careful examination; and (c) in the concluding paragraphs, she draws a rather striking normative consequence from her version of the relativist thesis.

The next selection is by A. L. *Kroeber* and C. *Kluckholn*, from their monograph, "Culture: A Critical Review of Concepts and Definitions." They, too, are anthropologists, and they, too, defend relativism. But they present a softer version of the thesis than does Benedict; and they approach the issue in a strikingly different way. In connection with this, several interesting features of their selection will catch your eye as you read it. First of all they argue that too much importance has been given (by people like Benedict) to the fact of cultural variability, to the neglect of an equally important "universality" of some cultural forms and even of some specific values. (The careful reader will notice that Kroeber and Kluckholn usually use the words *relativism* and *relativity* to refer to what Stace would prefer to call variability rather than to the relativist thesis per se!) So their first dispute with the hard line relativists is not a disagreement over the relativist thesis itself—it is a dispute about what the facts are and about which facts are relevant to a defense of the relativist thesis. Secondly, they are mostly concerned with finding a framework within which to explain how different cultures came to have *some* values that are *not* had by other cultures and *some* values that *are* had by *all* other cultures. In this connection they propose that anthropology ought to be done on the model of natural history. (Natural history is that part of biology concerned with the classification of organisms and with similarities among organisms.) So they come out with an explanation of these phenomena that is fundamentally evolutionary in character. Thirdly, Kroeber and Kluckholn are not content with using their evolutionary model to explain these phenomena—for they also use it to justify, on principle, the making of cross-cultural moral judgments. That is, they claim that their account of how groups come to have the values they do can also be used as a normative principle that could lie behind some moral judgments. Finally, this claim raises metaethical issues—issues with which Kroeber and Kluckholn do not explicitly deal. For, presumably they are presenting or assuming a kind of naturalist metaethical view in which moral terms are thought to refer to those beliefs and practices that have had survival value. Indeed it is our belief that they actually present such a view (rather than merely assuming it), although one has to read their article very carefully to detect it.

The last two selections are by philosophers who are explicitly dealing with some of the metaethical problems raised in the pieces by Benedict and Kroeber and Kluckholn. In effect, one could call Benedict's metaethical view a social form of subjectivism—the view that the word *good*, for example, means or is used to refer to that which a society has approved. With this view, when we say "X is good" we mean to be making the social "autobiographical" claim that we approve of X. In contrast, we have Kroeber and Kluckholn's implicit version of naturalism. Now, however, we turn to two other metaethical views: The first we shall call emotivism, the second is a different version of naturalism.

The fourth selection is by A. J. Ayer, from his book, *Language, Truth and Logic*. Ayer argues for a view of moral terms in which they are thought to be used to express emotions. After presenting some objections both to subjectivism and a version of naturalism that is similar to that of Kroeber and Kluckholn, Ayer argues for a third theory—emotivism—in which moral judgments and moral terms are assimilated to expressions of emotion and the words used in them. He then entertains an objection to his theory. This objection, originally raised by the philosopher G. E. Moore against subjectivism, claims that were Ayer's theory true, there could never be any genuine moral arguments. Ayer shows why that objection does hold against subjectivism, but he presents an ingenious argument to show the objection does not defeat his own emotivist theory.

The fifth and final selection is by Philippa *Foot,* from her article, "Moral Beliefs." We include this piece for two reasons. First, we believe her view is substantially on the right track. In addition the selection offers a fine example of the careful use of examples and analogies in philosophical reasoning. In the initial passages she directs attention to fundamental claims about the meaning of moral terms which underlie any version of emotivism. (But you might also notice that several of the crucial premises are also implicit in Benedict's social subjectivism and even Kroeber and Kluckholn's version of naturalism.) She then draws out two crucial assumptions that must be discussed carefully. The substance of her discussion from this point is to try to show that moral terms like *good* and *bad* cannot, logically speaking, be applied to just *any* beliefs or actions whatsoever. She argues that the logic of moral terms is much like that of the words *pride* and *fear;* and that it is clear that one cannot take pride in or fear just any objects or actions whatever. Without going into further detail about this selection, we can still safely say that Foot's conclusion is a view that not only directly undermines the appeal of Ayer's emotivism but also strikes deeply at the metaethical views of Benedict and Kroeber and Kluckholn. The reason for the latter claim is that to accept those views one must first believe that anything at all *could* be considered good; for, if one believes that *good* refers to or means "that which society approves" or "that which has survival value," there is no intrinsic reason why *any* event, trait, or action must be or must fail to be good.

Finally, neither of the last two selections explicitly addresses the relativism issue in any detail. But each has implications for that issue. For example, Ayer is quite clearly rejecting absolutism; but it is not altogether clear whether he is thereby committed to relativism. And even if he is, it is not clear to what *version* of relativism he would be committed. Again, in her concluding remarks, Foot suggests the lines of an argument against relativism. Whether it is a good argument needs to be discussed. And whether that argument would commit her to some version of absolutism, or perhaps would provide grounds for rejecting the entire issue as nonsensical, is also an area for further discussion.

What Is the Relativist Thesis?

W. T. STACE

THERE is an opinion widely current nowadays in philosophical circles which passes under the name of "ethical relativity." Exactly what this phrase means or implies is certainly far from clear. But unquestionably it stands

---

Reprinted with permission of Macmillan Publishing Co., Inc. from *The Concept of Morals* by W. T. Stace, Copyright 1937 by Macmillan Publishing Co., Inc., renewed 1965 by Walter T. Stace.

as a label for the opinions of a group of ethical philosophers whose position is roughly on the extreme left wing among the moral theorizers of the day. And perhaps one may best understand it by placing it in contrast with the opposite kind of extreme view against which, undoubtedly, it has arisen as a protest. For among moral philosophers one may clearly distinguish a left and a right wing. Those of the left wing are the ethical relativists. They are the revolutionaries, the clever young men, the up to date. Those of the right wing we may call the ethical absolutists. They are the conservatives and the old-fashioned.

Ethical Absolutism

According to the absolutists there is but one eternally true and valid moral code. This moral code applies with rigid impartiality to all men. What is a duty for me must likewise be a duty for you. And this will be true whether you are an Englishman, a Chinaman, or a Hottentot. If cannibalism is an abomination in England or America, it is an abomination in central Africa, notwithstanding that the African may think otherwise. The fact that he sees nothing wrong in his cannibal practices does not make them for him morally right. They are as much contrary to morality for him as they are for us. The only difference is that he is an ignorant savage who does not know this. There is not one law for one man or race of men, another for another. There is not one moral standard for Europeans, another for Indians, another for Chinese. There is but one law, one standard, one morality, for all men. And this standard, this law, is absolute and unvarying.

Moreover, as the one moral law extends its dominion over all the corners of the earth, so too it is not limited in its application by any considerations of time or period. That which is right now was right in the centuries of Greece and Rome, nay, in the very ages of the cave man. That which is evil now was evil then. If slavery is morally wicked today, it was morally wicked among the ancient Athenians, notwithstanding that their greatest men accepted it as a necessary condition of human society. Their opinion did not make slavery a moral good for them. It only showed that they were, in spite of their otherwise noble conceptions, ignorant of what is truly right and good in this matter.

The ethical absolutist recognizes as a fact that moral customs and moral ideas differ from country to country and from age to age. This indeed seems manifest and not to be disputed. We think slavery morally wrong, the Greeks thought it morally unobjectionable. The inhabitants of New Guinea certainly have very different moral ideas from ours. But the fact that the Greeks or the inhabitants of New Guinea think something right does not make it right, even for them. Nor does the fact that we think the same things wrong make them wrong. They are *in themselves* either right or wrong. What we have to do is to discover which they are. What anyone thinks makes no difference. It is here just as it is in matters of physical science. We believe the earth to be a globe. Our ancestors may have thought it flat. This does not show that it *was* flat, and is *now* a globe. What it shows is that men having in other ages been ignorant about the shape of the earth have now learned the truth. So if the Greeks thought slavery morally legitimate, this does not indicate that it was for them and in that age morally legitimate, but rather that they were ignorant of the truth of the matter.

The ethical absolutist is not indeed committed to the opinion that his own, or our own, moral code is the true one. Theoretically at least he might hold that slavery is ethically justifiable, that the Greeks knew better than we do about this, that ignorance of the true morality lies with us and not with them. All that he is actually committed to is the opinion that, whatever the true moral code may be, it is always the same for all men in all ages. His view is not at all inconsistent with the belief that humanity has still much to learn in moral matters. If anyone were to assert that in five hundred years the moral conceptions of the present day will appear as barbarous to the people of that age as the moral conceptions of the middle ages appear to us now, he need not deny it. If anyone were to assert that the ethics of Christianity are by no means final, and will be superseded in future ages by vastly nobler moral ideals, he need not deny this either. For it is of the essence of his creed to believe that morality is in some sense objective, not man-made, not produced by human opinion; that its principles are real truths about which men have to learn—just as they have to learn about the shape of the world—about which they may have been ignorant in the past, and about which therefore they may well be ignorant now.

Thus although absolutism is conservative in the sense that it is regarded by the more daring spirits as an out of date opinion, it is not necessarily conservative in the sense of being committed to the blind support of existing moral ideas and institutions. If ethical absolutists are sometimes conservative in this sense too, that is their personal affair. Such conservatism is accidental, not essential to the absolutist's creed. There is no logical reason, in the nature of the case, why an absolutist should not be a communist, an anarchist, a surrealist, or an upholder of free love. The fact that he is usually none of these things may be accounted for in various ways. But it has nothing to do with the sheer logic of his ethical position. The sole opinion to which he is committed is that whatever is morally right (or wrong)—be it free love or monogamy or slavery or cannibalism or vegetarianism—is morally right (or wrong) for all men at all times.

Usually the absolutist goes further than this. He often maintains, not merely that the moral law is the same for all the men on this planet—which is, after all, a tiny speck in space—but that in some way or in some sense it has application everywhere in the universe. He may express himself by saying that it applies to all "rational beings"—which would apparently include angels and the men on Mars (if they are rational). He is apt to think that the moral law is a part of the fundamental structure of the universe. But with this aspect of absolutism we need not, at the moment, concern ourselves. At present we may think of it as being simply the opinion that there is a single moral standard for all human beings. . . .

HISTORICAL CAUSES FOR THE ACCEPTANCE OF ABSOLUTISM. This brief and rough sketch of ethical absolutism is intended merely to form a background against which we may the more clearly indicate, by way of contrast, the theory of ethical relativity. Up to the present, therefore, I have not given any of the reasons which the absolutist can urge in favor of his case. It is sufficient for my purpose at the moment to state *what* he believes, without going into the question of *why* he believes it. But before proceeding to our next step—the explanation of ethical relativity—I think it will be helpful to indicate some of the historical causes (as distinguished from logical reasons) which have helped in the past to render absolutism a plausible interpretation of morality as understood by European peoples.

Our civilization is a Christian civilization. It has grown up, during nearly two thousand years, upon the soil of Christian monotheism. In this soil our whole outlook upon life, and consequently all our moral ideas, have their roots. They have been moulded by this influence. The wave of religious scepticism which, during the last half century, has swept over us, has altered this fact scarcely at all. The moral ideas even of those who most violently reject the dogmas of Christianity with their intellects are still Christian ideas. This will probably remain true for many centuries even if Christian theology, as a set of intellectual beliefs, comes to be wholly rejected by every educated person. It will probably remain true so long as our civilization lasts. A child cannot, by changing in later life his intellectual creed, strip himself of the early formative moral influences of his childhood, though he can no doubt modify their results in various minor ways. With the outlook on life which was instilled into him in his early days he, in large measure, lives and dies. So it is with a civilization. And our civilization, whatever religious or irreligious views it may come to hold or reject, can hardly escape within its lifetime the moulding influences of its Christian origin. Now ethical absolutism was, in its central ideas, the product of Christian theology.

The connection is not difficult to detect. For morality has been conceived, during the Christian dispensation, as issuing from the will of God. That indeed was its single and all-sufficient source. There would be no point, for the naïve believer in the faith, in the philosopher's questions regarding the foundations of morality and the basis of moral obligation. Even to ask such questions is a mark of incipient religious scepticism. For the true believer the author of the moral law is God. What pleases God, what God commands—that is the definition of right. What displeases God, what he forbids, that is the definition of wrong. Now there is, for the Christian monotheist, only one God ruling over the entire universe. And this God is rational, self-consistent. He does not act upon whims. Consequently his will and his commands must be the same everywhere. They will be unvarying for all peoples and in all ages. If the heathen have other moral ideas than ours—inferior ideas—that can only be because they live in ignorance of the true God. If they knew God and his commands, their ethical precepts would be the same as ours.

Polytheistic creeds may well tolerate a number of diverse moral codes. For the God of the western hemisphere might have different views from those entertained by the God of the eastern hemisphere. And the God of the north might issue to his worshippers commands at variance with the commands issued to other peoples by the God of the south. But a monotheistic religion implies a single universal and absolute morality.

This explains why ethical absolutism, until very recently, was not only believed by philosophers but *taken for granted without any argument.* The ideas of philosophers, like the ideas of everyone else, are largely moulded by the civilizations in which they live. Their philosophies are largely attempts to state in abstract terms and in self-consistent language the stock of ideas which they have breathed in from the atmosphere of their social environment. This accounts for the large number of so-called "unrecognized presuppositions" with which systems of philosophy always abound. These presuppositions are simply the ideas which the authors of the systems have breathed in with the intellectual atmospheres by which they happen to be surrounded—which they have taken over therefore as a matter of course, without argument, without criticism, without even a suspicion that they might be false.

It is not therefore at all surprising to find that Immanuel Kant, writing in the latter half of the eighteenth century, not only took the tenets of ethical absolutism for granted, but evidently considered that no instructed person would dispute them. It is a noticeable feature of his ethical philosophy that he gives no reasons whatever to support his belief in the existence of a universally valid moral law. He assumes as a matter of course that his readers will accept this view. And he proceeds at once to enquire what is the metaphysical foundation of the universal moral law. That alone is what interests him. *Assuming* that there does exist such a law, how, he asks, can this be the case, and what, in the way of transcendental truth, does it imply? It never occurs to him to reflect that any philosopher who should choose to question his fundamental assumption could outflank his whole ethical position; and that if this assumption should prove false his entire moral philosophy would fall to the ground like a pack of cards.

Definition of Ethical Relativity

We can now turn to the consideration of ethical relativity which is the proper subject of this chapter. The revolt of the relativists against absolutism is, I believe, part and parcel of the general revolutionary tendency of our times. In particular it is a result of the decay of belief in the dogmas of orthodox religion. Belief in absolutism was supported, as we have seen, by belief in Christian monotheism. And now that, in an age of widespread religious scepticism, that support is withdrawn, absolutism tends to collapse. Revolutionary movements are as a rule, at any rate in their first onset, purely negative. They attack and destroy. And ethical relativity is, in its essence, a purely negative creed. It is simply a denial of ethical absolutism. That is why the best way of explaining it is to begin by explaining ethical absolutism. If we understand that what the latter asserts the former denies, then we understand ethical relativity....

Any ethical position which denies that there is a single moral standard which is equally applicable to all men at all times may fairly be called a species of ethical relativity. There is not, the relativist asserts, merely one moral law, one code, one standard. There are many moral laws, codes, standards. What morality ordains in one place or age may be quite different from what morality ordains in another place or age. The moral code of Chinamen is quite different from that of Europeans, that of African savages quite different from both. Any morality, therefore, is relative to the age, the place, and the circumstances in which it is found. It is in no sense absolute.

This does not mean merely—as one might at first sight be inclined to suppose—that the very same kind of action which is *thought* right in one country and period may be *thought* wrong in another. This would be a mere platitude, the truth of which everyone would have to admit. Even the absolutist would admit this—would even wish to emphasize it—since he is well aware that different peoples have different sets of moral ideas, and his whole point is that some of these sets of ideas are false. What the relativist means to assert is, not this platitude, but that the very same kind of action which *is* right in one country and period may *be* wrong in another. And this, far from being a platitude, is a very startling assertion.

It is very important to grasp thoroughly the difference between the two ideas. For there is reason to think that many minds tend to find ethical relativity attractive because they fail to keep them clearly apart. It is so very obvious that moral ideas differ from country to country and from age to age. And it is so very easy, if you are mentally lazy, to suppose that to say this means the same as to say that no universal moral standard exists,—or in other words that it implies ethical relativity. We fail to see that the word "standard" is used in two different senses. It is perfectly true that, in one sense, there are many variable moral standards. We speak of judging a man by the standard of his time. And this implies that different times have different standards. And this, of course, is quite true. But when the word "standard" is used in this sense it means simply the set of moral ideas current during the period in question. It means what people *think* right, whether as a matter of fact it *is* right or not. On the other hand when the absolutist asserts that there exists a single universal moral "standard," he is not using the word in this sense at all. He means by "standard" what *is* right as distinct from what people merely think right. His point is that although what people think right varies in different countries and periods, yet what actually is right is everywhere and always the same. And it follows that when the ethical relativist disputes the position of the absolutist and denies that any universal moral standard exists he too means by "standard" what actually is right. But it is exceedingly easy, if we are not careful, to slip loosely from using the word in the first sense to using it in the second sense; and to suppose that the variability of moral beliefs is the same thing as the variability of what really is moral. And unless we keep the two senses of the word "standard" distinct, we are likely to think the creed of ethical relativity much more plausible than it actually is.

The genuine relativist, then, does not merely mean that Chinamen may think right what Frenchmen think wrong. He means that what *is* wrong for the Frenchman may *be* right for the Chinaman. And if one enquires how, in those circumstances, one is to know what actually is right in China or in France, the answer comes quite glibly. What is right in China is the same as what people think right in China; and what is right in France is the same as what people think right in France. So that, if you want to know what is moral in any particular country or age all you have to do is to ascertain what are the moral ideas current in that age or country. Those ideas are, *for that age or country*, right. Thus what is morally right is identified with what is thought to be morally right, and the distinction which we made above between these two is simply denied. To put the same thing in another way, it is denied that there can be or ought to be any distinction between the two senses of the word "standard." There is only one kind of standard of right and wrong, namely, the moral ideas current in any particular age or country.

Moral right *means* what people think morally right. It has no other meaning. What Frenchmen think right is, therefore, right *for Frenchmen.* And evidently one must conclude—though I am not aware that relativists are anxious to draw one's attention to such unsavoury but yet absolutely necessary conclusions from their creed—that cannibalism is right for people who believe in it, that human sacrifice is right for those races which practice it, and that burning widows alive was right for Hindus until the British stepped in and compelled the Hindus to behave immorally by allowing their widows to remain alive. . . .

When it is said that, according to the ethical relativist, what is thought right in any social group is right for that group, one must be careful not to misinterpret this. The relativist does not, of course, mean that there actually is an objective moral standard in France and a different objective standard in England, and that French and British opinions respectively give us correct information about these different standards. His point is rather that there are no objectively true moral standards at all. There is no single universal objective standard. Nor are there a variety of local objective standards. All standards are subjective. People's subjective feelings about morality are the only standards which exist. . . .

To sum up. The ethical relativist consistently denies, it would seem, whatever the ethical absolutist asserts. For the absolutist there is a single universal moral standard. For the relativist there is no such standard. There are only local, ephemeral, and variable standards. For the absolutist there are two senses of the word "standard." Standards in the sense of sets of current moral ideas are relative and changeable. But the standard in the sense of what is actually morally right is absolute and unchanging. For the relativist no such distinction can be made. There is only one meaning of the word standard, namely, that which refers to local and variable sets of moral ideas. Or if it is insisted that the word must be allowed two meanings, then the relativist will say that there is at any rate no actual example of a standard in the absolute sense, and that the word as thus used is an empty name to which nothing in reality corresponds;

so that the distinction between the two meanings becomes empty and useless. Finally—though this is merely saying the same thing in another way—the absolutist makes a distinction between what actually is right and what is thought right. The relativist rejects this distinction and identifies what is moral with what is thought moral by certain human beings or groups of human beings....

It is true that the relativist may object to my statement of his case on the ground that it does not specify precisely *who* the human beings are whose thinking makes what is right right and what is wrong wrong; and that he himself would not think of defining right as "that which people think right"—using the vague word "people" as if morality were determined by what chance persons, anyone or everyone, happen to think moral. We shall see later that there is a real and incurable ambiguity in the relativist's position here (and not merely in my statement of it), and that he himself has difficulty in saying who are the "people" whose ideas are to constitute moral standards. But he cannot deny, at any rate, that his creed does identify morality with the subjective thinking of human beings. And that is the only point which I am at present trying to make clear. To *what* human beings he means to refer will be a matter for our future discussion....

ARGUMENTS IN FAVOR OF ETHICAL RELATIVITY. There are, I think, four main arguments in favor of ethical relativity. The first is that which relies upon the actual varieties of moral "standards" found in the world. It was easy enough to believe in a single absolute morality in older times when there was no anthropology, when all humanity was divided clearly into two groups, Christian peoples and the "heathen." Christian peoples knew and possessed the one true morality. The rest were savages whose moral ideas could be ignored. But all this is changed. Greater knowledge has brought greater tolerance. We can no longer exalt our own morality as alone true, while dismissing all other moralities as false or inferior. The investigations of anthropologists have shown that there exist side by side in the world a bewildering variety of moral codes. On this topic endless volumes have been written, masses of evidence piled up. Anthropologists have ransacked the Melanesian Islands, the jungles of New Guinea, the steppes of Siberia, the deserts of Australia, the forests of central Africa, and have brought back with them countless examples of weird, extravagant, and fantastic "moral" customs with which to confound us. We learn that all kinds of horrible practices are, in this, that, or the other place, regarded as essential to virtue. We find that there is nothing, or next to nothing, which has always and everywhere been regarded as morally good by all men. Where then is our universal morality? Can we, in face of all this evidence, deny that it is nothing but an empty dream?

This argument, taken by itself, is a very weak one. It relies upon a single set of facts—the variable moral customs of the world. But this variability of moral ideas is admitted by both parties to the dispute, and is capable of ready explanation upon the hypothesis of either party. The relativist says that the facts are to be explained by the non-existence of any absolute moral standard. The absolutist says that they are to be explained by human ignorance of what the absolute moral standard is. And he can truly point out that men have differed widely in their opinions about all manner of topics including the subject-matters of the physical sciences—just as much as they differ about morals. And if the various different opinions which men have held about the shape of the earth do not prove that it has no one real shape, neither do the various opinions which they have held about morality prove that there is no one true morality.

Thus the facts can be explained equally plausibly on either hypothesis. There is nothing in the facts themselves which compels us to prefer the relativistic hypothesis to that of the absolutist. And therefore the argument fails to prove the relativist conclusion. If that conclusion is to be established, it must be by means of other considerations.

This is the essential point. But I will add some supplementary remarks. The work of the anthropologists, upon which ethical relativists seem to rely so heavily, has as a matter of fact added absolutely nothing *in principle* to what has always been known about the variability of moral ideas. Educated people have known all along that the Greeks tolerated sodomy, which in modern times has been regarded in some countries as an abominable crime; that the Hindus thought it a sacred duty to burn their widows; that trickery, now thought despicable, was once believed to be a virtue; that terrible torture was thought by our own ancestors only a few centuries ago to be a justifiable weapon of justice; that it was only yesterday that western peoples came to believe that slavery is immoral. Even the ancients knew very well that moral customs and ideas vary —witness the writings of Herodotus. Thus the principle of the variability of moral ideas was well understood long before modern anthropology was ever heard of. Anthropology has added nothing to the knowledge of this principle except a mass of new and extreme examples of it drawn from very remote sources. But to multiply examples of a principle already well known and universally admitted adds nothing to the argument which is built upon that principle. The discoveries of the anthropologists have no doubt been of the highest importance in their own sphere. But in my considered opinion they have thrown no new light upon the special problems of the moral philosopher.

Although the multiplication of examples has no logical bearing on the argument, it does have an immense *psychological* effect upon people's minds. These masses of anthropological learning are impressive. They are propounded in the sacred name of "science." If they are quoted in support of ethical relativity—as they often are—people *think* that they must prove something important. They bewilder and over-awe the simple-minded, batter down their resistance, make them ready to receive humbly the doctrine of ethical relativity from those who have acquired a reputation by their immense learning and their claims to be "scientific." Perhaps this is why so much ado is made by ethical relativists regarding the anthropological evidence. But we must refuse to be impressed. We must discount all this mass of evidence about the extraordinary moral customs of remote peoples. Once we have admitted—as everyone who is instructed must have admitted these last two thousand years without any anthropology at all—

the principle that moral ideas vary, all this new evidence adds nothing to the argument. And the argument itself proves nothing for the reasons already given.

Normality Is Relative

RUTH BENEDICT

MODERN social anthropology has become more and more a study of the varieties and common elements of cultural environment and the consequences of these in human behavior. For such a study of diverse social orders primitive people fortunately provide a laboratory not yet entirely vitiated by the spread of a standardized worldwide civilization. Dyaks and Hopis, Fijians and Yakuts are significant for psychological and sociological study because only among these simpler peoples has there been sufficient isolation to give opportunity for the development of localized social forms. In the higher cultures the standardization of custom and belief over a couple of continents has given a false sense of the inevitability of the particular forms that have gained currency, and we need to turn to a wider survey in order to check the conclusions we hastily base upon this near-universality of familiar customs. Most of the simpler cultures did not gain the wide currency of the one which, out of our experience, we identify with human nature, but this was for various historical reasons, and certainly not for any that gives us as its carriers a monopoly of social good or of social sanity. Modern civilization, from this point of view, becomes not a necessary pinnacle of human achievement but one entry in a long series of possible adjustments.

These adjustments, whether they are in mannerisms like the ways of showing anger, or joy, or grief in any society, or in major human drives like those of sex, prove to be far more variable than experience in any one culture would suggest. In certain fields, such as that of religion or of formal marriage arrangements, these wide limits of variability are well known and can be fairly described. In others it is not yet possible to give a generalized account, but that does not absolve us of the task of indicating the significance of the work that has been done and of the problems that have arisen.

One of these problems relates to the customary modern normal-abnormal categories and our conclusions regarding them. In how far are such categories culturally determined, or in how far can we with assurance regard them as absolute? In how far can we regard inability to function socially as diagnostic of abnormality, or in how far is it necessary to regard this as a function of the culture?

As a matter of fact, one of the most striking facts that emerges from a study of widely varying cultures is the ease with which our abnormals function in

Reprinted with permission of *The Journal Press* from "Anthropology and the Abnormal" by Ruth Benedict in *The Journal of General Psychology*, **10** (1934), 59–82.

other cultures. It does not matter what kind of "abnormality" we choose for illustration, those which indicate extreme instability, or those which are more in the nature of character traits like sadism or delusions of grandeur or of persecution, there are well-described cultures in which these abnormals function at ease and with honor, and apparently without danger or difficulty to the society.

The most notorious of these is trance and catalepsy. Even a very mild mystic is aberrant in our culture. But most peoples have regarded even extreme psychic manifestations not only as normal and desirable, but even as characteristic of highly valued and gifted individuals. Thus was true even in our own cultural background in that period when Catholicism made the ecstatic experience the mark of sainthood. It is hard for us, born and brought up in a culture that makes no use of the experience, to realize how important a rôle it may play and how many individuals are capable of it, once it has been given an honorable place in any society.

Some of the Indian tribes of California accorded prestige principally to those who passed through certain trance experiences. Not all of these tribes believed that it was exclusively women who were so blessed, but among the Shasta this was the convention. Their shamans were women, and they were accorded the greatest prestige in the community. They were chosen because of their constitutional liability to trance and allied manifestations. One day the woman who was so destined, while she was about her usual work, would fall suddenly to the ground. She had heard a voice speaking to her in tones of the greatest intensity. Turning, she had seen a man with a drawn bow and arrow. He commanded her to sing on pain of being shot through the heart by his arrow, but under the stress of the experience she fell senseless. Her family gathered. She was lying rigid, hardly breathing. They knew that for some time she had had dreams of a special character which indicated a shamanistic calling, dreams of escaping grizzly bears, falling off cliffs or trees, or of being surrounded by swarms of yellow jackets. The community knew therefore what to expect. After a few hours the woman began to moan gently and to roll about upon the ground, trembling violently. She was supposed to be repeating the song which she had been told to sing and which during the trance had been taught her by the spirit. As she revived her moaning became more and more clearly the spirit's song until at last she called out the name of the spirit itself, and immediately blood oozed from her mouth.

When the woman had come to herself after the first encounter with her spirit she danced that night her first initiatory shamanistic dance, holding herself by a rope that was swung from the ceiling. For three nights she danced, and on the third night she had to receive in her body her power from her spirit. She was dancing, and as she felt the approach of the moment she called out, "He will shoot me, he will shoot me." Her friends stood close, for when she reeled in a kind of cataleptic seizure, they had to seize her before she fell or she would die. From this time on she had in her body a visible materialization of her spirit's power, an icicle-like object which in her dances thereafter she would exhibit, producing it from one part of her body and returning it to another part. From this time on she continued to validate her supernatural power by further cataleptic demonstrations, and she was called upon in great emergencies of life and death, for curing and for divination and for counsel. She became in other words by this procedure a woman of great power and importance.[1]

It is clear that, so far from regarding cataleptic seizures as blots upon the family escutcheon and as evidences of dreaded disease, cultural approval had seized upon them and made of them the pathway to authority over one's fellows. They were the outstanding characteristic of the most respected social type, the type which functioned with most honor and reward in the community. It was precisely the cataleptic individuals who in this culture were singled out for authority and leadership....

It is clear that culture may value and make socially available even highly unstable human types. If it chooses to treat their peculiarities as the most valued variants of human behavior, the individuals in question will rise to the occasion and perform their social rôles without reference to our usual ideas of the types who can make social adjustments and those who cannot....

The most spectacular illustrations of the extent to which normality may be culturally defined are those cultures where an abnormality of our culture is the cornerstone of their social structure. It is not possible to do justice to these possibilities in a short discussion. A recent study of an island of northwest Melanesia by Fortune describes a society built upon traits which we regard as beyond the border of paranoia. In this tribe the exogamic groups look upon each other as prime manipulators of black magic, so that one marries always into an enemy group which remains for life one's deadly and unappeasable foes. They look upon a good garden crop as a confession of theft, for everyone is engaged in making magic to induce into his garden the productiveness of his neighbors'; therefore no secrecy in the island is so rigidly insisted upon as the secrecy of a man's harvesting of his yams. Their polite phrase at the acceptance of a gift is, "And if you now poison me, how shall I repay you this present?" Their preoccupation with poisoning is constant; no woman ever leaves her cooking pot for a moment untended. Even the great affinal economic exchanges that are characteristic of this Melanesian culture area are quite altered in Dobu since they are incompatible with this fear and distrust that pervades the culture. They go farther and people the whole world outside their own quarters with such malignant spirits that all-night feasts and ceremonials simply do not occur here. They have even rigorous religiously enforced customs that forbid the sharing of seed even in one family group. Anyone else's food is deadly poison to you, so that communality of stores is out of the question. For some months before harvest the whole society is on the verge of starvation, but if one falls to the

[1] In all cultures behavior which is socially rewarded attracts persons who are attracted by the possbility of leadership, and such individuals may simulate the required behavior. This is as true when society rewards prodigality as when it rewards catalepsy. For the present argument the amount of shamming is not considered though it is of obvious importance. It is a matter which cultures standardize quite as much as they standardize the type of rewarded behavior.

temptation and eats up one's seed yams, one is an outcast and a beachcomber for life. There is no coming back. It involves, as a matter of course, divorce and the breaking of social ties.

Now in this society where no one may work with another and no one may share with another, Fortune describes the individual who was regarded by all his fellows as crazy. He was not one of those who periodically ran amok and, beside himself and frothing at the mouth, fell with a knife upon anyone he could reach. Such behavior they did not regard as putting anyone outside the pale. They did not even put the individuals who were known to be liable to these attacks under any kind of control. They merely fled when they saw the attack coming on and kept out of the way. "He would be all right tomorrow." But there was one man of sunny, kindly disposition who liked work and liked to be helpful. The compulsion was too strong for him to repress it in favor of the opposite tendencies of his culture. Men and women never spoke of him without laughing; he was silly and simple and definitely crazy. Nevertheless, to the ethnologist used to a culture that has, in Christianity, made his type the model of all virtue, he seemed a pleasant fellow.

An even more extreme example, because it is of a culture that has built itself upon a more complex abnormality, is that of the North Pacific Coast of North America. The civilization of the Kwakiutl, at the time when it was first recorded in the last decades of the nineteenth century, was one of the most vigorous in North America. It was built up on an ample economic supply of goods, the fish which furnished their food staple being practically inexhaustible and obtainable with comparatively small labor, and the wood which furnished the material for their houses, their furnishings, and their arts being, with however much labor, always procurable. They lived in coastal villages that compared favorably in size with those of any other American Indians and they kept up constant communication by means of sea-going dug-out canoes.

It was one of the most vigorous and zestful of the aboriginal cultures of North America, with complex crafts and ceremonials, and elaborate and striking arts. It certainly had none of the earmarks of a sick civilization. The tribes of the Northwest Coast had wealth, and exactly in our terms. That is, they had not only a surplus of economic goods, but they made a game of the manipulation of wealth. It was by no means a mere direct transcription of economic needs and the filling of those needs. It involved the idea of capital, of interest, and of conspicuous waste. It was a game with all the binding rules of a game, and a person entered it as a child. His father distributed wealth for him, according to his ability, at a small feast or potlatch, and each gift the receiver was obliged to accept and to return after a short interval with interest that ran to about 100 per cent a year. By the time the child was grown, therefore, he was well launched, a larger potlatch had been given for him on various occasions of exploit or initiation, and he had wealth either out at usury or in his own possession. Nothing in the civilization could be enjoyed without validating it by the distribution of his wealth. Everything that was valued, names and songs as well as material objects, were passed down in family lines, but they were always publicly assumed with accompanying sufficient distributions of property. It was the game of validating and exercising all the privileges one could accumulate from one's various forbears, or by gift, or by marriage, that made the chief interest of the culture. Everyone in his degree took part in it, but many, of course, mainly as spectators. In its highest form it was played out between rival chiefs representing not only themselves and their family lines but their communities, and the object of the contest was to glorify oneself and to humiliate one's opponent. On this level of greatness the property involved was no longer represented by blankets, so many thousand of them to a potlatch, but by higher units of value. These higher units were like our bank notes. They were incised copper tablets, each of them named, and having a value that depended upon their illustrious history. This was as high as ten thousand blankets, and to possess one of them, still more to enhance its value at a great potlatch, was one of the greatest glories within the compass of the chiefs of the Northwest Coast.

The details of this manipulation of wealth are in many ways a parody on our own economic arrangements, but it is with the motivations that were recognized in this contest that we are concerned in this discussion. The drives were those which in our own culture we should call megalomaniac. There was an uncensored self-glorification and ridicule of the opponent that it is hard to equal in other cultures outside of the monologues of the abnormal. Any of the songs and speeches of their chiefs at a potlatch illustrate the usual tenor:

. . . .

Wa, out of the way. Wa, out of the way. Turn your faces that I may give way to my anger by striking my fellow chiefs.

Wa, great potlatch, greatest potlatch.[2] The little ones[3] only pretend, the little stubborn ones, they only sell one copper again and again and give it away to the little chiefs of the tribe.

Ah, do not ask in vain for mercy. Ah, do not ask in vain for mercy and raise your hands, you with lolling tongues! I shall break,[4] I shall let disappear the great copper that has the name Kentsegum, the property of the great foolish one, the great extravagant one, the great surpassing one, the one farthest ahead, the great Cannibal dancer among the chiefs.[5]

I am the great chief who makes people ashamed.
I am the great chief who makes people ashamed.
Our chief brings shame to the faces.
Our chief brings jealousy to the faces.
Our chief makes people cover their faces by what he is continually doing in this world, from the beginning to the end of the year,
Giving again and again oil feasts to the tribes.

I am the great chief who vanquishes.
I am the great chief who vanquishes.

[2] The feast he is now engaged in giving. [3] His opponents.

[4] To break a copper, showing in this way how far one rose above even the most superlatively valuable things, was the final mark of greatness.

[5] Himself.

Only at those who continue running round and round in this world, working hard, losing their tails,[6] I sneer, at the chiefs below the true chief.[7]
Have mercy on them! [8] Put oil on their dry heads with brittle hair, those who do not comb their hair!

I sneer at the chiefs below the true, real chief. I am the great chief who makes people ashamed.

. . . .

I am the only great tree, I the chief.
I am the only great tree, I the chief.
You are my subordinates, tribes.
You sit in the middle of the rear of the house, tribes.
Bring me your counter of property, tribes, that he may in vain try to count what is going to be given away by the great copper-maker, the chief.
Oh, I laugh at them, I sneer at them who empty boxes[9] in their houses, their potlatch houses, their inviting houses that are full only of hunger. They follow along after me like young sawbill ducks. I am the only great tree, I the chief.

. . . .

I have quoted a number of these hymns of self-glorification because by an association which psychiatrists will recognize as fundamental these delusions of grandeur were essential in the paranoid view of life which was so strikingly developed in this culture. All of existence was seen in terms of insult.[9a] Not only derogatory acts performed by a neighbor or an enemy, but all untoward events, like a cut when one's axe slipped, or a ducking when one's canoe overturned, were insults. All alike threatened first and foremost one's ego security, and the first thought one was allowed was how to get even, how to wipe out the insult. Grief was little institutionalized, but sulking took its place. Until he had resolved upon a course of action by which to save his face after any misfortune, whether it was the slipping of a wedge in felling a tree, or the death of a favorite child, an Indian of the Northwest Coast retired to his pallet with his face to the wall and neither ate nor spoke. He rose from it to follow out some course which according to the traditional rules should reinstate him in his own eyes and those of the community: to distribute property enough to wipe out the stain, or to go head-hunting in order that somebody else should be made to mourn. His activities in neither case were specific responses to the bereavement he had just passed through, but were elaborately directed toward getting even. If he had not the money to distribute and did not succeed in killing someone to humiliate another, he might take his own life. He had staked everything, in his view of life, upon a certain picture of the self, and, when the bubble of his self-esteem was pricked, he had no interest, no occupation to fall back on, and the collapse of his inflated ego left him prostrate.

[6] As salmon do. [7] Himself. [8] Irony, of course.

[9] Of treasure.

[9a] Insult is used here in reference to the intense susceptibility to shame that is conspicuous in this culture. All possible contingencies were interpreted as rivalry situations, and the gamut of emotions swung between triumph and shame.

Every contingency of life was dealt with in these two traditional ways. To them the two were equivalent. Whether one fought with weapons or "fought with property," as they say, the same idea was at the bottom of both. In the olden times, they say, they fought with spears, but now they fight with property. One overcomes one's opponents in equivalent fashion in both, matching forces and seeing that one comes out ahead, and one can thumb one's nose at the vanquished rather more satisfactorily at a potlatch than on a battlefield. Every occasion in life was noticed, not in its own terms, as a stage in the sex life of the individual or as a climax of joy or of grief, but as furthering this drama of consolidating one's own prestige and bringing shame to one's guests. Whether it was the occasion of the birth of a child, or a daughter's adolescence, or of the marriage of one's son, they were all equivalent raw material for the culture to use for this one traditionally selected end. They were all to raise one's own personal status and to entrench oneself by the humiliation of one's fellows. A girl's adolescence among the Nootka was an event for which her father gathered property from the time she was first able to run about. When she was adolescent he would demonstrate his greatness by an unheard of distribution of these goods, and put down all his rivals. It was not as a fact of the girl's sex life that it figured in their culture, but as the occasion for a major move in the great game of vindicating one's own greatness and humiliating one's associates.

In their behavior at great bereavements this set of the culture comes out most strongly. Among the Kwakiutl it did not matter whether a relative had died in bed of disease, or by the hand of an enemy, in either case death was an affront to be wiped out by the death of another person. The fact that one had been caused to mourn was proof that one had been put upon. A chief's sister and her daughter had gone up to Victoria, and either because they drank bad whiskey or because their boat capsized they never came back. The chief called together his warriors. "Now I ask you, tribes, who shall wail? Shall I do it or shall another?" The spokesman answered, of course, "Not you, Chief. Let some other of the tribes." Immediately they set up the war pole to announce their intention of wiping out the injury, and gathered a war party. They set out, and found seven men and two children asleep and killed them. "Then they felt good when they arrived at Sebaa in the evening."

The point which is of interest to us is that in our society those who on that occasion would feel good when they arrived at Sebaa that evening would be the definitely abnormal. There would be some, even in our society, but it is not a recognized and approved mood under the circumstances. On the Northwest Coast those are favored and fortunate to whom that mood under those circumstances is congenial, and those to whom it is repugnant are unlucky. This latter minority can register in their own culture only by doing violence to their congenial responses and acquiring others that are difficult for them. The person, for instance, who, like a Plains Indian whose wife has been taken from him, is too proud to fight, can deal with the Northwest Coast civilization only by ignoring its strongest bents. If he cannot achieve it, he is the deviant in that culture, their instance of abnormality.

This head-hunting that takes place on the Northwest Coast after a death is no matter of blood revenge or of organized vengeance. There is no effort to tie up the subsequent killing with any responsibility on the part of the victim for the death of the person who is being mourned. A chief whose son has died goes visiting wherever his fancy dictates, and he says to his host, "My prince has died today, and you go with him." Then he kills him. In this, according to their intepretation, he acts nobly because he has not been downed. He has thrust back in return. The whole procedure is meaningless without the fundamental paranoid reading of bereavement. Death, like all the other untoward accidents of existence, confounds man's pride and can only be handled in the category of insults.

Behavior honored upon the Northwest Coast is one which is recognized as abnormal in our civilization, and yet it is sufficiently close to the attitudes of our own culture to be intelligible to us and to have a definite vocabulary with which we may discuss it. The megalomaniac paranoid trend is a definite danger in our society. It is encouraged by some of our major preoccupations, and it confronts us with a choice of two possible attitudes. One is to brand it as abnormal and reprehensible, and is the attitude we have chosen in our civilization. The other is to make it an essential attribute of ideal man, and this is the solution in the culture of the Northwest Coast.

These illustrations, which it has been possible to indicate only in the briefest manner, force upon us the fact that normality is culturally defined. An adult shaped to the drives and standards of either of these cultures, if he were transported into our civilization, would fall into our categories of abnormality. He would be faced with the psychic dilemmas of the socially unavailable. In his own culture, however, he is the pillar of society, the end result of socially inculcated mores, and the problem of personal instability in his case simply does not arise.

No one civilization can possibly utilize in its mores the whole potential range of human behavior. Just as there are great numbers of possible phonetic articulations, and the possibility of language depends on a selection and standardization of a few of these in order that speech communication may be possible at all, so the possibility of organized behavior of any sort, from the fashions of local dress and houses to the dicta of a people's ethics and religion, depends upon a similar selection among the possible behavior traits. In the field of recognized economic obligations or sex tabus this selection is as nonrational and subconscious a process as it is in the field of phonetics. It is a process which goes on in the group for long periods of time and is historically conditioned by innumerable accidents of isolation or of contact of peoples. In any comprehensive study of psychology, the selection that different cultures have made in the course of history within the great circumference of potential behavior is of great significance.

Every society,[10] beginning with some slight inclination in one direction or

[10] This phrasing of the process is deliberately animistic. It is used with no reference to a group mind or a superorganic, but in the same sense in which it is customary to say, "Every art has its own canons."

another, carries its preference farther and farther, integrating itself more and more completely upon its chosen basis, and discarding those types of behavior that are uncongenial. Most of those organizations of personality that seem to us most incontrovertibly abnormal have been used by different civilizations in the very foundations of their institutional life. Conversely the most valued traits of our normal individuals have been looked on in differently organized cultures as aberrant. Normality, in short, within a very wide range, is culturally defined. It is primarily a term for the socially elaborated segment of human behavior in any culture; and abnormality, a term for the segment that that particular civilization does not use. The very eyes with which we see the problem are conditioned by the long traditional habits of our own society.

It is a point that has been made more often in relation to ethics than in relation to psychiatry. We do not any longer make the mistake of deriving the morality of our own locality and decade directly from the inevitable constitution of human nature. We do not elevate it to the dignity of a first principle. We recognize that morality differs in every society, and is a convenient term for socially approved habits. Mankind has always preferred to say, "It is a morally good," rather than "It is habitual," and the fact of this preference is matter enough for a critical science of ethics. But historically the two phrases are synonymous.

The concept of the normal is properly a variant of the concept of the good. It is that which society has approved. A normal action is one which falls well within the limits of expected behavior for a particular society. Its variability among different peoples is essentially a function of the variability of the behavior patterns that different societies have created for themselves, and can never be wholly divorced from a consideration of culturally institutionalized types of behavior.

Each culture is a more or less elaborate working-out of the potentialities of the segment it has chosen. In so far as a civilization is well integrated and consistent within itself, it will tend to carry farther and farther, according to its nature, its initial impulse toward a particular type of action, and from the point of view of any other culture those elaborations will include more and more extreme and aberrant traits.

Each of these traits, in proportion as it reinforces the chosen behavior patterns of that culture, is for that culture normal. Those individuals to whom it is congenial either congenitally, or as the result of childhood sets, are accorded prestige in that culture, and are not visited with the social contempt or disapproval which their traits would call down upon them in a society that was differently organized. On the other hand, those individuals whose characteristics are not congenial to the selected type of human behavior in that community are the deviants, no matter how valued their personality traits may be in a contrasted civilization.

The Dobuan who is not easily susceptible to fear of treachery, who enjoys work and likes to be helpful, is their neurotic and regarded as silly. On the Northwest Coast the person who finds it difficult to read life in terms of an insult contest will be the person upon whom fall all the difficulties of the culturally unprovided for. The person who does not find it easy to humiliate a neighbor, nor to see humiliation in his own experience, who is genial and loving, may, of course, find some unstandardized way of achieving satisfactions in his society, but not in the major patterned responses that his culture requires of him. If he is born to play an important rôle in a family with many hereditary privileges, he can succeed only by doing violence to his whole personality. If he does not succeed, he has betrayed his culture; that is, he is abnormal.

I have spoken of individuals as having sets toward certain types of behavior, and of these sets as running sometimes counter to the types of behavior which are institutionalized in the culture to which they belong. From all that we know of contrasting cultures it seems clear that differences of temperament occur in every society. The matter has never been made the subject of investigation, but from the available material it would appear that these temperament types are very likely of universal recurrence. That is, there is an ascertainable range of human behavior that is found wherever a sufficiently large series of individuals is observed. But the proportion in which behavior types stand to one another in different societies is not universal. The vast majority of the individuals in any group are shaped to the fashion of that culture. In other words, most individuals are plastic to the moulding force of the society into which they are born. In a society that values trance, as in India, they will have supernormal experience. In a society that institutionalizes homosexuality, they will be homosexual. In a society that sets the gathering of possessions as the chief human objective, they will amass property. The deviants, whatever the type of behavior the culture has institutionalized, will remain few in number, and there seems no more difficulty in moulding the vast malleable majority to the "normality" of what we consider an aberrant trait, such as delusions of reference, than to the normality of such accepted behavior patterns as acquisitiveness. The small proportion of the number of the deviants in any culture is not a function of the sure instinct with which that society has built itself upon the fundamental sanities, but of the universal fact that, happily, the majority of mankind quite readily take any shape that is presented to them.

The relativity of normality is not an academic issue. In the first place, it suggests that the apparent weakness of the aberrant is most often and in great measure illusory. It springs not from the fact that he is lacking in necessary vigor, but that he is an individual upon whom that culture has put more than the usual strain. His inability to adapt himself to society is a reflection of the fact that that adaptation involves a conflict in him that it does not in the so-called normal.

Therapeutically, it suggests that the inculcation of tolerance and appreciation in any society toward its less usual types is fundamentally important in successful mental hygiene. The complement of this tolerance, on the patients' side, is an education in self-reliance and honesty with himself. If he can be brought to realize that what has thrust him into his misery is despair at his lack of social backing he may be able to achieve a more independent and less tortured attitude and lay the foundation for an adequately functioning mode of existence.

Only Some Values Are Relative

A. A. KROEBER and C. KLUCKHOLN

WE KNOW by experience that sincere comparison of cultures leads quickly to recognition of their "relativity." What this means is that cultures are differently weighted in their values, hence are differently structured, and differ both in part-functioning and in total-functioning; and that true understanding of cultures therefore involves recognition of their particular value systems. Comparisons of cultures must not be simplistic in terms of an arbitrary or preconceived universal value system, but must be multiple, with each culture first understood in terms of its own particular value system and therefore its own idiosyncratic structure. After that, comparison can with gradually increasing reliability reveal to what degree values, significances, and qualities are common to the compared cultures, and to what degree distinctive. In proportion as common structures and qualities are discovered, the uniquenesses will mean more. And as the range of variability of differentiations becomes better known, it will add to the significance of more universal or common features—somewhat as knowledge of variability deepens significance of a statistical mean.

In attaining the recognition of the so-called relativity of culture, we have only begun to do what students of biology have achieved. The "natural classification" of animals and plants, which underlies and supplements evolutionary development, is basically relativistic. Biologists no longer group together plants by the simple but arbitrary factors of the number of their stamens and pistils, nor animals by the external property of living in sea, air, or land, but by degrees of resemblances in the totality of their structures. The relationship so established then proves usually also to correspond with the sequential developments of forms from one another. It is evident that the comparative study of cultures is aiming at something similar, a "natural history of culture"; and however imperfectly as yet, is beginning to attain it.

It will also be evident from this parallel why so much of culture investigation has been and remains historical in the sense in which we have defined that word. "A culture described in terms of its own structure" is in itself idiographic rather than nomothetic. And if a natural classification implicitly contains an evolutionary development—that is, a history—in the case of life, there is some presupposition that the same will more or less hold for culture. We should not let the customary difference in appelations disturb us. Just as we are in culture

---

Reprinted with permission of the Peabody Museum of Archaeology and Ethnology from "Culture: A Critical Review of Concepts and Definitions" by A. A. Kroeber and C. Kluckholn in *Peabody Museum Papers*, **47**, 1 (1952), 174–179.

de facto trying to work out a natural classification and a developmental history without usually calling them that, we may fairly say that the results attained in historical biology rest upon recognition of the "relativity" of organic structures. . . .

It is evident that as cultures are relativistically compared, both unique and common values appear, or, to speak less in extremes, values of lesser and greater frequency. Here an intellectual hazard may be predicted: an inclination to favor the commoner values as more nearly universal and therefore more "normal" or otherwise superior. This procedure may be anticipated because of the security sense promoted by refuge into absolutes or even majorities. Some attempts to escape from relativism are therefore expectable. The hazard lies in a premature plumping upon the commoner and nearer values and the forcing of these into false absolutes—a process of intellectual short-circuiting. The longer the quest for new absolute values can be postponed and the longer the analytic comparison of relative values can be prosecuted, the closer shall we come to re-emerging with at least near-absolutes. There will be talk in those days, as we are beginning to hear it already, that the principle of relativism is breaking down, that its own negativism is defeating it. There have been, admittedly, extravagances and unsound vulgarizations of cultural relativity. Actually, objective relativistic differences between cultures are not breaking down but being fortified. And relativism is not a negative principle except to those who feel that the whole world has lost its values when comparison makes their own private values lose their false absoluteness. Relativism may seem to turn the world fluid; but so did the concepts of evolution and of relativity in physics seem to turn the world fluid when they were new. Like them, cultural and value relativism is a potent instrument of progress in deeper understanding—and not only of the world but of man in the world.

On the other hand, the inescapable fact of cultural relativism does not justify the conclusion that cultures are in all respects utterly disparate monads and hence strictly noncomparable entities. If this were literally true, a comparative science of culture would be *ex hypothesi* impossible. It is, unfortunately the case that up to this point anthropology has not solved very satisfactorily the problem of describing cultures in such a way that objective comparison is possible. . . .

In principle, however, there is a generalized framework that underlies the more apparent and striking facts of cultural relativity. All cultures constitute so many somewhat distinct answers to essentially the same questions posed by human biology and by the generalities of the human situation. These are the considerations explored by Wissler under the heading of "the universal culture pattern" and by Murdock under the rubric of "the least common denominators of cultures." Every society's patterns for living must provide approved and sanctioned ways for dealing with such universal circumstances as the existence of two sexes; the helplessness of infants; the need for satisfaction of the elementary biological requirements such as food, warmth, and sex; the presence of individuals of different ages and of differing physical and other capacities. The basic similarities in human biology the world over are vastly more massive than the variations. Equally, there are certain necessities in social life for this kind of animal regardless of where that life is carried on or in what culture. Cooperation to obtain subsistence and for other ends requires a certain minimum of reciprocal behavior, of a standard system of communication, and indeed of mutually accepted values. The facts of human biology and of human group living supply, therefore, certain invariant points of reference from which cross-cultural comparison can start without begging questions that are themselves at issue. As Wissler pointed out, the broad outlines of the ground plan of all cultures is and has to be about the same because men always and everywhere are faced with certain unavoidable problems which arise out of the situation "given" by nature. Since most of the patterns of all cultures crystalize around the same foci, there are significant respects in which each culture is not wholly isolated, self-contained, disparate but rather related to and comparable with all other cultures.

Nor is the similarity between cultures, which in some ways transcends the fact of relativity, limited to the sheer forms of the universal culture pattern. There are at least some broad resemblances in content and specifically in value content. Considering the exhuberant variation of cultures in most respects, the circumstance that in some particulars almost identical values prevail throughout mankind is most arresting. No culture tolerates indiscriminate lying, stealing, or violence within the in-group. The essential universality of the incest taboo is well-known. No culture places a value upon suffering as an end in itself; as a means to the ends of the society (punishment, discipline, etc.), yes; as a means to the ends of the individual (purification, mystical exaltation, etc.), yes; but of and for itself, never. We know of no culture in either space or time, including the Soviet Russian, where the official idology denies an after-life, where the fact of death is not ceremonialized. Yet the more superficial conception of cultural relativity would suggest that at least one culture would have adopted the simple expedient of disposing of corpses in the same way most cultures do dispose of dead animals—i.e., just throwing the body out far enough from habitations so that the odor is not troubling. When one first looks rather carefully at the astonishing variety of cultural detail over the world one is tempted to conclude: human individuals have tried almost everything that is physically possible and nearly every individual habit has somewhere at some time been institutionalized in at least one culture. To a considerable degree this is a valid generalization—but not completely. In spite of loose talk (based upon an uncritical acceptance of an immature theory of cultural relativity) to the effect that the symptoms of mental disorder are completely relative to culture, the fact of the matter is that all cultures define as abnormal individuals who are permanently inaccessible to communication or who fail to maintain some degree of control over their impulse life. Social life is impossible without communication, without some measure of order: the behavior of any "normal" individual must be predictable—within a certain range—by his fellows and interpretable by them.

To look freshly at values of the order just discussed is very difficult because they are commonplaces. And yet it is precisely because they are *common*places that they are interesting and important. Their vast theoretical significance rests in the fact that despite all the influences that predispose toward cultural variation (biological variation, difference in physical environments, and the processes of history) all of the very many different cultures known to us have converged upon these universals. It is perfectly true (and for certain types of enquiry important) that the value "thou shalt not kill thy fellow tribesman" is not concretely identical either in its cognitive or in its affective aspects for a Navaho, an Ashanti, and a Chukchee. Nevertheless the central conception is the same, and there is understanding between representatives of different cultures as to the general intent of the prohibition. A Navaho would be profoundly shocked if he were to discover that there were no sanctions against in-group murder among the Ashanti.

There is nothing supernatural or even mysterious about the existences of these universalities in culture content. Human life is—and has to be—a moral life (up to a point) because it is a social life. It may safely be presumed that human groups which failed to incorporate certain values into their nascent cultures or which abrogated these values from their older tradition dissolved as societies or perished without record. Similarly, the biological sameness of the human animal (needs and potentialities) has also contributed to convergences.

The fact that a value is a universal does not, of course, make it an absolute. It is possible that changed circumstances in the human situation may lead to the gradual disappearance of some of the present universals. However, the mere existence of universals after so many millennia of cultural history and in such diverse environments suggests that they correspond to something extremely deep in man's nature and/or are necessary conditions to social life.

When one moves from the universals or virtual universals to values which merely are quite widespread, one would be on most shaky ground to infer "rightness" or "wrongness," "better" or "worse" from relative incidence. A value may have a very wide distribution in the world at a particular time just because of historical accidents such as the political and economic power of one nation at that time. Nations diffuse their culture into the areas their power reaches. Nevertheless this does not mean one must take all cultural values except universals as of necessarily equal validity. Slavery or cannibalism may have a place in certain cultures that is not evident to the ethnocentric Christian. Yet even if these culture patterns play an important part in the smooth functioning of these societies, they are still subject to a judgment which is alike moral and scientific. This judgment is not just a projection of values, local in time and space, that are associated with Western culture. Rather, it rests upon a *consensus gentium* and the best scientific evidence as to the nature of raw human nature —i.e., that human nature which all cultures mold and channel but never entirely remake. To say that certain aspects of Naziism were morally wrong—is not parochial arrogance. It is—or can be—an assertion based both upon cross-cultural evidence as to the universalities in human needs, potentialities, and fulfillments and upon natural science knowledge with which the basic assumptions of any philosophy must be congruent.

Any science must be adequate to explain both the similarities and the differences in the phenomena with which it deals. Recent anthropology has focussed its attention preponderantly upon the differences. They are there; they are very real and very important. Cultural relativism has been completely established and there must be no attempt to explain it away or to deprecate its importance because it is inconvenient, hard to take, hard to live with. Some values are almost purely cultural and draw their significance only from the matrix of that culture. Even the universal values have their special phrasings and emphases in accord with each distinct culture. And when a culture pattern, such as slavery, is derogated on the ground that it transgresses one of the more universal norms which in some sense and to some degree transcend cultural differences, one must still examine it not within a putatively absolutistic frame but in the light of cultural relativism.

At the same time one must never forget that cultural differences, real and important though they are, are still so many variations on themes supplied by raw human nature and by the limits and conditions of social life. In some ways culturally altered human nature is a comparatively superficial veneer. The common understandings between men of different cultures are very broad, very general, very easily obscured by language and many other observable symbols. True universals or near universals are apparently few in number. But they seem to be as deep-going as they are rare. Relativity exists only within a universal framework. Anthropology's facts attest that the phrase "a common humanity" is in no sense meaningless. This is also important.

Rapoport has recently argued that objective relativism can lead to the development of truly explicit and truly universal standards in science and in values:

In sum, cultures are distinct yet similar and comparable. As Steward has pointed out, the features that lend uniqueness are the secondary or variable ones. Two or more cultures can have a great deal of content—and even of patterning—in common and still there is distinctness; there are universals, but relativistic autonomy remains a valid principle. Both perspectives are true and important, and no false either-or antinomy must be posed between them. Once again there is a proper analogy between cultures and personalities. Each human being is unique in his concrete totality, and yet he resembles all other human beings in certain respects and some particular human beings a great deal. It is no more correct to limit each culture to its distinctive features and organization, abstracting out as "precultural" or as "conditions of culture" the likenesses that are universal, than to deny to each personality those aspects that derive from its cultural heritage and from participation in common humanity.

Moral Judgments Are Purely Emotive

A. J. AYER

THE ORDINARY system of ethics, as elaborated in the works of ethical philosophers, is very far from being a homogeneous whole. Not only is it apt to contain pieces of metaphysics, and analyses of non-ethical concepts: its actual ethical contents are themselves of very different kinds. We may divide them, indeed, into four main classes. There are, first of all, propositions which express definitions of ethical terms, or judgements about the legitimacy or possibility of certain definitions. Secondly, there are propositions describing the phenomena of moral experience, and their causes. Thirdly, there are exhortations to moral virtue. And, lastly, there are actual ethical judgements. It is unfortunately the case that the distinction between these four classes, plain as it is, is commonly ignored by ethical philosophers; with the result that it is often very difficult to tell from their works what it is that they are seeking to discover or prove.

In fact, it is easy to see that only the first of our four classes, namely that which comprises the propositions relating to the definitions of ethical terms, can be said to constitute ethical philosophy. The propositions which describe the phenomena of moral experience, and their causes, must be assigned to the science of psychology, or sociology. The exhortations to moral virtue are not propositions at all, but ejaculations or commands which are designed to provoke the reader to action of a certain sort. Accordingly, they do not belong to any branch of philosophy or science. As for the expressions of ethical judgements, we have not yet determined how they should be classified. But inasmuch as they are certainly neither definitions nor comments upon definitions, nor quotations, we may say decisively that they do not belong to ethical philosophy. A strictly philosophical treatise on ethics should therefore make no ethical pronouncements. But it should, by giving an analysis of ethical terms, show what is the category to which all such pronouncements belong. And this is what we are now about to do.

A question which is often discussed by ethical philosophers is whether it is possible to find definitions which would reduce all ethical terms to one or two fundamental terms. But this question, though it undeniably belongs to ethical philosophy, is not relevant to our present enquiry. We are not now concerned to discover which term, within the sphere of ethical terms, is to be taken as fundamental; whether, for example, "good" can be defined in terms of "right" or "right" in terms of "good," or both in terms of "value." What we are interested in is the possibility of reducing the whole sphere of ethical terms to non-ethical terms. We are enquiring whether statements of ethical value can be translated into statements of empirical fact.

Reprinted with permission of Victor Gollancz Ltd. from *Language, Truth and Logic* by A. J. Ayer, 1936, pp. 103–113.

That they can be so translated is the contention of those ethical philosophers who are commonly called subjectivists, and of those who are known as utilitarians. For the utilitarian defines the rightness of actions, and the goodness of ends, in terms of the pleasure, or happiness, or satisfaction, to which they give rise; the subjectivist, in terms of the feelings of approval which a certain person, or group of people, has towards them. Each of these types of definition makes moral judgements into a sub-class of psychological or sociological judgements; and for this reason they are very attractive to us. For, if either was correct, it would follow that ethical assertions were not generically different from the factual assertions which are ordinarily contrasted with them; and the account which we have already given of empirical hypotheses would apply to them also.

Nevertheless we shall not adopt either a subjectivist or a utilitarian analysis of ethical terms. We reject the subjectivist view that to call an action right, or a thing good, is to say that it is generally approved of, because it is not self-contradictory to assert that some actions which are generally approved of are not right, or that some things which are generally approved of are not good. And we reject the alternative subjectivist view that a man who asserts that a certain action is right, or that a certain thing is good, is saying that he himself approves of it, on the ground that a man who confessed that he sometimes approved of what was bad or wrong would not be contradicting himself. And a similar argument is fatal to utilitarianism. We cannot agree that to call an action right is to say that of all the actions possible in the circumstances it would cause, or be likely to cause, the greatest happiness, or the greatest balance of pleasure over pain, or the greatest balance of satisfied over unsatisfied desire, because we find that it is not self-contradictory to say that it is sometimes wrong to perform the action which would actually or probably cause the greatest happiness, or the greatest balance of pleasure over pain, or of satisfied over unsatisfied desire. And since it is not self-contradictory to say that some pleasant things are not good, or that some bad things are desired, it cannot be the case that the sentence "*x* is good" is equivalent to "*x* is pleasant," or to "*x* is desired." And to every other variant of utilitarianism with which I am acquainted the same objection can be made. And therefore we should, I think, conclude that the validity of ethical judgements is not determined by the felicific tendencies of actions, any more than by the nature of people's feelings; but that it must be regarded as "absolute" or intrinsic," and not empirically calculable.

If we say this, we are not, of course, denying that it is possible to invent a language in which all ethical symbols are definable in non-ethical terms, or even that it is desirable to invent such a language and adopt it in place of our own; what we are denying is that the suggested reduction of ethical to non-ethical statements is consistent with the conventions of our actual language. That is, we reject utilitarianism and subjectivism, not as proposals to replace our existing ethical notions by new ones, but as analyses of our existing ethical notions. Our contention is simply that, in our language, sentences which contain normative ethical symbols are not equivalent to sentences which express psychological propositions, or indeed empirical propositions of any kind.

It is advisable here to make it plain that it is only normative ethical symbols, and not descriptive ethical symbols, that are held by us to be indefinable in factual terms. There is a danger of confusing these two types of symbols, because they are commonly constituted by signs of the same sensible form. Thus a complex sign of the form "*x* is wrong" may constitute a sentence which expresses a moral judgement concerning a certain type of conduct, or it may constitute a sentence which states that a certain type of conduct is repugnant to the moral sense of a particular society. In the latter case, the symbol "wrong" is a descriptive ethical symbol, and the sentence in which it occurs expresses an ordinary sociological proposition; in the former case, the symbol "wrong" is a normative ethical symbol, and the sentence in which it occurs does not, we maintain, express an empirical proposition at all. It is only with normative ethics that we are at present concerned; so that whenever ethical symbols are used in the course of this argument without qualification, they are always to be interpreted as symbols of the normative type.

In admitting that normative ethical concepts are irreducible to empirical concepts, we seem to be leaving the way clear for the "absolutist" view of ethics—that is, the view that statements of value are not controlled by observation, as ordinary empirical propositions are, but only by a mysterious "intellectual intuition." A feature of this theory, which is seldom recognized by its advocates, is that it makes statements of value unverifiable. For it is notorious that what seems intuitively certain to one person may seem doubtful, or even false to another. So that unless it is possible to provide some criterion by which one may decide between conflicting intuitions, a mere appeal to intuition is worthless as a test of a proposition's validity. But in the case of moral judgements, no such criterion can be given. Some moralists claim to settle the matter by saying that they "know" that their own moral judgements are correct. But such an assertion is of purely psychological interest, and has not the slightest tendency to prove the validity of any moral judgement. For dissentient moralists may equally well "know" that their ethical views are correct. And, as far as subjective certainty goes, there will be nothing to choose between them. When such differences of opinion arise in connection with an ordinary empirical proposition, one may attempt to resolve them by referring to, or actually carrying out, some relevant empirical test. But with regard to ethical statements, there is, on the "absolutist" or "intuitionist" theory, no relevant empirical test. We are therefore justified in saying that on this theory ethical statements are held to be unverifiable. They are, of course, also held to be genuine synthetic propositions.

Considering the use which we have made of the principle that a synthetic proposition is significant only if it is empirically verifiable, it is clear that the acceptance of an "absolutist" theory of ethics would undermine the whole of our main argument. And as we have already rejected the "naturalistic" theories which are commonly supposed to provide the only alternative to "absolutism" in ethics, we seem to have reached a difficult position. We shall meet the difficulty by showing that the correct treatment of ethical statements is afforded by a third theory, which is wholly compatible with our radical empiricism.

We begin by admitting that the fundamental ethical concepts are unanalysable, inasmuch as there is no criterion by which one can test the validity of the judgements in which they occur. So far we are in agreement with the absolutists. But, unlike the absolutists, we are able to give an explanation of this fact about ethical concepts. We say that the reason why they are unanalysable is that they are mere pseudo-concepts. The presence of an ethical symbol in a proposition adds nothing to its factual content. Thus if I say to someone, "You acted wrongly in stealing that money," I am not stating anything more than if I had simply said, "You stole that money." In adding that this action is wrong I am not making any further statement about it. I am simply evincing my moral disapproval of it. It is as if I had said, "You stole that money," in a peculiar tone of horror, or written it with the addition of some special exclamation marks. The tone, or the exclamation marks, adds nothing to the literal meaning of the sentence. It merely serves to show that the expression of it is attended by certain feelings in the speaker.

If now I generalise my previous statement and say, "Stealing money is wrong," I produce a sentence which has no factual meaning—that is, expresses no proposition which can be either true or false. It is as if I had written "Stealing money!!"—where the shape and thickness of the exclamation marks show, by a suitable convention, that a special sort of moral disapproval is the feeling which is being expressed. It is clear that there is nothing said here which can be true or false. Another man may disagree with me about the wrongness of stealing, in the sense that he may not have the same feelings about stealing as I have, and he may quarrel with me on account of my moral sentiments. But he cannot, strictly speaking, contradict me. For in saying that a certain type of action is right or wrong, I am not making any factual statement, not even a statement about my own state of mind. I am merely expressing certain moral sentiments. And the man who is ostensibly contradicting me is merely expressing his moral sentiments. So that there is plainly no sense in asking which of us is in the right. For neither of us is asserting a genuine proposition.

What we have just been saying about the symbol "wrong" applies to all normative ethical symbols. Sometimes they occur in sentences which record ordinary empirical facts besides expressing ethical feeling about those facts: sometimes they occur in sentences which simply express ethical feeling about a certain type of action, or situation, without making any statement of fact. But in every case in which one would commonly be said to be making an ethical judgement, the function of the relevant ethical word is purely "emotive." It is used to express feeling about certain objects, but not to make any assertion about them.

It is worth mentioning that ethical terms do not serve only to express feeling. They are calculated also to arouse feeling, and so to stimulate action. Indeed some of them are used in such a way as to give the sentences in which they occur the effect of commands. Thus the sentence "It is your duty to tell the truth" may be regarded both as the expression of a certain sort of ethical feeling about truthfulness and as the expression of the command "Tell the truth." The sentence "You ought to tell the truth" also involves the command "Tell the truth," but here the tone of the command is less emphatic. In the sentence "It is good to tell the truth" the command has become little more than a suggestion. And thus the "meaning" of the word "good," in its ethical usage, is differentiated from that of the word "duty" or the word "ought." In fact we may define the meaning of the various ethical words in terms both of the different feelings they are ordinarily taken to express, and also the different responses which they are calculated to provoke.

We can now see why it is impossible to find a criterion for determining the validity of ethical judgements. It is not because they have an "absolute" validity which is mysteriously independent of ordinary sense-experience, but because they have no objective validity whatsoever. If a sentence makes no statement at all, there is obviously no sense in asking whether what it says is true or false. And we have seen that sentences which simply express moral judgements do not say anything. They are pure expressions of feeling and as such do not come under the category of truth and falsehood. They are unverifiable for the same reason as a cry of pain or a word of command is unverifiable—because they do not express genuine propositions.

Thus, although our theory of ethics might fairly be said to be radically subjectivist, it differs in a very important respect from the orthodox subjectivist theory. For the orthodox subjectivist does not deny, as we do, that the sentences of a moralizer express genuine propositions. All he denies is that they express propositions of a unique non-empirical character. His own view is that they express propositions about the speaker's feelings. If this were so, ethical judgements clearly would be capable of being true or false. They would be true if the speaker had the relevant feelings, and false if he had not. And this is a matter which is, in principle, empirically verifiable. Furthermore they could be significantly contradicted. For if I say, "Tolerance is a virtue," and someone answers, "You don't approve of it," he would, on the ordinary subjectivist theory, be contradicting me. On our theory, he would not be contradicting me, because, in saying that tolerance was a virtue, I should not be making any statement about my own feelings or about anything else. I should simply be evincing my feelings, which is not at all the same thing as saying that I have them.

The distinction between the expression of feeling and the assertion of feeling is complicated by the fact that the assertion that one has a certain feeling often accompanies the expression of that feeling, and is then, indeed, a factor in the expression of that feeling. Thus I may simultaneously express boredom and say that I am bored, and in that case my utterance of the words, "I am bored," is one of the circumstances which make it true to say that I am expressing or evincing boredom. But I can express boredom without actually saying that I am bored. I can express it by my tone and gestures, while making a statement about something wholly unconnected with it, or by an ejaculation, or without uttering any words at all. So that even if the assertion that one has a certain feeling always involves the expression of that feeling, the expression of a feeling assuredly does not always involve the assertion that one has it. And this is the important point to grasp in considering the distinction between our theory and the ordinary subjectivist theory. For whereas the subjectivist holds that ethical statements actually assert the existence of certain feelings, we hold that ethical statements are expressions and excitants of feeling which do not necessarily involve any assertions.

We have already remarked that the main objection to the ordinary subjectivist theory is that the validity of ethical judgements is not determined by the nature of their author's feelings. And this is an objection which our theory escapes. For it does not imply that the existence of any feelings is a necessary and sufficient condition of the validity of an ethical judgement. It implies, on the contrary, that ethical judgements have no validity.

There is, however, a celebrated argument against subjectivist theories which our theory does not escape. It has been pointed out by Moore that if ethical statements were simply statements about the speaker's feelings, it would be impossible to argue about questions of value.[1] To take a typical example: if a man said that thrift was a virtue, and another replied that it was a vice, they would not, on this theory, be disputing with one another. One would be saying that he approved of thrift, and the other that *he* didn't; and there is no reason why both these statements should not be true. Now Moore held it to be obvious that we do dispute about questions of value, and accordingly concluded that the particular form of subjectivism which he was discussing was false.

It is plain that the conclusion that it is impossible to dispute about questions of value follows from our theory also. For as we hold that such sentences as "Thrift is a virtue" and "Thrift is a vice" do not express propositions at all, we clearly cannot hold that they express incompatible propositions. We must therefore admit that if Moore's argument really refutes the ordinary subjectivist theory, it also refutes ours. But, in fact, we deny that it does refute even the ordinary subjectivist theory. For we hold that one really never does dispute about questions of value.

This may seem, at first sight, to be a very paradoxical assertion. For we certainly do engage in disputes which are ordinarily regarded as disputes about questions of value. But, in all such cases, we find, if we consider the matter closely, that the dispute is not really about a question of value, but about a question of fact. When someone disagrees with us about the moral value of a certain action or type of action, we do admittedly resort to argument in order to win him over to our way of thinking. But we do not attempt to show by our arguments that he has the "wrong" ethical feeling towards a situation whose nature he has correctly apprehended. What we attempt to show is that he is mistaken about the facts of the case. We argue that he has misconceived the agent's motive: or that he has misjudged the effects of the action, or its probable effects in view of the agent's knowledge; or that he has failed to take into account the special circumstances in which the agent was placed. Or else we employ more general arguments about the effects which actions of a certain

[1] cf. *Philosophical Studies,* "The Nature of Moral Philosophy."

type tend to produce, or the qualities which are usually manifested in their performance. We do this in the hope that we have only to get our opponent to agree with us about the nature of the empirical facts for him to adopt the same moral attitude towards them as we do. And as the people with whom we argue have generally received the same moral education as ourselves, and live in the same social order, our expectation is usually justified. But if our opponent happens to have undergone a different process of moral "conditioning" from ourselves, so that, even when he acknowledges all the facts, he still disagrees with us about the moral value of the actions under discussion, then we abandon the attempt to convince him by argument. We say that it is impossible to argue with him because he has a distorted or undeveloped moral sense; which signifies merely that he employs a different set of values from our own. We feel that our own system of values is superior, and therefore speak in such derogatory terms of his. But we cannot bring forward any arguments to show that our system is superior. For our judgement that it is so is itself a judgement of value, and accordingly outside the scope of argument. It is because argument fails us when we come to deal with pure questions of value, as distinct from questions of fact, that we finally resort to mere abuse.

In short, we find that argument is possible on moral questions only if some system of values is presupposed. If our opponent concurs with us in expressing moral disapproval of all actions of a given type *t*, then we may get him to condemn a particular action A, by bringing forward arguments to show that A is of type *t*. For the question whether A does or does not belong to that type is a plain question of fact. Given that a man has certain moral principles, we argue that he must, in order to be consistent, react morally to certain things in a certain way. What we do not and cannot argue about is the validity of these moral principles. We merely praise or condemn them in the light of our own feelings.

If anyone doubts the accuracy of this account of moral disputes, let him try to construct even an imaginary argument on a question of value which does not reduce itself to an argument about a question of logic or about an empirical matter of fact. I am confident that he will not succeed in producing a single example. And if that is the case, he must allow that its involving the impossibility of purely ethical arguments is not, as Moore thought, a ground of objection to our theory, but rather a point in favor of it.

Having upheld our theory against the only criticism which appeared to threaten it, we may now use it to define the nature of all ethical enquiries. We find that ethical philosophy consists simply in saying that ethical concepts are pseudo-concepts and therefore unanalysable. The further task of describing the different feelings that the different ethical terms are used to express, and the different reactions that they customarily provoke, is a task for the psychologist. There cannot be such a thing as ethical science, if by ethical science one means the elaboration of a "true" system of morals. For we have seen that, as ethical judgements are mere expressions of feeling, there can be no way of determining the validity of any ethical system, and, indeed, no sense in asking whether any such system is true. All that one may legitimately enquire in this connection is, What are the moral habits of a given person or group of people, and what causes them to have precisely those habits and feelings? And this enquiry falls wholly within the scope of the existing social sciences.

It appears, then, that ethics, as a branch of knowledge, is nothing more than a department of psychology and sociology. And in case anyone thinks that we are overlooking the existence of casuistry, we may remark that casuistry is not a science, but is a purely analytical investigation of the structure of a given moral system. In other words, it is an exercise in formal logic.

When one comes to pursue the psychological enquiries which constitute ethical science, one is immediately enabled to account for the Kantian and hedonistic theories of morals. For one finds that one of the chief causes of moral behavior is fear, both conscious and unconscious, of a god's displeasure, and fear of the enmity of society. And this, indeed, is the reason why moral precepts present themselves to some people as "categorical" commands. And one finds, also, that the moral code of a society is partly determined by the beliefs of that society concerning the conditions of its own happiness—or, in other words, that a society tends to encourage or discourage a given type of conduct by the use of moral sanctions according as it appears to promote or detract from the contentment of the society as a whole. And this is the reason why altruism is recommended in most moral codes and egotism condemned. It is from the observation of this connection between morality and happiness that hedonistic or eudæmonistic theories of morals ultimately spring, just as the moral theory of Kant is based on the fact, previously explained, that moral precepts have for some people the force of inexorable commands. As each of these theories ignores the fact which lies at the roof of the other, both may be criticized as being one-sided; but this is not the main objection to either of them. Their essential defect is that they treat propositions which refer to the causes and attributes of our ethical feelings as if they were definitions of ethical concepts. And thus they fail to recognise that ethical concepts are pseudo-concepts and consequently indefinable.

Not Just Anything Can Be Called Good

PHILIPPA FOOT

To many people it seems that the most notable advance in moral philosophy during the past 50 years or so has been the refutation of naturalism; and they are a little shocked that at this late date such an issue should be reopened. It is easy to understand their attitude: given certain apparently un-

Reprinted with permission of the Editor of The Aristotelian Society from "Moral Beliefs" by Philippa Foot in *Proceedings of Aristotelian Society, 1958–9*, 83–94.

questionable assumptions, it would be about as sensible to try to reintroduce naturalism as to try to square the circle. Those who see it like this have satisfied themselves that they know in advance that any naturalistic theory must have a catch in it somewhere, and are put out at having to waste more time exposing an old fallacy. This paper is an attempt to persuade them to look critically at the premisses on which their arguments are based.

It would not be an exaggeration to say that the whole of moral philosophy, as it is now widely taught, rests on a contrast between statements of fact and evaluations, which runs something like this: "The truth or falsity of statements of fact is shewn by means of evidence; and what counts as evidence is laid down in the meaning of the expressions occuring in the statement of fact. (For instance, the meaning of 'round' and 'flat' made Magellan's voyages evidence for the roundness rather than the flatness of the Earth; someone who went on questioning whether the evidence was evidence could eventually be shewn to have made some linguistic mistake.) It follows that no two people can make the same statement and count completely different things as evidence; in the end one at least of them could be convicted of linguistic ignorance. It also follows that if a man is given good evidence for a factual conclusion he cannot just refuse to accept the conclusion on the ground that in his scheme of things this evidence is not evidence at all. With evaluations, however, it is different. An evaluation is not connected logically with the factual statements on which it is based. One man may say that a thing is good because of some fact about it, and another may refuse to take that fact as any evidence at all, for nothing is laid down in the meaning of 'good' which connects it with one piece of 'evidence' rather than another. It follows that a moral eccentric could argue to moral conclusions from quite idiosyncratic premisses; he could say, for instance, that a man was a good man because he clasped and unclasped his hands, and never turned N.N.E. after turning S.S.W. He could also reject someone else's evaluation simply by denying that his evidence was evidence at all.

"The fact about 'good' which allows the eccentric still to use this term without falling into a morass of meaninglessness, is its 'action-guiding' or 'practical' function. This it retains; for like everyone else he considers himself bound to choose the things he calls 'good' rather than those he calls 'bad.' Like the rest of the world he uses 'good' in connexion only with a 'pro-attitude'; it is only that he has pro-attitudes to quite different things, and therefore calls them good."

There are here two assumptions about 'evaluations,' which I will call assumption (1) and assumption (2).

Assumption (1) is that some individual may, without logical error, base his beliefs about matters of value entirely on premisses which no one else would recognise as giving any evidence at all. Assumption (2) is that, given the kind of statement which other people regard as evidence for an evaluative conclusion, he may refuse to draw the conclusion because *this* does not count as evidence for *him*.

Let us consider assumption (1). We might say that this depends on the possibility of keeping the meaning of 'good' steady through all changes in the facts about anything which are to count in favor of its goodness. (I do not mean, of course, that a man can make changes as fast as he chooses; only that, whatever he has chosen, it will not be possible to rule him out of order.) But there is a better formulation, which cuts out trivial disputes about the meaning which 'good' happens to have in some section of the community. Let us say that the assumption is that the evaluative function of 'good' can remain constant through changes in the evaluative principle; on this ground it could be said that even if no one can call a man *good* because he clasps and unclasps his hands, he can commend him or express his *pro-attitude* towards him, and if necessary can invent a new moral vocabulary to express his unusual moral code.

Those who hold such a theory will naturally add several qualifications. In the first place, most people now agree with Hare, against Stevenson, that such words as 'good' only apply to individual cases through the application of general principles, so that even the extreme moral eccentric must accept principles of commendation. In the second place 'commending,' 'having a pro-attitude,' and so on, are supposed to be connected with doing and choosing, so that it would be impossible to say, *e.g.*, that a man was a good man only if he lived for a thousand years. The range of evaluation is supposed to be restricted to the range of possible action and choice. I am not here concerned to question these supposed restrictions on the use of evaluative terms, but only to argue that they are not enough.

The crucial question is this. Is it possible to extract from the meaning of words such as 'good' some element called 'evaluative meaning' which we can think of as externally related to its objects? Such an element would be represented, for instance, in the rule that when any action was 'commended' the speaker must hold himself bound to accept an imperative 'let me do these things.' This is externally related to its object because, within the limitation which we noticed earlier, to possible actions, it would make sense to think of anything as the subject of such 'commendation.' On this hypothesis a moral eccentric could be described as commending the clasping of hands as the action of a good man, and we should not have to look for some background to give the supposition sense. That is to say, on this hypothesis the clasping of hands could be commended without any explanation; it could be what those who hold such theories call 'an ultimate moral principle.'

I wish to say that this hypothesis is untenable, and that there is no describing the evaluative meaning of 'good,' evaluation, commending, or anything of the sort, without fixing the object to which they are supposed to be attached. Without first laying hands on the proper object of such things as evaluation, we shall catch in our net either something quite different such as accepting an order or making a resolution, or else nothing at all.

Before I consider this question, I shall first discuss some other mental attitudes and beliefs which have this internal relation to their object. By this I hope to clarify the concept of internal relation to an object, and incidentally, if my examples arouse resistance, but are eventually accepted, to show how easy it is to overlook an internal relation where it exists.

Consider, for instance, pride.

People are often surprised at the suggestion that there are limits to the things a man can be proud of, about which indeed he can feel pride. I do not know quite what account they want to give of pride; perhaps something to do with smiling and walking with a jaunty air, and holding an object up where other people can see it; or perhaps they think that pride is a kind of internal sensation, so that one might naturally beat one's breast and say 'pride is something I feel *here*.' The difficulties of the second view are well known; the logically private object cannot be what a name in the public language is the name of.[1] The first view is the more plausible, and it may seem reasonable to say that given certain behavior a man can be described as showing that he is proud of something, whatever that something may be. In one sense this is true, and in another sense not. Given any description of an object, action, personal characteristic, etc., it is not possible to rule it out as an object of pride. Before we can do so we need to know what would be said about it by the man who is to be proud of it, or feels proud of it; but if he does not hold the right beliefs about it then whatever his attitude is it is not pride. Consider, for instance, the suggestion that someone might be proud of the sky or the sea: he looks at them and what he feels is *pride*, or he puffs out his chest and gestures with *pride* in their direction. This makes sense only if a special assumption is made about his beliefs, for instance, that he is under some crazy delusion and believes that he has saved the sky from falling, or the sea from drying up. The characteristic object of pride is something seen (*a*) as in some way a man's own, and (*b*) as some sort of achievement or advantage; without this object pride cannot be described. To see that the second condition is necessary, one should try supposing that a man happens to feel proud because he has laid one of his hands on the other, three times in an hour. Here again the supposition that it is pride that he feels will make perfectly good sense if a special background is filled in. Perhaps he is ill, and it is an achievement even to do this; perhaps this gesture has some religious or political significance, and he is a brave man who will so defy the gods or the rulers. But with no special background there can be no pride, not because no one could psychologically speaking feel pride in such a case, but because whatever he did feel could not logically be pride. Of course, people can see strange things as achievements, though not just anything, and they can identify themselves with remote ancestors, and relations, and neighbours, and even on occasions with Mankind. I do not wish to deny there are many far-fetched and comic examples of pride.

We could have chosen many other examples of mental attitudes which are internally related to their object in a similar way. For instance, fear is not just trembling, and running, and turning pale; without the thought of some menacing evil no amount of this will add up to fear. Nor could anyone be said to feel dismay about something he did not see as bad; if his thoughts about it were that

[1] See Wittgenstein, *Philosophical Investigation*, especially §§243–315.

it was altogether a good thing, he could not say that (oddly enough) what he felt about it was dismay. "How odd, I feel dismayed when I ought to be pleased" is the prelude to a hunt for the adverse aspect of the thing, thought of as lurking behind the pleasant facade. But someone may object that pride and fear and dismay are feelings or emotions and therefore not a proper analogy for 'commendation,' and there will be an advantage in considering a different kind of example. We could discuss, for instance, the belief that a certain thing is dangerous, and ask whether this could logically be held about anything whatsoever. Like 'this is good,' 'this is dangerous' is an assertion, which we should naturally accept or reject by speaking of its truth or falsity; we seem to support such statements with evidence, and moreover there may seem to be a 'warning function' connected with the word 'dangerous' as there is supposed to be a 'commending function' connected with the word 'good.' For suppose that philosophers, puzzled about the property of dangerousness, decided that the word did not stand for a property at all, but was essentially a practical or action-guiding term, used for *warning*. Unless used in an 'inverted comma sense' the word 'dangerous' was used to warn, and this meant that anyone using it in such a sense committed himself to avoiding the things he called dangerous, to preventing other people from going near them, and perhaps to running in the opposite direction. If the conclusion were not obviously ridiculous, it would be easy to infer that a man whose application of the term was different from ours throughout might say that the oddest things were dangerous without fear of disproof; the idea would be that he could still be described as 'thinking them dangerous,' or at least as 'warning,' because by his attitude and actions he would have fulfilled the conditions for these things. This is nonsense because without its proper object *warning*, like *believing dangerous*, will not be there. It is logically impossible to warn about anything not thought of as threatening evil, and for danger we need a particular kind of serious evil such as injury or death.

There are, however, some differences between thinking a thing dangerous and feeling proud, frightened or dismayed. When a man says that something is dangerous he must support his statement with a special kind of evidence; but when he says that he feels proud or frightened or dismayed the description of the object of his pride or fright or dismay does not have quite this relation to his original statement. If he is shewn that the thing he was proud of was not his after all, or was not after all anything very grand, he may have to say that his pride was not justified, but he will not have to take back the statement that he was proud. On the other hand, someone who says that a thing is dangerous, and later sees that he made a mistake in thinking that an injury might result from it, has to go back on his original statement and admit that he was wrong. In neither case, however, is the speaker able to go on as before. A man who discovered that it was not his pumpkin but someone else's which had won the prize could only say that he still felt proud, if he could produce some other ground for pride. It is in this way that even feelings are logically vulnerable to facts.

It will probably be objected against these examples that for part of the way at least they beg the question. It will be said that indeed a man can only be proud of something he thinks a good action, or an achievement, or a sign of noble birth; as he can only feel dismay about something which he sees as bad, frightened at some threatened evil; similarly he can only warn if he is also prepared to speak, for instance, of injury. But this will only limit the range of possible objects of those attitudes and beliefs if the range of these terms is limited in its turn. To meet this objection I shall discuss the meaning of 'injury' because this is the simplest case. Anyone who feels inclined to say that anything could be counted as an achievement, or as the evil of which people were afraid, or about which they felt dismayed, should just try this out. I wish to consider the proposition that anything could be thought of as dangerous, because if it causes injury it is dangerous, and anything could be counted as an injury. I shall consider bodily injury because this is the injury connected with danger; it is not correct to put up a notice by the roadside reading 'Danger!' on account of bushes which might scratch a car. Nor can a substance be labelled 'dangerous' on the ground that it can injure delicate fabrics; although we can speak of the danger that it may do so, that is not the use of the word which I am considering here.

When a body is injured it is changed for the worse in a special way, and we want to know which changes count as injuries. First of all, it matters how an injury comes about; *e.g.*, it cannot be caused by natural decay. Then it seems clear that not just any kind of thing will do, for instance, any unusual mark on the body, however much trouble a man might take to have it removed. By far the most important class of injuries are injuries to a part of the body, counting as injuries because there is interference with the function of that part; injury to a leg, an eye, an ear, a hand, a muscle, the heart, the brain, the spinal cord. An injury to an eye is one that affects, or is likely to affect, its sight; an injury to a hand one which makes it less well able to reach out and grasp, and perform other operations of this kind. A leg can be injured because its movements and supporting power can be affected; a lung because it can become too weak to draw in the proper amount of air. We are most ready to speak of an injury where the function of a part of the body is to perform a characteristic operation, as in these examples. We might hesitate to say that a skull can be injured, and might prefer to speak of damage to it, since although there is indeed a function (a protective function) there is no operation. But thinking of the protective function of the skull we may want to speak of injury here. In so far as the concept of *injury* depends on that of *function* it is narrowly limited, since not even every use to which a part of the body is put will count as its function. Why is it that, even if it is the means by which they earn their living, we would never consider the removal of the dwarf's hump or the bearded lady's beard as a bodily injury? It will be tempting to say that these things are disfigurements, but this is not the point; if we suppose that a man who had some invisible extra muscle made his living as a court jester by waggling his ears, the ear would not have been injured if this were made to disappear. If it were natural to men to communicate by movements of the ear, then ears would have the function of signalling (we have no word for this kind of 'speaking') and an impairment of this function would be an injury; but things are not like this. This court jester would use his ears to make people laugh, but this is not the function of ears.

No doubt many people will feel impatient when such facts are mentioned, because they think that it is quite unimportant that this or that *happens* to be the case, and it seems to them arbitrary that the loss of the beard, the hump, or the ear muscle would not be called an injury. Isn't the loss of that by which one makes one's living a pretty catastrophic loss? Yet it seems quite natural that these are not counted as injuries if one thinks about the conditions of human life, and contrasts the loss of a special ability to make people gape or laugh with the ability to see, hear, walk, or pick things up. The first is only needed for one very special way of living; the other in any foreseeable future for any man. This restriction seems all the more natural when we observe what other threats besides that of injury can constitute danger: of death, for instance, or mental derangement. A shock which could cause mental instability or impairment of memory would be called dangerous, because a man needs such things as intelligence, memory, and concentration as he needs sight or hearing or the use of hands. Here we do not speak of injury unless it is possible to connect the impairment with some physical change, but we speak of danger because there is the same loss of a capacity which any man needs.

There can be injury outside the range we have been considering; for a man may sometimes be said to have received injuries where no part of his body has had its function interfered with. In general, I think that any blow which disarranged the body in such a way that there was lasting pain would inflict an injury, even if no other ill resulted, but I do not know of any other important extension of the concept.

It seems therefore that since the range of things which can be called injuries is quite narrowly restricted, the word 'dangerous' is restricted in so far as it is connected with injury. We have the right to say that a man cannot decide to call just anything dangerous, however much he puts up fences and shakes his head.

So far I have been arguing that such things as pride, fear, dismay, and the thought that something is dangerous have an internal relation to their object, and hope that what I mean is becoming clear. Now we must consider whether those attitudes or beliefs which are the moral philosopher's study are similar, or whether such things as 'evaluation' and 'thinking something good' and 'commendation' could logically be found in combination with any object whatsoever. All I can do here is to give an example which may make this suggestion seem implausible, and to knock away a few of its supports. The example will come from the range of trivial and pointless actions such as we were considering in speaking of the man who clasped his hands three times an hour, and we can point to the oddity of the suggestion that this can be called a good action. We are bound by the terms of our question to refrain from adding any special background, and it should be stated once more that the question is about what can count in favour of the goodness or badness of a man or an action, and not what could be, or be thought, good or bad with a special background. I believe that the view I am attacking often seems plausible only because the special background is surreptitiously introduced.

Someone who said that clasping the hands three times in an hour was a good action would first have to answer the question 'How do you mean?' For the sentence 'this is a good action' is not one which has a clear meaning. Presumably, since our subject is moral philosophy, it does not here mean 'that was a good thing to do' as this might be said of a man who had done something sensible in the course of any enterprise whatever; we are to confine our attention to 'the moral use of "good."' I am not clear that it makes sense to speak of 'a moral use of "good,"' but we can pick out a number of cases which raise moral issues. It is because these are so diverse and because 'this is a good action' does not pick out any one of them, that we must ask 'How do you mean?' For instance, some things that are done fulfil a duty, such as the duty of parents to children or children to parents. I suppose that when philosophers speak of good actions they would include these. Some come under the heading of a virtue such as charity, and they will be included too. Others again are actions which require the virtues of courage or temperance, and here the moral aspect is due to the fact that they are done in spite of fear or the temptation of pleasure; they must indeed be done for the sake of some real or fancied good, but not necessarily what philosophers would want to call a moral good. Courage is not *particularly* concerned with saving other people's lives, or temperance with leaving them their share of the food and drink, and the goodness of *what is done* may here be all kinds of usefulness. It is because there are these very diverse cases included (I suppose) under the expression 'a good action' that we should refuse to consider applying it without asking what is meant, and we should now ask what is intended when someone is supposed to say that 'clasping the hands three times in an hour is a good action.' Is it supposed that this action fulfils a duty? Then in virtue of what does a man have this duty, and to whom does he owe it? We have promised not to slip in a special background, but he cannot possibly have a *duty* to clasp his hands unless such a background exists. Nor could it be an act of charity, for it is not thought to do anyone any good, nor again a gesture of humility unless a special assumption turns it into this. The action could be courageous, but only if it were done both in the face of fear and for the sake of a good; and we are not allowed to put in special circumstances which could make this the case.

I am sure that the following objection will now be raised. "Of course clasping one's hand three times in an hour cannot be brought under one of the virtues which we recognise, but that is only to say that it is not a good action by our current moral code. It is logically possible that in a quite different moral code quite different virtues should be recognised, for which we have not even got a name." I cannot answer this objection properly, for that would need a satisfactory account of the concept of a virtue. But anyone who thinks it would be easy to describe a new virtue connected with clasping the hands three times in an hour should just try it. I think he will find that he has to cheat, and suppose that in the community concerned the clasping of hands has been given some special significance, or is thought to have some special effect. The difficulty is obviously connected with the fact that without a special background there is no possibility of answering the question 'What's the point?' It is no good saying that there would be a point in doing the action because the action was a morally good action: the question is how it can be given any such description if we cannot first speak about the point. And it is just as crazy to suppose that we can call *anything* the point of doing something without having to say what the point of *that* is. In clasping one's hands one may make a slight sucking noise, but what is the point of that? It is surely clear that moral virtues must be connected with human good and harm, and that it is quite impossible to call anything you like good or harm. Consider, for instance, the suggestion that a man might say he had been harmed because a bucket of water had been taken out of the sea. As usual it would be possible to think up circumstances in which this remark would make sense; for instance, when coupled with a belief in magical influences; but then the harm would consist in what was done by the evil spirits, not in the taking of the water from the sea. It would be just as odd if someone were supposed to say that harm had been done to him because the hairs of his head had been reduced to an even number.[2]

I conclude that assumption (1) is very dubious indeed, and that no one should be allowed to speak as if we can understand 'evaluation' 'commendation' or 'pro-attitude,' whatever the actions concerned.

[2] In face of this sort of example many philosophers take refuge in the thicket of aesthetics. It would be interesting to know if they are willing to let their whole case rest on the possibility that there might be aesthetic objections to what was done.

MORAL RELATIVISM

Stace

1. What does the relativist thesis maintain? What does the absolutist thesis maintain? What doesn't the absolutist thesis maintain?
2. Stace speaks at length about the facts of cultural variability. How would one state a thesis that could be called the variability thesis? How would it differ from the relativist thesis?
3. What is Stace's account of the ambiguity of the word *standards*? Is the word *standards* really ambiguous in the way Stace says it is? If it were, how would that help explain the apparent ease with which some people argue from the factual truth of the variability thesis to the relativist thesis?
4. What, according to Stace, is wrong with the popular anthropological argument in favor of relativism? What does this suggest to you about the nature of the problem of relativism?

Benedict

1. In what two general ways does Benedict believe that traits regarded as abnormal by our culture may be differently incorporated into the culture patterns of other cultures?
2. When Benedict speaks of "what is normal" for a culture, does she mean to refer merely to the *usual* behavioral traits exhibited by members of that culture; or does she mean to use the word *normal* in the sense it has in psychological evaluation? What is the connection, if any, between those two senses of *normal*?
3. What is Benedict's analogy between behavior traits and phonetic utterances supposed to show? In drawing the analogy does Benedict assume that any behavioral trait, in and of itself, is neither good nor bad?
4. What is Benedict's final judgment on the meaning of the terms *normal* and *good* and of sentences like "*x* is normal" and "*x* is good?" Can you think of any counterexamples to her account of the meaning of these expressions?
5. Benedict cites cases of behavior among some California and Northwest Indian tribes in which she describes these peoples as approving cataleptic seizures and paranoia. Given our ordinary understanding of the concepts of *catalepsy* and *paranoia* (concepts of illnesses) do you think she has correctly described the beliefs of these peoples?

Kroeber and Kluckholn

1. Would it not be fair to say that, for the most part, the way in which Kroeber and Kluckholn speak of cultural relativity suggests that they are referring to what Stace calls variability?
2. Kroeber and Kluckholn draw an analogy between cultural anthropology and natural history in order to show that the form of explanation in anthropology ought to be of the evolutionary type. How good is this analogy? Can you think of ways in which the analogy might seriously break down?
3. Kroeber and Kluckholn use this evolutionary model of explanation to account for both the universality of certain values and the "relativity" (variability) of others. How does this account go?
4. In that account they call attention (obliquely) to Benedict's claim that normality is variable. Do they agree with her claim? Why or why not?
5. In a crucial paragraph Kroeber and Kluckholn assert that cross-cultural judgments are possible which are "both scientific and *moral*" judgments. What thesis about the meaning of moral judgments must one hold in order to claim, as they go on to do, that a moral judgment can be based on a scientific understanding of a culture's value-patterns?
6. How might one use that theory, together with Kroeber and Kluckholn's explanation of the variability of certain values, to arrive at a limited version of the relativist thesis?
7. If one holds the view—as Kroeber and Kluckholn seem to—that "*x* is good" means something like "*x* has survival value for a culture," is one not also committed to the idea that no piece of behavior or behavioral trait is either good or bad in and of itself (but only becomes so if it has or fails to have survival value)? Can you think of counterexamples to this metaethical view?

Ayer

1. How does Ayer distinguish his view from those metaethical positions taken by the subjectivist and the utilitarian? What are his arguments against those views?
2. What is the importance of Ayer's insistence that he is attempting to give an account of

only normative uses of moral terms? Limited in this way, do Ayer's arguments actually affect the collective subjectivism of Benedict or the modified utilitarianism of Kroeber and Kluckholn? Note: we call Kroeber and Kluckholn's view a modified utilitarianism because they appear to believe that what makes something right or good is that it has utility—not for the promotion of happiness, as in classical utilitarianism, but for the promotion of cultural survival.

3. Ayer comments that he is not trying to explain the *meaning* of moral terms but only trying to describe their *use*. What's the difference? *Is* there a difference, in *this* context?
4. How might one deduce some version of the relativist thesis from Ayer's emotivist theory? Compare the relative strength and scope of that version to the versions found in Benedict and in Kroeber and Kluckholn.
5. Ayer responds to Moore's objection by asserting that there *are* no genuine moral disputes, and disputes that appear to be so are actually nothing more than disputes of fact—about, for example, the consequences of actions—between people who have the same emotional responses (and hence, the same moral codes). Can one describe the consequences of morally interesting actions in the purely factual manner Ayer envisions here?
6. Ayer argues that subjectivism and utilitarianism fail to count as correct descriptions of the *actual* use of moral terms. Is his own emotivist theory, which entails that there are no genuine *moral* disputes, a correct description of the *actual* use of moral terms?

Foot

1. The emotivist "assumption" that Foot discusses here is that someone may count anything at all as a reason for calling some action or practice good. How is this "assumption" entailed by emotivism as that view is explained by Ayer? Does it also follow from the view—which appears to be assumed both by Benedict and by Kroeber and Kluckholn—that no piece of behavior is good or bad in and of itself?
2. What does Foot have in mind by talking about a concept having an "internal" or an "external" relationship to its "object?" Which sort of relationship does she think moral concepts have to those actions, traits, and so on, that are the objects of these concepts?
3. How does her example of the concept of *pride* illustrate an internal relationship? Why does she think it necessary and/or useful to give the added example of the concept *dangerous*?
4. What exactly is Foot's argument that moral terms like *good* have an internal relationship to their objects?
5. Foot argues that the correct use of the term *good* requires that we have beliefs about the object of which the term is predicated; she also seems to argue that these must be certain *kinds* of beliefs. What *sorts* of things does Foot think we must believe about—for example, an action like clapping hands three times in an hour—in order to intelligibly call the action good.
6. How might one construct an antirelativist argument based on Foot's account of the meaning of moral terms? Do this for Benedict, Kroeber and Kluckholn, and for whatever version of relativism that is derivable from Ayer's view.
7. Look again at Stace's characterization of absolutism. In rejecting those metaethical theories that lead to relativism, is Foot automatically committed to absolutism? Why or why not? Note: We do not believe she is; and this, we think, should force us to ask whether the absolutism/relativism issue is a genuine issue at all or is instead a bogus issue that gets going because of some deeper philosophical confusion.

Abortion

The moral issue of abortion raises a number of philosophical problems that have their focus in what we have called normative ethics. You will recall that normative ethics is primarily concerned with questions about what may count as justifications for moral beliefs. Furthermore, there are two attitudes one may take here: one may think that the task of normative ethics is to provide some general theory about how we are to justify any moral beliefs; or one may see the task as essentially one of giving careful critical analyses of the lines of justification that are (or may be) used in the defense of some particular moral belief(s). The two attitudes are not incompatible—and frequently the adoption of one, in one context, leads to the adoption of the other, in some different context. However, the moral issue of abortion seems only to require (at least at first) the critical analysis of moral argument rather than normative theorizing. In any case that is the attitude we have taken in collecting the selections we present here.

The first piece is a selection from Justice *Blackmun*'s majority opinion for the U.S. Supreme Court in the case of Roe v. Wade. This is the Court's landmark decision in the legal controversy concerning abortion. We present this case not only because it is historically important but also because it exhibits very directly one way of dealing with the philosophical issues that arise concerning the moral problem of abortion. The Court addresses two of these problems head-on. The first problem is an apparently straightforward conceptual issue: "Is a fetus a person?" Blackmun's argument for the Court is that, if the issue is taken as a strictly legal question, the answer is "no." For the concept of a *person*, either in the language and intent of the Constitution or in civil law, has no prenatal application; nor do issues in law require that we give the concept a prenatal application. In addition, Blackmun reasons, if we take the issue to be a medical or a moral question, it is beyond the purview of the courts; and, in any case, since there is no consensus among doctors, biologists, theologians, and/or philosophers, the Court is in no position to speculate on the matter.

What is interesting about this maneuver is that the Court uses it to relegate the moral problem of abortion to the status of an issue in *private* morality. That is, in the Court's view, whether abortion is wrong is simply a matter for individual consciences to decide—usually it is between the pregnant woman and her doctor. Of course, if we took either the view that a fetus is a person or the view that a fetus is not a person, this maneuver of the Court's would be unacceptable. For, according to the first view, at least some abortions would have to be regarded as akin to murder—and whether murder is wrong is manifestly *not* a matter for individual consciences to decide. With the second view, similarly, a great many abortions would have to be regarded as no more morally problematic than, say, the removal of a cyst. Were that the case, there would be no moral issue here at all, neither a public nor a private moral issue.

The second question addressed by the Court is: "Given that the morality of abortion is a private matter, what grounds, if any, may a state have in interfering with the private moral decision (about abortion) of its citizens?" Blackmun reasons for the Court that there are two such grounds. The first is that a state may interfere in these private moral decisions because a decision to abort is a decision to undergo a certain medical operation, and states do have a legitimate interest in regulating medical practice. However, the Court argues, this interest does not become "compelling" until there are manifest dangers in the operation that call for regulation. Thus, the states may neither prohibit nor regulate abortions by licensed physicians until the second trimester of pregnancy when abortion operations come to involve very real dangers. The second ground the Court recognizes is that a state does have an interest in protecting what the Court calls "potential human life." However, the Court argues that this interest, too, is not absolute; and so it is only when this interest reaches a "compelling point" that states may act on the interest by restricting abortions or prohibiting abortions altogether. The compelling point of this interest is, according to Blackmun, that point at which a fetus could have a "meaningful life" outside the womb. This is sometimes called the point of fetal viability.

There are several problems with this handling of the issue of state interference in a private decision on abortion (assuming, for the moment, that this is a private matter). One wonders, for example, what is meant by the expression "potential human life." This is not a legal concept, nor is it a biological concept nor yet a moral concept. How then did the Court arrive at using it? Blackmun gives us no help here. How can one justify saying that a state has an interest in protecting potential life over and above its obvious interest in protecting the lives of persons? Again Blackmun says nothing here at all—it is just asserted that states have such an interest. Of course the reasons these questions occur to us is that it looks like the Court, which attempted to avoid the fetal-personhood issue, may just have done some of the speculation they said they would not do. Yet if they did speculate here, and if the expression "potential human life" as applied to postviable fetuses is just another word for *person* in a moral and civil sense, then the Court has undermined the entirety of its own position.

The second selection is a presentation, by Thomas J. *O'Donnell*, of the basic outlines of the traditional Roman Catholic objection to abortion. It is useful for all who enter into this debate to realize that, although the current position of the Church has been a long time in the making and even though the Church has from time to time entertained a wide spectrum of views on the matter, there has always been a *general* antiabortion attitude all the way through the Church's history. Thus, when O'Donnell presents the "traditional" objections, he is actually expressing the current *formulation* of the Church's long-held attitudes.

The basic attitudes involved here concern the humanity of fetuses and the moral malice of the taking of innocent human life. As O'Donnell notes, there has been some variation in the history of the Church on the crucial issue of when a fetus becomes a human being. There have also been some disputes concerning the *automatic* malice of killing a fetus—that is, some churchmen have argued for exceptions to the ban on abortion even though agreeing that a fetus is a person. However, the central position of Catholic *doctrine*—as opposed to theological *speculation* and to *canonical legislation*—has been more in line with the Church's current formulation.

To fully appreciate O'Donnell's remarks on fetal personhood, the student should note that very few churchmen have ever flatly denied that a fetus is a person. Instead what has been under dispute is the question: "*When* does a fetus *become* a person?" Thus, the current formulation of the Church, as presented by O'Donnell, is not an argument that a fetus *is* a person; instead it is an argument that a fetus is, in all probability, a person *from the moment of conception*. That is, it is an argument to *extend* the moral malice of abortion all the way to the point of conception.

What is perhaps most interesting in O'Donnell's view can be brought out by noticing the phrase "in all probability." O'Donnell argues that the question of when a fetus becomes a person cannot actually be decided at the present time! The view of Church doctrine then is that, since it is at least quite likely that a new human organism is a person from the moment of conception, the only practical moral stand to take is that directly killing a new human organism *at any time* is morally malicious.

A second interesting feature of O'Donnell's view arises in connection with his oft repeated phrase "directly killing." The unwary reader might suppose that, on O'Donnell's account of it, Church doctrine prohibits abortion altogether. But it is only the *direct* killing of innocent human life that is morally malicious. Of this, O'Donnell states that he has not discussed the reasons for thinking that such killing is morally wrong. Indeed one might wonder why such discussion should be needed in the first place! But what *does* want discussing is the implication in all this that there is such a thing as *indirect* killing, and that such killing is at least sometimes morally permissible. And that implication *is* accepted in Catholic doctrine, although O'Donnell omits any detailed account of it.

The Church does recognize instances where abortions are permissible. And Catholics, in order to justify such exceptions to the ban on abortion, have invoked a principle of moral reasoning that is extremely interesting from the philosopher's point of view. That principle, called the doctrine of the double effect, is (roughly) that if an action has two effects, one good and one evil, it is permissible to perform the action if: (a) the good effect equals or outweighs the evil; (b) the evil effect is not a *means* to the good; (c) the evil effect is not *intended* even if forseen; and (d) there is no other way of bringing about the good effect. In cases where a mother's life is really at stake the "good effect" of saving her life may be said to be at least equal to the "evil effect" of destroying the fetus; and of course if her life really is at stake abortion is the only way to bring about the "good effect." The question of the permissibility of abortions, in such cases, reduces to the question of whether the killing of the fetus is a *direct* killing—that is, whether the killing of the fetus is either a *means* to saving the mother's life or is really *intended* by the mother and her physician.

By this time the student will be awakened to the fact that the moral problem of abortion involves us in at least two philosophical problems involving what we have called normative ethics. The first question is: "If one takes the view that abortion is almost always morally wrong, can one use a line of justification like the doctrine of the double effect to permit abortions in some cases?" The second question is: "Is it necessary, or even helpful, to decide the question of fetal personhood in trying to settle the moral issue of abortion?" In the next two readings these questions are given careful scrutiny by two of the most perceptive philosophers currently working in ethical theory.

In her article. "The Problem of Abortion and the Doctrine of the Double Effect," Phillippa *Foot* argues that the doctrine is defective in at least two ways. First, while some sense probably can be given to the notions of *direct intention* and *oblique intention*, it is not clear what exactly that sense is. Her second, and more important, argument runs like this. The results of applying the doctrine do agree in many cases with our natural moral judgments, though there are some cases where by applying the doctrine we are led to judgments that conflict with our moral sense. If we look carefully at the cases where there *is* agreement we shall find that there are *other* and *stronger* considerations involved than those for which the doctrine allows. Specifically, those cases all seem to involve conflicts between positive duties and negative duties; and our natural moral judgment can be explained by the ways in which we assess the strictness with which the two kinds of duties oblige us. (For example, our negative duty to refrain from injuring another is usually more compelling than our positive duty to help those in need.) Furthermore, this line of justification leads us to conclusions that square with our moral sense in exactly those cases where the doctrine of the double effect comes up with morally odd results. Foot's conclusion then is that the doctrine is defective because: (a) it does not explain all that is important in those cases where we would naturally agree with the results of applying it and (b) it *cannot* explain what is involved in the other cases.

One important feature of this article is Foot's use of the common philosophical technique of using imaginative cases and anological argument to show clearly just what is at issue. Equally relevant is the fact that in the principle of the double effect, she steps back from the case of abortion where the status of the fetus is at issue to cases where this is not in question, although the principle of the double effect is very much in question. Then, after gaining some clarity about the principle in "easier" cases, she reapplies the new understanding of the principle to the case of abortion.

In the final article, "A Defense of Abortion," Judith J. *Thomson* critically examines the argument that, if the fetus is considered a person, no justification of abortion can be given, since no justification can be given for killing innocent humans. She begins her analysis by accepting, for the sake of argument, that the fetus is human but argues that the antiabortionist conclusion does not follow! The reason for this somewhat surprising conclusion is brilliant and yet simple: To say someone has the right to life is clearly not to say that, irrespective of the nature of the relationship between that person and another, that person has also a right to have his or her life *sustained* by another. Specifically, she argues that someone's having the right to life does not entail that he or she has the right to use another's body to sustain his or her life. That additional right, Thomson argues, can only be conferred by the other person in certain specific ways. So, even assuming fetal personhood, one is not automatically led to the antiabortion position.

Thomson is aware that her argument turns on what our understanding is, and can be, of the concept of the *right to life*. In the second half of her article she gives an interesting and perceptive account of what is involved in our use of that expression. In addition she has noted that we may still think that abortion is wrong because, although a fetus has no general claim of right against the woman for the use of her body, it would be morally indecent to refuse to sustain the life of a person who needs the use of her body. Although Thomson is willing to give some credit to this argument, she is quick to point out both that it is surely debatable whether we can justify using the sanctions of the law to force people to exhibit minimally decent behavior, and that most laws prior to the Supreme Court decision required pregnant women to be not just "minimally decent Samaritans" but *superlatively* decent. Thus, Thomson shows that, far from settling the moral issue of abortion, people who argue for fetal personhood have only *just* got into the enormous complexities of that moral problem. And it is not clear that asserting fetal personhood actually helps us to resolve anything about the moral problem at all.

The Court Decides

SUPREME COURT OF THE UNITED STATES

MR. JUSTICE BLACKMUN delivered the opinion of the Court.

This Texas federal appeal and its Georgia companion, *Doe* v. *Bolton, post* ——, present constitutional challenges to state criminal abortion legislation. The Texas statutes under attack here are typical of those that have been in effect in many States for approximately a century. . . .

We forthwith acknowledge our awareness of the sensitive and emotional nature of the abortion controversy, of the vigorous opposing views, even among physicians, and of the deep and seemingly absolute convictions that the subject inspires. One's philosophy, one's experiences, one's exposure to the raw edges of human existence, one's religious training, one's attitudes toward life and family and their values, and the moral standards one establishes and seeks to observe, are all likely to influence and to color one's thinking and conclusions about abortion.

Reprinted from *Roe* v. *Wade* in *The United States Law Week*, Syllabus No. 70-18, Vol. 41, No. 28, 1973.

In addition, population growth, pollution, poverty, and racial overtones tend to complicate and not to simplify the problem.

Our task, of course, is to resolve the issue by constitutional measurements free of emotion and predilection. We seek earnestly to do this, and, because we do, we have inquired into, and in this opinion place some emphasis upon, medical and medical-legal history and what that history reveals about man's attitudes toward the abortive procedure over the centuries. We bear in mind, too, Mr. Justice Holmes' admonition in his now vindicated dissent in *Lochner* v. *New York*, 198 U.S. 45, 76 (1905):

> It [the Constitution] is made for people of fundamentally differing views, and the accident of our finding certain opinions natural and familiar or novel and even shocking ought not to conclude our judgment upon the question whether statutes embodying them conflict with the Constitution of the United States.

The Texas statutes that concern us here are Arts. 1191–1194 and 1196 of the State's Penal Code. These make it a crime to "procure an abortion," as therein defined, or to attempt one, except with respect to "an abortion procured or attempted by medical advice for the purpose of saving the life of the mother." Similar statutes are in existence in a majority of the States.

Texas first enacted a criminal abortion statute in 1854. Texas Laws 1854.... This was soon modified into language that has remained substantially unchanged to the present time....

Jane Roe, a single woman who was residing in Dallas County, Texas, instituted this federal action in March 1970 against the District Attorney of the county. She sought a declaratory judgment that the Texas criminal abortion statutes were unconstitutional on their face, and an injunction restraining the defendant from enforcing the statutes.

Roe alleged that she was unmarried and pregnant; that she wished to terminate her pregnancy by an abortion "performed by a competent, licensed physician, under safe, clinical conditions"; that she was unable to get a "legal" abortion in Texas because her life did not appear to be threatened by the continuation of her pregnancy; and that she could not afford to travel to another jurisdiction in order to secure a legal abortion under safe conditions. She claimed that the Texas statutes were unconstitutionally vague and that they abridged her right of personal privacy, protected by the First, Fourth, Fifth, Ninth, and Fourteenth Amendments. By an amendment to her complaint Roe purported to sue "on behalf of herself and all other women" similarly situated.

James Hubert Hallford, a licensed physician, sought and was granted leave to intervene in Roe's action. In his complaint he alleged that he had been arrested previously for violations of the Texas abortion statutes and that two such prosecutions were pending against him. He described conditions of patients who came to him seeking abortions, and he claimed for many cases he, as a physician, was unable to determine whether they fell within or outside the exception recognized by Article 1196. He alleged that, as a consequence, the statutes were vague and uncertain, in violation of the Fourteenth Amendment, and that they violated his own and his patients' rights to privacy in the doctor-patient relationship and his own right to practice medicine, rights he claimed were guaranteed by the First, Fourth, Fifth, Ninth, and Fourteenth Amendments....

Three reasons have been advanced to explain historically the enactment of criminal abortion laws in the 19th century and to justify their continued existence.

It has been argued occasionally that these laws were the product of a Victorian social concern to discourage illicit sexual conduct. Texas, however, does not advance this justification in the present case, and it appears that no court or commentator has taken the argument seriously. The appellants and *amici* contend, moreover, that this is not a proper state purpose at all and suggest that, if it were, the Texas statutes are overbroad in protecting it since the law fails to distinguish between married and unwed mothers.

A second reason is concerned with abortion as a medical procedure. When most criminal abortion laws were first enacted, the procedure was a hazardous one for the woman. This was particularly true prior to the development of antisepsis. Antiseptic techniques, of course, were based on discoveries by Lister, Pasteur, and others first announced in 1867, but were not generally accepted and employed until about the turn of the century. Abortion mortality was high. Even after 1900, and perhaps until as late as the development of antibiotics in the 1940's, standard modern techniques such as dilation and curettage were not nearly so safe as they are today. Thus it has been argued that a State's real concern in enacting a criminal abortion law was to protect the pregnant woman, that is, to restrain her from submitting to a procedure that placed her life in serious jeopardy.

Modern medical techniques have altered this situation. Appellants and various *amici* refer to medical data indicating that abortion in early pregnancy, that is, prior to the end of first trimester, although not without its risk, is now relatively safe. Mortality rates for women undergoing early abortions, where the procedure is legal, appear to be as low as or lower than the rates for normal childbirth. Consequently, any interest of the State in protecting the woman from an inherently hazardous procedure, except when it would be equally dangerous for her to forgo it, has largely disappeared. Of course, important state interests in the area of health and medical standards do remain. The State has a legitimate interest in seeing to it that abortion, like any other medical procedure, is performed under circumstances that insure maximum safety for the patient. This interest obviously extends at least to the performing physician and his staff, to the facilities involved, to the availability of after-care, and to adequate provision for any complication or emergency that might arise. The prevalence of high mortality rates at illegal "abortion mills" strengthens, rather than weakens, the State's interest in regulating the conditions under which abortions are performed. Moreover, the risk to the woman increases as her pregnancy continues. Thus the State retains a definite interest in protecting the woman's own health and safety when an abortion is proposed at a late stage of pregnancy.

The third reason is the State's interest—some phrase it in terms of duty—in protecting prenatal life. Some of the argument for this justification rests on the theory that a new human life is present from the moment of conception. The State's interest and general obligation to protect life then extends, it is argued, to prenatal life. Only when the life of the pregnant mother herself is at stake, balanced against the life she carries within her, should the interest of the embryo or fetus not prevail. Logically, of course, a legitimate state interest in this area need not stand or fall on acceptance of the belief that life begins at conception or at some other point prior to live birth. In assessing the State's interest, recognition may be given to the less rigid claim that as long as at least *potential* life is involved, the State may assert interests beyond the protection of the pregnant woman alone.

Parties challenging state abortion laws have sharply disputed in some courts the contention that a purpose of these laws, when enacted, was to protect prenatal life. Pointing to the absence of legislative history to support the contention, they claim that most state laws were designed solely to protect the woman. Because medical advances have lessened this concern, at least with respect to abortion in early pregnancy, they argue that with respect to such abortions the laws can no longer be justified by any state interest. There is some scholarly support for this view of original purpose. The few state courts called upon to interpret their laws in the late 19th and early 20th centuries did focus on the State's interest in protecting the woman's health rather than in preserving the embryo and fetus. Proponents of this view point out that in many States, including Texas, by statute or judicial interpretation, the pregnant woman herself could not be prosecuted for self-abortion or for cooperating in an abortion performed upon her by another. They claim that adoption of the "quickening" distinction through received common law and state statutes tacitly recognizes the greater health hazards inherent in late abortion and impliedly repudiates the theory that life begins at conception.

It is with these interests, and the weight to be attached to them, that this case is concerned.

The Constitution does not explicitly mention any right of privacy. In a line of decisions, however, going back perhaps as far as *Union Pacific R. Co.* v. *Botsford*, 141 U.S. 250, 251 (1891), the Court has recognized that a right of personal privacy, or a guarantee of certain areas of zones of privacy, does exist under the Constitution. In varying contexts the Court or individual Justices have indeed found at least the roots of that right in the First Amendment,... in the Fourth and Fifth Amendments, in the penumbras of the Bill of Rights,... in the Ninth Amendment,... or in the concept of liberty guaranteed by the first section of the Fourteenth Amendment.... These decisions make it clear that only personal rights that can be deemed "fundamental" or "implicit in the concept of ordered liberty," ...are included in this guarantee of personal privacy. They also make it clear that the right has some extension to activities relating to marriage,... procreation,... contraception,... family relationships, ... and child rearing and education....

This right of privacy, whether it be founded in the Fourteenth Amendment's concept of personal liberty and restrictions upon state action, as we feel it is, or, as the District Court determined, in the Ninth Amendment's reservation of rights to the people, is broad enough to encompass a woman's decision whether or not to terminate her pregnancy. The detriment that the State would impose upon the pregnant woman by denying this choice altogether is apparent. Specific and direct harm medically diagnosable even in early pregnancy may be involved. Maternity, or additional off-spring, may force upon the woman a distressful life and future. Psychological harm may be imminent. Mental and physical health may be taxed by child care. There is also the distress, for all concerned, associated with the unwanted child, and there is the problem of bringing a child into a family already unable, psychologically and otherwise, to care for it. In other cases, as in this one, the additional difficulties and continuing stigma of unwed motherhood may be involved. All these are factors the woman and her responsible physician necessarily will consider in consultation.

On the basis of elements such as these, appellants and some *amici* argue that the woman's right is absolute and that she is entitled to terminate her pregnancy at whatever time, in whatever way, and for whatever reason she alone chooses. With this we do not agree. Appellants' arguments that Texas either has no valid interest at all in regulating the abortion decision, or no interest strong enough to support any limitation upon the woman's sole determination, is unpersuasive. The Court's decisions recognizing a right of privacy also acknowledge that some state regulation in areas protected by that right is appropriate. As noted above, a state may properly assert important interests in safeguarding health, in maintaining medical standards, and in protecting potential life. At some point in pregnancy, these respective interests become sufficiently compelling to sustain regulation of the factors that govern the abortion decision. The privacy right involved, therefore, cannot be said to be absolute. In fact, it is not clear to us that the claim asserted by some *amici* that one has an unlimited right to do with one's body as one pleases bears a close relationship to the right of privacy previously articulated in the Court's decisions. The Court has refused to recognize an unlimited right of this kind in the past....

We therefore conclude that the right of personal privacy includes the abortion decision, but that this right is not unqualified and must be considered against important state interests in regulation.

We note that those federal and state courts that have recently considered abortion law challenges have reached the same conclusion. A majority, in addition to the District Court in the present case, have held state laws unconstitutional, at least in part, because of vagueness or because of overbreadth and abridgement of rights....

Although the results are divided, most of these courts have agreed that the right of privacy, however based, is broad enough to cover the abortion decision;

that the right, nonetheless, is not absolute and is subject to some limitations; and that at some point the state interests as to protection of health, medical standards, and prenatal life, become dominant. We agree with this approach.

Where certain "fundamental rights" are involved, the Court has held that regulation limiting these rights may be justified only by a "compelling state interest." ...

In the recent abortion cases, cited above, courts have recognized these principles. Those striking down state laws have generally scrutinized the State's interest in protecting health and potential life and have concluded that neither interest justified broad limitations on the reasons for which a physician and his pregnant patient might decide that she should have an abortion in the early stages of pregnancy. Courts sustaining state laws have held that the State's determinations to protect health or prenatal life are dominant and constitutionally justifiable.

The District Court held that the appellee failed to meet his burden of demonstrating that the Texas statute's infringement upon Roe's rights was necessary to support a compelling state interest, and that, although the defendant presented "several compelling justifications for state presence in the area of abortions," the statutes outstripped these justifications and swept "far beyond any areas of compelling state interest." 314 F. Supp., at 1222–1223. Appellant and appellee both contest that holding. Appellant, as has been indicated, claims an absolute right that bars any state imposition of criminal penalties in the area. Appellee argues that the State's determination to recognize and protect prenatal life from and after conception constitutes a compelling state interest. As noted above, we do not agree fully with either formulation.

A. The appellee and certain *amici* argue that the fetus is a "person" within the language and meaning of the Fourteenth Amendment. In support of this they outline at length and in detail the well-known facts of fetal development. If this suggestion of personhood is established, the appellant's case, of course, collapses, for the fetus' right to life is then guaranteed specifically by the Amendment. The appellant conceded as much on reargument. On the other hand, the appellee conceded on reargument that no case could be cited that holds that a fetus is a person within the meaning of the Fourteenth Amendment.

The Constitution does not define "person" in so many words. Section 1 of the Fourteenth Amendment contains three references to "person." The first, in defining "citizens," speaks of "persons born or naturalized in the United States." The word also appears both in the Due Process Clause and in the Equal Protection Clause. "Person" is used in other places in the Constitution: in the listing of qualifications for representatives and senators,... in the Apportionment Clause,[1] ... in the Migration and Importation provision,... in the Emolument Clause,... in the Electors provisions; ... in the provision outlining qualifications for the office of President; ... in the Extradition provisions; ... and in the Fifth, Twelfth, and Twenty-second Amendments as well as in §§2 and 3 of

[1] We are not aware that in the taking of any census under this clause, a fetus has ever been counted.

the Fourteenth Amendment. But in nearly all these instances, the use of the word is such that it has application only postnatally. None indicates, with any assurance, that it has any possible pre-natal application.[2]

All this, together with our observation, *supra*, that throughout the major portion of the 19th century prevailing legal abortion practices were far freer than they are today, persuades us that the word "person," as used in the Fourteenth Amendment, does not include the unborn.[3] This is in accord with the results reached in those few cases where the issue has been squarely presented. . . .

This conclusion, however, does not of itself fully answer the contentions raised by Texas, and we pass on to other considerations.

B. The pregnant woman cannot be isolated in her privacy. She carries an embryo and, later, a fetus, if one accepts the medical definitions of the developing young in the human uterus.... The situation therefore is inherently different from marital intimacy, or bedroom possession of obscene material, or marriage, or procreation, or education.... As we have intimated above, it is reasonable and appropriate for a State to decide that at some point in time another interest, that of health of the mother or that of potential human life, becomes significantly involved. The woman's privacy is no longer sole and any right of privacy she possesses must be measured accordingly.

Texas urges that, apart from the Fourteenth Amendment, life begins at conception and is present throughout pregnancy, and that, therefore, the State has a compelling interest in protecting that life from and after conception. We need not resolve the difficult question of when life begins. When those trained in the respective disciplines of medicine, philosophy, and theology are unable to arrive at any consensus, the judiciary, at this point in the development of man's knowledge, is not in a position to speculate as to the answer.

It should be sufficient to note briefly the wide divergence of thinking on this most sensitive and difficult question. There has always been strong support for the view that life does not begin until live birth. This was the belief of the

[2] When Texas urges that a fetus is entitled to Fourteenth Amendment protection as a person, it faces a dilemma. Neither in Texas nor in any other State are all abortions prohibited. Despite broad proscription, an exception always exists. The exception contained in Art. 1196, for an abortion procured or attempted by medical advice for the purpose of saving the life of the mother, is typical. But if the fetus is a person who is not to be deprived of life without due process of law, and if the mother's condition is the sole determinant, does not the Texas exception appear to be out of line with the Amendment's command?

There are other inconsistencies between Fourteenth Amendment status and the typical abortion statute. It has already been pointed out, n. 49, *supra*, that in Texas the woman is not a principal or an accomplice with respect to an abortion upon her. If the fetus is a person, why is the woman not a principal or an accomplice? Further, the penalty for criminal abortion specified by Art. 1195 is significantly less than the maximum penalty for murder prescribed by Art. 1257 of the Texas Penal Code. If the fetus is a person, may the penalties be different?

[3] Cf. the Wisconsin abortion statute, defining "unbord child" to mean "a human being from the time of conception until it is born alive," Wis. Stat. §940.04 (6) (1969), and the new Connecticut statute, Public Act No. 1, May 1972 Special Session, declaring it to be the public policy of the State and the legislative intent "to protect and preserve human life from the moment of conception."

Stoics. It appears to be the predominant, though not the unanimous, attitude of the Jewish faith. It may be taken to represent also the position of a large segment of the Protestant community, insofar as that can be ascertained; organized groups that have taken a formal position on the abortion issue have generally regarded abortion as a matter for the conscience of the individual and her family. As we have noted, the common law found greater significance in quickening. Physicians and their scientific colleagues have regarded that event with less interest and have tended to focus either upon conception or upon live birth or upon the interim point at which the fetus becomes "viable," that is, potentially able to live outside the mother's womb, albeit with artificial aid. Viability is usually placed at about seven months (28 weeks) but may occur earlier, even at 24 weeks. The Aristotelian theory of "mediate animation," that held sway throughout the Middle Ages and the Renaissance in Europe, continued to be official Roman Catholic dogma until the 19th century, despite opposition to this "ensoulment" theory from those in the Church who would recognize the existence of life from the moment of conception. The latter is now, of course, the official belief of the Catholic Church. As one of the briefs *amicus* discloses, this is a view strongly held by many non-Catholics as well, and by many physicians. Substantial problems for precise definition of this view are posed, however, by new embryological data that purport to indicate that conception is a "process" over time, rather than an event, and by new medical techniques such as menstrual extraction, the "morning-after" pill, implantation of embryos, artificial insemination, and even artificial wombs.

In areas other than criminal abortion the law has been reluctant to endorse any theory that life, as we recognize it, begins before live birth or to accord legal rights to the unborn except in narrowly defined situations and except when the rights are contingent upon live birth. For example, the traditional rule of tort law had denied recovery for prenatal injuries even though the child was born alive. That rule has been changed in almost every jurisdiction. In most States recovery is said to be permitted only if the fetus was viable, or at least quick, when the injuries were sustained, though few courts have squarely so held. In a recent development, generally opposed by the commentators, some States permit the parents of a stillborn child to maintain an action for wrongful death because of prenatal injuries. Such an action, however, would appear to be one to vindicate the parents' interest and is thus consistent with the view that the fetus, at most, represents only the potentiality of life. Similarly, unborn children have been recognized as acquiring rights or interests by way of inheritance or other devolution of property, and have been represented by guardians *ad litem.* Perfection of the interests involved, again, has generally been contingent upon live birth. In short, the unborn have never been recognized in the law as persons in the whole sense.

In view of all this, we do not agree that, by adopting one theory of life, Texas may override the rights of the pregnant woman that are at stake. We repeat, however, that the State does have an important and legitimate interest in preserving and protecting the health of the pregnant woman, whether she be a resident of the State or a nonresident who seeks medical consultation and treatment there, and that it has still *another* important and legitimate interest in protecting the potentiality of human life. These interests are separate and distinct. Each grows in substantiality as the woman approaches term and, at a point during pregnancy, each becomes "compelling."

With respect to the State's important and legitimate interest in the health of the mother, the "compelling" point, in the light of present medical knowledge, is at approximately the end of the first trimester. This is so because of the now established and medical fact that until the end of the first trimester mortality in abortion is less than mortality in normal childbirth. It follows that, from and after this point, a State may regulate the abortion procedure to the extent that the regulation reasonably relates to the preservation and protection of maternal health. Examples of permissible state regulation in this area are requirements as to the qualifications of the person who is to perform the abortion; as to the licensure of that person; as to the facility in which the procedure is to be performed, that is, whether it must be a hospital or may be a clinic or some other place of less-than-hospital status; as to the licensing of the facility; and the like.

This means, on the other hand, that, for the period of pregnancy prior to this "compelling" point, the attending physician, in consultation with his patient, is free to determine, without regulation by the State, that in his medical judgment the patient's pregnancy should be terminated. If that decision is reached, the judgment may be effectuated by an abortion free of interference by the State.

With respect to the State's important and legitimate interest in potential life, the "compelling" point is at viability. This is so because the fetus then presumably has the capability of meaningful life outside the mother's womb. State regulation protective of fetal life after viability thus has both logical and biological justifications. If the State is interested in protecting fetal life after viability, it may go so far as to proscribe abortion during that period except when it is necessary to preserve the life or health of the mother.

Measured against these standards, Art. 1196 of the Texas Penal Code, in restricting legal abortions to those "procured or attempted by medical advice for the purpose of saving the life of the mother," sweeps too broadly. The statute makes no distinction between abortions performed early in pregnancy and those performed later, and it limits to a single reason, "saving" the mother's life, the legal justification for the procedure. The statute, therefore, cannot survive the constitutional attack made upon it here....

To summarize and to repeat:

1. A state criminal abortion statute of the current Texas type, that excepts from criminality only a *life saving* procedure on behalf of the mother, without regard to pregnancy stage and without recognition of the other interests involved, is violative of the Due Process Clause of the Fourteenth Amendment.

(a) For the stage prior to approximately the end of the first trimester, the abortion decision and its effectuation must be left to the medical judgment of the pregnant woman's attending physician.

(b) For the stage subsequent to approximately the end of the first trimester, the State, in promoting its interest in the health of the mother, may, if it chooses, regulate the abortion procedure in ways that are reasonably related to maternal health.

(c) For the stage subsequent to viability the State, in promoting its interest in the potentiality of human life, may, if it chooses, regulate, and even proscribe, abortion except where it is necessary, in appropriate medical judgment, for the preservation of the life or health of the mother.

2. The State may define the term "physician," as it has been employed in the preceding numbered paragraphs of this Part XI of this opinion, to mean only a physician currently licensed by the State, and may proscribe any abortion by a person who is not a physician as so defined.

In *Doe* v. *Bolton, post*, procedural requirements contained in one of the modern abortion statutes are considered. That opinion and this one, of course, are to be read together.

This holding, we feel, is consistent with the relative weights of the respective interests involved, with the lessons and example of medical and legal history, with the lenity of the common law, and with the demands of the profound problems of the present day. The decision leaves the State free to place increasing restrictions on abortion as the period of pregnancy lengthens, so long as those restrictions are tailored to the recognized state interests. The decision vindicates the right of the physician to administer medical treatment according to his professional judgment up to the points where important state interests provide compelling justifications for intervention. Up to those points the abortion decision in all its aspects is inherently, and primarily, a medical decision, and basic responsibility for it must rest with the physician. If an individual practitioner abuses the privilege of exercising proper medical judgment, the usual remedies, judicial and intra-professional, are available.

Abortion Is a Case of Moral Malice

THOMAS J. O'DONNELL

I WILL try to clarify two aspects of the traditional Catholic view on abortion: firstly, what the doctrine of the church has been and is now, and secondly, the components of the doctrine which have been most frequently misinterpreted or misunderstood.

As the nascent Christian church emerged from Galilee and Judea and began to carry the good news of the gospel into the heart of the Roman Empire, it immediately encountered certain mores which were inconsistent with the meaning of the message. It is not surprising that the new evangel—that men should know and love the one eternal God as Father and love each other as true

Reprinted with permission of the Association for the Study of Abortion.

brothers—might find some practices of pagan culture quite inconsistent with this new law of love; for this Christian love was to be, above all, a well-ordered and enlightened love. One of the very first of these moral problems encountered by the early church was the Roman disregard for the life of the unborn child. This disregard was reflected not only in the classical literature of Rome (as in both Juvenal and Ovid), but even in the Roman law condemning abortion, which did so with an eye more to the damage done to the expectant father than to the unborn infant.

Thus the first-century Christian *Didache* condemned abortion, as did several classic second-century Christian writings. This condemnation was picked up by Tertullian and Cyprian, among others, in the third century and was canonized by the Council of Elvira around the year 300 and by the Council of Ancyra. So it was that at the dawn of the Christian era one of the earliest moral imperatives to take form was against abortion because, as many of these writers phrased it, abortion of the human fetus was murder of the innocent.

It is true that to describe the destruction of the unborn child as the murder of the innocent is not a very euphemistic turn of phrase, but that is the way the theologians put it then—and that is the way it stands in Catholic doctrine, even today. This is, and always has been, the teaching of the Catholic church, reiterated in our own time by each of the twentieth-century popes and by the recent Second Vatican Council. Even the gentle John XXIII wrote regarding abortion: "Human life is sacred—all men must recognize that fact. From its very inception it reveals the creating hand of God. Those who violate His laws not only offend the divine majesty and degrade themselves and humanity, they also sap the vitality of the political community of which they are members" (Mater et Magistra, May 15, 1961), and the Second Vatican Council, in 1965, reunderlined the fact that in Catholic doctrine "abortion and infanticide are unspeakable crimes."

There are, however, three important modifications of this theme which have emerged throughout the long history of the church and are no less pertinent today. While they do not change the basic doctrine of the church on abortion, we must consider them briefly lest they be totally misunderstood. The first is the history of the theological speculation on abortion, the second is the variation in canonical discipline as distinct from moral doctrine, and the third is the extension of the moral malice of abortion even to the moment of conception.

Before turning our attention to these, however, we would do well to make some comment on the yet unanswered question: "When do the products of human conception become human?" or "At what stage of its development is the embryo, or fetus, a human being?"

Hippocrates, Aristotle, and Galen all struggled with the problem of the moment of specifically human animation, as did Tertullian and Apollinaris, Basil and Gregory of Nyssa, Jerome and Augustine, and Thomas Aquinas. The most common theory, that the conceptus passed through a vegetative and animal stage, finally becoming human about the fortieth day in the case of males and about the eightieth day in the case of females, is by no means bizarre against the background of the scientific method of the times. Men have generally concluded that things are probably what they appear to be. To the naked eye, a conceptus in its early stages does look like a sea anemone, and by the time an embryo is observable it looks almost like any animal embryo. At about forty days the phallic tubercule makes the embryo look more like a human male than a female, and the external genitalia of the female are not clearly discernible to the naked eye until about the eightieth day. With the theory accepted medically, it is not surprising that some contemporary theologians thought they saw confirmatory references in Leviticus (12:2–5), where the purification period of the parturient similarly varies according to the sex of the child.

While the moment of new human life still evades any known investigative process, it is interesting to note that the same scientific method of observation, aided today by modern microscopy, indicates chromosomal patterns in the nuclei of the earliest stages of cell division as specifically human and indeed already personally individualized, thus seeming to support the likelihood that from the moment of conception John is John, and not George.

The bearing which these considerations have had, and still have, on the doctrine of the Catholic church will become more explicit as we proceed.

I have already referred to three modifications of the basic doctrine on abortion—the first being the history of theological speculation on the subject. My report on the basic doctrine as the constant teaching of the church over her long history does not mean to imply that the theologians have never speculated on the subject, nor sought to defend the licitness of abortion under some extreme circumstances. Some have held that very early abortion was permissible under the delayed animation theory when this theory was a commonly accepted medical premise. Some few have even sought to defend late abortion under the principle of the unjust aggressor, or as the lesser of two evils, or as a necessity for baptizing the fetus, or even under the presumed willingness of the unborn child to sacrifice its right to life in favor of the safety of its mother. But all of these theories have been shown to be erroneous and deficient, and in the history of Catholic thinking they were never accepted by the church as Catholic doctrine.

The second modification to which I have referred is the variation in canonical discipline as distinct from moral doctrine. The canonical discipline of the church, imposing ecclesiastical penalties for certain public crimes, is not a moral code and only a lack of scholarship would interpret it as such. When the canon law prescribes an ecclesiastical penalty for a certain crime, or certain modalities of a crime, there is no implication that other modalities of the same crime, or similar crimes which are not mentioned in the law, are morally acceptable or even any less morally reprehensible. The fact that even at this moment contemporary canonical legislation inflicts the penalty of excommunication on those who "procure abortion," but not on those who perform embryotomy, in no way implies an approval of the latter form of infanticide, or even suggests a different degree of moral malice in the two acts. Nor is this type of legalism, though ecclesiastical, inappropriate within the context of external penal law. To view this type of canonical legislation as identified with, or even suggesting, a nuance of moral doctrine is to misunderstand completely the distinction between the two entities. This matter merits particular stress because some contemporary writers, insufficiently familiar with the structure of the church, have obviously mistaken changes in canonical legislation for doctrinal variations in the matter of abortion.

The third modification to which I have referred is the extension of the moral malice of abortion even to the moment of conception. This is a point of utmost importance for the clear and correct understanding of the Catholic position. At this juncture we should note that, although in some early instances there was a certain community of principle viewed as interrelating the questions of contraception and abortion, in the light of modern embryology this is no longer the case. Abortion is a question completely distinct from, and indeed unrelated to, the notion of contraception. The still unanswered question of the moment of ensoulment figures very large in this picture. If, for example, it could be conclusively shown that prior to the second trimester the fetus is not even probably a human being, the whole question of the morality of abortion in the first trimester would be a distinct problem in Catholic theology today.

You will recall that the Catholic church identifies the wrongness of abortion in the destruction of innocent human life. Quite obviously, then, if it were possible to verify the moment of ensoulment as later than the moment of conception, an abortion prior to ensoulment would not be the destruction of an innocent human life.

But since it is at least quite *probable* that ensoulment does coincide with the very earliest stages of embryonic life, the only practical working premise, from a moral viewpoint, is to treat the human conceptus as if the moment of a new and distinct human life were certainly the moment of conception. Since a new and distinct human life may very likely be present from that moment, directly to destroy the products of human conception, even at a very early stage of development, is at least very likely the destruction of an innocent human life.

One who does even this has already discarded from his moral code the inviolability of human life and the human person and falls far short of that regard for the dignity and rights of the individual which is basic to the entire Judeo-Christian theology and tradition. Such an action is identified with the moral malice of murder since it implies a willingness to take a human life.

As early as the fourth century, Basil pointed out the same analysis of the malice of abortion and wrote, regarding the fetus, that "any fine distinction as to its being completely formed or unformed is not admissible among us," and referred to those who procure abortion as "murderers."

In this essay I have reviewed the constant teaching of the Catholic church on abortion as the murder of the innocent. I have made some comment on the theories of ensoulment in relation to this doctrine, and I have commented briefly on three distinct facets of the doctrine which are frequently misunderstood. I have not, indeed, commented on the reasons why the Catholic church views the direct destruction of innocent human life as morally wrong. If some explanation of this moral stance is in order, suffice it to say that the Catholic church recognizes the echo of sound Catholic doctrine in those immortal words of the American Declaration of Independence so basic to our American way of life: "We hold these truths to be self-evident, that all men are created equal, that they are endowed by their Creator with certain unalienable Rights"—and that among these is the right to Life.

The Doctrine of the Double Effect

PHILIPPA FOOT

ONE OF the reasons why most of us feel puzzled about the problem of abortion is that we want, and do not want, to allow to the unborn child the rights that belong to adults and children. When we think of a baby about to be born it seems absurd to think that the next few minutes or even hours could make so radical a difference to its status; yet as we go back in the life of the foetus we are more and more reluctant to say that this is a human being and must be treated as such. No doubt this is the deepest source of our dilemma, but it is not the only one. For we are also confused about the general question of what we may and may not do where the interests of human beings conflict. We have strong intuitions about certain cases; saying, for instance, that it is all right to raise the level of education in our country, though statistics allow us to predict that a rise in the suicide rate will follow, while it is not all right to kill the feeble-minded to aid cancer research. It is not easy, however, to see the principles involved, and one way of throwing light on the abortion issue will be by setting up parallels involving adults or children once born. So we will be able to isolate the "equal rights" issue, and should be able to make some advance.

I shall not, of course, discuss all the principles that may be used in deciding what to do where the interest or rights of human beings conflict. What I want to do is to look at one particular theory, known as the "doctrine of the double effect" which is invoked by Catholics in support of their views on abortion but supposed by them to apply elsewhere. As used in the abortion argument this doctrine has often seemed to non-Catholics to be a piece of complete sophistry. In the last number of the *Oxford Review* it was given short shrift by Professor Hart.[1] And yet this principle has seemed to some non-Catholics as well as to Catholics to stand as the only defence against decisions on other issues that are quite unacceptable. It will help us in our difficulty about abortion if this conflict can be resolved.

The doctrine of the double effect is based on a distinction between what a

[1] H. L. A. Hart, "Intention and Punishment," *Oxford Review*, Number 4, Hilary 1967. I owe much to this article and to a conversation with Professor Hart, though I do not know whether he will approve of what follows.

Reprinted with permission of the author from the *Oxford Review*, 1967, 29–41.

man foresees as a result of his voluntary action and what, in the strict sense, he intends. He intends in the strictest sense both those things that he aims at as ends and those that he aims at at means to his ends. The latter may be regretted in themselves but nevertheless desired for the sake of the end, as we may intend to keep dangerous lunatics confined for the sake of our safety. By contrast a man is said not strictly, or directly, to intend the foreseen consequences of his voluntary actions where these are neither the end at which he is aiming nor the means to this end. Whether the word "intention" should be applied in both cases is not of course what matters: Bentham spoke of "oblique intention," contrasting it with the "direct intention" of ends and means, and we may as well follow his terminology. Everyone must recognize that some such distinction can be made, though it may be made in a number of different ways, and it is the distinction that is crucial to the doctrine of the double effect. The words "double effect" refer to the two effects that an action may produce: the one aimed at, and the one foreseen but in no way desired. By "the doctrine of the double effect" I mean the thesis that it is sometimes permissible to bring about by oblique intention what one may not directly intend. Thus the distinction is held to be relevant to moral decision in certain difficult cases. It is said for instance that the operation of hysterectomy involves the death of the foetus as the foreseen but not strictly or directly intended consequence of the surgeon's act, while other operations kill the child and count as the direct intention of taking an innocent life, a distinction that has evoked particularly bitter reactions on the part of non-Catholics. If you are permitted to bring about the death of the child, what does it matter how it is done? The doctrine of the double effect is also used to show why in another case, where a woman in labour will die unless a craniotomy operation is performed, the intervention is not to be condoned. There, it is said, we may not operate but must let the mother die. We foresee her death but do not directly intend it, whereas to crush the skull of the child would count as direct intention of its death.[2]

This last application of the doctrine has been queried by Professor Hart on the ground that the child's death is not strictly a means to saving the mother's life and should logically be treated as an unwanted but foreseen consequence by those who make use of the distinction between direct and oblique intention. To interpret the doctrine in this way is perfectly reasonable given the language that has been used; it would, however, make nonsense of it from the beginning. A certain event may be desired under one of its descriptions, unwanted under another, but we cannot treat these as two different events, one of which is aimed at and the other not. And even if it be argued that there are here two different events—the crushing of the child's skull and its death—the two are obviously much too close for an application of the doctrine of the double effect. To see how odd it would be to apply the principle like this we may consider the story,

[2] For discussions of the Catholic doctrine on abortion see Glanville Williams, *The Sanctity of Life and the Criminal Law* (New York, 1957); also N. St. John Stevas, *The Right to Life* (London, 1963).

well known to philosophers, of the fat man stuck in the mouth of the cave. A party of potholers have imprudently allowed the fat man to lead them as they make their way out of the cave, and he gets stuck, trapping the others behind him. Obviously the right thing to do is to sit down and wait until the fat man grows thin; but philosophers have arranged that flood waters should be rising within the cave. Luckily (luckily?) the trapped party have with them a stick of dynamite with which they can blast the fat man out of the mouth of the cave. Either they use the dynamite or they drown. In one version the fat man, whose head is *in* the cave, will drown with them; in the other he will be rescued in due course.[3] Problem: may they use the dynamite or not? Later we will find parallels to this example. Here it is introduced for light relief and because it will serve to show how ridiculous one version of the doctrine of the double effect would be. For suppose that the trapped explorers were to argue that the death of the fat man might be taken as a merely foreseen consequence of the act of blowing him up. ("We didn't want to kill him . . . only to blow him into small pieces" or even ". . . only to blast him out of the mouth of the cave.") I believe that those who use the doctrine of the double effect would rightly reject such a suggestion, though they will, of course, have considerable difficulty in explaining where the line is to be drawn. What is to be the criterion of "closeness" if we say that anything very close to what we are literally aiming at counts as if part of our aim?

Let us leave this difficulty aside and return to the arguments for and against the doctrine, supposing it to be formulated in the way considered most effective by its supporters, and ourselves bypassing the trouble by taking what must on any reasonable definition be clear cases of "direct" or "oblique" intention.

The first point that should be made clear, in fairness to the theory, is that no one is suggesting that it does not matter what you bring about as long as you merely foresee and do not strictly intend the evil that follows. We might think, for instance, of the (actual) case of wicked merchants selling, for cooking, oil they knew to be poisonous and thereby killing a number of innocent people, comparing and contrasting it with that of some unemployed gravediggers, desperate for custom, who got hold of this same oil and sold it (or perhaps *they* secretly gave it away) in order to create orders for graves. They strictly (directly) intend the deaths they cause, while the merchants could say that it was not part of their *plan* that anyone should die. In morality, as in law, the merchants, like the gravediggers, would be considered as murderers; nor are the supporters of the doctrine of the double effect bound to say that there is the least difference between them in respect of moral turpitude. What they are committed to is the thesis that *sometimes* it makes a difference to the permissibility of an action involving harm to others that this harm, although foreseen, is not part of the agent's direct intention. An end such as earning one's living is clearly not such as to justify *either* the direct or oblique intention of the death of innocent

[3] It was Professor Hart who drew my attention to this distinction.

people, but in certain cases one is justified in bringing about knowingly what one could not directly intend.

It is now time to say why this doctrine should be taken seriously in spite of the fact that it sounds rather odd, that there are difficulties about the distinction on which it depends, and that it seemed to yield one sophistical conclusion when applied to the problem of abortion. The reason for its appeal is that its opponents have often *seemed* to be committed to quite indefensible views. Thus the controversy has raged around examples such as the following. Suppose that a judge or magistrate is faced with rioters demanding that a culprit be found for a certain crime and threatening otherwise to take their own bloody revenge on a particular section of the community. The real culprit being unknown, the judge sees himself as able to prevent the bloodshed only by framing some innocent person and having him executed. Beside this example is placed another in which a pilot whose aeroplane is about to crash is deciding whether to steer from a more to a less inhabited area. To make the parallel as close as possible it may rather be supposed that he is the driver of a runaway tram which he can only steer from one narrow track on to another; five men are working on one track and one man on the other; anyone on the track he enters is bound to be killed. In the case of the riots the mob have five hostages, so that in both the exchange is supposed to be one man's life for the lives of five. The question is why we should say, without hesitation, that the driver should steer for the less occupied track, while most of us would be appalled at the idea that the innocent man could be framed. It may be suggested that the special feature of the latter case is that it involves the corruption of justice, and this is, of course, very important indeed. But if we remove that special feature, supposing that some private individual is to kill an innocent person and pass him off as the criminal we still find ourselves horrified by the idea. The doctrine of the double effect offers us a way out of the difficulty, insisting that it is one thing to steer towards someone foreseeing that you will kill him and another to aim at his death as part of your plan. Moreover there is one very important element of good in what is here insisted. In real life it would hardly ever be certain that the man on the narrow track would be killed. Perhaps he might find a foothold on the side of the tunnel and cling on as the vehicle hurtled by. The driver of the tram does *not* then leap off and brain him with a crowbar. The judge, however, needs the death of the innocent man for his (good) purposes. If the victim proves hard to hang he must see to it that he dies another way. To choose to execute him is to choose that this evil *shall come about*, and this must therefore count as a *certainty* in weighing up the good and evil involved. The distinction between direct and oblique intention is crucial here, and is of great importance in an uncertain world. Nevertheless this is no way to defend the doctrine of the double effect. For the question is whether the difference between aiming at something and obliquely intending it is *in itself* relevant to moral decisions; not whether it is important when correlated with a difference of certainty in the balance of good and evil. Moreover we are particularly interested in the application of the doctrine of the double effect to the question of abortion, and no one can deny that in medicine there are sometimes certainties so complete that it would be a mere quibble to speak of the "probable outcome" of this course of action or that. It is not, therefore, with a merely philosophical interest that we should put aside the uncertainty and scrutinize the examples to test the doctrine of the double effect. Why can we not argue from the case of the steering driver to that of the judge?

Another pair of examples poses a similar problem. We are about to give a patient who needs it to save his life a massive dose of a certain drug in short supply. There arrive, however, five other patients each of whom could be saved by one-fifth of that dose. We say with regret that we cannot spare our whole supply of the drug for a single patient, just as we should say that we could not spare the whole resources of a ward for one dangerously ill individual when ambulances arrive bringing in the victims of a multiple crash. We feel bound to let one man die rather than many if that is our only choice. Why then do we not feel justified in killing people in the interests of cancer research or to obtain, let us say, spare parts for grafting on to those who need them? We can suppose, similarly, that several dangerously ill people can be saved only if we kill a certain individual and make a serum from his dead body. (These examples are not over fanciful considering present controversies about prolonging the life of mortally ill patients whose eyes or kidneys are to be used for others.) Why cannot we argue from the case of the scarce drug to that of the body needed for medical purposes? Once again the doctrine of the double effect comes up with an explanation. In one kind of case but not the other we aim at the death of the innocent man.

A further argument suggests that if the doctrine of the double effect is rejected this has the consequence of putting us hopelessly in the power of bad men. Suppose for example that some tyrant should threaten to torture five men if we ourselves would not torture one. Would it be our duty to do so, supposing we believed him, because this would be no different from choosing to rescue five men from his tortures rather than one? If so anyone who wants us to do something we think wrong has only to threaten that otherwise he himself will do something we think worse. A mad murderer, known to keep his promises, could thus make it our duty to kill some innocent citizen to prevent him from killing two. From this conclusion we are again rescued by the doctrine of the double effect. If we refuse, we foresee that the greater number will be killed but we do not intend it: it is he who intends (that is strictly or directly intends) the death of innocent persons; we do not.

At one time I thought that these arguments in favour of the doctrine of the double effect were conclusive, but I now believe that the conflict should be solved in another way. The clue that we should follow is that the strength of the doctrine seems to lie in the distinction it makes between what we *do* (equated with direct intention) and what we allow (thought of as obliquely intended). Indeed it is interesting that the disputants tend to argue about whether we are to be held responsible for what we allow as we are for what we do.[4] Yet it is not obvious that this is what they should be discussing, since the distinction between what one does and what one allows to happen is not the same as that between direct and oblique intention. To see this one has only to consider that it is possible *deliberately* to allow something to happen, aiming at it either for its own sake or as part of one's plan for obtaining something else. So one person might want another person dead, and deliberately allow him to die. And again one may be said to *do* things that one does not aim at, as the steering driver would kill the man on the track. Moreover there is a large class of things said to be brought about rather than either done or allowed, and either kind of intention is possible. So it is possible to *bring about* a man's death by getting him to go to sea in a leaky boat, and the intention of his death may be either direct or oblique.

Whatever it may, or may not, have to do with the doctrine of the double effect, the idea of *allowing* is worth looking into in this context. I shall leave aside the special case of giving permission, which involves the idea of authority, and consider the two main divisions into which cases of allowing seem to fall. There is firstly the allowing which is forbearing to prevent. For this we need a sequence thought of as somehow already in train, and something that the agent could do to intervene. (The agent must be able to intervene, but does not do so.) So, for instance, he could warn someone, but *allows* him to walk into a trap. He could feed an animal but *allows* it to die for lack of food. He could stop a leaking tap but *allows* the water to go on flowing. This is the case of allowing with which we shall be concerned, but the other should be mentioned. It is the kind of allowing which is roughly equivalent to *enabling*; the root idea being the removal of some obstacle which is, as it were, holding back a train of events. So someone may remove a plug and *allow* water to flow; open a door and *allow* an animal to get out; or give someone money and *allow* him to get back on his feet.

The first kind of allowing requires an omission, but there is no other general correlation between omission and allowing, commission and bringing about or doing. An actor who fails to turn up for a performance will generally spoil it rather than allow it to be spoiled. I mention the distinction between omission and commission only to set it aside.

Thinking of the first kind of allowing (forbearing to prevent), we should ask whether there is any difference, from the moral point of view, between what one does or causes and what one merely allows. It seems clear that on occasions one is just as bad as the other, as is recognized in both morality and law. A man may murder his child or his aged relatives, by allowing them to die of starvation as well as by giving poison; he may also be convicted of murder on either account. In another case we would, however, make a distinction. Most of us allow people to die of starvation in India and Africa, and there is surely

[4] See, e.g., J. Bennett, "Whatever the Consequences," *Analysis*, January 1966, and G. E. M. Anscombe's reply in *Analysis*, June 1966. See also Miss Anscombe's "Modern Moral Philosophy" in *Philosophy*, January 1958.

something wrong with us that we do; it would be nonsense, however, to pretend that it is only in law that we make a distinction between allowing people in the underdeveloped countries to die of starvation and sending them poisoned food. There is worked into our moral system a distinction between what we owe people in the form of aid and what we owe them in the way of non-interference. Salmond, in his *Jurisprudence*, expressed as follows the distinction between the two.

> A positive right corresponds to a positive duty, and is a right that he on whom the duty lies shall do some positive act on behalf of the person entitled. A negative right corresponds to a negative duty, and is a right that the person bound shall refrain from some act which would operate to the prejudice of the person entitled. The former is a right to be positively benefited; the latter is merely a right not to be harmed.[5]

As a general account of rights and duties this is defective, since not all are so closely connected with benefit and harm. Nevertheless for our purposes it will do well. Let us speak of negative duties when thinking of the obligation to refrain from such things as killing or robbing, and of the positive duty, e.g., to look after children or aged parents. It will be useful, however, to extend the notion of positive duty beyond the range of things that are strictly called duties, bringing acts of charity under this heading. These are owed only in a rather loose sense, and some acts of charity could hardly be said to be *owed* at all, so I am not following ordinary usage at this point.

Let us now see whether the distinction of negative and positive duties explains why we see differently the action of the steering driver and that of the judge, of the doctors who withhold the scarce drug and those who obtain a body for medical purposes, of those who choose to rescue the five men rather than one man from torture and those who are ready to torture the one man themselves in order to save five. In each case we have a conflict of duties, but what kind of duties are they? Are we, in each case, weighing positive duties against positive, negative against negative, or one against the other? Is the duty to refrain from injury, or rather to bring aid?

The steering driver faces a conflict of negative duties, since it is his duty to avoid injuring five men and also his duty to avoid injuring one. In the circumstances he is not able to avoid both, and it seems clear that he should do the least injury he can. The judge, however, is weighing the duty of not inflicting injury against the duty of bringing aid. He wants to rescue the innocent people threatened with death but can do so only by inflicting injury himself. Since one does not *in general* have the same duty to help people as to refrain from injuring them, it is not possible to argue to a conclusion about what he should do from the steering driver case. It is interesting that, even where the strictest duty of positive aid exists, this still does not weigh as if a negative duty were involved. It is not, for instance, permissible to commit a murder to bring one's starving children food. If the choice is between inflicting injury on one or many there

[5] J. Salmond, *Jurisprudence*, 11th edition, p. 283.

seems only one rational course of action; if the choice is between aid to some at the cost of injury to others, and refusing to inflict the injury to bring the aid, the whole matter is open to dispute. So it is not inconsistent of us to think that the driver must steer for the road on which only one man stands while the judge (or his equivalent) may not kill the innocent person in order to stop the riots. Let us now consider the second pair of examples, which concern the scarce drug on the one hand and on the other the body needed to save lives. Once again we find a difference based on the distinction between the duty to avoid injury and the duty to provide aid. Where one man needs a massive dose of the drug and we withhold it from him in order to save five men, we are weighing aid against aid. But if we consider killing a man in order to use his body to save others, we are thinking of doing him injury to bring others aid. In an interesting variant of the model, we may suppose that instead of killing someone we deliberately let him die. (Perhaps he is a beggar to whom we are thinking of giving food, but then we say "No, they need bodies for medical research.") Here it does seem relevant that in allowing him to die we are aiming at his death, but presumably we are inclined to see this as a violation of negative rather than positive duty. If this is right, we see why we are unable in either case to argue to a conclusion from the case of the scarce drug.

In the examples involving the torturing of one man or five men, the principle seems to be the same as for the last pair. If we are bringing aid (rescuing people about to be tortured by the tyrant), we must obviously rescue the larger rather than the smaller group. It does not follow, however, that we would be justified in inflicting the injury, or getting a third person to do so, in order to save the five. We may therefore refuse to be forced into acting by the threats of bad men. To refrain from inflicting injury ourselves is a stricter duty than to prevent other people from inflicting injury, which is not to say that the other is not a very strict duty indeed.

So far the conclusions are the same as those at which we might arrive following the doctrine of the double effect, but in others they will be different, and the advantage seems to be all on the side of the alternative. Suppose, for instance, that there are five patients in a hospital whose lives could be saved by the manufacture of a certain gas, but that this inevitably releases lethal fumes into the room of another patient whom for some reason we are unable to move. His death, being of no use to us, is clearly a side effect, and not directly intended. Why then is the case different from that of the scarce drug, if the point about that is that we foresaw but did not strictly intend the death of the single patient? Yet it surely is different. The relatives of the gassed patient would presumably be successful if they sued the hospital and the whole story came out. We may find it particularly revolting that someone should be *used* as in the case where he is killed or allowed to die in the interest of medical research, and the fact of *using* may even determine what we would decide to do in some cases, but the principle seems unimportant compared with our reluctance to bring such injury for the sake of giving aid.

My conclusion is that the distinction between direct and oblique intention plays only a quite subsidiary role in determining what we say in these cases, while the distinction between avoiding injury and bringing aid is very important indeed. I have not, of course, argued that there are no other principles. For instance it clearly makes a difference whether our positive duty is a strict duty or rather an act of charity: feeding our own children or feeding those in far away countries. It may also make a difference whether the person about to suffer is one thought of as uninvolved in the threatened disaster, and whether it is his presence that constitutes the threat to the others. In many cases we find it very hard to know what to say, and I have not been arguing for any general conclusion such as that we may never, whatever the balance of good and evil, bring injury to one for the sake of aid to others, even when this injury amounts to death. I have only tried to show that even if we reject the doctrine of the double effect we are not forced to the conclusion that the size of the evil must always be our guide.

Let us now return to the problem of abortion, carrying out our plan of finding parallels involving adults or children rather than the unborn. We must say something about the different cases in which abortion might be considered on medical grounds.

First of all there is the situation in which nothing that can be done will save the life of child and mother, but where the life of the mother can be saved by killing the child. This is parallel to the case of the fat man in the mouth of the cave who is bound to be drowned with the others if nothing is done. Given the certainty of the outcome, as it was postulated, there is no serious conflict of interests here, since the fat man will perish in either case, and it is reasonable that the action that will save someone should be done. It is a great objection to those who argue that the direct intention of the death of an innocent person is never justifiable that the edict will apply even in this case. The Catholic doctrine on abortion must here conflict with that of most reasonable men. Moreover we would be justified in performing the operation whatever the method used, and it is neither a necessary nor a good justification of the special case of hysterectomy that the child's death is not directly intended, but rather a foreseen consequence of what is done. What difference could it make as to how the death is brought about?

Secondly we have the case in which it is possible to perform an operation which will save the mother and kill the child or kill the mother and save the child. This is parallel to the famous case of the shipwrecked mariners who believed that they must throw someone overboard if their boat was not to founder in a storm, and to the other famous case of the two sailors, Dudley and Stephens, who killed and ate the cabin boy when adrift on the sea without food. Here again there is no conflict of interests so far as the decision to act is concerned; only in deciding whom to save. Once again it would be reasonable to act, though one would respect someone who held back from the appalling action either because he preferred to perish rather than do such a thing or because he held on past the limits of reasonable hope. In real life the certainties postulated by philosophers hardly ever exist, and Dudly and Stephens were rescued not long after their ghastly meal. Nevertheless if the certainty were absolute, as it might be in the abortion case, it would seem better to save one than none. Probably we should decide in favour of the mother when weighing her life against that of the unborn child, but it is interesting that, a few years later, we might easily decide it the other way.

The worst dilemma comes in the third kind of example where to save the mother we must kill the child, say by crushing its skull, while if nothing is done the mother will perish but the child can be safely delivered after her death. Here the doctrine of the double effect has been invoked to show that we may not intervene, since the child's death would be directly intended while the mother's would not. On a strict parallel with cases not involving the unborn we might find the conclusion correct though the reason given was wrong. Suppose, for instance, that in later life the presence of a child was certain to bring death to the mother. We would surely not think ourselves justified in ridding her of it by a process that involved its death. For in general we do not think that we can kill one innocent person to rescue another, quite apart from the special care that we feel is due to children once they have prudently got themselves born. What we would be prepared to do when a great many people were involved is another matter, and this is probably the key to one quite common view of abortion on the part of those who take quite seriously the rights of the unborn child. They probably feel that if *enough* people are involved one must be sacrificed, and they think of the mother's life against the unborn child's life as if it were many against one. But of course many people do not view it like this at all, having no inclination to accord to the foetus or unborn child anything like ordinary human status in the matter of rights. I have not been arguing for or against these points of view but only trying to discern some of the currents that are pulling us back and forth. The levity of the examples is not meant to offend.

A Defence of Abortion[1]

JUDITH J. THOMSON

MOST opposition to abortion relies on the premise that the fetus is a human being, a person, from the moment of conception. The premise is argued for, but, as I think, not well. Take, for example, the most common argument. We are asked to notice that the development of a human being from conception through birth into childhood is continuous; then it is said that to

[1] I am very much indebted to James Thomson for discussion, criticism, and many helpful suggestions.

draw a line, to choose a point in this development and say "before this point the thing is not a person, after this point it is a person" is to make an arbitrary choice, a choice for which in the nature of things no good reason can be given. It is concluded that the fetus is, or anyway that we had better say it is, a person from the moment of conception. But this conclusion does not follow. Similar things might be said about the development of an acorn into an oak tree, and it does not follow that acorns are oak trees, or that we had better say they are. Arguments of this form are sometimes called "slippery slope arguments"—the phrase is perhaps self-explanatory—and it is dismaying that opponents of abortion rely on them so heavily and uncritically.

I am inclined to agree, however, that the prospects for "drawing a line" in the development of the fetus look dim. I am inclined to think also that we shall probably have to agree that the fetus has already become a human person well before birth. Indeed, it comes as a surprise when one first learns how early in its life it begins to acquire human characteristics. By the tenth week, for example, it already has a face, arms and legs, fingers and toes; it has internal organs, and brain activity is detectable.[2] On the other hand, I think that the premise is false, that the fetus is not a person from the moment of conception. A newly fertilized ovum, a newly implanted clump of cells, is no more a person than an acorn is an oak tree. But I shall not discuss any of this. For it seems to me to be of great interest to ask what happens if, for the sake of argument, we allow the premise. How, precisely, are we supposed to get from there to the conclusion that abortion is morally impermissible? Opponents of abortion commonly spend most of their time establishing that the fetus is a person, and hardly any time explaining the step from there to the impermissibility of abortion. Perhaps they think the step too simple and obvious to require much comment. Or perhaps instead they are simply being economical in argument. Many of those who defend abortion rely on the premise that the fetus is not a person, but only a bit of tissue that will become a person at birth; and why pay out more arguments than you have to? Whatever the explanation, I suggest that the step they take is neither easy nor obvious, that it calls for closer examination than it is commonly given, and that when we do give it this closer examination we shall feel inclined to reject it.

I propose, then, that we grant that the fetus is a person from the moment of conception. How does the argument go from here? Something like this, I take it. Every person has a right to life. So the fetus has a right to life. No doubt the mother has a right to decide what shall happen in and to her body; everyone would grant that. But surely a person's right to life is stronger and more stringent than the mother's right to decide what happens in and to her body,

[2] Daniel Callahan, *Abortion: Law, Choice and Morality* (New York, 1970), p. 373. This book gives a fascinating survey of the available information on abortion. The Jewish tradition is surveyed in David M. Feldman, *Birth Control in Jewish Law* (New York, 1968), Part 5, the Catholic tradition in John T. Noonan, Jr., "An Almost Absolute Value in History," in *The Morality of Abortion*, ed. John T. Noonan, Jr. Cambridge, Mass., 1970).

and so outweighs it. So the fetus may not be killed; an abortion may not be performed.

It sounds plausible. But now let me ask you to imagine this. You wake up in the morning and find yourself back to back in bed with an unconscious violinist. A famous unconscious violinist. He has been found to have a fatal kidney ailment, and the Society of Music Lovers has canvassed all the available medical records and found that you alone have the right blood type to help. They have therefore kidnapped you, and last night the violinist's circulatory system was plugged into yours, so that your kidneys can be used to extract poisons from his blood as well as your own. The director of the hospital now tells you, "Look, we're sorry the Society of Music Lovers did this to you—we would never have permitted it if we had known. But still, they did it, and the violinist now is plugged into you. To unplug you would be to kill him. But never mind, it's only for nine months. By then he will have recovered from his ailment, and can safely be unplugged from you." Is it morally incumbent on you to accede to this situation? No doubt it would be very nice of you if you did, a great kindness. But do you *have* to accede to it? What if it were not nine months, but nine years? Or longer still? What if the director of the hospital says, "Tough luck, I agree, but you've now got to stay in bed, with the violinist plugged into you, for the rest of your life. Because remember this. All persons have a right to life, and violinists are persons. Granted you have a right to decide what happens in and to your body, but a person's right to life outweighs your right to decide what happens in and to your body. So you cannot ever be unplugged from him." I imagine you would regard this as outrageous, which suggests that something really is wrong with that plausible-sounding argument I mentioned a moment ago.

In this case, of course, you were kidnapped; you didn't volunteer for the operation that plugged the violinist into your kidneys. Can those who oppose abortion on the ground I mentioned make an exception for a pregnancy due to rape? Certainly. They can say that persons have a right to life only if they didn't come into existence because of rape; or they can say that all persons have a right to life, but that some have less of a right to life than others, in particular, that those who came into existence because of rape have less. But these statements have a rather unpleasant sound. Surely the question of whether you have a right to life at all, or how much of it you have, shouldn't turn on the question of whether or not you are the product of a rape. And in fact the people who oppose abortion on the ground I mentioned do not make this distinction, and hence do not make an exception in case of rape.

Nor do they make an exception for a case in which the mother has to spend the nine months of her pregnancy in bed. They would agree that would be a great pity, and hard on the mother; but all the same, all persons have a right to life, the fetus is a person, and so on. I suspect, in fact, that they would not make an exception for a case in which miraculously enough, the pregnancy went on for nine years, or even the rest of the mother's life.

Some won't even make an exception for a case in which continuation of the pregnancy is likely to shorten the mother's life; they regard abortion as impermissible even to save the mother's life. Such cases are nowadays very rare, and many opponents of abortion do not accept this extreme view. All the same, it is a good place to begin: a number of points of interest come out in respect to it.

1. Let us call the view that abortion is impermissible even to save the mother's life "the extreme view." I want to suggest first that it does not issue from the argument I mentioned earlier without the addition of some fairly powerful premises. Suppose a woman has become pregnant, and now learns that she has a cardiac condition such that she will die if she carries the baby to term. What may be done for her? The fetus, being a person, has a right to life, but as the mother is a person too, so has she a right to life. Presumably they have an equal right to life. How is it supposed to come out that an abortion may not be performed? If mother and child have an equal right to life, shouldn't we perhaps flip a coin? Or should we add to the mother's right to life her right to decide what happens in and to her body, which everybody seems to be ready to grant—the sum of her rights now outweighing the fetus' right to life?

The most familiar argument here is the following. We are told that performing the abortion would be directly killing[3] the child, whereas doing nothing would not be killing the mother, but only letting her die. Moreover, in killing the child, one would be killing an innocent person, for the child has committed no crime, and is not aiming at his mother's death. And then there are a variety of ways in which this might be continued. (1) But as directly killing an innocent person is always and absolutely impermissible, an abortion may not be performed. Or, (2) as directly killing an innocent person is murder, and murder is always and absolutely impermissible, an abortion may not be performed.[4] Or, (3) as one's duty to refrain from directly killing an innocent person is more stringent than one's duty to keep a person from dying, an abortion may not be performed. Or (4) if one's only options are directly killing an innocent person or letting a person die, one must prefer letting the person die, and thus an abortion may not be performed.[5]

Some people seem to have thought that these are not further premises which must be added if the conclusion is to be reached, but that they follow from the

[3] The term "direct" in the arguments I refer to is a technical one. Roughly what is meant by "direct killing" is either killing as an end in itself or killing as a means to some end, for example, the end of saving someone else's life, see note 6, below, for an example of its use.

[4] Cf. *Encyclical Letter of Pope Pius XI on Christian Marriage*, St. Paul Editions (Boston, n.d.), p. 32: "however much we may pity the mother whose health and even life is gravely imperiled in the performance of the duty allotted to her by nature, nevertheless what could ever be a sufficient reason for excusing in any way the direct murder of the innocent? This is precisely what we are dealing with here." Noonan (*The Morality of Abortion*, p. 43) reads this as follows: "What cause can ever avail to excuse in any way the direct killing of the innocent? For it is a question of that."

[5] The thesis in (4) is in an interesting way weaker than those in (1), (2), and (3): they rule out abortion even in cases in which both mother *and* child will die if the abortion is not performed. By contrast, one who held the view expressed in (4) could consistently say that one needn't prefer letting two persons die to killing one.

very fact that an innocent person has a right to life.[6] But this seems to me to be a mistake, and perhaps the simplest way to show this is to bring out that while we must certainly grant that innocent persons have a right to life, the theses in (1) through (4) are all false. Take (2), for example. If directly killing an innocent person is murder, and thus is impermissible, then the mother's directly killing the innocent person inside her is murder, and thus is impermissible. But it cannot seriously be thought to be murder if the mother performs an abortion on herself to save her life. It cannot seriously be said that she *must* refrain, that she *must* sit passively by and wait for her death. Let us look again at the case of you and the violinist. There you are, in bed with the violinist, and the director of the hospital says to you, "It's all most distressing, and I deeply sympathize, but you see this is putting an additional strain on your kidneys, and you'll be dead within the month. But you *have* to stay where you are all the same. Because unplugging you would be directly killing an innocent violinist, and that's murder, and that's impermissible." If anything in the world is true, it is that you do not commit murder, you do not do what is impermissible, if you reach around to your back and unplug yourself from that violinist to save your life.

The main focus of attention in writings on abortion has been on what a third party may or may not do in answer to a request from a woman for an abortion. This is in a way understandable. Things being as they are, there isn't much a woman can safely do to abort herself. So the question asked is what a third party may do, and what the mother may do, if it is mentioned at all, is deduced, almost as an afterthought, from what it is concluded that third parties may do. But it seems to me that to treat the matter in this way is to refuse to grant to the mother that very status of person which is so firmly insisted on for the fetus. For we cannot simply read off what a person may do from what a third party may do. Suppose you find yourself trapped in a tiny house with a growing child. I mean a very tiny house, and a rapidly growing child—you are already up against the wall of the house and in a few minutes you'll be crushed to death. The child on the other hand won't be crushed to death; if nothing is done to stop him from growing he'll be hurt, but in the end he'll simply burst open the house and walk out a free man. Now I could well understand it if a bystander were to say, "There's nothing we can do for you. We cannot choose between your life and his, we cannot be the ones to decide who is to live, we cannot intervene." But it cannot be concluded that you too can do nothing, that you cannot attack it to save your life. However innocent the child may be, you do not have to wait passively while it crushes you to death. Perhaps a pregnant

[6] Cf. the following passage from Pius XII, *Address to the Italian Catholic Society of Midwives*: "The baby in the maternal breast has the right to life immediately from God.—Hence there is no man, no human authority, no science, no medical, eugenic, social, economic or moral 'indication' which can establish or grant a valid juridical ground for a direct deliberate disposition of an innocent human life, that is a disposition which looks to its destruction either as an end or as a means to another end perhaps in itself not illicit.—The baby, still not born, is a man in the same degree and for the same reason as the mother" (quoted in Noonan, *The Morality of Abortion*, p. 45).

woman is vaguely felt to have the status of house, to which we don't allow the right of self-defense. But if the woman houses the child, it should be remembered that she is a person who houses it.

I should perhaps stop to say explicitly that I am not claiming that people have a right to do anything whatever to save their lives. I think, rather, that there are drastic limits to the right of self-defense. If someone threatens you with death unless you torture someone else to death, I think you have not the right, even to save your life, to do so. But the case under consideration here is very different. In our case there are only two people involved, one whose life is threatened, and one who threatens it. Both are innocent: the one who is threatened is not threatened because of any fault, the one who threatens does not threaten because of any fault. For this reason we may feel that we bystanders cannot intervene. But the person threatened can.

In sum, a woman surely can defend her life against the threat to it posed by the unborn child, even if doing so involves its death. And this shows not merely that the theses in (1) through (4) are false; it shows also that the extreme view of abortion is false, and so we need not canvass any other possible ways of arriving at it from the argument I mentioned at the outset.

2. The extreme view could of course be weakened to say that while abortion is permissible to save the mother's life, it may not be performed by a third party, but only by the mother herself. But this cannot be right either. For what we have to keep in mind is that the mother and the unborn child are not like two tenants in a small house which has, by an unfortunate mistake, been rented to both: the mother *owns* the house. The fact that she does adds to the offensiveness of deducing that the mother can do nothing from the supposition that third parties can do nothing. But it does more than this: it casts a bright light on the supposition that third parties can do nothing. Certainly it lets us see that a third party who says "I cannot choose between you" is fooling himself if he thinks this is impartiality. If Jones has found and fastened on a certain coat, which he needs to keep him from freezing, but which Smith also needs to keep him from freezing, then it is not impartiality that says "I cannot choose between you" when Smith owns the coat. Women have said again and again "This body is *my* body!" and they have reason to feel angry, reason to feel that it has been like shouting into the wind. Smith, after all, is hardly likely to bless us if we say to him, "Of course it's your coat, anybody would grant that it is. But no one may choose between you and Jones who is to have it."

We should really ask what it is that says "no one may choose" in the face of the fact that the body that houses the child is the mother's body. It may be simply a failure to appreciate this fact. But it may be something more interesting, namely the sense that one has a right to refuse to lay hands on people, even where it would be just and fair to do so, even where justice seems to require that somebody do so. Thus justice might call for somebody to get Smith's coat back from Jones, and yet you have a right to refuse to be the one to lay hands on Jones, a right to refuse to do physical violence to him. This, I think, must be granted. But then what should be said is not "no one may choose," but only "*I* cannot choose," and indeed not even this, but "*I* will not *act*," leaving it open that somebody else can or should, and in particular that anyone in a position of authority, with the job of securing people's rights, both can and should. So this is no difficulty. I have not been arguing that any given third party must accede to the mother's request that he perform an abortion to save her life, but only that he may.

I suppose that in some views of human life the mother's body is only on loan to her, the loan not being one which gives her any prior claim to it. One who held this view might well think it impartiality to say "I cannot choose." But I shall simply ignore this possibility. My own view is that if a human being has any just, prior claim to anything at all, he has a just, prior claim to his own body. And perhaps this needn't be argued for here anyway, since, as I mentioned, the arguments against abortion we are looking at do grant that the woman has a right to decide what happens in and to her body.

But although they do grant it, I have tried to show that they do not take seriously what is done in granting it. I suggest the same thing will reappear even more clearly when we turn away from cases in which the mother's life is at stake, and attend, as I propose we now do, to the vastly more common cases in which a woman wants an abortion for some less weighty reason than preserving her own life.

3. Where the mother's life is not at stake, the argument I mentioned at the outset seems to have a much stronger pull. "Everyone has a right to life, so the unborn person has a right to life." And isn't the child's right to life weightier than anything other than the mother's own right to life, which she might put forward as ground for an abortion?

This argument treats the right to life as if it were unproblematic. It is not, and this seems to me to be precisely the source of the mistake.

For we should now, at long last, ask what it comes to, to have a right to life. In some views having a right to life includes having a right to be given at least the bare minimum one needs for continued life. But suppose that what in fact *is* the bare minimum a man needs for continued life is something he has no right at all to be given? If I am sick unto death, and the only thing that will save my life is the touch of Henry Fonda's cool hand on my fevered brow, then all the same, I have no right to be given the touch of Henry Fonda's cool hand on my fevered brow. It would be frightfully nice of him to fly in from the West Coast to provide it. It would be less nice, though no doubt well meant, if my friends flew out to the West Coast and carried Henry Fonda back with them. But I have no right at all against anybody that he should do this for me. Or again, to return to the story I told earlier, the fact that for continued life that violinist needs the continued use of your kidneys does not establish that he has a right to be given the continued use of your kidneys. He certainly has no right against you that *you* should give him continued use of your kidneys. For nobody has any right to use your kidneys unless you give him such a right; and nobody has the right against you that you shall give him this right—if you do allow him to go on using your kidneys, this is a kindness on your part, and not something he can claim from you as his due. Nor has he any right against anybody else that *they* should give him continued use of your kidneys. Certainly he had no right against the Society of Music Lovers that they should plug him into you in the first place. And if you now start to unplug yourself, having learned that you will otherwise have to spend nine years in bed with him, there is nobody in the world who must try to prevent you, in order to see to it that he is given something he has a right to be given.

Some people are rather stricter about the right to life. In their view it does not include the right to be given anything, but amounts to and only to, the right not to be killed by anybody. But here a related difficulty arises. If everybody is to refrain from killing that violinist, then everybody must refrain from doing a great many different sorts of things. Everybody must refrain from slitting his throat, everybody must refrain from shooting him—and everybody must refrain from unplugging you from him. But does he have a right against everybody that they shall refrain from unplugging you from him? To refrain from doing this is to allow him to continue to use your kidneys. It could be argued that he has a right against us that *we* should allow him to continue to use your kidneys. That is, while he had no right against us that we should give him the use of your kidneys, it might be argued that he anyway has a right against us that we shall not now intervene and deprive him of the use of your kidneys. I shall come back to third-party interventions later. But certainly the violinist has no right against you that *you* shall allow him to continue to use your kidneys. As I said, if you do allow him to use them, it is a kindness on your part, and not something you owe him.

The difficulty I point to here is not peculiar to the right to life. It reappears in connection with all the other natural rights; and it is something which an adequate account of rights must deal with. For present purposes it is enough just to draw attention to it. But I would stress that I am not arguing that people do not have a right to life—quite to the contrary, it seems to me that the primary control we must place on the acceptability of an account of rights is that it should turn out in that account to be a truth that all persons have a right to life. I am arguing only that having a right to life does not guarantee having either a right to be given the use of or a right to be allowed continued use of another person's body—even if one needs it for life itself. So the right to life will not serve the opponents of abortion in the very simple and clear way in which they seem to have thought it would.

4. There is another way to bring out the difficulty. In the most ordinary sort of case, to deprive someone of what he has a right to is to treat him unjustly. Suppose a boy and his small brother are jointly given a box of chocolates for Christmas. If the older boy takes the box and refuses to give his brother any of the chocolates, he is unjust to him, for the brother has been given a right to half of them. But suppose that, having learned that otherwise it means nine years in bed with that violinist, you unplug yourself from him. You surely are not being unjust to him, for you gave him no right to use your kidneys, and no one else can have given him any such right. But we have to notice that in

unplugging yourself, you are killing him; and violinists, like everybody else, have a right to life, and thus in the view we were considering just now, the right not to be killed. So here you do what he supposedly has a right you shall not do, but you do not act unjustly to him in doing it.

The emendation which may be made at this point is this: the right to life consists not in the right not to be killed, but rather in the right not to be killed unjustly. This runs a risk of circularity, but never mind: it would enable us to square the fact that the violinist has a right to life with the fact that you do not act unjustly toward him in unplugging yourself, thereby killing him. For if you do not kill him unjustly, you do not violate his right to life, and so it is no wonder you do him no injustice.

But if this emendation is accepted, the gap in the argument against abortion stares us plainly in the face: it is by no means enough to show that the fetus is a person, and to remind us that all persons have a right to life—we need to be shown also that killing the fetus violates its right to life, i.e., that abortion is unjust killing. And is it?

I suppose we may take it as a datum that in a case of pregnancy due to rape the mother has not given the unborn person a right to the use of her body for food and shelter. Indeed, in what pregnancy could it be supposed that the mother has given the unborn person such a right? It is not as if there were unborn persons drifting about the world, to whom a woman who wants a child says "I invite you in."

But it might be argued that there are other ways one can have acquired a right to the use of another person's body than by having been invited to use it by that person. Suppose a woman voluntarily indulges in intercourse, knowing of the chance it will issue in pregnancy, and then she does become pregnant; is she not in part responsible for the presence, in fact the very existence, of the unborn person inside her? No doubt she did not invite it in. But doesn't her partial responsibility for its being there itself give it a right to the use of her body?[7] If so, then her aborting it would be more like the boy's taking away the chocolates, and less like your unplugging yourself from the violinist—doing so would be depriving it of what it does have a right to, and thus would be doing it an injustice.

And then, too, it might be asked whether or not she can kill it even to save her own life: If she voluntarily called it into existence, how can she now kill it, even in self-defense?

The first thing to be said about this is that it is something new. Opponents of abortion have been so concerned to make out the independence of the fetus, in order to establish that it has a right to life, just as its mother does, that they have tended to overlook the possible support they might gain from making out that the fetus is *dependent* on the mother, in order to establish that she has a special kind of responsibility for it, a responsibility that gives it rights against

[7] The need for a discussion of this argument was brought home to me by members of the Society for Ethical and Legal Philosophy, to whom this paper was originally presented.

her which are not possessed by any independent person—such as an ailing violinist who is a stranger to her.

On the other hand, this argument would give the unborn person a right to its mother's body only if her pregnancy resulted from a voluntary act, undertaken in full knowledge of the chance a pregnancy might result from it. It would leave out entirely the unborn person whose existence is due to rape. Pending the availability of some further argument, then, we would be left with the conclusion that unborn persons whose existence is due to rape have no right to the use of their mothers' bodies, and thus that aborting them is not depriving them of anything they have a right to and hence is not unjust killing.

And we should also notice that it is not at all plain that this argument really does go even as far as it purports to. For there are cases and cases, and the details make a difference. If the room is stuffy, and I therefore open a window to air it, and a burglar climbs in, it would be absurd to say, "Ah, now he can stay, she's given him a right to the use of her house—for she is partially responsible for his presence there, having voluntarily done what enabled him to get in, in full knowledge that there are such things as burglars, and that burglars burgle." It would be still more absurd to say this if I had had bars installed outside my windows, precisely to prevent burglars from getting in, and a burglar got in only because of a defect in the bars. It remains equally absurd if we imagine it is not a burglar who climbs in, but an innocent person who blunders or falls in. Again, suppose it were like this: people-seeds drift about in the air like pollen, and if you open your windows, one may drift in and take root in your carpets or upholstery. You don't want children, so you fix up your windows with fine mesh screens, the very best you can buy. As can happen, however, and on very, very rare occasions does happen, one of the screens is defective; and a seed drifts in and takes root. Does the person-plant who now develops have a right to the use of your house? Surely not—despite the fact that you voluntarily opened your windows, you knowingly kept carpets and upholstered furniture, and you knew that screens were sometimes defective. Someone may argue that you are responsible for its rooting, that it does have a right to your house, because after all you *could* have lived out your life with bare floors and furniture, or with sealed windows and doors. But this won't do—for by the same token anyone can avoid a pregnancy due to rape by having a hysterectomy, or anyway by never leaving home without a (reliable!) army.

It seems to me that the argument we are looking at can establish at most that there are *some* cases in which the unborn person has a right to the use of its mother's body, and therefore *some* cases in which abortion is unjust killing. There is room for much discussion and argument as to precisely which, if any. But I think we should sidestep this issue and leave it open, for at any rate the argument certainly does not establish that all abortion is unjust killing.

5. There is room for yet another argument here, however. We surely must all grant that there may be cases in which it would be morally indecent to detach a person from your body at the cost of his life. Suppose you learn that what the violinist needs is not nine years of your life, but only one hour: all you need

do to save his life is to spend one hour in that bed with him. Suppose also that letting him use your kidneys for that one hour would not affect your health in the slightest. Admittedly you were kidnapped. Admittedly you did not give anyone permission to plug him into you. Nevertheless it seems to me plain you *ought* to allow him to use your kidneys for that hour—it would be indecent to refuse.

Again, suppose pregnancy lasted only an hour, and constituted no threat to life or health. And suppose that a woman becomes pregnant as a result of rape. Admittedly she did not voluntarily do anything to bring about the existence of a child. Admittedly she did nothing at all which would give the unborn person a right to the use of her body. All the same it might well be said, as in the newly emended violinist story, that she *ought* to allow it to remain for that hour—that it would be indecent in her to refuse.

Now some people are inclined to use the term "right" in such a way that it follows from the fact that you ought to allow a person to use your body for the hour he needs, that he has a right to use your body for the hour he needs, even though he has not been given that right by any person or act. They may say that it follows also that if you refuse, you act unjustly toward him. This use of the term is perhaps so common that it cannot be called wrong; nevertheless it seems to me to be an unfortunate loosening of what we would do better to keep a tight rein on. Suppose that box of chocolates I mentioned earlier had not been given to both boys jointly, but was given only to the older boy. There he sits, stolidly eating his way through the box, his small brother watching enviously. Here we are likely to say "You ought not to be so mean. You ought to give your brother some of those chocolates." My own view is that it just does not follow from the truth of this that the brother has any right to any of the chocolates. If the boy refuses to give his brother any, he is greedy, stingy, callous—but not unjust. I suppose that the people I have in mind will say it does follow that the brother has a right to some of the chocolates, and thus that the boy does act unjustly if he refuses to give his brother any. But the effect of saying this is to obscure what we should keep distinct, namely the difference between the boy's refusal in this case and the boy's refusal in the earlier case, in which the box was given to both boys jointly, and in which the small brother thus had what was from any point of view clear title to half.

A further objection to so using the term "right" that from the fact that A ought to do a thing for B, it follows that B has a right against A that A do it for him, is that it is going to make the question of whether or not a man has a right to a thing turn on how easy it is to provide him with it; and this seems not merely unfortunate, but morally unacceptable. Take the case of Henry Fonda again. I said earlier that I had no right to the touch of his cool hand on my fevered brow, even though I needed it to save my life. I said it would be frightfully nice of him to fly in from the West Coast to provide me with it, but that I had no right against him that he should do so. But suppose he isn't on the West Coast. Suppose he has only to walk across the room, place a hand briefly on my brow—and lo, my life is saved. Then surely he ought to do it, it would be indecent to refuse. Is it to be said "Ah, well, it follows that in this case she has a right to the touch of his hand on her brow, and so it would be an injustice in him to refuse?" So that I have a right to it when it is easy for him to provide it, though no right when it's hard? It's rather a shocking idea that anyone's rights should fade away and disappear as it gets harder and harder to accord them to him.

So my own view is that even though you ought to let the violinist use your kidneys for the one hour he needs, we should not conclude that he has a right to do so—we should say that if you refuse, you are, like the boy who owns all the chocolates and will give none away, self-centered and callous, indecent in fact, but not unjust. And similarly, that even supposing a case in which a woman pregnant due to rape ought to allow the unborn person to use her body for the hour he needs, we should not conclude that he has a right to do so; we should conclude that she is self-centered, callous, indecent, but not unjust, if she refuses. The complaints are no less grave; they are just different. However, there is no need to insist on this point. If anyone does wish to deduce "he has a right" from "you ought," then all the same he must surely grant that there are cases in which it is not morally required of you that you allow that violinist to use your kidneys, and in which he does not have a right to use them, and in which you do not do him an injustice if you refuse. And so also for mother and unborn child. Except in such cases as the unborn person has a right to demand it—and we were leaving open the possibility that there may be such cases—nobody is morally *required* to make large sacrifices, of health, of all other interests and concerns, of all other duties and commitments, for nine years, or even for nine months, in order to keep another person alive.

6. We have in fact to distinguish between two kinds of Samaritan: the Good Samaritan and what we might call the Minimally Decent Samaritan. The story of the Good Samaritan, you will remember, goes like this:

> A certain man went down from Jerusalem to Jericho, and fell among thieves, which stripped him of his raiment and wounded him, and departed, leaving him half dead.
>
> And by chance there came down a certain priest that way; and when he saw him, he passed by on the other side.
>
> And likewise a Levite, when he was at the place, came and looked on him, and passed by on the other side.
>
> But a certain Samaritan, as he journeyed, came where he was; and when he saw him he had compassion on him.
>
> And went to him, and bound up his wounds, pouring in oil and wine, and set him on his own beast, and brought him to an inn, and took care of him.
>
> And on the morrow, when he departed, he took out two pence, and gave them to the host, and said unto him, "Take care of him; and whatsoever thou spendest more, when I come again, I will repay thee." (Luke 10:30-35)

The Good Samaritan went out of his way, at some cost to himself, to help one in need of it. We are not told what the options were, that is, whether or not the priest and the Levite could have helped by doing less than the Good Samaritan did, but assuming they could have, then the fact they did nothing at all shows they were not even Minimally Decent Samaritans, not because they were not Samaritans, but because they were not even minimally decent.

These things are a matter of degree, of course, but there is a difference, and it comes out perhaps most clearly in the story of Kitty Genovese, who, as you will remember, was murdered while thirty-eight people watched or listened, and did nothing at all to help her. A Good Samaritan would have rushed out to give direct assistance against the murderer. Or perhaps we had better allow that it would have been a Splendid Samaritan who did this, on the ground that it would have involved a risk of death for himself. But the thirty-eight not only did not do this, they did not even trouble to pick up a phone to call the police. Minimally Decent Samaritanism would call for doing at least that, and their not having done it was monstrous.

After telling the story of the Good Samaritan, Jesus said "Go, and do thou likewise." Perhaps he meant that we are morally required to act as the Good Samaritan did. Perhaps he was urging people to do more than is morally required of them. At all events it seems plain that it was not morally required of any of the thirty-eight that he rush out to give direct assistance at the risk of his own life, and that it is not morally required of anyone that he give long stretches of his life—nine years or nine months—to sustaining the life of a person who has no special right (we were leaving open the possibility of this) to demand it.

Indeed, with one rather striking class of exceptions, no one in any country in the world is *legally* required to do anywhere near as much as this for anyone else. The class of exceptions is obvious. My main concern here is not the state of the law in respect to abortion, but it is worth drawing attention to the fact that in no state in this country is any man compelled by law to be even a Minimally Decent Samaritan to any person; there is no law under which charges could be brought against the thirty-eight who stood by while Kitty Genovese died. By contrast, in most states in this country women are compelled by law to be not merely Minimally Decent Samaritans, but Good Samaritans to unborn persons inside them. This doesn't by itself settle anything one way or the other, because it may well be argued that there should be laws in this country—as there are in many European countries—compelling at least Minimally Decent Samaritanism.[8] But it does show that there is a gross injustice in the existing state of the law. And it shows also that the groups currently working against liberalization of abortion laws, in fact working toward having it declared unconstitutional for a state to permit abortion, had better start working for the adoption of Good Samaritan laws generally, or earn the charge that they are acting in bad faith.

I should think, myself, that Minimally Decent Samaritan laws would be one thing, Good Samaritan laws quite another, and in fact highly improper. But we

[8] For a discussion of the difficulties involved, and a survey of the European experience with such laws, see *The Good Samaritan and the Law*, ed. James M. Ratcliffe (New York, 1966).

are not here concerned with the law. What we should ask is not whether anybody should be compelled by law to be a Good Samaritan, but whether we must accede to a situation in which somebody is being compelled—by nature, perhaps—to be a Good Samaritan. We have, in other words, to look now at third-party interventions. I have been arguing that no person is morally required to make large sacrifices to sustain the life of another who has no right to demand them, and this even where the sacrifices do not include life itself; we are not morally required to be Good Samaritans or anyway Very Good Samaritans to one another. But what if a man cannot extricate himself from such a situation? What if he appeals to us to extricate him? It seems to me plain that there are cases in which we can, cases in which a Good Samaritan would extricate him. There you are, you were kidnapped, and nine years in bed with that violinist lie ahead of you. You have your own life to lead. You are sorry, but you simply cannot see giving us so much of your life to the sustaining of his. You cannot extricate yourself, and ask us to do so. I should have thought that—in light of his having no right to the use of your body—it was obvious that we do not have to accede to your being forced to give up so much. We can do what you ask. There is no injustice to the violinist in our doing so.

7. Following the lead of the opponents of abortion, I have throughout been speaking of the fetus merely as a person, and what I have been asking is whether or not the argument we began with, which proceeds only from the fetus' being a person, really does establish its conclusion. I have argued that it does not.

But of course there are arguments and arguments, and it may be said that I have simply fastened on the wrong one. It may be said that what is important is not merely the fact that the fetus is a person, but that it is a person for whom the woman has a special kind of responsibility issuing from the fact that she is its mother. And it might be argued that all my analogies are therefore irrelevant—for you do not have that special kind of responsibility for that violinist, Henry Fonda does not have that special kind of responsibility for me. And our attention might be drawn to the fact that men and women both *are* compelled by law to provide support for their children.

I have in effect dealt (briefly) with this argument in section 4 above; but a (still briefer) recapitulation now may be in order. Surely we do not have any such "special responsibility" for a person unless we have assumed it, explicitly or implicitly. If a set of parents do not try to prevent pregnancy, do not obtain an abortion, and then at the time of birth of the child do not put it out for adoption, but rather take it home with them, then they have assumed responsibility for it, they have given it rights, and they cannot *now* withdraw support from it at the cost of its life because they now find it difficult to go on providing for it. But if they have taken all reasonable precautions against having a child, they do not simply by virtue of their biological relationship to the child who comes into existence have a special responsibility for it. They may wish to assume responsibility for it, or they may not wish to. And I am suggesting that if assuming responsibility for it would require large sacrifices, then they may refuse. A Good Samaritan would not refuse—or anyway, a Splendid Samaritan, if the sacrifices that had to be made were enormous. But then so would a Good Samaritan assume responsibility for that violinist; so would Henry Fonda, if he is a Good Samaritan, fly in from the West Coast and assume responsibility for me.

8. My argument will be found unsatisfactory on two counts by many of those who want to regard abortion as morally permissible. First, while I do argue that abortion is not impermissible, I do not argue that it is always permissible. There may well be cases in which carrying the child to term requires only Minimally Decent Samaritanism of the mother, and this is a standard we must not fall below. I am inclined to think it a merit of my account precisely that it does *not* give a general yes or a general no. It allows for and supports our sense that, for example, a sick and desperately frightened fourteen-year-old schoolgirl, pregnant due to rape, may of *course* choose abortion, and that any law which rules this out is an insane law. And it also allows for and supports our sense that in other cases resort to abortion is even positively indecent. It would be indecent in the woman to request an abortion, and indecent in a doctor to perform it, if she is in her seventh month, and wants the abortion just to avoid the nuisance of postponing a trip abroad. The very fact that the arguments I have been drawing attention to treat all cases of abortion, or even all cases of abortion in which the mother's life is not at stake, as morally on a par ought to have made them suspect at the outset.

Secondly, while I am arguing for the permissibility of abortion in some cases, I am not arguing for the right to secure the death of the unborn child. It is easy to confuse these two things in that up to a certain point in the life of the fetus it is not able to survive outside the mother's body; hence removing it from her body guarantees its death. But they are importantly different. I have argued that you are not morally required to spend nine months in bed, sustaining the life of that violinist; but to say this is by no means to say that if, when you unplug yourself, there is a miracle and he survives, you then have a right to turn round and slit his throat. You may detach yourself even if this costs him his life; you have no right to be guaranteed his death, by some other means, if unplugging yourself does not kill him. There are some people who will feel dissatisfied by this feature of my argument. A woman may be utterly devastated by the thought of a child, a bit of herself, put out for adoption and never seen or heard of again. She may therefore want not merely that the child be detached from her, but more, that it die. Some opponents of abortion are inclined to regard this as beneath contempt—thereby showing insensitivity to what is surely a powerful source of despair. All the same, I agree that the desire for the child's death is not one which anybody may gratify, should it turn out to be possible to detach the child alive.

At this place, however, it should be remembered that we have only been pretending throughout that the fetus is a human being from the moment of conception. A very early abortion is surely not the killing of a person, and so is not dealt with by anything I have said here.

INTRODUCTION TO ETHICS / Study Questions

ABORTION

The Supreme Court

1. As Blackmun presents it, what exactly were the arguments before the Court and who brought the original suits?
2. What, historically, have been the reasons for enactment of abortion laws, according to Blackmun? What is the Court's response to each of these reasons?
3. Whence does Blackmun derive the "right to privacy" and how does he argue that it extends to "encompass a woman's decision whether or not to terminate her pregnancy?"
4. Is this right, according to Blackmun, absolute? What does this mean?
5. What considerations may be brought to limit this right? That is, what state interests may be invoked in order to regulate abortions?
6. How does Blackmun argue that the concept of a *person* has no prenatal application in the Constitution? How does he argue that the Court need not resolve the extra legal question of fetal personhood? How does he argue that in areas of law other than those dealing with abortion, "the unborn have never been recognized . . . as persons in the whole sense"?
7. From the point of view of the question of whether abortion is a public or a private moral issue, what is the significance of the arguments you have just reviewed?
8. What is the substance, finally, of the Court's decision? What are the "compelling points" of the two interests states may have in regulating abortions?
9. What does it mean to say a fetus is "viable"? Is this clear? Are premature infants viable"? How many tubes does a fetus have to be plugged into before it is no longer viable? (That is, would a fetus being grown *in vitro*, attached to an artificial "placenta," be "viable"?)
10. The Court gives no reasons for asserting that states have an interest in protecting *potential* human life. Some reasons we might give for this would be: (a) that the interest is derived from the interest in protecting human life; (b) that the interest is derived from civil law precedents (see question 7); or (c) that the interest is derived from considerations about preserving an on-going citizenry. Can you think of other reasons? Which, among these reasons, seems to involve us again in the fetal-personhood question? Among those that do not, is there any one that gives us a reason for choosing "viability" as the compelling point of the states' interest?

O'Donnell

1. On what grounds does O'Donnell reject the idea that a new human organism is not really human until it looks human? Is there more than one sense of the word *human* involved in that discussion?
2. By using such words as *probability* and *likelihood*, O'Donnell seems to suggest that the question of fetal personhood is an *empirical* question; that is, a question of how much information we have. Is that correct? In evaluating this it might be helpful to ask how much the facts aobut "chromosomal patterns in the nuclei of the earliest stages of cell division" can actually show us. Can they show us (a) that a given embryo belongs to the species of human beings? (b) that a given human embryo is different from any other? (c) that a given unique human embryo is a person in the civil and moral sense, i.e., that it has rights?

3. What *does* make John John and not George?
4. Suppose someone responded to O'Donnell by saying the issue was not entirely empirical but required resolution of the question: "What do we mean when we speak of some individual as a *person*?" How could you respond for O'Donnell? For example, would O'Donnell be willing to say that his criterion for calling an individual a *person* is simply that the individual is biologically human? Would *you* be willing to say that? Can you imagine a case in which *you would* accord rights to an individual who (which?) was not biologically human; e.g., a very nice "man" from outer space?
5. O'Donnell claims that, since a fetus is *very likely* "a human" from the moment of conception, the only morally safe course is to prohibit the killing of any product of human conception. Can one always determine *the* morally safe course of action by appeal to probabilities like this? Assume, for the sake of argument, that O'Donnell is right that this is an empirical matter; suppose we were to discover next year that the conceptus is not "human." The consequence of this would be that we had condemned many mothers to mental disorder, physical illness and many children to growing up in hostile environments. *Could* we not, in retrospect, have serious doubts about whether our previous ban on abortion was "*the only* practical working premise, from a moral viewpoint"? What other morally safe courses might still be open to someone who agrees with O'Donnell that the new organism is very likely "a human"? Or, do you think there would be no clear way to decide what really would be morally safe here?
6. If as O'Donnell says, the direct killing of an innocent human being is morally wrong, might an *indirect* killing be permissible? What do you think an "indirect" killing is? What do you think is meant by referring to some human beings as "innocent"? What sense of the word *innocent* do you think is employed here? Is murder in self-defense a killing of an innocent human being? Is voluntary manslaughter a case of this type? Would either of these count as "indirect" killings? Relate your discussion of these points to the abortion question, assuming for the argument's sake, that a fetus is a person. (Then go on to read the article by Phillippa Foot.)

Foot

1. According to Foot, what is Hart's objection to the traditional application of the doctrine of the double effect to fetal craniotomy cases? How would his objection entail the meaninglessness of the entire doctrine? How does Foot respond to that line of reasoning?
2. What, according to Foot, is the first reason that the doctrine has been taken seriously? How do the cases of the magistrate and the train driver seem to support that reason? What is the second reason, and how do the cases of the tyrant and the mad murderer seem to support it?
3. Why does the fact that one may "deliberately allow" some harm to occur pose serious difficulties for the doctrine?
4. What are the two senses of *allowing* to which Foot calls attention? Which one is relevant to this issue? With respect to that sense, what is the distinction between positive and negative duties?
5. How does Foot reason that this distinction, together with an analysis of which sorts of duties are being weighed against each other, helps us explain the relation between the train driver and the magistrate cases? Do we in general, according to Foot, have a stronger duty to refrain from injuring people than we have to bring people aid?

6. What sorts of cases does Foot think her analysis deals with in a better way than can the doctrine of the double effect?
7. What is Foot's concluding assessment of the role played by the distinction between direct and oblique intention in our evaluation of those cases where the doctrine of the double effect seemed to get most of its support?
8. In detail, how does the analysis given by Foot (of the weighing of positive and negative duties) apply to the problem of abortion?

Thomson

1. According to Thomson, how is the claim that abortion is always wrong supposed to follow from the premise that a fetus is a person? How does the "famous violinist" case show that the premise, by itself, does not justify the antiabortion position?
2. What extra premises must be added to make the argument work? What, in detail, is Thomson's evaluation of those premises?
3. Suppose one used these claims to prove only that a third party may not perform an abortion. How does Thomson criticize that line; how does her discussion of the "Smith's coat" case illuminate her argument?
4. According to Thomson, what are two unacceptable views of the concept of a right to life? Why are they unacceptable? What is an acceptable view of this right; and how does its analysis reveal a gap in the antiabortion argument?
5. Thomson argues that to show that abortion is an unjust killing one must claim not only that the fetus has a right to life but also that it has a right to the use of the woman's body. In what ways might that further right be granted to the fetus? How does Thomson's "people-seeds" case illuminate her discussion of this issue?
6. What are the differences between a moral requirement to behave decently and the requirement to respect somone's rights? Can one derive the claim that a fetus has a right to use a woman's body from the claim that she ought (out of decency) to allow the fetus to use her body?
7. What is Thomson's distinction between a Good Samaritan and a Minimally Decent Samaritan? How does Thomson use her discussion of this distinction to criticize antiabortion laws? Note: Thomson's article was written before the Supreme Court's January, 1974, decision in the case of *Roe v. Wade.*

SUGGESTED FURTHER READINGS / Introduction to Ethics

GENERAL

Brandt, Richard. *Ethical Theory.* Englewood Cliffs, N.J.: Prentice-Hall, Inc., 1959.
Frankena, William. *Ethics.* Englewood Cliffs, N.J.: Prentice-Hall, Inc., 1963.
Jones, W. T., Frederick Sontag, Morton Beckner, and Robert J. Fogelin eds. *Approaches to Ethics.* New York: McGraw-Hill Book Company, 1962, rev. ed., 1969.
Mabbott, J. D. *An Introduction to Ethics.* London: Hutchinson & Company, 1966.
Nowell-Smith, Patrick. *Ethics.* Baltimore: Penguin Books, 1954.
Pahel, Kenneth, and Marvin Schiller, eds. *Readings in Contemporary Ethical Theory.* Englewood Cliffs, N.J.: Prentice-Hall, Inc., 1970.
Sellars, Wilfrid, and John Hospers. *Readings in Ethical Theory.* New York: Appleton-Century-Croffs, 1970.

Taylor, Paul W. *Problems of Moral Philosophy*. Belmont, Calif.: Dickenson Pub. Co., Inc., 1967.

Thompson, J. J., and G. Dworkin. *Ethics*. New York: Harper & Row, Publishers, 1968.

CULTURAL RELATIVISM

Benedict, Ruth. *Patterns of Culture*. New York: Pelican Books, 1947.

Kluckholn, Clyde. *Culture and Behavior*. New York: The Free Press, 1962.

Stace, W. T. *The Concept of Morals*. New Haven: Yale University Press, 1963.

Sumner, William G. *Folkways*. Boston: Ginn and Company, 1934.

Westermarck, Edward. *Ethical Relativity*. New York: Harcourt Brace Jovanovich, Inc., 1932.

ABORTION

Feinberg, Joel. *The Problem of Abortion*. Belmont, Calif.: Wadsworth Publishing Co., Inc., 1973.

Hall, Robert E., ed. *Abortion in a Changing World*, vol. I. New York: Columbia University Press, 1970.

Noonan, John T., Jr., ed. *The Morality of Abortion, Legal and Historical Perspectives*. Cambridge: Harvard University Press, 1970.

Smith, David T., ed. *Abortion and The Law*. Cleveland, Ohio: The Press of Case Western Reserve University, 1967.

PART 2

Introduction to Metaphysics

A general introduction to that branch of philosophy called "metaphysics" is no easier to give than a brief, accurate, and intelligible account of philosophy itself. Indeed, two of the definitions we gave of philosophy in our introductory article "What Is Philosophy?" were in fact definitions of metaphysics.

The first comes from *Aristotle*:

> Philosophy is the "science which investigates being as being and the attributes which belong to this in virtue of its own nature. . . . Now this is not the same as any of the so-called special sciences. . . . [And] since we are seeking the first principles and highest causes, clearly there must be something to which these belong in virtue of its own nature. . . . Therefore it is of being as being that we must also grasp the first causes.

The second is C. D. *Broad*'s definition of philosophy that also characterized metaphysics:

> It's [philosophy's] object is to take over the results of the various sciences, to add to them the results of the religious and ethical experiences of mankind, and then to reflect upon the whole. The hope is that, by this means, we may be able to reach some general conclusions as to the nature of the universe, and as to our position and prospects in it.

We face here in trying to understand what metaphysics is the same difficulty that we have in understanding philosophy. The short accounts don't seem to be very enlightening. Here, as in our introductory remarks about philosophy, we will suggest the same solution. That is, we will try to understand metaphysics by working our way through two representative metaphysical questions.

Before we go into these particular problems, however, a few remarks may be worthwhile. The aforementioned quotations show two general tendencies in traditional metaphysics. Aristotle saw metaphysics as the investigation of what he called the "first principles" of the special sciences. In Aristotle's philosophy each of the special sciences —astronomy, biology, psychology, and so on—investigates a certain class of objects or substances, the way in which these things change, and the causes of those changes. Metaphysics, by contrast, investigates the nature of substance, change, and causality *in general*, the principles said to underlie the various particular sciences. The second traditional conception of metaphysics, illustrated in Broad's account, perceives it as a kind of superscience to which the various special sciences are subordinate. The task of the metaphysician, as Broad sees it, is to construct a big picture of the universe as a whole by drawing on the results of the sciences and correlating and reconciling their findings with the insights of morality and religion. Broad, like the majority of metaphysicians, is especially interested in arriving at a theory about the nature of man and his place in the world as a whole.

Traditional metaphysics thus conceived its task as one of arriving at very general *factual* descriptions of the world. The possibility of providing this kind of factual description of the world has from time to time been questioned and never more seriously than in the present century. In the nineteen twenties a group of scientists and philosophers associated with the university of Vienna objected to metaphysics on the grounds that its alleged "factual" descriptions were in fact literal nonsense. These men of the so-called Vienna Circle, later known as logical positivists, based their objection upon a theory of meaning. They held that the only statements that are meaningful are (a) analytic statements and (b) statements that are empirically verifiable. An analytic statement is one that is true by virtue of the meaning of the words or symbols that it contains or by virtue of the logical form of the statement. "Triangles have three sides" is an example of an analytic statement where it is clear that the word "triangle" means simply "three-sided figure." Although such statements are undeniably true, they are also empty of factual content and can tell us nothing at all about the world. The logical positivists thought that all the statements of logic and mathematics are analytic statements. The only statements that can give us information about the world are empirically verifiable ones, that is, ones whose truth or falsity can be determined, at least in principle, by observation and scientific experiment.

The logical positivists thus had a test for the meaningfulness of claims about the way the world is, factual claims, that came to be called the Verifiability Criterion. It was primarily this criterion that the logical positivists applied to representative metaphysical statements. The result, they concluded, was that such statements were not false, but unintelligible. Subsequently, however, the distinction between analytic and empirical statements and the Verifiability Criterion of meaning were themselves attacked. Specifically, it was argued that some sentences, for example, expressions of pain and expressions of attitude are neither analytic nor empirically verifiable and yet are undoubtedly meaningful. Secondly, some philosophical statements made by the positivists themselves failed to meet their own standards of meaning. The most notorious example being the Verifiable Criterion! In whatever way it could be stated it turned out to be both nonanalytic and not empirically verifiable.

This breakdown of the positivistic theory of meaning seems to reopen the door to all manner of excessive mataphysical speculations and claims, but in fact it does not. All that has to follow is that the Verifiability Criterion is too restrictive and that there are more types of meaningful expressions in language than either analytic ones or empirical ones. Although the distinction between analytic and empirical statements and the Verifiability Criterion for the meaningfulness of empirical statements may be perfectly all right, the *statement* of that distinction and the Criterion belong to some other type of meaningful discourse. Generally speaking, such philosophical statements are now construed as being about the proper picturing of some portion of our conceptual schemes, of our language. That is, they are remarks about the meaning of certain words. The Verifiability Criterion, for example, may be taken as a remark about the interrelationships among the words *fact, true, false, test,* and so on—and what it claims is that one cannot apply the word *factual* to a sentence unless one can explain what would count as a test (in the ordinary sense) for the truth or falsity of the sentence.

Now this maneuver—regarding certain philosophical claims as being remarks about our conceptual schemes—does open the door to the rephrasing of traditional metaphysical theses. They no longer have to be represented as strange and untestable speculations about the hidden structure of the universe, nor do they have to be dismissed as so much sheer nonsense. Understood in the new way they can direct our attention to important and even unsuspected conceptual features of our language and their adequacy can be checked by looking very carefully at our language and how it works.

We have chosen two problems as illustrative of metaphysics, the freedom-determinism question and the mind-body problem. Both are typical of metaphysical issues and both have important implications outside of philosophy proper, the former with matters of law and morality and the latter with the science of psychology. In both cases, the selection of readings will also exemplify the significant changes in the conception of metaphysics and philosophical method that have taken place in recent years.

Freedom or Determinism

The question of whether men do freely any of the things they do is one that engages us practically as well as theoretically. The practical importance of the freedom-determinism issue is the result of the connection between the ideas of freedom and determinism on the one hand and that of responsibility on the other. If it can be shown, in a court of law, for example, that what someone did was the result of a push, coercion, insanity, or other forces beyond his control he can often be absolved of responsibility for what he did. The famous trial lawyer,

Clarence Darrow, was quite successful in winning acquittals for his clients by convincing the jury that his clients were compelled to perform their deeds. He would argue that certain factors in the defendant's background, such as heredity, environment, temperament, and upbringing, over which he had no control, were such that his actions were the inevitable result. Since the defendant had no control over his actions, Darrow would insist that he could not be held responsible for them. How far can such a contention be pushed? What changes in the way we live our lives would have to come about if people were never held responsible for their actions? Some of the implications are obvious: No one would ever be blamed or praised, no one would go to jail, and no one would ever be rewarded. You are invited to think out some of the other consequences in order to appreciate the importance of clear thinking about the freedom-determinism issue. No proponent of philosophical determinism, however, is content to offer the obvious truism that sometimes we are moved by forces beyond our control and so act in ways that are not wholly free. The philosophical determinist advances the more radical and interesting thesis that *all* human actions are determined and that no human being has ever acted freely nor can act freely. We will undertake to investigate the philosophical thesis of determinism as a prime example of a metaphysical question and of our changing conception of the nature of such questions.

Limitations of space prevent us from pursuing the practical consequences of determinism for our ideas of responsibility. As the authors of the first two selections clearly understood, the thesis of determinism makes the notions of moral and legal responsibility unintelligible. Although some determinists have been quite willing to accept this consequence of their thesis, others have tried to reconcile their determinism with ideas of responsibility. The student may want to ask himself, as a logical exercise, how this might be done, or even whether it can be done at all.

The first selection is from Baron *d'Holbach*. The most distinctive feature of d'Holbach's milieu, the intellectual landscape of seventeenth- and eighteenth-century Europe, was the rise of modern science. Theological explanations, philosophical speculations, and many superstitions fell into disrepute before the advance of scientific observation, hypotheses, and explanation. In particular, the success of the science of mechanics led many philosophers and scientists to attempt to generalize its results and construct out of it a theory of the universe as a whole. Thus, the world came to be regarded as a great machine and everything in it as working parts of the machine; everything was to be understood in mechanical terms.

Although d'Holbach did not originate the view called determinism, his is a classical statement of it. As a matter of fact, d'Holbach's work was prefigured by that of *Descartes* in at least two ways. In the first place, Descartes, impressed by the certainties possible in mathematics, urged that the methods of mathematics be generalized and that all knowledge be put into mathematical form. d'Holbach, like Descartes, was also impressed by the success of a single discipline and suggested that all knowledge be expressed in terms of and developed along the lines of that discipline. Only for d'Holbach the favored discipline was mechanics rather than mathematics. In the second place, Descartes' view of man was that of a machine—a body—inhabited by a soul that served to direct the body-machine. Descartes thought of animals other than man as simply very complex machines, far more intricate than clockwork, to be sure, but nevertheless explainable by the same principles. d'Holbach accepted Descartes' account of man with the modification that he claims the "soul" was nothing but a "modification of the brain" and that men, in fact, are nothing other than Descartes' body-machines.

d'Holbach's version of determinism claims that the actions of men are amenable to the same kind of explanation that we give for the rest of nature. That is, we can explain the actions of persons in exactly the same way that we explain, say, the trajectory of a cannonball as the resultant of the sum of the forces acting upon it. For d'Holbach a man's actions are the result of the strongest motive that acts upon him. Since the forces acting upon a person are not under his control, he cannot be said to be free. d'Holbach understands full well that his thesis of determinism entails that it is nonsense to suppose that men are responsible for their actions. By means of a striking example, d'Holbach claims that the man who jumps out of a window is no more free and no more responsible for what he does than is the man who is thrown out of the window by someone else. In both cases, says d'Holbach, the action is the result of forces outside the control of the person involved.

Today we may smile at d'Holbach's naive understanding of mechanics and what appear to us to be his crude "erector set" metaphors for men and their actions. But the determinist position can easily be brought up to date as John *Hospers* does in his article, "Meaning and Free Will." Hospers, for the most part, gives up the mechanical account of our actions and substitutes the more modern account of psychoanalysis. Now he can conceive the forces acting on us as psychological rather than mechanical. He invokes the notions of unresolved complexes, repressed wishes, and forgotten traumas in place of the pushes and pulls of d'Holbach's account of motivation. But the conclusion is the same: Not only are our actions determined by forces outside our control, but even our thoughts, wishes, dreams, and reasons are the inevitable result of unconscious forces. The language and metaphors of mechanics are exchanged for those of Freudian depth psychology.

Both d'Holbach and Hospers see themselves as making factual claims about the nature of man. Both authors attempt to offer what they consider evidence for their claims. d'Holbach offers the example of the man dying of thirst and Hospers offers data from psycholanalytic casebooks. But in the writings of neither do we find any *arguments* for the truth of determinism nor anything that could count as genuine empirical *evidence*. The student should note that the descriptions in the psychoanalyst's casebooks *presuppose* the conceptual scheme of psychoanalysis and the very theory of determinism for which they are supposed to be evidence. Thus, we should be no more surprised to find the people in these examples acting out their repressed wishes and doing the bidding of the "id" than we would be to find in a book of the lives of the saints that they acted "because of actual grace" or "in accordance with the will of God."

The selection from the psychologist, Robert *Bolles*, comes from the introduction to his book, *Theory of Motivation*. It is included because it exemplifies the importance of this metaphysical question for those outside of philosophy. It should be obvious that what is really at issue here is how men and their actions should be described. Since it is the business of psychology to explain human behavior, including human action, an answer to this philosophical question is presupposed by anyone who sets himself to do psychology. Bolles says that "the naive and traditional explanation of human behavior is that we act because we have reasons for acting. . . . We attribute a man's behavior to events going on in his mind." He goes on to reject this account of human behavior on the grounds that it is teleological and untestable. Without arguing the matter in detail, we would like to point out that Bolles' view rests on a serious misunderstanding of what is going on when we give reasons for our actions. He pictures giving a reason as making reference to a special kind of cause, a secret, mental cause. Of course, if it were, then Bolles' criticism of explaining an action by pointing to the agent's reasons for doing it would be more to the mark.

Our fourth selection is by R. S. *Peters*, from the first chapter of the *Concept of Motivation*. Peters carefully explains the difference between a causal explanation and an explanation by reference to reasons. This selection should serve to clear up the difficulty raised in the Bolles reading as well as point out some of the conceptual confusions underlying the whole question of freedom or determinism. In short, to explain most human actions, says Peters, we must put them in a context of purposeful, rule-following behavior. When we are puzzled about what a person is doing, his behavior is explained by showing why he is doing what he is doing (his purpose) and why he is doing it just that way. We look for a causal explanation only when an intentional account cannot be given. Contrary to Bolles' claim that only a causal explanation is a true explanation, Peters claims that a causal explanation of *human* behavior can at most be of use only where an intentional explanation fails.

The selection we have chosen from the influential contemporary French philosopher, Jean-Paul *Sartre*, shows that he also shares the change in our understanding of metaphysical questions. He begins by stating, "It is strange that philosophers have been able to argue endlessly about determinism and free-will, to cite examples in favor of one or the other thesis without ever attempting first to make explicit the structures contained in the very idea of *action*." His contention is that we cannot go on endlessly debating whether human action is determined without first inquiring into what we mean by *action*. He goes on to give an account of the concept that shows that the determinist thesis is unintelligible and that, therefore, the whole debate has been wide of the mark.

Sartre offers an analysis of the concept *action* and insists "that an action is on principle intentional." He then argues that no state of affairs by itself can serve as a reason for doing something. Rather, a state of affairs has to be seen in a certain light before it becomes a reason for an action. It must be seen as not necessary; that is, it must be seen against a background of other possible states of affairs: It must also be seen as lacking some desirable features present in other possible states of affairs. There is nothing in any particular state of affairs that requires that we see it against one background rather than another; and so, says Sartre, no particular social condition, no historical occurrence, no political event, can, by itself, be a reason for doing something else. Sartre offers the building of Constantinople and a workers' revolt as examples of his claims about the concepts of action and intention. Whether his particular analysis is correct or whether it can be generalized to cover all cases requires careful scrutiny. Our point here is that we now see metaphysical questions as requiring an understanding of certain key concepts in the descriptions of ourselves and our doings rather than general quasi-descriptive claims about human nature and the universe. This particular metaphysical question began with the claim that men are not free since all of their actions are the inevitable result of antecedent causes. This claim was treated as if it was descriptive and empirical and its proponents tried to offer evidence in favor of it. Its opponents attempted to invalidate particular pieces of evidence or to restrict the scope of the claim. Our view is that nothing could count as evidence for a claim such as this for two reasons. First, the claim of determinism was presupposed in the description of the evidence. For example, the psychoanalyst prepares a case history, describing the patient's complexes and repressed wishes, analyzing his dreams, and, in general, employing the language of psychoanalysis. Therefore, this case history cannot be used as proof of the psychoanalytical claims; it presupposed them. Secondly, we cannot say what will count as evidence when we are totally unclear about that for which it is supposed to be evidence. If we find the determinist's claim puzzling, we must first clearly understand just what is being claimed before we can argue that so-and-so is evidence for it and such-and-such is evidence against it.

We make a significant advance in understanding what philosophy is when we understand that much philosophy consists in clarifying the nature of the questions we ask and determining what is relevant to answering them. Frequently, the philosophical issue is in the question itself rather than the alleged answers to it.

Man Is a Physical Machine

BARON PAUL HENRI D'HOLBACH

IN WHATEVER manner man is considered, he is connected to universal nature, and submitted to the necessary and immutable laws that she imposes on all beings she contains, according to their peculiar essences or to the respective properties with which, without consulting them, she endows each particular species. Man's life is a line that nature commands him to describe upon the

---

Excerpted from *System of Nature*, Chaps. XI and XII, by Baron Paul Henri d'Holbach.

surface of the earth, without his ever being able to swerve from it, even for an instant. He is born without his own consent; his organization does innowise depend upon himself; his ideas come to him involuntarily; his habits are in the power of those who cause him to contract them; he is unceasingly modified by causes, whether visible or concealed, over which he has no control, which necessarily regulate his mode of existence, give the hue to his way of thinking, and determine his manner of acting. He is good or bad, happy or miserable, wise or foolish, reasonable or irrational, without his will being for anything in these various states. Nevertheless, in spite of the shackles by which he is bound, it is pretended he is a free agent, or that independent of the causes by which he is moved, he determines his own will, and regulates his own condition.

However slender the foundation of his opinion, of which everything ought to point out to him the error, it is current at this day and passes for an incontestable truth with a great number of people, otherwise extremely enlightened; it is the basis of religion, which supposing relations between man and the unknown being she has placed above nature, has been incapable of imagining how man could merit reward or deserve punishment from this being, if he was not a free agent. Society has been believed interested in this system; because an idea has gone abroad, that if all the actions of man were to be contemplated as necessary, the right of punishing those who injure their associates would no longer exist. At length human vanity accommodated itself to a hypothesis which, unquestionably, appears to distinguish man from all other physical beings, by assigning to him the special privilege of a total independence of all other causes, but of which a very little reflection would have shown him the impossibility....

The will, as we have elsewhere said, is a modification of the brain, by which it is disposed to action, or prepared to give play to the organs. This will is necessarily determined by the qualities, good or bad, agreeable or painful, of the object or the motive that acts upon his sense, or of which the idea remains with him, and is resuscitated by his memory. In consequence, he acts necessarily, his action is the result of the impulse he receives either from the motive, from the object, or from the idea which has modified his brain, or disposed his will. When he does not act according to this impulse, it is because there comes some new cause, some new motive, some new idea, which modified his brain in a different manner, gives him a new impulse, determines his will in another way, by which the action of the former impulse is suspended: thus, the sight of an agreeable object, or its idea, determines his will to set him in action to procure it; but if a new object or a new idea more powerfully attracts him, it gives a new direction to his will, annihilates the effect of the former, and prevents the action by which it was to be procured. This is the mode in which reflection, experience, reason, necessarily arrests or suspends the action of man's will: without this he would of necessity have followed the anterior impulse which carried him towards a then desirable object. In all this he always acts according to necessary laws from which he has no means of emancipating himself.

If when tormented with violent thirst, he figures to himself in idea, or really perceives a fountain, whose limpid streams might cool his feverish want, is he sufficient master of himself to desire or not to desire the object competent to satisfy so lively a want? It will no doubt be conceded, that it is impossible he should not be desirous to satisfy it; but it will be said—if at this moment it is announced to him that the water he so ardently desires is poisoned, he will, notwithstanding his vehement thirst, abstain from drinking it: and it has, therefore, been falsely concluded that he is a free agent. The fact, however, is, that the motive in either case is exactly the same: his own conservation. The same necessity that determined him to drink before he knew the water was deleterious upon this new discovery equally determined him not to drink; the desire of conserving himself either annihilates or suspends the former impulse; the second motive becomes stronger than the preceding, that is, the fear of death, or the desire of preserving himself, necessarily prevails over the painful sensation caused by his eagerness to drink: but, it will be said, if the thirst is very parching, an inconsiderate man without regarding the danger will risk swallowing the water. Nothing is gained by this remark: in this case, the anterior impulse only regains the ascendancy; he is persuaded that life may possibly be longer preserved, or that he shall derive a greater good by drinking the poisoned water than by enduring the torment, which, to his mind, threatens instant dissolution: thus the first becomes the strongest and necessarily urges him on to action. Nevertheless, in either case, whether he partakes of the water, or whether he does not, the two actions will be equally necessary; they will be the effect of that motive which finds itself most puissant; which consequently acts in the most coercive manner upon his will.

This example will serve to explain the whole phenomena of the human will. This will, or rather the brain, finds itself in the same situation as a bowl, which, although it has received an impulse that drives it forward in a straight line, it deranged in its course whenever a force superior to the first obliges it to change its direction. The man who drinks the poisoned water appears a madman; but the actions of fools are as necessary as those of the most prudent individuals. The motives that determine the voluptuary and the debauchee to risk their health, are as powerful, and their actions are as necessary, as those which decide the wise man to manage his. But, it will be insisted, the debauchee may be prevailed on to change his conduct: this does not imply that he is a free agent; but that motives may be found sufficiently powerful to annihilate the effect of those that previously acted upon him; then these new motives determine his will to the new mode of conduct he may adopt as necessarily as the former did to the old mode....

The errors of philosophers on the free agency of man, have arisen from their regarding his will as the *primum mobile*, the original motive of his actions; for want of recurring back, they have not perceived the multiplied, the complicated causes which, independently of him, give motion to the will itself; or which dispose and modify his brain, whilst he himself is purely passive in the motion he receives. Is he the master of desiring or not desiring an object that appears desirable to him? Without doubt it will be answered, no: but he is the master of resisting his desire, if he reflects on the consequences. But, I ask, is he capable of reflecting on these consequences, when his soul is hurried along by a very lively passion, which entirely depends upon his natural organization, and the causes by which he is modified? Is it in his power to add to these consequences all the weight necessary to counterbalance his desire? Is he the master of preventing the qualities which render an object desirable from residing in it? I shall be told: he ought to have learned to resist his passions; to contract a habit of putting a curb on his desires. I agree to it without any difficulty. But in reply, I again ask, is his nature susceptible of this modification? Does his boiling blood, his unruly imagination, the igneous fluid that circulates in his veins, permit him to make, enable him to apply true experience in the moment when it is wanted? And even when his temperament has capacitated him, has his education, the examples set before him, the ideas with which he has been inspired in early life, been suitable to make him contract this habit of repressing his desires? Have not all these things rather contributed to induce him to seek with avidity, to make him actually desire those objects which you say he ought to resist.

The *ambitious man* cries out: you will have me resist my passion; but have they not unceasingly repeated to me that rank, honors, power, are the most desirable advantages in life? Have I not seen my fellow citizens envy them, the nobles of my country sacrifice every thing to obtain them? In the society in which I live, am I not obliged to feel, that if I am deprived of these advantages, I must expect to languish in contempt; to cringe under the rod of oppression?

The *miser* says: you forbid me to love money, to seek after the means of acquiring it: alas! does not every thing tell me that, in this world, money is the greatest blessing; that it is amply sufficient to render me happy? In the country I inhabit, do I not see all my fellow citizens covetous of riches? but do I not also witness that they are little scrupulous in the means of obtaining wealth? As soon as they are enriched by the means which you censure, are they not cherished, considered and respected? by what authority, then, do you defend me from amassing treasure? what right have you to prevent my using means, which, although you call them sordid and criminal, I see approved by the sovereign? Will you have me renounce my happiness?

The *voluptuary* argues: you pretend that I should resist my desires; but was I the maker of my own temperament, which unceasingly invites me to pleasure? You call my pleasures disgraceful; but in the country in which I live, do I not witness the most dissipated men enjoying the most distinguished rank? Do I not behold that no one is ashamed of adultery but the husband it has outraged? do not I see men making trophies of their debaucheries, boasting of their libertinism, rewarded with applause?

The *choleric man* vociferates: you advise me to put a curb on my passions, and to risk the desire of avenging myself: but can I conquer my nature? Can I alter the received opinions of the world? Shall I not be forever disgraced, infallibly dishonoured in society, if I do not wash out in the blood of my fellow creatures the injuries I have received?

The *zealous enthusiast* exclaims: you recommend me mildness; you advise me to be tolerant; to be indulgent to the opinions of my fellow men; but is not my temperament violent? Do I not ardently love my God? Do they not assure me, that zeal is pleasing to him; that sanguinary inhuman persecutors have been his friends? As I wish to render myself acceptable in his sight, I therefore adopt the same means.

In short, the actions of man are never free; they are always the necessary consequence of his temperament, of the received ideas, and of the notions, either true or false, which he has formed to himself of happiness; of his opinions, strengthened by example, by education, and by daily experience. So many crimes are witnessed on the earth only because every thing conspires to render man vicious and criminal; the religion he has adopted, his government, his education, the examples set before him, irresistibly drive him on to evil: under these circumstances, morality preaches virtue to him in vain. In those societies where vice is esteemed, where crime is crowned, where venality is constantly recompense, where the most dreadful disorders are punished only in those who are too weak to enjoy the privilege of committing them with impunity, the practice of virtue is considered nothing more than a painful sacrifice of happiness. Such societies chastise, in the lower orders, those excesses which they respect in the higher ranks; and frequently have the injustice to condemn those in the penalty of death, whom public prejudices, maintained by constant example, have rendered criminal.

Man, then, is not a free agent in any one instant of his life; he is necessarily guided in each step by those advantages, whether real or fictitious, that he attaches to the objects by which his passions are roused: these passions themselves are necessary in a being who unceasingly tends towards his own happiness; their energy is necessary, since that depends on his temperament; his temperament is necessary, because it depends on the physical elements which enter into his composition; the modification of this temperament is necessary, as it is the infallible and inevitable consequence of the impulse he receives from the incessant action of moral and physical beings.

Choice Does Not Prove Freedom

In spite of these proofs of the want of free agency in man, so clear to unprejudiced minds, it will perhaps be insisted upon with no small feeling of triumph, that if it be proposed to any one, to move or not to move his hand, an action in the number of those called indifferent, he evidently appears to be the master of choosing; from which it is concluded that evidence has been offered of free agency. The reply is, this example is perfectly simple; man in performing some action which he is resolved on doing, does not by any means prove his free agency: the very desire of displaying this quality, excited by the dispute, becomes a necessary motive, which decides his will either for the one or the other of these actions: What deludes him in this instance, or that which persuades him he is a free agent at this moment, is, that he does not discern the true motive which sets him in action, namely, the desire of convincing his opponent: if in the heat of the dispute he insists and asks, "Am I not the master of throwing myself out of the window?" I shall answer him, no; that whilst he preserves his reason there is no probability that the desire of proving his free agency, will become a motive sufficiently powerful to make him sacrifice his life to the attempt: if, notwithstanding this, to prove he is a free agent, he should actually precipitate himself from the window, it would not be a sufficient warranty to conclude he acted freely, but rather that it was the violence of his temperament which spurred him on to this folly. Madness is a state, that depends upon the heat of the blood, not upon the will. A fanatic or a hero, braves death as necessarily as a more phlegmatic man or a coward flies from it.

There is, in point of fact, no difference between the man that is cast out of the window by another, and the man who throws himself out of it, except that the impulse in the first instance comes immediately from without whilst that which determines the fall in the second case, springs from within his own peculiar machine, having its more remote cause also exterior. When Mutius Scaevola held his hand in the fire, he was as much acting under the influence of necessity (caused by interior motives) that urged him to this strange action, as if his arm had been held by strong men: pride, despair, the desire of braving his enemy, a wish to astonish him, an anxiety to intimidate him, etc., were the invisible chains that held his hand bound to the fire. The love of glory, enthusiasm for their country, in like manner caused Codrus and Decius to devote themselves for their fellow-citizens. The Indian Colanus and the philosopher Peregrinus were equally obliged to burn themselves, by desire of exciting the astonishment of the Grecian assembly.

It is said that free agency is the absence of those obstacles competent to oppose themselves to the actions of man, or to the exercise of his faculties: it is pretended that he is a free agent whenever, making use of these faculties, he produces the effect he has proposed to himself. In reply to this reasoning, it is sufficient to consider that it in nowise depends upon himself to place or remove the obstacles that either determine or resist him; the motive that causes his action is no more in his own power than the obstacle that impedes him, whether this obstacle or motive be within his own machine or exterior of his person: he is not master of the thought presented to his mind, which determines his will; this thought is excited by some cause independent of himself.

To be undeceived on the system of his free agency, man has simply to recur to the motive by which his will is determined; he will always find this motive is out of his own control. It is said: that in consequence of an idea to which the mind gives birth, man acts freely if he encounters no obstacle. But the question is, what gives birth to this idea in his brain? was he the master either to prevent it from presenting itself, or from renewing itself in his brain? Does not this idea depend either upon objects that strike him exteriorly and in despite of himself, or upon causes, that without his knowledge, act within himself and modify his brain? Can he prevent his eyes, cast without design upon any object whatever, from giving him an idea of this object, and from moving his brain? He is not more master of the obstacles; they are the necessary effects of either interior or exterior causes, which always act according to their given properties. A man insults a coward; this necessarily irritates him against his insulter; but his will cannot vanquish the obstacle that cowardice places to the object of his desire, because his natural conformation, which does not depend upon himself, prevents his having courage. In this case, the coward is insulted in spite of himself; and against his will is obliged patiently to brook the insult he has received.

Absence of Restraint Is Not Absence of Necessity

The partisans of the system of free agency appear ever to have confounded constraint with necessity. Man believes he acts as a free agent, every time he does not see any thing that places obstacles to his actions; he does not perceive that the motive which causes him to will, is always necessary and independent of himself. A prisoner loaded with chains is compelled to remain in prison; but he is not a free agent in the desire to emancipate himself; his chains prevent him from acting, but they do not prevent him from willing; he would save himself if they would loose his fetters; but he would not save himself as a free agent; fear or the idea of punishment would be sufficient motives for his action.

Man may, therefore, cease to be restrained, without, for that reason, becoming a free agent: in whatever manner he acts, he will act necessarily, according to motives by which he shall be determined. He may be compared to a heavy body that finds itself arrested in its descent by any obstacle whatever: take away this obstacle, it will gravitate or continue to fall; but who shall say this dense body is free to fall or not? Is not its descent the necessary effect of its own specific gravity? The virtuous Socrates submitted to the laws of his country, although they were unjust; and though the doors of his jail were left open to him, he would not save himself; but in this he did not act as a free agent: the invisible chains of opinion, the secret love of decorum, the inward respect for the laws, even when they were iniquitous, the fear of tarnishing his glory, kept him in his prison; they were motives sufficiently powerful with this enthusiast for virtue, to induce him to wait death with tranquillity; it was not in his power to save himself, because he could find no potential motive to bring him to depart, even for an instant, from those principles to which his mind was accustomed.

Man, it is said, frequently acts against his inclination, from whence it is falsely concluded he is a free agent; but when he appears to act contrary to his inclination, he is always determined to it by some motive sufficiently efficacious to vanquish this inclination. A sick man, with a view to his cure, arrives at conquering his repugnance to the most disgusting remedies: the fear of pain, or the dread of death, then become necessary motives; consequently this sick man cannot be said to act freely.

When it is said, that man is not a free agent, it is not pretended to compare him to a body moved by a simple impulsive cause: he contains within himself causes inherent to his existence; he is moved by an interior organ, which has its own peculiar laws, and is itself necessarily determined in consequence of ideas formed from perception resulting from sensation which it receives from exterior objects. As the mechanism of these sensations, of these perceptions, and the manner they engrave ideas on the brain of man, are not known to him; because he is unable to unravel all these motions; because he cannot perceive the chain of operations in his soul, or the motive principle that acts within him, he supposes himself a free agent; which literally translated, signifies, that he moves himself by himself; that he determines himself without cause: when he rather ought to say, that he is ignorant how or why he acts in the manner he does. It is true the soul enjoys an activity peculiar to itself: but it is equally certain that this activity would never be displayed, if some motive or some cause did not put it in a condition to exercise itself: at least it will not be pretended that the soul is able either to love or to hate without being moved, without knowing the objects, without having some idea of their qualities. Gunpowder has unquestionably a particular activity, but this activity will never display itself, unless fire be applied to it; this, however, immediately sets it in motion.

The Complexity of Human Conduct and the Illusion of Free Agency

It is the great complication of motion in man, it is the variety of his action, it is the multiplicity of causes that move him, whether simultaneously or in continual succession, that persuades him he is a free agent: if all his motions were simple, if the causes that move him did not confound themselves with each other, if they were distinct, if his machine were less complicated, he would perceive that all his actions were necessary, because he would be enabled to recur instantly to the cause that made him act. A man who should be always obliged to go towards the west, would always go that side; but he would feel that, in so going, he was not a free agent: if he had another sense, as his actions or his motion, augmented by a sixth, would be still more varied and much more complicated, he would believe himself still more a free agent than he does with his five senses.

It is, then for want of recurring to the causes that move him; for want of being able to analyze, from not being competent to decompose the complicated motion of his machine, that man believes himself a free agent: it is only upon his own ignorance that he founds the profound yet deceitful notion he has of his free agency; that he builds those opinions which he brings forward as a striking proof of his pretended freedom of action. If, for a short time, each man was willing to examine his own peculiar actions, search out their true motives to discover their concatenation, he would remain convinced that the sentiment he has of his natural free agency, is a chimera that must speedily be destroyed by experience.

Nevertheless it must be acknowledged that the multiplicity and diversity of the causes which continually act upon man, frequently without even his knowledge, render it impossible, or at least extremely difficult for him to recur to the true principles of his own peculiar actions, much less the actions of others: they frequently depend upon causes so fugitive, so remote from their effects, and which, superficially examined, appear to have so little analogy, so slender a relation with them, that it requires singular sagacity to bring them into light. This is what renders the study of the moral man a task of such difficulty; this is the reason why his heart is an abyss, of which it is frequently impossible for him to fathom the depth....

If he understood the play of his organs, if he were able to recall to himself all the impulsions they have received, all the modifications they have undergone, all the effects they have produced, he would perceive that all his actions are submitted to that fatality, which regulates his own particular system, as it does the entire system of the universe: no one effect in him, any more than in nature, produces itself by chance; this, as has been before proved, is word void of sense. All that passes in him; all that is done by him; as well as all that happens in nature, or that is attributed to her, is derived from necessary causes, which act according to necessary laws, and which produce necessary effects from whence necessarily flow others.

Fatality, is the eternal, the immutable, the necessary order, established in nature; or the indispensable connexion of causes that act, with the effects they operate. Conforming to this order, heavy bodies fall; light bodies rise; that which is analogous in matter reciprocally attracts; that which is heterogeneous mutally repels; man congregates himself in society, modifies each his fellow; becomes either virtuous or wicked; either contributes to his mutual happiness, or reciprocates his misery; either loves his neighbour, or hates his companion necessarily, according to the manner in which the one acts upon the other. From whence it may be seen, that the same necessity which regulates the physical, also regulates the moral world, in which every thing is in consequence submitted to fatality. Man, in running over, frequently without his knowledge, often in spite of himself, the route which nature has marked out for him, resembles a swimmer who is obliged to follow the current that carries him along: he believes himself a free agent, because he sometimes consents, sometimes does not consent, to glide with the stream, which, notwithstanding, always hurries him forward; he believes himself the master of his condition, because he is obliged to use his arms under the fear of sinking.

Man Is a Psychological Machine

JOHN HOSPERS

PERHAPS the most obvious conception of freedom is this: an act is free if and only if it is a voluntary act. A response that occurs spontaneously, not as a result of your willing it, such as a reflex action, is not a free act. I do not know

Reprinted with permission of the International Phenomenological Society from "Meaning and Free Will" by John Hospers in *Philosophy and Phenomenological Research,* **10**, 3 (1950), 313–330.

that this view is ever held in its pure form, but it is the basis for other ones. As it stands, of course, it is ambiguous: does "voluntary" entail "premeditated?" are acts we perform semi-automatically through habit to be called free acts? To what extent is a conscious decision to act required for the act to be classified as voluntary? What of sudden outbursts of feeling? They are hardly premeditated or decided upon, yet they may have their origin in the presence or absence of habit-patterns due to self-discipline which may have been consciously decided upon. Clearly the view needs to be refined.

Now, however we may come to define "voluntary," it is perfectly possible to maintain that all voluntary acts are free acts and vice versa; after all, it is a matter of what meaning we are giving to the word "free" and we can give it this meaning if we choose. But it soon becomes apparent that this is not the meaning which most of us *want* to give it: for there *are* classes of actions which we want to refrain from calling "free" even though they are voluntary (not that we have this denial in mind when we use the word "free"—still, it is significant that we do not use the word in some situations in which the act in question is nevertheless voluntary).

When a man tells a state secret under torture, he does choose voluntarily between telling and enduring more torture; and when he submits to a bandit's command at the point of a gun, he voluntarily chooses to submit rather than to be shot. And still such actions would not generally be called free; it is clear that they are performed under compulsion. Voluntary acts performed under compulsion would not be called free; and the cruder view is to this extent amended.

For some persons, this is as far as we need to go. Schlick, for example, says that the free-will issue is the scandal of philosophy and nothing but so much wasted ink and paper, because the whole controversy is nothing but an inexcusable confusion between compulsion and universal causality.[1] The free act is the uncompelled act, says Schlick, and controversies about causality and determinism have nothing to do with the case. When one asks whether an act done of necessity is free, the question is ambiguous: if "of necessity" means "by compulsion," then the answer is no; if, on the other hand, "of necessity" is a way of referring to "causal uniformity" in nature—the sense in which we may misleadingly speak of the laws of nature as "necessary" simply because there are no exceptions to them—then the answer is clearly yes; every act is an instance of some causal law (uniformity) or other, but this has nothing to do with its being free in the sense of uncompelled.

For Schlick, this is the end of the matter. Any attempt to discuss the matter further simply betrays a failure to perceive the clarifying distinctions that Schlick has made.

> Freedom means the opposite of compulsion; a man is *free* if he does not act under *compulsion*, and he is compelled or unfree when he is hindered from without in the realization of his natural desires. Hence he is unfree when he is locked

[1] Moritz Schlick, *The Problems of Ethics*, Chapter VII.

> up, or chained, or when someone forces him at the point of a gun to do what otherwise he would not do. This is quite clear, and everyone will admit that the everyday or legal notion of the lack of freedom is thus correctly interpreted, and that a man will be considered quite free . . . if no such external compulsion is exerted upon him.[2]

This all seems clear enough. And yet if we ask whether it ends the matter, whether it states what we "really mean" by "free," many of us will feel qualms. We remember statements about human beings being pawns of their environment, victims of conditions beyond their control, the result of causal influences stemming from parents, etc., and we think, "Still, are we really free?" We do not want to say that the uniformity of nature itself binds us or renders us unfree; yet is there not something in what generations of wise men have said about man being fettered? Is there not something too facile, too sleight-of-hand, in Schlick's cutting of the Gordian knot?

It will be noticed that we have slipped from talking about acts as being free into talking about human beings as free. Both locutions are employed, I would say about 50-50. Sometimes an attempt is made to legislate definitely between the two: Stebbing, for instance, says that one must never call acts free, but only the doers of the acts.[3]

Let us pause over this for a moment. If it is we and not our acts that are to be called free, the most obvious reflection to make is that we are free to do some things and not free to do other things; we are free to lift our hands but not free to lift the moon. We cannot simply call ourselves free or unfree *in toto*; we must say at best that we are free in respect of certain actions only. G. E. Moore states the criterion as follows: we are free to do an act if we can do it *if* we want to; that which we can do if we want to is what we are free to do.[4] Some things certain people are free to do while others are not: most of us are free to move our legs, but paralytics are not; some of us are free to concentrate on philosophical reading matter for three hours at a stretch while others are not. In general, we could relate the two approaches by saying that a *person* is free *in respect of* a given action if he can do it if he wants to, and in this case his *act* is free.

Moore himself, however, has reservations that Schlick has not. He adds that there *is* a sense of "free" which fulfills the criterion he has just set forth; but that there may be *another* sense in which man cannot be said to be free in all the situations in which he could rightly be said to be so in the first sense.

And surely it is not necessary for me to multiply examples of the sort of thing we mean. In practice most of us would not call free many persons who behave voluntarily and even with calculation aforethought, and under no compulsion either of any obvious sort. A metropolitan newspaper headlines an article with the words "Boy Killer Is Doomed Long before He Is Born,"[5] and then goes

[2] *Ibid.*, p. 150.

[3] L. Susan Stebbing, *Philosophy and the Physicists*, p. 242.

[4] G. E. Moore, *Ethics*, p. 205.

[5] *New York Post*, Tuesday, May 18, 1948, p. 4.

on to describe how a twelve-year-old boy has just been sentenced to thirty years in Sing Sing for the murder of a girl; his family background includes records of drunkenness, divorce, social maladjustment, epilepsy, and paresis. He early displays a tendency to sadistic activity to hide an underlying masochism and "prove that he's a man"; being coddled by his mother only worsens this tendency, until, spurned by a girl in his attempt on her, he kills her—not simply in a fit of anger, but calculatingly, deliberately. Is he free in respect of his criminal act, or for that matter in most of the acts of his life? Surely to ask this question is to answer it in the negative. Perhaps I have taken an extreme case; but it is only to show the superficiality of the Schlick analysis the more clearly. Though not everyone has criminotic tendencies, everyone has been moulded by influences which in large measure at least determine his present behavior; he is literally the product of these influences, stemming from periods prior to his "years of discretion," giving him a host of character traits that he cannot change now even if he would. So obviously does what a man is depend upon how a man comes to be, that it is small wonder that philosophers and sages have considered man far indeed from being the master of his fate. It is not as if a man's will were standing high and serene above the flux of events that have moulded him; it is itself caught up in this flux, itself carried along on the current. An act is free when it is determined by the man's character, say moralists; but when there was nothing the man could do to shape his character, and even the degree of will power available to him in shaping his habits and disciplining himself to overcome the influence of his early environment is a factor over which he has no control, what are we to say of this kind of "freedom?" Is it not rather like the freedom of the machine to stamp labels on cans when it has been devised for just that purpose? Some machines can do so more efficiently than others, but only because they have been better constructed.

It is not my purpose here to establish this thesis in general, but only in one specific respect which has received comparatively little attention, namely, the field referred to by psychiatrists as that of unconscious motivation. In what follows I shall restrict my attention to it because it illustrates as clearly as anything the points I wish to make.

Let me try to summarize very briefly the psychoanalytic doctrine on this point.[6] The conscious life of the human being, including the conscious decisions and volitions, is merely a mouthpiece for the unconscious—not directly for the enactment of unconscious drives, but of the compromise between unconscious drives and unconscious reproaches. There is a Big Three behind the scenes which the automaton called the conscious personality carries out: the id, an "eternal

[6] I am aware that the theory presented below is not accepted by all practicing psychoanalysts. Many non-Freudians would disagree with the conclusions presented below. But I do not believe that this fact affects my argument, as long as the concept of unconscious motivation is accepted. I am aware, too, that much of the language employed in the following descriptions is animistic and metaphorical; but as long as I am presenting a view I would prefer to "go the whole hog" and present it in its strongest possible light. The theory can in any case be made clearest by the use of such language, just as atomic theory can often be made clearest to students with the use of models.

gimme," presents its wish and demands its immediate satisfaction; the super-ego says no to the wish immediately upon presentation, and the unconscious ego, the mediator between the two, tries to keep peace by means of compromise.[7]

To go into examples of the functioning of these three "bosses" would be endless; psychoanalytic case books supply hundreds of them. The important point for us to see in the present context is that it is the unconscious that determines what the conscious impulse and the conscious action shall be. Hamlet, for example, had a strong Oedipus wish, which was violently counteracted by super-ego reproaches; these early wishes were vividly revived in an unusual adult situation in which his uncle usurped the coveted position from Hamlet's father and won his mother besides. This situation evoked strong strictures on the part of Hamlet's super-ego, and it was this that was responsible for his notorious delay in killing his uncle. A dozen times Hamlet could have killed Claudius easily; but every time Hamlet "decided" not to: a free choice, moralists would say—but no, listen to the super-ego: "What you feel such hatred toward your uncle for, what you are plotting to kill him for, is precisely the crime which you yourself desire to commit: to kill your father and replace him in the affections of your mother. Your fate and your uncle's are bound up together." This paralyzes Hamlet into inaction. Consciously all he knows is that he is unable to act; this conscious inability he rationalizes, giving a different excuse each time.[8]

We have always been conscious of the fact that we are not masters of our fate in every respect—that there are many things which we cannot do, that nature is more powerful than we are, that we cannot disobey laws without danger of reprisals, etc. Lately we have become more conscious, too, though novelists and dramatists have always been fairly conscious of it, that we are not free with respect to the emotions that we feel—whom we love or hate, what types we admire, and the like. More lately still we have been reminded that there are unconscious motivations for our basic attractions and repulsions, our compulsive actions or inabilities to act. But what is not welcome news is that our very acts of volition, and the entire train of deliberations leading up to them, are but facades for the expression of unconscious wishes, or rather, unconscious compromises and defenses....

A student at a university, possessing wealth, charm, and all that is usually considered essential to popularity, begins to develop the following personality-pattern: although well taught in the graces of social conversation, he always makes a *faux pas* somewhere, and always in the worst possible situation; to his friends he makes cutting remarks which hurt deeply—and always apparently aimed in such a way as to hurt the most: a remark that would not hurt A but would hurt B he invariably makes to B rather than to A, and so on. None of this is conscious. Ordinarily he is considerate of people, but he contrives always

[7] This view is very clearly developed in Edmund Bergler, *Divorce Won't Help*, especially Chapter I.

[8] See *The Basic Writings of Sigmund Freud*, Modern Library Edition, p. 310. (In *The Interpretation of Dreams.*) Cf. also the essay by Ernest Jones, "A Psycho-analytical Study of Hamlet."

(unconsciously) to impose on just those friends who would resent it most, and at just the times when he should know that he should not impose: at 3 o'clock in the morning, without forewarning, he phones a friend in a near-by city demanding to stay at his apartment for the weekend; naturally the friend is offended, but the person himself is not aware that he has provoked the grievance ("common sense" suffers a temporary eclipse when the neurotic pattern sets in, and one's intelligence, far from being of help in such a situation, is used in the interest of the neurosis), and when the friend is cool to him the next time they meet, he wonders why and feels unjustly treated. Aggressive behavior on his part invites resentment and aggression in turn, but all that he consciously sees is other's behavior toward him—and he considers himself the innocent victim of an unjustified "persecution."

Each of these choices is, from the moralist's point of view, free: he chose to phone his friend at 3 a.m.; he chose to make the cutting remark that he did, etc. What he does not know is that an ineradicable masochistic pattern has set in. His unconscious is far more shrewd and clever than is his conscious intellect; it sees with uncanny accuracy just what kind of behavior will damage him most, and unerringly forces him into that behavior. Consciously, the student "doesn't know why he did it"—he gives different "reasons" at different times, but they are all, once again, rationalizations cloaking the unconscious mechanism which propels him willy-nilly into actions that his "common sense" eschews.

The more of this sort of thing you see, the more you can see what the psychoanalyst means when he talks about "the illusion of free-will." And the more of a psychiatrist you become, the more you are overcome with a sense of what an illusion this precious free-will really is. In some kinds of cases most of us can see it already: it takes no psychiatrist to look at the epileptic and sigh with sadness at the thought that soon this person before you will be as one possessed, not the same thoughtful intelligent person you knew. But people are not aware of this in other contexts, for example when they express surprise at how a person whom they have been so good to could treat them so badly. Let us suppose that you help a person financially or morally or in some other way, so that he is in your debt; suppose further that he is one of the many neurotics who unconsciously identify kindness with weakness and aggression with strength, then he will unconsciously take your kindness to him as weakness and use it as the occasion for enacting some aggression against you. He can't help it, he may regret it himself later; still, he will be driven to do it. If we gain a little knowledge of psychiatry, we can look at him with pity, that a person otherwise so worthy should be so unreliable—but we will exercise realism too and be aware that there are some types of people that you cannot be good to in "free" acts of their conscious volition, they will use your own goodness against you.

Sometimes the persons themselves will become dimly aware that "something behind the scenes" is determining their behavior. The divorcee will sometimes view herself with detachment, as if she were some machine (and indeed the psychoanalyst does call her a "repeating-machine"): "I know I'm caught in a net, that I'll fall in love with this guy and marry him and the whole ridiculous merry-go-round will start all over again."

We talk about free will, and we say, yes, the person is free to do so-and-so if he can do so *if* he wants to—and we forget that his wanting to is itself caught up in the stream of determinism, that unconscious forces drive him into the wanting or not wanting to do the thing in question. The idea of the puppet whose motions are manipulated from behind the invisible wires, or better still, by springs inside, is no mere figure of speech. The analogy is a telling one at almost every point.

And the pity of it is that it all started so early, before we knew what was happening. The personality-structure is inelastic after the age of five, and comparatively so in most cases after the age of three. Whether one acquires a neurosis or not is determined by that age—and just as involuntarily as if it had been a curse of God. If, for example, a masochistic pattern was set up, under pressure of hyper-narcissism combined with real or fancied infantile deprivation, then the masochistic snowball was on its course downhill long before we or anybody else knew what was happening, and long before anyone could do anything about it. To speak of human beings as "puppets" in such a context is no mere metaphor, but a stark rendering of a literal fact: only the psychiatrist knows what puppets people really are; and it is no wonder that the protestations of philosophers that "the act which is the result of a volition, a deliberation, a conscious decision, is free" leave these persons, to speak mildly, somewhat cold.

But, one may object, all the states thus far described have been abnormal, neurotic ones. The well-adjusted (normal) person at least is free.

Leaving aside the question of how clearly and on what grounds one can distinguish the neurotic from the normal, let me use an illustration of a proclivity that everyone would call normal, namely, the decision of a man to support his wife and possibly a family, and consider briefly its genesis.[9]

Every baby comes into the world with a full-fledged case of megalomania—interested only in himself, naively assuming that he is the center of the universe and that others are present only to fulfill his wishes, and furious when his own wants are not satisfied immediately no matter for what reason. Gratitude, even for all the time and worry and care expended on him by the mother, is an emotion entirely foreign to the infant, and as he grows older it is inculcated in him only with the greatest difficulty; his natural tendency is to assume that everything that happens to him is due to himself, except for denials and frustrations, which are due to the "cruel, denying" outer world, in particular the mother; and that he owes nothing to anyone, is dependent on no one. This omnipotence-complex, or illusion of non-dependence, has been called the "autarchic fiction." Such a conception of the world is actually fostered in the child by the conduct of adults, who automatically attempt to fulfill the infant's every wish concerning nourishment, sleep, and attention. The child misconceives causality and sees

9 Edmund Bergler, *The Battle of the Conscience*, Chapter I.

in these wish-fulfillments not the results of maternal kindness and love, but simply the result of his own omnipotence.

This fiction of omnipotence is gradually destroyed by experience, and its destruction is probably the deepest disappointment of the early years of life. First of all, the infant discovers that he is the victim of organic urges and necessities: hunger, defecation, urination. More important, he discovers that the maternal breast, which he has not previously distinguished from his own body (he has not needed to, since it was available when he wanted it), is not a part of himself after all, but of another creature upon whom he is dependent. He is forced to recognize this, e.g., when he wants nourishment and it is at the moment not present; even a small delay is most damaging to the "autarchic fiction." Most painful of all is the experience of weaning, probably the greatest tragedy in every baby's life, when his dependence is most cruelly emphasized; it is a frustrating experience because what he wants is no longer there at all; and if he has been able to some extent to preserve the illusion of non-dependence heretofore, he is not able to do so now—it is plain that the source of his nourishment is not dependent on him, but he on it. The shattering of the autarchic fiction is a great disillusionment to every child, a tremendous blow to his ego which he will, in one way or another, spend the rest of his life trying to repair. How does he do this?

First of all, his reaction to frustration is anger and fury; and he responds by kicking, biting, etc., the only ways he knows. But he is motorically helpless, and these measures are ineffective, and only serve to emphasize his dependence the more. Moreover, against such responses of the child the parental reaction is one of prohibition, generally accompanied by physical force of some kind. Generally the child soon learns that this form of rebellion is profitless, and brings him more harm than good. He wants to respond to frustration with violent aggression, and at the same time learns that he will be punished for such aggression, and that in any case the latter is ineffectual. What face-saving solution does he find? Since he must "face facts," since he must in any case "conform" if he is to have any peace at all, he tries to make it seem as if he himself is the source of the commands and prohibitions: the *external* prohibitive force is *internalized*—and here we have the origin of conscience. By making the prohibitive agency seem to come from within himself, the child can "save face"—as if saying, "The prohibition comes from within me, not from outside, so I'm not subservient to external rule, I'm only obeying rules I've set up myself," thus to some extent saving the autarchic fiction, and at the same time avoiding unpleasant consequences directed against himself by complying with parental commands.

Moreover, the boy[10] has unconsciously never forgiven the mother for his dependence on her in early life, for nourishment and all other things. It has upset his illusion of non-dependence. These feelings have been repressed and are not remembered; but they are acted out in later life in many ways—e.g., in

[10] The girl's development after this point is somewhat different. Society demands more aggressiveness of the adult male, hence there are more super-ego strictures on tendencies toward passivity in the male; accordingly his defenses must be stronger.

the constant deprecation man has for woman's duties such as cooking and housework of all sorts ("All she does is stay at home and get together a few meals, and she calls that work"), and especially in the man's identification with the mother in his sex experiences with women. By identifying with someone one cancels out in effect the person with whom he identifies—replacing that person, unconsciously denying his existence, and the man, identifying with his early mother, playing the active role in "giving" to his wife as his mother has "given" to him, is in effect the denial of his mother's existence, a fact which is narcissistically embarrassing to his ego because it is chiefly responsible for shattering his autarchic fiction. In supporting his wife, he can unconsciously deny that his mother gave to him, and that he was dependent on her giving. Why is it that the husband plays the provider, and wants his wife to be dependent on no one else, although twenty years before he was nothing but a parasitic baby? This is a face-saving device on his part: he can act out the reasoning "See, I'm not the parasitic baby, on the contrary I'm the provider, the giver." His playing the provider is a constant face-saving device, to deny his early dependence which is so embarrassing to his ego. It is no wonder that men generally dislike to be reminded of their babyhood, when they were dependent on woman.

Thus we have a perfectly normal adult reaction which is unconsciously motivated. The man "chooses" to support a family—and his choice is as unconsciously motivated as anything could be. (I have described here only the "normal" state of affairs, uncomplicated by the well-nigh infinite number of variations that occur in actual practice.)

Now, what of the notion of responsibility? What happens to it on our analysis? . . .

We speak of a machine turning out good products most of the time but every once in a while it turns out a "lemon." We do not, of course, hold the product responsible for this, but the machine, and via the machine, its maker. Is it silly to extend to inanimate objects the idea of responsibility? Of course. But is it any less silly to employ the notion in speaking of human creatures? Are not the two kinds of cases analogous in countless important ways? Occasionally a child turns out badly too, even when his environment and training are the same as that of his brothers and sisters who turn out "all right." He is the "bad penny." His acts of rebellion against parental discipline in adult life (such as the case of the gambler, already cited) are traceable to early experiences of real or fancied denial of infantile wishes. Sometimes the denial has been real, though many denials are absolutely necessary if the child is to grow up to observe the common decencies of civilized life; sometimes, if the child has an unusual quantity of narcissism, every event that occurs is interpreted by him as a denial of his wishes, and nothing a parent could do, even granting every humanly possible wish, would help. In any event, the later neurosis can be attributed to this. Can the person himself be held responsible? Hardly. If he engages in activities which are a menace to society, he must be put into prison, of course, but responsibility is another matter. The time when the events occurred which rendered his neurotic behavior inevitable was a time long before he was capable of thought and decision. As an adult, he is a victim of a world he never made—only this world is inside him.

What about the children who turn out "all right"? All we can say is that "it's just lucky for them" that what happened to their unfortunate brother didn't happen to them; *through no virtue of their own* they are not doomed to the life of unconscious guilt, expiation, conscious depression, terrified ego-gestures for the appeasement of a tyrannical super-ego that he is. The machine turned them out with a minimum of damage. But if the brother cannot be blamed for his evils, neither can they be praised for their good. It will take society a long time to come round to this attitude. We do not blame people for the color of their eyes, but we have not attained the same attitude toward their socially significant activities.

We all agree that machines turn out "lemons," we all agree that nature turns out misfits in the realm of biology—the blind, the crippled, the diseased; but we hesitate to include the realm of the personality, for here, it seems, is the last retreat of our dignity as human beings. Our ego can endure anything but this; this island at least must remain above the encroaching flood. But may not precisely the same analysis be made here also? Nature turns out psychological "lemons" too, in far greater quantities than any other kind; and indeed all of us are "lemons" in some respect or other, the difference being one of degree. Some of us are lucky enough not to have a gambling-neurosis or criminotic tendencies or masochistic mother-attachment or overdimensional repetition-compulsion to make our lives miserable, but most of our actions, those usually considered the most important, are unconsciously dominated just the same. And, if a neurosis may be likened to a curse of God, let those of us, the elect, who are enabled to enjoy a measure of life's happiness without the hell-fire of neurotic guilt, take this, not as our own achievement, but simply for what it is—a gift of God.

Let us, however, quit metaphysics and put the situation schematically in the form of a deductive argument.

1. An occurrence over which we had no control is something we cannot be held responsible for.
2. Events E, occurring during our babyhood, were events over which we had no control.
3. Therefore events E were events which we cannot be held responsible for.
4. But if there is something we cannot be held responsible for, neither can we be held responsible for something that inevitably results from it.
5. Events E have as inevitable consequence Neurosis N, which in turn has an inevitable consequence Behavior B.
6. Since N is the inevitable consequence of E and B is the inevitable consequence of N, B is the inevitable consequence of E.
7. Hence, not being responsible for E, we cannot be responsible for B.

In Samuel Butler's Utopian satire *Erewhon* there occurs the following passage, in which a judge is passing sentence on a prisoner:

> It is all very well for you to say that you came of unhealthy parents, and had a severe accident in your childhood which permanently undermined your constitution; excuses such as these are the ordinary refuge of the criminal; but they cannot for one moment be listened to by the ear of justice. I am not here to enter upon curious metaphysical questions as to the origin of this or that—questions to which there would be no end were their introduction once tolerated, and which would result in throwing the only guilt on the tissues of the primordial cell, or on the elementary gases. There is no question of how you came to be wicked, but only this—namely, are you wicked or not? This has been decided in the affirmative, neither can I hesitate for a single moment to say that it has been decided justly. You are a bad and dangerous person, and stand branded in the eyes of your fellow countrymen with one of the most heinous known offenses.[11]

As moralists read this passage, they may perhaps nod with approval. But the joke is on them. The sting comes when we realize what the crime is for which the prisoner is being sentenced: namely, consumption. The defendant is reminded that during the previous year he was sentenced for aggravated bronchitis, and is warned that he should profit from experience in the future. Butler is employing here his familiar method of presenting some human tendency (in this case, holding people responsible for what isn't their fault) to a ridiculous extreme and thereby reducing it to absurdity. How soon will mankind appreciate the keen edge of Butler's bitter irony? How long will they continue to read such a passage, but fail to smile, or yet to wince?

Our discussion thus far has developed into a kind of double-headed monster. We started to talk about analysis of meaning, and we have ended by taking a journey into the realm of the unconscious. Can we unite the two heads into one, or at least make them look at each other?

I think the second possibility is not a remote one. Surely we have shown that the "meaning of a word" is not the same as "what we had in mind in using the word," and the word "free" is a concrete illustration of this. The psychoanalytic examples we have adduced have (if one was not acquainted with them before) added, so to speak, a new dimension to the term "free." In our ordinary use of this word we probably had nothing in mind as concrete as the sort of thing brought to light in our examples; but now that we have, we hesitate to label many actions as free which previously we had so labeled without hesitation. And we would, I think, call people "free" in far fewer respects than we would have previously.

Can human beings, in the light of psychiatric knowledge, be called "free" in any respect at all?

We must remember that every term that can be significantly used must have a significant opposite. If the opposite cannot significantly be asserted, neither can its original. If the term "unfree" can be significantly used, so can the term "free." Even though there may be no actual denotation of a term naming an opposite, one must know what it would be like—what it would mean to speak

[11] Samuel Butler, *Erewhon* (Modern Library edition), p. 107.

of it; even though there are no white crows, it must be significant, as indeed it is, to speak of them. Now is the case of freedom like that of the white crows that don't exist but can be significantly spoken of, or like the black crows that do exist and can be significantly spoken of as well?

Unless "freedom" is taken to mean the same as "lack of cause" and a principle of universal causality is taken for granted, I think the latter must be the case.

If we asked the psychoanalysts for their opinion on this, they would doubtless reply somewhat as follows. They would say that they were not accustomed to using the term "free" at all, but that if they had to suggest a criterion for distinguishing the free from the unfree, they would say that a person's freedom occurs in inverse proportion to his neuroticism; the more he is compelled in his behavior by a *malevolent* unconscious, the less free he is. We speak of degrees of freedom—and the psychologically normal and well-adjusted individual is comparatively the freest, even though most of his behavior is determined by his unconscious.

But suppose it is the determination of his behavior by his unconscious, no matter what kind, that we balk at? We may then say that a man is free only to the extent that his behavior is *not* unconsciously motivated at all. If this be our criterion, most of our behavior could not be called free: everything, including both impulses and volitions, having to do with our basic attitudes toward life, the general tenor of our tastes, whether we become philosophers or artists or business men, our whole affective life including our preferences for blondes or brunettes, active or passive, older or younger, has its inevitable basis in the unconscious. Only those comparatively vanilla-flavored aspects of life—such as our behavior toward people who don't really matter to us—are exempted from this rule.

These, I think, are the two principal criteria for distinguishing freedom from the lack of it which we might set up on the basis of psychoanalytic knowledge. Conceivably we might set up others. In every case, of course, it remains trivially true that "it all depends on how we choose to use the word." The facts are what they are, regardless of how we choose to label them. But if we choose to label facts in a way which is out of accordance with people's deep-seated and traditional methods of labeling them, as we would be doing if we labeled "free" human actions which we know as much about as we now do through modern psychiatry, then we shall only be manipulating words to mislead our fellow creatures.

Behaviorism and Determinism

ROBERT BOLLES

> The notion of cause is replaced by the notion of law. Instead of causal relation, we have the conception of a continuous succession of events logically connected with one another by an underlying principle . . .
>
> SIR EDMUND WHITTAKER

ONLY rarely is motivation said to be a fact of human experience, that is, a mental event, which determines the course of action. The idea of motivation does not originate from what men say either about their own experience or about their own behavior. It is not one of the "indigenous problems" of psychology.

Nor is motivation a fact of behavior. There is not one feature or aspect or characteristic of behavior to which we invariably have reference when we say that some behavior is motivated. Although some writers have suggested behavioral criteria to define motivation, these attempts to specify what is meant by motivation are not very compelling. There is little agreement among the different proposals about what the defining criteria should be. We may say, for example, that an animal that has been deprived of food is hungry, or that it has a hunger drive, or that it "looks" motivated. But even though we may agree on this, it is not so clear that we can agree on what characteristic of its behavior makes the animal look motivated.

What one proposes as a definition of motivated behavior seems to depend more upon his theoretical commitments than upon anything in the behavior itself. Any solution to the problem of what it is about a particular behavior that makes it appear motivated will therefore depend upon how we regard behavior in general and how we explain it in general. Thus, motivation seems to be neither a fact of experience nor a fact of behavior, but rather an idea or concept we introduce when we undertake to explain behavior.

The Explanation of Behavior

Sometimes we are fortunate enough to observe behavior occurring as a direct response to prevailing stimulus conditions in the environment. In such cases no very elaborate explanation is necessary; we may simply cite the eliciting conditions. In these cases of reflexive responses, the behavior of the organism becomes nearly as predictable as the behavior of simple physical systems, and our explanation can be correspondingly simple. More frequently, though, no identifiable external stimulus can be specified for a certain act. In this case behavior might be explained indirectly as the result of stimuli that have been effective in the past or it might be explained indirectly as a result of the physical structure

---

of the individual, or of its prior experience. But all such explanations would be relatively indirect compared with the simple idea that there is a single active internal agency which, if it could be located, would provide a direct explanation. If such an internal agency or cause of behavior could be found, our explanation of all behavior could then be as simple as it is in the case of the reflex. Typically, the search for such an agency is fruitless, and it is then that we take the much easier course of hypothesizing the existence of an appropriate agency.[1] Different theories of motivation are distinguished primarily by the different sorts of motivating agencies that they hypothesize.

In this sense the most enduring theory of motivation is that which attributes a man's behavior to the results of his own mental processes. We can designate this traditional approach to the problem of explaining behavior by any name we wish, since it has no accepted name (prevailing doctrines often don't). Let us call it rationalism or, more precisely, traditional rationalism.

TRADITIONAL RATIONALISM. The naive and traditional explanation of human behavior is that we act because we have reasons for acting. Because we have free will, our reasons constitute a sufficient account of the whole matter. Such was the common view of the Greek philosophers, and such is the common view of the layman today. Traditional rationalism, of course, receives considerable support from our continuing use of it in our day-to-day contact with people. We hold our fellow man personally responsible as the author of his actions, and society expects him to describe his own actions in terms of intention, awareness, and purpose. We teach our children to use these words by making our transactions with them contingent upon what we consider to be their proper usage. We all do this, even the most behavioristic of us, because that is, in turn, what we have learned to do.

We attribute a man's behavior to events going on in his mind. This is the common and familiar variety of explanation which provides the point of departure for all other theories of motivation. All alternative conceptions of motivation and all alternative motivation constructs arise as reactions to this traditional rationalistic doctrine.

There are two distinguishing characteristics of traditional rationalistic explanations of behavior. These explanations are almost invariably (1) teleological and (2) untestable.

TELEOLOGY. When we speak in everyday language about the reasons for some behavior or about its purpose, we usually have reference to the mind, and more specifically to the conscious intentions of the person behaving. And to the extent that the individual has some purpose or intention that is focused upon the future, such an explanation is said to be teleological. Today we tend to re-

[1] Skinner makes the point this way: "A rat does not always respond to food placed before it, and a factor called its 'hunger' is invoked by way of explanation. The rat is said to eat only when it is hungry. It is because eating is not inevitable that we are led to hypothesize an internal state to which we may assign the variability. Where there is a no variability, no state is needed. Since the rat usually responds to a shock to its foot by flexing its leg, no 'flexing drive' comparable to hunger is felt to be required" (Skinner, 1938, p. 341).

strict teleological explanations to human behavior because of our conviction that only man can foresee the consequences of his actions. The idea that purpose always implies intention and that some reasoning intellect, either man's or God's, must be the author of the intention is a feature of Christian philosophy; it was formalized by Augustine and the other codifiers of Christian theology.[2] By contrast, Greek philosophers found it possible to consider purpose, and even reason as characteristics of nature quite apart from any conscious intention on the part of man. Thus, Aristotle proclaims that in some cases an event is explained when we know what end it serves.

> Another sort of cause is that on account of which a thing is done. For example, bodily health is a cause of walking exercise. Why does a man take exercise? We say it is in order to have good health; in this way we mean to specify the cause of walking.[3]

This earlier teleological concept, the idea of final cause as something apart from intention, was most suited to processes of growth, development, and fulfillment. For example, a block of stone becomes a statue with the sculptor as a causal agent or a child grows up and becomes a man. The stone and the child represent the unfulfilled but potential matter to which the statue and the man give form and fulfillment. They in turn are the final causes of their respective developments.

Whether we speak of purpose in the sense of final cause or purpose in the sense of intentions, both usages have a common element; some events are explained for some people when a justification for them is found. Justification is one variety of explanation. Some, like Aristotle, insist that there are certain events in the world that can be given meaning only in terms of the reasons for which they occur. But the meaning that is found in these instances is invariably evaluative; it is justification. Consider as an example the ancient argument that the appearance of purpose throughout nature is proof of the existence of a Creator. Aside from the difficulty that the argument presupposes what it purports to prove (i.e., the existence of purpose), it has the additional difficulty that after invoking a Creator such an explanation, or justification, stops with its account of nature as though nothing more were of interest. Invoking a Creator perhaps justifies creation but tells us nothing about creation; it has only restated the problem.[4] So, too, when we demand of a person the reason for his actions,

[2] The idea that man is personally, morally responsible for his own acts is also due to the early Church Fathers. The blamable part of the human personality was called the soul. The Greeks, on the assumption that man always sought to do good, attributed evil to human error or ignorance.

[3] Aristotle's views on causation are given in *Physics*, Book 2, ch. 3, and *de Anima*, Book 2, ch. 4. He believed a phenomenon was not fully explained until its purpose, its final form, and its physical causes had all been accounted for.

[4] The point was made by Hume (1779) when he said that the argument (for the existence of God) from design was invalid because it involves the assumption that the existence of a creator was a sufficient cause of creation, whereas at most the existence of a creator is only necessary. The argument itself is that the world presents endless indications of means adapting themselves to ends, which could only have occurred as the deliberate action of a powerful intellect.

his statement that he behaved as he did for such and such a reason only restates the problem; at best, we still have to explain why he had the reason he had. In the meantime, however, we may attach blame or praise to his purposes, and, indeed, it is probably just the evaluative freedom we have with another person's motives that gives us such a sense that his purposes are important. If we were to give up the notion of purpose as the cause of action we would lose one of the principal objects of our own affections and aggressions.

UNTESTABILITY. The most serious limitation of traditional rationalism is not that its explanations are teleological, but that they are inherently untestable. The events that are presumed to explain behavior are supposed to occur in the mind and be available only to the individual himself. Others have no ready or certain access to the hypothesized events. Moreover, there are no explicit hypotheses about how the mind is supposed to work so as to produce behavior; the relationships between these inaccessible mental events and observable behavior are so ill-defined and elusive that we cannot lay down any rules to indicate how the mind itself works. How does an intention to act (granting that an intention to act can produce the action) itself arise from the individual's perceptions, knowledge, feelings, and so on? There are no rules to guide us.

We should note that it is not just the case that such rules have not been found; typically, the proponents of traditional rationalism insist that there are no such rules. They say that the mind of man cannot be bound by lawfulness; it operates creatively and dynamically rather than according to fixed, predictable principles. Plato said that the psyche is that which moves itself; it has laws of its own being and needs no others. Similar statements about the inherent unpredictability, the untrammeled freedom of the human mind have come rattling down the ages. These assertions are, in fact, a crucial part of the traditional rationalistic doctrine and it is for this reason, as we will see later in this chapter, that traditional rationalism does not constitute a "theory" of motivation; nor does it provide an explanation of behavior in any real sense. That is, it is not a coherent, consistent, testable set of propositions about behavior; indeed, it is in large measure a denial that such a set of propositions can be found.

Mechanism

In his restless quest for understanding and certainty man has sought to find the causes of all natural events, including, sometimes, human behavior. One of the oldest and most time-honored alternatives to the traditional rationalistic approach to explanation is mechanism or physicalism. To summarize it briefly, this is the doctrine that all natural events have physical causes, and that if we knew enough about physical and mechanical systems we would then be able to explain, at least in principle, all natural phenomena. The mechanist has the faith that when all the mechanical factors have been accounted for there will be nothing else left to explain.

This faith is supported in part by the predictability of physical objects in everyday life. We throw rocks and we observe that they behave in a reasonably predictable manner. If we make our observations on a billiard table we find that the predictability of the balls appears to be limited only by our skill in applying energy to them. The mechanist starts on the basis of a number of such observations and proceeds by analogy to the hypothesis that all events in nature have a similar machine-like predictability.

The doctrine of mechanism is based upon several distinct precepts, and it is important not to confuse them. Mechanism views all the phenomena of nature in the same light; while the rationalist makes a special case of man's ability to reason, the mechanist is concerned with finding principles that will include the behavior of man among the other phenomena of nature. Man's ability to reason provides no grounds for introducing exceptions to the laws of nature. His intellectual activity must be derived somehow from other, simpler principles.

The mechanist is also a determinist. While the rationalist assumes free will, the mechanist assumes that there are systematic laws of behavior that can be discovered. He assumes that if these laws were known they would permit behavior to be predicted. He may or may not involve the mind of man in his explanatory schemes, but if the mind is included, then it too must follow determinate laws.

The third distinguishing characteristic of the mechanist is his assumption that the world of physical events not only provides the pattern of what is natural and what is lawfully determined in nature but also provides the substance for all phenomena. Thus, he is a materialist. Behavior is not only a natural phenomenon, and lawfully determined, but is determined by precisely the same physical laws and forces that apply throughout nature. The ultimate and only reality, it is assumed, is physical in character.

There were Greek mechanists, but they were a minority group, and their influence was small compared with that of either Plato or Aristotle. Any substantial gains for the mechanistic position had to await its development and success in the physical realm itself; this occurred only in the seventeenth century through the work of such giants as Galileo and Newton. Wider scientific acceptance of mechanism had to wait still longer until it had been applied to the phenomena of the biological sciences.

Faith in the mechanistic doctrine has usually extended far beyond its usefulness in explaining the phenomena to which it has been applied. For example, most and perhaps all of our motivational concepts, such as drive and incentive, were developed and popularized during the interval between the introduction of mechanistic assumptions into psychology and the time when these concepts were put to empirical test. As a consequence, our theorizing made considerable use of drives and incentives and their postulated properties long before the usefulness of these concepts had been demonstrated by their ability to explain behavior. Indeed, virtually the entire history of motivation theory is devoted to declarations by this or that theorist that we must find the forces underlying behavior and the physiological causes of behavior if we are ever to explain it. The urgency with which this program has been proclaimed has, unfortunately, not always been matched by the development of what we now consider to be the proper fruits of science, namely, adequate explanatory theories. We will consider shortly what is meant by an adequate explanatory theory, but first we must note some objections that have been raised to the mechanistic doctrine.

Empirical Determinism

The traditional difference of opinion regarding what constitutes an adequate explanation of any natural phenomenon has centered about purpose and teleology. The scientist has always been reluctant to admit that there are purposes operating in nature, preferring to rely upon what he views as the "real" or physical causes of things. On the other hand, rationalists, humanists, the clergy, and most thoughtful laymen have felt most at ease with, or even insisted upon, teleological accounts of certain natural phenomena, such as human behavior. The question at issue has traditionally been whether physical causes provide a total explanation, or whether teleological principles had to be added for some phenomena. Before David Hume (1739) did so, no one seemed to question whether physical causes were necessary, but only whether they were sufficient. Hume asked, How can we know the nature of causation? How can we know if causes really produce their effects? Hume's skeptical epistemology led him to the realization that the best evidence we can ever obtain is that two events invariably occur together, one preceding the other, always in the same order, and neither occurring alone. The imputation of causation, the abstract conception that the prior event necessitates the subsequent event, is an inference which goes beyond the evidence. There may be such a thing as physical or material causation, of course, but we can never be sure whether nature operates mechanistically since all we can know is the successive experience of successive events. It is in the nature of the human mind, Hume asserted, to transcend the data and infer a causal relationship between the two events if we invariably experience them one before the other.

Although scientists have characteristically operated in an empirical and pragmatic manner, philosophers, even philosophers of science, have tended to lag conceptually behind. Hence, for many years Hume's point was regarded as undue skepticism or as mere sophistry. Most men felt bound to commit themselves metaphysically either to a rationalistic position, to a mechanistic position, or to some dualistic combination of the two.

As far as science is concerned, its object is not to discover the ultimate nature of reality, but rather to explore empirical relationships and derive useful generalizations from them. The question of what sort of causation is involved in explanation is an unnecessary impediment, a philosophical encumbrance, to the conduct of science. It is futile for the scientist to be concerned with whether an event occurred because some other event compelled it to occur; much more to the point is that an event occurs and its occurrence can be correlated with certain sets of conditions. Of course we wish to refine our observations and improve our ability to control conditions until a point is reached where perfect or near-perfect correlations are possible and where very powerful general descriptive laws can be found.[5] But science does not wait for the final solution of the causation problem. We must proceed to view empirical correlations as the subject matter of science without committing ourselves to either a teleological, purposive, or materialistic philosophy. Nor do we need to go as far as Hume and say that we can never transcend empirical correlations. We may believe that, or we may take the more optimistic position that the empirical correlations we observe will ultimately be undergirded by a more profound understanding of causation. By adhering to a descriptive or correlational approach we may at least leave the way open for such a possibility.

The empirical approach is noncommittal; it provides a convenient vantage point from which we may survey other, more highly committed approaches. Psychology, particularly the area of motivation, is confused enough by the practice of regarding motives, or drives, or instincts, or needs, as the causes of behavior. If we are to describe behavior from a point of view which does not restrict us to any particular theoretical or philosophical position, then it is necessary that we adopt a terminology which leaves these questions open. Thus the relationship which exists, for example, between a stimulus and a response will be described throughout, not in causal terms, but in neutral and descriptive terms. We will say that deprivation and stimulus conditions *determine* behavior, or that some behavior is under the *control* of some stimulus.

The crucial insight here is that the empirical attitude does not imply a rejection of the principle of determinism. Quite the contrary; it will be argued that behavior is determined, not because forces act on the organism to make it behave, nor because the behavior was willed by some reasoning intellect, but is determined simply in the sense that it is intrinsically predictable. Behavior is determined in that it is lawful.

The doctrine that I have called empirical determinism thus keeps the first two propositions of the mechanistic doctrine, namely, that behavior is a natural phenomenon and that it is determined, and rejects only its mechanistic or materialistic bias. It will be argued that a "causeless" account of a phenomenon can constitute an explanation of it even though it fails to provide any justification, or indicate its physical basis. It will also be argued that accordance with an empirical law constitutes just the kind of explanation we want, provided only that the empirical law is contained in a systematic theory. Before proceeding with this argument let us digress briefly to consider some objections that might be raised to this position.

Hempel and Oppenheim (1948) have discussed a number of such objections. They consider, for example, the argument that a strictly empirical explanatory system is not applicable to behavior in humans because of the enormous complexity of the human subject and the unique character of his

[5] Recent scholars have sought to analyze more carefully the meaning of terms like "cause," "effect," and "necessitate" (Bunge, 1959; Smith, 1960). Usually, the conditions of temporal and spacial contiguity between cause and effect call for their most serious consideration. These considerations are serious, weighty, and highly involved logically—particularly when contrasted with the elegance of the empirical laws to which they are purported to be relevant.

behavior. Hempel and Oppenheim contend that the only real question here is whether phenomena as complex as human behavior are susceptible to adequate explanation. This is an empirical question; can laws of sufficient breadth and generality be discovered and can sufficient precision be obtained in specifying the appropriate antecedent conditions? The uniqueness and the irrepeatability of observations do not distinguish behavior from other observable phenomena. Irrepeatability is no less a problem in physics, or even astronomy, than it is in psychology; all observations are unique. The only strategy by which science can proceed at all is to concern itself with common features of and abstractions from unique observations.

Is such a system of explanation applicable to psychological phenomena in view of the fact that so many of the theoretical entities in psychology are not directly observable? The answer, again, is that psychological phenomena and theoretical constructs do not differ appreciably from those in physics or from those in any other science in this respect. So long as there are methods for determining with reasonable clarity and precision the hypothesized variables there is no special problem here at all. The only real question is whether psychological theories are to be based entirely upon empirical observations or whether they are to be based partly upon other, "transempirical," sources of knowledge.

Another question is whether psychological explanations, which have historically involved reference to purposive behavior, call for a different mode of explanation. If "purposive" pertains to Divine purpose or to some inscrutable intention on the part of the individual, then, it is true, the approach fails to provide an adequate explanation. But if these kinds of purpose really have no empirical reference, then it is not clear that behavior which is purposive in this sense is susceptible to any sort of explanation. On the other hand, if we mean by "purposive behavior" only that form of behavior which is highly correlated with its consequences, i.e., if we use the phrase in a purely descriptive or empirical manner, then there is no difference in principle between purposive behavior and any other kind of phenomena.

Perhaps the most fundamental practical objection that might be raised to empirical determinism is that it fails to tell *why* an event occurs; it only describes how and when events occur. When all is said and done a phenomenon is explained when it is put into terms with which we are familiar and shown to be an instance of a principle with which we are familiar. As Bridgman (1932) has said, an explanation is that kind of account that puts the curiosity at rest. We may ask what is the frame of mind of a man whose curiosity is only "put at rest" by an account of why things happen. What are such men really looking for? In the case of behavior, there seem to be two different kinds of accounts that men may be seeking when they ask "why?" One is justification, and the other is an application of the mechanistic doctrine. Thus, some of the time when someone is asked "why did you do that?", what is expected is a justification of the action. At other times it seems clear that what is demanded is an understanding of the physiological or neurological machinery that produced the effect.

In general, a satisfactory answer to a "why" question is a statement involving terms with which the inquirer is familiar. The difficulty of explanation in psychology is that those who ask the psychologist "why" come to him quite familiar with justifying action and quite familiar with the reality of the physical body and seek some explanation in these terms. On the other hand, the scientist, who is familiar with the empirical regularities in his science, does not seek the why of them. Insofar as the psychologist asks why, it is because he is curious about moral questions of justification or about the mysteries of neurology, either of which he may have legitimate reasons for wanting to relate to behavior. But the psychologist asks why only when he wants to transcend or extend the boundaries of his science and not when he is working within them.

How Actions Are Explained

R. S. PETERS

> Whether a given proposition is true or false, significant or meaningless, depends upon what questions it was meant to answer.
>
> R. G. COLLINGWOOD

Types of Explanation in Psychological Theories

Introductory

EVER since Hobbes was fired by the imaginative idea that *all* human behaviour might be explained in terms of mechanical principles, there have been sporadic attempts to provide over-all theories of human behaviour. Such theories have been instigated more by the desire to develop an ambitious theory than by puzzlement about concrete problems of human behaviour. This was true of Hobbes who pictured himself doing for psychology what Harvey had done for physiology by extending the new science of motion to the most intimate spheres of human thought and endeavour. It was also true of later theorists who, under the influence of Darwin rather than of Galileo, were excited by the thought that men were animals as well as mere bodies. McDougall, for instance, did not provide any startling answers to concrete questions about human behaviour; rather he concocted a sort of dynamic atomism to show that man's social behaviour could be explained in terms of biological principles. In fact the inspiration behind theorizing in psychology has been, in the main, the success of other sciences like physiology, chemistry, and mechanics, and the idea that there could be an all-inclusive theory of human behaviour if psychology were to adopt the postulates and methods of other sciences.

A contributory factor, too, has been the understandable determination of psychologists to make their enquiries 'scientific.' This had led them to cast their

---

Reprinted with permission of Humanities Press, Inc., New Jersey, and Routledge & Kegan Paul Ltd. from *The Concept of Motivation* by R. S. Peters, chapter one.

theories in a mould dictated by the current conception of scientific method. For a long time this was thought to be the method of induction; and so systems of psychology like introspectionism and behaviourism, developed, which were products of what Popper calls 'inductivism'—attempts to build up generalizations on the basis of carefully scrutinized data. (Peters, 1951). The methodologists then proclaimed that scientific method was really deductive. So an enormity like Hull's *Principles of Behaviour* emerged, scientifically impeccable because it was a hypothetico-deductive system. Hull (1943) boldly proclaimed his programme of starting from 'colourless movements and mere receptor impulses as such' and eventually explaining everything in terms of such concepts—

> familial behaviour, individual adaptive efficiency (intelligence), the formal educative processes, psychogenic disorders, social control and delinquency, character and personality, culture and acculturation, magic and religious practices, custom law and jurisprudence, politics and government and many other specialized fields of behaviour.

In fact Hull developed some simple postulates which gave dubious answers to limited questions about particular species of rats. He never asked, let alone tried to answer, any concrete questions about human behaviour. He was in love with the idea of a science of behaviour; he was not acutely worried about concrete questions of explaining *human* behaviour.

Freud was perhaps the great exception. For he was genuinely puzzled about concrete phenomena and developed some very fertile assumptions to explain them. Also, in his early work especially, he was very much aware of the limitations of his assumptions and defined carefully the types of phenomena that could be explained by the postulation of unconscious mental processes. In other words he seemed to be aware of the *sort* of questions about human behaviour which he was answering. For there are many *different* sorts of questions which can be asked about human behaviour and the differences, as I shall hope to show, are such that an all-embracing theory is inappropriate. These different sorts of questions are especially confused in theories of motivation. It is this thesis which I now hope to substantiate.

Types of questions about human behaviour

(A) 'HIS REASON' EXPLANATIONS. The over-riding aim of a scientist should be explanation. This sounds rather obvious, but it has many important consequences in relation to psychological theorizing. For the general question 'Why did Jones do that?' is capable of being asked and answered in a variety of different ways. The particular formula employed in asking the question usually dictates the sort of answer which is expected and which counts as an explanation.[1] The paradigm case of a human action is when something is done in order to bring about an end. So the usual way of explaining an action is to describe it as an action of a certain sort by indicating the end which Jones had in mind. We therefore ask the 'why' question in a more specific form. We ask what was

[1] I am indebted to J. O. Urmson (1952) for some of these distinctions.

his *reason* for doing that or what was the *point* of it, what *end* he had in mind. If we asked why Jones walked across the road, the obvious answer will be something like 'To buy tobacco.' Instead of saying this we could say 'because he wanted some tobacco.' This is, logically speaking, another way of giving the same sort of answer; for the answer 'to buy some tobacco' is only an explanation because we assume in Jones some sort of directive disposition—a general tendency to obtain and use tobacco (Peters, 1952).

Even in this very simple sort of explanation in terms of a man's reason for doing something, there are, as a matter of fact, concealed assumptions. We assume, for instance, that walking across the street is an efficient way of getting to the tobacconist. This counts as an explanation not simply because Jones envisaged walking across the street as a means to getting the tobacco but because it really is a means to getting it. We assume, too, that a man who has this information will act on it if he wants some tobacco. We assume that men are rational in that they will take means which lead to ends if they have the information and want the ends. 'His reason' is an explanation in terms of what Popper (1945) calls 'the logic of the situation.'

But it is not only norms of efficiency and consistency that are implicit in the concept of 'his reason.' There are also norms or standards of social appropriateness. After all Jones might have crawled or run across the road. But 'to get some tobacco' would be a very odd answer to the question 'Why did Jones *run* across the road?' Yet running would be quite an efficient way of getting across the road. It would, however, be socially odd as a way of crossing the road to get some tobacco. *Man is a rule-following animal.* His actions are not simply directed towards ends; they also conform to social standards and conventions, and unlike a calculating machine he acts because of his knowledge of rules and objectives. For instance, we ascribe to people *traits* of character like honesty, punctuality, considerateness and meanness. Such terms do not, like ambition or hunger or sexual desire, indicate the sorts of goals that a man tends to pursue; rather they indicate the type of regulation that he imposes on his conduct whatever his goals may be. A man who is ruthless, selfish, punctual, considerate, persistent, and honest, does not have any particular goals; rather he pursues whatever goals he has in particular sorts of ways.

This simple purposive model of a man taking means to bring about an end is further complicated by the fact that norms enter into and often entirely define the end. Ends like passing an examination, getting married, becoming a professor, and reading a paper, explain quite adequately a great deal of the goings on in the precincts of a university; yet they are defined almost entirely by social convention. It is a gross over-simplification to think of ends merely as terminating points of activity. Actually even a rat, after eating or achieving some other end, will continue being active in a variety of ways—sniffing, preening, and so on. If eating can be regarded as an end this is not because it is a definite terminating point of activity but because activity *previous* to it varies concomitantly with changes in the conditions necessary to define it as an end. The concept of means is just as necessary to bring out what is meant by an end as the concept of end is to bring out what is meant by a means. Ends are not given as natural terminating points like a chain of oases distributed across a desert. And, to a large extent, what counts as falling within a means-to-end explanatory framework is determined by convention. Even those ends, like eating and sexual intercourse, which are universal and which have an obvious biological basis, can scarcely be specified without recourse to norms. For there are countless ways of performing the acts which can be regarded as ends and in every culture a few particular ways are stamped with the hallmark of conventionality. Eating is not just getting food into the stomach. Jones' movements across the road are classifiable as means to the end of buying tobacco because of a vast system of norms defining 'buying tobacco' as an end as well as a system of norms regulating what is an efficient and socially appropriate way of attaining it.

My reasons for stressing this rule-following purposive pattern into which we fit our common-sense explanations are twofold. In the first place I want to insist that most of our explanations are couched in terms of this model and our predictions of people's behaviour presuppose it. We know what the parson will do when he begins to walk towards the pulpit because we know the conventions regulating church services. And we can make such predictions without knowing anything about the *causes* of people's behaviour unless we include under 'causes' things like the parson's training and grasp of the rules, which are things of a different order from 'causes' in the sense of antecedent movements. Man in society is like a chess-player writ large. Requests for explanation are usually reflections of our ignorance about the particular rule or goal which is relevant to the behaviour in question. We usually know the general pattern but are unsure which part of it is relevant. Sometimes, of course, we are in the position of a free-thinker at a Roman Catholic mass. The question 'Why did X do that?' is then usually a request for an elucidation of the whole pattern of conventions. In explaining human actions we, like anthropologists, must all, in the first place be structuralists. Indeed I would go so far as to say that anthropology or sociology must be the basic sciences of human action in that they exhibit the systematic framework of norms and goals which are necessary to classify actions as being of a certain sort. They both—like classical economics—presuppose the purposive, rule-following model; in this respect they are quite unlike sciences which imply a mechanical model of explanation.

In the second place this rule-following purposive pattern of explanation must be sketched in some detail because a proper understanding of what is meant by a human action has very important logical consequences. It shows, for instance, as I shall argue, that human actions cannot be sufficiently explained in terms of causal concepts like 'colourless movements.' Indeed to claim that we are confronted with an action is *ipso facto* to rule out such mechanical explanations, as being sufficient.

(B) 'THE REASON' EXPLANATIONS. But, of course, as psychologists will be the first to point out, people often invent reasons for doing things or delude themselves into thinking that the reasons they offer for their actions are operative reasons. We therefore often say of a man that *his* reason may have been x but *the* reason why he acted like that was y. For instance we might say that Jones said that he crossed the road in order to buy some tobacco but the reason why he did it was not really his desire for tobacco; it was sex. There was a pretty girl looking in the window of the tobacconist. This explanation may of course be erroneous. For instance a psychologist once told me that I delayed crossing the road to College because of an aversion to getting down to work. I replied, and I think more convincingly, that I stayed on the other side in order to look at the row of glistening cars drawn up opposite. But whether the explanation in question is correct or incorrect does not much matter; the point is that to speak of *the* reason why a person does something is different in that it is a way of calling attention to the law or assumed law that a given case actually falls under. *His* reason may coincide with *the* reason. *The* reason why Jones crossed the road might in fact be his desire for tobacco. He might also be aware that he wanted to inspect the girl at close quarters, but was concealing this by the camouflage of buying tobacco. This would then be his *real* reason. But whereas *his* reason—whether real or not—entails that a man is conscious of his objective, the reason why he did it does not.[2] *The* reason why he did it might well be sex or aversion to work; yet the individual might be quite unaware of pursuing or avoiding the relevant goals. And whereas to say that *he* had a reason for doing something is more or less to rule out a causal explanation, to give *the* reason why he did it is sometimes to subsume it under a law-like proposition of a causal kind. This is not necessarily so. For we can say that sex or aversion to work was *the* reason why he did it and simply be insisting that a different directive disposition is being exercised. But *the* reason why he did it might also be that he was pushed or assailed by an attack of giddiness. These would be causal explanations which would rebut the suggestion that he had a reason for crossing the road. Causal explanations, in other words, can count as *the* reason why a person does something; but they are only one type of answer to the question 'What was *the* reason why he did it?'

(C) CAUSAL EXPLANATIONS. There are, however, other questions about particular goings on—I omit to say actions on purpose—to which answers in causal terms are appropriate. Instead of the omnibus question 'Why did Jones do that?' we often ask what made, drove, or possessed him to do it. These are usually cases of lapses from action or failure to act—when there is some kind of *deviation* from the purposive rule-following model, when people, as it were, get it wrong. This may be in respect of an efficiency norm—for example, when a person refuses to take the only quick route to his destination by underground train, or when he can't remember a well-known name when he is performing

[2] Hamlyn has pointed out to me the use of "the reason for his action" as well as "the reason why he did it." "The reason for" seems to be similar to "his reason" but to imply a coincidence between "his reason" and "the reason why he did it." I am not here concerned with the use of "reason" in the context of *justification* as when we say that *a* reason for giving up smoking is that it causes lung cancer. "His reason" and "the reason for" can be used in contexts both of justification and of explanation. Needless to say "the reason why he did it" is reserved for contexts of explanation with which I am here concerned.

an introduction. Or the behaviour may go wrong in respect of a norm governing social appropriateness—as with a business man who runs to work when he is not late or a tutor who crawls round the room sniffing while listening to an undergraduate essay. Or behaviour may go wrong by being deflected towards a peculiar goal as with a married man who suddenly makes an advance to a choir boy. In such cases it is as if the man suffers something rather than does something. It is because things seem to be happening to him that it is appropriate to ask what made, drove, or possessed him to do that. The appropriate answer in such cases may be in terms of causal theory.

These cases of particular goings on which look like breakdowns of action are very similar to a whole class of general activities which seem to have no point or a very odd point—dreams, hallucinations, obsessions, anxieties and perversions. In such cases the Greeks suggested that the gods intervene and take possession of the individual's mind. Very often recourse is made to crude physiological explanations. It was not till the advent of Freud that any systematic explanation of such goings-on was offered in psychological terms. Indeed Freud claimed in 1913 that the main contribution of psycho-analysis to general psychology was to link together and to give psychological explanations for happenings which had previously been left to physiology or to folk-lore. Many have claimed that Freud, by reclaiming these phenomena for psychology, was in fact extending the model of purposive rule-following behaviour to cover the unconscious. He showed, it is argued, that we have reasons for acts which were previously only explained in terms of causes. I shall argue later that this thesis is mistaken. Freud showed, perhaps, that the concept of 'wish' has a wider application than was previously thought. But his account of the working of the primary processes creaks with causality. In maintaining that in the unconscious there is no sense of causal or logical connexion he was *ipso facto* denying that the model of 'his reason,' implying norms of efficiency and social appropriateness, was relevant. Freud, I shall argue, provides the classic case of giving quasi-causal explanations where causal explanations seem *prima facie* appropriate.

I shall also argue that Freud in fact only intended to explain by reference to unconscious mental processes cases where the purposive rule-following model breaks down or is inappropriate. He did not think—and often explicitly denied—that this sort of explanation can be appropriately given for everything—for cases where a man acts as well as for cases where something happens to a man. In this respect Freud was, from the point of view of my argument, on the side of the angels. For my case is not simply that causal explanations are otiose when we know the point of a person's action in that, life being short and time limited, we no longer feel inclined to ask 'why' once we have accommodated a piece of behaviour within the rule-following purposive model. It is also that if we are in fact confronted with a case of a genuine action (i.e., an act of doing something as opposed to suffering something), then causal explanations are *ipso facto* inappropriate as sufficient explanations. Indeed they may rule out rule-following purposive explanations. To ask what made Jones do something is at least to suggest that he had no good reason for doing it. Similarly to ascribe a point to his action is *ipso facto* to deny that it can be *sufficiently explained* in terms of causes, though, of course, there will be many causes in the sense of *necessary* conditions. A story can always be told about the underlying mechanisms; but this does not add up to a sufficient explanation, if it is an action that has to be explained.

To give a causal *explanation* of an event involves at least showing that other conditions being presumed unchanged a change in one variable is a *sufficient* condition for a change in another. In the mechanical conception of 'cause' it is also demanded that there should be spatial and temporal contiguity between the movements involved. Now the trouble about giving this sort of explanation of human actions is that we can never specify an action exhaustively in terms of movements of the body or within the body (Hamlyn, 1953). It is therefore impossible to state sufficient conditions in terms of antecedent movements which may vary concomitantly with subsequent movements. 'Signing a contract,' for instance, is a typical example of a human action. The movements involved are grouped together because they are seen by the agent to be efficient and appropriate means to an end. But it would be impossible to stipulate exhaustively what the movements *must* be. For if this is a case of a human action the agent must be presumed to be intelligent and he will, accordingly, vary his movements in a great variety of ways. He may hold the pen slightly differently, vary the size of his writing according to the space available, and so on, depending on the sort of ink, paper, and pen available. But provided that he produces a signature which confirms to rough and ready criteria—e.g., it must not be typed—more or less *any* movements will do. I suppose he could sign a contract by holding the pen between his toes. A very general range of movements could perhaps be specified, but no specific movements of the muscles, limbs, or nervous system, which *must* occur before it would be conceded that a contract had been signed. This is tantamount to saying that the concept of an action is inseparable from that of intelligence; for part of what we mean by 'intelligence' is the ability to vary movements relative to a goal in a way which is appropriate to changes in the situation necessary to define it as a goal and in the conditions relevant to attaining it. So we could never give a sufficient explanation of an action in causal terms because we could never stipulate the movements which would have to count as dependent variables. A precise functional relationship could never be established. Of course, just as we could stipulate a general range of movements necessary to define signing a contract, so also we could lay down certain very general *necessary* conditions. We could, for instance, say that a man could not sign a contract unless he had a brain and nervous system. Such physiological knowledge *might* enable us to predict *bodily movements*. And *if* we had bridging laws to correlate such physiological findings with descriptions of actions we might *indirectly predict* actions. But we would *first* have to grasp concepts connected with action like 'knowing what we are doing' and 'grasp of means to an end.' As such concepts have no application at the level of mere movement, such predictions would not count as sufficient *explanations* of *actions*.

Furthermore, as I have already argued, general standards or rules are implicit in the concept of an action. We can therefore say that a man is doing something efficiently, correctly, and so on, if he knowingly varies what he does in accordance with changes in the situation conventionally singled out as the goal and the conditions perceived as relevant to attaining it. It only makes sense to talk of actions in this way, not of cases where something happens to a man. A man's action may break down because of a causal condition like a lesion in his brain. But all that can be said of such causal conditions is that they just occur. Movements *qua* movements are neither intelligent, efficient, nor correct. They only become so in the context of an action. There cannot therefore be a sufficient explanation of actions in causal terms because, as Popper has put it, there is a logical gulf between nature and convention. Statements implying norms and standards cannot be deduced from statements about mere movements which have no such normative implications. The contention that man is a rule-following animal must, if taken seriously, entail that the transition from nature to convention occurs whenever we try to give a sufficient explanation of human actions in causal terms. There is, however, no objection to such explanations of what *happens* to a man; for happenings cannot be characterized as intelligent or unintelligent, correct or incorrect, efficient or inefficient. *Prima facie* they are just occurrences. Perhaps Freud showed that some lapses and breakdowns may not be *just* occurrences. But this is another story. The point is that there is a *prima facie* case for treating them as such.

To make explicit the implications of my thesis for psychological theories: If the question is 'Why did Jones walk across the road?' a *sufficient* explanation can only be given in terms of the rule-following purposive model—if this is a case of an action rather than of something happening to him. Answers in terms of causal concepts like 'receptor impulses' and 'colourless movement,' are either not explanations because they state not sufficient but only necessary conditions, or they are ways of denying that what has to be explained is a human action. If we ask 'Why did Jones *jump* while he was crossing the road?' it might be appropriate to say 'because of a twinge in his stomach' or 'because a car backfired.' The stimulus-response sort of model would perhaps be appropriate and the causal type of explanation in terms of internal or external stimulation might be sufficient because the assumption might be that Jones was suffering something rather than performing an action. This sort of jump would then be quite different from the jump he might perform while competing in an athletic contest.

This is not to deny that causal explanations are *relevant* to human actions. It is only to deny that they are sufficient explanations of them. Causal theories have at least three jobs to do in this context. Firstly they can state *necessary* conditions for human actions to occur. Hebb's physiological speculations, for instance, might well provide a sketch of a typical class of necessary conditions. But this does not mean that such speculations *explain* human actions. Secondly, as a corollary, they could show that some individual differences in performance are dependent on slight differences in such necessary conditions. Hebb's hypothesis of the relationship between the size of the association areas of the brain and the possibility of late learning would be such a hypothesis. Thirdly such theories could be used to give *sufficient* conditions for breakdowns in performance, as in the case of brain lesions, by indicating a necessary condition which was absent. Alternatively lapses and breakdowns could be explained by the postulation of special disrupting conditions—e.g., Freud's theory of the unconscious wish.

(D) END-STATE EXPLANATIONS. There are, of course, all sorts of higher level questions which can be asked about human actions, most of which are irrelevant to psychology in general and theories of motivation in particular. Questions, for instance, can be raised about the conventions in accordance with which a man acts or which determine his goals. We can ask why Jones is mean or why he eats fish. The way it would be answered would depend on the context. It might be answered in terms of a rule-following type of explanation like 'because he is a Scotsman' or 'because he is a Roman Catholic.' This would assume some *established set of norms* and a system of training for handing them on. It would be radically different from the explanation 'because he is an anal character' or 'because he is an oral character.' For these explanations would presuppose that Jones was in some way a deviant from the norm of the circle in which he had been trained. It would state special conditions in his upbringing which occasioned his deviation. Whether or not such explanations, which presuppose fixation at certain periods of development, are causal or not, will have to be considered later.

Another way of answering the question 'Why does Jones eat fish?' would be to state in a tough-minded way 'because he likes it,' or 'because it satisfies him.' This could be simply an impatient way of terminating the discussion or it could be an answer to the even more general question 'Why does a man eat anything?' At a common-sense level this is a very odd question; for 'a man must eat' is regarded as a decisive way of terminating a discussion. If pressed still further common-sense might reach rock-bottom with the truism that a man would die if he did not eat. The implication is the Hobbesian axiom that every man is afraid of death and that it makes no further sense to ask 'why?'

A variant on this type of answer is the assertion that a man needs food, which is very much like saying that a man *must* eat. For, at a common-sense level, the term 'need' is mainly normative. It prescribes one of a set of standard goals. It usually functions as a diagnostic term with remedial implications. It implies that something is wrong with a person if certain conditions are absent. We say things like 'The trouble with Jones is that he needs a wife' or 'Every child needs at least ten hours sleep.' The implication is that there is a state of affairs the absence of which is or is likely to be damaging to the individual in question. The individual, like a patient, may well be unaware of what this state of affairs is. Indeed, when we say that a person needs something, we are often indicating a discrepancy between what he actually does and what he ought to be doing. In other words the notion of 'need' in ordinary language is seldom *explanatory*. It is used to point out what a person ought to be doing rather than to explain what he is doing. It would only be an observer grossly over-sophisticated by

Freudian theory who would say of a man leaping around in a Morris ring that old Jones obviously needs a woman, and who would think that he had *explained* his performance by pointing to the reality beneath the appearances. Reference to needs implies a standard pattern of prescribed goals; but it does not explain actions by reference to them. Whereas causal theories explain deviations from a norm, reference to needs prescribes the norms whose absence is thought to be injurious. It redirects attention to the accepted content of the rule-following purposive model.

Often we hear of 'basic needs' and 'need-reduction' in the context of explanatory theories in psychology. What has happened here is that conditions whose absence is thought to occasion injury have been interpreted in terms of a biological or physiological model. The answer to questions like 'Why does a man eat?' is provided by picturing an organism whose activities are directed towards survival or the preservation of equilibrium or some other such desirable and completely general end-state. This, of course, has to be broken down by giving an account of the particular conditions whose absence is thought to be injurious. Homeostasis, for instance, has to be described in terms of *particular* states like the temperature of the body and the level of blood-sugar. And, no doubt, postulating such conditions restored by various movements of the body in part explains them if the conditions restored are not part of what is meant by the description given to the movements. Sweating, for instance, may be a method of bringing about an optimum level of temperature in the body; but restoration of this level is not part of what is meant when we call certain movements 'sweating.' So saying that people sweat because it lowers the temperature of the body is explanatory.

But all too often this type of functional or end-state explanation is redescriptive rather than explanatory—especially when it is used for voluntary rather than for involuntary movements. This is when the conditions restored are part of what is meant by the activity to be explained. For instance it might be said that people dominate others because it reduces a need in them to do so. But what is the condition restored apart from that of the presence of others being dominated? What in this type of case is the equivalent of the temperature level which is restored by sweating? The homeo-static model of explanation is retained; but in the absence of specific states required to define what constitutes the equilibrium, it becomes entirely metaphysical. It is true that recourse is made to vague states of quiescence which the activity of dominating or acquiring money is alleged to bring about. But as there are no rules for identifying such states, their explanatory value is nil. Indeed in such cases need-reduction looks like a redescription of goal-seeking in terms which have the normative function of stressing the importance of conventionally prescribed pursuits. It is a justification masquerading as a high-level explanation.

Need-reduction explanations are a particular instance of a very common sort of explanation which will be termed 'explanations in terms of end-states.' For supervenient states of quiescence and satisfaction abound in psychological theories of motivation. It will probably be found that all such explanations share the logical features revealed in the specific case of need-reduction. These are (*i*) the generalization of a type of explanation that applies properly only to a very limited class of phenomena and (*ii*) the use of a term with highly general normative implications which obscure its emptiness as a highly general *explanation*.

The term 'end-state' has been chosen advisedly rather than the term 'end.' For one of the first things to be pointed out about these highly general sorts of explanation is that the ends postulated are not ends in the sense of 'end' or 'goal' employed in the purposive rule-following model. They are not—or should not be—postulated as answers to questions like 'Why did Jones walk across the road?' but as answers to questions like 'Why does a man eat?' or 'Why does a man smoke?'. They are therefore inappropriate as answers to lower order questions. For a man does not eat *in order to* reduce a need or relieve a tension. By eating, so the theories say, he in fact brings about such an end-state. Such explanations then do not give a man's reason for eating but the reason why he eats. But they differ from other cases of directed behaviour where we contrast *his* reason with *the* reason. For in other such cases—e.g. explanations in terms of unconscious wishes—we imply a goal *of the same sort* as that implied in *his* reason explanations, but we add the rider that the man does not envisage this goal as a conscious objective. We say, for instance, that *the* reason why he was unintentionally rude to his employer was because of his unconscious desire to injure a man like his father. But end-states are not goals like hurting a man, marrying a girl, or becoming Prime Minister. They are more mysterious states of quiescence, satisfaction, tension-reduction, and so on.

The theoretical interest of these types of explanation is that they are regarded as explaining *all* behaviour, whether of the rule-following sort or where there is a breakdown in behaviour and a cause is assigned, or when an activity—like dreaming—is of a sort such that it makes no sense to say 'What is the point of it?' Freud's pleasure principle is a good example; for he claimed

> In the theory of psycho-analysis we have no hesitation in assuming that the course taken by mental events is automatically regulated by the pleasure principle. We believe, that is to say, that the course of these events is invariably set in motion by an unpleasurable tension, and that it takes a direction such that its final outcome coincides with a lowering of that tension—that is with an avoidance of unpleasure or a production of pleasure.

Some such homeostatic principle is so common in modern psychology that it has reached the standard text-books. To quote a typical case—Stagner and Karwoski (1952):

> The organism is endowed with an automatic equilibrium maintaining tendency which helps to preserve existence in the face of many kinds of environmental obstacles and difficulties.

It is assumed that everything we do can somehow be subsumed under this very general principle. This assumption is so widespread and is so important to the claim that an over-all theory of motivation can be developed, that much more must be said about its appropriateness.

The assumption, to repeat, is that the reason why men eat, sleep, eliminate, and so on, is that achieving such goals relieves tension, restores equilibrium, produces satisfaction, and other such variations on a theme. This assumption is usually extended to cover all goal-directed behaviour—the pursuit of riches and foxes as well as the pursuit of water and women.

I will defer for a moment the problem of whether the postulation of such end-states is *ever* explanatory. For the issue is whether it *always* is. And this seems plainly false. For many goal-directed actions like posting letters, travelling to work, and passing the salt to one's neighbour do not seem invariably to be followed by such end-states. Indeed usually when we *say* that we get satisfaction or pleasure from doing something, we are not referring to some extra subsequent state of mind which we have become aware of by introspection. Rather we are saying two general sorts of things about it. In the first place we are saying that we were not bored, irritated, or distracted while we did it. We put our mind to the job in hand and concentrated on bringing about the required state of affairs. We were absorbed. The reference to satisfaction is not, in this case, an *explanation* of the pursuit of a goal, but a way of emphasizing that it really was a goal in the sense that our movements flowed towards it in an unimpeded and co-ordinated manner. Secondly the reference to satisfaction can be a way of stressing that the activity in question was done for its own sake and not as a means to something else. If a husband insists doggedly that he does the gardening because of the satisfaction he gets out of it he may simply be denying that he does it in order to help his wife with the housekeeping. He is not claiming necessarily that he glows and enters into a beatific state when the peas have been staked and the lawn cut. In other words, just as reference to need-reduction is a way of emphasizing the importance of some goals for the avoidance of injury, so reference to satisfaction is often a way of singling out others which are worth pursuing for their own sake. In a context of justification 'Because it satisfies him' is as final as 'Because he needs it.' What follows the 'because' are different facets of the bed-rock of justification. Psychologists have mistaken this bed-rock of justification for the apex of explanation.

Is it to be assumed, then, that reference to such end-states is *never* explanatory? All we have shown is that it is not *always* so. Clearly some such reference is reasonable in answering certain questions about the *body*, as was seen in the case of need-reduction. Cannon, in his *Wisdom of the Body*, was indicating the evidence for bodily mechanisms of regulation and adjustment. The transition to using this type of explanation for voluntary actions rather than for the automatic adjustments of the body, comes about because it is suggested, e.g. by Freud—that types of stimulation brought about by departures from these optimum levels or end-states can only be mitigated by contact with the environment. The baby's hunger, for instance, is relieved only by contact with its mother's breast or with some equivalent source of supply. Its movements are at first random; but eventually, through the association of relief of tension with contact with the breast, a directed tendency develops which is activated by the stimulation of hunger. It is therefore concluded, probably erroneously, that whenever we find a case of such directed behaviour, it must be sandwiched in between tension and the reduction of tension. Yet even if such tension-reduction were an explanation of *acquiring* such a directed disposition, it would not follow that it also explained its *activation* later on after it had been acquired.

It is, however, significant that the sort of phenomena which have seemed to psychologists to require some sort of an end-state explanation, are those connected with learning and experimental types of situation. Thorndike's Law of Effect, for instance, postulated that successful responses were stamped in because of the satisfaction associated with contact with the correct goal. The pleasure-principle could well be vacuous as an all-embracing postulate, as envisaged by Freud; but it might well be part of the explanation of why certain directed sequences of behaviour are *learnt.* And surely it would here coincide with the use of 'feeling of satisfaction' in ordinary speech which cannot be analysed purely in the way described above. For in exploratory and experimental stages of an activity, before a habit has been formed, or when we are confronted with obstacles that impede habitual routines, we do speak of a feeling of satisfaction or a sense of achievement. If we are learning to swim or to play golf or to walk after a long illness, we do get a feeling of satisfaction or sense of achievement on attaining the goal. This is not exactly a supervenient state extra to attaining the goal. The feeling of satisfaction when one hits a good drive is different from that attendant on hitting a good niblick shot; and both are quite different from that attendant on writing a good sentence or doing a good dive. In the same way a hungry man gets satisfaction from eating a beef-steak; but the type of satisfaction is specific to the beef-steak. The end-states are not exactly supervenient; rather they are descriptions of the attainment of certain sorts of goals under certain sorts of conditions. So in some cases which approximate in varying degrees to a learning, experimental or obstacle type of situation, the postulated sequence of tension, persistent and directed behaviour, and relief of tension may well occur. But as most of our days are spent in carrying out habits and routines, they do not occur whenever there is a case of directed behaviour. Indeed part of what we want to deny when we call a piece of behaviour a habit is that it is a case of the varied, experimental, obstacle-ridden type of behaviour.

My point is therefore not that the reduction of tension type of explanation is never relevant, but that it explains the directedness of behaviour only under certain limited sorts of conditions. My objection to it is that it is so often used as an all-inclusive principle. For most psychological theories seem to accommodate their purposive or causal explanations under some such homeostatic postulate. The quasi-causal concept of drive, for instance, is usually subsumed under the general postulate of homeostasis; so is the purposive concept of the Freudian wish. But the relationship between these types of explanation and a homeostatic postulate is not of this deductive sort. It seems, to say the least of it, misleading to assimilate dreams and playing chess to shivering and sweating by maintaining that they are all particular cases of the maintenance of equilibrium

—especially when the theorists, like Stagner and Karwoski, have to go on to distinguish static from dynamic homeostasis to make the suggestion even sound plausible! The quest for an all-inclusive explanation has led repeatedly to the obscuring of important differences by stressing trivial and highly speculative similarities.

Freedom: The First Condition of Action

JEAN-PAUL SARTRE

It is strange that philosophers have been able to argue endlessly about determinism and free-will, to cite examples in favor of one or the other thesis without ever attempting first to make explicit the structures contained in the very idea of *action.* The concept of an act contains, in fact, numerous subordinate notions which we shall have to organize and arrange in a hierarchy: to act is to modify the *shape* of the world; it is to arrange means in view of an end; it is to produce an organized instrumental complex such that by a series of concatenations and connections the modification effected on one of the links causes modifications throughout the whole series and finally produces an anticipated result. But this is not what is important for us here. We should observe first that an action is on principle *intentional.* The careless smoker who has through negligence caused the explosion of a powder magazine has not *acted.* On the other hand the worker who is charged with dynamiting a quarry and who obeys the given orders has acted when he has produced the expected explosion; he knew what he was doing or, if you prefer, he intentionally realized a conscious project.

This does not mean, of course, that one must foresee all the consequences of his act. The emperor Constantine when he established himself at Byzantium, did not foresee that he would create a center of Greek culture and language, the appearance of which would ultimately provoke a schism in the Christian Church and which would contribute to weakening the Roman Empire. Yet he performed an act just in so far as he realized his project of creating a new residence for emperors in the Orient. Equating the result with the intention is here sufficient for us to be able to speak of action. But if this is the case, we establish that the action necessarily implies as its condition the recognition of a "desideratum"; that is, of an objective lack or again of a *négatité. The intention* of providing a rival for Rome can come to Constantine only through the apprehension of an objective lack: Rome lacks a counterweight; to this still profoundly pagan city ought to be opposed a Christian city which at the moment is *missing.* Creating Constantinople is understood as an *act* only if first the conception of a new city has preceded the action itself or at least if this conception serves as an organizing

Reprinted with the permission of Philosophical Library, Inc. From *Being and Nothingness* by Jean-Paul Sartre. pp. 433–438 and 483–484.

theme for all later steps. But this conception can not be the pure representation of the city as *possible.* It apprehends the city in its essential characteristic, which is to be a *desirable* and not yet realized possible.

This means that from the moment of the first conception of the act, consciousness has been able to withdraw itself from the full world of which it is consciousness and to leave the level of being in order frankly to approach that of non-being. Consciousness in so far as it is considered exclusively in its being, is perpetually referred from being to being and can not find in being any motive for revealing non-being. The imperial system with Rome as its capital functions positively and in a certain real way which can be easily discovered. Will someone say that the taxes are collected badly, that Rome is not secure from invasions, that it does not have the geographical location which is suitable for the capital of a Mediterranean empire which is threatened by barbarians, that its corrupt morals make the spread of the Christian religion difficult? How can anyone fail to see that all these considerations are *negative*; that is, that they aim at what is not, not at what is. To say that sixty per cent of the anticipated taxes have been collected can pass, if need be for a positive appreciation of the situation *such as it is.* To say that they are *badly* collected is to consider the situation across a situation which is posited as an absolute end but which precisely *is not.* To say that the corrupt morals at Rome hinder the spread of Christianity is not to consider this diffusion for what it is; that is, for a propagation at a rate which the reports of the clergy can enable us to determine. It is to posit the diffusion in itself as insufficient; that is, as suffering from a secret nothingness. But it appears as such only if it is surpassed toward a limiting-situation posited *a priori* as a value (for example, toward a certain rate of religious conversions, toward a certain mass morality). This limiting-situation can not be conceived in terms of the simple consideration of the real state of things; for the most beautiful girl in the world can offer only what she *has*, and in the same way the most miserable situation can by itself be designated only as it *is* without any reference to an ideal nothingness.

In so far as man is immersed in the historical situation, he does not even succeed in conceiving of the failures and lacks in a political organization or determined economy; this is not, as it is stupidly said, because he "is accustomed to it," but because he apprehends it in its plenitude of being and because he can not even imagine that he can exist in it otherwise. For it is necessary here to reverse common opinion and on the basis of what it is not, to acknowledge the harshness of a situation or the sufferings which it imposes, both of which are motives for conceiving of another state of affairs in which things would be better for everybody. It is on the day that we can conceive of a different state of affairs that a new light falls on our troubles and our suffering and that we *decide* that these are unbearable. A worker in 1830 is capable of revolting if his salary is lowered, for he easily conceives of a situation in which his wretched standard of living would be not as low as the one which is about to be imposed on him. But he does not represent his sufferings to himself as unbearable; he adapts himself to them not through resignation but because he lacks the education and reflection necessary for him to conceive of a social state in which these sufferings would not exist. Consequently *he does not act.* Masters of Lyon following a riot, the workers at Croix-Rousse do not know what to do with their victory; they return home bewildered, and the regular army has no trouble in overcoming them. Their misfortunes do not appear to them "habitual" but rather *natural*; they are, that is all, and they constitute the worker's condition. They are not detached; they are not seen in the clear light of day, and consequently they are integrated by the worker with his being. He suffers without considering his suffering and without conferring value upon it. To suffer and to *be* are one and the same for him. His suffering is the pure affective tenor of his non-positional consciousness, but he does not *contemplate* it. Therefore this suffering can not be in itself a *motive*[1] for his acts. Quite the contrary, it is after he has formed the project of changing the situation that it will appear intolerable to him. This means that he will have had to give himself room, to withdraw in relation to it, and will have to have effected a double nihilation: on the one hand, he must posit an ideal state of affairs as a pure *present* nothingness; on the other hand, he must posit the actual situation as nothingness in relation to this state of affairs. He will have to conceive of a happiness attached to his class as a pure possible—that is, presently as a certain nothingness—and on the other hand, he will return to the present situation in order to illuminate it in the light of this nothingness and in order to nihilate it in turn by declaring: "I *am not* happy."

Two important consequences result. (1) No factual state whatever it may be (the political and economic structure of society, the psychological "state," etc.) is capable by itself of motivating any act whatsoever. For an act is a projection of the for-itself toward what is not, and what is can in no way determine by itself what is not. (2) No factual state can determine consciousness to apprehend it as a *négatité* or as a lack. Better yet no factual state can determine consciousness to define it and to circumscribe it since, as we have seen, Spinoza's statement, "Omnis determinatio est negatio," remains profoundly true. Now every action has for its express condition not only the discovery of a state of affairs as "lacking in——," *i.e.*, as a *négatité*—but also, and before all else, the constitution of the state of things under consideration into an isolated system. There *is* a factual state—satisfying or not—only by means of the nihilating power of the for-itself. But this power of nihilation can not be limited to realizing a simple *withdrawal* in relation to the world. In fact in so far as consciousness is "invested" by being, in so far as it simply suffers what is, it must be included in being. It is the organized form—worker-finding-his-suffering-natural—which must be surmounted and denied in order for it to be able to form the object of a revealing contemplation. This means evidently that it is

[1] In this and following sections Sartre makes a sharp distinction between mo*tif* and mo*bile.* The English word "motive" expresses sufficiently adequately the French mo*bile*, which refers to an inner subjective fact or attitude. For *motif t*here is no true equivalent. Since it refers to an external fact or situation, I am translating it by "cause." The reader must remember, however, that this carries with it no idea of determinism. Sartre emphatically denies the existence of any cause in the usual deterministic sense. Tr.

by a pure wrenching away from himself and the world that the worker can posit his suffering as unbearable suffering and consequently can *make of it the motive* for his revolutionary action. This implies for consciousness the permanent possibility of effecting a rupture with its own past, of wrenching itself away from its past so as to be able to consider it in the light of a non-being and so as to be able to confer on it the meaning which *it has* in terms of the project of a meaning which it *does not have.* Under no circumstances can the past in any way by itself produce *an act*; that is, the positing of an end which turns back upon itself so as to illuminate it. That is what Hegel caught sight of when he wrote that "the mind is the negative," although he seems not to have remembered this when he came to presenting his own theory of action and of freedom. In fact as soon as one attributes to consciousness this negative power with respect to the world and itself, as soon as the nihilation forms an integral part of the *positing* of an end, we must recognize that the indispensable and fundamental condition of all action is the freedom of the acting being.

Thus at the outset we can see what is lacking in those tedious discussions between determinists and the proponents of free will. The latter are concerned to find cases of decision for which there exists no prior cause, or deliberations concerning two opposed acts which are equally possible and possess causes (and motives) of exactly the same weight. To which the determinists may easily reply that there is no action without a cause and that the most insignificant gesture (raising the right hand rather than the left hand, etc.) refers to causes and motives which confer its meaning upon it. Indeed the case could not be otherwise since every action must be *intentional*; each action must, in fact, have an end, and the end in turn is referred to a cause. Such indeed is the unity of the three temporal ekstases; the end or temporalization of my future implies a cause (or motive); that is, it points toward my past, and the present is the upsurge of the act. To speak of an act without a cause is to speak of an act which would lack the intentional structure of every act; and the proponents of free will by searching for it on the level of the act which is in the process of being performed can only end up by rendering the act absurd. But the determinists in turn are weighting the scale by stopping their investigation with the mere designation of the cause and motive. The essential question in fact lies beyond the complex organization "cause-intention-act-end"; indeed we ought to ask how a cause (or motive) can be constituted as such.

Now we have just seen that if there is no act without a cause, this is not in the sense that we can say that there is no phenomenon without a cause. In order to be a *cause*, the *cause* must be *experienced* as such. Of course this does not mean that it is to be thematically conceived and made explicit as in the case of deliberation. But at the very least it means that the for-itself must confer on it its value as cause or motive. And, as we have seen, this constitution of the cause as such can not refer to another real and positive existence; that is, to a prior cause. For otherwise the very nature of the act as engaged intentionally in non-being would disappear. The motive is understood only by the end; that is, by the non-existent. It is therefore in itself a négatité. If I accept a niggardly salary it is doubtless because of fear; and fear is a motive. But it is *fear of dying from starvation*; that is, this fear has meaning only outside itself in an end ideally posited, which is the preservation of a life which I apprehend as "in danger." And this fear is understood in turn only in relation to the *value which I* implicitly give to this life; that is, it is referred to that hierarchal system of ideal objects which are values. Thus the motive makes itself understood as what it is by means of the ensemble of beings which "are not," by ideal existences, and by the future. Just as the future turns back upon the present and the past in order to elucidate them, so it is the ensemble of my projects which turns back in order to confer upon the *motive* its structure as a motive. It is only because I escape the in-itself by nihilating myself toward my possibilities that this in-itself can take on value as cause or motive. Causes and motives have meaning only inside a projected ensemble which is precisely an ensemble of non-existents. And this ensemble is ultimately myself as transcendence; it is Me in so far as I have to be myself outside of myself.

If we recall the principle which we established earlier—namely that it is the apprehension of a revolution as possible which gives to the workman's suffering its value as a motive—we must thereby conclude that it is by fleeing a situation toward our possibility of changing it that we organize this situation into complexes of causes and motives. The nihilation by which we achieve a withdrawal in relation to the situation is the same as the ekstasis by which we project ourselves toward a modification of this situation. The result is that it is in fact impossible to find an act without a motive but that this does not mean that we must conclude that the motive causes the act; the motive is an integral part of the act. For as the resolute project toward a change is not distinct from the act, the motive, the act, and the end are all constituted in a single upsurge. Each of these three structures claims the two others as its meaning. But the organized totality of the three is no longer explained by any particular structure, and its upsurge as the pure temporalizing nihilation of the in-itself is one with freedom. It is the act which decides its ends and its motives, and the act is the expression of freedom. . . .

In addition it is necessary to point out to "common sense" that the formula "to be free" does not mean "to obtain what one has wished" but rather "by oneself to determine oneself to wish" (in the broad sense of choosing). In other words success is not important to freedom. The discussion which opposes common sense to philosophers stems here from a misunderstanding: the empirical and popular concept of "freedom" which has been produced by historical, political, and moral circumstances is equivalent to "the ability to obtain the ends chosen." The technical and philosophical concept of freedom, the only one which we are considering here, means only the autonomy of choice. It is necessary, however, to note that the choice, being identical with acting, supposes a commencement of realization in order that the choice may be distinguished from the dream and the wish. Thus we shall not say that a prisoner is always free to go out of prison, which would be absurd, nor that he is always free to long for release, which would be an irrelevant truism, but that he is always free to try to escape (or get himself liberated); that is, that whatever his condition may be, he can project his escape and learn the value of his project by undertaking some action. Our description of freedom, since it does not distinguish between choosing and doing, compels us to abandon at once the distinction between the intention and the act. The intention can no more be separated from the act than thought can be separated from the language which expresses it; and as it happens that our speech informs us of our thought, so our acts will inform us of our intentions—that is, it will enable us to disengage our intentions, to schematize them, and to make objects of them instead of limiting us to living them—*i.e.*, to assume a non-thetic consciousness of them. This essential distinction between the freedom of choice and the freedom of obtaining was certainly perceived by Descartes, following Stoicism. It puts an end to all arguments based on the distinction between "willing" and "being able," which are still put forth today by the partisans and the opponents of freedom.

INTRODUCTION TO METAPHYSICS / Study Questions

FREEDOM OR DETERMINISM

d'Holbach

1. Describe d'Holbach's conception of the will. In what way is the conception physiological and/or mechanical?
2. Is the will the ultimate cause of human action? What influences can determine a man's will?
3. How does d'Holbach argue that choice does not prove the existence of free will?
4. Explain the distinction d'Holbach draws between restraint and necessity. How does he use this distinction in his argument?
5. Why does d'Holbach believe that men think they are free?
6. Explain the general view of nature that underlies d'Holbach's theory of human action.
7. What does it mean to say, in d'Holbach's terms, that one motive is stronger than another? Is it informative to say that a man acts upon his strongest motive?
8. How does one *find out* what motive(s) the person has in d'Holbach's case of the thirsty man? If one has to see some behavior (the machine at work, so to speak) to find out what the motive was, could one ever know what the motive is *in advance of* the action, so as to predict what the behavior will be? Compare this with the case of the errant bowl and the forces acting on it (where prediction *is* possible). What does this suggest to you about the machine-model of explaining human action?

Hospers

1. What difficulties does Hospers see in trying to understand free acts as voluntary acts?
2. Is it important to distinguish between talking about *acts* as free and *human beings* as free?
3. Explain the author's criticism of Schlick.
4. Summarize the psychoanalytic doctrine on the issue of freedom.
5. Is Hospers justified in generalizing his account of abnormal behavior to cover *all* behavior?

6. In what ways is Hospers' position a restatement of d'Holbach's thesis in the modern dress of Freudian psychoanalysis?
7. What views about the relation between freedom and determinism on the one hand and responsibility on the other are shared by d'Holbach and Hospers?
8. Hospers says that for a term to be "significantly used" it "must have a significant opposite." What is the importance of this remark for the entire "free will or determinism" issue? How could it be used against d'Holbach? What role does it play in the two criteria "for distinguishing the free from the unfree" which Hospers develops out of psychoanalytic theory? What are those two criteria, and in what respects do they differ?
9. Will Hospers' schematic representation of his argument still work if we leave out any reference to Neurosis N as a link between Events E and Behavior B and claim simply that B is the inevitable consequence of E? If the argument still works, would that tend to show that perhaps the reference to neuroses has no explanatory value?
10. Is there a logical problem about what will count as evidence for the truth of Hospers' version of determinism? Is there, perhaps, something suspicious in his reliance on psychoanalytic case studies?
11. At both the beginning and the end of this piece Hospers says that this is an issue involving the possible meanings of the word *free*. He also states that one can choose to mean what one wants here, although it might be misleading to do so. If one can always just *choose* to mean what one wants, how are we to show which uses of a word are misleading and which are not?
12. Why is it mistaken to hold someone responsible for having a disease, according to Hospers? How could we explain the mistake *as* Hospers does if a person is almost never really "at fault" for what he does? It may be tempting here to suggest that, on Hospers' view, a person *can* be truly responsible for actions of a trivial nature, where unconscious drives are not brought into play; so one must now ask whether it would ever make sense to hold someone responsible—"at fault"—for such *trivial* action. If not, has Hospers actually provided criteria "for distinguishing the free from the unfree" which meet his own test of the significance of opposite terms?

Bolles

1. According to Bolles what is the role of the concept of *motivation*?
2. What is "traditional rationalism?" How does Bolles criticize it?
3. What is "mechanism?" How is this theory related to that of other authors in this section? How can it be criticized?
4. What is "empirical determinism?" What is Bolles' stance on determinism relative to this theory? Compare Bolles' position with that of other authors in this section.
5. What distinction between "how?" questions and "why?" questions does Bolles want to draw? Why does he think this distinction is important? Can such a distinction, in fact, be nicely drawn? For instance, imagine a case in which someone wants to know what another person is doing and is given an answer: To what extent can we separate, in the answer, that element which tells us "how" the individual came to do the thing in question from that element which tells us "why" the person did it?

Peters

1. What different kinds of questions about human behavior does Peters point out can be asked?

2. List the important features of "his reason" explanations and contrast them with features of the other kinds.
3. What important differences does Peters show between *bodily movements* and *actions*? Does the recognition of this distinction undercut the theory of, say, d'Holbach?
4. Why are causal explanations not *sufficient* explanations of human behavior? In what ways might appeals to causes be used in explaining *some* human behavior?
5. Why is the question, "Why does a man eat anything?" an odd question? What does this tend to show about end-state explanations?
6. How would Peters criticize the claim made by psychologists such as Bolles that reference to peoples' intentions and purposes is never explanatory of their behavior?
7. What is the importance of Peters' initial remarks about "ambitious theories" and their relationship (if any) to "concrete problems" about human behavior? Do you think that any version of determinism which you have read in this section can escape Peters' implied charge that any "science" which is founded upon a philosophical picture of science, rather than getting its start in attempting to answer concrete questions about the phenomena, is doomed to fail of becoming an explanatory science?

Sartre

1. What philosophical issue does Sartre think underlies the freedom-determinism question?
2. How does Sartre arrive at his claim that all action is intentional? Is he correct in this claim? What about the case of the careless smoker?
3. What does Sartre mean by "*négatité*"? What is its importance in his theory of action?
4. Explain Sartre's diagnosis of what is lacking in the freedom-determinism debate.
5. How does Sartre distinguish between the *cause* of an act and the *motive* of an act?
6. In Sartre's terms how are we to distinguish choice from dream or wish? Must we be successful in accomplishing what we set out to do in order to be free?

The Mind-Body Problem

The problem that philosophers call the mind-body problem arises in modern times out of the work of René *Descartes*. Descartes concluded that a human being is composed of a physical body inhabited by a nonphysical mind. In the *First Meditation* (see Part 3) he argued that it is conceivable that all our perceptions are illusory and that there are no physical objects at all. This, of course, includes our own bodies. In the *Second Meditation* (a selection from which is included here) he goes on to argue that we cannot, however, doubt that we exist. That is, while we may doubt that we have bodies, in order even to entertain such doubts we must exist. Thus, Descartes is arguing that we are conscious, thinking beings—in a word, we have minds—and it is possible for minds to exist without bodies.

According to Descartes physical objects, including the human body, are characterized by size, shape, motion, and position. Descartes' physics was very crudely mechanical, but we can easily bring it up to date and add to the list of physical properties those of mass as well as chemical and electromagnetic properties. The mind, on the other hand, has no physical properties at all, but is characterized by thought. It is clear that Descartes uses the word "thinking" as a covering term for anything that could be called a state of consciousness, or is psychological or mental in nature. This would include perception, sensation, emotion, memory, reasoning, and so on. Descartes' conclusion is that the concepts of mind and body, as he understands them, are *logically independent* of one another. This means that there is no inconsistency in supposing that minds can exist without bodies or bodies without minds. It also means that no *fact* about a body entails any *fact* about a mind and conversely.

Before going on, one consequence of the cartesian theory must be mentioned. While physical objects are presumably public, that is, they are there for anyone to observe, this is not true of minds. Minds and their states of consciousness are inherently private; each of us is said to be immediately aware of his own states of consciousness, but can never be aware of the mental states of another person. All that I can observe of another is his body and its movements; given the logical independence of body and mind just mentioned, no conclusions about his mental states can be reached from any information about his bodily behavior. It is quite consistent with the cartesian theory that another "person" is only a physiological automaton and possesses no mind at all. All of this is part of what philosophers call the problem of *other minds*. We shall not include any detailed discussion of this problem here, but it is important that you notice that there is such a problem and that it is easily derived from any view on which minds and bodies are thought to be logically independent. What makes all this a problem, of course, is just the simple fact that we do seem to be able to know when another person is angry, has certain intentions, feels morose or glad, and so on. Yet the view in question denies that such things ever could be known.

There are several possible reactions to the cartesian dualism of minds and bodies. Two such reactions have typically been called monism. One type of monism claims to find something incoherent both in the very idea of physical objects and in the idea that we could have knowledge of them and concludes that there are only minds. According to this view, the world around us, including our own bodies, is a creation of the mind by which we attempt to explain our sensations; but that world has no more reality than any other convenient fiction we create to suit our purposes. We have not included selections on this type of monism, called idealism, for the simple reason that, although these views are historically important, they do not have much currency now and do not capture the fancy of many of our students. The other type of monism, called materialism, *is* represented here. With this view, all this talk about "minds," "mental states," "mental events," and so on is just so much superstitious talk about things that on principle are unobservable. The materialist, then, tries to solve both the other minds and mind-body problem by ignoring one half of the cartesian dualism, the mental half. Two versions of materialism are presented here; one that arises out of the needs of psychology and one that, to a large degree, has been inspired by developments in brain physiology. We shall discuss these in turn.

Before going on, it will be helpful to point out that in both of these materialist views we have the beginning of a shift in the understanding of what is at issue.

Descartes has given us an account of the nature of human beings based on two sets of alleged facts, first, "facts" about what we can know, that is, be justified in believing as true, and second, very general "facts" about the nature of bodies and minds, for example, that they do not have certain physical properties, and so on. But in the two versions of materialism presented here the issue shifts from being about the composition of human beings—as though that issue could be settled by an appeal to facts—to being about the nature of the explanation of human behavior. And the form that the issue takes concerns what sort of language about human beings can best effect scientific explanation of human behavior. Both forms of materialism hold that mentalistic language, as it is commonly understood, is defective for that task. Thus, of course, some other language or part of our language must be the adequate one; and the question then becomes one of trying to show how that part of our language does enable us to describe and explain human behavior scientifically.

The first version of materialism we will look at is the psychological theory of behaviorism. It will help if we comment briefly on the influence of cartesianism on the history of psychology. Descartes' dualism of mind and body became the basis for the subsequent division of the sciences into the physical and biological sciences on the one hand and psychology on the other. Just as there are chemistry and physics that describe the laws governing the physical world so there must be a comparable science of psychology to investigate the nature of mind. Psychological theory down to the present day has to be understood against the background of cartesianism. When psychology developed as an independent discipline in the second half of the nineteenth century it assumed this cartesian conception of mind. Minds, as we know this theory to hold, are not publically observable as are physical objects, therefore the psychologist thought he must study his subject matter indirectly by means of the reports that people give him about their mental states. This was called the method of introspection. The subject was supposed to "introspect"—somehow to observe—his own mental states, and then relate what is going on in his mind to the investigator.

As a method of scientific investigation this method of introspection was said to be inadequate because the alleged subject matter of psychology was not open to public inspection and because the introspective reports of subjects could never be checked for accuracy. For these, among other reasons, psychologists early in this century argued that psychology must be put on a sound scientific basis by restricting its subject matter to what is publically observable. The obvious candidate for the subject matter of the new psychology was bodily behavior. As a matter of fact, the behaviorists were of two minds about mind. Sometimes they tended to say that there is no such thing as a mind and at other times they were willing to admit that minds might exist after all. In either case, however, they agreed that whether there be minds or not, the only proper study of psychology is human behavior. Thus the psychological theory of behaviorism was born. That theory is represented here by selections from John B. *Watson*, generally considered the founder of behaviorism, and from the well-known American psychologist B. F. *Skinner*. There are two themes manifested in both Watson and Skinner that are crucial to our discussion of the mind-body problem. One is that our ordinary, mentalistic, explanations of human behavior are basically superstitious in that they appeal to happenings that can never in principle be observed. The other is that mentalistic language can be explained away or defined operationally in terms of bodily behavior. Watson attempts to do this in terms of the notion of a conditioned reflex, a notion that Skinner argues is inadequate and seeks to replace by the notion of operant conditioning. Note that both Watson and Skinner agree that purposes, intentions, thoughts, and the like have no place in scientific explanations of human behavior. Not only do they need to be, but they can be eliminated from science.

The second, and quite different, materialist attempt at solving the mind-body problem is provided here by J. J. C. *Smart* in his article, "Sensations and Brain Processes." Smart argues that what we call mental events, states of mind, and so on are in fact really identical with physiological processes in and states of the brain. This materialist answer to cartesianism is called the mind-brain indentity theory and it has been one of the most widely discussed philosophical theories of recent years. It has had wide support not only within philosophy, but also among theorists within computer science and mathematics as well; and it seems to open up fascinating possibilities for speculation about robots and artificial intelligence. For the purposes of this introduction to the mind-body problem, however, it will be useful for you to focus on two things. First, Smart argues—largely by implication—that mentalistic language is an archaic and superstitious way of referring to what we now know are goings-on in the brain. Thus, unlike the behaviorist, he does not appear to suggest that mentalistic language *cannot* afford explanations of human behavior. Rather, he suggests that those explanations are merely outmoded and prescientific. Secondly, and again unlike the behaviorist, Smart does not think that terms ostensibly referring to mental states and events and terms referring to brain states and events (the *material* in this materialism) *mean* the same thing. This point can best be brought out in the following way.

Descartes' dualism of mind and body suggests a corresponding dualism in our language. Many of the words of our language are used to refer to and describe physical things and events. Other words are used to refer to and describe our states of mind. The mind-body problem can be reinterpreted as a conceptual problem about how these two languages fit together. Descartes, committed to the logical independence of mind and body, would have to say that these two vocabularies are altogether independent of one another. The behaviorist claims that mental words can be defined in terms of words descriptive of the body and its behavior. Smart claims that although words for mental states and words referring to brain processes have different meanings, that is, they cannot be defined in terms of one another, they nevertheless refer to the same things. You might notice, however, that Smart is here appealing to an idea of "referring to the same thing" that demands far more explanation than he gives us.

In the next selection, "Scientific Materialism and the Identity Theory," Norman *Malcolm* launches a sharp criticism of Smart's view. There are several distinct elements in Malcolm's criticism that need to be kept separate. After an initial note in which he declares that he will discuss Smart's view as it might apply to having a sudden thought, Malcolm sets for himself three questions. (a) What exactly is this "strict identity" of which Smart speaks; and could having a sudden thought intelligibly be said to be "strictly identical" with having a brain process? Malcolm shows that Smart's examples of "strict identity" should convince us that his assertion of mind/brain identity requires that we be able to give a spatio-temporal location to the having of a thought, such that it could be discovered that some brain process has the same location and, so, is identical with the having of the thought. The problem with this, in Malcolm's view, is that giving spatio-temporal locations for the having of thoughts is completely unintelligible. (b) What are the criteria for our saying that some behavior is indicative of the having of a sudden thought; and could we intelligibly think of those criteria as also being indicative of someone's having a certain brain process? As to the first half of this issue, Malcolm urges that those criteria involve talk of "practices, rules, and agreements." It is, then, difficult to see how the presence of such things as these could be sufficient conditions for the occurrence of brain processes. This is made all the more difficult if one were also to hold, as Smart does, to a kind of scientific materialism that pictures everything in the world as consisting of "the ultimate particles of physics." For, it is surely unclear "what it would mean to say, for example, that [a] *rule* . . . is a configuration of ultimate particles." (c) Even if we were to be able to give some sense to the mind/brain identity theory, would it follow that we could reduce all explanations (including explanations of human thought and action) to just one *kind* of explanation—namely, that sort used in physics? The "fact" that it does follow is, of course, one of the strong points in favor of the identity theory, according to Smart. Yet Malcolm, in an ingenious use of one of Smart's own arguments, shows that it does not actually follow. That being the case, a crucial motive for holding the identity theory suddenly evaporates.

The article, "Human Beings," by John W. *Cook* is, we believe, one of the most penetrating and illuminating pieces in recent philosophy. Cook's intention is to provide an elucidation of the contribution of Ludwig Wittgenstein to the mind-body problem. While the article is a masterful exposition of Wittgenstein's thought and succeeds in correcting a number of misunderstandings, its importance for our purposes lies in what gets said about the mind-body problem rather than in what gets said about Wittgenstein.

Cook's strategy is not to provide another solution to the mind-body problem, but is rather to show that the cartesian dualism that generates the problem is the result of certain confusions and misunderstandings about our language and the way that we describe human beings. Cook's claim is that cartesianism is not a false theory, but is an unintelligible one. He also makes clear that behaviorism is really a version of cartesianism and shares certain of its assumptions about mind and body. But if cartesianism is infected with conceptual confusion, then so is any theory that is logically parasitic upon it, for example, behaviorism. Cook shows that neither the cartesian nor his intellectual bedfellow, the behaviorist, can understand human behavior. What is needed, Cook will say, is not theorizing about human beings and human behavior, but a very careful look at the relevant concepts embedded in the language with which we talk about, describe, and explain people and their doings. What he says about human behavior also serves to call into question, by implication, speculations about robots and artificial intelligence and, in addition, has far reaching consequences for psychology and the behavioral sciences generally.

The Mind Is Distinct from the Body

RENÉ DESCARTES

Of the Nature of the Human Mind; and that it is more easily known than the Body

THE MEDITATION of yesterday filled my mind with so many doubts that it is no longer in my power to forget them. And yet I do not see in what manner I can resolve them; and, just as if I had all of a sudden fallen into very deep water, I am so disconcerted that I can neither make certain of setting my feet on the bottom, nor can I swim and so support myself on the surface. I shall nevertheless make an effort and follow anew the same path as that on which I yesterday entered, i.e. I shall proceed by setting aside all that in which the least doubt could be supposed to exist, just as if I had discovered that it was absolutely false; and I shall ever follow in this road until I have met with something which is certain, or at least, if I can do nothing else, until I have learned for certain that there is nothing in the world that is certain. Archimedes, in order that he might draw the terrestrial globe out of its place, and transport it elsewhere, demanded only that one point should be fixed and immoveable; in the same way I shall have the right to conceive high hopes if I am happy enough to discover one thing only which is certain and indubitable.

I suppose, then, that all the things that I see are false; I persuade myself that nothing has ever existed of all that my fallacious memory represents to me. I consider that I possess no senses; I imagine that body, figure, extension, movement and place are but the fictions of my mind. What, then, can be esteemed as true? Perhaps nothing at all, unless that there is nothing in the world that is certain.

But how can I know there is not something different from those things that I have just considered, of which one cannot have the slightest doubt? Is there not some God, or some other being by whatever name we call it, who puts these reflections into my mind? That is not necessary, for is it not possible that I am capable of producing them myself? I myself, am I not at least something? But I have already denied that I had senses and body. Yet I hesitate, for what follows from that? Am I so dependent on body and senses that I cannot exist without these? But I was persuaded that there was nothing in all the world, that

---

Reprinted from *Meditations On First Philosophy* by René Descartes, Meditation II.

there was no heaven, no earth, that there were no minds, nor any bodies: was I not then likewise persuaded that I did not exist? Not at all; of a surety I myself did exist since I persuaded myself of something [or merely because I thought of something]. But there is some deceiver or other, very powerful and very cunning, who ever employs his ingenuity in deceiving me. Then without doubt I exist also if he deceives me, and let him deceive me as much as he will, he can never cause me to be nothing so long as I think that I am something. So that after having reflected well and carefully examined all things, we must come to the definite conclusion that this proposition: I am, I exist, is necessarily true each time that I pronounce it, or that I mentally conceive it.

But I do not yet know clearly enough what I am, I who am certain that I am; and hence I must be careful to see that I do not imprudently take some other object in place of myself, and thus that I do not go astray in respect of this knowledge that I hold to be the most certain and most evident of all that I have formerly learned. That is why I shall now consider anew what I believed myself to be before I embarked upon these last reflections; and of my former opinions I shall withdraw all that might even in a small degree be invalidated by the reasons which I have just brought forward, in order that there may be nothing at all left beyond what is absolutely certain and indubitable.

What then did I formerly believe myself to be? Undoubtedly I believed myself to be a man. But what is a man? Shall I say a reasonable animal? Certainly not; for then I should have to inquire what an animal is, and what is reasonable; and thus from a single question I should insensibly fall into an infinitude of others more difficult; and I should not wish to waste the little time and leisure remaining to me in trying to unravel subtleties like these. But I shall rather stop here to consider the thoughts which of themselves spring up in my mind, and which were not inspired by anything beyond my own nature alone when I applied myself to the consideration of my being. In the first place, then, I considered myself as having a face, hands, arms, and all that system of members composed of bones and flesh as seen in a corpse which I designated by the name of body. In addition to this I considered that I was nourished, that I walked, that I felt, and that I thought, and I referred all these actions to the soul: but I did not stop to consider what the soul was, or if I did stop, I imagined that it was something extremely rare and subtle like a wind, a flame, or an ether, which was spread throughout my grosser parts. As to body I had no manner of doubt about its nature, but thought I had a very clear knowledge of it; and if I had desired to explain it according to the notions that I had then formed of it, I should have described it thus: By the body I understand all that which can be defined by a certain figure: something which can be confined in a certain place, and which can fill a given space in such a way that every other body will be excluded from it; which can be perceived either by touch, or by sight, or by hearing, or by taste, or by smell: which can be moved in many ways not, in truth, by itself, but by something which is foreign to it, by which it is touched [and from which it receives impressions]: for to have the power of self-movement, as also of feeling or of thinking, I did not consider to appertain to the nature of body: on the contrary, I was rather astonished to find that faculties similar to them existed in some bodies.

But what am I, now that I suppose that there is a certain genius which is extremely powerful, and, if I may say so, malicious, who employs all his powers in deceiving me? Can I affirm that I possess the least of all those things which I have just said pertain to the nature of body? I pause to consider, I revolve all these things in my mind, and I find none of which I can say that it pertains to me. It would be tedious to stop to enumerate them. Let us pass to the attributes of soul and see if there is any one which is in me? What of nutrition or walking [the first mentioned]? But if it is so that I have no body it is also true that I can neither walk nor take nourishment. Another attribute in sensation. But one cannot feel without body, and besides I have thought I perceived many things during sleep that I recognized in my waking moments as not having been experienced at all. What of thinking? I find here that thought is an attribute that belongs to me; it alone cannot be separated from me. I am, I exist, that is certain. But how often? Just when I think; for it might possibly be the case if I ceased entirely to think, that I should likewise cease altogether to exist. I do not now admit anything which is not necessarily true: to speak accurately I am not more than a thing which thinks, that is to say a mind or a soul, or an understanding, or a reason, which are terms whose significance was formerly unknown to me. I am, however, a real thing and really exist; but what thing? I have answered: a thing which thinks.

And what more? I shall exercise my imagination [in order to see if I am not something more]. I am not a collection of members which we call the human body: I am not a subtle air distributed through these members, I am not a wind, a fire, a vapour, a breath, nor anything at all which I can imagine or conceive; because I have assumed that all these were nothing. Without changing that supposition I find that I only leave myself certain of the fact that I am somewhat. But perhaps it is true that these same things which I supposed were non-existent because they are unknown to me, are really not different from the self which I know. I am not sure about this, I shall not dispute it now; I can only give judgment on things that are known to me. I know that I exist, and I inquire what I am, I whom I know to exist. But it is very certain that the knowledge of my existence taken in its precise significance does not depend on things whose existence is not yet known to me; consequently it does not depend on those which I can feign in imagination. And indeed the very term *feign* in imagination[1] proves to me my error, for I really do this if I imagine myself a something, since to imagine is nothing else than to contemplate the figure or image of a corporeal thing. But I already know for certain that I am, and that it may be that all these images, and, speaking generally, all things that relate to the nature of body are nothing but dreams [and chimeras]. For this reason I see clearly that I have as little reason to say, 'I shall stimulate my imagination in order to know more distinctly what I am,' than if I were to say, 'I am now awake, and I per-

[1] Or 'form an image' (effingo).

ceive somewhat that is real and true: but because I do not yet perceive it distinctly enough, I shall go to sleep of express purpose, so that my dreams may represent the perception with greatest truth and evidence.' And, thus, I know for certain that nothing of all that I can understand by means of my imagination belongs to this knowledge which I have of myself, and that it is necessary to recall the mind from this mode of thought with the utmost diligence in order that it may be able to know its own nature with perfect distinctness.

But what then am I? A thing which thinks. What is a thing which thinks? It is a thing which doubts, understands, [conceives], affirms, denies, wills, refuses, which also imagines and feels.

Certainly it is no small matter if all these things pertain to my nature. But why should they not so pertain? Am I not that being who now doubts nearly everything, who nevertheless understands certain things, who affirms that one only is true, who denies all the others, who desires to know more, is averse from being deceived, who imagines many things, sometimes indeed despite his will, and who perceives many likewise, as by the intervention of the bodily organs? Is there nothing in all this which is as true as it is certain that I exist, even though I should always sleep and though he who has given me being employed all his ingenuity in deceiving me? Is there likewise any one of these attributes which can be distinguished from my thought, or which might be said to be separated from myself? For it is so evident of itself that it is I who doubts, who understands, and who desires, that there is no reason here to add anything to explain it. And I have certainly the power of imagining likewise; for although it may happen (as I formerly supposed) that none of the things which I imagine are true, nevertheless this power of imagining does not cease to be really in use, and it forms part of my thought. Finally, I am the same who feels, that is to say, who perceives certain things, as by the organs of sense, since in truth I see light, I hear noise, I feel heat. But it will be said that these phenomena are false and that I am dreaming. Let it be so; still it is at least quite certain that it seems to me that I see light, that I hear noise and that I feel heat. That cannot be false; properly speaking it is what is in me called feeling; and used in this precise sense that is no other thing than thinking.

What Is Behaviorism?

JOHN B. WATSON

TWO OPPOSED points of view are still dominant in American psychological thinking—introspective or subjective psychology, and behaviorism or objective psychology. Until the advent of behaviorism in 1912, introspective psychology completely dominated American university psychological life.

The conspicuous leaders of introspective psychology in the first decade of the twentieth century were E. B. Titchener of Cornell and William James of Harvard. The death of James in 1910 and the death of Titchener in 1927 left introspective psychology without emotional leadership. Although Titchener's psychology differed in many points from that of William James, their fundamental assumptions were the same. In the first place, both were of German origin. In the second place, and of more importance, both claimed that *consciousness is the subject matter of psychology.*

Behaviorism, on the contrary, holds that the subject matter of human psychology *is the behavior of the human being.* Behaviorism claims that consciousness is neither a definite nor a usable concept. The behaviorist, who has been trained always as an experimentalist, holds, further, the belief in the existence of consciousness goes back to the ancient days of superstition and magic.

The great mass of the people even today has not yet progressed very far away from savagery—it wants to believe in magic. The savage believes that incantations can bring rain, good crops, good hunting, that an unfriendly voodoo doctor can bring disaster to a person or to a whole tribe; that an enemy who has obtained a nail paring or a lock of your hair can cast a harmful spell over you and control your actions. There is always interest and news in magic. Almost every era has its new magic, black or white, and its new magician. Moses had his magic: he smote the rock and water gushed out. Christ had his magic: he turned water into wine and raised the dead to life. Coué had his magic word formula. Mrs. Eddy had a similar one.

Magic lives forever. As time goes on, all of these critically undigested, innumerably told tales get woven into the folk lore of the people. Folk lore in turn gets organized into religions. Religions get caught up into the political and economic network of the country. Then they are used as tools. The public is forced to accept all of the old wives' tales, and it passes them on as gospel to its children's children.

The extent to which most of us are shot through with a savage background is almost unbelievable. Few of us escape it. Not even a college education seems to correct it. If anything, it seems to strengthen it, since the colleges themselves are filled with instructors who have the same background. Some of our greatest biologists, physicists, and chemists, when outside of their laboratories, fall back upon folk lore which has become crystallized into religious concepts. These concepts—these heritages of a timid savage past—have made the emergence and growth of scientific psychology extremely difficult.

An Example of Such Concepts

One example of such a religious concept is that every individual has a *soul* which is separate and distinct from the *body.* This soul is really a part of a supreme being. This ancient view led to the philosophical platform called "dualism." This dogma has been present in human psychology from earliest antiquity. No one has ever touched a soul, or seen one in a test tube, or has in any way come into relationship with it as he has with the other objects of his daily experience. Nevertheless, to doubt its existence is to become a heretic and once might possibly even have led to the loss of one's head. Even today the man holding a public position dare not question it.

With the development of the physical sciences which came with the renaissance, a certain release from this stifling soul cloud was obtained. A man could think of astronomy, of the celestial bodies and their motions, of gravitation and the like, without involving soul. Although the early scientists were as a rule devout Christians, nevertheless they began to leave soul out of their test tubes.

Psychology and philosophy, however, in dealing as they thought with non-material objects, found it difficult to escape the language of the church, and hence the concept of mind or soul as distinct from the body came down almost unchanged in essence to the latter part of the nineteenth century.

Wundt, the real father of experimental psychology, unquestionably wanted in 1879 a scientific psychology. He grew up in the midst of a dualistic philosophy of the most pronounced type. He could not see his way clear to a solution of the mind-body problem. His psychology, which has reigned supreme to the present day, is necessarily a compromise. He substituted the term *consciousness* for the term soul. Consciousness is not quite so unobservable as soul. We observe it by peeking in suddenly and catching it unawares as it were (*introspection*).

Wundt had an immense following. Just as now it is fashionable to go to Vienna to study psycho-analysis under Freud, just so was it fashionable some 40 years ago to study at Leipzig with Wundt. The men who returned founded the laboratories at Johns Hopkins University, the University of Pennsylvania, Columbia, Clark and Cornell. All were equipped to do battle with the elusive (almost soul-like) thing called consciousness.

To show how unscientific is the main concept behind this great German-American school of psychology, look for a moment at William James' definition of psychology. "Psychology is the description and explanation of states of consciousness as such." Starting with a definition which *assumes* what he starts out to prove, he escapes his difficulty by an *argumentum ad hominem.* Consciousness—Oh, yes, everybody must know what this "consciousness" is. When we have a sensation of red, a perception, a thought, when we *will* do something, or when we *purpose* to do something, or when we desire to do something, we are being *conscious.*

All other introspectionists are equally illogical. In other words, they do not tell us what consciousness is, but merely begin to put things into it by assumption; and then when they come to analyze consciousness, naturally they find in it just what they put into it. Consequently, in the analyses of consciousness made by certain of the psychologists you find such elements as *sensations* and their ghosts, the *images.* With others you find not only sensations, but so-called *affective elements*; in still others you find such elements as *will*—the so-called *conative element* in consciousness. With some psychologists you find many hundreds of sensations of a certain type; others maintain that only a few of that type exist. And so it goes. Literally hundreds of thousands of printed pages have been published on the minute analysis of this intangible something called "consciousness." And how do we begin work upon it? Not by analyzing it as we would a chemical compound, or the way a plant grows. No, those things are material things. This thing we call consciousness can be analyzed only by *introspection*—a looking in on what takes place inside of us.

As a result of this major assumption that there is such a thing as consciousness and that we can analyze it by introspection, we find as many analyses as there are individual psychologists. There is no way of experimentally attacking and solving psychological problems and standardizing methods.

The Advent of the Behaviorists

In 1912 the objective psychologists or behaviorists reached the conclusion that they could no longer be content to work with Wundt's formulations. They felt that the 30 odd barren years since the establishment of Wundt's laboratory had proved conclusively that the so-called introspective psychology of Germany was founded upon wrong hypotheses—that no psychology which included the religious mind-body problem could ever arrive at verifiable conclusions. They decided either to give up psychology or else to make it a natural science. They saw their brother-scientists making progress in medicine, in chemistry, in physics. Every new discovery in those fields was of prime importance; every new element isolated in one laboratory could be isolated in some other laboratory; each new element was immediately taken up in the warp and woof of science as a whole. One need only mention wireless, radium, insulin, thyroxin, to verify this. Elements so isolated and methods so formulated immediately began to function in human achievement.

In his first efforts to get uniformity in subject matter and in methods the behaviorist began his own formulation of the problem of psychology by sweeping aside all mediaeval conceptions. He dropped from his scientific vocabulary all subjective terms such as sensation, perception, image, desire, purpose, and even thinking and emotion as they were subjectively defined.

The Behaviorist's Platform

The behaviorist asks: Why don't we make what we can *observe* the real field of psychology? Let us limit ourselves to things that can be observed, and formulate laws concerning only those things. Now what can we observe? We can observe *behavior—what the organism does or says.* And let us point out at once: that *saying* is doing—that is, *behaving.* Speaking overtly or to ourselves (thinking) is just as objective a type of behavior as baseball.

The rule, or measuring rod, which the behaviorist puts in front of him always is: Can I describe this bit of behavior I see in terms of "stimulus and response?" By stimulus we mean any object in the general environment or any change in the tissues themselves due to the physiological condition of the animal, such as the change we get when we keep an animal from sex activity, when we keep it from feeding, when we keep it from building a nest. By response we mean anything the animal does—such as turning toward or away from a light, jumping at a sound, and more highly organized activities such as building a skyscraper, drawing plans, having babies, writing books, and the like.

Some Specific Problems of the Behaviorists

You will find, then, the behaviorist working like any other scientist. His sole object is to gather facts about behavior—verify his data—subject them both to logic and to mathematics (the tools of every scientist). He brings the new-born individual *into his experimental nursery* and begins to set problems: What is the baby doing now? What is the stimulus that makes him behave this way? He finds that the stimulus of tickling the cheek brings the response of turning the mouth to the side stimulated. The stimulus of the nipple brings out the sucking response. The stimulus of a rod placed on the palm of the hand brings closure of the hand and the suspension of the whole body by that hand and arm if the rod is raised. Stimulating the infant with a rapidly moving shadow across the eye will not produce blinking until the individual is sixty-five days of age. Stimulating the infant with an apple or stick of candy or any other object will not call out attempts at reaching until the baby is around 120 days of age. Stimulating a properly brought up infant at any age with snakes, fish, darkness, burning paper, birds, cats, dogs, monkeys, will not bring out that type of response which we call "fear" (which to be objective we might call reaction "X") which is a catching of the breath, a stiffening of the whole body, a turning away of the body from the source of stimulation, a running or crawling away from it.

On the other hand, there are just two things which will call out a fear response, namely, a loud sound, and loss of support.

Now the behaviorist finds from observing children brought up *outside of his nursery* that hundreds of these objects will call out fear responses. Consequently, the scientific question arises: If at birth only two stimuli will call out fear, how do all these other things ever finally come to call it out? Please note that the question is not a speculative one. It can be answered by experiments, and the experiments can be reproduced and the same findings can be had in every other laboratory if the original observation is sound. Convince yourself of this by making a simple test.

If you will take a snake, mouse or dog and show it to a baby who has never seen these objects or been frightened in other ways, he begins to manipulate it, poking at this, that or the other part. Do this for ten days until you are logically certain that the child will always go toward the dog and never run away from it (positive reaction) and that it does not call out a fear response at any time. In contrast to this, pick up a steel bar and strike upon it loudly behind the infant's head. Immediately the fear response is called forth. Now try this: At the instant you show him the animal and just as he begins to reach for it, strike the steel bar behind his head. Repeat the experiment three or four times. A new and important change is apparent. The animal now calls out the same response as the steel bar, namely a fear response. We call this, in behavioristic psychology, the *conditioned emotional response*—a form of *conditioned reflex.*

Our studies of conditioned reflexes make it easy for us to account for the child's fear of the dog on a thoroughly natural science basis without lugging in consciousness or any other so-called mental process. A dog comes toward the child rapidly, jumps upon him, pushes him down and at the same time barks loudly. Oftentimes one such combined stimulation is all that is necessary to make the baby run away from the dog the moment it comes within his range of vision....

Does This Behavioristic Approach Leave Anything Out of Psychology?

After so brief a survey of the behavioristic approach to the problems of psychology, one is inclined to say: "Why, yes, it is worth while to study human behavior in this way, but the study of behavior is not the whole of psychology. It leaves out too much. Don't I have sensations, perceptions, conceptions? Do I not forget things and remember things, imagine things, have visual images and auditory images of things I once have seen and heard? Can I not see and hear things that I have never seen or heard in nature? Can I not be attentive or inattentive? Can I not will to do a thing or will not do it, as the case may be? Do not certain things arouse pleasure in me, and others displeasure? Behaviorism is trying to rob us of everything we have believed in since earliest childhood."

Having been brought up on introspective psychology, as most of us have, you naturally ask these questions and you will find it hard to put away the old terminology and begin to formulate your psychological life in terms of behaviorism. Behaviorism is new wine and it will not go into old bottles. It is advisable for the time being to allay your natural antagonism and accept the behavioristic platform at least until you get more deeply into it. Later you will find that you have progressed so far with behaviorism that the questions you now raise will answer themselves in a perfectly satisfactory natural science way. Let me hasten to add that if the behaviorist were to ask you what you mean by the subjective terms you have been in the habit of using he could soon make you tongue-tied with contradictions. He could even convince you that you do not know what you mean by them. You have been using them uncritically as a part of your social and literary tradition....

What Is a Stimulus?

If I suddenly flash a strong light in your eye, your pupil will contract rapidly. If I were suddenly to shut off all light in the room in which you are sitting, the pupil would begin to widen. If a pistol shot were suddenly fired behind you, you would jump and possibly turn your head around. If hydrogen sulphide were suddenly released in your sitting room you would begin to hold your nose and possibly even seek to leave the room. If I suddenly made the room very warm, you would begin to unbutton your coat and perspire. If I suddenly made it cold, another response would take place.

Again, on the inside of us we have an equally large realm in which stimuli can exert their effect. For example, just before dinner the muscles of your stomach begin to contract and expand rhythmically because of the absence of food. As soon as food is eaten those contractions cease. By swallowing a small balloon and attaching it to a recording instrument we can easily register the response of the stomach to lack of food and note the lack of response when food is present. In the male, at any rate, the pressure of certain fluids (semen) may lead to sex activity. In the case of the female possibly the presence of certain chemical bodies can lead in a similar way to overt sex behavior. The muscles of our arms and legs and trunk are not only subject to stimuli coming from the blood; they are also stimulated by their own responses—that is, the muscle is under constant tension; any increase in that tension, as when a movement is made, gives rise to a stimulus which leads to another response in that same muscle or in some distant part of the body; any decrease in that tension, as when the muscle is relaxed, similarly gives rise to a stimulus. . . .

General Classification of Response

The two commonsense classifications of response are "external" and "internal"—or possibly the terms "overt" (explicit) and "implicit" are better. By external or overt responses we mean the ordinary doings of the human being: he stoops to pick up a tennis ball, he writes a letter, he enters an automobile and starts driving, he digs a hole in the ground, he sits down to write a lecture, or dances, or flirts with a woman, or makes love to his wife. We do not need instruments to make these observations. On the other hand, responses may be wholly confined to the muscular and glandular systems inside the body. A child or hungry adult may be standing stock still in front of a window filled with pastry. Your first exclamation may be "He isn't doing anything" or "He is just looking at the pastry." An instrument would show that his salivary glands are pouring out secretions, that his stomach is rhythmically contracting and expanding, and that marked changes in blood pressure are taking place—that the endocrine glands are pouring substances into the blood. The internal or implicit responses are difficult to observe, not because they are inherently different from the external or overt responses, but merely because they are hidden from the eye.

Advances In Behaviorism

B. F. SKINNER

The Consequences of Behavior

REFLEXES, conditioned or otherwise, are mainly concerned with the internal physiology of the organism. We are most often interested, however, in behavior which has some effect upon the surrounding world. Such behavior raises most of the practical problems in human affairs and is also of particular theoretical interest because of its special characteristics. The consequences of behavior may "feed back" into the organism. When they do so, they may change the probability that the behavior which produced them will occur again. The English language contains many words, such as "reward" and "punishment," which refer to this effect, but we can get a clear picture of it only through experimental analysis.

Learning Curves

One of the first serious attempts to study the changes brought about by the consequences of behavior was made by E. L. Thorndike in 1898. His experiments arose from a controversy which was then of considerable interest. Darwin, in insisting upon the continuity of species, had questioned the belief that man was unique among the animals in his ability to think. Anecdotes in which lower animals seemed to show the "power of reasoning" were published in great numbers. But when terms which had formerly been applied only to human behavior were thus extended, certain questions arose concerning their meaning. Did the observed facts point to mental processes, or could these apparent evidences of thinking be explained in other ways? Eventually it became clear that the assumption of inner thought-processes was not required. Many years were to pass before the same question was seriously raised concerning human behavior, but Thorndike's experiments and his alternative explanation of reasoning in animals were important steps in that direction.

If a cat is placed in a box from which it can escape only by unlatching a door, it will exhibit many different kinds of behavior, some of which may be effective in opening the door. Thorndike found that when a cat was put into such a box again and again, the behavior which led to escape tended to occur sooner and sooner until eventually escape was as simple and quick as possible. The cat had solved its problem as well as if it were a "reasoning" human being, though perhaps not so speedily. Yet Thorndike observed no "thought-process" and argued that none was needed by way of explanation. He could describe his results simply by saying that a part of the cat's behavior was "stamped in" because it was followed by the opening of the door.

The fact that behavior is stamped in when followed by certain consequences, Thorndike called "The Law of Effect." What he had observed was that certain behavior occurred more and more readily in comparison with other behavior characteristic of the same situation. By noting the successive delays in getting out of the box and plotting them on a graph, he constructed a "learning curve." This early attempt to show a quantitative process in behavior, similar to the processes of physics and biology, was heralded as an important advance. It revealed a process which took place over a considerable period of time and which was not obvious to casual inspection. Thorndike, in short, had made a discovery. Many similar curves have since been recorded and have become the substance of chapters on learning in psychology texts....

Operant Conditioning

To get at the core of Thorndike's Law of Effect, we need to clarify the notion of "probability of response." This is an extremely important concept; unfortunately, it is also a difficult one. In discussing human behavior, we often refer to "tendencies" or "predispositions" to behave in particular ways. Almost every theory of behavior uses some such term as "excitatory potential," "habit strength," or "determining tendency." But how do we observe a tendency? And how can we measure one?

If a given sample of behavior existed in only two states, in one of which it always occurred and in the other never, we should be almost helpless in following a program of functional analysis. An all-or-none subject matter lends itself only to primitive forms of description. It is a great advantage to suppose instead that the *probability* that a response will occur ranges continuously between these all-or-none extremes. We can then deal with variables which, unlike the eliciting stimulus, do not "cause a given bit of behavior to occur" but simply make the occurrence more probable. We may then proceed to deal, for example, with the combined effect of more than one such variable.

The everyday expressions which carry the notion of probability, tendency, or predisposition describe the frequencies with which bits of behavior occur. We never observe a probability as such. We say that someone is "enthusiastic" about bridge when we observe that he plays bridge often and talks about it often. To be "greatly interested" in music is to play, listen to, and talk about music a good deal. The "inveterate" gambler is one who gambles frequently. The camera "fan" is to be found taking pictures, developing them, and looking at pictures made by himself and others. The "highly sexed" person frequently engages in sexual behavior. The "dipsomaniac" drinks frequently.

In characterizing a man's behavior in terms of frequency, we assume certain standard conditions: he must be able to execute and repeat a given act, and other behavior must not interfere appreciably. We cannot be sure of the extent of a man's interest in music, for example, if he is necessarily busy with other things. When we come to refine the notion of probability of response for scientific use, we find that here, too, our data are frequencies and that the conditions under which they are observed must be specified. The main technical problem in designing a controlled experiment is to provide for the observation and interpretation of frequencies. We eliminate, or at least hold constant, any condition which encourages behavior which competes with the behavior we are to study. An organism is placed in a quiet box where its behavior may be observed through a one-way screen or recorded mechanically. This is by no means an environmental vacuum, for the organism will react to the features of the box in many ways; but its behavior will eventually reach a fairly stable level, against which the frequency of a selected response may be investigated.

To study the process which Thorndike called stamping in, we must have a "consequence." Giving food to a hungry organism will do. We can feed our subject conveniently with a small food tray which is operated electrically. When the tray is first opened, the organism will probably react to it in ways which interfere with the process we plan to observe. Eventually, after being fed from the tray repeatedly, it eats readily, and we are then ready to make this consequence contingent upon behavior and to observe the result.

We select a relatively simple bit of behavior which may be freely and rapidly repeated, and which is easily observed and recorded. If our experimental subject is a pigeon, for example, the behavior of raising the head above a given height is convenient. This may be observed by sighting across the pigeon's head at a scale pinned on the far wall of the box. We first study the height at which the head is normally held and select some line on the scale which is reached only infrequently. Keeping our eye on the scale we then begin to open the food tray very quickly whenever the head rises above the line. If the experiment is conducted according to specifications, the result is invariable: we observe an immediate change in the frequency with which the head crosses the line. We also observe, and this is of some importance theoretically, that higher lines are now being crossed. We may advance almost immediately to a higher line in determining when food is to be presented. In a minute or two, the bird's posture has changed so that the top of the head seldom falls below the line which we first chose.

When we demonstrate the process of stamping in this relatively simple way, we see that certain common interpretations of Thorndike's experiment are superfluous. The expression "trial-and-error learning," which is frequently associated with the Law of Effect, is clearly out of place here. We are reading something into our observations when we call any upward movement of the head a "trial," and there is no reason to call any movement which does not achieve a specified consequence an "error." Even the term "learning" is misleading. The statement that the bird "learns that it will get food by stretching its neck" is an inaccurate report of what has happened. To say that it has acquired the "habit" of stretching its neck is merely to resort to an explanatory fiction, since our only evidence of the habit is the acquired tendency to perform the act. The barest possible statement of the process is this: we make a given consequence contingent upon certain physical properties of behavior (the upward movement of the head), and the behavior is then observed to increase in frequency.

It is customary to refer to any movement of the organism as a "response." The word is borrowed from the field of reflex action and implies an act which, so to speak, answers a prior event—the stimulus. But we may make an event contingent upon behavior without identifying, or being able to identify, a prior stimulus. We did not alter the environment of the pigeon to *elicit* the upward movement of the head. It is probably impossible to show that any single stimulus invariably precedes this movement. Behavior of this sort may come under the control of stimuli, but the relation is not that of elicitation. The term "response" is therefore not wholly appropriate but is so well established that we shall use it in the following discussion.

A response which has already occurred cannot, of course, be predicted or controlled. We can only predict that *similar* responses will occur in the future. The unit of a predictive science is, therefore, not a response but a class of responses. The word "operant" will be used to describe this class. The term emphasizes the fact that the behavior *operates* upon the environment to generate consequences. The consequences define the properties with respect to which responses are called similar. The term will be used both as an adjective (operant behavior) and as a noun to designate the behavior defined by a given consequence.

A single instance in which a pigeon raises its head is a *response.* It is a bit of history which may be reported in any frame of reference we wish to use. The behavior called "raising the head," regardless of when specific instances occur, is an *operant.* It can be described, not as an accomplished act, but rather as a set of acts defined by the property of the height to which the head is raised. In this sense an operant is defined by an effect which may be specified in physical terms; the "cutoff" at a certain height is a property of behavior.

The term "learning" may profitably be saved in its traditional sense to describe the reassortment of responses in a complex situation. Terms for the process of stamping in may be borrowed from Pavlov's analysis of the conditioned reflex. Pavlov himself called all events which strengthened behavior "reinforcement" and all the resulting changes "conditioning." In the Pavlovian experiment, however, a reinforcer is paired with a *stimulus*; whereas in operant behavior it is contingent upon a *response.* Operant reinforcement is therefore a separate process and requires a separate analysis. In both cases, the strengthening of behavior which results from reinforcement is appropriately called "conditioning." In operant conditioning we "strengthen" an operant in the sense of making a response more probable or, in actual fact, more frequent. In Pavlovian or "respondent" conditioning we simply increase the magnitude of the response elicited by the conditioned stimulus and shorten the time which elapses between stimulus and response. (We note, incidentally, that these two cases exhaust the possibilities: an organism is conditioned when a reinforcer [1] accompanies another stimulus or [2] follows upon the organism's own behavior. Any event which does neither has no effect in changing a probability of response.) In the pigeon experiment, then, food is the *reinforcer* and presenting food when a response is emitted is the *reinforcement.* The *operant* is defined by the property upon which reinforcement is contingent—the height to which the head must be raised. The change in frequency with which the head is lifted to this height is the process of *operant conditioning.*

While we are awake, we act upon the environment constantly, and many of the consequences of our actions are reinforcing. Through operant conditioning the environment builds the basic repertoire with which we keep our balance, walk, play games, handle instruments and tools, talk, write, sail a boat, drive a car, or fly a plane. A change in the environment—a new car, a new friend, a new field of interest, a new job, a new location—may find us unprepared, but our behavior usually adjusts quickly as we acquire new responses and discard old....

The Control of Operant Behavior

The experimental procedure in operant conditioning is straightforward. We arrange a contingency of reinforcement and expose an organism to it for a given period. We then explain the frequent emission of the response by pointing to this history. But what improvement has been made in the prediction and control of the behavior in the future? What variables enable us to predict whether or not the organism will respond? What variables must we now control in order to induce it to respond?

We have been experimenting with a *hungry* pigeon. . . . this means a pigeon which has been deprived of food for a certain length of time or until its usual body-weight has been slightly reduced. Contrary to what one might expect, experimental studies have shown that the magnitude of the reinforcing effect of food may not depend upon the degree of such deprivation. But the frequency of response which results from reinforcement depends upon the degree of deprivation at the time the response is observed. Even though we have conditioned a pigeon to stretch its neck, it does not do this if it is not hungry. We have, therefore, a new sort of control over its behavior: in order to get the pigeon to stretch its neck, we simply make it hungry. A selected operant has been added to all those things which a hungry pigeon will do. Our control over the response has been pooled with our control over food deprivation. . . . an operant may also come under the control of an external stimulus, which is another variable to be used in predicting and controlling the behavior. We should note, however, that both these variables are to be distinguished from operant reinforcement itself.

Operant Extinction

When reinforcement is no longer forthcoming, a response becomes less and less frequent in what is called "operant extinction." If food is withheld, the pigeon will eventually stop lifting its head. In general when we engage in behavior which no longer "pays off," we find ourselves less inclined to behave in that way again. If we lose a fountain pen, we reach less and less often into the pocket which formerly held it. If we get no answer to telephone calls, we eventually stop telephoning. If our piano goes out of tune, we gradually play it less and less. If our radio becomes noisy or if programs become worse, we stop listening.

Since operant extinction takes place much more slowly than operant conditioning, the process may be followed more easily. Under suitable conditions smooth curves are obtained in which the rate of response is seen to decline slowly, perhaps over a period of many hours. The curves reveal properties which could not possibly be observed through casual inspection. We may "get the impression" that an organism is responding less and less often, but the orderliness of the change can be seen only when the behavior is recorded. The curves suggest that there is a fairly uniform process which determines the output of behavior during extinction.

Under some circumstances the curve is disturbed by an emotional effect. The failure of a response to be reinforced leads not only to operant extinction but also to a reaction commonly spoken of as frustration or rage. A pigeon which has failed to receive reinforcement turns away from the key, cooing, flapping its wings, and engaging in other emotional behavior. . . . The human organism shows a similar double effect. The child whose tricycle no longer responds to pedaling not only stops pedaling but engages in a possibly violent emotional display. The adult who finds a desk drawer stuck may soon stop pulling, but he may also pound the desk, exclaim "Damn it!," or exhibit other signs of rage. Just as the child eventually goes back to the tricycle, and the adult to the drawer, so the pigeon will turn again to the key when the emotional response has subsided. As other responses go unreinforced, another emotional episode may ensue. Extinction curves under such circumstances show a cyclic oscillation as the emotional response builds up, disappears, and builds up again. If we eliminate the emotion by repeated exposure to extinction, or in other ways, the curve emerges in a simpler form.

Behavior during extinction is the result of the conditioning which has preceded it, and in this sense the extinction curve gives an additional measure of the effect of reinforcement. If only a few responses have been reinforced, extinction occurs quickly. A long history of reinforcement is followed by protracted responding. The resistance to extinction cannot be predicted from the probability of response observed at any given moment. We must know the history of reinforcement. For example, though we have been reinforced with an excellent meal in a new restaurant, a bad meal may reduce our patronage to zero; but if we have found excellent food in a restaurant for many years, several poor meals must be eaten there, other things being equal, before we lose the inclination to patronize it again.

There is no simple relation between the number of responses reinforced and the number which appear in extinction. . . . the resistance to extinction generated by *intermittent* reinforcement may be much greater than if the same number of reinforcements are given for consecutive responses. Thus if we only occasionally reinforce a child for good behavior, the behavior survives after we discontinue reinforcement much longer than if we had reinforced every instance up to the same total number of reinforcements. This is of practical importance where the available reinforcers are limited. Problems of this sort arise in education, industry, economics, and many other fields. Under some schedules of intermittent reinforcement as many as 10,000 responses may appear in the behavior of a pigeon before extinction is substantially complete.

Extinction is an effective way of removing an operant from the repertoire of an organism. It should not be confused with other procedures designed to have the same effect. The currently preferred technique is punishment, which . . . involves different processes and is of questionable effectiveness. Forgetting is frequently confused with extinction. In forgetting, the effect of conditioning is lost simply as time passes, whereas extinction requires that the response be emitted without reinforcement. Ususally forgetting does not take place quickly; sizeable extinction curves have been obtained from pigeons as long as six years after the response had last been reinforced. Six years is about half the normal life span of the pigeon. During the interval the pigeons lived under circumstances in which the response could not possibly have been reinforced. In human behavior skilled responses generated by relatively precise contingencies frequently survive unused for as much as half a lifetime. The assertion that early experiences determine the personality of the mature organism assumes that the effect of operant reinforcement is long-lasting. Thus if, because of early childhood experiences, a man marries a woman who resembles his mother, the effect of certain reinforcements must have survived for a long time. . . .

What Events Are Reinforcing?

In dealing with our fellow men in everyday life and in the clinic and laboratory, we may need to know just how reinforcing a specific event is. We often begin by noting the extent to which our own behavior is reinforced by the same event. This practice frequently miscarries; yet it is still commonly believed that reinforcers can be identified apart from their effects upon a particular organism. As the term is used here, however, the only defining characteristic of a reinforcing stimulus is that it reinforces.

The only way to tell whether or not a given event is reinforcing to a given organism under given conditions is to make a direct test. We observe the frequency of a selected response, then make an event contingent upon it and observe any change in frequency. If there is a change, we classify the event as reinforcing to the organism under the existing conditions. There is nothing circular about classifying events in terms of their effects; the criterion is both empirical and objective. It would be circular, however, if we then went on to assert that a given event strengthens an operant *because* it is reinforcing. We achieve a certain success in guessing at reinforcing powers only because we have in a sense made a crude survey; we have gauged the reinforcing effect of a stimulus upon ourselves and assume the same effect upon others. We are successful only when we resemble the organism under study and when we have correctly surveyed our own behavior.

Events which are found to be reinforcing are of two sorts. Some reinforcements consist of *presenting* stimuli, of adding something—for example, food, water, or sexual contact—to the situation. These we call *positive* reinforcers. Others consist of *removing* something—for example, a loud noise, a very bright light, extreme cold or heat, or electric shock—from the situation. These we call *negative* reinforcers. In both cases the effect of reinforcement is the same—the probability of response is increased. We cannot avoid this distinction by arguing that what is reinforcing in the negative case is the *absence* of the bright light, loud noise, and so on; for it is absence after presence which is effective, and this is only another way of saying that the stimulus is removed. The difference between the two cases will be clearer when we consider the *presentation* of a *negative* reinforcer or the *removal* of a *positive.* These are the consequences which we call punishment.

A survey of the events which reinforce a given individual is often required in the practical application of operant conditioning. In every field in which human behavior figures prominently—education, government, the family, the clinic, industry, art, literature, and so on—we are constantly changing probabilities of response by arranging reinforcing consequences. The industrialist who wants employees to work consistently and without absenteeism must make certain that their behavior is suitably reinforced—not only with wages but with suitable working conditions. The girl who wants another date must be sure that her friend's behavior in inviting her and in keeping the appointment is suitably reinforced. To teach a child to read or sing or play a game effectively, we must work out a program of educational reinforcement in which appropriate responses "pay off" frequently. If the patient is to return for further counsel, the psychotherapist must make sure that the behavior of coming to him is in some measure reinforced.

We evaluate the strength of reinforcing events when we attempt to discover what someone is "getting out of life." What consequences are responsible for his present repertoire and for the relative frequencies of the responses in it? His responses to various topics of conversation tell us something, but his everyday behavior is a better guide. We infer important reinforcers from nothing more unusual than his "interest" in a writer who deals with certain subjects, in stores or museums which exhibit certain objects, in friends who participate in certain kinds of behavior, in restaurants which serve certain kinds of food, and so on. The "interest" refers to the probability which results, at least in part, from the consequences of the behavior of "taking an interest." We may be more nearly sure of the importance of a reinforcer if we watch the behavior come and go as the reinforcer is alternately supplied and withheld, for the change in probability is then less likely to be due to an incidental change of some other sort. The behavior of associating with a particular friend varies as the friend varies in supplying reinforcement. If we observe this covariation, we may then be fairly sure of "what this friendship means" or "what our subject sees in his friend."

This technique of evaluation may be improved for use in clinical and laboratory investigation. A direct inventory may be made by allowing a subject to look at an assortment of pictures and recording the time he spends on each. The behavior of looking at a picture is reinforced by what is seen in it. Looking at one picture may be more strongly reinforced than looking at another, and the times will vary accordingly. The information may be valuable if it is necessary for any reason to reinforce or extinguish our subject's behavior.

Literature, art, and entertainment, are contrived reinforcers. Whether the public buys books, tickets to performances, and works of art depends upon whether those books, plays, concerts, or pictures are reinforcing. Frequently the artist confines himself to an exploration of what is reinforcing to himself. When he does so his work "reflects his own individuality," and it is then an accident (or a measure of his universality) if his book or play or piece of music or picture is reinforcing to others. Insofar as commercial success is important, he may make a direct study of the behavior of others.

We cannot dispense with this survey simply by asking a man what reinforces him. His reply may be of some value, but it is by no means necessarily reliable. A reinforcing connection need not be obvious to the individual reinforced. It is often only in retrospect that one's tendencies to behave in particular ways are seen to be the result of certain consequences, and . . . , the relation may never be seen at all even though it is obvious to others.

There are, of course, extensive differences between individuals in the events which prove to be reinforcing. The differences between species are so great as scarcely to arouse interest; obviously what is reinforcing to a horse need not be reinforcing to a dog or man. Among the members of a species, the extensive differences are less likely to be due to hereditary endowment, and to that extent may be traced to circumstances in the history of the individual. The fact that organisms evidently inherit the capacity to be reinforced by certain kinds of events does not help us in predicting the reinforcing effect of an untried stimulus. Nor does the relation between the reinforcing event and deprivation or any other condition of the organism endow the reinforcing event with any particular physical property. It is especially unlikely that events which have *acquired* their power to reinforce will be marked in any special way. Yet such events are an important species of reinforcer. . . .

Why Is a Reinforcer Reinforcing?

The Law of Effect is not a theory. It is simply a rule for strengthening behavior. When we reinforce a response and observe a change in its frequency, we can easily report what has happened in objective terms. But in explaining *why* it has happened we are likely to resort to theory. Why does reinforcement reinforce? One theory is that an organism repeats a response because it finds the consequences "pleasant" or "satisfying." But in what sense is this an explanation within the framework of a natural science? "Pleasant" or "satisfying" apparently do not refer to physical properties of reinforcing events, since the physical sciences use neither these terms nor any equivalents. The terms must refer to some effect upon the organism, but can we define this in such a way that it will be useful in accounting for reinforcement?

It is sometimes argued that a thing is pleasant if an organism approaches or maintains contact with it and unpleasant if the organism avoids it or cut it short. There are many variations on this attempt to find an objective definition, but they are all subject to the same criticism: the behavior specified may be merely another product of the reinforcing effect. To say that a stimulus is pleasant in the sense that an organism tends to approach or prolong it may be only another way of saying that the stimulus has reinforced the behavior of approaching or prolonging. Instead of defining a reinforcing effect in terms of its effect upon behavior in general, we have simply specified familiar behavior which is almost inevitably reinforced and hence generally available as an indicator of reinforcing power. If we then go on to say that a stimulus is reinforcing, *because* it is pleasant, what purports to be an explanation in terms of two effects is in reality a redundant description of one.

An alternative approach is to define "pleasant" and "unpleasant" (or "satisfying" and "annoying") by asking the subject how he "feels" about certain events. This assumes that reinforcement has two effects—it strengthens behavior and generates "feelings"—and that one is a function of the other. But the functional relation may be in the other direction. When a man reports that an event is pleasant, he may be merely reporting that it is the sort of event which reinforces him or toward which he finds himself tending to move because it has reinforced such movement. . . . one could probably not acquire verbal responses with respect to pleasantness as a purely private fact unless something like this were so. In any case, the subject himself is not at an especially good point of vantage for making such observations. "Subjective judgments" of the pleasantness or satisfaction provided by stimuli are usually unreliable and inconsistent. As the doctrine of the unconscious has emphasized, we may not be able to report at all upon events which can be shown to be reinforcing to us or we may make a report which is in direct conflict with objective observations; we may report as unpleasant a type of event which can be shown to be reinforcing. Examples of this anomaly range from masochism to martyrdom.

It is sometimes argued that reinforcement is effective because it reduces a state of deprivation. Here at least is a collateral effect which need not be confused with reinforcement itself. It is obvious that deprivation is important in operant conditioning. We used a *hungry* pigeon in our experiment, and we could not have demonstrated operant conditioning otherwise. The hungrier the bird, the oftener it responds as the result of reinforcement. But in spite of this connection it is not true that reinforcement always reduces deprivation. Conditioning may occur before any substantial change can take place in the deprivation measured in other ways. All we can say is that the *type* of event which reduces deprivation is also reinforcing.

The connection between reinforcement and satiation must be sought in the process of evolution. We can scarcely overlook the great biological significance of the primary reinforcers. Food, water, and sexual contact, as well as escape from injurious conditions . . . are obviously connected with the well-being of the organism. An individual who is readily reinforced by such events will acquire highly efficient behavior. It is also biologically advantageous if the behavior due to a given reinforcement is especially likely to occur in an appropriate state of deprivation. Thus it is important, not only that any behavior which leads to the receipt of food should become an important part of a repertoire, but that this behavior should be particularly strong when the organism is hungry. These two advantages are presumably responsible for the fact that an organism can be reinforced in specific ways and that the result will be observed in relevant conditions of deprivation.

Some forms of stimulation are positively reinforcing although they do not appear to elicit behavior having biological significance. A baby is reinforced, not only by food, but by the tinkle of a bell or the sparkle of a bright object. Behavior which is consistently followed by such stimuli shows an increased probability. It is difficult, if not impossible, to trace these reinforcing effects to a history of conditioning. Later we may find the same individual being reinforced by an orchestra or a colorful spectacle. Here it is more difficult to make sure that the reinforcing effect is not conditioned. However, we may plausibly argue that a capacity to be reinforced by any feed-back from the environment would be biologically advantageous, since it would prepare the organism to manipulate the environment successfully before a given state of deprivation developed. When the organism generates a tactual feed-back, as in feeling the texture of a piece of cloth or the surface of a piece of sculpture, the conditioning is commonly regarded as resulting from sexual reinforcement, even when the area stimulated is not primarily sexual in function. It is tempting to suppose that other forms of stimulation produced by behavior are similarly related to biologically important events.

When the environment changes, a capacity to be reinforced by a given event may have a biological *disadvantage.* Sugar is highly reinforcing to most members of the human species, as the ubiquitous candy counter shows. Its effect in this respect far exceeds current biological requirements. This was not true before sugar had been grown and refined on an extensive scale. Until a few hundred years ago, the strong reinforcing effect of sugar must have been a biological advantage. The environment has changed, but the genetic endowment of the organism has not followed suit. Sex provides another example. There is no longer a biological advantage in the great reinforcing effect of sexual contact, but we need not go back many hundreds of years to find conditions of famine and pestilence under which the power of sexual reinforcement offered a decisive advantage.

A biological explanation of reinforcing power is perhaps as far as we can go in saying why an event is reinforcing. Such an explanation is probably of little help in a functional analysis, for it does not provide us with any way of identifying a reinforcing stimulus as such before we have tested its reinforcing power upon a given organism. We must therefore be content with a survey in terms of the effects of stimuli upon behavior. . . .

Goals, Purposes, and Other Final Causes

It is not correct to say that operant reinforcement "strengthens the response which precedes it." The response has already occurred and cannot be changed. What is changed is the future probability of responses in the same *class.* It is the operant as a class of behavior, rather than the response as a particular instance, which is conditioned. There is, therefore, no violation of the fundamental principle of science which rules out "final causes." But this principle is violated when it is asserted that behavior is under the control of an "incentive" or "goal" which the organism has not yet achieved or a "purpose" which it has not yet fulfilled. Statements which use such words as "incentive" or "purpose" are usually reducible to statements about operant conditioning, and only a slight change is required to bring them within the framework of a natural science. Instead of saying that a man behaves because of the consequences which *are* to follow his behavior, we simply say that he behaves because of the consequences which *have* followed similar behavior in the past. This is, of course, the Law of Effect or operant conditioning.

It is sometimes argued that a response is not fully described until its purpose is referred to as a current property. But what is meant by "describe?" If we observe someone walking down the street, we may report this event in the language of physical science. If we then add that "his purpose is to mail a letter," have we said anything which was not included in our first report? Evidently so, since a man may walk down the street "for many purposes" and in the same physical way in each case. But the distinction which needs to be made is not between instances of behavior; it is between the variables of which behavior is a function. Purpose is not a property of the behavior itself; it is a way of referring to controlling variables. If we make our report after we have seen our subject mail his letter and turn back, we attribute "purpose" to him from the event which brought the behavior of walking down the street to an end. This event "gives meaning" to his performance, not by amplifying a description of the behavior as such, but by indicating an independent variable of which it may have been a function. We cannot see his "purpose" before seeing that he mails a letter, unless we have observed similar behavior and similar consequences before. Where we have done this, we use the term simply to predict that he will mail a letter upon this occasion.

Nor can our subject see his own purpose without reference to similar events. If we ask him why he is going down the street or what his purpose is and he says, "I am going to mail a letter," we have not learned anything new about his behavior but only about some of its possible causes. The subject himself, of course, may be in an advantageous position in describing these variables because he has had an extended contact with his own behavior for many years. But his statement is not therefore in a different class from similar statements made by others who have observed his behavior upon fewer occasions. . . . he is simply making a plausible prediction in terms of his experiences with himself. Moreover, he may be wrong. He may report that he is "going to mail a letter," and he may indeed carry an unmailed letter in his hand and may mail it at the end of the street, but we may still be able to show that his behavior is primarily determined by the fact that upon past occasions he has encountered someone who is important to him upon just such a walk. He may not be "aware of this purpose" in the sense of being able to say that his behavior is strong for this reason.

The fact that operant behavior seems to be "directed toward the future" is misleading. Consider, for example, the case of "looking for something." In what sense is the "something" which has not yet been found relevant to the behavior? Suppose we condition a pigeon to peck a spot on the wall of a box and then, when the operant is well established, remove the spot. The bird now goes to the usual place along the wall. It raises its head, cocks its eye in the usual direction, and may even emit a weak peck in the usual place. Before extinction is very far advanced, it returns to the same place again and again in similar behavior. Must we say that the pigeon is "looking for the spot"? Must we take the "looked for" spot into account in explaining the behavior?

It is not difficult to interpret this example in terms of operant reinforcement. Since visual stimulation from the spot has usually preceded the receipt of food, the spot has become a conditioned reinforcer. It strengthens the behavior of looking in given directions from different positions. Although we have undertaken to condition only the pecking response, we have in fact strengthened many different kinds of precurrent behavior which bring the bird into positions from which it sees the spot and pecks it. These responses continue to appear, even though we have removed the spot, until extinction occurs. The spot that is "being looked for" is the spot which has occurred in the past as the immediate reinforcement of the behavior of looking. In general, looking for something consists of emitting responses which in the past have produced "something" as a consequence.

The same interpretation applies to human behavior. When we see a man moving about a room opening drawers, looking under magazines, and so on, we may describe his behavior in fully objective terms: "Now he is in a certain part of the room; he has grasped a book between the thumb and forefinger of his right hand; he is lifting the book and bending his head so that any object under the book can be seen." We may also "interpret" his behavior or "read a meaning into it" by saying that "he is looking for something" or, more specifically, that "he is looking for his glasses." What we have added is not a further description of his behavior but an inference about some of the variables responsible for it. There is no *current* goal, incentive, purpose, or meaning to be taken into account. This is so even if we ask him what he is doing and he says, "I am looking for my glasses." This is not a further description of his behavior but of the variables of which his behavior is a function; it is equivalent to "I have lost my glasses," "I shall stop what I am doing when I find my glasses," or "When I have done this in the past, I have found my glasses." These translations may seem unnecessarily roundabout, but only because expressions involving goals and purposes are abbreviations.

Very often we attribute purpose to behavior as another way of describing its biological adaptability. This issue has already been discussed, but one point may be added. In both operant conditioning and the evolutionary selection of behavioral characteristics, consequences alter future probability. Reflexes and other innate patterns of behavior evolve because they increase the chances of survival of the *species.* Operants grow strong because they are followed by important consequences in the life of the *individual.* Both processes raise the question of purpose for the same reason, and in both the appeal to a final cause may be rejected in the same way. A spider does not possess the elaborate behavioral repertoire with which it constructs a web because that web will enable it to capture the food it needs to survive. It possesses this behavior because similar behavior on the part of spiders in the past has enabled *them* to capture the food *they* needed to survive. A series of events have been relevant to the behavior of web-making in its earlier evolutionary history. We are wrong in saying that we observe the "purpose" of the web when we observe similar events in the life of the individual.

The Mind and the Brain Are Identical

J. J. C. SMART

THIS paper takes its departure from arguments to be found in U. T. Place's "Is Consciousness a Brain Process?"[1] I have had the benefit of discussing Place's thesis in a good many universities in the United States and Australia, and I hope that the present paper answers objections to his thesis which Place has not considered and that it presents his thesis in a more nearly unobjectionable form. This paper is meant also to supplement the paper "The 'Mental' and the 'Physical,'" by H. Feigl,[2] which in part argues for a similar thesis to Place's.

Suppose that I report that I have at this moment a roundish, blurry-edged after-image which is yellowish towards its edge and is orange towards its center. What is it that I am reporting? One answer to this question might be that I am not reporting anything, that when I say that it looks to me as though there is a roundish yellowy-orange patch of light on the wall I am expressing some sort

1 *British Journal of Psychology*, XLVII (1956), 44–50.

2 *Minnesota Studies in the Philosophy of Science*, Vol. II (Minneapolis: University of Minnesota Press, 1958), pp. 370–497.

This is a very slightly revised version of a paper which was first published in the *Philosophical Review*, LXVIII (1959), 141–156. [Reprinted by permission of the author and the editors of the *Philosophical Review*.]

of *temptation*, the temptation to say that there *is* a roundish yellowy-orange patch on the wall (though I may know that there is not such a patch on the wall). This is perhaps Wittgenstein's view in the *Philosophical Investigations* (see §§ 367,370). Similarly, when I "report" a pain, I am not really reporting anything (or, if you like, I am reporting in a queer sense of "reporting"), but am doing a sophisticated sort of wince. (See § 244: "The verbal expression of pain replaces crying and does not describe it." Nor does it describe anything else?)[3] I prefer most of the time to discuss an after-image rather than a pain, because the word "pain" brings in something which is irrelevant to my purpose: the notion of "distress." I think that "he is in pain" entails "he is in distress," that is, that he is in a certain agitation-condition.[4] Similarly, to say "I am in pain" may be to do more than "replace pain behavior": it may be partly to report something, though this something is quite nonmysterious, being an agitation-condition, and so susceptible of behavioristic analysis. The suggestion I wish if possible to avoid is a different one, namely that "I am in pain" is a genuine report, and that what it reports is an irreducibly psychical something. And similarly the suggestion I wish to resist is also that to say "I have a yellowish-orange after-image" is to report something irreducibly psychical.

Why do I wish to resist this suggestion? Mainly because of Occam's razor. It seems to me that science is increasingly giving us a viewpoint whereby organisms are able to be seen as physico-chemical mechanisms:[5] it seems that even the behavior of man himself will one day be explicable in mechanistic terms. There does seem to be, so far as science is concerned, nothing in the world but increasingly complex arrangements of physical constituents. All except for one place: in consciousness. That is, for a full description of what is going on in a man you would have to mention not only the physical processes in his tissues, glands, nervous system, and so forth, but also his states of consciousness: his visual, auditory, and tactual sensations, his aches and pains. That these should be *correlated* with brain processes does not help, for to say that they are *correlated* is to say that they are something "over and above." You cannot correlate something with itself. You correlate footprints with burglars, but not Bill Sikes the burglar with Bill Sikes the burglar. So sensations, states of consciousness, do seem to be the one sort of thing left outside the physicalist picture, and for various reasons I just cannot believe that this can be so. That everything should be explicable in terms of physics (together of course with descriptions of the ways in which the

[3] Some philosophers of my acquaintance, who have the advantage over me in having known Wittgenstein, would say that this interpretation of him is too behavioristic. However, it seems to me a very natural interpretation of his printed words, and whether or not it is Wittgenstein's real view it is certainly an interesting and important one. I wish to consider it here as a possible rival both to the "brain-process" thesis and to straight-out old-fashioned dualism.

[4] See Ryle, *The Concept of Mind* (London: Hutchinson's University Library, 1949), p. 93.

[5] On this point see Paul Oppenheim and Hilary Putnam, "Unity of Science as a Working Hypothesis," in *Minnesota Studies in the Philosophy of Science*, Vol. II (Minneapolis: University of Minnesota Press, 1958), pp. 3–36.

parts are put together—roughly, biology is to physics as radio-engineering is to electromagnetism) except the occurrence of sensations seems to me to be frankly unbelievable. Such sensations would be "nomological danglers," to use Feigl's expression.[6] It is not often realized how odd would be the laws whereby these nomological danglers would dangle. It is sometimes asked, "Why can't there be psychophysical laws which are of a novel sort, just as the laws of electricity and magnetism were novelties from the standpoint of Newtonian mechanics?" Certainly we are pretty sure in the future to come across new ultimate laws of a novel type, but I expect them to relate simple constituents: for example, whatever ultimate particles are then in vogue. I cannot believe that ultimate laws of nature could relate simple constituents to configurations consisting of perhaps billions of neurons (and goodness knows how many billion billions of ultimate particles) all put together for all the world as though their main purpose in life was to be a negative feedback mechanism of a complicated sort. Such ultimate laws would be like nothing so far known in science. They have a queer "smell" to them. I am just unable to believe in the nomological danglers themselves, or in the laws whereby they would dangle. If any philosophical arguments seemed to compel us to believe in such things, I would suspect a catch in the argument. In any case it is the object of this paper to show that there are no philosophical arguments which compel us to be dualists.

The above is largely a confession of faith, but it explains why I find Wittgenstein's position (as I construe it) so congenial. For on this view there are, in a sense, no sensations. A man is a vast arrangement of physical particles, but there are not, over and above this, sensations or states of consciousness. There are just behavioral facts about this vast mechanism, such as that it expresses a temptation (behavior disposition) to say "there is a yellowish-red patch on the wall" or that it goes through a sophisticated sort of wince, that is, says "I am in pain." Admittedly Wittgenstein says that though the sensation "is not a something," it is nevertheless "not a nothing either" (§ 304), but this need only mean that the word "ache" has a use. An ache is a thing, but only in the innocuous sense in which the plain man, in the first paragraph of Frege's *Foundations of Arithmetic*, answers the question "What is the number one?" by "a thing." It should be noted that when I assert that to say "I have a yellowish-orange after-image" is to express a temptation to assert the physical-object statement "There is a yellowish-orange patch on the wall," I mean that saying "I have a yellowish-orange after-image" is (partly) the exercise of the disposition[7] which is the temptation. It is not to *report* that I have the temptation, any more than is "I love you"

[6] Feigl, *op. cit.,* p. 428. Feigl uses the expression "nomological danglers" for the laws whereby the entities dangle: I have used the expression to refer to the dangling entities themselves.

[7] Wittgenstein did not like the word "disposition." I am using it to put in a nutshell (and perhaps inaccurately) the view which I am attributing to Wittgenstein. I should like to repeat that I do not wish to claim that my interpretation of Wittgenstein is correct. Some of those who knew him do not interpret him in this way. It is merely a view which I find myself extracting from his printed words and which I think is important and worth discussing for its own sake.

normally a report that I love someone. Saying "I love you" is just part of the behavior which is the exercise of the disposition of loving someone.

Though for the reasons given above, I am very receptive to the above "expressive" account of sensation statements, I do not feel that it will quite do the trick. Maybe this is because I have not thought it out sufficiently, but it does seem to me as though, when a person says "I have an after-image," he *is* making a genuine report, and that when he says "I have a pain," he *is* doing more than "replace pain-behavior," and that "this more" is not just to say that he is in distress. I am not so sure, however, that to admit this is to admit that there are nonphysical correlates of brain processes. Why should not sensations just be brain processes of a certain sort? There are, of course, well-known (as well as lesser-known) philosophical objections to the view that reports of sensations are reports of brain-processes, but I shall try to argue that these arguments are by no means as cogent as is commonly thought to be the case.

Let me first try to state more accurately the thesis that sensations are brain-processes. It is not the thesis that, for example, "after-image" or "ache" means the same as "brain process of sort X" (where "X" is replaced by a description of a certain sort of brain process). It is that, in so far as "after-image" or "ache" is a report of a process, it is a report of a process that *happens to be* a brain process. It follows that the thesis does not claim that sensation statements can be translated into statement about brain processes.[8] Nor does it claim that the logic of a sensation statement is the same as that of a brain-process statement. All it claims is that in so far as a sensation statement is a report of something, that something is in fact a brain process. Sensations are nothing over and above brain processes. Nations are nothing "over and above" citizens, but this does not prevent the logic of nation statements being very different from the logic of citizen statements, nor does it insure the translatability of nation statements into citizen statements. (I do not, however, wish to assert that the relation of sensation statements to brain-process statements is very like that of nation statements to citizen statements. Nations do not just *happen to be* nothing over and above citizens, for example. I bring in the "nations" example merely to make a negative point: that the fact that the logic of A-statements is different from that of B-statements does not insure that A's are anything over and above B's.)

Remarks on Identity. When I say that a sensation is a brain process or that lightning is an electric discharge, I am using "is" in the sense of strict identity. (Just as in the—in this case necessary—proposition "7 is identical with the smallest prime number greater than 5.") When I say that a sensation is a brain process or that lightning is an electric discharge I do not mean just that the sensation is somehow spatially or temporally continuous with the brain process or that the lightning is just spatially or temporally continuous with the discharge. When on the other hand I say that the successful general is the same person as the small boy who stole the apples I mean only that the successful

[8] See Place, *of cit.*, p. 45, and Feigl, *op. cit.*, p. 390, near top.

general I see before me is a time slice[9] of the same four-dimensional object of which the small boy stealing apples is an earlier time slice. However, the four-dimensional object which has the general-I-see-before-me for its late time slice is identical in the strict sense with the four-dimensional object which has the small-boy-stealing-apples for an early time slice. I distinguish these two senses of "is identical with" because I wish to make it clear that the brain-process doctrine asserts identity in the *strict* sense.

I shall now discuss various possible objections to the view that the processes reported in sensation statements are in fact processes in the brain. Most of us have met some of these objections in our first year as philosophy students. All the more reason to take a good look at them. Others of the objections will be more recondite and subtle.

Objection 1. Any illiterate peasant can talk perfectly well about his after-images, or how things look or feel to him, or about his aches and pains, and yet he may know nothing whatever about neurophysiology. A man may, like Aristotle, believe that the brain is an organ for cooling the body without any impairment of his ability to make true statements about his sensations. Hence the things we are talking about when we describe our sensations cannot be processes in the brain.

Reply. You might as well say that a nation of slugabeds, who never saw the Morning Star or knew of its existence, or who had never thought of the expression "the Morning Star," but who used the expression "the Evening Star" perfectly well, could not use this expression to refer to the same entity as we refer to (and describe as) "the Morning Star."[10]

You may object that the Morning Star is in a sense not the very same thing as the Evening Star, but only something spatiotemporally continuous with it. That is, you may say that the Morning Star is not the Evening Star in the strict sense of "identity" that I distinguished earlier.

There is, however, a more plausible example. Consider lightning.[11] Modern physical science tells us that lightning is a certain kind of electrical discharge due to ionization of clouds of water vapor in the atmosphere. This, it is now believed, is what the true nature of lightning is. Note that there are not two things: a flash of lightning and an electrical discharge. There is one thing, a flash of lightning, which is described scientifically as an electrical discharge to the earth from a cloud of ionized water molecules. The case is not at all like that of explaining a footprint by reference to a burglar. We say that what lightning really is, what its true nature as revealed by science is, is an electrical discharge. (It is not the true nature of a footprint to be a burglar).

To forestall irrelevant objections, I should like to make it clear that by

[9] See J. H. Woodger, *Theory Construction*, International Encyclopedia of Unified Science, II, No. 5 (Chicago: University of Chicago Press, 1939), 38. I here permit myself to speak loosely. For warnings against possible ways of going wrong with this sort of talk, see my note "Spatialising Time," *Mind*, LXIV (1959), 239–41.

[10] Cf. Feigl, *op. cit.*, p. 439.

[11] See Place, *op. cit.*, p. 48; also Feigl, *op. cit.*, p. 438.

"lightning" I mean the publicly observable physical object, lightning, not a visual sense-datum of lightning. I say that the publicly observable physical object lightning is in fact the electrical discharge, not just a correlate of it. The sense-datum, or rather the having of the sense-datum, the "look" of lightning, may well in my view be a correlate of the electrical discharge. For in my view it is a brain state *caused* by the lightning. But we should no more confuse sensations of lightning with lightning than we confuse sensations of a table with the table.

In short, the reply to Objection 1 is that there can be contingent statements of the form "A is identical with B," and a person may well know that something is an A without knowing that it is a B. An illiterate peasant might well be able to talk about his sensations without knowing about his brain processes, just as he can talk about lightning though he knows nothing of electricity.

Objection 2. It is only a contingent fact (if it is a fact) that when we have a certain kind of sensation there is a certain kind of process in our brain. Indeed it is possible, though perhaps in the highest degree unlikely, that our present physiological theories will be as out of date as the ancient theory connecting mental processes with goings on in the heart. It follows that when we report a sensation we are not reporting a brain-process.

Reply. The objection certainly proves that when we say "I have an after-image" we cannot *mean* something of the form "I have such and such a brain-process." But this does not show that what we report (having an after-image) is not *in fact* a brain process. "I see lightning" does not *mean* "I see an electrical discharge." Indeed, it is logically possible (though highly unlikely) that the electrical discharge account of lightning might one day be given up. Again, "I see the Evening Star" does not *mean* the same as "I see the Morning Star," and yet "The Evening Star and the Morning Star are one and the same thing" is a contingent proposition. Possibly Objection 2 derives some of its apparent strengh from a "Fido"–Fido theory of meaning. If the meaning of an expression were what the expression named, then of course it *would* follow from the fact that "sensation" and "brain-process" have different meanings that they cannot name one and the same thing.

Objection 3.[12] Even if Objection 1 and 2 do not prove that sensations are something over and above brain-processes, they do prove that the qualities of sensations are something over and above the qualities of brain-processes. That is, it may be possible to get out of asserting the existence of irreducibly psychic *properties.* For suppose we identify the Morning Star with the Evening Star. Then there must be some properties which logically imply that of being the Morning Star, and quite distinct properties which entail that of being the Evening Star. Again, there must be some properties (for example, that of being a yellow flash) which are logically distinct from those in the physicalist story.

[12] I think this objection was first put to me by Professor Max Black. I think it is the most subtle of any of those I have considered, and the one which I am least confident of having satisfactorily met.

Indeed, it might be thought that the objection succeeds at one jump. For consider the property of "being a yellow flash." It might seem that this property lies inevitably outside the physicalist framework within which I am trying to work (either by "yellow" being an objective emergent property of physical objects, or else by being a power to produce yellow sense-data where "yellow," in this second instantiation of the word, refers to a purely phenomenal or introspectible quality). I must therefore digress for a moment and indicate how I deal with secondary qualities. I shall concentrate on color.

First of all, let me introduce the concept of a normal percipient. One person is more a normal percipient than another if he can make color discriminations that the other cannot. For example, if A can pick a lettuce leaf out of a heap of cabbage leaves, whereas B cannot though he can pick a lettuce leaf out of a heap of beetroot leaves, then A is more normal than B. (I am assuming that A and B are not given time to distinguish the leaves by their slight difference in shape, and so forth.) From the concept of "more normal than" it is easy to see how we can introduce the concept of "normal." Of course, Eskimos may make the finest discriminations at the blue end of the spectrum, Hottentots at the red end. In this case the concept of a normal percipient is a slightly idealized one, rather like that of "the mean sun" in astronomical chronology. There is no need to go into such subtleties now. I say that "This is red" means something roughly like "A normal percipient would not easily pick this out of a clump of geranium petals though he would pick it out of a clump of lettuce leaves." Of course it does not exactly mean this: a person might know the meaning of "red" without knowing anything about geraniums, or even about normal percipients. But the point is that a person can be *trained* to say "This is red" of objects which would not easily be picked out of geranium petals by a normal percipient, and so on. (Note that even a color-blind person can reasonably assert that something is red, though of course he needs to use another human being, not just himself, as his "color meter.") This account of secondary qualities explains their unimportance in physics. For obviously the discriminations and lack of discriminations made by a very complex neurophysiological mechanism are hardly likely to correspond to simple and nonarbitrary distinctions in nature.

I therefore elucidate colors as powers, in Locke's sense, to evoke certain sorts of discriminatory responses in human beings. They are also, of course, powers to cause sensations in human beings (an account still nearer Locke's). But these sensations, I am arguing, are identifiable with brain processes.

Now how do I get over the objection that a sensation can be identified with a brain process only if it has some phenomenal property, not possessed by brain processes, whereby one-half of the identification may be, so to speak, pinned down?

Reply. My suggestion is as follows. When a person says, "I see a yellowish-orange after-image," he is saying something like this: "*There is something going on which is like what is going on when* I have my eyes open, am awake, and there is an orange illuminated in good light in front of me, that is, when I really see an orange." (And there is no reason why a person should not say the same thing when he is having a veridical sense-datum, so long as we construe "like" in the last sentence in such a sense that something can be like itself.) Notice that the italicized words, namely "there is something going on which is like what is going on when," are all quasilogical or topic-neutral words. This explains why the ancient Greek peasant's reports about his sensations can be neutral between dualistic metaphysics or my materialistic metaphysics. It explains how sensations can be brain-processes and yet how a man who reports them need know nothing about brain-processes. For he reports them only very abstractly as "something going on which is like what is going on when. . . ." Similarly, a person may say "someone is in the room," thus reporting truly that the doctor is in the room, even though he has never heard of doctors. (There are not two people in the room: "someone" *and* the doctor.) This account of sensation statements also explains the singular elusiveness of "raw feels"—why no one seems to be able to pin any properties on them.[13] Raw feels, in my view, are colorless for the very same reason that *something* is colorless. This does not mean that sensations do not have plenty of properties, for if they are brain-processes they certainly have lots of neurological properties. It only means that in speaking of them as being like or unlike one another we need not know or mention these properties.

This, then, is how I would reply to Objection 3. The strength of my reply depends on the possibility of our being able to report that one thing is like another without being able to state the respect in which it is like. I do not see why this should not be so. If we think cybernetically about the nervous system we can envisage it as able to respond to certain likenesses of its internal processes without being able to do more. It would be easier to build a machine which would tell us, say on a punched tape, whether or not two objects were similar, than it would be to build a machine which would report wherein the similarities consisted.

Objection 4. The after-image is not in physical space. The brain-process is. So the after-image is not a brain-process.

Reply. This is an *ignoratio elenchi.* I am not arguing that the after-image is a brain-process, but that the experience of having an after-image is a brain-process. It is the *experience* which is reported in the introspective report. Similarly, if it is objected that the after-image is yellowy-orange, my reply is that it is the experience of seeing yellowy-orange that is being described, and this experience is not a yellowy-orange something. So to say that a brain-process cannot be yellowy orange is not to say that a brain-process cannot in fact be the experience of having a yellowy-orange after-image. There is, in a sense, no such thing as an after-image or a sense-datum, though there is such a thing as the experience of having an image, and this expereince is described indirectly in material object language, not in phenomenal language, for there is no such

13 See B. A. Farrell, "*Experience*," *Mind*, LIX (1950), 170–98.

thing.[14] We describe the experience by saying, in effect, that it is like the experience we have when, for example, we really see a yellowy-orange patch on the wall. Trees and wallpaper can be green, but not the experience of seeing or imagining a tree or wallpaper. (Or if they are described as green or yellow this can only be in a derived sense.)

Objection 5. It would make sense to say of a molecular movement in the brain that it is swift or slow, straight or circular, but it makes no sense to say this of the experience of seeing something yellow.

Reply. So far as we have not given sense to talk of experiences as swift or slow, straight or circular. But I am not claiming that "experience" and "brain-process" mean the same or even that they have the same logic. "Somebody" and "the doctor" do not have the same logic, but this does not lead us to suppose that talking about somebody telephoning is talking about someone over and above, say, the doctor. The ordinary man when he reports an experience is reporting that something is going on, but he leaves it open as to what sort of thing is going on, whether in a material solid medium or perhaps in some sort of gaseous medium, or even perhaps in some sort of nonspatial medium (if this makes sense). All that I am saying is that "experience" and "brain-process" may in fact refer to the same thing, and if so we may easily adopt a convention (which is not a change in our present rules for the use of experience words but an addition to them) whereby it would make sense to talk of an experience in terms appropriate to physical processes.

Objection 6. Sensations are private, brain processes are *public.* If I sincerely say, "I see a yellowish-orange after-image," and I am not making a verbal mistake, then I cannot be wrong. But I can be wrong about a brain-process. The scientist looking into my brain might be having an illusion. Moreover, it makes sense to say that two or more people are observing the same brain-process but not that two or more people are reporting the same inner experience.

Reply. This shows that the language of introspective reports has a different logic from the language of material processes. It is obvious that until the brain-process theory is much improved and widely accepted there will be no *criteria* for saying "Smith has an experience of such-and-such a sort" *except* Smith's introspective reports. So we have adopted a rule of language that (normally) what Smith says goes.

Objection 7. I can imagine myself turned to stone and yet having images, aches, pains, and so on.

Reply. I can imagine that the electrical theory of lightning is false, that light-

[14] Dr. J. R. Smythies claims that a sense-datum language could be taught independently of the material object language ("A Note on the Fallacy of the 'Phenomenological Fallacy,' " *British Journal of Psychology*, XLVIII [1957], 141–44). I am not so sure of this: there must be some public criteria for a person having got a rule wrong before we can teach him the rule. I suppose someone might *accidentally* learn color words by Dr. Smythie's procedure. I am not, of course, denying that we can learn a sense-datum language in the sense that we can learn to report our experience. Nor would Place deny it.

ning is some sort of purely optical phenomenon. I can imagine that lightning is not an electrical discharge. I can imagine that the Evening Star is not the Morning Star. But it is. All the objection shows is that "experience" and "brain-process" do not have the same meaning. It does not show that an experience is not in fact a brain-process.

This objection is perhaps much the same as one which can be summed up by the slogan: "What can be composed of nothing cannot be composed of anything."[15] The argument goes as follows: on the brain-process thesis the identity between the brain-process and the experience is a contingent one. So it is logically possible that there should be no brain-process, and no process of any other sort either (no heart process, no kidney process, no liver process). There would be the experience but no "corresponding" physiological process with which we might be able to identify it empirically.

I suspect that the objector is thinking of the experience as a ghostly entity. So it is composed of something, not of nothing, after all. On his view it is composed of ghost stuff, and on mine it is composed of brain stuff. Perhaps the counter-reply will be[16] that the experience is simple and uncompounded, and so it is not composed of anything after all. This seems to be a quibble, for, if it were taken seriously, the remark "What can be composed of nothing cannot be composed of anything" could be recast as an a priori argument against Democritus and atomism and for Descartes and infinite divisibility. And it seems odd that a question of this sort could be settled a priori. We must therefore construe the word "composed" in a very weak sense, which would allow us to say that even an indivisible atom is composed of something (namely, itself). The dualist cannot really say that an experience can be composed of nothing. For he holds that experiences are something over and above material processes, that is, that they are a sort of ghost stuff. (Or perhaps ripples in an underlying ghost stuff.) I say that the dualist's hypothesis is a perfectly intelligible one. But I say that experiences are not to be identified with ghost stuff but with brain stuff. This is another hypothesis, and in my view a very plausible one. The present argument cannot knock it down a priori.

Objection 8. The "beetle in the box" objection (see Wittgenstein, *Philosophical Investigations*, § 293). How could descriptions of experiences, if these are genuine reports, get a foothold in language? For any rule of language must have public criteria for its correct application.

Reply. The change from describing how things are to describing how we feel is just a change from uninhibitedly saying "this is so" to saying "this looks so." That is, when the naïve person might be tempted to say, "There is a patch of light on the wall which moves whenever I move my eyes" or "A pin is being stuck into me," we have learned how to resist this temptation and say "It *looks as though* there is a patch of light on the wallpaper" or "It *feels as though*

15 I owe this objection to Dr. C. B. Martin. I gather that he no longer wishes to maintain this objection, at any rate in its present form.

16 Martin did not make this reply, but one of his students did.

someone were sticking a pin into me." The introspective account tells us about the individual's state of consciousness in the same way as does "I see a patch of light" or "I feel a pin being stuck into me": it differs from the corresponding perception statement in so far as it withdraws any claim about what is actually going on in the external world. From the point of view of the psychologist, the change from talking about the environment to talking about one's perceptual sensations is simply a matter of disinhibiting certain reactions. These are reactions which one normally suppresses because one has learned that in the prevailing circumstances they are unlikely to provide a good indication of the state of the environment.[17] To say that something looks green to me is simply to say that my experience is like the experience I get when I see something that really is green. In my reply to Objection 3, I pointed out the extreme openness or generality of statements which report experiences. This explains why there is no language of private qualities. (Just as "someone," unlike "the doctor," is a colorless word.)[18]

If it is asked what is the difference between those brain processes which, in my view, are experiences and those brain processes which are not, I can only reply that it is at present unknown. I have been tempted to conjecture that the difference may in part be that between perception and reception (in D. M. MacKay's terminology) and that the type of brain process which is an experience might be identifiable with MacKay's active "matching response."[19] This, however, cannot be the whole story, because sometimes I can perceive something unconsciously, as when I take a handkerchief out of a drawer without being aware that I am doing so. But at the very least, we can classify the brain processes which are experiences as those brain processes which are, or might have been, causal conditions of those pieces of verbal behavior which we call reports of immediate experience.

I have now considered a number of objections to the brain-process thesis. I wish now to conclude with some remarks on the logical status of the thesis itself. U. T. Place seems to hold that it is a straight-out scientific hypothesis.[20] If so, he is partly right and partly wrong. If the issue is between (say) a brain-process thesis and a heart thesis, or a liver thesis, or a kidney thesis, then the issue is a purely empirical one, and the verdict is overwhelmingly in favor of the brain. The right sorts of things don't go on in the heart, liver, or kidney, nor

17 I owe this point to Place, in correspondence.

18 The "beetle in the box" objection is, *if it is sound*, an objection to *any* view, and in particular the Cartesian one, that introspective reports are genuine reports. So it is no objection to a weaker thesis that I would be concerned to uphold, namely, that if introspective reports of "experiences" are genuinely reports, then the things they are reports of are in fact brain processes.

19 See his article "Towards in Information-Flow Model of Human Behaviour," *British Journal of Psychology*, XLVII (1956), 30–43.

20 *Op. cit.* For a further discussion of this, in reply to the original version of the present paper, see Place's note "Materialism as a Scientific Hypothesis," *Philosophical Review*, LXIX (1960), 104–4.

do these organs possess the right sort of complexity of structure. On the other hand, if the issue is between a brain-or-liver-or-kidney thesis (that is, some form of materialism) on the one hand and epiphenomenalism on the other hand, then the issue is not an empirical one. For there is no conceivable experiment which could decide between materialism and epiphenomenalism. This latter issue is not like the average straight-out empirical issue in science, but like the issue between the nineteenth-century English naturalist Philip Gosse[21] and the orthodox geologists and paleontologists of his day. According to Gosse, the earth was created about 4000 B.C. exactly as described in *Genesis*, with twisted rock strata, "evidence" of erosion, and so forth, and all sorts of fossils, all in their appropriate strata, just as if the usual evolutionist story had been true. Clearly this theory is in a sense irrefutable: no evidence can possibly tell against it. Let us ignore the theological setting in which Philip Gosse's hypothesis had been placed, thus ruling out objections of a theological kind, such as "what a queer God who would go to such elaborate lengths to deceive us." Let us suppose that it is held that the universe just *began* in 4004 B.C. with the initial conditions just everywhere as they were in 4004 B.C., and in particular that our own planet began with sediment in the rivers, eroded cliffs, fossils in the rocks, and so on. No scientist would ever entertain this as a serious hypothesis, consistent though it is with all possible evidence. The hypothesis offends against the principles of parsimony and simplicity. There would be far too many brute and inexplicable facts. Why are pterodactyl bones just as they are? No explanation in terms of the evolution of pterodactyls from earlier forms of life would any longer be possible. We would have millions of facts about the world as it was in 4004 B.C. that just have to be *accepted.*

This issue between the brain-process theory and epiphenomenalism seems to be of the above sort. (Assuming that a behavioristic reduction of introspective reports is not possible.) If it be agreed that there are no cogent philosophical arguments which force us into accepting dualism, and if the brain process theory and dualism are equally consistent with the facts, then the principles of parsimony and simplicity seem to me to decide overwhelmingly in favor of the brain-process theory. As I pointed out earlier, dualism involves a large number of irreducible psychophysical laws (whereby the "nomological danglers" dangle) of a queer sort, that just have to be taken on trust, and are just as difficult to swallow as the irreducible facts about the paleontology of the earth with which we are faced on Philip Gosse's theory.

[21] See the entertaining account of Gosse's book *Omphalos* by Martin Gardner in *Fads and Fallacies in the Name of Science*, 2nd ed. (New York: Dover, 1957), pp. 124–27.

The Identity Theory Is Incoherent

NORMAN MALCOLM

I

MY MAIN topic will be, roughly speaking, the claim that mental events or conscious experiences or inner experiences are brain processes.[1] I hasten to say, however, that I am not going to talk about "mental events" or "conscious experiences" or "inner experiences." These expressions are almost exclusively philosophers' terms, and I am not sure that I have got the hang of any of them. Philosophers are not in agreement in their use of these terms. One philosopher will say, for example, that a pain in the foot is a mental event, whereas another will say that a pain *in the foot* certainly is not a *mental* event.

I will avoid these expressions, and concentrate on the particular example of *sudden thoughts.* Suddenly remembering an engagement would be an example of suddenly thinking of something. Suddenly realizing, in a chess game, that moving this pawn would endanger one's queen, would be another example of a sudden thought. Professor Smart says that he wishes to "elucidate thought as an inner process,"[2] and he adds that he wants to identify "such inner processes with brain processes." He surely holds, therefore, that thinking and thoughts, including sudden thoughts, are brain processes. He holds also that conscious experiences, (pp. 656 and 657), illusions (p. 659), and aches and pains (p. 654) are brain processes, and that love (p. 652) is a brain state. I will restrict my discussion, however, to sudden thoughts.

My first inclination, when I began to think on this topic, was to believe that Smart's view is false—that a sudden thought certainly is not a brain process. But now I think that I do not know what it *means* to say that a sudden thought is a brain process. In saying this I imply, of course, that the proponents of this view also do not know what it means. This implication is risky for it might turn out, to my surprise and gratification, that Smart will explain his view with great clarity.

In trying to show that there is real difficulty in seeing what his view means, I will turn to Smart's article "Sensations and Brain Processes."[3] He says there that

[1] This paper was read at the Sixtieth Annual Meeting of the American Philosophical Association, Eastern Division. It is a reply to Professor J. J. C. Smart's essay, "Materialism," published in *The Journal of Philosophy*, Vol. LX, No. 22: October, 1963.

[2] Smart, *op. cit.*, p. 657.

[3] J. J. Smart, "Sensations and Brain Processes," *The Philosophical Review,* April 1959; republished in *The Philosophy of Mind*, ed. V. C. Chappell, Prentice-Hall 1962. Page references will be to the latter.

Reprinted with permission of the author from "Scientific Materialism and the Identity Theory" *Dialogue:* Canadian Philosophical Review, 3, 2 (1964), 115–125.

in holding that a sensation is a brain process he is "using 'is' in the sense of strict identity" (p. 163). "I wish to make it clear," he says, "that the brain process doctrine asserts identity in the *strict* sense" (p. 164). I assume that he wishes to say the same about the claimed identity of a thought with a brain process. Unfortunately he does not attempt to define this "strict sense of identity," and so we have to study his examples.

One of his examples of a "strict identity" is this: 7 is identical with the smallest prime number greater than 5 (p. 163). We must remember, however, that one feature of "the identity theory," as I shall call it, is that the alleged identity between thoughts, sensations, etc., and brain processes, is held to be *contingent.* Since the identity of 7 with the smallest prime greater than 5 is *a priori* and relates to timeless objects, it does not provide me with any clue as to how I am to apply the notion of "strict identity" to temporal events that are *contingently* related. The example is unsatisfactory, therefore, for the purpose of helping me to deal with the question of whether thoughts are or are not "strictly identical" with certain brain processes.

Let us move to another example. Smart tells us that the sense in which the small boy who stole apples is the same person as the victorious general, is *not* the "strict" sense of "identity" (p. 164). He thinks there is a mere spatio-temporal continuity between the apple-stealing boy and the general who won the war. From this *non*-example of "strict identity" I think I obtain a clue as to what he means by it. Consider the following two sentences: "General De Gaulle is the tallest Frenchman"; "The victorious general is the small boy who stole apples." Each of these sentences might be said to express an identity: yet we can see a difference between the two cases. Even though the victorious general *is* the small boy who stole apples, it is possible for the victorious general to be in this room at a time when there is *no* small boy here. In contrast, if General De Gaulle *is* the tallest Frenchman, then General De Gaulle is not in this room unless the tallest Frenchman is here. It would be quite natural to say that this latter identity (if it holds) is a *strict* identity, and that the other one is not. I believe that Smart would say this. This suggests to me the following rule for his "strict identity": If something, x, is in a certain place at a certain time, then something, y, is strictly identical with x only if y is in that same place at that same time.

If we assume that Smart's use of the expression "strict identity" is governed by the necessary condition I have stated, we can possibly understand why he is somewhat hesitant about whether to say that the Morning Star is strictly identical with the Evening Star. Smart says to an imaginary opponent: "You may object that the Morning Star is in a sense not the very same thing as the Evening Star, but only something spatio-temporally continuous with it. That is, you may say that the Morning Star is not the Evening Star in the strict sense of 'identity' that I distinguished earlier" (p. 164). Instead of rebutting this objection, Smart moves on to what he calls "a more plausible example" of strict identity. This suggests to me that Smart is not entirely happy with the case of the Stars as an example of strict identity. Why not? Perhaps he has some inclination to feel that the planet that is both the Morning and Evening Star, is not the Morning Star *at the same time* it is the Evening Star. If this were so, the suggested necessary condition for "strict identity" would not be satisfied. Smart's hesitation is thus a further indication that he wants his use of the expression "strict identity" to be governed by the rule I have stated.

Let us turn to what Smart calls his "more plausible" example of strict identity. It is this: Lightning is an electric discharge. Smart avows that this is truly a strict identity (p. 163 and pp. 164–165). This example provides additional evidence that he wants to follow the stated rule. If an electrical discharge occurred in one region of the sky and a flash of lightning occurred simultaneously in a different region of the sky, Smart would have no inclination to assert (I think) that the lightning was strictly identical with the electric discharge. Or if electrical discharges and corresponding lightning flashes occurred in the same region of the sky, but not at the same time, there normally being a perceptible interval of time between a discharge and a flash, then Smart (I believe) would not wish to hold that there was anything more strict than a systematic correlation (perhaps causal) between electric discharges and lightning.[4]

I proceed now to take up Smart's claim that a sudden thought is strictly identical with some brain process. It is clear that a brain process has spatial location. A brain process would be a mechanical, chemical or electrical process in the brain substance, or an electric discharge from the brain mass, or something of the sort. As Smart puts it, brain processes take place "inside our skulls."[5]

Let us consider an example of a sudden thought. Suppose that when I am in my house I hear the sound of a truck coming up the driveway and it suddenly occurs to me that I have not put out the milk bottles. Now is this sudden thought (which is also a sudden memory) literally inside my skull? I think that in our ordinary use of the terms "thought" and "thinking," we attach no meaning to the notion of determining the bodily location of a thought. We do not seriously debate whether someone's sudden thought occurred in his heart, or his throat, or his brain. Indeed, we should not know what the question meant. We should have no idea what to look for to settle this "question." We do say such a thing as "He can't get the thought out of his head"; but this is not taken as giving the location of a thought, any more than the remark "He still has that girl on the brain," is taken as giving the location of a girl.

4 Mr. U. T. Place, in his article "Is Consciousness A Brain Process?" (*The Philosophy of Mind*, V. C. Chappell, ed., Prentice-Hall 1962) also defends the identity theory. An example that he uses to illustrate the sense of identity in which, according to him, "consciousness" could turn out to be a brain process is this: "A cloud is a mass of water droplets or other particles in suspension" (*loc. cit.*, pp. 103 and 105). I believe that Place would not be ready to hold that this is a genuine identity, *as contrasted with* a systematic and/or causal correlation, if he did not assume that in the very same region of space occupied by a cloud there is, at the very same time, a mass of particles in suspension.

5 "Materialism," *loc. cit.*, p. 654.

It might be replied that *as things are* the bodily location of thoughts is not a meaningful notion; but if massive correlations were discovered between thoughts and brain processes then we might *begin* to locate thoughts in the head. To this I must answer that our philosophical problem *is* about how things are. It is a question about our *present* concepts of thinking and thought, not about some conjectured future concepts.[6]

The difficulty I have in understanding Smart's identity theory is the following. Smart wants to use a concept of "strict identity." Since there are a multitude of uses of the word "is," from the mere fact that he tells us that he means "is" in the sense of "strict identity," it does not follow that he has explained which use of "is" he intends. From his examples and non-examples, I surmise that his so-called "strict identity" is governed by the necessary condition that if x occurs in a certain place at a certain time, then y is strictly identical with x only if y occurs in the same place at the same time. But if x is a brain process and y is a sudden thought, then this condition for strict identity is not (and cannot be) satisfied. Indeed, it does not even make sense to set up a test for it. Suppose we had determined, by means of some instrument, that a certain process occurred inside my skull at the exact moment I had the sudden thought about the milk bottles. How do we make the further test of whether my *thought* occurred inside my skull? For it would have to be a *further* test: it would have to be logically independent of the test for the presence of the brain process, because Smart's thesis is that the identity is *contingent.* But no one has any notion of what it would mean to test for the occurrence of the thought inside my skull *independently* of testing for a brain process. The idea of such a test is not intelligible. Smart's thesis, as I understand it, requires this unintelligible idea. For he is not satisfied with holding that there is a systematic correlation between sudden thoughts and certain brain processes. He wants to take the additional step of holding that there is a "strict identity." Now his concept of strict identity either embodies the necessary condition I stated previously, or it does not. If it does not, then I do not know what he means by "strict identity," over and above systematic correlation. If his concept of strict identity does embody that necessary condition, then his concept of strict identity cannot be meaningfully applied to the relationship between sudden thoughts and brain processes. My conclusion is what I said in the beginning: the identity theory has no clear meaning.

[6] Mr. Jerome Shaffer proposes an ingenious solution to our problem ("Could Mental Sates Be Brain Processes?", *The Journal of Philosophy*, Vol. LVIII, No. 26: December 21, 1961). He allows that at present we do not attach any meaning to a bodily location of thoughts. As he puts it, we have no "rules" for asserting or denying that a particular thought occurred in a certain part of the body. But why could we not *adopt* a rule, he asks? Supposing that there was discovered to be a one-to-one correspondence between thoughts and brain processes, we could *stipulate* that a thought is located where the corresponding brain process is located. Nothing would then stand in the way of saying that thoughts are *identical* with those brain processes! Although filled with admiration for this philosophical technique, I disagree with Shaffer when he says (*ibid.*, p. 818) that the adopted convention for the location of thoughts would not have to be merely an elliptical way of speaking of the location of the corresponding brain processes. Considering the origin of the convention, how could it amount to anything else?

II

I turn now to a different consideration. A thought requires circumstances or, in Wittgenstein's word, "surroundings" (Umgebung). Putting a crown on a man's head is a coronation, only in certain circumstances.[7] The behavior of exclaiming, "Oh, I have not put out the milk bottles," or the behavior of suddenly jumping up, rushing to the kitchen, collecting the bottles and carrying them outside—such behavior expresses the thought that one has not put out the milk bottles, *only in certain circumstances.*

The circumstances necessary for this simple thought are complex. They include the existence of an organized community, of a practice of collecting and distributing milk, of a rule that empty bottles will not be collected unless placed outside the door, and so on. These practices, arrangements and rules could exist only if there was a common language; and this in turn would presuppose shared activities and agreement in the use of language. The thought about the milk bottles requires a background of mutual purpose, activity and understanding.

I assume that if a certain brain process were strictly identical with a certain thought, then the occurrence of that brain process would be an absolutely sufficient condition for the occurrence of that thought. If this assumption is incorrect, then my understanding of what Smart means by "strict identity" is even *less* than I have believed. In support of this assumption I will point out that Smart has never stated his identity theory in the following way: *In certain circumstances* a particular brain process is identical with a particular thought. His thesis has not carried such a qualification. I believe his thesis is the following: A particular brain process is, *without qualification*, strictly identical with a particular thought. If this thesis were true it would appear to follow that the occurrence of that brain process would be an absolutely sufficient condition for the occurrence of that thought.

I have remarked that a necessary condition for the occurrence of my sudden thought about the milk bottles is the previous existence of various practices, rules and agreements. If the identity theory were true, then the surroundings that are necessary for the existence of my sudden thought would also be necessary for the existence of the brain process with which it is identical.[8] That brain process would not have occurred unless, for example, there was or had been a practice of delivering milk.

This consequence creates a difficulty for those philosophers who, like Smart, hold both to the identity theory and also to the viewpoint that I shall call "scientific materialism." According to the latter viewpoint, the furniture of the

7 *Investigations*, Sec. 584.

8 It is easy to commit a fallacy here. The circumstances that I have mentioned are *conceptually* necessary for the occurrence of my thought. If the identity theory were true it would not follow that they were *conceptually* necessary for the occurrence of the brain process that is identical with that thought. But it would follow that those circumstances were necessary for the occurrence of the brain process *in the sense* that the brain process *would not* have occurred in the absence of those circumstances.

world "in the last resort" consists of "the ultimate entities of physics."[9] Smart holds that everything in the world is "explicable in terms of physics."[10] It does not seem to me that this can be true. My sudden thought about the milk bottles was an occurrence in the world. That thought required a background of common practices, purposes and agreements. But a reference to a practice of (*e.g.*) delivering milk could not appear in a proposition of physics. The word "electron" is a term of physics, but the phrase "a practice of delivering milk" is not. There could not be an explanation of the occurrence of my thought (an explanation taking account of all the necessary circumstances) which was stated solely in terms of the entities and laws of physics.

My sudden thought about the milk bottles is not unique in requiring surroundings. The same holds for any other thought. No thought would be explicable wholly in the terms of physics (and/or biology) because the circumstances that form the "stage-setting" for a thought cannot be described in the terms of physics.

Now if I am right on this point, and if the identity theory were true, it would follow that none of those *brain processes* that are identical with thoughts could be given a purely physical explanation. A philosopher who holds both to the identity theory and to scientific materialism is forced, I think, into the self-defeating position of conceding that many brain processes are not explicable solely in terms of physics.[11] The position is self-defeating because such a philosopher regards a brain process as a *paradigm* of something wholly explicable in terms of physics.

A defender of these two positions might try to avoid this outcome by claiming that the circumstances required for the occurrence of a thought, do themselves consist of configurations of ultimate particles (or of their statistical properties, or something of the sort). I doubt, however, that anyone knows what it would mean to say, for example, that the *rule* that milk bottles will not be collected unless placed outside the door, is a configuration of ultimate particles. At the very least, this defence would have to assume a heavy burden of explanation.

III

There is a further point connected with the one just stated. At the foundation of Smart's monism there is, I believe, the desire for a homogeneous system of explanation. Everything in the world, he feels, should be capable of the same *kind* of explanation, namely, one in terms of the entities and laws of physics.

9 "Materialism," *loc. cit.*, p. 651.

10 "Sensations and Brain Processes," *loc. cit.*, p. 161.

11 I believe this argument is pretty similar to a point made by J. T. Stevenson, in his "Sensations and Brain Processes: A Reply to J. J. C. Smart," *The Philosophical Review*, October 1960, p. 507. Smart's view, roughly speaking, is that unless sensations are identical with brain processes they are "nomological danglers," Stevenson's retort is that by insisting that sensations are identical with brain processes we have not got rid of any nomological danglers. He says: "Indeed, on Smart's thesis it turns out that brain processes are danglers, for now brain processes have all those properties that made sensations danglers."

He thinks we advance toward this goal when we see that sensations, thoughts, etc., are identical with brain processes.

Smart has rendered a service to the profession by warning us against a special type of fallacy. An illustration of this fallacy would be to argue that a sensation is not a brain process because a person can be talking about a sensation and yet not be talking about a brain process.[12] The verb "to talk about" might be called an "intentional" verb, and this fallacy committed with it might be called "the intentional fallacy." Other intentional verbs would be "to mean," "to intend," "to know," "to predict," "to describe," "to notice," and so on.

It is easy to commit the intentional fallacy, and I suspect that Smart himself has done so. The verb "to explain" is also an intentional verb and one must beware of using it to produce a fallacy. Suppose that the Prime Minister of Ireland is the ugliest Irishman. A man might argue that this cannot be so, because someone might be explaining the presence of the Irish Prime Minister in New York and yet not be explaining the presence in New York of the ugliest Irishman. It would be equally fallacious to argue that since the Irish Prime Minister and the ugliest Irishman *are* one and the same person, therefore, to explain the presence of the Prime Minister *is* to explain the presence of the ugliest Irishman.

I wonder if Smart has not reasoned fallaciously, somewhat as follows: If a sudden thought *is* a certain brain process, then to *explain* the occurrence of the brain process *is* to explain the occurrence of the thought. Thus there will be just one kind of explanation for both thoughts and brain processes.

The intentional fallacy here is transparent. If a thought is identical with a brain process, it does not follow that to explain the occurrence of the brain process is to explain the occurrence of the thought. And in fact, an explanation of the one differs in *kind* from an explanation of the other. The explanation of why someone *thought* such and such, involves different assumptions and principles and is guided by different interests than is an explanation of why this or that process occurred in his brain. These explanations belong to different *systems* of explanation.

I conclude that even if Smart were right in holding that thoughts are strictly identical with brain processes (a claim that I do not yet find intelligible) he would not have established that there is one and the same explanation for the occurrence of the thoughts and for the occurrence of the brain processes. If he were to appreciate this fact then, I suspect, he would no longer have any *motive* for espousing the identity theory. For this theory, even if true, would not advance us one whit toward the single, homogeneous system of explanation that is the goal of Smart's materialism.

IV

I shall close by taking note of Smart's conceptual experiment with a human brain kept alive in *vitro*.[13] What is supposed to be proved by this experiment? That for thinking, pain, and so-called "mental experience" in general, what

12 Smart, "Sensations and Brain Processes," *loc. cit.*, p. 164.

13 "Materialism," *loc. cit.*, pp. 659–660.

goes on in the brain is more "important" or "essential" than behavior. How is this proved? By the supposed fact that the experimental brain has thoughts, illusions, pains, and so on, although separated from a human body.

Could this supposed fact be a fact? Could a *brain* have thoughts, illusions or pains? The senselessness of the supposition seems so obvious that I find it hard to take it seriously. No experiment could establish this result for a brain. Why not? The fundamental reason is that a brain does not sufficiently resemble a human being.[14]

What can have led Smart to suppose that a brain can have thoughts? The only explanation which occurs to me is that he thinks that if my thought is in my brain, then my brain has a thought. This would be like thinking that if my invitation to dinner is in my pocket, then my pocket has an invitation to dinner. One bad joke deserves another.

[14] Cf. Wittgenstein, *Investigations*, section 281 and 283.

Human Beings

JOHN W. COOK

> Only of a living human being and what resembles (behaves like) a living human being can one say: it has sensations; it sees; is blind; hears; is deaf; is conscious or unconscious.
>
> WITTGENSTEIN

IT SEEMS fair to say that there is no very general agreement on what exactly Wittgenstein has contributed to our understanding of the problem of other minds. Some will attribute this to the perplexing nature of Wittgenstein's style, and perhaps there is some justice in this. On the other hand, it may be that the difficulties that we find in his style are partly the result of preconceptions that we bring to our reading of him. When it comes to the problem of other minds there is surely a readiness on our part to find the main lines of his position running along certain well-known paths. We expect to find some element of Cartesianism or some element of behaviourism in his position, for these seem to divide up the field without remainder. True, he may have disavowed certain consequences, such as the idea of a private language, that others thought they saw in these alternatives, but he cannot have rejected both in their entirety. Perhaps he struck a compromise by adopting elements of each. Against this way of reading Wittgenstein I will try to show that he did indeed reject both Cartesianism and behaviourism in their entirety. He rejects an element that these alternatives fundamentally share, namely, a certain way of saying what a human being is. In order to bring this element into the open, I will begin by

Reprinted with permission of Humanities Press, Inc., New Jersey and Routledge & Kegan Paul Ltd. from "Human Beings" by John W. Cook in *Studies in Philosophy of Wittgenstein*, Peter Winch, ed., 1969, pp. 117–128 and 149–151.

reviewing those features of philosophical scepticism that give rise to the problems of other minds.

I

In his First Meditation Descartes makes clear the following features of philosophical scepticism: the sceptic is to set aside doubts about particular cases ('Has the cat been put out?', 'Is the gun loaded?') and instead is to search out grounds for calling in question an entire class of judgements. This is to be accomplished by undercutting in some way the ordinary sort of justifications we give for judgements of the class in question. Now scepticism thus understood has given rise to a set of demands that philosophers have usually tried to honour in the answers they have given to the sceptic. First, in answering the sceptic we are debarred from merely appealing to justifications of the ordinary sort ('I looked'), for it is precisely these that he purports to have undercut. (This is what Moore seemed so often to disregard.) Secondly, if the sceptic is to be answered on his own terms and we are to progress from merely moral certainty to metaphysical certainty, as Descartes would have put it, we must begin from premisses that do not themselves have questionable presuppositions of any sort. We must find some way of grounding our ordinary judgements in what have been called 'protocol statements.' (For simplicity of exposition I will retain this phrase, drawing on the etymological significance of 'proto.') Thirdly, this grounding of our ordinary judgements is to be accomplished by either (i) a justification of some extraordinary sort for making inferences from protocol statements, e.g., Descartes' appeal to the veracity of God, or (ii) a construction (in letter if not in spirit) of our ordinary judgements out of protocol sentences by purely formal means. (I will call these the demands of scepticism.) Philosophers, as I said, have usually honoured these demands. There have been exceptions, such as Moore and Thomas Reid, but their responses to the sceptic have proved to be more puzzling than helpful. Accordingly, modern philosophy has been chiefly a contest for finding suitable ways of meeting the sceptic's third demand. Thus, we have witnessed a succession of reductionists, on the one hand, and those they call metaphysicians, on the other. These are the lines, then, between which the skirmishes are carried on. Every so often a philosopher has tried to find middle ground, but the others call 'Foul' and the contest goes on with added subtleties.

This, in outline, is the background against which we read Wittgenstein. It will be well to review, then, the content of the sceptic's demands as regards the problem of other minds. The first demand requires that we set aside our ordinary justifications for the statements we make about other people's mental states, events, and processes, such as 'I know she is worried; I've been talking to her,' 'I could see he was in pain; he was grimacing and holding his elbow,' etc. (These must be excluded, if for no other reason, because 'She told me' and 'He was grimacing' seem to be, at least implicitly, statements of the sort the sceptic means to be calling in question.) The second demand is now the requirement that the protocol statements on which we ground any statements about other people's mental (or 'mental') states, events, and processes are to be statements about human bodies. (Behaviorists sometimes talk about descriptions of 'colourless movements.') We might put this demand most graphically by saying that the protocol statements are to be free of any suggestion that the subjects to which they apply are essentially different from automata. The third demand is most commonly met either (i) by the argument from analogy, which is allowed to be less than what the sceptic will settle for but the best we can do if we are Cartesians, or (ii) by some form of behaviourism. Now let us ask where Wittgenstein is supposed to stand in response to the sceptic. There seem to be three interpretations: either Wittgenstein is trying to meet the third demand with his notion of criteria and is thus, despite his disclaimers, a subtle behaviourist; or he is carrying on, in a sophisticated way, Moore's tradition of refusing to accede to the first demand and is thus what might be called an 'ordinary language Cartesian'; or he is attempting to combine somehow these seemingly antithetical approaches and is thus perhaps the first crypto-Cartaviourist. What no one seems to have considered in all of this is what Wittgenstein has to say about the second demand and in particular the idea of 'body' or 'bodily movements' from which the whole problem begins. If in fact he advanced substantial considerations against this very root of the problem, he will have done something very different from anything suggested by current interpretations. It will be my claim in this essay that Wittgenstein struck at the root.

In order to make clear what such an approach to the problem would involve, it will be well to review the status of the second demand in the problem about the external world. There the demand is that we begin from protocol statements about sense-data or, more leniently, about appearances. I think it would now be widely conceded that the notion of sense-data is hopelessly confused and also that although we do understand and commonly make remarks about the appearances of things, these could not serve as the logical-epistemological foundation for our statements about such things as chocolate bars ('It's melted') and footballs ('It has a leak'). Some of the reasons for this can be stated briefly. First of all, it is obvious that children do not first master the language of appearances and then move on to construct or derive physical object statements. Moreover, there are good grounds for holding that there is a great deal in our physical object statements, e.g. words like 'melted' and 'leak,' that could not occur in descriptions of appearances, and in any case learning the language of appearances logically presupposes a mastery of the language used in talking about physical objects. Indeed, the language of appearances is a highly sophisticated use of words. Who, after all, can easily describe hues and highlights and shadows and apparent convergence of lines and the like? And when do we take notice of such things? Children's drawings do not suggest that they take much notice of appearances. For these and other reasons the idea that the language of appearances constitutes an epistemologically basic language has now been pretty well abandoned. One of the additional reasons for this is that we no longer find plausible those sceptical arguments, such as the argument from illusion, that seemed to create the need for—and to give us the very idea of—a protocol language. (No one thought there were sense-data before they found such arguments appealing.) I make particular mention of this point because it illustrates the essential connexion between sceptical arguments and the idea of a basic description or protocol language of the sort the sceptic demands. Thus, philosophers who would answer the sceptic on his own terms by meeting the third demand in some way share an assumption that is far more fundamental than the differences there may be between their opposing ways of meeting the third demand. In the problem of other minds this means that behaviourism and the argument from analogy are brothers under the skin: both rest upon the assumption that we are forced to recognize descriptions (or observations) of bodily movements as being epistemologically basic in our knowledge of other persons. Now it is just this assumption that Wittgenstein rejects. I refer especially to sections 281–7 of *Philosophical Investigations*, where he first introduces questions about bodies, souls, and human beings, and also to the way in which he follows this up in sections 288–316 with an attack on the idea of an inward or private identification of pain or thinking.[1] What I want to bring out is the connexion between these two groups of passages. In order to do this, however, it will be necessary to begin by working back through the problem itself, for much of the published discussion of Wittgenstein's views is simply the result of having got the problem of other minds badly out of focus. I will begin, then, by asking what this problem is.

II

Consider how we are to state the problem of other minds. We might ask: 'Do other people have a mental life, as I do?' But this clearly won't do, for they are not people, surely, if they do not have thoughts, emotions, sensations, desires, and so on. After all, we do not mean to be asking in the ordinary way whether this or that person is in a coma or something of the sort. So we had better retreat to this formulation: 'Are the things that I take to be people really people, that is, do they have thoughts and emotions and so on?' But this, too, is unsatisfactory, for it is left unspecified what distinction we are being asked to make. If the question is whether they are people or not, we must ask: 'People as opposed to *what*?' And here the answer is not at all clear. If I look at my son playing near by and ask, 'What else might he be?', no answer readily suggests itself. He is

[1] At section 316 the discussion does not end but is given a new turn; the investigation of the concept *thinking* and others in sections 316–76 should be seen as containing a further account of the way in which Wittgenstein means to oppose the idea of an inward or private identification of a mental state or process. He makes this connexion explicit in the next group of passages, 377–97, and then in section 398 the discussion returns to the question raised in 281–7 about the nature of the *subject* of pain or thought. Here he first discusses (398–413) puzzles about the first person pronoun and the idea that the 'self' is discerned by an inward gaze, and he then concludes the discussion of the whole topic by taking up questions about human beings, souls, and automata (414–27). He comes back to the topic in Part II, p. 178.

clearly not a statue, nor is he an animated doll of the sort we sometimes see looking very lifelike. He is my own child, my own flesh and blood.[2]

The problem of other minds seems to be in danger of foundering at the outset. It is clear, at least, that we cannot get the problem stated so long as we allow the concept *human being* (or *person* or *child*) to have its usual place. Somehow we must shunt it aside by setting some other concept over against it. Descartes sought to raise a doubt about the furniture of the world by supposing that he dreamed, and in this way he could talk not only of ships and shoes and beeswax but also of dreams of these. It is just such a move that is required if we are to launch the problem of other minds. But this move, too, ought to be found in the *Meditations*, for wasn't it Descartes himself who launched the problem? *Sum res cogitans.* How did Descartes manage this?

He began with the following reminder about himself: 'As though I were not a man who habitually sleeps at night and has the same impressions (or even wilder ones) in sleep as these [mad]men do when awake!' The reminder is that he goes to sleep and dreams. But then he continues: 'When I reflect more carefully on this, I am bewildered; and my very bewilderment confirms the idea of my being asleep.' This provides Descartes with that challenge to his former opinions that he was looking for: he may be only dreaming that he sees and hears. It is the next sentence, however, that approaches our present problem: 'Well, suppose I am dreaming, and these particulars, that I open my eyes, shake my head, put out my hand, are incorrect; suppose even that I have no such hand, no such body. . . .'[3] Here we have the beginning of an answer to our question: with the supposition that he is dreaming Descartes sees a place to enter a wedge between himself and his body, a wedge that is driven further in the remaining Meditations. But there is a difficulty here. Descartes begins by reminding himself that he is 'a man who habitually sleeps at night' and dreams, and he adds that these dreams occur while 'I am undressed and lying in bed.' This is Descartes' beginning and the point at which we must grasp what he says. There is no difficulty, of course, in understanding at least a part of this. People go to bed, usually undressed; they sleep, calmly or restlessly, and they dream. Dreams, of course, are what people tell when they wake up or perhaps write in a diary or keep to themselves. So a dreamer here (and this includes Descartes) is a human being: he gets dressed and undressed, sleeps on a bed or pallet, tells dreams while eating breakfast, and so on. If this is what we are to understand by Descartes' opening remark, we need not put up resistance yet. But then comes the wedge: 'suppose even that I have no such hand, no such body.' Here we must call a halt. We were to think of Descartes as a man who, undressed and in bed, often dreams. It was only with that understanding that we were able to take his first step with him. Does this still stand? If so, what is this 'body' that he now supposes himself not to have? Can he, without this 'body,' sleep, either calmly or

[2] See *Philosophical Investigations*, p. 178.

[3] *Descartes: Philosophical Writings* (Edinburgh, 1954), eds. G. E. M. Anscombe and P. T. Geach.

restlessly, and dream? Or has Descartes unwittingly contradicted himself here? Has he appealed to the possibility of dreaming only to take back something that the very possibility of dreaming itself requires? This does appear to be the case. But if that is so, then we can go no further with him. Either we are to think of him—and he is to think of himself—as a man who, undressed and in bed, often dreams, and then we understand him, or he takes this back and wipes out all he has said. And this holds for the remaining Meditations, for everything that Descartes goes on to say in the *Meditations* is said under the supposition that he may be dreaming. Whatever sort of philosophical doubts this may raise, there is at least one thing certain; if he should ask himself 'What am I?', he can answer that he is a man who sleeps, undressed and in bed, and often dreams. To take back this beginning is to take back everything.

So the wedge that Descartes would drive between himself and his body is never really driven. Or rather, no place is found for the wedge to enter. For it is not that we understand about Descartes *and his body.* We understand only about Descartes, that philosopher who habitually undressed and went to bed at night and whose dreams, by his own testimony, were sometimes wilder than the fantasies of madmen. But this is not to say that we understand only about his body. No, to say that we understand only about Descartes is to say neither more nor less than we mean, for no place has been found yet for the word 'body'—at least not in the special sense (if it is a sense) that Descartes requires. This is a point we tend to forget. Descartes introduced a highly extraordinary use of the word 'body.' He has to be understood to be using it always in the context of his distinction between *himself* and his body. So his use of the word is not at all like these: 'His body was covered with mosquito bites,' 'His body was found at the bottom of the cliff,' 'He has a strong body but no brains,' and so on. In saying such things as these we do not use 'body' as the one side of a Cartesian distinction. We are not saying, for instance, 'His body, but not his mind, was covered with mosquito bites.' That would be utter nonsense. If I say that someone's body was covered with mosquito bites, I could also say 'He was covered, etc.' The word 'body' comes in here as part of the emphasis: not just his ankles and wrists, but his back and stomach, too. Again, in speaking of a corpse we can say either 'His body was found, etc.' or 'He was found dead, etc.' The word 'body' in the first of these is used to make the contrast between dead and alive. No special ontology need come in here. As for the third sentence in the above list, it might be found in a requested letter of recommendation, and from it we should take the warning that the man can do heavy work but should not be expected to go at his work with much intelligence. In these and in other ordinary cases our understanding of the word 'body' is tied to particular contexts to a variety of particular distinctions of the kind just illustrated, and none of these provides a place to drive a conceptual wedge between Descartes and his body. But once again, this should not lead us to conclude: Then Descartes was *only* a body. For what distinction would that be making? It was not, after all, a corpse that wrote the *Meditations.*

There is a bit of a clue, in what Descartes says, to how he may have failed to realize that he was introducing an extraordinary use of the word 'body.' He says: 'suppose even that I have no hand, no such body,' and thus it looks as though he supposed that 'hand' and 'body' are words of the same sort or that 'hand' and 'body' are related as 'shirt' and 'clothing' are, so that one could work up from supposing that you had no hand, no foot, etc. to supposing that you had no body, as you might work up from supposing you had no shirt, no coat, etc. to supposing that you had no clothing. This would perhaps be encouraged by the fact that we do use both the expressions 'my whole body' and 'my whole suit of clothing,' and we also say 'He lost a hand' as well as 'He lost a shirt.' But the parallel fails just where it is crucial for Descartes. I could understand, given a certain context, a man's believing that he had no right hand, that he was a one-armed man, but I can make no sense of a man's believing that he has no body, that he has never had a body. I might have occasion to worry about a child being born with no hands, but there is no occasion to worry about a child being born with no body. And this is not merely because bodies are required for birth. Bodies are not born; they are stillborn. What are born are babies, human beings.

We may summarize our results as follows: Descartes' use of the word 'body' presupposes that he has driven his wedge, that he has provided the right sort of contrast between 'I' and 'my body,' but on the other hand there seems to be no place for his wedge to be driven unless his use of the word 'body' is itself presupposed, and these requirements are incompatible. (If anyone should wonder about the locution 'my body' and ask what the body belongs to if not the mind, he need only remind himself of the locution 'my mind.')[4]

We began by trying to formulate the problem of other minds and encountered a difficulty in discovering what could be contrasted with a human being in such a way as to allow the problem to arise. In turning to Descartes we hoped to find the required contrast in his use of the word 'body,' but it now appears that this has only further exposed the difficulty. Is the case hopeless, then? To answer this it is necessary to take notice of a reply that might be made to the foregoing arguments. The reply is this. Names of mental states, events, and processes, including the word 'dreaming,' get their meaning from private ostensive definitions. For this reason it does not follow that if Descartes begins from the reminder that he dreams, he must allow ever after that he is a man who goes to bed and sleeps. To speak of dreaming carries no such implication, for the state we call 'dreaming' is something known to us by means of introspection or inner sense, and introspection discloses nothing of a bodily nature.[5]

It is to this account of words like 'dream' and 'pain' and 'thinking' that we

[4] Frank Ebersole once remarked in another context that philosophers often talk of people as if they were speaking of zombies, which the dictionary describes as corpses that, by sorcery, are made to move and act as if alive. At the time I did not fully appreciate the significance of this remark, but very likely it did something to help focus my thoughts for the present essay. (See also the excellent chapter on human actions in Ebersole's book, *Things We Know* (Eugene, Oregon, 1967), pp. 282–304).

[5] See Descartes' *Principles*, I, xlvi, lxviii, where he maintains that what is clearly and distinctly perceived as a sensation is something that 'takes place within ourselves' and involves nothing of a corporeal nature.

must ultimately trace the problem of other minds. Putting the matter in unabashed metaphor, it is the idea that since the inner sense that reveals our mental states does not discover anything bodily, it must be possible to conceptually skim off a mental side of our nature leaving a physical remainder called 'the body.'[6] It is this idea of a physical remainder, the 'senseless body' which some mind may 'have,' that gives us our problem, for it is a consequence of this idea that when we look at another person all that we really see is something that, in itself, is no more an appropriate subject of pain or thought than a stone is. Philosophers have puzzled over the question 'Why shouldn't we regard a complicated automaton as we do a person,' but what ought to puzzle us is the question 'If all that we see of other "people" are "senseless bodies," how could we have got as far as connecting the concepts of thought and sensation with them at all?' The argument from analogy should not impress us here unless, as Wittgenstein saw (283), we are willing to go a step further and allow that perhaps stones have pains and machines think. For if I identify pain and thinking inwardly, if I do not learn these concepts in learning a common language, then my concepts *pain* and *thinking* are not essentially related to living human beings (in the ordinary sense), and so my body might turn to stone or into a pillar of salt while my pain continues. But in that case I should allow that the pebbles I walk on may be in pain, too. It would be gratuitous to restrict the concept to human beings and to what more or less resemble (behave like) them.[7] But the real difficulty here is not to account for our restricting our concept of pain to human beings but to account for how we extend it beyond our own case. For on the supposition we are here considering (that I learn what 'pain' means from my own pains) it will not do to say that I extend the concept to others by simply supposing that they sometimes have the same thing that I have so often had, since this explanation presupposes the very use of words, namely, 'same sensation,' that we ought to be explaining (350–2). But this means that I could never get as far as using the argument from analogy or anything like it. I could not even understand the question whether there are other beings that feel what I call 'pain.' The only recourse here is to admit that I cannot extend the use of 'pain' from myself to others and to hold to a strict logical behaviourism: when I say that other people are in pain, I am merely speaking of the movements of

[6] This idea is seldom made as explicit as it was by C. J. Ducasse, who wrote: 'What thought, desire, sensation, and other mental states are like, each of us can observe directly by introspection; and what introspection reveals is that they do not in the least resemble muscular contraction, or glandular secretion, or any other known bodily events. No tampering with language can alter the observable fact that thinking is one thing and muttering quite another; that the feeling called anger has no resemblance to the bodily behavior which usually goes with it; or that an act of will is not in the least like anything we find when we open the skull and examine the brain. Certain mental events are doubtless connected in some way with bodily events, but they are not those bodily events themselves,' *Is Life After Death Possible?* (Berkeley, 1948), p. 7.

[7] Locke was bold enough to draw this conclusion. Having said (*Essay* II, I, 4) that we get the ideas of the operations of our own minds from 'internal sense', he can later see 'no contradiction' in the supposition that God might give to some 'systems of matter' the powers to think, feel, and enjoy. (*Essay* IV, III, 6.)

those senseless bodies that I see. What this would fail to account for, of course, is my pity or concern for them. Since I can no more think of my children as *suffering*, in the sense that applies to me, then I could think this of a stone, my pity for them should strike me as a logical incongruity. It's as if I were to fall passionately in love with a fleck of dust.

It should now be possible to get an understanding of Wittgenstein's discussion of the problem of other minds. In particular, we can see the connexion between those passages (281–7) in which he first introduces questions about bodies, souls, and human beings and the next group of passages (288–316) in which he attacks the idea of an inward or private identification of mental states, events, and processes. The essential point is that if there is confusion in the idea of an inward, private, identification, then there is also confusion in the idea of conceptually skimming off a mental side of our nature, leaving a physical remainder called 'the body.' The philosophical idea of a 'senseless body' must be dropped. But in that case we must also reject the idea that when we look at another person we see only a 'body,' i.e., something which is no more a possible subject of pain or thinking than a stone would be. And finally, in rejecting *that* idea, we eliminate the only grounds of scepticism with regard to other 'minds' and in this way eliminate, too, the only source of the plausibility of behaviourism. In short, by rejecting the idea of a private identification, we get back our ordinary concept of a living human being. In place of 'colourless bodily movements' we now have human actions and reactions; we are back in the world of people running from danger, telling us their woes, nursing painful bruises, grimacing, frowning in disapproval, and so on. Thus, Wittgenstein's primary contribution to the problem of other minds was his attack on the idea of a private language, of a private identification of mental states and processes. Although he has a number of other important things to say about such words as 'pain' and 'thinking,' these cannot be understood apart from a grasp of his primary contribution. His reminders about such words will be of no use until we have eliminated the philosophical notion of 'body' and have brought human beings back into our discussions. I will return later on to consider some of these reminders and in particular to consider the objection that may now have occurred to the reader, that it must be a question-begging move to make the concept *human beings* primary in any account of mental predicates.

At the beginning of this essay I remarked that our difficulty in understanding Wittgenstein's contribution to the problem of other minds might be the result of preconceptions that we bring to our reading of him. These preconceptions should now be clear. The philosophical ideas of 'body' and 'bodily movement' have simply become unquestioned notions; they set for us what we take to be the problem of other minds. The problem, as we understand it, is that of grounding or justifying our ascriptions of mental states and processes on observations of bodily movements. Thus, when Wittgenstein speaks of 'behaviour,' we inevitably read into this our own concession to the sceptic; we think of Wittgenstein as trying to solve the same problem that others have tried to solve with behaviourism or the argument from analogy, only it is not clear what his own solution comes to. In struggling with this people have seen that he allows no place for the argument from analogy or at least that he makes no appeal to such an argument, and this has given rise to suggestions that, despite all he says to the contrary, Wittgenstein settled for some form of behaviourism. In defence of this suggestion interpreters have fastened on his concept of criteria and have argued that he puts forth a "criteriological' theory of meaning that could not amount to anything but a subtle form of behaviourism. I believe that I have already given sufficient reasons for dismissing this interpretation, but because the misunderstandings about the rôle of criteria have run so deep, I will digress from my main topic to say something about this.

. . . .

VI

I should now like to return to Descartes once again to ferret out one further source of the whole problem. In the following passage in the Second Meditation he gives us what we can now see to be a metaphysical redescription of a human being. He writes:

> First came the thought that I had a face, hands, arms,—in fact the whole structure of limbs that is observable also in a corpse, and that I called 'the body'. Further, that I am nourished, that I move, that I have sensations, that I am conscious: these acts I assigned to the soul. . . . As regards 'body' I had no doubt, and I thought I distinctly understood its nature; if I had tried to describe my conception, I might have given this explanation: 'By *body* I mean whatever is capable of being bounded by some shape, and comprehended by some place, and of occupying space in such a way that all other bodies are excluded; moreover of being perceived by touch, sight, hearing, taste or smell; and further, of being moved in various ways not of itself but by some other body that touches it.' For the power of self-movement, and the further powers of sensation and consciousness, I judged not to belong in any way to the essence of body . . .; indeed, I marvelled even that there were some bodies in which such faculties were found.[8]

Now in one respect Descartes is quite right about this last part: a corpse is not the sort of thing of which we can say that it has sensations, sees, is blind, is conscious or unconscious. And if a soul is that of which we *can* say these things, then of course a living human being is a soul.

The difficulty in Descartes' remarks lies in the move that looks quite innocent, namely, in 'I have a body.' And I think we can now see a further source of this move. Descartes' redescription is a kind of rehearsal of two quite different kinds of language-games. On the one hand, there are those in which human beings are central (complaining of aches and pains, telling dreams, guessing at a man's motives, etc.), and on the other hand, there are those in which human beings have roughly the same status as sticks and stones (weighing and measuring, etc.). This is a difference that stands out in sharpest relief; it is manifested in hundreds of ways. (Compare: 'I am as tall as this tree' and 'The rock hit a tree, so no one got hurt.') Now when we come to reflect on this difference it is surely

[8] Descartes, *op. cit.*, pp. 67–8.

inevitable that we will treat this difference in the use of words, that is, the special status of human beings in the one case and their non-special status in the other, as marking out two different sorts of things composing a human being. This, of course, is the Cartesian account. Behaviourism, then, starting from this account, rejects the language-games in which human beings have a special status. Unlike either of these, Wittgenstein rejects the first step, which escaped unnoticed: the redescription of a human being. We can now express this result as follows: these two kinds of language-games *taken together* mark off human beings from sticks and stones. If someone now should want to re-open the question, asking: 'But how can something that lies undressed in bed at night, something of a certain height and weight, have thoughts and sensations?' we shall have to say, as Wittgenstein suggests (284, 412, 421): Look at someone engaged in a conversation or think of a child just stung by a bee and ask yourself what better subject there could be for thoughts and sensations. In this way we are brought back to earth, turned aside from misleading pictures, and we will find nothing odd in saying that these creatures are thinking or in pain.

Getting these two language-games back together—and in the right way—is not, of course, a simple matter. The problem is rather like that of getting substance and quality to lie down together again: the separation has been so prolonged as now to seem virtually in the nature of things. In each case the difficulty seems to be that we have saddled ourselves with a pair of spurious entities. In the latter case it is the 'bare particular' and qualities designed to 'clothe' it; in the former case it is the 'body' and 'private objects.' It is only if we let go of these that we can find those 'real connexions' that Hume was looking for.—Yet other matters are bound to intrude here. One of these Wittgenstein mentions when he remarks that 'religion teaches that the soul can exist when the body has disintegrated' (p. 178). Seen in the context of the philosophical problem we have been considering, it is natural to think of this teaching as requiring an interpretation along lines that now seem impossible. It is natural, that is, to think of this teaching as requiring a Cartesian ontology. Yet it would be obtuse to insist on this, for, as Wittgenstein goes on to remark, the teaching has, after all, a point. It is one way of announcing the promise of a life everlasting. And that promise does not itself specify a Cartesian ontology. If we do not at once see how a non-Cartesian account of the matter is possible, then we can only confess ignorance.[9] In any case, it would seem presumptuous of a believer to insist that the promise shall be fulfilled in the way that he has been accustomed to thinking of it. At the same time, it would be equally presumptuous of a non-believer to boggle at this talk of soul and body. After all, we all still speak of the sun rising and setting, and no one is the worse off for that. Indeed, it seems unlikely that we shall ever speak otherwise.

9 Wittgenstein says that he 'can imagine plenty of things in connexion with' the teaching and here we should bear in mind that the promise has been filled out with an account of 'resurrection bodies'. On this point I have been greatly benefited by conversations with my colleague Robert Herbert. See his essay 'Puzzle Cases and Earthquakes', *Analysis*, January, 1968.

INTRODUCTION TO METAPHYSICS / Study Questions

THE MIND-BODY PROBLEM

Descartes

1. What is the status of Descartes' beliefs at the beginning of this second meditation?
2. How does Descartes conclude that he exists?
3. What did he formerly believe himself to be? Why does he think this former belief is wrong?
4. What is his conception of body?
5. What kind of a thing does Descartes believe he is?
6. What does Descartes include under the term *thought*?
7. In what ways would Descartes say that minds differ from bodies?

Watson

1. What is introspective psychology and what is its method? Why does Watson think it a superstitious belief? What is the connection between introspectionism and cartesianism?
2. What problems with older theories of psychology led to behaviorism? How does behaviorism intend to meet these problems?
3. Explain the notion of conditioned reflex.
4. What connection does Watson see between the psychological theory of introspectionism and our everyday talk about people, their thoughts, feelings, and so on.
5. Why does Watson say we do not really understand the "subjective" terms in our language?
6. Explain Watson's concepts of *stimulus* and *response*. What serious ambiguity is built into these notions?
7. What cartesian assumptions does Watson share?

Skinner

1. Explain Thorndike's "Law of Effect."
2. Explain operant conditioning. How does it differ from Pavlov's (and Watson's) concept of conditioning?
3. What methodological problems does Skinner think are involved in determining why reinforcers reinforce?
4. How does Skinner propose to understand statements referring to goals and purposes? Why must a thinker like Skinner be suspicious of such notions?
5. Skinner says that purposes are not features of behavior. What, then, are features of behavior? How is a piece of behavior to be properly described? Is there an easy distinction to be made between describing behavior and "interpreting" it?

Smart

1. Why does Smart object to thinking of reports of pains, after-images, and so on, as reports of things that are irreducibly psychical?
2. State the identity thesis.
3. Explain Smart's contention that the word *after-image* does not mean the same as "brain process of sort x." In what way are these remarks about meaning relevant to his identity thesis?
4. What does Smart mean by "strict identity?"
5. Can Smart's examples of identity, for example, lightening-electric discharge and Morning Star-Evening Star, illuminate the alleged sensation-brain process identity?

6. Is Smart's distinction between an after-image and the experience of having an after-image an intelligible distinction?
7. What is Smart's view of the logical status of his identity thesis?

Malcolm

1. How does Malcolm characterize Smart's notion of "strict identity?"
2. Why should Malcolm say that we attach no meaning to the notion of determining the bodily location of a thought?
3. In the light of the answers to questions (1) and (2) why does it make no sense to say that a sudden thought might be strictly identical to a brain process?
4. Explain what Malcolm means when he points out that a thought requires circumstances or surroundings.
5. In the light of Malcolm's remark about the circumstances of a thought why cannot the occurrence of a brain process be a sufficient condition for the occurrence of a thought?
6. Explain Malcolm's objection to the materialist's contention that everything in the world is explicable in terms of physics.
7. What is the intentional fallacy? How does Malcolm accuse Smart of committing it? If Malcolm is right about this, how does it destroy the motive for Smart's materialism?
8. Malcolm says that it is nonsense to suppose that a brain has thoughts, and so on, although he does not really argue for it. How might it be argued for?

Cook

1. What are the three demands of scepticism? How do these demands apply to the other-minds problem?
2. How do these sceptical demands and the possible responses to them define the cartesian and behavioristic positions? In what way does this show how cartesianism and behaviorism are brothers under the skin?
3. Why does Cook say that there is a problem in the very statement of the other-minds problem? What is required to get the problem started?
4. Why has Descartes failed to drive his wedge between mind and body?
5. What account of the meaning of words such as *dream, pain, thinking,* and so on, must be given in order to get the other-minds problem going?
6. According to Cook, what was Wittgenstein's primary contribution to the other-minds problem?
7. Why is the introduction of the concept *human being* not a question-begging move?
8. Explain Cook's final characterization of cartesianism, the behaviorist response to it, and Wittgenstein's rejection of both.
9. How do Cook's arguments and conclusions undercut the entire traditional treatment of the mind-body problem? What implications do you see this having for the science of psychology?

SUGGESTED FURTHER READING / Introduction to Metaphysics

GENERAL

Ayer, A. J. *Language, Truth and Logic.* New York: Oxford University Press, 1936.
Baylis, Charles A., ed., *Metaphysics.* New York: Macmillan Publishing Co., Inc., 1965.
Taylor, A. E. *Elements of Metaphysics.* London: Methuen & Co., Ltd., 1903.
Taylor, Richard. *Metaphysics.* Englewood Cliffs, N.J.: Prentice-Hall, Inc., 1963.

FREEDOM OR DETERMINISM

Anscombe, G. E. M. *Intention*. Oxford, England: Basil Blackwell, 1957.

Care, N. S., and C. Landsman, eds. *Readings in the Theory of Action*. Bloomington: University of Indiana Press, 1968.

Dworkin, G., ed. *Determinism, Free Will, and Moral Responsibility*. Englewood Cliffs, N.J.: Prentice-Hall, Inc., 1970.

Hook, S., ed. *Determinism and Freedom in the Age of Modern Science*. New York: Crowell Collier and Macmillan, Inc., 1961.

Lehrer, K., ed. *Freedom and Determinism*. New York: Random House, Inc., 1966.

Melden, A. I. *Free Action*. New York: Routledge & Kegan Paul, 1961.

Morganbesser, S., and J. Walse, eds. *Free Will*. Englewood Cliffs, N.J.: Prentice-Hall, Inc., 1962.

Peters, R. S. *The Concept of Motivation*. London: Routledge & Kegan Paul, 1958.

Skinner, B. F. *Walden Two*. New York: Macmillan Publishing Co., Inc., 1948.

MIND-BODY PROBLEM

Chappell, V. C., ed. *The Philosophy of Mind*. Englewood Cliffs, N.J.: Prentice-Hall, Inc., 1962.

Malcolm, Norman. *Problems of Mind*. New York: Harper & Row, Publishers, 1971.

Wisdom, John. *Other Minds*. Oxford, England: Basil Blackwell and Mott, Ltd., 1952.

Wittgenstein, Ludwig. *Philosophical Investigations*. Oxford, England: Basil Blackwell and Mott, Ltd., 1953.

PART 3

Introduction to Epistemology

The word *epistemology* is derived from the Greek and means "theory of knowledge." In one of its traditional conceptions philosophy was thought of as the attempt to provide a general description and explanation of the world as a whole. Rather early on in the history of this attempt it was realized that if we are to arrive at an adequate philosophical theory of the world, we are going to have to begin by investigating the nature of the knowledge that we can have of the world. Thus did epistemology come into being. Contemporary philosophers, however, by and large have little concern with epistemology as a necessary first step in a grander metaphysical enterprise. They are concerned with the theory of knowledge for the intrinsic interest and importance of its problems. These problems can be sorted very roughly into two kinds: first, there are problems about the *concept* of knowledge and its relations to other concepts such as belief, doubt, certainty, learning, and truth and second, there are problems about how knowledge is acquired.

The first group of selections in this part considers some of the conceptual connections between knowledge, learning, and truth. We have all learned how to do a number of things and have learned that certain things are so. Having *learned* these things we can be said to *know* them. Thus we know how to do various things and we know that certain things are so. Gilbert *Ryle*, in his influential book, *The Concept of Mind*, has drawn our attention to this useful distinction between "knowing how" and "knowing that." A sentence of the form "I know (have learned) how . . ." is frequently completed by an infinitive phrase such as ". . . to swim" or ". . . to ride a bicycle" while a sentence of the form "I know that . . ." is completed by a clause that can stand by itself as a statement such as ". . . George Washington was the first president of the United States" or ". . . salt is a compound of sodium and chlorine". Someone may know how to do any number of things without necessarily being able to give any account of what it is he can do or how he goes about doing it, but the kind of knowledge that we want to examine here cannot be disconnected from the ability to say what it is that one knows, the ability to make statements. Now a statement, in contrast to other kinds of sentences, for example, questions, imperatives, exclamations, always has a truth value; that is, a statement must be either true or false. Thus, when I claim to know something, I am claiming that some statement is true. When I claim to know that George Washington was the first president of the United States I am, in effect, claiming that the statement "George Washington was the first president of the United States" is true. Let "S" be the statement in question and the foregoing point can be represented in this way: If I know that S, then "S" is true. Of course, if it is shown to me that "S" is in fact false, then I will have to retract my claim to have known.

It is instructive to contrast the concept of knowledge with that of belief on this score. It is possible to have false belief, but not false knowledge. When it is pointed out to me that what I said I believe is false, although I can no longer believe it, nevertheless it remains true that I *did* believe it. It is, however, unintelligible to insist of what is shown to be false that nevertheless I *did* know it.

These remarks are intended to suggest that there are intimate conceptual relations between knowledge, learning, and truth and that no account of knowledge can be complete that does not also concern itself with what it means to learn and what it means for a statement to be true.

The second sort of problem in epistemology is the one about how knowledge is acquired and how it is that we determine that any particular statement is true. It is this question that has undoubtedly dominated the history of the theory of knowledge. The problem has sometimes been phrased in its most general form: How do we know? Let us look at the following instances of this question.
How do I know that

1. there is coffee in the pot?
2. salt is a compound of sodium and chlorine?
3. the interior angles of a triangle equal two right angles?
4. abortion is wrong?
5. another man is angry?
6. God exists?

Question (1) can be answered very simply; I find out there is coffee in the pot merely by looking in the pot. However, (2) cannot be answered *merely* by looking; the necessary observations must be made in connection with laboratory experiments undertaken within the context of a scientific theory. Question (3) is not to be settled by any kind of observation or experiment at all but rather by geometrical proof that is a species of logical deduction. In this section, however, we are not going to be concerned with the nature of mathematical and logical knowledge, fascinating and important as that subject is. Neither are we going to be concerned with the issues raised by questions (4), (5) and (6), issues that take us into ethics, the philosophy of mind, and the philosophy of religion. These issues are dealt with in other parts of this book. Students may be interested in noting how many of the topics touched on in this book involve in one way or another matters that can be thought of as belonging to epistemology.

A great deal of our knowledge of the world is based upon observation where observation is construed in the widest possible sense to include the perceptions of all our senses. This is true both of our everyday awareness of things in the world as well as of scientific knowledge. Both the philosopher and the scientist are concerned with observation, but in rather different ways. The scientist must naturally be concerned with the methodology of his inquiries. He knows, as we all do, that some observations are more reliable than others; he knows that unusual lighting conditions, possible distortions in optical instruments, fatigue, and so on can mitigate against seeing things as they really are and he tries to make measurements and to design experiments that will minimize the possibility of inaccurate observation. The philosopher, on the other hand, is not really concerned with the details of methodology and experimental design. The questions about observation that he asks seem to have a deeper character. The philosopher raises certain very general questions about the nature of our perception of the world and then goes on to ask the really puzzling question that is the subject of the second group of articles in this part: Is the distinction that both scientists and laymen draw between accurate and inaccurate observation really well founded? Can perception really give us any knowledge of the world at all?

Learning, Knowledge, and Truth

It is natural to suppose that college and university students should be interested in learning for, after all, that is presumably what they are involved in doing. We believe they also ought to be interested in certain philosophical questions about learning, that is, they also ought to be interested in the *concept* of *learning*. It is perhaps unfortunate that when learning is talked about in the university it is usually done so in the context of courses in either empirical psychology or educational theory intended for the training of school teachers. We would argue for a wider consideration of the topic on the grounds that (a) many of the interesting questions about learning are conceptual rather than empirical and that (b) the issue is sufficiently important that it ought to be placed before students generally rather than only those pursuing curricula in what is called professional education. Thus, we think it appropriate to begin this section with a review of current theories of learning drawn from a textbook of educational psychology.

Let us begin with the typically philosophical question, "What is learning?" K. *Lovell* offers an answer to this question in the form of a definition making use of the notion of changes in behavior. This definition is characteristic of much educational theory and is derived from work in psychology and the behavioral sciences. There is doubtless something correct about this definition, for a person who has learned can now do things that he could not before, for example, play the piano, work problems in arithmetic, speak French. Nevertheless this definition must be very carefully examined if for no other reason than the fact that the educational theory it represents can have far reaching consequences, by means of teacher training, for what goes on in our schools. If there is something right about the definition, there may also be something dreadfully wrong. Suppose that in a game of football I injure my leg in such a way that I now must limp. This is a permanent change in my behavior that results from an activity and as such fits Lovell's definition of learning. But in no sense of the word could I be said to have *learned* to limp. This absurd conclusion makes it clear that something has been left out of Lovell's account of learning.

We do not have to look far to see what has been left out. It is the concepts of *knowing, understanding*, and *getting things right*. These notions are missing from Lovell's general definition of learning and they are clearly missing from what he calls Stimulus-Response Association theories, although Field Cognition theories may fare somewhat better in this respect.

These shortcomings can be highlighted by a comparison with Gilbert *Ryle*'s article, "Teaching and Training." Ryle's discussion has an important point of contact with Lovell's definition in that he, too, insists upon education's involving changes in behavior; the essential thing in teaching, Ryle tells us, is teaching people how to do various things. What Ryle goes on to say about this, however, is quite opposed to anything in Lovell's account and that makes the juxtaposition of the two selections interesting. Ryle makes clear that teaching someone how to do something is not at all like conditioning him to respond in a prearranged way to a prearranged stimulus; rather, it involves teaching him techniques and methods that will allow him to fend for himself successfully and correctly when faced with new situations and new questions. He makes clear how being able to do various things is a necessary part of understanding and knowing, whether it be a matter of simple arithmetic, riding a bicycle, or philosophy.

The selection from *Plato*'s dialogue, *Gorgias*, can also be construed as an attack on the conception of education held by Lovell. In the process of arriving at an adequate description of Gorgias' art of rhetoric, it is shown that rhetoric is the art of persuasion, the art of causing people to have whatever beliefs the rhetorician wants them to have. But, as Socrates points out in a neat argument, belief and knowledge are different things and if the rhetorician's concern with the techniques of persuasion is divorced from any concern for knowledge and truth, then the art of persuasion is no more than the art of manipulating people and the rhetorician is no teacher.

There is a tone of moral earnestness running through this dialogue—as indeed there is in all of Plato's dialogues. In the Greece of Socrates and Plato there was a class of professional rhetoricians—Gorgias and Polus were real people—who advertised themselves as experts in very nearly everything and undertook to teach aspiring politicians the art of persuasion. Both Socrates and Plato were opposed to what they saw as a pernicious disregard for knowledge and truth in favor of persuasion, that is, manipulation, especially in ethics and politics where it matters most.

It is not difficult to see Socrates' objections to rhetoric applying to Lovell's definition of learning. If teaching and learning are matters only of bringing about changes in behavior with notions of knowing and understanding apparently ignored, then it is not easy to escape the conclusion that the kind of learning theory derived from recent behavioral science is simply the art or science of manipulating people. It is perhaps not merely chance that in Lovell's chapter there is no tone of moral earnestness or other indication that what is being talked about is of supreme human importance.

Neither Ryle nor Plato have provided an answer to the question, "What is learning?" in the sense of stating a definition or a full-scale theory of learning. Nevertheless something important has emerged: The concepts of *education*, *teaching*, and *learning* cannot be understood unless we have an understanding of the concept of *knowledge*. In a selection from another of his dialogues, *Theaetetus*, Plato raises the question, "What is knowledge?" In the course of discussing that question it is found that the closely related concept of *truth* must also be introduced. The remaining three articles shift the focus of this first group of selections from the concept of *education*, by way of the concept of *knowledge*, to that of *truth*.

Historically, philosophers have recognized three principal theories of truth—the correspondence theory, the coherence theory, and the pragmatic theory. We have chosen to consider only the latter. There are two reasons for this apart from the obvious ones of limitations of both time and space. First, an adequate investigation of the first two theories would soon involve rather technical issues in logic and the philosophy of language unsuitable for beginning students in philosophy, although some important things can be said about the pragmatic theory in a nontechnical way. Secondly, it is our belief that many students, and not a few of their instructors as well, are inclined to subscribe to something very much like the pragmatic theory, thereby giving it a kind of relevance that the others perhaps do not have. This belief is strengthened by the numerous occasions upon which we have heard students suggest the relativity of truth by remarking that what is true for one person may well not be true for another.

The pragmatic theory is stated by the American philosopher William *James*. James, as his style shows, has to be one of the most engaging of philosophical writers while at the same time unfortunately being possibly one of the least consistent of thinkers. As a result it is sometimes difficult to figure out exactly what the thesis is that he is advocating. Nevertheless what does emerge from his chapter is a picture of truth as something that changes historically and is thus relative to time and place and maybe even to individuals. It is this idea of the relativity of truth that is critically examined and attacked by both Plato and Montague.

Plato, in *Theaetetus*, examines the idea of the relativity of truth by way of the dictum of Protagoras that "man is the measure of all things." In response to Socrates' request for a definition of knowledge the young Theaetetus responds that knowledge is perception. Socrates then goes on to develop this idea by identifying it with the theory of Protagoras. As a matter of historical fact we know very little about Protagoras and that mostly at second hand. We do know that he is supposed to have said that man is the measure of all things, but we don't know exactly what he had in mind by this or how he would have gone on to elaborate his own theory. Socrates offers an interpretation of the saying that begins by recognizing the relativity of sense perception and then goes on to develop a theory of knowledge and truth as equally relative. Whether this is an historically accurate interpretation of the Protagorean theory is not the point. What is important is the adequacy of the theory itself as an account of knowledge and truth regardless of who advances it. It is clear that Socrates believes it to be a grossly mistaken theory that must be gotten out of the way before an adequate theory of knowledge can be constructed. In fact the theory seems to be a remarkable anticipation of the pragmatic theory of truth, and students should be interested in examining the extent to which the objections Socrates brings against Protagoras are equally telling against James.

The selection from *Montague* speaks directly to James' theory of truth. Montague begins by pointing out how James borrowed much in his theory from the very important American philosopher, C. S. Peirce, although modifying it in significant ways and, in so doing, possibly misunderstanding Peirce. Montague goes on to argue against James' theory; his principal argument is that James has confused believing a statement to be true with that statement's being true. We find this argument to be telling and believe, along with Montague, that what plausibility the relativist's theory has probably rests on some such failure to keep the concepts of *belief, knowledge,* and *truth* straight. Thus, we would conclude that the relativist's contention that what is true for one may not be true for another is unintelligible.

We would be less than candid if we did not admit that this section is to a large extent polemical in intent. We think it is important to remind students that there are genuine distinctions between truth and falsity, between knowing and merely believing, and between an honest man and a liar. That there are intellectual virtues and that knowledge and truth are desirable things to be sought might seem sufficiently obvious to render our insistence inappropriate; and indeed it would be were it not for the fact that these things are under attack from so many quarters. The sources of these attacks need not be catalogued here and the reader can be left free to assemble his own list; examples shall not be wanting. A tradition of respect for intellectual values has painfully developed in Western culture over the last 2,500 years and we intend to do what we can to perpetuate it against those who would debase the coinage of truth and understanding, whether from sinister motives of personal or political gain or from loftier motives of well-meaning (although misplaced) tolerance. It is also worth reminding students that these intellectual values are inseparable from moral values and that to blur the distinction between the true and the false, between getting things right and getting them wrong, is to make of honesty no virtue and of the liar no scoundrel.

A Definition of Learning

K. LOVELL

Learning

WE MAY define learning as a change in behaviour which is more or less permanent in nature, and which results from activity, training or observation. To say that learning must have taken place when there is a change in behaviour is not enough; such a change must persist for a while. Momentary changes in behaviour due to sensory adaptation may take place but learning is not necessarily involved. We must also specify that the changes are due to activity, training or observation to distinguish them from the changes brought about by maturation discussed in the previous chapter. Learning occurs in many different situations; for example, in connection with memorization, the acquisition of physical or intellectual skills, solving problems, learning by trial and error, rather sudden or 'insightful' learning, the establishment of attitudes, interests and character traits, and the acquisition of mannerisms and gestures.

THE TWO MAIN APPROACHES TO LEARNING THEORY. Although we are going to discuss some theories on how learning is brought about, it must be made clear at the outset that most of our knowledge about learning has been determined empirically and has not been derived from any psychological theory. The experiments of psychologists have certainly taught us a great deal about how animals and children learn, but none of their theories are yet comprehensive enough to tie together all the known facts, or to answer all the questions that we would like to ask. Such information as we have about learning can, however, be put to good use even if we have no complete theory to explain the process, in the same way we can put electricity to excellent use although we do not have, as yet, any comprehensive theory to explain its nature.[1]

At present, then, there are two main approaches to learning theory. One of

[1] For an account of the theoretical approaches to the psychology of learning see: Hilgard, E. R., *Theories of Learning*. London: Methuen, 1958, Second Edition. Hall, F. W., *Learning: A Survey of Psychological Interpretations*. London: University Paperbacks, 1963. For an advanced and critical account of theories of learning see Lunzer, E. A. In *Development in Learning—2. The Regulation of Behaviour*. London: Staples, 1968.

Reprinted with permission of The University of London Press from *Educational Psychology and Children*, by Kenneth Lovell, 1967, pp. 125–139.

these is the Stimulus-Response Associationist type of theory and the other is the Field-Cognition type of theory. These terms may seem somewhat technical but in the following two sections we hope to make them clear.

STIMULUS-RESPONSE ASSOCIATION[2] THEORIES. On many occasions in everyday life one event follows closely upon another, for example, lightning and thunder. In such situations, we are said to associate one event with another, and the basic principle of associationism is that if A and B are presented together in space or in time the subsequent presentation of A tends to evoke B. Moreover, the strength of the association between A and B will depend upon the frequency, recency and vividness of previous associations. Our symbols A and B include amongst other things, ideas, perceptions, moods, and emotions. Associationism has been a topic of great interest to philosophers and thinkers from the time of Plato, but we can consider here only the more recent and relevant aspects of the problem.

In 1896 E. L. Thorndike began his studies of animals. In his well-known experiments with cats, he would place a young, lively, and hungry animal into a cage and put a piece of fish outside. Plenty of action on the part of the cat would be observed; it would push its claws through the bars, bite the bars and try to squeeze through them. Sooner or later it would touch the button which held the cage door, the door would swing open and the cat get out. When the animal, still hungry, was replaced in the cage, it would still attempt a 'trial and error,' or 'trial and success,' approach to the problem, but there were fewer actions and the door was opened sooner. With further trials the successful movements were 'stamped in' and useless ones eliminated, so that on being placed in the cage once more the animal got out in a couple of seconds.

As a result of his many experiments, Thorndike was led to formulate, in the early years of this century, his three famous laws. These are:

a. *Law of Exercise.* The response to a situation becomes associated with that situation, and the more it is used in a given situation, the more strongly it becomes associated with it. On the other hand, disuse of the response weakens the association.
b. *Law of Effect.* Responses that are accompanied or closely followed by satisfaction are more likely to happen again when the situation recurs, while responses accompanied or closely followed by discomfort will be less likely to recur.
c. *Law of Intensity.* The greater the satisfaction or discomfort, the greater will be the strengthening or weakening of the bond between the situation and the response.

It will be seen that the Law of Exercise really embodies the principle of association applied to the situation and response. The Law of Effect is also one of association, for it really states that the satisfactory or unsatisfactory outcome of an act respectively strengthens or weakens the association already existing. Note

[2] It seems that associations are due to linkages formed in the cerebral cortex, between nerve cells and their ramifications.

carefully that the cat was motivated; it was learning more quickly since it was acting under the influence of the hunger drive. Later, in 1932 and 1933, Thorndike[3] made a fresh study of the Law of Effect, using human beings instead of animals. His new evidence led him to give much greater weight to reward than to punishment. The latter did not so much break the bond between the situation and the response; rather it caused the learner to try other moves which would bring him reward. Some psychologists think that the Law of Effect is the most important single principle in learning theory today.

Also working with animals at the beginning of this century was I. P. Pavlov (1849–1936), the Russian physiologist. He found that saliva flowed from a dog's mouth not only when food was placed in it, but also when the dog heard the approaching footsteps of the person bringing food, or if he heard a bell[4] rung just before food was brought. Now the normal flow of saliva when food is in the mouth is a reflex action and we may write:

Unconditioned stimulus→	Unconditioned response
(food in mouth)	(reflex action of saliva)

But when the animal learns to associate the sound of a bell with food soon to be eaten, and commences to salivate before food is actually in the mouth, we may say that the complete sequence is:

Conditioned stimulus→	Conditioned response→
(Sound of bell or footsteps)	(Advanced flow of saliva)
→Unconditioned stimulus→	Conditioned Response
(food in mouth)	(Reflex action of saliva)

This learning took place because of *reinforcement*, that is, because food was always given after the bell had sounded. By conditioning, then, we mean that the organism learns to respond to a secondary or neutral stimulus which has become associated in time with a primary stimulus. We may, therefore, regard conditioning as a special case of association by contiguity.

Among other important findings, Pavlov showed that if the conditioned stimulus is an electric bell, and is replaced by, say, a buzzer, conditioned responses are still evoked but they are weaker. The fact that other stimuli, more or less similar to the original conditioned stimulus, can bring about the same conditioned response is known as *stimulus generalization.*

Pavlov was of the opinion that in the animal, knowledge of the external world is obtained almost exclusively by stimuli which come into the special cells of the sense organs which receive incoming signals, and the changes which these signals cause in the cerebral cortex. This type of signal activity must also play a great part in the life of man. But in human beings there is an important addition, for arising out of his social life and work, there has developed what Pavlov

[3] Thorndike, E. L., *The Fundamentals of Learning.* New York: Teachers College, Columbia University, 1932. Thorndike, E. L., *An Experimental Study of Rewards.* New York: Teachers College, Columbia University, 1933.

[4] The stimulus must be of a nature to attract the animal's attention.

called *second order* signals, in the form of oral and written language. Thus speech or written words represent an abstraction from reality and allow of generalizations and the build-up of concepts. In Pavlov's view laws established in the work of the first signal system should also govern the second signal system.

We may now explain in terms of Pavlovian theory how a child comes to use, say, the word 'horse' correctly:

Father says 'horse'→Child says 'horse'—an imitative response.
Sight of *horse* plus the word 'horse,' frequently said by father,→
Child says 'horse.' (This sequence repeated many times).
Sight of *horse*→Child says 'horse'—a conditioned response.

For a long time it was thought that Thorndike's trial-and-error learning was quite different from the conditioned response of Pavlov. Later, however, Clark Hull[5] worked out a very elaborate theory of learning which, while taking into account stimulus-response theory, also makes use of Thorndike's Law of Effect. He maintains that learning will not take place without reinforcement[6] or reward, and that it depends on a reduction in the individual's needs, primary or secondary, in accordance with the Law of Effect. Thus if a response reduces a need, say, hunger, which is strong at the time, then the same stimulus will bring about the same response in the future. This can be illustrated simply by considering a rat placed in a maze which has a number of blind alleys but also a correct path which leads to food. At first the rat will be seen to explore by trial and error, but eventually it reaches food and is rewarded. Next day if, when hungry, it is put in the maze again, it finds the food rather more quickly. Its correct choices are rewarded by food and its 'errors' (going up blind alleys) are penalised by its being temporarily denied food. After being put into the maze a few more times, it will go along the correct path without error. Thus Hull's theory of reinforcement provides a neat hypothesis of why learning takes place. Hull has made a great contribution to learning theory, and he modified his view from time to time as experimental evidence demanded. But these views are still controversial and their ultimate value must be decided by future research.

Summing up this section, we may say that in the Stimulus-Response Associationist type of learning theory, learning takes place through the establishment or strengthening of bonds between the stimulating conditions and the response. But for this to happen the stimulus, the response and the reinforcement must take place together in time. Responses which are followed by reductions of needs tend to be repeated, and those not followed by reward or need-reduction tend to disappear.

THE FIELD-COGNITION TYPE OF THEORY. Consider once more the rat placed in the maze. On the first few occasions, when it goes up blind alleys, its behaviour would be regarded by Tolman as a kind of exploration rather than as 'errors.'

5 Hull, C. L., *Principles of Behaviour: An Introduction to Behaviour Theory.* New York: Appleton Century, 1943.

6 'Reinforcement' is here used in the more restricted sense of reward or drive-reduction.

Even on the first run through the maze the rat appears to learn something, for on the second run less exploration is necessary. In a way, then, the rat becomes *aware* of his surroundings, and on later runs he behaves as though he was aware that certain responses would bring him to food, that is, as if he was guided by a kind of *cognitive theory.*

For Tolman,[7] learning depends upon what he calls 'cognitive maps,' which are built out of experience. The previous association of environmental events appearing in time suggest to the individual that by responding in a certain way to a particular situation, other specific events will follow. As a result of experience, the learner builds up new expectancies, realizations or cognitions; that is, he learns 'what will lead to what.' These 'cognitive maps' may be simple or comprehensive, depending upon the structure of the brain, motivation, relevant experience and practice, and the nature of the external stimuli. The more comprehensive the map, the more likely it is that transfer of training will take place. Tolman questions the whole notion of trial and error learning which appears to operate without meaning and purpose. When animals are put into a situation in which they can respond in different ways, he claims that they show systematic if not appropriate behaviour. If one type of systematic attack does not bring the animal to its goal, say a food box, then another kind of systematic attack is used. Indeed, the animal seems to act in accordance with a series of 'hypotheses' (so called by Krechevsky) or 'provisional maps.' Each of these hypotheses is linked with the one that went before it, so that as each is tried out the number of potential approaches is cut down until the problem is finally solved.

Field theorists like Lewin and Tolman believe that all behaviour is 'purposive' or 'goal directed.' Their theories are connected historically with Gestalt theory, which in turn suggests that the psychological field is always organised as well as possible. This is sometimes difficult as there may be conflicting factors in the field, but even so we do as well as we can. Thus in learning, field theory opposes the idea of blindness or randomness in the organism's movement. Even when the individual's responses are badly adapted to the environment (as in the neurotic), field theory maintains that there is an attempt to deal with the environmental situation, and that the attempt is purposeful to the individual concerned.

INSIGHT. Learning to solve problems is a matter of great interest to everyone connected with education. In this kind of learning some goal has to be reached but the way is not immediately clear. The individual often makes use of some of the following: the observation of relations, reasoning, generalization, and what the Gestalt psychologists call 'insight.' This term requires some explanation and to understand it we must go back to Thorndike's experiments mentioned before. It will be remembered that Thorndike believed that the cat used a purely 'trial and error' approach when attempting to get out of the box to eat

[7] Tolman, E. C., *Collected Papers in Psychology*. Berkeley, Calif., University of California Press, 1951. Also Tolman, E. C., 'Cognitive Maps in Rats and Men." *Psychol. Rev.*, 1948, **55**, 189–208.

the fish. Kohler,[8] however, in 1927, pointed out that Thorndike's problems were so arranged that it was hardly possible for the animal to solve them without such activity. A comparable situation for a human being would be to put him in a room, the door of which could be opened only by his treading on a small electric switch in the floor, the whole of the floor being covered by a carpet. The man would not be able to see at first even how to set about the problem, and a certain amount of examining the door, lock, walls, floor and so forth would be necessary however intelligent the man might be. Kohler maintained that, had the animal been able to survey the whole problem right from the start, in order to obtain a grasp of the situation as a whole from the beginning, then it would have been in a position to solve the problem.

In his own experiments, Kohler found that a chimpanzee, after looking at a problem for a while would suddenly solve it at a first attempt without making any false moves. This Kohler called *insight.* Thus a chimpanzee quickly learnt, after studying the situation, how to use a box as a stool from which to reach up to a suspended banana; but the stacking of several boxes to reach a higher object proved much more difficult for many of the animals. Even if they reached the objects, the boxes were often stacked in such a manner that they were unstable. In other words some had sufficient insight to solve the problem geographically but even so they could not always solve it mechanically.

One characteristic of good insight is *reproducibility*, that is, the animal when confronted with the situation once more, will quickly resort to the same solution. Another characteristic is the capacity to transfer the method of attack to other similar problems. Gestalt psychologists have generally spoken disparagingly of 'trial and error' behaviour, although they admit that such activity may change the situation in some ways so that a clearer view of the whole problem is obtained. Actually it seems that 'trial and error' behaviour is a necessary component of most problem-solving, though it may take place as a mental event rather than as overt behaviour. Gestalt theory holds that the organism *does* always organise its psychological field, and that the exploration and manipulation observed in 'trial and error' learning helped in such organisation. After each move, the psychological field is again reorganised until insight suddenly occurs. Looking at the matter another way, we may say that the animal sets up a series of 'provisional maps' or 'hypotheses' to solve the problem. Many of these may be tried out by behaviour internal to the animal which cannot be detected by the observer; others have to be tried out by external 'trial and error' behaviour. Note that previous relevant experience is of help; it permits of more comprehensive 'hypotheses' on which the animal can work.

LEARNING IN CHILDREN. We have seen, then, that there are two main schools of learning theory. Field cognition theorists suggest that the active learner attempts to give meaning to his experiences, and the insight that he is able to display is as 'good' as it can be in the circumstances. The function of the teacher is to present situations to his pupils in which the relationships involved

[8] Kohler's criticism had been anticipated by Hobhouse in 1901.

are not beyond their power of mental organisation. The children will then learn by direct insight. But the associationist would suggest that the job of the teacher is the forming of bonds of association and the 'stamping in' of those associations by repetition. Hence there is an emphasis on drill work and the need for motivating the learner. Each school has something to contribute to learning and teaching in the classroom where the children are mainly engaged in cognitive activities.

There is no doubt that the establishment of many simple habits like feeding, elimination, and sleeping, can be explained in terms of conditioning. Attempts have also been made to solve certain behaviour problems in children by means of conditioned response procedures. For example, a few experimenters have used a technique involving conditioning in curing enuresis (bed wetting).[9] In a typical study wire mesh sheets, separated by gauze, were placed in an electric circuit which included a bell. When the child commenced to urinate the gauze became wet and acted as a conductor of electricity; at the same time the bell rang (unconditioned stimulus). The child was awakened and went to the toilet to complete the passing of urine. After a number of trials bladder tension (now the conditioned stimulus) was enough to wake the child before the urination began. One worker reports that thirty cases between 3 and 13 years of age were cured by this means within two to three months. This technique would be most likely to be successful when enuresis is due to faulty training and not to emotional maladjustment. But in the usual classroom situation, the learning process is much more complex and cannot be explained on conditioning alone. Indeed, there is usually an interplay of associationist and field cognition theories.

It is possible for almost all children to have some degree of insight. If apes can show insight so can the dull child. Since Pavlov's dog organised its field of experience and noted relevant experiences in a situation that first appeared vague and meaningless, so insightful behaviour is possible at all levels of intelligence in children, provided the learning task is at the correct level of difficulty. On this view, the task of the teacher is to start from whatever insight his pupils possess and to direct them to new situations of the appropriate complexity which they can solve by insight. Essentially the new situation must be so arranged that the children are stimulated to ask themselves the right questions and to find for themselves the correct answers. They thereby tend to look upon themselves as organisers of their own environment and gain self-confidence. This helps children to think well of themselves and acts as a source of motivation. It is quite true that drill work will often be necessary, for successive repetition may bring 'partial insights,' and each of these may in turn provide opportunities for further acts of insight. In other words drill often helps to reduce the complexity of the overall situation and through a succession of partial insights we get complete insight—in short we piece together a number of small cues. This is very different from regarding the function of repetition as the mere 'stamping in' of correct associations. Again, once there has been some

9 Compare Mowrer, O. H., and Mowrer, W. M. Enuresis, a Method for its Study and Treatment,' *Amer. J. Orthopsychiat.*, 1938, **8**, 436–459.

understanding of the situation, or some achievement in solving the problem, repetition does away with conscious attention to the repeated act and leaves the child free to turn his attention to more complex issues.

Duncker,[10] Wertheimer[11] and many other psychologists have stressed that the most effective thinking occurs when use is made of insightful learning and their suggestions should be carefully noted by teachers. On the other hand, there will be occasions when the teacher will have to give the greater part of the material to his pupils in direct fashion, and learning will be likely to take place in the manner suggested by Hull.[12] Learning then depends upon adequate motivation. Indeed, when entirely new material has to be learnt in which the child has no sophistication at all, then learning seems to take place along the lines suggested by Hull, and reinforcement has to be immediate and informative. But if the child finds himself in a situation, fairly simple for him, and he has a rich background relative to the situation, then learning will take place using a field cognitive approach.

Skemp[13] has drawn attention to the fact that *schemata*—organisation of past impressions, and themselves the result of experience and learning—give meaning in all future learning. He points out that when a child first enters a new field, the elementary schemata first built up are of great consequence to all future learning in that field. Schematic learning is more efficient than rote learning, for at each stage the child builds a platform from which further advance may be made. The problem, practically, is how best to help a child to build adequate schemata at the beginning of a new learning situation. If such schemata could be built then we should certainly have more efficient learning, more effective recall, and a preparation for future learning. Moreover, while stimulus-response association theories may well account for some learning of content *within* any of the stages of thought, they seem unable to explain the move from one stage of thinking to the next. Likewise it seems that such theories are unable to explain how the child acquires adult language structures.

The way in which children actually solve problems is of great interest to teachers. Very often the solution depends upon their discovering some underlying principle or recognising some relationship. Many different types of experiments have been devised in this field, ranging from puzzle problems involving the use of apparatus, to problems demanding abstract reasoning; and ranging from simple to insoluble problems. The upshot of such investigations is that some sort of exploratory or manipulative behaviour is frequently used, helped by verbalization. But in other instances the various hypotheses are tested

10 Duncker, K., 'On Problem Solving,' *Psychol. Monogr.*, 1945, **58**, No. 270.

11 Wertheimer, M. *Productive Training.* Revised Edition. London: Tavistock, 1961.

12 The more formal type of teaching which proceeds logically from one step to the next and attempts to build up in the child's mind a coherent body of knowledge seems to be founded, even unconsciously, on associationism.

13 Skemp, R. R., 'The Need for a Schematic Theory of Learning', *Brit. J. Educ. Psychol.*, 1962, **32**, 133–142.

covertly; there is much transfer from other situations, and the child works out the correct moves.[14]

The following are among the most important factors influencing the learning process in children. These have been found by experiment and are not deduced from learning theory:

(*a*) *Intelligence.* The more intelligent the child, the more easily will he spot relevant relationships between objects or ideas, and apply them to new but similar situations. Thus we find, as we should expect, that bright children are superior to dull children in trial and error learning, and their superiority is even greater in insightful learning.

(*b*) *Age.* Mental Age increases with chronological age up to about 15–16 years. Thus learning takes place with increasing facility up to the school leaving age providing motivation is maintained. In some instances, mental age increases after 16 years.

(*c*) *Relevant experience.* The greater the relevant experience in some field, the easier in general will be the learning of fresh material in that particular field or in one closely allied to it.

(*d*) *Motivation.* The extent to which a child is motivated determines the energy he will put into the learning process. Either primary or secondary needs may be involved. Further, unless he is motivated (even if only to avoid punishment) he cannot be rewarded, hence there can be no reinforcement. Indeed, it is no exaggeration to say that one of our chief problems is to discover the best ways of motivating children so that they will learn.

(*e*) *Observation.* Noting the characteristic features of the learning situation, or spotting the exact nature of the stimuli, is essential. Furthermore, observation of results is important, since these results act as a reinforcement and serve as a guide towards better performance.

(*f*) *Reinforcement.* Reward plays a great part in determining which activities will be learnt. If a learnt activity is not rewarded, that activity tends not to reappear in future behaviour. The form that the reward can take depends upon the motivation, at that instant, of the particular child. Learnt behaviour that is rewarded by the teacher with praise or a 'star' will tend to recur, and learnt behaviour that brings blame will tend to disappear. The desire for recognition is a particularly strong motive in most children, especially in early school years. Reinforcement seems to be particularly important when children establish their moral-social values.

(*g*) *Repetition.* The learning of very simple activities may be accomplished on the first occasion when they are attempted. But with more complex activities, repetitions, suitably spaced, help the learning process considerably.

(*h*) *Concern.* There is evidence that a pupil's concern for the outcome of his study brings about conditions that help learning. We do not, of course, want anxiety in our pupils, let alone neurotic anxiety, but when they do not feel

14 See Duncker, K., *op. cit.*

uncomfortable in 'not knowing' they are unlikely to learn. Indeed, there can be little reinforcement. The concern or tension must, of course, be relieved after making the correct response.

PROGRAMMED INSTRUCTION. In recent years there has been a great increase of interest in the use of programmed instruction. Some of the approaches originate from the work of B. F. Skinner in the training of animals. In a way he stands in the tradition of Thorndike, and his rules for training may be stated briefly as follows:

a. Reinforce the desired behaviour as quickly and as frequently as possible.
b. Shape the behaviour in the desired way through a series of small steps.
c. Reinforce as far as possible by reward rather than by punishing. Some forms of automated teaching put these principles into effect.

In a typical teaching machine, there passes in front of the pupil a number of items illustrating, say, printed materials, diagrammatic materials demonstrating principles, statements of fact etc., and a question is asked about each. In the Skinner type of programme the student has to make up his response (a creative response) to each question, which he can then evaluate against the correct response given by the machine. Moreover, the step between each item is so small and well graded that the pupil can scarcely go wrong. In the type of programme devised by Crowder, however, there is a multiple-choice type of response. If the subject is correct he moves on to the next item; if he is wrong he has to work through a further item (selected by the machine) that will eradicate his error.

Wittrock and Twelker[15] studied the effects of prompting, i.e. the giving of extra information or prompting before the subject makes his response; also the effect of the giving of information after the response has been made, i.e. knowledge of correct response or reinforcement. It was found that prompted rules produced an effect on learning, retention, transfer, and time taken to learn. When little prompting had been given, knowledge of correct response also enhanced learning, where knowledge of correct response added to prompting did little to learning, retention and transfer, although it did not appear to reduce these. Such findings suggest that it is the initial presentation of the material that is important. They also run counter to the view that material should be so presented that learners make few mistakes *and* that it should receive immediate reinforcement.

The programmed textbook is another form of automated teaching. The correct response to each question appears on a later page together with the next item in the sequence. The instructions to the student might well read, 'Read each item, write your response on a separate sheet of paper, and turn to the page to see if the answer is correct.' Programmed textbooks are devised along the lines of either Skinner or Crowder. In the latter type of text an incorrect answer leads to a new piece of information related to, or a further discussion of, the

[15] Wittrock, M. C. and Twelker, P. A., 'Prompting and Feedback in the Learning, Retention, and Transfer of Concepts,' *Brit. J. Educ. Psychol.*, 1964, **34**, 10–18.

question just asked, while a correct answer leads to new information and another question.

Programmed instruction in school is probably better for structured subjects like mathematics; it may also have a future in further education, such as instruction in industry or the services. At the moment programmed textbooks are much cheaper than teaching machines. Simple but comprehensive surveys of the principles underlying automated teaching, including forms of such teaching which are developments beyond those of the 'linear' approach of Skinner and the 'branching' approach of Crowder, are listed below.[16] Moreover, these references review much relevant research.

There have been, of course, many critics of programmed instruction. Cronbach[17] has pointed out that automated teaching is the antithesis of the discovery method, while Wohlwill[18] has criticised the movement on the grounds that the programmers do not come to grips with what it is the child learns. Progressive steps in a programme are not related to each other by virtue of similarity of appearance or location (as in training animals). Rather, the steps are arranged in supposedly meaningful sequence, governed by the internal structure of the material to be learned and the semantic and syntactical characteristics of the verbal stimulation of which they are composed. It is an assumption that the principles that govern learning in the former situation, govern it in the latter. It is unlikely, however, that Cronbach's criticism is now valid. It seems possible to develop programmes that contain sufficient intuitive content of data and enough variety of actions to be performed by the child to facilitate the acquisition of new coordinating schemes using this term in the Piagetian sense.[19]

Programmed instruction of some kind has come to stay; it is both likely to prove a valuable aid in schools and to be of particular help in areas where teachers are in short supply. It seems likely that it must be considered in perspective along with other educational techniques and aids, each having its own advantages (or disadvantages) for specific tasks. Perhaps research should be directed towards the discovery of ways in which automated teaching can be

16 Green, E. J., *The Learning Process and Programmed Instruction.* New York: Holt, Rinehart and Winston, 1962. See also the *Times Educational Supplement*, 19th April 1963, 803–808. Another useful series of articles by Williams, J. D., Curr, W., Peel, E. A., Leith, G. O. M., under the general title 'Aspects of Programmed Instruction,' can be found in *Educ. Res.*, 1963, **5**, 163–99. A guide to the writing of programmes, including matrix construction and flow diagrams, is given in Thomas, C. A. *et al., Programmed Learning in Perspective.* London: City Publicity Services, 1963. Also *Educational Review*, Vol. 16, 1964 and its Supplements. Austwick, K. (Editor). *Teaching Machines and Programming.* Oxford: Pergamon Press, 1964. DeCecco, J. P., *Educational Technology.* New York, Holt, Rinehart and Winston, 1964. Leedham, J. & Unwin D., *Programmed Learning in the Schools.* London: Longmans, 1965. Kay, H., 'Programmed Instruction.' In *Educational Research in Britain* (Ed. Butcher, H. J.). London: University of London Press Ltd., 1968.

17 Cronbach, L. J. *Child and Education.* Copenhagen: Munksgaard, 1962, 145–146.

18 Wohlwill, J. F., 'The Teaching Machine: Psychology's new Hobbyhorse.' *Teachers College Record*, November 1962, 139–146.

19 Compare Leith, G. 'Developments in Programmed Learning.' *Trends in Education*, 1966, April, 20–26.

combined with other educational methods so as to provide the best possible instruction for different tasks and different student characteristics.[20]

COMPUTER AIDED INSTRUCTION (CAI). At a number of centres in the U.S.A. computer aided instruction is in use, at least on an experimental basis, even if the experience gained so far under practical classroom conditions is limited. A beginning in this field has also been made at the University of Leeds.

In essence CAI consists of information or a problem being displayed to the child, his response being evaluated by the computer, and a feedback message sent automatically to the child and a new item displayed. This new data may contain remedial material if his response was incorrect, or help if the child requested this, or it may be new information or a fresh problem. The information given to the subject can be by teletype or a cathode ray tube, while the computer can control a slide projector and a tape recorder. Thus while the slide is projecting fresh information or a new problem on the screen, the appropriate information can be given orally as well. The child for his part, can make his response by typing, pointing with a 'light pen' on a cathode ray tube, or use other rather sophisticated devices. Moreover, the large computers now available allow a number of subjects to work at the same time, each having his own teletype, cathode ray tube, etc.

CAI can use different logics depending upon the teaching strategy it is wished to employ. For example, material can be presented which merely requires the child to respond. Another logic presents problems which the child has to solve; but he may require additional information and so has to question the computer, which in turn responds by giving the help requested. The success of CAI is largely dependent upon the skill of the person who writes the lessons. He has to specify the teaching strategies that will cause the computer to select appropriate sequences of instruction to match each child's pattern of responses.

The computer can also make an analysis of the path each child took through the programme, the frames he used, the questions asked, the help requested, and the time taken. Indeed, the computer can present a wealth of detail about each pupil's path, performance and progress that no other means could provide so quickly and accurately. Such information is likely to throw light on children's learning and on their problem-solving strategies; also to pin-point specific difficulties for each child and thus enable a remedial programme to be written where this is necessary.

It must not be thought that CAI will be a panacea. There are many psychological problems involved in CAI, computers are expensive to purchase and service, and programmes take much skill and time to write. But it appears that it might play a major role in educational technology in the future.[21]

[20] See Coulson, J. E., 'Programmed Instruction: a Perspective.' *The Journal of Teacher Education,* 1963, **14**, 372–378.

[21] Coulson, J. E. 'Computer-Based Instruction.' *Int. Rev. of Education*, 1968, **14**, 140–152. See also *Programmed Learning and Educational Technology*, 1968, 5, whole number. Also Apter, M. J. *The New Technology in Education.* London: Macmillan, 1968.

NEUROTICISM, INTROVERSION AND LEARNING. Earlier evidence suggests that among both school children and students, the capacity for sustained work—and thus for good educational achievement—may be associated with a somewhat greater degree of neuroticism and introversion.[22] This had been found by comparing individuals of good and poor educational achievement. It must be stressed, however, that the position was not altogether clear in respect of the optimum degree of neuroticism for maximum scholastic attainment.

A later study by Entwistle and Cunningham[23] involved 2,707 children aged around 13 years in Aberdeen schools. Their evidence showed a linear relationship (i.e. a straight line relationship) between school attainment and neuroticism scores, the correlation coefficient being —·16. Thus children with high neuroticism scores tend to be less successful in scholastic attainments than children with low scores, although the size of the correlation is small. The finding was, however, true for both boys and girls. Further, Entwistle and Cunningham found that girls who are 'stable extraverts' and boys who are 'stable introverts' show the highest mean attainment scores. This data can, perhaps, be treated with more confidence than the earlier findings, which were often obtained from small and unrepresentative samples.

[22] Lynn, R., 'Individual Differences in Introversion-Extraversion, Reactive Inhibition and Reading Attainment.' *J. Educ. Psychol.*, 1960, 51, 318–321.
Lynn, R., and Gordon, I. E., 'The Relation of Neuroticism and Extraversion to Intelligence and Educational Attainment,' *Brit. J. Educ. Psychol.*, 1961, 31, 194-203. But Child, while finding a positive correlation between stable introversion and attainment in school examinations, found neither high nor moderate neuroticism advantageously related to attainment. See Child, D., 'The Relationship between Introversion, Extraversion, Neuroticism and performance in School Examinations.' *Brit. J. Educ. Psychol.*, 1964, 34, 187–196. See also Evans, E. G. S., 'Reasoning Ability and Personality Differences Among Student-Teachers.' *Brit. J. Educ. Psychol.*, 1964, 34, 305–314.

[23] Entwistle, N. J. and Cunningham, S. 'Neuroticism and School Attainment—a Linear Relationship,' *Brit. J. Educ. Psychol.*, 1968, **38**, 123–133.

Teaching and Training

GILBERT RYLE

I HAVE no teaching tricks or pedagogic maxims to impart to you, and I should not impart them to you if I had any. What I want to do is to sort out and locate a notion which is cardinal to the notions of teaching, training, education, etc. about which too little is ordinarily said. This notion is that of *teaching oneself* which goes hand in glove with the notion of *thinking for oneself*. You will all agree, I think, the teaching fails, that is, either the teacher is a failure or the pupil is a failure if the pupil does not sooner or later become able and apt to

Reprinted with permission of Humanities Press, Inc., New Jersey and Routledge & Kegan Paul Ltd. from "Teaching and Training" by Gilbert Ryle in *The Concept of Education* by R. S. Peters, ed., 1967, pp. 451–463.

arrive at his own solutions to problems. But how, in logic, can anyone be taught to do untaught things? I repeat, how, in logic, can anyone be taught to do untaught things?

To clear the air, let me begin by quickly putting on one side an unimportant but familiar notion, that of the self-taught man. Normally when we describe someone as a self-taught man we think of a man who, having been deprived of tuition from other teachers, tries to make himself an historian, say, or a linguist or an astronomer, without criticism, advice or stimulation from anyone else, save from the authors of such textbooks, encyclopaedia articles and linguaphone records as he may happen to hit on. He hits on these, of course, randomly, without having anyone or anything to tell him whether they are good ones, silly ones, old-fashioned ones or cranky ones. We admire the devotion with which he studies, but, save for the rare exception, we pity him for having been the devoted pupil only of that solitary and untrained teacher, himself. However, I am not interested in him.

What I am interested in is this. Take the case of an ordinary unbrilliant, unstupid boy who is learning to read. He has learned to spell and read monosyllables like 'bat,' 'bad,' 'at,' 'ring,' 'sing,' etc. and some two-syllable words like 'running,' 'dagger' and a few others. We have never taught him, say, the word 'batting.' Yet we find him quite soon reading and spelling unhesitantly the word 'batting.' We ask him who taught him this word and, if he remembers, he says that he had found it out for himself. He has learned from himself how the word 'batting' looks in print, how to write it down on paper and how to spell it out aloud, so in a sense he has taught himself this word—taught it to himself without yet knowing it. How can this be? How can a boy who does not know what 'b-a-t-t-i-n-g' spells teach himself what it spells?

In real life we are not a bit puzzled. It is just what we expect of a not totally stupid child. Yet there is the semblance of a conceptual paradox here, for we seem to be describing him as at a certain stage being able to teach himself something new, which *ipso facto* was not yet in his repertoire to teach. Here his teacher was as ignorant as the pupil, for they were the same boy. So how can the one learn something from the other?

What should we say? Well, clearly we want to say that the prior things that we *had* taught him, namely words like 'bat,' 'bad,' 'rat' and longer words like 'butter,' 'running' etc. enabled him and perhaps encouraged him to make a new bit of independent, uncoached progress on his own. We had taught him *how* to read some monosyllables, *how* to run some of them together in dissyllables, and so on. We had taught him a way or some ways of coping with combinations of printed letters, though not in their particular application to this new word 'batting.' He had made this particular application himself. So to speak, we had previously from the deck shown him the ropes and now he climbs one of them with his own hands and feet; that is to say, not being totally stupid, he was able and ready to employ this slightly general knowledge that we had given to him on a new concrete and particular problem that we had not solved for him. We had given him the wherewithal with which to think it out for himself—and this thinking out was his doing and not ours. I could just as well have taken an example from the much more sophisticated stratum where a brilliant undergraduate makes a good philosophical move that no one else has ever taught him, and maybe no one else has ever made.

Naturally, most often the boy or the undergraduate, if asked Who taught you that? would reply not that he had taught it to himself or that he had learned it from himself, but rather that he had found it out or thought it out or worked it out for himself. Just this brings out a big part of what interests me, namely, that though in one way it is obviously impossible for one person's own discovery, whether trivial or important, to be simply what someone else had previously taught him—since it would then not be his discovery—, yet in another way it is and ought to be one main business of a teacher precisely to get his pupils to advance beyond their instructions and to discover new things for themselves, that is, to get them to think things out for themselves. I teach Tommy to read a few words like 'bat,' 'run' and 'running' in order that he may then, of his own motion, find out how to read lots and lots of other words, like 'batting,' that we have not taught to him. Indeed we do not deem him really able to spell or read until he can spell and read things that he has not been introduced to. Nor, to leave the school-room for the moment, do I think that Tommy has learned to bicycle until he can do things on his own bicycle far more elaborate, speedy, tricky and delicate than the things I drilled him in on the first morning. I taught him the few elements on the first morning just in order that he might then find out for himself how to cope with hosts of non-elementary tasks. I gave him a few stereotyped exercises, and, as I had hoped and expected, in a couple of days he had developed for himself on this basis a fair wealth of boyish skills and dexterities, though he acquired these while I was away in London.

However, there remains a slight feeling of a puzzle or paradox here, and it comes, I think, from this source. A familiar and indispensable part or sort of teaching consists in teaching by rote lists of truths or facts, for example the proposition that 7 × 7 is 49, etc., the proposition that Waterloo was fought in 1815, etc., and the proposition that Madrid is the capital of Spain, etc. That the pupil has learned a lesson of this propositional sort is shown, in the first instance, by his being able and reasonably ready to reproduce word-perfectly these pieces of information. He gets them by heart, and he can come out with them on demand. Now every teacher knows that only a vanishingly small fraction of his teaching-day really consists in simply reciting lists of such snippets of information to pupils, but very unfortunately, it happens to be the solitary part which unschooled parents, sergeant-majors, some silly publicists and some educationalists always think of when they think of teaching and learning. They think or half-think that the request 'Recite what you have learned in school today, Tommy' is a natural and proper one, as if all that Tommy could or should have learned is a number of memorizable propositions; or as if to have learned anything consisted simply in being able to echo it, like a gramophone. As you all know, most teaching has nothing whatsoever in common with this crude, semi-surgical picture of teaching as the forcible insertion into the pupil's memory of strings of officially approved propositions; and I hope to show before long that even that small and of course indispensable part of instruction which is the imparting of factual information is grossly mis-pictured when pictured as literal cramming. Yet, bad as the picture is, it has a powerful hold over people's general theorizing about teaching and learning. Even Tommy's father, after spending the morning in teaching Tommy to swim, to dribble the football or to diagnose and repair what is wrong with the kitchen clock, in the afternoon cheerfully writes to the newspapers letters which take it for granted that all lessons are strings of memorizable propositions. His practice is perfectly sensible, yet still his theory is as silly as it could be.

Perhaps the prevalence of this very thin and partial notion of teaching and learning inherits something from the teaching and learning that are done in the nursery, where things such as 'Hickory Dickory Dock' and simple tunes are learned by heart from that mere vocal repetition which enables the parrot to pick them up too.

Well, in opposition to this shibboleth, I want to switch the centre of gravity of the whole topic onto the notions of Teaching-to so and so, and Learning-to so and so, that is, on to the notion of the development of abilities and competences. Let us forget for a while the memorization of truths, and, of course, of rhymes and tunes, and attend, instead, to the acquisition of skills, knacks and efficiencies. Consider, for example, lessons in drawing, arithmetic and cricket—and, if you like, in philosophy. These lessons cannot consist of and cannot even contain much of dictated propositions. However many true propositions the child has got by heart, he has not begun to learn to draw or play cricket until he has been given a pencil or a bat and a ball and has practised doing things with them; and even if he progresses magnificently in these arts, he will have little or nothing to reply to his parents if they ask him in the evening to recite to them the propositions that he has learned. He can *exhibit* what he has begun to master, but he cannot *quote* it. To avoid the ambiguity between 'teach' in the sense of 'teach that' and 'teach' in the sense of 'teach to' or 'teach how to,' I shall now sometimes use the word 'train.' The drawing-master, the language-teacher or the cricket-coach *trains* his pupils in drawing or in French pronunciation or in batting or bowling, and this training incorporates only a few items of quotable information. The same is true of philosophy.

Part, but only part of this notion of training is the notion of drilling, i.e. putting the pupil through stereotyped exercises which he masters by sheer repetition. Thus the recruit learns to slope arms just by going through the same sequence of motions time after time, until he can, so to speak, perform them in his sleep. Circus dogs and circus seals are trained in the same way. At the start piano-playing, counting and gear-changing are also taught by simple habituation. But disciplines do not reduce to such sheer drills. Sheer drill, though it is the indispensable beginning of training, is, for most abilities, only their very beginning. Having become able to do certain low-level things automatically and without thinking, the pupil is expected to advance beyond this point and to employ his inculcated automatisms in higher-level tasks which are not automatic and cannot be done without thinking. Skills, tastes and scruples are more than mere habits, and the disciplines and the self-disciplines which develop them are more than mere rote-exercises.

His translators and commentators have been very unjust to Aristotle on this matter. Though he was the first thinker, and is still the best, systematically to study the notions of ability, skill, training, character, learning, discipline, self-discipline, etc., the translators of his works nearly always render his key-ideas by such terms as 'habit' and 'habituation'—as if, for example, a person who has been trained and self-trained to play the violin, or to behave scrupulously in his dealings with other people acts from sheer habit, in the way in which I do tie up my shoelaces quite automatically and without thinking what I am doing or how to do it. Of course Aristotle knew better than this, and the Greek words that he used are quite grossly mistranslated when rendered merely by such words as 'habit' and 'habituation.' The well-disciplined soldier, who does indeed slope arms automatically, does not also shoot automatically or scout by blind habit or read maps like a marionette.

Nor is Tommy's control of his bicycle merely a rote-performance, though he cannot begin to control his bicycle until he has got some movements by rote. Having learned through sheer habit-formation to keep his balance on his bicycle with both hands on the handlebars, Tommy can now try to ride with one hand off, and later still with both hands in his pockets and his feet off the pedals. He now progresses by experimentation. Or, having got by heart the run of the alphabet from ABC through to XYZ, he can now, but not without thinking, tell you what three letters run *backwards* from RQP, though he has never learned by heart this reversed sequence.

I suggest that our initial seeming paradox, that a learner can sometimes of himself, after a bit of instruction, better his instructions, is beginning to seem less formidable. The possibility of it is of the same pattern as the familiar fact that the toddler who has this morning taken a few aided steps tries this afternoon with or without success to take some unaided steps. The swimmer who can now keep himself up in salt water, comes by himself, at first with a bit of extra splashing, to keep himself up in fresh water. How do any formerly difficult things change into now easy things? Or any once untried things into now feasible ones? The answer is just in terms of the familiar notions of the development of abilities by practice, that is trying and failing and then trying again and not failing so often or so badly, and so on.

Notoriously a very few pupils are, over some tasks, so stupid, idle, scared, hostile, bored or defective that they make no efforts of their own beyond those imposed on them as drill by their trainer. But to be non-stupid, vigorous and interested *is* to be inclined to make, if only as a game, moves beyond the drilled moves, and to practice of oneself, e.g. to multiply beyond 12×12, to run through the alphabet backwards, to bicycle with one hand off the handlebar, or to slope arms in the dark with a walking-stick when no drill-sergeant is there. As Aristotle says, 'The things that we have got to do when we have learned to do them, we learn to do by doing them.' What I can do today I could not do easily or well or successfully yesterday; and the day before I could not even try to do them; and if I had not tried unsuccessfully yesterday, I should not be succeeding today.

Before returning to go further into some of these key notions of ability, practice, trying, learning to, teaching to, and so on, I want to look back for a moment to the two over-influential notions of teaching *that* so and so, i.e. telling or informing, and of learning *that* so and so, i.e. the old notion of propositional cramming. In a number of nursery, school and university subjects, there are necessarily some or many true propositions to be accumulated by the student. He must, for example, learn that Oslo is the capital of Norway, Stockholm is the capital of Sweden and Copenhagen is the capital of Denmark. Or he must learn that the Battle of Trafalgar was fought in 1805 and that of Waterloo in 1815. Or that $7 + 5 = 12, 7 + 6 = 13, 7 + 7 = 14$, etc.

At the very start, maybe, the child just memorizes these strings of propositions as he memorizes 'Hickory Dickory Dock,' the alphabet or 'Thirty days hath September.' But so long as parroting is all he can do, he does not yet know the geographical fact, say, that Stockholm is the capital of Sweden, since if you ask him what Stockholm is the capital of, or whether Madrid is the capital of Sweden, he has no idea how to move. He can repeat, but he cannot yet use the memorized dictum. All he can do is to go through the memorized sequence of European capitals from start through to the required one. He does not qualify as knowing that Stockholm is the capital of Sweden until he can detach this proposition from the memorized rigmarole; and can, for example, answer new-type questions like 'Of which country out of the three, Italy, Spain and Sweden, is Stockholm the capital?' or 'Here is Stockholm on the globe—whereabouts is Sweden?' and so on. To know the geographical fact requires having taken it in, i.e. being able and ready to operate with it, from it, around it and upon it. To possess a piece of information is to be able to mobilize it apart from its rote-neighbours and out of its rote-formulation in unhackneyed and *ad hoc* tasks. Nor does the pupil know that $7 + 7 = 14$ while this is for him only a still undetachable bit of a memorized sing-song, but only when, for example, he can find fault with someone's assertion that $7 + 8 = 14$, or can answer the new-type question How many 7s are there in 14? or the new-type question 'If there are seven boys and seven girls in a room, how many children are in the room?' etc. Only then has he taken it in.

In other words, even to have learned the piece of information *that something is so* is more than merely to be able to parrot the original telling of it—somewhat as to have digested a biscuit is more than merely to have had it popped into one's mouth. Can he or can he not infer from the information that Madrid is the capital of Spain that Madrid is not in Sweden? Can he or can he not tell us what sea-battle occurred ten years before Waterloo?

Notice that I am not in the least deprecating the inculcation of rotes like the alphabet, the figures of the syllogism, 'Hickory Dickory Dock,' the dates of the Kings of England, or sloping arms. A person who has not acquired such rotes cannot progress from and beyond them. All that I am arguing is that he does not qualify as knowing even that Waterloo was fought in 1815 if all that he can do is to sing out out this sentence inside the sing-song of a memorized string of such sentences. If he can only echo the syllables that he has heard, he has not yet taken in the information meant to be conveyed by them. He has not grasped it if he cannot handle it. But if he could not even echo things told to him, *a fortiori* he could not operate with, from or upon their informative content. One cannot digest a biscuit unless it is first popped into one's mouth. So we see that even to have learned a true proposition is to have learned *to do* things other than repeating the words in which the truth had been dictated. To have learned even a simple geographical fact is to have become able to cope with some unhabitual geographical tasks, however elementary.

We must now come back to our central question: How is it possible that a person should learn from himself something which he previously did not know, and had not, e.g. been taught by someone else? This question is or embodies the apparently perplexing question: How can one person teach another person to think things out for himself, since if he gives him, say, the new arithmetical thoughts, then they are not the pupil's own thoughts; or if they are his own thoughts, then he did not get them from his teacher? Having led the horse to the water, how can we make him drink? But I have, I hope, shifted the centre of gravity of this seeming puzzle, by making the notions of *learning-to* and *teaching-to* the primary notions. In its new form the question is: How, on the basis of some tuition, can a person today get himself to do something which he had not been able to do yesterday or last year? How can competences, abilities and skills develop? How can trying ever succeed? We are so familiar, in practice, with the fact that abilities do develop, and that trying can succeed that we find little to puzzle us in the idea that they do.

Looked at from the end of the teacher the question is: How can the teacher get his pupil to make independent moves of his own? If this question is tortured into the shape: How can the teacher make or force his pupil to do things which he is not made or forced to do? i.e. How can the teacher be the initiator of the pupil's initiatives? the answer is obvious. He cannot. I cannot compel the horse to drink thirstily. I cannot coerce Tommy into doing spontaneous things. Either he is not coerced, or they are not spontaneous.

As every teacher, like every drill-sergeant or animal trainer knows in his practice, teaching and training have virtually not yet begun so long as the pupil is too young, too stupid, too scared or too sulky to respond—and to respond is not just to yield. Where there is a modicum of alacrity, interest or anyhow docility in the pupil, where he tries, however faintheartedly, to get things right rather than wrong, fast rather than slow, neat rather than awkward, where even, he registers even a slight contempt for the poor performances of others or chagrin at his own, pleasure at his own successes and envy of those of others, then he is, in however slight a degree, cooperating and so self-moving. He is doing something, though very likely not much, and is not merely having things done to him. He is, however unambitiously and however desultorily, attempting the still difficult. He has at least a little impetus of his own. A corner, however small a corner, of his heart is now in the task. The eager pupil is, of course, the one who, when taught, say, to read or spell a few words like 'at,' 'bat' and 'mat' travels home on the bus trying out, just for fun, all the other monosyllables that rhyme with 'at,' to see which of them are words. When taught to read and spell a dissyllable or two, he tries his hand, just for fun and often but not always unsuccessfully, on the polysyllables on the advertisement hoardings; and just for fun he challenges his father to spell long words when he gets home. He does this for fun; but like much play it is spontaneous self-practising. When he returns to school after the holidays, although his spelling and reading are now far in advance of their peak of last term, he will stoutly deny that he has done any work during the holidays. It has not been work, it has been absorption in a new hobby, like exercising a new limb.

His over-modest teacher may say that he has taught this boy next to nothing—nor has he, save for the very beginnings of everything.

However, we should remember that although a total absence of eagerness or even willingness spells total unteachability, the presence of energy, adventurousness and self-motion is not by itself enough. The wild guesser and the haphazard plunger have freedom of movement of a sort, but not of the best sort. Learning how to do new and therefore more or less difficult things does indeed require trying things out for oneself, but if this trying-out is not controlled by any testing or making sure, then its adventurousness is recklessness and not enterprise. He is like the gambler, not like the investor. The moves made, though spontaneous, are irresponsible and they yield no dividends. Nothing can be learned by him from their unsuccesses or from their occasional fortuitous successes. He shoots away, but learns nothing from his misses—or from his fluke hits.

It is just here, with the notion of taking care when taking risks, that there enters on the scenes the cardinal notion of *method*, i.e. of techniques, *modi operandi*, rules, canons, procedures, knacks, and even tricks of the trade. In doing a thing that he has never done before, a person may, but need not, operate according to a method, sometimes even according to a sheer drill that he has adhered to before. If he does, then his action is still an innovation, although the pattern of his action is a familiar and inculcated one. The poet composes a sonnet, taking care to adhere to the regulation 14 lines, to the regulation rhyming scheme, to the regulation metrical pattern, or else perhaps to one of the several permitted patterns—yet, nonetheless, his sonnet is a new one. No one has ever composed *it* before. His teacher who taught him how to compose sonnets had not and could not have made him compose this sonnet, else it would be the teacher's and not the pupil's sonnet. Teaching people how to do things just *is* teaching them methods or *modi operandi*; and it is just because it is one thing to have learned a method and another thing to essay a new application of it that we can say without paradox that the learner's new move is his own move and yet that he may have learned the *how* of making it from someone else. The cook's pudding is a new one and piping hot, but its recipe was known to Mrs. Beeton in the days of Queen Victoria.

Well, then, what sort of a thing is a method? First for what it is not. Despite what many folk would say, a method is not a stereotyped sequence-pattern or routine of actions, inculcatable by pure rote, like sloping arms or going through the alphabet. The parrot that can run through 'Hickory Dickory Dock' has not learned how to do anything or therefore how not to do it. There is nothing that he takes care not to do.

A method is a learnable way of doing something, where the word 'way' connotes more than mere rote, or routine. A way of doing something, or a *modus operandi*, is something general, and general in at least two dimensions. First, the way in which you do a thing, say mount your bicycle, can be the way or a way in which some other people or perhaps most other people mount or try to mount their bicycles. Even if you happen to be the only person who yet does something in a certain way, it is possible that others should in future learn from you or find out for themselves the very same way of doing it. *Modi operandi* are, in principle, public property, though a particular action performed in this way is my action and not yours, or else it is your action and not mine. We mount our bicycles in the same way, but my bicycle-mounting is my action and not yours. You do not make my mince pies, even though we both follow the same Victorian recipe.

The second way in which a method is something general is the obvious one, that there is no limit to the number of actions that may be done in that way. The method is, roughly, applicable anywhere and anywhen, as well as by anyone. For, however many people are known by me to have mounted their bicycles in a certain way, I know that there could have been and there could be going to be any number of other bicycle-mountings performed by myself and others in the same way.

Next, methods can be helpfully, if apparently cynically, thought of as systems of avoidances or as patterns of *don'ts.* The rules, say, of English grammar do not tell us positively what to say or write; they tell us negatively not to say or write such things as 'A dog *are* . . .' and 'The dogs *is* . . . ,' and learning the art of rock-climbing or tree-climbing is, among hundreds of other things, learning never, or hardly ever, to trust one's whole weight to an untried projection or to a branch that is leafless in summer time.

People sometimes grumble at the Ten Commandments on the score that most of them are prohibitions, and not positive injunctions. They have not realized that the notice 'Keep off the grass' licenses us to walk anywhere else we choose; where the notice 'Keep to the gravel' leaves us with almost no freedom of movement. Similarly to have learned a method is to have learned to take care against certain specified kinds of risk, muddle, blind alley, waste, etc. But carefully keeping away from this cliff and from that morass leaves the rest of the countryside open for us to walk lightheartedly in. If I teach you even twenty kinds of things that would make your sonnet a bad sonnet or your argument a bad argument, I have still left you an indefinite amount of elbow-room within which you can construct your own sonnet or argument, and this sonnet or argument of yours, whether brilliant or ordinary or weak, will at least be free of faults of those twenty kinds.

There exists in some quarters the sentimental idea that the teacher who teaches his pupils how to do things is hindering them, as if his apron-strings coerced their leg-movements. We should think of the inculcation of methods rather as training the pupils to avoid specified muddles, blockages, sidetracks and thin ice by training them to recognize these for what they are. Enabling them to avoid troubles, disasters, nuisances and wasted efforts is helping them to move where they want to move. Road signs are not, for the most part, impediments to the flow of traffic. They are preventives of impediments to the flow of traffic.

Of course we can easily think of silly ways of doing things which continue to be taught by grown-ups to children and adhered to by the grown-ups themselves. Not all methods are good methods, or all recipes good recipes. For example, the traditional ban on splitting the infinitive was a silly rule. But the gratuitous though trivial bother of conforming to this particular veto was negligible compared with the handicap that would be suffered by the child who had never been taught or had never picked up for himself any of the procedures for composing or construing sentences. He would have been kept back at the level of total infancy. He could not say or follow anything at all if, for example, he had not mastered conjunctions, or even verbs, and mastering them involves learning how *not* to make hashes of them.

How does one teach methods or ways of doing things? Well, there is no simple answer to this. Different arts and crafts require different kinds of disciplines; and in some one particular field, say drawing, one teacher works very differently from another. Sometimes a little, sometimes a lot can be told; there is much that cannot be told, but can be shown by example, by caricature and so on. But one thing is indispensable. The pupil himself must, whether under pressure or from interest or ambition or conscientiousness, practise doing what he is learning how to do. Whether in his exercises in the art he religiously models his strokes after Bradman, or whether he tries to win the praise or avoid the strictures or sarcasms of a feared, respected or loved coach, he learns by performing and improves by trying to better his own and his fellows' previous performances by eradicating their faults. The methods of operating taught to him become his personal methods of operating by his own criticized and self-criticized practice. Whether in spelling, in Latin grammar, fencing, arithmetic or philosophy, he learns the ropes, not much by gazing at them or hearing about them, but by trying to climb them—and by trying to climb them less awkwardly, slowly and riskily today than he did yesterday.

So far I have been, for simplicity, dividing the contributions of the teacher and the pupil by saying that the teacher in teaching how to so and so is teaching a method or way of operating, while the pupil keeps his initiative by making his own, at the start somewhat arduous, because new, applications of that method.

The teacher introduces the pupil to the ropes, but it is for the pupil to try to climb them.

But now we should pay some attention to the fact that pretty soon the pupil has become familiar with the quite general fact that for lots and lots of widely different kinds of operations—spelling, say, skating and bowling at cricket—there exist different *modi operandi.* There are spelling-mistakes and there are bowling-faults, and neither spelling nor bowling can go right unless these faults are systematically avoided. So now, when he undertakes an altogether new kind of operation, canoeing, say, he from the start expects there to be *modi operandi* here too. This too will be a thing that he will have to learn how to do, partly by learning how not to do it. But this time, it may be, there is no one to teach him, and not even any other canoeist to imitate. He has got to find out for himself the way, or anyhow a way, of balancing, propelling and steering his canoe. Well, at first he tries a lot of random things, and nearly all of them end in immersion or collision; but he does after a time find out some ways of managing his craft. He may not achieve elegance or speed, but he does find out how not to topple over and how not to run into obstacles. He is trained, this time purely self-trained, regularly to avoid some kinds of faulty watermanship. But it is because he had previously learned by practice, coaching and imitation the 'hows' of lots of other things such as tree-climbing, spelling and skating that he now takes it for granted that canoeing has its 'hows' as well, which similarly can be learned by practice, trial and error, and looking for ways of avoiding the repetition of errors. Here, as elsewhere, he has to study in order to improve; but this time he has nothing to study save his own unsuccesses and successes.

His more reckless and impatient brother, though full of go, just makes a dash at it, and then another quite different dash at it, and learns nothing or almost nothing from the failures which generally result, or even from the successes which sometimes just happen to result. He is not a self-trainer.

The third brother is uninterested, slow in the uptake, scared or idle. He never chances his arm. He tries nothing, and so initiates nothing either successfully or unsuccessfully. So he never learns to canoe; never, perhaps, even regrets not having learned it or envies those who have. There is no question of his training himself in this particular art, or even, if he is a very bad case, of his being trained by anyone else; just as there was fifty years ago no real question of me training myself or of my being trained by anyone else in the arts of cricket or music.

The supreme reward of the teacher is to turn out from time to time the student who comes to be not merely abreast of his teacher but ahead of him, the student, namely, who advances his subject or his craft not just by adding to it further applications of the established ways of operating but by discovering new methods or procedures of types which no one could have taught to him. He has given to his subject or his craft a new idea or a battery of new ideas. He is original. He himself, if of a grateful nature, will say that his original idea just grew of itself out of what he had learned from his teachers, his competitors and his colleagues; while they, if of a grateful nature, will say that the new idea was his discovery. Both will be right. His new idea is the fruit of a tree that others had planted and pruned. It is really his own fruit and he is really their tree.

We started off with the apparent paradox that though the teacher in teaching is doing something to his pupil, yet the pupil has learned virtually nothing unless he becomes able and ready to do things of his own motion other than what the teacher exported to him. We asked: How in logic can the teacher dragoon his pupil into thinking for himself, impose initiative upon him, drive him into self-motion, conscript him into volunteering, enforce originality upon him, or make him operate spontaneously? The answer is that he cannot—and the reason why we half felt that he must do so was that we were unwittingly enslaved by the crude, semi-hydraulic idea that in essence to teach is to pump propositions, like 'Waterloo, 1815' into the pupils' ears, until they regurgitate them automatically.

When we switched from the notion of 'hydraulic injection' to the notion of 'teaching to' or 'teaching how to,' the paradox began to disappear. I can introduce you to a way or the way of doing something, and still your actual essays in the exercise of this craft or competence are yours and not mine. I do not literally make you do them, but I do enable you to do them. I give you the *modus operandi*, but your operatings or tryings to operate according to this *modus* are your own doings and not my inflictings and the practising by which you master the method is your exertion and not mine. I have given you some equipment against failing, *if* you try. But that you try is not something that I can coerce. Teaching is not gate-shutting but gate-opening, yet still the dull or the scared or the lame calf does not walk out into the open field. All this does not imply the popular sentimental corollary that teachers should never be strict, demanding, peremptory or uncondoning. It is often the hard task-master who alone succeeds in instilling mistrust of primrose paths. The father may enlarge the child's freedom of movement by refusing to hold his hand, and the boxing-instructor or the philosophy-tutor may enlarge his pupil's powers of defence and attack by hitting him hard and often. It is not the chocolates and the sponge-cakes that strengthen the child's jaw-muscles. They have other virtues, but not this one.

Teaching Is Not Persuading

PLATO

Persons of the Dialogue

CALLICLES SOCRATES CHAEREPHON GORGIAS POLUS

SCENE:—*The house of Callicles*

Callicles. The wise man, as the proverb says, is late for a fray, but not for a feast.

Socrates. And are we late for a feast?

Excerpted from *Gorgias* by Plato.

Cal. Yes, and a delightful feast; for Gorgias has just been exhibiting to us many fine things.

Soc. It is not my fault, Callicles; our friend Chaerephon is to blame; for he would keep us loitering in the Agora.

Chaerephon. Never mind, Socrates; the misfortune of which I have been the cause I will also repair; for Gorgias is a friend of mine, and I will make him give the exhibition again either now, or, if you prefer, at some other time.

Cal. What is the matter, Chaerephon—does Socrates want to hear Gorgias?

Chaer. Yes, that was our intention in coming.

Cal. Come into my house, then; for Gorgias is staying with me, and he shall exhibit to you.

Soc. Very good, Callicles; but will he answer our questions? for I want to hear from him what is the nature of his art, and what it is which he professes and teaches; he may, as you [Chaerephon] suggest, defer the exhibition to some other time.

Cal. There is nothing like asking him, Socrates: and indeed to answer questions is a part of his exhibition, for he was saying only just now, that any one in my house might put any question to him, and that he would answer.

Soc. How fortunate! will you ask him, Chaerephon—?

Chaer. What shall I ask him?

Soc. Ask him who he is.

Chaer. What do you mean?

Soc. I mean such a question as would elicit from him, if he had been a maker of shoes, the answer that he is a cobbler. Do you understand?

Chaer. I understand, and will ask him: Tell me, Gorgias, is our friend Callicles right in saying that you undertake to answer any questions which you are asked?

Gorgias. Quite right, Chaerephon: I was saying as much only just now; and I may add, that many years have elapsed since any one has asked me a new one.

Chaer. Then you must be very ready, Gorgias.

Gor. Of that, Chaerephon, you can make trial.

Polus. Yes, indeed, and if you like, Chaerephon, you may make trial of me too, for I think that Gorgias, who has been talking a long time, is tired.

Chaer. And do you, Polus, think that you can answer better than Gorgias?

Pol. What does that matter if I answer well enough for you?

Chaer. Not at all:—and you shall answer if you like.

Pol. Ask:—

Chaer. My question is this: If Gorgias had the skill of his brother Herodicus, what ought we to call him? Ought he not to have the name which is given to his brother?

Pol. Certainly.

Chaer. Then we should be right in calling him a physician?

Pol. Yes.

Chaer. And if he had the skill of Aristophon the son of Aglaophon, or of his brother Polygnotus, what ought we to call him?

Pol. Clearly, a painter.

Chaer. But now what shall we call him—what is the art in which he is skilled?

Pol. O Chaerephon, there are many arts among mankind which are experimental, and have their origin in experience, for experience makes the days of men to proceed according to art, and inexperience according to chance, and different persons in different ways are proficient in different arts, and the best persons in the best arts. And our friend Gorgias is one of the best, and the art in which he is a proficient is the noblest.

Soc. Polus has been taught how to make a capital speech, Gorgias; but he is not fulfilling the promise which he made to Chaerephon.

Gor. What do you mean, Socrates?

Soc. I mean that he has not exactly answered the question which he was asked.

Gor. Then why not ask him yourself?

Soc. But I would much rather ask you, if you are disposed to answer: for I see, from the few words which Polus has uttered, that he has attended more to the art which is called rhetoric than to dialectic.

Pol. What makes you say so, Socrates?

Soc. Because, Polus, when Chaerephon asked you what was the art which Gorgias knows, you praised it as if you were answering some one who found fault with it, but you never said what the art was.

Pol. Why, did I not say that it was the noblest of arts?

Soc. Yes, indeed, but that was no answer to the question: nobody asked what was the quality, but what was the nature, of the art, and by what name we were to describe Gorgias. And I would still beg you briefly and clearly, as you answered Chaerephon when he asked you at first, to say what this art is, and what we ought to call Gorgias: Or rather, Gorgias, let me turn to you, and ask the same question,—what are we to call you, and what is the art which you profess?

Gor. Rhetoric, Socrates, is my art.

Soc. Then I am to call you a rhetorician?

Gor. Yes, Socrates, and a good one too, if you would call me that which, in Homeric language, 'I boast myself to be.'

Soc. I should wish to do so.

Gor. Then pray do.

Soc. And are we to say that you are able to make other men rhetoricians?

Gor. Yes, that is exactly what I profess to make them, not only at Athens, but in all places.

Soc. And will you continue to ask and answer questions, Gorgias, as we are at present doing, and reserve for another occasion the longer mode of speech which Polus was attempting? Will you keep your promise, and answer shortly the questions which are asked of you?

Gor. Some answers, Socrates, are of necessity longer; but I will do my best to make them as short as possible; for a part of my profession is that I can be as short as any one.

Soc. That is what is wanted, Gorgias; exhibit the shorter method now, and the longer one at some other time.

Gor. Well, I will; and you will certainly say, that you never heard a man use fewer words.

Soc. Very good then; as you profess to be a rhetorician, and a maker of rhetoricians, let me ask you, with what is rhetoric concerned: I might ask with what is weaving concerned, and you would reply (would you not?), with the making of garments?

Gor. Yes.

Soc. And music is concerned with the composition of melodies?

Gor. It is.

Soc. By Herè, Gorgias, I admire the surpassing brevity of your answers.

Gor. Yes, Socrates, I do think myself good at that.

Soc. I am glad to hear it; answer me in like manner about rhetoric: with what is rhetoric concerned?

Gor. With discourse.

Soc. What sort of discourse, Gorgias?—such discourse as would teach the sick under what treatment they might get well?

Gor. No.

Soc. Then rhetoric does not treat of all kinds of discourse?

Gor. Certainly not.

Soc. And yet rhetoric makes men able to speak?

Gor. Yes.

Soc. And to understand that about which they speak?

Gor. Of course.

Soc. But does not the art of medicine, which we were just now mentioning, also make men able to understand and speak about the sick?

Gor. Certainly.

Soc. Then medicine also treats of discourse?

Gor. Yes.

Soc. Of discourse concerning diseases?

Gor. Just so.

Soc. And does not gymnastic also treat of discourse concerning the good or evil condition of the body?

Gor. Very true.

Soc. And the same, Gorgias, is true of the other arts:—all of them treat of discourse concerning the subjects with which they severally have to do.

Gor. Clearly.

Soc. Then why, if you call rhetoric the art which treats of discourse, and all the other arts treat of discourse, do you not call them arts of rhetoric?

Gor. Because, Socrates, the knowledge of the other arts has only to do with some sort of external action, as of the hand; but there is no such action of the hand in rhetoric which works and takes effect only through the medium of discourse. And therefore I am justified in saying that rhetoric treats of discourse.

Soc. I am not sure whether I entirely understand you, but I dare say I shall soon know better; please to answer me a question:—you would allow that there are arts?

Gor. Yes.

Soc. As to the arts generally, they are for the most part concerned with doing, and require little or no speaking; in painting, and statuary, and many other arts, the work may proceed in silence; and of such arts I suppose you would say that they do not come within the province of rhetoric.

Gor. You perfectly conceive my meaning, Socrates.

Soc. But there are other arts which work wholly through the medium of language, and require either no action or very little, as, for example, the arts of arithmetic, of calculation, of geometry, and of playing draughts; in some of these speech is pretty nearly co-extensive with action, but in most of them the verbal element is greater—they depend wholly on words for their efficacy and power: and I take your meaning to be that rhetoric is an art of this latter sort?

Gor. Exactly.

Soc. And yet I do not believe that you really mean to call any of these arts rhetoric; although the precise expression which you used was, that rhetoric is an art which works and takes effect only through the medium of discourse; and an adversary who wished to be captious might say, 'And so, Gorgias, you call arithmetic rhetoric.' But I do not think that you really call arithmetic rhetoric any more than geometry would be so called by you.

Gor. You are quite right, Socrates, in your apprehension of my meaning.

Soc. Well, then, let me now have the rest of my answer:—seeing that rhetoric is one of those arts which works mainly by the use of words, and there are other arts which also use words, tell me what is that quality in words with which rhetoric is concerned:—Suppose that a person asks me about some of the arts which I was mentioning just now; he might say, 'Socrates, what is arithmetic?' and I should reply to him, as you replied to me, that arithmetic is one of those arts which take effect through words. And then he would proceed to ask: 'Words about what?' and I should reply, Words about odd and even numbers, and how many there are of each. And if he asked again: 'What is the art of calculation?' I should say, That also is one of the arts which is concerned wholly with words. And if he further said, 'Concerned with what?' I should say, like the clerks in the assembly, 'as aforesaid' of arithmetic, but with a difference, the difference being that the art of calculation considers not only the quantities of odd and even numbers, but also their numerical relations to themselves and to one another. And suppose, again, I were to say that astronomy is only words—he would ask, 'Words about what, Socrates?' and I should answer, that astronomy tells us about the motions of the stars and sun and moon, and their relative swiftness.

Gor. You would be quite right, Socrates.

Soc. And now let us have from you, Gorgias, the truth about rhetoric: which you would admit (would you not?) to be one of those arts which act always and fulfil all their ends through the medium of words?

Gor. True.

Soc. Words which do what? I should ask. To what class of things do the words which rhetoric uses relate?

Gor. To the greatest, Socrates, and the best of human things.

Soc. That again, Gorgias, is ambiguous; I am still in the dark: for which are the greatest and best of human things? I dare say that you have heard men singing at feasts the old drinking song, in which the singers enumerate the goods of life, first health, beauty next, thirdly, as the writer of the song says, wealth honestly obtained.

Gor. Yes, I know the song; but what is your drift?

Soc. I mean to say, that the producers of those things which the author of the song praises, that is to say, the physician, the trainer, the money-maker, will at once come to you, and first the physician will say: 'O Socrates, Gorgias is deceiving you, for my art is concerned with the greatest good of men and not his.' And when I ask, Who are you? he will reply, 'I am a physician.' What do you mean? I shall say. Do you mean that your art produces the greatest good? 'Certainly,' he will answer, 'for is not health the greatest good? What greater good can men have, Socrates?' And after him the trainer will come and say, 'I too, Socrates, shall be greatly surprised if Gorgias can show more good of his art than I can show of mine.' To him again I shall say, Who are you, honest friend, and what is your business? 'I am a trainer,' he will reply, 'and my business is to make men beautiful and strong in body.' When I have done with the trainer, there arrives the money-maker, and he, as I expect, will utterly despise them all. 'Consider, Socrates,' he will say, 'whether Gorgias or any one else can produce any greater good than wealth.' Well, you and I say to him, and are you a creator of wealth? 'Yes,' he replies. And who are you? 'A money-maker.' And do you consider wealth to be the greatest good of man? 'Of course,' will be his reply. And we shall rejoin: Yes; but our friend Gorgias contends that his art produces a greater good than yours. And then he will be sure to go on and ask, 'What good? Let Gorgias answer.' Now I want you, Gorgias, to imagine that this question is asked of you by them and by me; What is that which, as you say, is the greatest good of man, and of which you are the creator? Answer us.

Gor. That good, Socrates, which is truly the greatest, being that which gives to men freedom in their own persons, and to individuals the power of ruling over others in their several states.

Soc. And what would you consider this to be?

Gor. What is there greater than the word which persuades the judges in the courts, or the senators in the council, or the citizens in the assembly, or at any other political meeting?—if you have the power of uttering this word, you will have the physician your slave, and the trainer your slave, and the money-maker of whom you talk will be found to gather treasures, not for himself, but for you who are able to speak and to persuade the multitude.

Soc. Now I think, Gorgias, that you have very accurately explained what you conceive to be the art of rhetoric; and you mean to say, if I am not mistaken, that rhetoric is the artificer of persuasion, having this and no other business, and that this is her crown and end. Do you know any other effect of rhetoric over and above that of producing persuasion?

Gor. No: the definition seems to me very fair, Socrates: for persuasion is the chief end of rhetoric.

Soc. Then hear me, Gorgias, for I am quite sure that if there ever was a man who entered on the discussion of a matter from a pure love of knowing the truth, I am such a one, and I should say the same of you.

Gor. What is coming, Socrates?

Soc. I will tell you: I am very well aware that I do not know what, according to you, is the exact nature, or what are the topics of that persuasion of which you speak, and which is given by rhetoric; although I have a suspicion about both the one and the other. And I am going to ask—what is this power of persuasion which is given by rhetoric, and about what? But why, if I have a suspicion, do I ask instead of telling you? Not for your sake, but in order that the argument may proceed in such a manner as is most likely to set forth the truth. And I would have you observe, that I am right in asking this further question: If I asked, 'What sort of a painter is Zeuxis?' and you said, 'The painter of figures,' should I not be right in asking, 'What kind of figures, and where do you find them?'

Gor. Certainly.

Soc. And the reason for asking this second question would be, that there are other painters besides, who paint many other figures?

Gor. True.

Soc. But if there had been no one but Zeuxis who painted them, then you would have answered very well?

Gor. Quite so.

Soc. Now I want to know about rhetoric in the same way;—is rhetoric the only art which brings persuasion, or do other arts have the same effect? I mean to say—Does he who teaches anything persuade men of that which he teaches or not?

Gor. He persuades, Socrates,—there can be no mistake about that.

Soc. Again, if we take the arts of which we were just now speaking:—do not arithmetic and the arithmeticians teach us the properties of number?

Gor. Certainly.

Soc. And therefore persuade us of them?

Gor. Yes.

Soc. Then arithmetic as well as rhetoric is an artificer of persuasion?

Gor. Clearly.

Soc. And if any one asks us what sort of persuasion, and about what,—we shall answer, persuasion which teaches the quantity of odd and even; and we shall be able to show that all the other arts of which we were just now speaking are artificers of persuasion, and of what sort, and about what.

Gor. Very true.

Soc. Then rhetoric is not the only artificer of persuasion?

Gor. True.

Soc. Seeing, then, that not only rhetoric works by persuasion, but that other arts do the same, as in the case of the painter, a question has arisen which is a very fair one: Of which persuasion is rhetoric the artificer, and about what?—is not that a fair way of putting the question?

Gor. I think so.

Soc. Then, if you approve the question, Gorgias, what is the answer?

Gor. I answer, Socrates, that rhetoric is the art of persuasion in courts of law and other assemblies, as I was just now saying, and about the just and unjust.

Soc. And that, Gorgias, was what I was suspecting to be your notion; yet I would not have you wonder if by-and-by I am found repeating a seemingly plain question; for I ask not in order to confute you, but as I was saying that the argument may proceed consecutively, and that we may not get the habit of anticipating and suspecting the meaning of one another's words; I would have you develop your own views in your own way, whatever may be your hypothesis.

Gor. I think that you are quite right, Socrates.

Soc. Then let me raise another question; there is such a thing as 'having learned'?

Gor. Yes.

Soc. And there is also 'having believed'?

Gor. Yes.

Soc. And is the 'having learned' the same as 'having believed,' and are learning and belief the same things?

Gor. In my judgment, Socrates, they are not the same.

Soc. And your judgment is right, as you may ascertain in this way:—if a person were to say to you, 'Is there, Gorgias, a false belief as well as a true?'—you would reply, if I am not mistaken, that there is.

Gor. Yes.

Soc. Well, but is there a false knowledge as well as a true?

Gor. No.

Soc. No, indeed; and this again proves that knowledge and belief differ.

Gor. Very true.

Soc. And yet those who have learned as well as those who have believed are persuaded?

Gor. Just so.

Soc. Shall we then assume two sorts of persuasion,—one which is the source of belief without knowledge, as the other is of knowledge?

Gor. By all means.

Soc. And which sort of persuasion does rhetoric create in courts of law and other assemblies about the just and unjust, the sort of persuasion which gives belief without knowledge, or that which gives knowledge?

Gor. Clearly, Socrates, that which only gives belief.

Soc. Then rhetoric, as would appear, is the artificer of a persuasion which creates belief about the just and unjust, but gives no instruction about them?

Gor. True.

Soc. And the rhetorician does not instruct the courts of law or other assemblies about things just and unjust, but he creates belief about them; for no one can be supposed to instruct such a vast multitude about such high matters in a short time?

Gor. Certainly not.

Soc. Come, then, and let us see what we really mean about rhetoric; for I do not know what my own meaning is as yet. When the assembly meets to elect a physician or a shipwright or any other craftsman, will the rhetorician be taken into counsel? Surely not. For at every election he ought to be chosen who is most skilled; and, again, when walls have to be built or harbours or docks to be constructed, not the rhetorician but the master workman will advise; or when generals have to be chosen and an order of battle arranged, or a proposition taken, then the military will advise and not the rhetoricians: what do you say, Gorgias? Since you profess to be a rhetorician and a maker of rhetoricians, I cannot do better than learn the nature of your art from you. And here let me assure you that I have your interest in view as well as my own. For likely enough some one or other of the young men present might desire to become your pupil, and in fact I see some, and a good many too, who have this wish, but they would be too modest to question you. And therefore when you are interrogated by me, I would have you imagine that you are interrogated by them. 'What is the use of coming to you, Gorgias?' they will say—'about what will you teach us to advise the state?—about the just and unjust only, or about those other things also which Socrates has just mentioned?' How will you answer them?

Gor. I like your way of leading us on, Socrates, and I will endeavour to reveal to you the whole nature of rhetoric. You must have heard, I think, that the docks and the walls of the Athenians and the plan of the harbour were devised in accordance with the counsels, partly of Themistocles, and partly of Pericles, and not at the suggestion of the builders.

Soc. Such is the tradition, Gorgias, about Themistocles; and I myself heard the speech of Pericles when he advised us about the middle wall.

Gor. And you will observe, Socrates, that when a decision has to be given in such matters the rhetoricians are the advisers; they are the men who win their point.

Soc. I had that in my admiring mind, Gorgias, when I asked what is the nature of rhetoric, which always appears to me, when I look at the matter in this way, to be a marvel of greatness.

Gor. A marvel, indeed, Socrates, if you only knew how rhetoric comprehends and holds under her sway all the inferior arts. Let me offer you a striking example of this. On several occasions I have been with my brother Herodicus or some other physician to see one of his patients, who would not allow the physician to give him medicine, or apply a knife or hot iron to him; and I have persuaded him to do for me what he would not do for the physician just by the use of rhetoric. And I say that if a rhetorician and a physician were to go to any city, and had there to argue in the Ecclesia or any other assembly as to which of them should be elected state-physician, the physician would have no chance;

but he who could speak would be chosen if he wished; and in a contest with a man of any other profession the rhetorician more than any one would have the power of getting himself chosen, for he can speak more persuasively to the multitude than any of them, and on any subject. Such is the nature and power of the art of rhetoric! And yet, Socrates, rhetoric should be used like any other competitive art, not against everybody,—the rhetorician ought not to abuse his strength any more than a pugilist or pancratiast or other master of fence;—because he has powers which are more than a match either for friend or enemy, he ought not therefore to strike, stab, or slay his friends. Suppose a man to have been trained in the palestra and to be a skilful boxer,—he in the fulness of his strength goes and strikes his father or mother or one of his familiars or friends; but that is no reason why the trainers or fencing-masters should be held in detestation or banished from the city;—surely not. For they taught their art for a good purpose, to be used against enemies and evil-doers, in self-defence not in aggression, and others have perverted their instructions, and turned to a bad use their own strength and skill. But not on this account are the teachers bad, neither is the art in fault, or bad in itself; I should rather say that those who make a bad use of the art are to blame. And the same argument holds good of rhetoric; for the rhetorician can speak against all men and upon any subject,—in short, he can persuade the multitude better than any other man of anything which he pleases, but he should not therefore seek to defraud the physician or any other artist of his reputation merely because he has the power; he ought to use rhetoric fairly, as he would also use his athletic powers. And if after having become a rhetorician he makes a bad use of his strength and skill, his instructor surely ought not on that account to be held in detestation or banished. For he was intended by his teacher to make a good use of his instructions, but he abuses them. And therefore he is the person who ought to be held in detestation, banished, and put to death, and not his instructor.

Soc. You, Gorgias, like myself, have had great experience of disputations, and you must have observed, I think, that they do not always terminate in mutual edification, or in the definition by either party of the subjects which they are discussing: but disagreements are apt to arise—somebody says that another has not spoken truly or clearly; and then they get into a passion and begin to quarrel, both parties conceiving that their opponents are arguing from personal feeling only and jealousy of themselves, not from any interest in the question at issue. And sometimes they will go on abusing one another until the company at last are quite vexed at themselves for ever listening to such fellows. Why do I say this? Why, because I cannot help feeling that you are now saying what is not quite consistent or accordant with what you were saying at first about rhetoric. And I am afraid to point this out to you, lest you should think that I have some animosity against you, and that I speak, not for the sake of discovering the truth, but from jealousy of you. Now if you are one of my sort, I should like to cross-examine you, but if not I will let you alone. And what is my sort? you will ask. I am one of those who are very willing to be refuted if I say anything which is not true, and very willing to refute any one else who says what is not true, and quite as ready to be refuted as to refute; for I hold that this is the greater gain of the two, just as the gain is greater of being cured of a very great evil than of curing another. For I imagine that there is no evil which a man can endure so great as an erroneous opinion about the matters of which we are speaking, and if you claim to be one of my sort, let us have the discussion out, but if you would rather have done, no matter;—let us make an end of it.

Gor. I should say, Socrates, that I am quite the man whom you indicate; but, perhaps, we ought to consider the audience, for, before you came, I had already given a long exhibition, and if we proceed the argument may run on to a great length. And therefore I think that we should consider whether we may not be detaining some part of the company when they are wanting to do something else.

Chaer. You hear the audience cheering, Gorgias and Socrates, which shows their desire to listen to you; and for myself, Heaven forbid that I should have any business on hand which would take me away from a discussion so interesting and so ably maintained.

Cal. By the gods, Chaerephon, although I have been present at many discussions, I doubt whether I was ever so much delighted before, and therefore if you go on discoursing all day I shall be the better pleased.

Soc. I may truly say, Callicles, that I am willing, if Gorgias is.

Gor. After all this, Socrates, I should be disgraced if I refused, especially as I have promised to answer all comers; in accordance with the wishes of the company, then, do you begin, and ask of me any question which you like.

Soc. Let me tell you then, Gorgias, what surprises me in your words; though I dare say that you may be right, and I may have misunderstood your meaning. You say that you can make any man, who will learn of you, a rhetorician?

Gor. Yes.

Soc. Do you mean that you will teach him to gain the ears of the multitude on any subject, and this not by instruction but by persuasion?

Gor. Quite so.

Soc. You were saying, in fact, that the rhetorician will have greater powers of persuasion than the physician even in a matter of health?

Gor. Yes, with the multitude,—that is.

Soc. You mean to say, with the ignorant; for with those who know he cannot be supposed to have greater powers of persuasion.

Gor. Very true.

Soc. But if he is to have more power of persuasion than the physician, he will have greater power than he who knows?

Gor. Certainly.

Soc. Although he is not a physician:—is he?

Gor. No.

Soc. And he who is not a physician must, obviously, be ignorant of what the physician knows.

Gor. Clearly.

Soc. Then, when the rhetorician is more persuasive than the physician, the ignorant is more persuasive with the ignorant than he who has knowledge?—is not that the inference?

Gor. In the case supposed:—Yes.

Soc. And the same holds of the relation of rhetoric to all the other arts; the rhetorician need not know the truth about things; he has only to discover some way of persuading the ignorant that he has more knowledge than those who know?

Gor. Yes, Socrates, and is not this a great comfort?—not to have learned the other arts, but the art of rhetoric only, and yet to be in no way inferior to the professors of them?

Soc. Whether the rhetorician is or is not inferior on this account is a question which we will hereafter examine if the enquiry is likely to be of any service to us; but I would rather begin by asking whether he is or is not as ignorant of the just and unjust, base and honourable, good and evil, as he is of medicine and the other arts; I mean to say, does he really know anything of what is good and evil, base or honourable, just or unjust in them; or has he only a way with the ignorant of persuading them that he not knowing is to be esteemed to know more about these things than some one else who knows? Or must the pupil know these things and come to you knowing them before he can acquire the art of rhetoric? If he is ignorant, you who are the teacher of rhetoric will not teach him—it is not your business; but you will make him seem to the multitude to know them, when he does not know them; and seem to be a good man, when he is not. Or will you be unable to teach him rhetoric at all, unless he knows the truth of these things first? What is to be said about all this? By heavens, Gorgias, I wish that you would reveal to me the power of rhetoric, as you were saying that you would.

Gor. Well, Socrates, I suppose that if the pupil does chance not to know them, he will have to learn of me these things as well.

Soc. Say no more, for there you are right; and so he whom you make a rhetorician must either know the nature of the just and unjust already, or he must be taught by you.

Gor. Certainly.

Soc. Well, and is not he who has learned carpentering a carpenter?

Gor. Yes.

Soc. And he who has learned music a musician?

Gor. Yes.

Soc. And he who has learned medicine is a physician, in like manner? He who has learned anything whatever is that which his knowledge makes him.

Gor. Certainly.

Soc. And in the same way, he who has learned what is just is just?

Gor. To be sure.

Soc. And he who is just may be supposed to do what is just?

Gor. Yes.

Soc. And must not the just man always desire to do what is just?

Gor. That is clearly the inference.

Soc. Surely, then, the just man will never consent to do injustice?

Gor. Certainly not.

Soc. And according to the argument the rhetorician must be a just man?

Gor. Yes.

Soc. And will therefore never be willing to do injustice?

Gor. Clearly not.

Soc. But do you remember saying just now that the trainer is not to be accused or banished if the pugilist makes a wrong use of his pugilistic art; and in like manner, if the rhetorician makes a bad and unjust use of rhetoric, that is not to be laid to the charge of his teacher, who is not to be banished, but the wrong-doer himself who made a bad use of his rhetoric—he is to be banished—was not that said?

Gor. Yes, it was.

Soc. But now we are affirming that the aforesaid rhetorician will never have done injustice at all?

Gor. True.

Soc. And at the very outset, Gorgias, it was said that rhetoric treated of discourse, not [like arithmetic] about odd and even, but about just and unjust? Was not this said?

Gor. Yes.

Soc. I was thinking at the time, when I heard you saying so, that rhetoric, which is always discoursing about justice, could not possibly be an unjust thing. But when you added, shortly afterwards, that the rhetorician might make a bad use of rhetoric I noted with surprise the inconsistency into which you had fallen; and I said, that if you thought, as I did, that there was a gain in being refuted, there would be an advantage in going on with the question, but if not, I would leave off. And in the course of our investigations, as you will see yourself, the rhetorician has been acknowledged to be incapable of making an unjust use of rhetoric, or of willingness to do injustice. By the dog, Gorgias, there will be a great deal of discussion, before we get at the truth of all this.

The True Is the Useful

WILLIAM JAMES

WHEN Clerk-Maxwell was a child it is written that he had a mania for having everything explained to him, and that when people put him off with vague verbal accounts of any phenomenon he would interrupt them impatiently by saying, 'Yes; but I want you to tell me the *particular go* of it!' Had his question been about truth, only a pragmatist could have told him the particular go of it. I believe that our contemporary pragmatists, especially Messrs. Schiller

Reprinted from "Pragmatism's Conception of Truth" in *Pragmatism* by William James, New York: David Mckay, 1909, pp. 131–156.

and Dewey, have given the only tenable account of this subject. It is a very ticklish subject, sending subtle rootlets into all kinds of crannies, and hard to treat in the sketchy way that alone befits a public lecture. But the Schiller-Dewey view of truth has been so ferociously attacked by rationalistic philosophers, and so abominably misunderstood, that here, if anywhere, is the point where a clear and simple statement should be made.

I fully expect to see the pragmatist view of truth run through the classic stages of a theory's career. First, you know, a new theory is attacked as absurd; then it is admitted to be true, but obvious and insignificant; finally it is seen to be so important that its adversaries claim that they themselves discovered it. Our doctrine of truth is at present in the first of these three stages, with symptoms of the second stage having begun in certain quarters. I wish that this lecture might help it beyond the first stage in the eyes of many of you.

Truth, as any dictionary will tell you, is a property of certain of our ideas. It means their 'agreement,' as falsity means their disagreement, with 'reality.' Pragmatists and intellectualists both accept this definition as a matter of course. They begin to quarrel only after the question is raised as to what may precisely be meant by the term 'agreement,' and what by the term 'reality,' when reality is taken as something for our ideas to agree with.

In answering these questions the pragmatists are more analytic and painstaking, the intellectualists more off-hand and irreflective. The popular notion is that a true idea must copy its reality. Like other popular views, this one follows the analogy of the most usual experience. Our true ideas of sensible things do indeed copy them. Shut your eyes and think of yonder clock on the wall, and you get just such a true picture or copy of its dial. But your idea of its 'works' (unless you are a clockmaker) is much less of a copy, yet it passes muster, for it in no way clashes with the reality. Even though it should shrink to the mere word 'works,' that word still serves you truly; and when you speak of the 'time-keeping function' of the clock, or of its spring's elasticity,' it is hard to see exactly what your ideas can copy.

You perceive that there is a problem here. Where our ideas cannot copy definitely their object, what does agreement with that object mean? Some idealists seem to say that they are true whenever they are what God means that we ought to think about that object. Others hold the copy-view all through, and speak as if our ideas possessed truth just in proportion as they approach to being copies of the Absolute's eternal way of thinking.

These views, you see, invite pragmatistic discussion. But the great assumption of the intellectualists is that truth means essentially an inert static relation. When you've got your true idea of anything, there's an end of the matter. You're in possession; you *know;* you have fulfilled your thinking destiny. You are where you ought to be mentally; you have obeyed your categorical imperative; and nothing more need follow on that climax of your rational destiny. Epistemologically you are in stable equilibrium.

Pragmatism, on the other hand, asks its usual question. "Grant an idea or belief to be true," it says, "what concrete difference will its being true make in any one's actual life? How will the truth be realized? What experiences will be different from those which would obtain if the belief were false? What, in short, is the truth's cash-value in experiential terms?"

The moment pragmatism asks this question, it sees the answer: *True ideas are those that we can assimilate, validate, corroborate and verify. False ideas are those that we can not.* That is the practical difference is makes to us to have true ideas; that, therefore, is the meaning of truth, for it is all that truth is known-as.

This thesis is what I have to defend. The truth of an idea is not a stagnant property inherent in it. Truth *happens* to an idea. It *becomes* true, is *made* true by events. Its verity *is* in fact an event, a process: the process namely of its verifying itself, its veri-*fication.* Its validity is the process of its valid-*ation.*

But what do the words verification and validation themselves pragmatically mean? They again signify certain practical consequences of the verified and validated idea. It is hard to find any one phrase that characterizes these consequences better than the ordinary agreement-formula—just such consequences being what we have in mind whenever we say that our ideas 'agree' with reality. They lead us, namely, through the acts and other ideas which they instigate, into or up to, or towards, other parts of experience with which we feel all the while —such feeling being among our potentialities—that the original ideas remain in agreement. The connexions and transitions come to us from point to point as being progressive, harmonious, satisfactory. This function of agreeable leading is what we mean by an idea's verification. Such an account is vague and it sounds at first quite trivial, but it has results which it will take the rest of my hour to explain.

Let me begin by reminding you of the fact that the possession of true thoughts means everywhere the possession of invaluable instruments of action; and that our duty to gain truth, so far from being a blank command from out of the blue, or a 'stunt' self-imposed by our intellect, can account for itself by excellent practical reasons.

The importance to human life of having true beliefs about matters of fact is a thing too notorious. We live in a world of realities that can be infinitely useful or infinitely harmful. Ideas that tell us which of them to expect count as the true ideas in all this primary sphere of verification, and the pursuit of such ideas is a primary human duty. The possession of truth, so far from being here an end in itself, is only a preliminary means towards other vital satisfactions. If I am lost in the woods and starved, and find what looks like a cow-path, it is of the utmost importance that I should think of a human habitation at the end of it, for if I do so and follow it, I save myself. The true thought is useful here because the house which is its object is useful. The practical value of true ideas is thus primarily derived from the practical importance of their objects to us. Their objects are, indeed, not important at all times. I may on another occasion have no use for the house; and then my idea of it, however verifiable, will be practically irrelevant, and had better remain latent. Yet since almost any object may some day become temporarily important, the advantage of having a general stock of *extra* truths, of ideas that shall be true of merely possible situations, is obvious. We store such extra truths away in our memories, and with the overflow we fill our books of reference. Whenever such an extra truth becomes practically relevant to one of our emergencies, it passes from cold-storage to do work in the world and our belief in it grows active. You can say of it then either that 'it is useful because it is true' or that 'it is true because it is useful.' Both these phrases mean exactly the same thing, namely that here is an idea that gets fulfilled and can be verified. True is the name for whatever idea starts the verification-process, useful is the name for its completed function in experience. True ideas would never have been singled out as such, would never have acquired a class-name, least of all a name suggesting value, unless they had been useful from the outset in this way.

From this simple cue pragmatism gets her general notion of truth as something essentially bound up with the way in which one moment in our experience may lead us towards other moments which it will be worth while to have been led to. Primarily, and on the common-sense level, the truth of a state of mind means this function of *a leading that is worth while.* When a moment in our experience, of any kind whatever, inspires us with a thought that is true, that means that sooner or later we dip by that thought's guidance into the particulars of experience again and make advantageous connexion with them. This is a vague enough statement, but I beg you to retain it, for it is essential.

Our experience meanwhile is all shot through with regularities. One bit of it can warn us to get ready for another bit, can 'intend' or be 'significant of' that remoter object. The object's advent is the significance's verification. Truth, in these cases, meaning nothing but eventual verification, is manifestly incompatible with waywardness on our part. Woe to him whose beliefs play fast and loose with the order which realities follow in his experience; they will lead him nowhere or else make false connexions.

By 'realities' or 'objects' here, we mean either things of common sense, sensibly present, or else common-sense relations, such as dates, places, distances, kinds, activities. Following our mental image of a house along the cow-path, we actually come to see the house; we get the image's full verification. *Such simply and fully verified leadings are certainly the originals and prototypes of the truth-process.* Experience offers indeed other forms of truth-process, but they are all conceivable as being primary verifications arrested, multiplied or substituted one for another.

Take, for instance, yonder object on the wall. You and I consider it to be a 'clock,' altho no one of us has seen the hidden works that make it one. We let our notion pass for true without attempting to verify. If truths mean verification-process essentially, ought we then to call such unverified truths as this abortive? No, for they form the overwhelmingly large number of the truths we live by. Indirect as well as direct verifications pass muster. Where circumstantial evidence is sufficient, we can go without eye-witnessing. Just as we here assume Japan to exist without ever having been there, because it *works* to do so, everything we know conspiring with the belief, and nothing interfering, so we assume that thing to be a clock. We *use* it as a clock, regulating the length of our lecture by it. The verification of the assumption here means its leading to no frustration or contradiction. Verifi*ability* of wheels and weights and pendulum is as good as verification. For one truth-process completed there are a million in our lives that function in this state of nascency. They turn us *towards* direct verification; lead us into the *surroundings* of the objects they envisage; and then, if everything runs on harmoniously, we are so sure that verification is possible that we omit it, and are usually justified by all that happens.

Truth lives, in fact, for the most part on a credit system. Our thoughts and beliefs 'pass,' so long as nothing challenges them, just as bank-notes pass so long as nobody refuses them. But this all points to direct face-to-face verifications somewhere, without which the fabric of truth collapses like a financial system with no cash-basis whatever. You accept my verification of one thing, I yours of another. We trade on each other's truth. But beliefs verified concretely by *somebody* are the posts of the whole superstructure.

Another great reason—beside economy of time—for waiving complete verification in the usual business of life is that all things exist in kinds and not singly. Our world is found once for all to have that peculiarity. So that when we have once directly verified our ideas about one specimen of a kind, we consider ourselves free to apply them to other specimens without verification. A mind that habitually discerns the kind of thing before it, and acts by the law of the kind immediately, without pausing to verify, will be a 'true' mind in ninety-nine out of a hundred emergencies, proved so by its conduct fitting everything it meets, and getting no refutation.

Indirectly or only potentially verifying processes may thus be true as well as full verification-processes. They work as true processes would work, give us the same advantages, and claim our recognition for the same reasons. All this on the common-sense level of matters of fact, which we are alone considering.

But matters of fact are not our only stock in trade. *Relations among purely mental ideas* form another sphere where true and false beliefs obtain, and here the beliefs are absolute, or unconditional. When they are true they bear the name either of definitions or of principles. It is either a principle or a definition that 1 and 1 make 2, that 2 and 1 make 3, and so on; that white differs less from gray than it does from black; that when the cause begins to act the effect also commences. Such propositions hold of all possible 'ones,' of all conceivable 'whites' and 'grays' and 'causes.' The objects here are mental objects. Their relations are perceptually obvious at a glance, and no sense-verification is necessary. Moreover, once true, always true, of those same mental objects. Truth here has an 'eternal' character. If you can find a concrete thing anywhere that is 'one' or 'white' or 'gray' or an 'effect,' then your principles will everlastingly apply to it. It is but a case of ascertaining the kind, and then applying the law of its kind to the particular object. You are sure to get truth if you can but name the kind rightly, for your mental relations hold good of everything of that kind without exception. If you then, nevertheless, failed to get truth concretely, you would say that you had classed your real objects wrongly.

In this realm of mental relations, truth again is an affair of leading. We relate one abstract idea with another, framing in the end great systems of logical and mathematical truth, under the respective terms of which the sensible facts of experience eventually arrange themselves, so that our eternal truths hold good of realities also. This marriage of fact and theory is endlessly fertile. What we say is here already true in advance of special verification, *if we have subsumed our objects rightly.* Our ready-made ideal framework for all sorts of possible objects follows from the very structure of our thinking. We can no more play fast and loose with these abstract relations than we can do so with our sense-experiences. They coerce us; we must treat them consistently, whether or not we like the results. The rules of addition apply to our debts as rigorously as to our assets. The hundredth decimal of π, the ratio of the circumference to its diameter, is predetermined ideally now, tho no one may have computed it. If we should ever need the figure in our dealings with an actual circle we should need to have it given rightly, calculated by the usual rules; for it is the same kind of truth that those rules elsewhere calculate.

Between the coercions of the sensible order and those of the ideal order, our mind is thus wedged tightly. Our ideas must agree with realities, be such realities concrete or abstract, be they facts or be they principles, under penalty of endless inconsistency and frustration.

So far, intellectualists can raise no protest. They can only say that we have barely touched the skin of the matter.

Realities mean, then, either concrete facts, or abstract kinds of thing and relations perceived intuitively between them. They furthermore and thirdly mean, as things that new ideas of ours must no less take account of, the whole body of other truths already in our possession. But what now does 'agreement' with such threefold realities mean?—to use again the definition that is current.

Here it is that pragmatism and intellectualism begin to part company. Primarily, no doubt, to agree means to copy, but we saw that the mere word 'clock' would do instead of a mental picture of its works, and that of many realities our ideas can only be symbols and not copies. 'Past time,' 'power,' 'spontaneity,'—how can our mind copy such realities?

To 'agree' in the widest sense with a reality *can only mean to be guided either straight up to it or into its surroundings, or to be put into such working touch with it as to handle either it or something connected with it better than if we disagreed.* Better either intellectually or practically! And often agreement will only mean the negative fact that nothing contradictory from the quarter of that reality comes to interfere with the way in which our ideas guide us elsewhere. To copy a reality is, indeed, one very important way of agreeing with it, but it is far from being essential. The essential thing is the process of being guided. Any idea that helps us to *deal*, whether practically or intellectually, with either the reality or its belongings, that doesn't entangle our progress in frustrations, that *fits*, in fact, and adapts our life to the reality's whole setting, will agree sufficiently to meet the requirement. It will hold true of that reality.

Thus, *names* are just as 'true' or 'false' as definite mental pictures are. They set up similar verification-processes, and lead to fully equivalent practical results.

All human thinking gets discursified; we exchange ideas; we lend and borrow verifications, get them from one another by means of social intercourse. All truth thus gets verbally built out, stored up, and made available for every one. Hence, we must *talk* consistently just as we must *think* consistently: for both in talk and thought we deal with kinds. Names are arbitrary, but once understood they must be kept to. We mustn't now call Abel 'Cain' or Cain 'Abel.' If we do, we ungear ourselves from the whole book of Genesis, and from all its connexions with the universe of speech and fact down to the present time. We throw ourselves out of whatever truth that entire system of speech and fact may embody.

The overwhelming majority of our true ideas admit of no direct or face-to-face verification—those of past history, for example, as of Cain and Abel. The stream of time can be remounted only verbally, or verified indirectly by the present prolongations or effects of what the past harbored. Yet if they agree with these verbalities and effects, we can know that our ideas of the past are true. *As true as past time itself was*, so true was Julius Caesar, so true were antediluvian monsters, all in their proper dates and settings. That past time itself was, is guaranteed by its coherence with everything that's present. True as the present *is*, the past *was* also.

Agreement thus turns out to be essentially an affair of leading—leading that is useful because it is into quarters that contain objects that are important. True ideas lead us into useful verbal and conceptual quarters as well as directly up to useful sensible termini. They lead to consistency, stability and flowing human intercourse. They lead away from eccentricity and isolation, from foiled and barren thinking. The untrammelled flowing of the leading-process, its general freedom from clash and contradiction, passes for its indirect verification; but all roads lead to Rome, and in the end and eventually, all true processes must lead to the face of directly verifying sensible experiences *somewhere*, which somebody's ideas have copied.

Such is the large loose way in which the pragmatist interprets the word agreement. He treats it altogether practically. He lets it cover any process of conduction from a present idea to a future terminus, provided only it run prosperously. It is only thus that 'scientific' ideas, flying as they do beyond common sense, can be said to agree with their realities. It is, as I have already said, as if reality were made of ether, atoms or electrons, but we mustn't think so literally. The term 'energy' doesn't even pretend to stand for anything 'objective.' It is only a way of measuring the surface of phenomena so as to string their changes on a simple formula.

Yet in the choice of these man-made formulas we can not be capricious with impunity any more than we can be capricious on the common-sense practical level. We must find a theory that will *work;* and that means something extremely difficult; for our theory must mediate between all previous truths and certain new experiences. It must derange common sense and previous belief as little as possible, and it must lead to some sensible terminus or other that can be verified exactly. To 'work' means both these things; and the squeeze is so tight that there is little loose play for any hypothesis. Our theories are wedged and controlled as nothing else is. Yet sometimes alternative theoretic formulas are equally compatible with all the truths we know, and then we choose between them for subjective reasons. We choose the kind of theory to which we are already partial; we follow 'elegance' or 'economy.' Clerk-Maxwell somewhere says it would be 'poor scientific taste' to choose the more complicated of two equally well-evidenced conceptions; and you will all agree with him. Truth in science is what gives us the maximum possible sum of satisfactions, taste included, but consistency both with previous truth and with novel fact is always the most imperious claimant.

I have led you through a very sandy desert. But now, if I may be allowed so vulgar an expression, we begin to taste the milk in the cocoanut. Our rationalist critics here discharge their batteries upon us, and to reply to them will take us out from all this dryness into full sight of a momentous philosophical alternative.

Our account of truth is an account of truths in the plural, of processes of leading, realized *in rebus*, and having only this quality in common, that they *pay.* They pay by guiding us into or towards some part of a system that dips at numerous points into sense-percepts, which we may copy mentally or not, but with which at any rate we are now in the kind of commerce vaguely designated as verification. Truth for us is simply a collective name for verification-processes, just as health, wealth, strength, etc., are names for other processes connected with life, and also pursued because it pays to pursue them. Truth is *made*, just as health, wealth and strength are made, in the course of experience.

Here rationalism is instantaneously up in arms against us. I can imagine a rationalist to talk as follows:

"Truth is not made," he will say; "it absolutely obtains, being a unique relation that does not wait upon any process, but shoots straight over the head of experience, and hits its reality every time. Our belief that yon thing on the wall is a clock is true already, altho no one in the whole history of the world should verify it. The bare quality of standing in that transcendent relation is what makes any thought true that possesses it, whether or not there be verification. You pragmatists put the cart before the horse in making truth's being reside in verification-processes. These are merely signs of its being, merely our lame ways of ascertaining after the fact, which of our ideas already has possessed the wondrous quality. The quality itself is timeless, like all essences and natures. Thoughts partake of it directly, as they partake of falsity or of irrelevancy. It can't be analyzed away into pragmatic consequences."

The whole plausibility of this rationalist tirade is due to the fact to which we have already paid so much attention. In our world, namely, abounding as it does in things of similar kinds and similarly associated, one verification serves for others of its kind, and one great use of knowing things is to be led not so much to them as to their associates, especially to human talk about them. The quality of truth, obtaining *ante rem*, pragmatically means, then, the fact that in such a world innumerable ideas work better by their indirect or possible than by their direct and actual verification. Truth *ante rem* means only verifiability, then; or else it is a case of the stock rationalist trick of treating the *name* of a concrete phenomenal reality as an independent prior entity, and placing it behind the reality as its explanation. Professor Mach quotes somewhere an epigram of Lessing's:

> *Sagt Hänschen Schlau zu Vetter Fritz,*
> *"Wie kommt es, Vetter Fritzen,*
> *Dass grad' die Reichsten in der Welt,*
> *Das meiste Geld besitzen?"*

Hänschen Schlau here treats the principle 'wealth' as something distinct from the facts denoted by the man's being rich. It antedates them; the facts become only a sort of secondary coincidence with the rich man's essential nature.

In the case of 'wealth' we all see the fallacy. We know that wealth is but a name for concrete processes that certain men's lives play a part in, and not a natural excellence found in Messrs. Rockefeller and Carnegie, but not in the rest of us.

Like wealth, health also lives *in rebus.* It is a name for processes, as digestion, circulation, sleep, etc., that go on happily, tho in this instance we are more inclined to think of it as a principle and to say the man digests and sleeps so well *because* he is so healthy.

With 'strength' we are, I think, more rationalistic still, and decidedly inclined to treat it as an excellence pre-existing in the man and explanatory of the herculean performances of his muscles.

With 'truth' most people go over the border entirely, and treat the rationalistic account as self-evident. But really all these words in *th* are exactly similar. Truth exists *ante rem* just as much and as little as the other things do.

The scholastics, following Aristotle, made much of the distinction between habit and act. Health *in actu* means, among other things, good sleeping and digesting. But a healthy man need not always be sleeping, or always digesting, any more than a wealthy man need be always handling money, or a strong man always lifting weights. All such qualities sink to the status of 'habits' between their times of exercise; and similarly truth becomes a habit of certain of our ideas and beliefs in their intervals of rest from their verifying activities. But those activities are the root of the whole matter, and the condition of there being any habit to exist in the intervals.

'The true,' to put it very briefly, is only the expedient in the way of our thinking, just as 'the right' is only the expedient in the way of our behaving. Expedient in almost any fashion; and expedient in the long run and on the whole

of course; for what meets expediently all the experience in sight won't necessarily meet all farther experiences equally satisfactorily. Experience, as we know, has ways of *boiling over*, and making us correct our present formulas.

The 'absolutely' true, meaning what no farther experience will ever alter, is that ideal vanishing-point towards which we imagine that all our temporary truths will some day converge. It runs on all fours with the perfectly wise man, and with the absolutely complete experience; and, if these ideals are ever realized, they will all be realized together. Meanwhile we have to live to-day by what truth we can get to-day, and be ready to-morrow to call it falsehood. Ptolemaic astronomy, euclidean space, aristotelian logic, scholastic metaphysics, were expedient for centuries, but human experience has boiled over those limits, and we now call these things only relatively true, or true within those borders of experience. 'Absolutely' they are false; for we know that those limits were casual, and might have been transcended by past theorists just as they are by present thinkers.

When new experiences lead to retrospective judgments, using the past tense, what these judgments utter *was* true, even tho no past thinker had been led there. We live forwards, a Danish thinker has said, but we understand backwards. The present sheds a backward light on the world's previous processes. They may have been truth-processes for the actors in them. They are not so for one who knows the later revelations of the story.

This regulative notion of a potential better truth to be established later, possibly to be established some day absolutely, and having powers of retroactive legislation, turns its face, like all pragmatist notions, towards concreteness of fact, and towards the future. Like the half-truths, the absolute truth will have to be *made*, made as a relation incidental to the growth of a mass of verification-experience, to which the half-true ideas are all along contributing their quota.

I have already insisted on the fact that truth is made largely out of previous truths. Men's beliefs at any time are so much experience *funded.* But the beliefs are themselves parts of the sum total of the world's experience, and become matter, therefore, for the next day's funding operations. So far as reality means experienceable reality, both it and the truths men gain about it are everlastingly in process of mutation—mutation towards a definite goal, it may be—but still mutation.

Mathematicians can solve problems with two variables. On the Newtonian theory, for instance, acceleration varies with distance, but distance also varies with acceleration. In the realm of truth-processes facts come independently and determine our beliefs provisionally. But these beliefs make us act, and as fast as they do so, they bring into sight or into existence new facts which re-determine the beliefs accordingly. So the whole coil and ball of truth, as it rolls up, is the product of a double influence. Truths emerge from facts; but they dip forward into facts again and add to them; which facts again create or reveal new truth (the word is indifferent) and so on indefinitely. The 'facts' themselves meanwhile are not *true.* They simply *are.* Truth is the function of the beliefs that start and terminate among them.

The case is like a snowball's growth, due as it is to the distribution of the snow on the one hand, and to the successive pushes of the boys on the other, with these factors co-determining each other incessantly.

The most fateful point of difference between being a rationalist and being a pragmatist is now fully in sight. Experience is in mutation, and our psychological ascertainments of truth are in mutation—so much rationalism will allow; but never that either reality itself or truth itself is mutable. Reality stands complete and ready-made from all eternity, rationalism insists, and the agreement of our ideas with it is that unique unanalyzable virtue in them of which she has already told us. As that intrinsic excellence, their truth has nothing to do with our experiences. It adds nothing to the content of experience. It makes no difference to reality itself; it is supervenient, inert, static, a reflexion merely. It doesn't *exist*, it *holds* or *obtains*, it belongs to another dimension from that of either facts or fact-relations, belongs, in short, to the epistemological dimension—and with that big word rationalism closes the discussion.

Thus, just as pragmatism faces forward to the future, so does rationalism here again face backward to a past eternity. True to her inveterate habit, rationalism reverts to 'principles,' and thinks that when an abstraction once is named, we own an oracular solution.

The tremendous pregnancy in the way of consequences for life of this radical difference of outlook will only become apparent in my later lectures. I wish meanwhile to close this lecture by showing that rationalism's sublimity does not save it from inanity.

When, namely, you ask rationalists, instead of accusing pragmatism of desecrating the notion of truth, to define it themselves by saying exactly what *they* understand by it, the only positive attempts I can think of are these two:

1. "Truth is the system of propositions which have an unconditional claim to be recognized as valid."
2. Truth is a name for all those judgments which we find ourselves under obligation to make by a kind of imperative duty.

The first thing that strikes one in such definitions is their unutterable triviality. They are absolutely true, of course, but absolutely insignificant until you handle them pragmatically. What do you mean by 'claim' here, and what do you mean by 'duty'? As summary names for the concrete reasons why thinking in true ways is overwhelmingly expedient and good for mortal men, it is all right to talk of claims on reality's part to be agreed with, and of obligations on our part to agree. We feel both the claims and the obligations, and we feel them for just those reasons.

But the rationalists who talk of claim and obligation *expressly say that they have nothing to do with our practical interests or personal reasons.* Our reasons for agreeing are psychological facts, they say, relative to each thinker, and to the accidents of his life. They are his evidence merely, they are no part of the life of truth itself. That life transacts itself in a purely logical or epistemological, as distinguished from a psychological, dimension, and its claims antedate and exceed all personal motivations whatsoever. Tho neither man nor God should ever ascertain truth, the word would still have to be defined as that which *ought* to be ascertained and recognized.

There never was a more exquisite example of an idea abstracted from the concretes of experience and then used to oppose and negate what it was abstracted from.

Philosophy and common life abound in similar instances. The 'sentimentalist fallacy' is to shed tears over abstract justice and generosity, beauty, etc., and never to know these qualities when you meet them in the street, because the circumstances make them vulgar. Thus I read in the privately printed biography of an eminently rationalistic mind: "It was strange that with such admiration for beauty in the abstract, my brother had no enthusiasm for fine architecture, for beautiful painting, or for flowers." And in almost the last philosophic work I have read, I find such passages as the following: "Justice is ideal, solely ideal. Reason conceives that it ought to exist, but experience shows that it can not. . . . Truth, which ought to be, can not be. . . . Reason is deformed by experience. As soon as reason enters experience it becomes contrary to reason."

The rationalist's fallacy here is exactly like the sentimentalist's. Both extract a quality from the muddy particulars of experience, and find it so pure when extracted that they contrast it with each and all its muddy instances as an opposite and higher nature. All the while it is *their* nature. It is the nature of truths to be validated, verified. It pays for our ideas to be validated. Our obligation to seek truth is part of our general obligation to do what pays. The payments true ideas bring are the sole why of our duty to follow them. Identical whys exist in the case of wealth and health.

Truth makes no other claim and imposes no other kind of ought than health and wealth do. All these claims are conditional; the concrete benefits we gain are what we mean by calling the pursuit a duty. In the case of truth, untrue beliefs work as perniciously in the long run as true beliefs work beneficially. Talking abstractly, the quality 'true' may thus be said to grow absolutely precious and the quality 'untrue' absolutely damnable: the one may be called good, the other bad, unconditionally. We ought to think the true, we ought to shun the false, imperatively.

But if we treat all this abstraction literally and oppose it to its mother soil in experience, see what a preposterous position we work ourselves into.

We can not then take a step forward in our actual thinking. When shall I acknowledge this truth and when that? Shall the acknowledgment be loud? —or silent? If sometimes loud, sometimes silent, which *now?* When may a truth go into cold-storage in the encyclopedia? and when shall it come out for battle? Must I constantly be repeating the truth 'twice two are four' because of its eternal claim on recognition? or is it sometimes irrelevant? Must my thoughts dwell night and day on my personal sins and blemishes, because I truly have them?—or may I sink and ignore them in order to be a decent social unit, and not a mass of morbid melancholy and apology?

It is quite evident that our obligation to acknowledge truth, so far from being unconditional, is tremendously conditioned. Truth with a big T, and in the singular, claims abstractly to be recognized, of course; but concrete truths in the plural need be recognized only when their recognition is expedient. A truth must always be preferred to a falsehood when both relate to the situation; but when neither does, truth is as little of a duty as falsehood. If you ask me what o'clock it is and I tell you that I live at 95 Irving Street, my answer may indeed be true, but you don't see why it is my duty to give it. A false address would be as much to the purpose.

With this admission that there are conditions that limit the application of the abstract imperative, *the pragmatistic treatment of truth sweeps back upon us in its fulness.* Our duty to agree with reality is seen to be grounded in a perfect jungle of concrete expediencies.

When Berkeley had explained what people meant by matter, people thought that he denied matter's existence. When Messrs. Schiller and Dewey now explain what people mean by truth, they are accused of denying *its* existence. These pragmatists destroy all objective standards, critics say, and put foolishness and wisdom on one level. A favorite formula for describing Mr. Schiller's doctrines and mine is that we are persons who think that by saying whatever you find it pleasant to say and calling it truth you fulfil every pragmatistic requirement.

I leave it to you to judge whether this be not an impudent slander. Pent in, as the pragmatist more than any one else sees himself to be, between the whole body of funded truths squeezed from the past and the coercions of the world of sense about him, who so well as he feels the immense pressure of objective control under which our minds perform their operations? If any one imagines that this law is lax, let him keep its commandment one day, says Emerson. We have heard much of late of the uses of the imagination in science. It is high time to urge the use of a little imagination in philosophy. The unwillingness of some of our critics to read any but the silliest of possible meanings into our statements is as discreditable to their imaginations as anything I know in recent philosophic history. Schiller says the true is that which 'works.' Thereupon he is treated as one who limits verification to the lowest material utilities. Dewey says truth is what gives 'satisfaction.' He is treated as one who believes in calling everything true which, if it were true, would be pleasant.

Our critics certainly need more imagination of realities. I have honestly tried to stretch my own imagination and to read the best possible meaning into the rationalist conception, but I have to confess that it still completely baffles me. The notion of a reality calling on us to 'agree' with it, and that for no reasons, but simply because its claim is 'unconditional' or 'transcendent,' is one that I can make neither head nor tail of. I try to imagine myself as the sole reality in the world, and then to imagine what more I would 'claim' if I were allowed to. If you suggest the possibility of my claiming that a mind should come into being from out of the void inane and stand and *copy* me, I can indeed imagine what the copying might mean, but I can conjure up no motive. What good it would do me to be copied, or what good it would do that mind to copy me, if further consequences are expressly and in principle ruled out as motives for the claim (as they are by our rationalist authorities) I can not fathom. When the Irishman's admirers ran him along to the place of banquet in a sedan chair with no bottom, he said, "Faith, if it wasn't for the honor of the thing, I might as well have come on foot." So here: but for the honor of the thing, I might as well have remained uncopied. Copying is one genuine mode of knowing (which for some strange reason our contemporary transcendentalists seem to be tumbling over each other to repudiate); but when we get beyond copying, and fall back on unnamed forms of agreeing that are expressly denied to be either copyings or leadings or fittings, or any other process pragmatically definable, the *what* of the 'agreement' claimed becomes as unintelligible as the why of it. Neither content nor motive can be imagined for it. It is an absolutely meaningless abstraction.

Surely in this field of truth it is the pragmatists and not the rationalists who are the more genuine defenders of the universe's rationality.

Knowledge and Truth Are Not Relative

PLATO

Soc. Then now is the time, my dear Theaetetus, for me to examine, and for you to exhibit; since although Theodorus has praised many a citizen and stranger in my hearing, never did I hear him praise any one as he has been praising you.

Theaet. I am glad to hear it, Socrates; but what if he was only in jest?

Soc. Nay, Theodorus is not given to jesting; and I cannot allow you to retract your consent on any such pretence as that. If you do, he will have to swear to his words; and we are perfectly sure that no one will be found to impugn him. Do not be shy then, but stand to your word.

Theaet. I suppose I must, if you wish it.

Soc. In the first place, I should like to ask what you learn of Theodorus: something of geometry, perhaps?

Theaet. Yes.

Soc. And astronomy and harmony and calculation?

Theaet. I do my best.

Soc. Yes, my boy, and so do I: and my desire is to learn of him, or of anybody who seems to understand these things. And I get on pretty well in general; but there is a little difficulty which I want you and the company to aid me in investigating. Will you answer me a question: 'Is not learning growing wiser about that which you learn?'

Excerpted from *Theaetetus* by Plato.

Theaet. Of course.

Soc. And by wisdom the wise are wise?

Theaet. Yes.

Soc. And is that different in any way from knowledge?

Theaet. What?

Soc. Wisdom; are not men wise in that which they know?

Theaet. Certainly they are.

Soc. Then wisdom and knowledge are the same?

Theaet. Yes.

Soc. Herein lies the difficulty which I can never solve to my satisfaction—What is knowledge? Can we answer that question? What say you? which of us will speak first? whoever misses shall sit down, as at a game of ball, and shall be donkey, as the boys say; he who lasts out his competitors in the game without missing, shall be our king, and shall have the right of putting to us any questions which he pleases. . . . Why is there no reply? I hope, Theodorus, that I am not betrayed into rudeness by my love of conversation? I only want to make us talk and be friendly and sociable. . . . Once more, then, Theaetetus, I repeat my old question, 'What is knowledge?'—and do not say that you cannot tell; but quit yourself like a man, and by the help of God you will be able to tell.

Theaet. At any rate, Socrates, after such an exhortation I should be ashamed of not trying to do my best. Now he who knows perceives what he knows, and, as far as I can see at present, knowledge is perception.

Soc. Bravely said, boy; that is the way in which you should express your opinion. And now, let us examine together this conception of yours, and see whether it is a true birth or a mere wind-egg:—You say that knowledge is perception?

Theaet. Yes.

Soc. Well, you have delivered yourself of a very important doctrine about knowledge; it is indeed the opinion of Protagoras, who has another way of expressing it. Man, he says, is the measure of all things, of the existence of things that are, and of the non-existence of things that are not:—You have read him?

Theaet. O yes, again and again.

Soc. Does he not say that things are to you such as they appear to you, and to me such as they appear to me, and that you and I are men?

Theaet. Yes, he says so.

Soc. A wise man is not likely to talk nonsense. Let us try to understand him: the same wind is blowing, and yet one of us may be cold and the other not, or one may be slightly and the other very cold?

Theaet. Quite true.

Soc. Now is the wind, regarded not in relation to us but absolutely, cold or not; or are we to say, with Protagoras, that the wind is cold to him who is cold, and not to him who is not?

Theaet. I suppose the last.

Soc. Then it must appear so to each of them?

Theaet. Yes.

Soc. And 'appears to him' means the same as 'he perceives.'

Theaet. True.

Soc. Then appearing and perceiving coincide in the case of hot and cold, and in similar instances; for things appear, or may be supposed to be, to each one such as he perceives them?

Theaet. Yes.

Soc. Then perception is always of existence, and being the same as knowledge is unerring? . . .

Soc. Let us not leave the argument unfinished, then; for there still remains to be considered an objection which may be raised about dreams and diseases, in particular about madness, and the various illusions of hearing and sight, or of other senses. For you know that in all these cases the *esse-percipi* theory appears to be unmistakably refuted, since in dreams and illusions we certainly have false perceptions; and far from saying that everything is which appears, we should rather say that nothing is which appears.

Theaet. Very true, Socrates.

Soc. But then, my boy, how can any one contend that knowledge is perception, or that to every man what appears is?

Theaet. I am afraid to say, Socrates, that I have nothing to answer, because you rebuked me just now for making this excuse; but I certainly cannot undertake to argue that madmen or dreamers think truly, when they imagine, some of them that they are gods, and others that they can fly, and are flying in their sleep.

Soc. Do you see another question which can be raised about these phenomena, notably about dreaming and waking?

Theaet. What question?

Soc. A question which I think that you must often have heard persons ask:—How can you determine whether at this moment we are sleeping, and all our thoughts are a dream; or whether we are awake, and talking to one another in the waking state?

Theaet. Indeed, Socrates, I do not know how to prove the one any more than the other, for in both cases the facts precisely correspond; and there is no difficulty in supposing that during all this discussion we have been talking to one another in a dream; and when in a dream we seem to be narrating dreams, the resemblance of the two states is quite astonishing.

Soc. You see, then, that a doubt about the reality of sense is easily raised, since there may even be a doubt whether we are awake or in a dream. And as our time is equally divided between sleeping and waking, in either sphere of existence the soul contends that the thoughts which are present to our minds at the time are true; and during one half of our lives we affirm the truth of the one, and, during the other half, of the other; and are equally confident of both.

Theaet. Most true.

Soc. And may not the same be said of madness and other disorders? the difference is only that the times are not equal.

Theaet. Certainly.

Soc. And is truth or falsehood to be determined by duration of time?

Theaet. That would be in many ways ridiculous.

Soc. But can you certainly determine by any other means which of these opinions is true?

Theaet. I do not think that I can. . . .

Soc. Then my perception is true to me, being inseparable from my own being; and, as Protagoras says, to myself I am judge of what is and what is not to me.

Theaet. I suppose so.

Soc. How then, if I never err, and if my mind never trips in the conception of being or becoming, can I fail of knowing that which I perceive?

Theaet. You cannot.

Soc. Then you were quite right in affirming that knowledge is only perception; and the meaning turns out to be the same, whether with Homer and Heracleitus, and all that company, you say that all is motion and flux, or with the great sage Protagoras, that man is the measure of all things; or with Theaetetus, that, given these premises, perception is knowledge. Am I not right, Theaetetus, and is not this your new-born child, of which I have delivered you? What say you?

Theaet. I cannot but agree, Socrates.

Soc. Then this is the child, however he may turn out, which you and I have with difficulty brought into the world. And now that he is born, we must run round the hearth with him, and see whether he is worth rearing, or is only a wind-egg and a sham. Is he to be reared in any case, and not exposed? or will you bear to see him rejected, and not get into a passion if I take away your first-born?

Theod. Theaetetus will not be angry, for he is very good-natured. But tell me, Socrates, in heaven's name, is this, after all, not the truth?

Soc. You, Theodorus, are a lover of theories, and now you innocently fancy that I am a bag full of them, and can easily pull one out which will overthrow its predecessor. But you do not see that in reality none of these theories come from me; they all come from him who talks with me. I only know just enough to extract them from the wisdom of another, and to receive them in a spirit of fairness. And now I shall say nothing myself, but shall endeavour to elicit something from our young friend.

Theod. Do as you say, Socrates; you are quite right.

Soc. Shall I tell you, Theodorus, what amazes me in your acquaintance Protagoras?

Theod. What is it?

Soc. I am charmed with his doctrine, that what appears is to each one, but I wonder that he did not begin his book on Truth with a declaration that a pig or a dog-faced baboon, or some other yet stranger monster which has sensation, is the measure of all things; then he might have shown a magnificent contempt for our opinion of him by informing us at the outset that while we were reverencing him like a God for his wisdom he was no better than a tadpole, not to speak of his fellow-men—would not this have produced an overpowering effect? For if truth is only sensation, and no man can discern another's feelings better than he, or has any superior right to determine whether his opinion is true or false, but each, as we have several times repeated, is to himself the sole judge, and everything that he judges is true and right, why, my friend, should Protagoras be preferred to the place of wisdom and instruction, and deserve to be well paid, and we poor ignoramuses have to go to him, if each one is the measure of his own wisdom? Must he not be talking 'ad captandum' in all this? I say nothing of the ridiculous predicament in which my own midwifery and the whole art of dialectic is placed; for the attempt to supervise or refute the notions or opinions of others would be a tedious and enormous piece of folly, if to each man his own are right; and this must be the case if Protagoras' Truth is the real truth, and the philosopher is not merely amusing himself by giving oracles out of the shrine of his book.

Theod. He was a friend of mine, Socrates, as you were saying, and therefore I cannot have him refuted by my lips, nor can I oppose you when I agree with you; please, then, to take Theaetetus again; he seemed to answer very nicely.

Soc. If you were to go into a Lacedaemonian palestra, Theodorus, would you have a right to look on at the naked wrestlers, some of them making a poor figure, if you did not strip and give them an opportunity of judging of your own person?

Theod. Why not, Socrates, if they would allow me, as I think you will, in consideration of my age and stiffness; let some more supple youth try a fall with you, and do not drag me into the gymnasium.

Soc. Your will is my will, Theodorus, as the proverbial philosophers say, and therefore I will return to the sage Theaetetus: Tell me, Theaetetus, in reference to what I was saying, are you not lost in wonder, like myself, when you find that all of a sudden you are raised to the level of the wisest of men, or indeed of the gods?—for you would assume the measure of Protagoras to apply to the gods as well as men?

Theaet. Certainly I should, and I confess to you that I am lost in wonder. At first hearing, I was quite satisfied with the doctrine, that whatever appears is to each one, but now the face of things has changed.

Soc. Why, my dear boy, you are young, and therefore your ear is quickly caught and your mind influenced by popular arguments. Protagoras, or some one speaking on his behalf, will doubtless say in reply,—Good people, young and old, you meet and harangue, and bring in the gods, whose existence or non-existence I banish from writing and speech, or you talk about the reason of man being degraded to the level of the brutes, which is a telling argument with the multitude, but not one word of proof or demonstration do you offer. All is probability with you, and yet surely you and Theodorus had better reflect whether you are disposed to admit of probability and figures of speech in matters of such importance. He or any other mathematician who argued from probabilities and likelihoods in geometry, would not be worth an ace.

Theaet. But neither you nor we, Socrates, would be satisfied with such arguments.

Soc. Then you and Theodorus mean to say that we must look at the matter in some other way?

Theaet. Yes, in quite another way.

Soc. And the way will be to ask whether perception is or is not the same as knowledge; for this was the real point of our argument, and with a view to this we raised (did we not?) those many strange questions.

Theaet. Certainly.

Soc. Shall we say that we know every thing which we see and hear? for example, shall we say that not having learned, we do not hear the language of foreigners when they speak to us? or shall we say that we not only hear, but know what they are saying? Or again, if we see letters which we do not understand, shall we say that we do not see them? or shall we aver that, seeing them, we must know them?

Theaet. We shall say, Socrates, that we know what we actually see and hear of them—that is to say, we see and know the figure and colour of the letters, and we hear and know the elevation or depression of the sound of them; but we do not perceive by sight and hearing, or know, that which grammarians and interpreters teach about them.

Soc. Capital, Theaetetus; and about this there shall be no dispute, because I want you to grow; but there is another difficulty coming, which you will also have to repulse.

Theaet. What is it?

Soc. Some one will say, Can a man who has ever known anything, and still has and preserves a memory of that which he knows, not know that which he remembers at the time when he remembers? I have, I fear, a tedious way of putting a simple question, which is only, whether a man who has learned, and remembers, can fail to know?

Theaet. Impossible, Socrates; the supposition is monstrous.

Soc. Am I talking nonsense, then? Think: is not seeing perceiving, and is not sight perception?

Theaet. True.

Soc. And if our recent definition holds, every man knows that which he has seen?

Theaet. Yes.

Soc. And you would admit that there is such a thing as memory?

Theaet. Yes.

Soc. And is memory of something or of nothing?

Theaet. Of something, surely.

Soc. Of things learned and perceived, that is?

Theaet. Certainly.

Soc. Often a man remembers that which he has seen?

Theaet. True.

Soc. And if he closed his eyes, would he forget?

Theaet. Who, Socrates, would dare to say so?

Soc. But we must say so, if the previous argument is to be maintained.

Theaet. What do you mean? I am not quite sure that I understand you, though I have a strong suspicion that you are right.

Soc. As thus: he who sees knows, as we say, that which he sees; for perception and sight and knowledge are admitted to be the same.

Theaet. Certainly.

Soc. But he who saw, and has knowledge of that which he saw, remembers, when he closes his eyes, that which he no longer sees.

Theaet. True.

Soc. And seeing is knowing, and therefore not-seeing is not-knowing?

Theaet. Very true.

Soc. Then the inference is, that a man may have attained the knowledge of something, which he may remember and yet not know, because he does not see; and this has been affirmed by us to be a monstrous supposition.

Theaet. Most true.

Soc. Thus, then, the assertion that knowledge and perception are one, involves a manifest impossibility?

Theaet. Yes.

Soc. Then they must be distinguished?

Theaet. I suppose that they must.

Soc. Once more we shall have to begin, and ask 'What is knowledge?' and yet, Theaetetus, what are we going to do?

Theaet. About what?

Soc. Like a good-for-nothing cock, without having won the victory, we walk away from the argument and crow.

Theaet. How do you mean?

Soc. After the manner of disputers,[1] we were satisfied with mere verbal consistency, and were well pleased if in this way we could gain an advantage. Although professing, not to be mere Eristics, but philosophers, I suspect that we have unconsciously fallen into the error of that ingenious class of persons.

Theaet. I do not as yet understand you.

Soc. Then I will try to explain myself: just now we asked the question, whether a man who had learned and remembered could fail to know, and we showed that a person who had seen might remember when he had his eyes shut and could not see, and then he would at the same time remember and not know. But this was an impossibility. And so the Protagorean fable came to nought, and yours also, who maintained that knowledge is the same as perception.

Theaet. True.

Soc. And yet, my friend, I rather suspect that the result would have been different if Protagoras, who was the father of the first of the two brats, had been alive; he would have had a great deal to say on their behalf. But he is dead, and we insult over his orphan child; and even the guardians whom he left, and of whom our friend Theodorus is one, are unwilling to give any help, and therefore I suppose that I must take up his cause myself, and see justice done?

Theod. Not I, Socrates, but rather Callias, the son of Hipponicus, is guardian of his orphans. I was too soon diverted from the abstractions of dialectic to geometry. Nevertheless, I shall be grateful to you if you assist him.

[1] Lys. 216 A; Phaedo 90 B, 101 E; Rep. V, 453 E ff.

Soc. Very good, Theodorus; you shall see how I will come to the rescue. If a person does not attend to the meaning of terms as they are commonly used in argument, he may be involved even in greater paradoxes than these. Shall I explain this matter to you or to Theaetetus?

Theod. To both of us, and let the younger answer; he will incur less disgrace if he is discomfited.

Soc. Then now let me ask the awful question, which is this:—Can a man know and also not know that which he knows?

Theod. How shall we answer, Theaetetus?

Theaet. He cannot, I should say.

Soc. He can, if you maintain that seeing is knowing. When you are imprisoned in a well, as the saying is, and the self-assured adversary closes one of your eyes with his hand, and asks whether you can see his cloak with the eye which he has closed, how will you answer the inevitable man?

Theaet. I should answer, 'Not with that eye but with the other.'

Soc. Then you see and do not see the same thing at the same time.

Theaet. Yes, in a certain sense.

Soc. None of that, he will reply; I do not ask or bid you answer in what sense you know, but only whether you know that which you do not know. You have been proved to see that which you do not see; and you have already admitted that seeing is knowing, and that not-seeing is not-knowing: I leave you to draw the inference.

Theaet. Yes, the inference is the contradictory of my assertion.

Soc. Yes, my marvel, and there might have been yet worse things in store for you, if an opponent had gone on to ask whether you can have a sharp and also a dull knowledge, and whether you can know near, but not at a distance, or know the same thing with more or less intensity, and so on without end. Such questions might have been put to you by a light-armed mercenary, who argued for pay. He would have lain in wait for you, and when you took up the position, that sense is knowledge, he would have made an assault upon hearing, smelling, and the other senses;—he would have shown you no mercy; and while you were lost in envy and admiration of his wisdom, he would have got you into his net, out of which you would not have escaped until you had come to an understanding about the sum to be paid for your release. Well, you ask, and how will Protagoras reinforce his position? Shall I answer for him?

Theaet. By all means.

Soc. He will repeat all those things which we have been urging on his behalf, and then he will close with us in disdain, and say:—The worthy Socrates asked a little boy, whether the same man could remember and not know the same thing, and the boy said No, because he was frightened, and could not see what was coming, and then Socrates made fun of poor me. The truth is, O slatternly Socrates, that when you ask questions about any assertion of mine, and the person asked is found tripping, if he has answered as I should have answered, then I am refuted, but if he answers something else, then he is refuted and not I. For do you really suppose that any one would admit the memory which a man has of an impression which has passed away to be the same with that which he experienced at the time? Assuredly not. Or would he hesitate to acknowledge that the same man may know and not know the same thing? Or, if he is afraid of making this admission, would he ever grant that one who has become unlike is the same as before he became unlike? Or would he admit that a man is one at all, and not rather many and infinite as the changes which take place in him? I speak by the card in order to avoid entanglements of words. But, O my good sir, he will say, come to the argument in a more generous spirit; and either show, if you can, that our sensations are not relative and individual, or, if you admit them to be so, prove that this does not involve the consequence that the appearance becomes, or, if you will have the word, is, to the individual only. As to your talk about pigs and baboons, you are yourself behaving like a pig, and you teach your hearers to make sport of my writings in the same ignorant manner; but this is not to your credit. For I declare that the truth is as I have written, and that each of us is a measure of existence and of non-existence. Yet one man may be a thousand times better than another in proportion as different things are and appear to him. And I am far from saying that wisdom and the wise man have no existence; but I say that the wise man is he who makes the evils which appear and are to a man, into goods which are and appear to him. And I would beg you not to press my words in the letter, but to take the meaning of them as I will explain them. Remember what has been already said,—that to the sick man his food appears to be and is bitter, and to the man in health the opposite of bitter. Now I cannot conceive that one of these men can be or ought to be made wiser than the other: nor can you assert that the sick man because he has one impression is foolish, and the healthy man because he has another is wise; but the one state requires to be changed into the other, the worse into the better. As in education, a change of state has to be effected, and the sophist accomplishes by words the change which the physician works by the aid of drugs. Not that any one ever made another think truly, who previously thought falsely. For no one can think what is not, or think anything different from that which he feels; and this is always true. But as the inferior habit of mind has thoughts of kindred nature, so I conceive that a good mind causes men to have good thoughts; and these which the inexperienced call true, I maintain to be only better, and not truer than others. And, O my dear Socrates, I do not call wise men tadpoles: far from it; I say that they are the physicians of the human body, and the husbandmen of plants—for the husbandmen also take away the evil and disordered sensations of plants, and infuse into them good and healthy sensations—aye and true ones, and the wise and good rhetoricians make the good instead of the evil to seem just to states; for whatever appears to a state to be just and fair, so long as it is regarded as such, is just and fair to it; but the teacher of wisdom causes the good to take the place of the evil, both in appearance and in reality. And in like manner the Sophist who is able to train his pupils in this spirit is a wise man, and deserves to be well paid by them. And so one man is wiser than another; and no one thinks falsely, and you, whether you will or not, must endure to be a measure. On these foundations the argument stands firm, which you, Socrates, may, if you please, overthrow by an opposite argument, or if you like you may put questions to me—a method to which no intelligent person will object, quite the reverse. But I must beg you to put fair questions: for there is great inconsistency in saying that you have a zeal for virtue, and then always behaving unfairly in argument. The unfairness of which I complain is that you do not distinguish between mere disputation and dialectic: the disputer may trip up his opponent as often as he likes, and make fun; but the dialectician will be in earnest, and only correct his adversary when necessary, telling him the errors into which he has fallen through his own fault, or that of the company which he has previously kept. If you do so, your adversary will lay the blame of his own confusion and perplexity on himself, and not on you. He will follow and love you, and will hate himself, and escape from himself into philosophy, in order that he may become different from what he was. But the other mode of arguing, which is practised by the many, will have just the opposite effect upon him; and as he grows older, instead of turning philosopher, he will come to hate philosophy. I would recommend you, therefore, as I said before, not to encourage yourself in this polemical and controversial temper, but to find out, in a friendly and congenial spirit, what we really mean when we say that all things are in motion, and that to every individual and state what appears, is. In this manner you will consider whether knowledge and sensation are the same or different, but you will not argue, as you were just now doing, from the customary use of names and words, which the vulgar pervert in all sorts of ways, causing infinite perplexity to one another. Such, Theodorus, is the very slight help which I am able to offer to your old friend; had he been living, he would have helped himself in a far more gloriose style.

Theod. You are jesting, Socrates; indeed, your defence of him has been most valorous.

Soc. Thank you, friend; and I hope that you observed Protagoras bidding us be serious, as the text, 'Man is the measure of all things,' was a solemn one; and he reproached us with making a boy the medium of discourse, and said that the boy's timidity was made to tell against his argument; he also declared that we made a joke of him.

Theod. How could I fail to observe all that, Socrates?

Soc. Well, and shall we do as he says?

Theod. By all means.

Soc. But if his wishes are to be regarded, you and I must take up the argument, and in all seriousness, and ask and answer one another, for you see that the rest of us are nothing but boys. In no other way can we escape the imputation, that in our fresh analysis of his thesis we are making fun with boys.

Theod. Well, but is not Theaetetus better able to follow a philosophical enquiry than a great many men who have long beards?

Soc. Yes, Theodorus, but not better than you; and therefore please not to imagine that I am to defend by every means in my power your departed friend; and that you are to defend nothing and nobody. At any rate, my good man, do not sheer off until we know whether you are a true measure of diagrams, or whether all men are equally measures and sufficient for themselves in astronomy and geometry, and the other branches of knowledge in which you are supposed to excel them.

Theod. He who is sitting by you, Socrates, will not easily avoid being drawn into an argument; and when I said just now that you would excuse me, and not, like the Lacedaemonians, compel me to strip and fight, I was talking nonsense—I should rather compare you to Scirrhon, who threw travellers from the rocks; for the Lacedaemonian rule is 'strip or depart,' but you seem to go about your work more after the fashion of Antaeus: you will not allow any one who approaches you to depart until you have stripped him, and he has been compelled to try a fall with you in argument.

Soc. There, Theodorus, you have hit off precisely the nature of my complaint; but I am even more pugnacious than the giants of old, for I have met with no end of heroes; many a Heracles, many a Theseus, mighty in words, has broken my head; nevertheless I am always at this rough exercise, which inspires me like a passion. Please, then, to try a fall with me, whereby you will do yourself good as well as me.

Theod. I consent; lead me whither you will, for I know that you are like destiny; no man can escape from any argument which you may weave for him. But I am not disposed to go further than you suggest.

Soc. Once will be enough; and now take particular care that we do not again unwittingly expose ourselves to the reproach of talking childishly.

Theod. I will do my best to avoid that error.

Soc. In the first place, let us return to our old objection, and see whether we were right in blaming and taking offence at Protagoras on the ground that he assumed all to be equal and sufficient in wisdom; although he admitted that there was a better and worse, and that in respect of this, some who as he said were the wise excelled others.

Theod. Very true.

Soc. Had Protagoras been living and answered for himself, instead of our answering for him, there would have been no need of our reviewing or reinforcing the argument. But as he is not here, and some one may accuse us of speaking without authority on his behalf, had we not better come to a clearer agreement about his meaning, for a great deal may be at stake?

Theod. True.

Soc. Then let us obtain, not through any third person, but from his own statement and in the fewest words possible, the basis of agreement.

Theod. In what way?

Soc. In this way:—His words are, 'What seems to a man, is to him.'

Theod. Yes, so he says.

Soc. And are not we, Protagoras, uttering the opinion of man, or rather of all mankind, when we say that every one thinks himself wiser than other men in some things, and their inferior in others? In the hour of danger, when they are in perils of war, or of the sea, or of sickness, do they not look up to their commanders as if they were gods, and expect salvation from them, only because they excel them in knowledge? Is not the world full of men in their several employments, who are looking for teachers and rulers of themselves and of the animals? and there are plenty who think that they are able to teach and able to rule. Now, in all this is implied that ignorance and wisdom exist among them, at least in their own opinion.

Theod. Certainly.

Soc. And wisdom is assumed by them to be true thought, and ignorance to be false opinion.

Theod. Exactly.

Soc. How then, Protagoras, would you have us treat the argument? Shall we say that the opinions of men are always true, or sometimes true and sometimes false? In either case, the result is the same, and their opinions are not always true, but sometimes true and sometimes false. For tell me, Theodoras, do you suppose that you yourself, or any other follower of Protagoras, would contend that no one deems another ignorant or mistaken in his opinion?

Theod. The thing is incredible, Socrates.

Soc. And yet that absurdity is necessarily involved in the thesis which declares man to be the measure of all things.

Theod. How so?

Soc. Why, suppose that you determine in your own mind something to be true, and declare your opinion to me; let us assume, as he argues, that this is true to you. Now, if so, you must either say that the rest of us are not the judges of this opinion or judgment of yours, or that we judge you always to have a true opinion? But are there not thousands upon thousands who, whenever you form a judgment, take up arms against you and are of an opposite judgment and opinion, deeming that you judge falsely?

Theod. Yes, indeed, Socrates, thousands and tens of thousands, as Homer says, who give me a world of trouble.

Soc. Well, but are we to assert that what you think is true to you and false to the ten thousand others?

Theod. No other inference seems to be possible.

Soc. And how about Protagoras himself? If neither he nor the multitude thought, as indeed they do not think, that man is the measure of all things, must it not follow that the truth of which Protagoras wrote would be true to no one? But if you suppose that he himself thought this, and that the multitude does not agree with him, you must begin by allowing that in whatever proportion the many are more than one, in that proportion his truth is more untrue than true.

Theod. That would follow if the truth is supposed to vary with individual opinion.

Soc. And the best of the joke is, that he acknowledges the truth of their opinion who believe his own opinion to be false; for he admits that the opinions of all men are true.

Theod. Certainly.

Soc. And does he not allow that his own opinion is false, if he admits that the opinion of those who think him false is true?

Theod. Of course.

Soc. Whereas the other side do not admit that they speak falsely?

Theod. They do not.

Soc. And he, as may be inferred from his writings, agrees that this opinion is also true.

Theod. Clearly.

Soc. Then all mankind, beginning with Protagoras, will contend, or rather, I should say that he will allow, when he concedes that his adversary has a true opinion—Protagoras, I say, will himself allow that neither a dog nor any ordinary man is the measure of anything which he has not learned—am I not right?

Theod. Yes.

Soc. And the truth of Protagoras being doubted by all, will be true neither to himself nor to any one else?

Theod. I think, Socrates, that we are running my old friend too hard.

Soc. But I do not know that we are going beyond the truth. Doubtless, as he is older, he may be expected to be wiser than we are. And if he could only just get his head out of the world below, he would have overthrown both of us again and again, me for talking nonsense and you for assenting to me, and have been off and underground in a trice. But as he is not within call, we must make the best use of our own faculties, such as they are, and speak out what appears to us to be true. And one thing which no one will deny is, that there are great differences in the understandings of men.

Theod. In that opinion I quite agree.

Soc. And is there not most likely to be firm ground in the distinction which we were indicating on behalf of Protagoras, viz. that most things, and all immediate sensations, such as hot, dry, sweet, are only such as they appear; if however difference of opinion is to be allowed at all, surely we must allow it in respect of health or disease? for every woman, child, or living creature has not such a knowledge of what conduces to health as to enable them to cure themselves.

Theod. I quite agree.

Soc. Or again, in politics, while affirming that just and unjust, honourable and disgraceful, holy and unholy, are in reality to each state such as the state thinks and makes lawful, and that in determining these matters no individual or state is wiser than another, still the followers of Protagoras will not deny that in determining what is or is not expedient for the community one state is wiser and one counsellor better than another—they will scarcely venture to maintain, that what a city enacts in the belief that it is expedient will always be really expedient. But in the other case, I mean when they speak of justice and injustice, piety and impiety, they are confident that in nature these have no existence or essence of their own—the truth is that which is agreed on at the time of the agreement, and as long as the agreement lasts; and this is the philosophy of many who do not altogether go along with Protagoras. Here arises a new question, Theodorus, which threatens to be more serious than the last. . . .

Soc. Had we not reached the point at which the partisans of the perpetual flux, who say that things are as they seem to each one, were confidently maintaining that the ordinances which the state commanded and thought just, were just to the state which imposed them, while they were in force; this was especially asserted of justice; but as to the good, no one had any longer the hardihood to contend of any ordinances which the state thought and enacted to be good that these, while they were in force, were really good;—he who said so would be playing with the name 'good,' and would not touch the real question —it would be a mockery, would it not?

Theod. Certainly it would.

Soc. He ought not to speak of the name, but of the thing which is contemplated under the name.

Theod. Right.

Soc. Whatever be the term used, the good or expedient is the aim of legislation, and as far as she has an opinion, the state imposes all laws with a view to the greatest expediency; can legislation have any other aim?

Theod. Certainly not.

Soc. But is the aim attained always? do not mistakes often happen?

Theod. Yes, I think that there are mistakes.

Soc. The possibility of error will be more distinctly recognised, if we put the question in reference to the whole class under which the good or expedient falls. That whole class has to do with the future, and laws are passed under the idea that they will be useful in after-time; which, in other words, is the future.

Theod. Very true.

Soc. Suppose now, that we ask Protagoras, or one of his disciples, a question: —O, Protagoras, we will say to him, Man is, as you declare, the measure of all things—white, heavy, light: of all such things he is the judge; for he has the criterion of them in himself, and when he thinks that things are such as he experiences them to be, he thinks what is and is true to himself. Is it not so?

Theod. Yes.

Soc. And do you extend your doctrine, Protagoras (as we shall further say), to the future as well as to the present; and has he the criterion not only of what in his opinion is but of what will be, and do things always happen to him as he expected? For example, take the case of heat:—When an ordinary man thinks that he is going to have a fever, and that this kind of heat is coming on, and another person, who is a physician, thinks the contrary, whose opinion is likely to prove right? Or are they both right?—he will have a heat and fever in his own judgment, and not have a fever in the physician's judgment?

Theod. How ludicrous!

Soc. And the vinegrower, if I am not mistaken, is a better judge of the sweetness or dryness of the vintage which is not yet gathered than the harp-player?

Theod. Certainly.

Soc. And in musical composition the musician will know better than the training master what the training master himself will hereafter think harmonious or the reverse?

Theod. Of course.

Soc. And the cook will be a better judge than the guest, who is not a cook, of the pleasure to be derived from the dinner which is in preparation; for of present or past pleasure we are not as yet arguing; but can we say that every one will be to himself the best judge of the pleasure which will seem to be and will be to him in the future?—nay, would not you, Protagoras, better guess which arguments in a court would convince any one of us than the ordinary man?

Theod. Certainly, Socrates, he used to profess in the strongest manner that he was the superior of all men in this respect.

Soc. To be sure, friend: who would have paid a large sum for the privilege of talking to him, if he had really persuaded his visitors that neither a prophet nor any other man was better able to judge what will be and seem to be in the future than every one could for himself?

Theod. Who indeed?

Soc. And legislation and expediency are all concerned with the future; and every one will admit that states, in passing laws, must often fail of their highest interests?

Theod. Quite true.

Soc. Then we may fairly argue against your master, that he must admit one man to be wiser than another, and that the wiser is a measure: but I, who know nothing, am not at all obliged to accept the honour which the advocate of Protagoras was just now forcing upon me, whether I would or not, of being a measure of anything.

Theod. That is the best refutation of him, Socrates; although he is also caught when he ascribes truth to the opinions of others, who give the lie direct to his own opinion.

Soc. There are many ways, Theodorus, in which the doctrine that every opinion of every man is true may be refuted.

Epistemological Relativism Rests on a Confusion

W. MONTAGUE

Introductory and Historical

IN THE *Popular Science Monthly* of January 1878 there appeared a paper by Mr. Charles Peirce entitled "How to Make Our Ideas Clear." Mr. Peirce, distinguished for the originality of his contributions to symbolic logic and to general philosophy, in this paper set forth a new method for ascertaining the meaning of concepts and judgments which he later named "Pragmatism," and still later "Pragmaticism," to distinguish it from the newer forms of pragmatic

---

Reprinted with permission of Allen & Unwin, Ltd. from "The Method of Pragmatism" in *The Ways of Knowing* by W. Montague, 1925, pp. 131–133 and 156–167.

philosophy. According to Mr. Peirce, the real meaning of an idea is to be found in its concrete results, and especially in its practical consequences for human action. In the article just mentioned Peirce expresses his principle as follows: "consider what effects which might conceivably have practical bearings we conceive the object of our conception to have. Then our conception of these effects is the whole of our conception of the object."

It is interesting to note that Mr. Peirce offers his pragmatic principle as a criterion for ascertaining, not the *truth* of an idea or proposition, but its *meaning.* He opposes his conception to the Leibnitzian conceptions of what constitutes clearness and distinctness of ideas. According to Peirce, in order to understand the meaning of a thought, it is not sufficient to mark it off from other ideas, nor is it necessary to analyse its logical essence. What is both necessary and sufficient is to discover all its consequences both actual and possible. One might question whether this identification of the meaning of a proposition with its effects did not leave the proposition itself rather devoid of meaning. But it is more relevant to our present purpose to point out the great difference between Peirce's use of practical consequences as a way of defining and discovering *meanings* from the later pragmatists' use of the *satisfactoriness* of practical consequences as a way of defining and discovering *truths.* I think it was Professor Dewey who pointed out that the characteristic generosity of William James caused him to over-estimate his debt to Peirce, and to under-estimate the originality of his own pragmatism. Consequences do, to be sure, however used, imply a prospective attitude; and the prospective suggests the conative or voluntaristic interest in the good. This in turn might have suggested that the good consequences of holding a proposition were a sign of its truth, and even that truth consisted in satisfaction. But to Peirce himself the proper method of verifying a belief as set forth in other papers of his series of "Illustrations of the Logic of Science" had nothing to do with the goodness or badness of the consequences, but consisted entirely in the use of observation and experiment, supplemented by a use of the theory of probability. As explaining his epistemological theory of the meaning of truth, as well as his logical theory of how we should verify our beliefs, the following passage is of interest:

"The opinion which is fated to be ultimately agreed to by all who investigate is what we mean by truth and the object represented in this opinion is the real." This passage from the article above cited might appear to have a slightly subjective flavour, but if we interpret it in the light of a passage in a preceding article of the series on "Illustrations of the Logic of Science," we shall see that the "fated agreement" in belief was to be brought about by purely objective factors. The article to which I am referring was published in the *Popular Science Monthly* for November 1877, and the significant passage reads as follows: "To satisfy our doubts, therefore, it is necessary that a method should be found by which our beliefs may be caused by nothing human but by some external permanency, something upon which our thinking has no effect. . . . It must be something which affects or might affect every man. And though these effects are necessarily as various as are individual conditions, yet the method must be such that the ultimate conclusions of every man be the same. Such is the method of science. Its fundamental hypothesis restated in more familiar language is this: There are real things whose characters are entirely independent of our opinions about them; those realities affect our senses according to regular laws. And though our sensations are as different as our relations to the objects, yet by taking advantage of the laws of perception we can ascertain by reasoning how things really are. And any man if he have sufficient experience and reason enough about it will be led to the one true conclusion."

In view of the subjectivism and relativism with which pragmatism appears to many of us to be infected, it has seemed worth while to show by these somewhat extended quotations that the prophet of the movement at least was sufficiently committed to a realistic theory of knowledge.

The novel and interesting doctrine of Peirce seems to have attracted little notice until in 1898 it was expounded and developed in a new form by William James in an address to the Philosophical Union of the University of California. James followed this address with many articles in which he set forth various phases of the pragmatic theory; and in 1907 he published his *Pragmatism*, which, together with its sequel *The Meaning of Truth*, constitutes a fairly complete presentation of the Pragmatic philosophy in the form in which James held it. . . .

Pragmatism as Relativism

The third of the major phases or tendencies of pragmatism I have called, for want of a better name, Relativism. Like Futurism and Practicalism, it is to be found in some form and to a greater or less extent in all who call themselves pragmatists. But while futurism is mainly significant for ethics, education, and social philosophy, and while practicalism in all of its three phases is mainly significant for genetic psychology and for the problem as to the proper criteria for attaining truth, relativism, in distinction from the other parts of the philosophy of pragmatism, is concerned primarily with epistemology, *i.e.* the branch of methodology that addresses itself to the problem, not of how knowledge is and should be attained, but of how the meaning of knowledge or truth when once attained should be interpreted. And as was pointed out in the introduction, the question as to the meaning of truth turns upon the question as to the manner in which the objects of knowledge are related to the minds that know them. The systematic treatment of the problems of epistemology is reserved for Part II; but because of the intimate manner in which the practicalist logic of pragmatism is bound up with its relativistic epistemology, it seems best to discuss them together. This somewhat irregular procedure is further justified by the arrogant claim of the epistemological relativist that his interpretation of the meaning of truth is so superior as to render meaningless and artificial all of the traditional answers to the epistemological problem. And this attitude of arrogance is carried so far by the relativist that he does not even like to call his particular species of epistemology by the generic name. He prefers to regard his doctrine as a substitute for epistemology rather than as a form of it, and as a means of escaping the whole set of puzzles involved in the relation of the knowing subject to the objects known.

This relativistic epistemology of pragmatism can be best understood if we treat it as an outgrowth of its practicalistic logic. Hence, before criticizing the relativistic conception of the meaning of truth, I should like to say something about the manner in which it has developed from the practicalist conception of the method of attaining and testing truth. At the outset, let us remember that at least one of the beginnings of pragmatism was the attempt to apply evolutionary biology to the domain of psychology. This results in what James called a "teleological" interpretation of mental processes. And if every phase of mental life is interpreted teleologically, as a dynamic process aimed at the satisfaction of individual needs, it is natural to take the further step of subsuming the logical interest in attaining cognitive satisfaction under the ethical interest in attaining practical satisfaction.

Now, the empirically-minded founders of pragmatism were naturally in strong sympathy with the ethical Utilitarianism of Mill; hence their affiliation of logic with ethics meant that logical value or truth was to be interpreted by the utilitarian principle of expediency. If the morally good is the expedient or satisfactory in the way of conduct, then also the logically true is the expedient or satisfactory in the way of belief. And as utilitarianism in ethics means a relativistic conception of the good, the pragmatic extension of Utilitarianism to logic will mean a relativistic conception of the true. William James's dedication of his *Pragmatism* to the memory of John Stuart Mill voiced with beautiful precision the mission of the new philosophy. The Utilitarians had abolished the notion of a Good that was absolute and independent of the changing desires of individuals. The pragmatists were to abolish the conception of a Truth that was absolute and independent of the changing beliefs of individuals. The utilitarians had substituted for the absolutistic conception of an independent good the relativistic theory that whatever satisfied desires was in so far forth good. The pragmatists would substitute for the absolutistic conception of the true the relativistic theory that whatever satisfies individual beliefs is in so far forth true. And as the utilitarians had answered the charge that their theory meant mere anarchy in ethics, by declaring that the highest good was what was most satisfactory to the desires of the greatest number, so the pragmatists can answer the charge that their theory means mere anarchy in logic by declaring that the highest truth is what proves most satisfactory to the beliefs of the greatest number. *It is the essence of each theory to deny that the good and the true, respectively, possesses any absolute content apart from the interests of individuals.*

It has been customary in recent years for various groups of philosophers to criticize the utilitarians for their somewhat artificial hedonistic psychology; but at least among the empirically-minded of such critics there can be found few if any who will deny the tremendous service which utilitarianism rendered to the whole vast domain of the moral sciences. So much of the spiritual energies of men had been spent in devotion to abstract rules and principles of conduct which had lost their relevance to actual human wants, that there was need for a new ethical gospel which should sweep away antiquated taboos and fine-sounding slogans and call on all lovers of the good for a single-hearted devotion to such measures and only such measures as would increase human well-being. These advocates of the new dispensation appraised any and all codes of morality by the sole criterion of their efficacy to satisfy human needs; and to the service of that supreme ideal they unhesitatingly conscripted the resources of organized knowledge, physical and psychological. Their aim in brief was to make ethics a science, and to substitute the co-operative and experimental methods of intelligence for the sterile competitions of sentiment and dialectic.

Now, the inheritors of this great and clarifying movement of utilitarianism are the pragmatists of to-day. And we cannot properly estimate the strength and weakness of their doctrine of epistemological relativism unless we keep in mind their inheritance of ethical relativism from Bentham and Mill. All pragmatists are in a broad sense utilitarians, and because their relativism in the theory of values is useful and valid they and their friends have assumed that their relativism in the theory of knowledge must be equally useful and valid. I feel sure that it is this extension of relativity from the field of the good to the field of the true that constitutes the principal cause for the success of pragmatism to-day. And I feel equally sure that this contention of pragmatism, that relativity of value implies relativity of truth, is as false in reality as it is plausible in appearance. It is plausible in appearance because the methods applicable to the moral and social sciences seem to be and in many cases actually are the same as those applicable to the other branches of science. The leaders of pragmatism deserve much credit in the fields of law, education, and political and economic reform, for making the methods of procedure more flexible and efficient and more relevant to the concrete questions at issue. Hence it is natural enough to suppose that their principles will be equally sound in other fields. If it has proved beneficial to conceive the ethically desirable or good as relative to individuals, why should it not prove equally beneficial to conceive the cognitively desirable or true as equally relative to individuals? But this identification, though plausible in appearance, is false in reality because of that profound contrast between the good and the true which we have noted above. We can only express once more our conviction that the adjustment between the individual and his environment, which is the goal of the cognitive interest in truth, is an adjustment in which the environment is the primary and independent variable, the individual's ideas and judgments being secondary and dependent for their validity upon their agreement with objective facts. On the other hand, the goal of the conative interest in the good is an adjustment between the individual and the environment in which individual desires and sentiments constitute the primary and independent variables, the environment being secondary and dependent for its goodness on its agreement with individual needs. The cognitive equilibrium of truth is cosmocentric and absolute, while the conative equilibrium of goodness is anthropocentric and relative. Because of this contrast, to recognize that what is really and not merely apparently good for one may be really and not merely apparently bad for another is very sound ethics; while for the same reason, to claim that what is really and not merely apparently true for one may be really and not merely apparently false for another is very unsound logic. Ideas are *true* only when they conform to objective facts; but facts are *good* only when they conform to subjective needs.

In explaining the manner in which the relativism of the pragmatists has developed from their practicalism we were led to a statement and criticism of the first and principal argument in support of that relativism, *viz.* the apparent similarity between the cognitive satisfaction of human beliefs and the conative satisfaction of human needs. The latter being relative to individuals, it was falsely argued that the former was equally relative; and that consequently pragmatism could clarify the concept of *truth* in the same fashion that utilitarianism had clarified the concept of *good.*

In addition to its supposed agreement with utilitarianism, there are, I believe, three further reasons for the growth of pragmatic relativism: (1) its apparent connection with the doctrine of evolution; (2) its apparent connection with the attitude of scepticism; (3) an ambiguity of the term "truth." Let us consider these reasons in turn.

The theory of evolution has made us familiar with the extent to which the universe is pervaded by change; even the things that appear to be most permanent, such as the heavenly bodies, the seas and mountains, and the species of plants and animals, are in a process of change. Human institutions and human beliefs that at one time seemed eternal are now being revised. It is natural for us to suppose that this evolutionary process to which all existing things are subject should extend to the realm of logical meaning; and consequently we tend to regard the notion of an unchangeable system of truth as a relic of the pre-Darwinian age. Yet while the extension of the notion of change from the things of physics to the things of logic may be natural, it is absolutely unjustifiable and leads only to confusion. In the first place, change itself has no meaning unless the terms of the process remain fixed. I cannot speak of a man changing from youth to age, or of a species changing from simian to human, unless the terms "youth," "age," "simian," "human," are supposed to preserve their meanings unchanged. What holds true of logical terms holds true equally of propositions which are relations between terms. If the proposition that the earth has been spherical for the ten billion years prior to the year 1900 is true at this moment, then that proposition will always be true on pain of losing its meaning as a proposition. The earth might change to-morrow from a globe to a disc without changing the truth of the above proposition. In short, the maxims: *True for one, true for all*, and *once true, always true*, apply not only to all abstract or non-existential propositions, but to all other propositions in so far as they are made thoroughly unambiguous with respect to the time and space of the facts asserted. Change resides only in physical processes and in the psychological processes by which we become aware of physical processes. But between those processes and the logical relations which they reveal there is fixed a gulf which no change can cross.

Let us turn now to the second of the three causes for the spread of the doctrine of relativism, *viz.* its connection with scepticism. And here the relativistic pragmatist can make out a somewhat better case. We may imagine him to speak to us as follows: "You talk about an absolute truth, independent of anyone's belief in it or knowledge of it. Well, supposing that there were such a thing, we could never attain it; or at least if we did attain it, we could never recognize it for what it was. All that we can know in the way of truth is something that is believed. Each man calls his own belief by the eulogistic name of *truth*, and with respect to this as an absolute standard, he describes his neighbour's opinions by such uncomplimentary names as 'apparent truths' or 'subjective beliefs.' Consequently, we pragmatists, recognizing this universal shortcoming of human nature, are frank enough to say that there is no truth with a capital T; no absolute impersonal objective reality, not even our own, and that whether we like it or not we have to put up with *the best in the way of belief.* We may still use the word truth in this semi-subjective sense, and it is in this sense that truth is relative to different persons and subject to change."

Now, the only trouble with this reply of the pragmatist is that it is a virtual confession that the relativistic feature of his doctrine, when freed from ambiguities, reduces to pure scepticism. For scepticism is the theory that truth in its objective sense is unattainable by any means within our power. The only difference between pragmatic relativism and scepticism is that the former doctrine uses the word "truth" in a purely subjective sense that is different from the sense in which it is used by the other methodological theories. The thoroughgoing sceptic believes with the relativist that we possess beliefs which we prefer to those of our neighbours, but he gives himself no false verbal comfort by calling these preferred beliefs "truth." He reserves that word for the objective reality which he thinks lies beyond the reach of our knowledge. But whether he is right or wrong in holding to his pessimistic and negative attitude towards the methodological problem, we cannot discuss until the next chapter.

The third of the reasons for the popularity of Epistemological relativism may be stated as follows: *All truth depends upon or is in part created by individuals. It is, therefore, inseparable from them and relative to them; and as such, it changes as they change.* Now there are two meanings involved in this statement of relativism which depend upon the two meanings that can be given to the word truth. By "truth" may be meant (1) whatever is believed, or (2) whatever is real or is a fact. If the word is taken in the first or subjective sense, then the relativistic principle that truth changes becomes a truism, for it means only that *people's beliefs change as people's minds change.* If truth is taken in the second or objective sense, the relativistic principle ceases to be a truism and becomes a paradox, for it then means that *the facts or realities of the world change as people's minds change.* We may illustrate the difference by the following example: " 'That the earth is flat' was for the ancients an obvious truth; 'that the earth is round' is for us an established truth. Their truth was not our truth. Truth, therefore, is relative and changing, and what is true for one may be false for another." These statements sound pretty well, and we should probably pass them over unchallenged, because we should take for granted that the word "truth" was being used in its subjective sense as a synonym of belief. It is a truism that people's beliefs can differ, that one can believe what another disbelieves; and it is a commonplace that a change in beliefs took place with regard to the shape of the earth. The ancients believed it to be flat, and we believe it to be round. But if we were told that the author of the statements cited meant "truth" to be taken in the objective sense, we should suppose that he had been indulging in either a geological or a logical paradox. If he meant that the flatness of the earth was a truth (fact) in ancient times and also that its roundness was a truth (fact) in modern times, we should assume that he believed that the earth's shape had undergone a marvellous geological change from a disc to a globe. If in still adhering to the objective meaning of the term "truth" he denied that he intended any such geological absurdity as the above, we should have to assume that he was committing the still greater logical absurdity of supposing that the shape of the earth could be both flat and spherical at once.

The pragmatic doctrine of the relativity of truth is thus seen to owe some of its plausibility to an ambiguity. Before the ambiguity is revealed, the truism and the paradox conceal one another and unite to produce the appearance of a novel and important discovery. In exactly the same way a black cardboard seen through white tissue paper appears to be a single surface of grey. When we look at the thing edgewise, however, the effect of grey disappears and we see only the black and the white. So, when once we recognize the ambiguity of the term "truth," and insist upon the relativistic pragmatist using the word in one sense or the other, we find only an ill-looking juxtaposition of the paradox that facts depend upon people believing them, and the truism that our beliefs about facts change and vary. In case the illustration chosen fails to satisfy the reader, I would suggest that he make up for himself examples of statements which can loosely be regarded as cases of "truth changing" or of "true for one but false for another," and see for himself whether a little analysis of the meanings involved in all such statements will not disclose the above-mentioned ambiguity or duplicity of the "truth" in question.

In concluding this analysis of the relativistic epistemology of pragmatism I should like to call attention to a very real disaster which threatens the study and teaching of philosophy, and which is likely to be brought nearer by the spread of the doctrine we have been considering.

There is a certain type of "up-to-date" student to whom the humility involved in honourable scepticism is intolerable. These students, eager, earnest, and not consciously insincere, will study for a time the problems of Being and Knowing which have been raised by the great philosophers. They do their best, but they become confused. They disagree with the idealistic conclusions of Berkeley and Kant, but cannot refute the reasoning on which those conclusions are based. They are piqued and stirred by such vitalistic criticisms of the current scientific naturalism as are made by Driesch and Bergson, but they lack the knowledge of the elements of natural science that would make possible even a tentative appraisal of those criticisms. It is inevitable that the less scrupulous and more confused of these students, when placed in such a situation, will seize with avidity upon any device, no matter how hollow, which will serve to conceal their failure even from themselves, and enable them to gain a sense of superiority over the great philosophers of the past. There is grave danger that the relativistic form of pragmatism will be adopted to meet such needs. For to the relativist with his covert suggestion that "truth" is only the best that we attain in the way of belief, all questions about the nature of objective reality will appear as "artificial." And if there is no objective reality apart from human interests and beliefs, it may seem unnecessary to bother oneself about the problems of traditional philosophy. Philistine minds will be tempted to mask their incompetency with the boast that the puzzles that they have failed to solve were "unreal," "old-fashioned," "dialectical" subtleties with which a practical man in a practical age need not concern himself. Like the fox in the fable, if we fail to get the grapes we can save our face by calling them sour.

INTRODUCTION TO EPISTEMOLOGY / Study Questions

LEARNING, KNOWLEDGE, AND TRUTH

Lovell

1. How does Lovell define learning? How might he have found out that this is what learning really is?
2. Can you think of any examples that fit the definition but are clearly not cases to which the word *learning* applies?
3. Describe the two main kinds of theories of learning discussed.
4. Can Pavlov's dogs correctly be described as having *learned* to salivate?
5. Is it plausible to suppose that a child can be *conditioned* to learn a language? To learn arithmetic? To appreciate a work of art? To understand a moral situation?
6. Can the notion of insight serve as an *explanation* of learning?
7. Do the notions of "organization of the psychological field," "provisional maps," or "hypotheses" have any explanatory value? How, for example, could it be determined that the "psychological field" of an animal had been organized in a certain way so that fact could be cited as an explanation of its behaving as it does?
8. A person who has learned a language is able to construct and understand sentences he has never heard before. Similarly, a person who has learned arithmetic can do sums he has never seen before. Can these facts be explained either by *conditioning* or *insight?* (Recall the kinds of examples used to explain insight.)
9. In a programmed textbook what is the criterion of a "correct response?"
10. Is the conception of teaching and learning that is bound up with the talk about conditioning, reinforcement, programmed tests, and so on, consistent with the imparting of complete misinformation?
11. Can one learn what is false? (Note that this is a question about the logical relations between the *concepts* of *learning* and *truth* and *falsity*.)

Ryle

1. What is the problem that Ryle wants to investigate?
2. What examples does Ryle offer of finding out something for oneself?
3. Why does there seem to be a paradox in the idea of teaching oneself something new?

4. What is the point of Ryle's claim that it is the business of the teacher to get his pupils to advance beyond their instruction?
5. What may be improper about the request "Recite what you have learned in school today, Tommy?"
6. What is the mistaken picture of teaching to which Ryle is opposed? Is this picture embodied in the theories reviewed by Lovell?
7. Why does Ryle put emphasis on the notions of "teaching-to" and "learning-to?"
8. What connection does Ryle see between drill and thinking? Can the theories discussed by Lovell make sense of this connection?
9. What difference does Ryle see between being able to parrot facts and knowing facts? Can the theories discussed by Lovell take account of this?
10. How does Ryle resolve the paradox referred to in question 3?
11. How does Ryle describe a *method?* How are methods taught?
12. Discuss your own education in the light of Ryle's article.

Plato (Gorgias)

1. What does Socrates want to learn from Gorgias? What is the motivation behind his question?
2. How does Polus misunderstand the question about Gorgias?
3. What is the art of Gorgias?
4. How does Gorgias compare the occupation of the rhetorician with other occupations such as medicine or physical culture?
5. In what ways does Socrates find this account unclear?
6. What revised account of rhetoric does Gorgias then offer? With what conception of human value does this account seem bound up?
7. What connection does Socrates make between teaching and persuasion?
8. State the argument by means of which Socrates distinguishes between knowledge and belief.
9. Explain clearly the conceptual relations Socrates establishes between *teaching, learning, belief, knowledge,* and *rhetoric.*
10. What is Gorgias' view about the moral responsibility of the teacher of rhetoric? How does Socrates show an inconsistency in the view?
11. If what Socrates says about teaching, knowledge, and belief is embarrassing to Gorgias' position, ought it to be equally embarrassing to the theories of learning discussed by Lovell?

James

1. According to James, what is the dictionary definition of truth?
2. In what part of this definition do both pragmatists and intellectualists (rationalists) agree? In what do they disagree?
3. James speaks of *ideas* as being true or false and under this heading seems to include things as diverse as mental images, words, and beliefs. Is there a possible source of confusion here?
4. Why does James think there is a problem about ideas copying or agreeing with their objects?
5. What question about truth does the pragmatist want to ask?
6. James says that "True ideas are those that we can . . . verify." Is this an informative statement? (What does the word *verify* mean?)

7. What is James' pragmatic account of verification?
8. Is it possible to know what experiences will verify a statement unless we have a conception of what it is for that statement to be true that is independent of that process of verification?
9. At some points James wants to connect the notion of truth with that of "a world of realities" and at other places with the notion of utility. Is this consistent?
10. Is it true to say that "it is useful because it is true" and "it is true because it is useful" mean exactly the same thing?
11. Does James believe that every statement we are willing to call true has in fact been verified?
12. What account does James give of mathematical and logical truth?
13. How does James propose to deal with statements about the past?
14. James says that the word *truth* denotes a process. Is this the way the word is in fact used in our language? Do we use it to denote anything at all?
15. How does James represent the rationalist's criticism of his theory? Does he adequately refute this criticism? What is the point of the examples of *wealth, health,* and *strength?*
16. James says that "*'The true' . . . is only the expedient in our way of thinking. . . .*" What does this mean? Is it consistent with his characterization of truth as a process?
17. Make a catalogue of all the ways in which James describes truth. Are these descriptions consistent?
18. James charges his critics with offering silly interpretations of the pragmatic theory of truth. Have pragmatists left themselves open to this charge?

Plato (Theaetetus)

1. What is the question that Socrates puts to Theaetetus and how does Theaetetus answer?
2. How does Socrates link what Theaetetus says with the theory of Protagoras?
3. In what way are the objects of sense perception said to be relative to the perceiver? Is what is true of the sensations of hot and cold also true of other sense perceptions, color, for example?
4. How does Socrates suggest that Protagoras' conclusions are inconsistent with the purpose of his own book?
5. State the arguments that Socrates presents against the identification of perception with knowledge based on the use of such words as *see, know,* and *remember.*
6. How does Socrates undertake to defend the theory of Protagoras? What does this defense involve doing with the concepts of *wisdom, truth,* and *falsity*?
7. Is the position that Socrates works out on behalf of Protagoras in any way an anticipation of James' pragmatic theory of truth?
8. Would Protagoras be better off to give up the concepts of *truth* and *falsity* and to banish those words from his vocabulary? Would the same apply to James?
9. Must Protagoras accept the assumption that one man may have more knowledge than another? What are the implications of this assumption for the truth and falsity of judgments?
10. What are the consequences of the Protagorean theory of truth for the truth of the theory itself?
11. What is the application of Protagoras' theory of morality and politics? What account of moral and political value is being assumed and how does Socrates use this account to argue against Protagoras?

relative? That moral values are relative?

12. Has Socrates been successful in refuting the thesis that knowledge and truth are

Montague

1. Describe Peirce's theory of pragmatism. What is it a theory about? In what way, according to Montague, did James modify the theory?
2. What does Montague claim is the connection between pragmatism and utilitarianism? What is Montague's view of the respective merits of utilitarianism and pragmatism?
3. What does Montague cite as the three reasons for the growth of pragmatic relativism?
4. How does "the extension of the notion of change from the things of physics to the things of logic" lead to confusion?
5. What is meant by the claim that *truth* is only a eulogistic name for certain beliefs?
6. How does Montague argue that the pragmatist is committed to scepticism? Does scepticism entail the relativity of truth?
7. What is the ambiguity in the meaning of the word *truth* that Montague says pragmatism trades upon?
8. Why is it important to distinguish between a proposition's being true and someone's belief that it is true?
9. Can any sense at all be made of a sentence such as "What is true for you may not be true for me?"

Scepticism and Perception

Problems about knowledge and perception had been raised in antiquity although these problems never dominated the thinking of either the Greeks or the philosophers of the middle ages. These questions were reopened in the first half of the seventeenth century as a result of the impetus given by the new scientific developments brought about by the work of men such as Kepler, Galileo, and *Descartes.* Dissatisfaction with the view of the world inherited from the middle ages led the seventeenth-century pioneers of modern science to search for the correct method of scientific inquiry. It was generally agreed that science had to proceed by direct observation of nature and natural phenomena. Indeed, no one today would think of doubting that scientific knowledge, as well as our everyday and commonsense knowledge of things is based on observation, that is, on what we can see, hear, taste, smell, and touch.

It was Descartes who was largely responsible for reopening the question about the adequacy of sense experience and as a result of his influence this epistemological issue became perhaps the central one for philosophy for the next three hundred years. In the first of his *Meditations*, Descartes concludes that it is possible that all our sense preceptions are illusory and, hence, that it is possible that things are not as they appear to us to be and that it is altogether possible that there are no things at all, no "external world," of which our senses could be aware. Note that Descartes does not claim that our senses *are* always mistaken, only that they *may* be mistaken. Descartes' position here is one of *scepticism:* At this stage in the investigation there is no way to know that our senses do not deceive us because it is possible to doubt that any experience we choose to consider is veridical.

Descartes supports his sceptical conclusion with three arguments, the argument about "things that are hardly perceptible or, very far away," the dream argument, and the evil genius argument. The intended result of these arguments is for us to conclude that although we are apparently seeing and hearing things, there may be nothing at all in the world corresponding to these experiences and, indeed, there may be no world at all. But we nevertheless seem to see things; if there is nothing to be seen (or heard, touched, and so on) what, then, are the things we seem to be seeing, hearing, and so on? Seventeenth century philosophers termed these alleged objects of immediate perception "ideas in the mind"; the twentieth century has substituted the term "sense data." The conclusion Descartes wants us to draw from his three sceptical arguments, then, is that the only things we can be immediately conscious of are our own sense data and that from this awareness of sense data alone we can reach no conclusion at all about whether our sense data correspond to, or give us any information about, things in the world.

Some philosophers have tried to argue that at least some of our sense data do represent the world to us by being like copies or pictures of the real things in the world. This theory about the relation between sense data and the physical world has been called the representational theory of perception. However, very little reflection is enough to show that this kind of theory is, on its own terms, utterly implausible. How could anyone know that his sense data do, in fact, give him a correct picture of the world? In order to find out that one thing—a photograph for example—is an accurate representation of something else, say Aunt Lucy, we must be able to compare the two things, Aunt Lucy with her photo. We can, of course, compare Aunt Lucy to her photo and thereby find out whether it is a good likeness. What we cannot do, however, is to compare our sense data with the things of the world for there can be no awareness of these things independently of our awareness of sense data. It would seem that we can never know what the world is like or even if there is a world apart from our own sense data. Thus we would seem to be trapped in scepticism.

Contemporary philosophical strategy has not been to try to solve the problem posed by scepticism by searching for some as yet unsuspected link that will guarantee a correspondence between our sense data and the physical world, but has been rather to show that the arguments designed to lead to the sceptical conclusions do not in fact entail those consequences and, in addition, has been to suggest that the hypothesis of scepticism may not even be intelligible.

In his paper, "Descartes' Evil Genius," O. K. *Bouwsma* questions the intelligibility of the evil genius hypothesis and the concomitant claim that all beliefs might be false and all experiences illusory. If Bouwsma is correct in understanding scepticism as he does, then Descartes' whole program collapses; for instead of an epistemological problem needing a solution there was only a conceptual confusion needing straightening out.

In his chapter from *Foundations of Empirical Knowledge*, A. J. *Ayer* provides us with another argument for the sense datum theory of perception. Ayer calls this argument the argument from illusion and he elaborates it carefully and in considerable detail. This argument might be thought of as a spelling out of some of the things suggested in Descartes' first sceptical argument about things that are hardly perceptible, an argument that Descartes does not develop at all. Although Ayer says in his conciuding paragraph that we may be allowed to have indirect knowledge of material things by way of our experience of sense data, we would question, given the terms of the sense datum theory, whether such a claim has any justification whatsoever.

The selection from M. D. *Vernon* is introduced to clearly show that these problems about knowledge and perception are not the property of philosophers alone, but arise, although frequently unacknowledged, in the work of psychologists as well as other thinkers in other disciplines. The account of perception that she gives us begins with a consideration of the physiological facts of perception about how patterns of nerve stimulation are set up and conveyed to the brain and what processes then result in the brain itself. It is concluded that we are not directly aware of physical objects in the world, but rather that our perception of the world is in some way constructed out of bits of information provided by these processes in the nervous system and brain. It will be recognized that this account of perception is essentially that found in most standard psychology textbooks.

This description of perception suggests strongly that we are aware of the world in very much the same kind of way that the warship's radar operator is "aware" of the other ships and aircraft about him. From his station in the bowels of the vessel the radarman cannot directly see these other ships, but must construct a picture of what is going on out of the blips on the radar screen. The important thing to note here is that this account of perception is in reality only another version of the representational theory of perception. A little reflection will again suffice to show there is no conceivable way, given this theory, that our perceptions can be checked for accuracy in the way that the radarman's reports can be verified by direct observation of sea and sky. This kind of psychological theory can only end in scepticism and this scepticism has to apply equally to the very physiological facts upon which the theory was supposed to rest. Note that as philosophers we cannot question any of the facts of physiology and should have no desire to do so. We do not want to question the facts, only the conclusions that may be incorrectly drawn from the facts. The theory just described can make no sense of there even being any physiological facts; it has sawed off the limb it wants to sit on.

The last selection offers one kind of diagnosis of how the argument from illusion and the sense datum theory get started. In his discussion of Ayer's chapter, J. L. *Austin* seeks to show how Ayer has lead us down "the garden path" by an initial misrepresentation of the ordinary man's views about perception. Austin wants us to realize that the term *material thing* is not part of the ordinary man's conceptual furniture since it was introduced to serve as a foil for the philosopher's term *sense datum*. Austin echoes Bouwsma's point that talk about deception makes sense only against a background of possible nondeception that is never supplied by Ayer, and then goes on to charge that Ayer is able to attach no sense to his contrast of direct with indirect perception. The sense datum theory, Austin is arguing, is a confusion from the beginning.

We have included no discussion of Descartes' dream argument as a ground for scepticism in this section. Students may want to look at John Cook's subtle examination of the argument in his article, "Human Beings," included in Part 2.

Do Our Senses Always Deceive Us?

RENÉ DESCARTES

Meditation I

Of the things which may be brought within the sphere of the doubtful

IT IS now some years since I detected how many were the false beliefs that I had from my earliest youth admitted as true, and how doubtful was everything I had since constructed on this basis; and from that time I was convinced that I must once for all seriously undertake to rid myself of all the opinions which I had formerly accepted, and commence to build anew from the foundation, if I wanted to establish any firm and permanent structure in the sciences. But as this enterprise appeared to be a very great one, I waited until I had attained an age so mature that I could not hope that at any later date I should be better fitted to execute my design. This reason caused me to delay so long that I should feel that I was doing wrong were I to occupy in deliberation the time that yet remains to me for action. To-day, then, since very opportunely for the plan I have in view I have delivered my mind from every care [and am happily agitated by no passions] and since I have procured for myself an assured leisure in a peaceable retirement, I shall at last seriously and freely address myself to the general upheaval of all my former opinions.

Now for this object it is not necessary that I should show that all of these are false—I shall perhaps never arrive at this end. But inasmuch as reason already persuades me that I ought no less carefully to withhold my assent from matters which are not entirely certain and indubitable than from those which appear to me manifestly to be false, if I am able to find in each one some reason to doubt, this will suffice to justify my rejecting the whole. And for that end it will not be requisite that I should examine each in particular, which would be an endless undertaking; for owing to the fact that the destruction of the foundations of necessity brings with it the downfall of the rest of the edifice, I shall only in the first place attack those principles upon which all my former opinions rested.

Reprinted from *Meditations on First Philosophy* by René Descartes, Meditation I.

All that up to the present time I have accepted as most true and certain I have learned either from the senses or through the senses; but it is sometimes proved to me that these senses are deceptive, and it is wiser not to trust entirely to any thing by which we have once been deceived.

But it may be that although the senses sometimes deceive us concerning things which are hardly perceptible, or very far away, there are yet many others to be met with as to which we cannot reasonably have any doubt, although we recognise them by their means. For example, there is the fact that I am here, seated by the fire, attired in a dressing gown, having this paper in my hands and other similar matters. And how could I deny that these hands and this body are mine, were it not perhaps that I compare myself to certain persons, devoid of sense, whose cerebella are so troubled and clouded by the violent vapours of black bile, that they constantly assure us that they think they are kings when they are really quite poor, or that they are clothed in purple when they are really without covering, or who imagine that they have an earthenware head or are nothing but pumpkins or are made of glass. But they are mad, and I should not be any the less insane were I to follow examples so extravagant.

At the same time I must remember that I am a man, and that consequently I am in the habit of sleeping, and in my dreams representing to myself the same things or sometimes even less probable things, than do those who are insane in their waking moments. How often has it happened to me that in the night I dreamt that I found myself in this particular place, that I was dressed and seated near the fire, whilst in reality I was lying undressed in bed! At this moment it does indeed seem to me that it is with eyes awake that I am looking at this paper; that this head which I move is not asleep, that it is deliberately and of set purpose that I extend my hand and perceive it; what happens in sleep does not appear so clear nor so distinct as does all this. But in thinking over this I remind myself that on many occasions I have in sleep been deceived by similar illusions, and in dwelling carefully on this reflection I see so manifestly that there are no certain indications by which we may clearly distinguish wakefulness from sleep that I am lost in astonishment. And my astonishment is such that it is almost capable of persuading me that I now dream.

Now let us assume that we are asleep and that all these particulars, e.g. that we open our eyes, shake our head, extend our hands, and so on, are but false delusions; and let us reflect that possibly neither our hands nor our whole body are such as they appear to us to be. At the same time we must at least confess that the things which are represented to us in sleep are like painted representations which can only have been formed as the counterparts of something real and true, and that in this way those general things at least, i.e. eyes, a head, hands, and a whole body, are not imaginary things, but things really existent. For, as a matter of fact, painters, even when they study with the greatest skill to represent sirens and satyrs by forms the most strange and extraordinary, cannot give them natures which are entirely new, but merely make a certain medley of the members of different animals; or if their imagination is extravagant enough to invent something so novel that nothing similar has ever before been seen, and that then their work represents a thing purely fictitious and absolutely false, it is certain all the same that the colours of which this is composed are necessarily real. And for the same reason, although these general things, to wit, [a body], eyes, a head, hands, and such like, may be imaginary, we are bound at the same time to confess that there are at least some other objects yet more simple and more universal, which are real and true; and of these just in the same way as with certain real colours, all these images of things which dwell in our thoughts, whether true and real or false and fantastic are formed.

To such a class of things pertains corporeal nature in general, and its extension, the figure of extended things, their quantity or magnitude and number, as also the place in which they are, the time which measures their duration, and so on.

That is possibly why our reasoning is not unjust when we conclude from this that Physics, Astronomy, Medicine and all other sciences which have as their end the consideration of composite things, are very dubious and uncertain; but that Arithmetic, Geometry and other sciences of that kind which only treat of things that are very simple and very general, without taking great trouble to ascertain whether they are actually existent or not, contain some measure of certainty and an element of the indubitable. For whether I am awake or asleep, two and three together always form five, and the square can never have more than four sides, and it does not seem possible that truths so clear and apparent can be suspected of any falsity [or uncertainty].

Nevertheless I have long had fixed in my mind the belief that an all-powerful God existed by whom I have been created such as I am. But how do I know that He has not brought it to pass that there is no earth, no heaven, no extended body, no magnitude, no place, and that nevertheless [I possess the perceptions of all these things and that] they seem to me to exist just exactly as I now see them? And, besides, as I sometimes imagine that others deceive themselves in the things which they think they know best, how do I know that I am not deceived every time that I add two and three, or count the sides of a square, or judge things yet simpler, if anything simpler can be imagined? But possibly God has not desired that I should be thus deceived, for He is said to be supremely good. If, however, it is contrary to His goodness to have made me such that I constantly deceive myself, it would also appear to be contrary to His goodness to permit me to be sometimes deceived, and nevertheless I cannot doubt that He does permit this.

There may indeed be those who would prefer to deny the existence of a God so powerful, rather than believe that all other things are uncertain. But let us not oppose them for the present, and grant that all that is here said of a God is a fable; nevertheless in whatever way they suppose that I have arrived at the state of being that I have reached—whether they attribute it to fate or to accident, or make out that it is by a continual succession of antecedents, or by some other method—since to err and deceive oneself is a defect, it is clear that the greater will be the probability of my being so imperfect as to deceive myself ever, as is the Author to whom they assign my origin the less powerful. To these reasons I have certainly nothing to reply, but at the end I feel constrained to confess that there is nothing in all that I formerly believed to be true, of which I cannot in some measure doubt, and that not merely through want of thought or through levity, but for reasons which are very powerful and maturely considered; so that henceforth I ought not the less carefully to refrain from giving credence to these opinions than to that which is manifestly false, if I desire to arrive at any certainty [in the sciences].

But it is not sufficient to have made these remarks, we must also be careful to keep them in mind. For these ancient and commonly held opinions still revert frequently to my mind, long and familiar custom having given them the right to occupy my mind against my inclination and rendered them almost masters of my belief; nor will I ever lose the habit of deferring to them or of placing my confidence in them, so long as I consider them as they really are, i.e. opinions in some measure doubtful, as I have just shown, and at the same time highly probable, so that there is much more reason to believe in than to deny them. That is why I consider that I shall not be acting amiss, if, taking of set purpose a contrary belief, I allow myself to be deceived, and for a certain time pretend that all these opinions are entirely false and imaginary, until at last, having thus balanced my former prejudices with my latter [so that they cannot divert my opinions more to one side than to the other], my judgment will no longer be dominated by bad usage or turned away from the right knowledge of the truth. For I am assured that there can be neither peril nor error in this course, and that I cannot at present yield too much to distrust, since I am not considering the question of action, but only of knowledge.

I shall then suppose, not that God who is supremely good and the fountain of truth, but some evil genius not less powerful than deceitful, has employed his whole energies in deceiving me; I shall consider that the heavens, the earth, colours, figures, sound, and all other external things are nought but the illusions and dreams of which this genius has availed himself in order to lay traps for my credulity; I shall consider myself as having no hands, no eyes, no flesh, no blood, nor any senses, yet falsely believing myself to possess all these things; I shall remain obstinately attached to this idea, and if by this means it is not in my power to arrive at the knowledge of any truth, I may at least do what is in my power [i.e. suspend my judgment], and with firm purpose avoid giving credence to any false thing, or being imposed upon by this arch deceiver, however powerful and deceptive he may be. But this task is a laborious one, and insensibly a certain lassitude leads me into the course of my ordinary life. And just as a captive who in sleep enjoys an imaginary liberty, when he begins to suspect that his liberty is but a dream, fears to awaken, and conspires with these agreeable illusions that the deception may be prolonged, so insensibly of my own accord I fall back into my former opinions, and I dread awakening from this slumber, lest the laborious wakefulness which would follow the tranquillity of this repose should have to be spent not in daylight, but in the excessive darkness of the difficulties which have just been discussed.

Descartes' Evil Genius

O. K. BOUWSMA

THERE was once an evil genius who promised the mother of us all that if she ate of the fruit of the tree, she would be like God, knowing good and evil. He promised knowledge. She did eat and she learned, but she was disappointed, for to know good and evil and not to be God is awful. Many an Eve later, there was rumor of another evil genius. This evil genius promised no good, promised no knowledge. He made a boast, a boast so wild and so deep and so dark that those who heard it cringed in hearing it. And what was that boast? Well, that apart from a few, four or five, clear and distinct ideas, he could deceive any son of Adam about anything. So he boasted. And with some result? Some indeed! Men going about in the brightest noonday would look and exclaim: "How obscure!" and if some careless merchant counting his apples was heard to say: "Two and three are five," a hearer of the boast would rub his eyes and run away. This evil genius still whispers, thundering, among the leaves of books, frightening people, whispering: "I can. Maybe I will. Maybe so, maybe not." The tantalizer! In what follows I should like to examine the boast of this evil genius.

I am referring, of course, to that evil genius of whom Descartes writes:

> I shall then suppose, not that God who is supremely good and the fountain of truth, but some evil genius not less powerful than deceitful, has employed his whole energies in deceiving me; I shall consider that the heavens, the earth, the colors, figures, sound, and all other external things are nought but illusions and dreams of which this evil genius has availed himself, in order to lay traps for my credulity; I shall consider myself as having no hands, no eyes, no flesh, no blood, nor any senses, yet falsely believing myself to possess all these things.[1]

This then is the evil genius whom I have represented as boasting that he can deceive us about all these things. I intend now to examine this boast, and to understand how this deceiving and being deceived are to take place. I expect to discover that the evil genius may very well deceive us, but that if we are wary, we need not be deceived. He will deceive us, if he does, by bathing the word "illusion" in a fog. This then will be the word to keep our minds on. In order to accomplish all this, I intend to describe the evil genius carrying out his boast in two adventures. The first of these I shall consider a thoroughly transparent case of deception. The word "illusion" will find a clear and familiar application. Nevertheless in this instance the evil genius will not have exhausted "his whole energies in deceiving us." Hence we must aim to imagine a further trial of the boast, in which the "whole energies" of the evil genius are exhausted. In this

[1] *Philosophical Works of Descartes*, trans. E. S. Haldane and G. R. T. Ross (2 vols.; Cambridge: Cambridge University Press, 1912), I, 147.

instance I intend to show that the evil genius is himself befuddled, and that if we too exhaust some of our energies in sleuthing after the peculiarities in his diction, then we need not be deceived either.

Let us imagine the evil genius then at his ease meditating that very bad is good enough for him, and that he would let bad enough alone. All the old pseudos, pseudo names and pseudo statements, are doing very well. But today it was different. He took no delight in common lies, everyday fibs, little ones, old ones. He wanted something new and something big. He scratched his genius; he uncovered an idea. And he scribbled on the inside of his tattered halo, "Tomorrow, I will deceive," and he smiled, and his words were thin and like fine wire. "Tomorrow I will change everything, everything, everything. I will change flowers, human beings, trees, hills, sky, the sun, and everything else into paper. Paper alone I will not change. There will be paper flowers, paper human beings, paper trees. And human beings will be deceived. They will think that there are flowers, human beings, and trees, and there will be nothing but paper. It will be gigantic. And it ought to work. After all men have been deceived with much less trouble. There was a sailor, a Baptist I believe, who said that all was water. And there was no more water then than there is now. And there was a pool-hall keeper who said that all was billiard balls. That's a long time ago of course, a long time before they opened one, and listening, heard that it was full of the sound of a trumpet. My prospects are good. I'll try it."

And the evil genius followed his own directions and did according to his words. And this is what happened.

Imagine a young man, Tom, bright today as he was yesterday, approaching a table where yesterday he had seen a bowl of flowers. Today it suddenly strikes him that they are not flowers. He stares at them troubled, looks away, and looks again. Are they flowers? He shakes his head. He chuckles to himself. "Huh! that's funny. Is this a trick? Yesterday there certainly were flowers in that bowl." He sniffs suspiciously, hopefully, but smells nothing. His nose gives no assurance. He thinks of the birds that flew down to peck at the grapes in the picture and of the mare that whinnied at the likeness of Alexander's horse. Illusions! The picture oozed no juice, and the likeness was still. He walked slowly to the bowl of flowers. He looked, and he sniffed, and he raised his hand. He stroked a petal lightly, lover of flowers, and he drew back. He could scarcely believe his fingers. They were not flowers. They were paper.

As he stands, perplexed, Milly, friend and dear, enters the room. Seeing him occupied with the flowers, she is about to take up the bowl and offer them to him, when once again he is overcome with feelings of strangeness. She looks just like a great big doll. He looks more closely, closely as he dares, seeing this may be Milly after all. Milly, are you Milly?—that wouldn't do. Her mouth clicks as she opens it, speaking, and it shuts precisely. Her forehead shines, and he shudders at the thought of Mme Tussaud's. Her hair is plaited, evenly, perfectly, like Milly's but as she raises one hand to guard its order, touching it, preening, it whispers like a newspaper. Her teeth are white as a genteel monthly. Her gums are pink, and there is a clapper in her mouth. He thinks of mama dolls, and of the rubber doll he used to pinch; it had a misplaced navel right in the pit of the back, that whistled. Galatea in paper! Illusions!

He noted all these details, flash by flash by flash. He reaches for a chair to steady himself and just in time. She approaches with the bowl of flowers, and, as the bowl is extended towards him, her arms jerk. The suppleness, the smoothness, the roundness of life is gone. Twitches of a smile mislight up her face. He extends his hand to take up the bowl and his own arms jerk as hers did before. He takes the bowl, and as he does so sees his hand. It is pale, fresh, snowy. Trembling, he drops the bowl, but it does not break, and the water does not run. What a mockery!

He rushes to the window, hoping to see the real world. The scene is like a theatre-set. Even the pane in the window it drawn very thin, like cellophane. In the distance are the forms of men walking about and tossing trees and houses and boulders and hills upon the thin cross section of a truck that echoes only echoes of chugs as it moves. He looks into the sky upward, and it is low. There is a patch straight above him, and one seam is loose. The sun shines out of the blue like a drop of German silver. He reaches out with his pale hand, crackling the cellophane, and his hand touches the sky. The sky shakes and tiny bits of it fall, flaking his white hand with confetti.

Make-believe!

He retreats, crinkling, creaking, hiding his sight. As he moves he misquotes a line of poetry: "Those are perils that were his eyes," and he mutters, "Hypocritical pulp!" He goes on: "I see that the heavens, the earth, colors, figures, sound, and all other external things, flowers, Milly, trees and rocks and hills are paper, paper laid as traps for my credulity. Paper flowers, paper Milly, paper sky!" Then he paused, and in sudden fright he asked "And what about me?" He reaches to his lip and with two fingers tears the skin and peels off a strip of newsprint. He looks at it closely, grim. "I shall consider myself as having no hands, no eyes, no flesh, no blood, or any senses." He lids his paper eyes and stands dejected. Suddenly he is cheered. He exclaims: "*Cogito me papyrum esse, ergo sum.*" He has triumphed over paperdom.

I have indulged in this phantasy in order to illustrate the sort of situation which Descartes' words might be expected to describe. The evil genius attempts to deceive. He tries to mislead Tom into thinking what is not. Tom is to think that these are flowers, that this is the Milly that was, that those are trees, hills, the heavens, etc. And he does this by creating illusions, that is, by making something that looks like flowers, artificial flowers; by making something that looks like and sounds like and moves like Milly, an artificial Milly. An illusion is something that looks like or sounds like, so much like, something else that you either mistake it for something else, or you can easily understand how someone might come to do this. So when the evil genius creates illusions intending to deceive he makes things which might quite easily be mistaken for what they are not. Now in the phantasy as I discovered it Tom is not deceived. He does experience the illusion, however. The intention of this is not to cast any reflection upon the deceptive powers of the evil genius. With such refinements in the paper art as we now know, the evil genius might very well have been less unsuccessful. And that in spite of his rumored lament: "And I made her of the best paper!" No, that Tom is not deceived, that he detects the illusion, is introduced in order to remind ourselves how illusions are detected. That the paper flowers are illusory is revealed by the recognition that they are paper. As soon as Tom realizes that though they look like flowers but are paper, he is acquainted with, sees through the illusion, and is not deceived. What is required, of course, is that he know the difference between flowers and paper, and that when presented with one or the other he can tell the difference. The attempt of the evil genius also presupposes this. What he intends is that though Tom knows this difference, the paper will look so much like flowers that Tom will not notice the respect in which the paper is different from the flowers. And even though Tom had actually been deceived and had not recognized the illusion, the evil genius himself must have been aware of the difference, for this is involved in his design. This is crucial, as we shall see when we come to consider the second adventure of the evil genius.

As you will remember I have represented the foregoing as an illustration of the sort of situation which Descartes' words might be expected to describe. Now, however, I think that this is misleading. For though I have described a situation in which there are many things, nearly all of which are calculated to serve as illusions, this question may still arise. Would this paper world still be properly described as a world of illusions? If Tom says: "These are flowers," or "These look like flowers" (uncertainly), then the illusion is operative. But if Tom says: "These are paper," then the illusion has been destroyed. Descartes uses the words: "And all other external things are nought but illusions." This means that the situation which Descartes has in mind is such that if Tom says: "These are flowers," he will be wrong, but he will be wrong also if he says: "These are paper," and it won't matter what sentence of that type he uses. If he says: "These are rock"—or cotton or cloud or wood—he is wrong by the plan. He will be right only if he says: "These are illusions." But the project is to keep him from recognizing the illusions. This means that the illusions are to be brought about not by anything so crude as paper or even cloud. They must be made of the stuff that dreams are made of.

Now let us consider this second adventure.

The design then is this. The evil genius is to create a world of illusions. There are to be no flowers, no Milly, no paper. There is to be nothing at all, but Tom is every moment to go on mistaking nothing for something, nothing at all for flowers, nothing at all for Milly, etc. This is, of course, quite different from mistaking paper for flowers, paper for Milly. And yet all is to be arranged in such a way that Tom will go on just as we now do, and just as Tom did before the paper age, to see, hear, smell the world. He will love the flowers, he will kiss Milly, he will blink at the sun. So he thinks. And in thinking about these things he will talk and argue just as we do. But all the time he will be mistaken. There are no flowers, there is no kiss, there is no sun. Illusions all. This then is the end at which the evil genius aims.

How now is the evil genius to attain this end? Well, it is clear that a part of what he aims at will be realized if he destroys everything. Then there will be no flowers, and if Tom thinks that there are flowers he will be wrong. There will be no face that is Milly's and no tumbled beauty on her head, and if Tom thinks that there is Milly's face and Milly's hair, he will be wrong. It is necessary then to see to it that there are none of these things. So the evil genius, having failed with paper, destroys even all paper. Now there is nothing to see, nothing to hear, nothing to smell, etc. But this is not enough to deceive. For though Tom sees nothing, and neither hears nor smells anything, he may also think that he sees nothing. He must also be misled into thinking that he does see something, that there are flowers and Milly, and hands, eyes, flesh, blood, and all other senses. Accordingly the evil genius restores to Tom his old life. Even the memory of that paper day is blotted out, not a scrap remains. Witless Tom lives on, thinking, hoping, loving as he used to, unwitted by the great destroyer. All that seems so solid, so touchable to seeming hands, so biteable to apparent teeth, is so flimsy that were the evil genius to poke his index at it, it would curl away save for one tiny trace, the smirch of that index. So once more the evil genius has done according to his word.

And now let us examine the result.

I should like first of all to describe a passage of Tom's life. Tom is all alone, but he doesn't know it. What an opportunity for methodologico-metaphysico-solipsimo! I intend, in any case, to disregard the niceties of his being so alone and to borrow his own words, with the warning that the evil genius smiles as he reads them. Tom writes:

> Today, as usual, I came into the room and there was the bowl of flowers on the table. I went up to them, caressed them, and smelled over them. I thank God for flowers! There's nothing so real to me as flowers. Here the genuine essence of the world's substance, as its gayest and most hilarious speaks to me. It seems unworthy even to think of them as erect, and waving on pillars of sap. Sap! Sap!

There was more in the same vein, which we need not bother to record. I might say that the evil genius was a bit amused, snickered in fact, as he read the words "so real," "essence," "substance," etc., but later he frowned and seemed puzzled. Tom went on to describe how Milly came into the room, and how glad he was to see her. They talked about the flowers. Later he walked to the window and watched the gardener clearing a space a short distance away. The sun was shining, but there were a few heavy clouds. He raised the window, extended his hand and four large drops of rain wetted his hand. He returned to the room and quoted to Milly a song from *The Tempest.* He got all the words right, and was well pleased with himself. There was more he wrote, but this was enough to show how quite normal everything seems. And, too, how successful the evil genius is.

And the evil genius said to himself, not quite in solipsimo, "Not so, not so, not at all so."

The evil genius was, however, all too human. Admiring himself but unadmired, he yearned for admiration. To deceive but to be unsuspected is too little glory. The evil genius set about then to plant the seeds of suspicion. But how to do this? Clearly there was no suggestive paper to tempt Tom's confidence. There was nothing but Tom's mind, a stream of seemings and of words to make the seemings seem no seemings. The evil genius must have words with Tom and must engage the same seemings with him. To have words with Tom is to have the words together, to use them in the same way, and to engage the same seemings is to see and to hear and to point to the same. And so the evil genius, free spirit, entered in at the door of Tom's pineal gland and lodged there. He floated in the humors that flow, glandwise and sensewise, everywhere being as much one with Tom as difference will allow. He looked out of the same eyes, and when Tom pointed with his finger, the evil genius said "This" and meant what Tom, hearing, also meant, seeing. Each heard with the same ear what the other heard. For every sniffing of the one nose there were two identical smells, and there were two tactualities for every touch. If Tom had had a toothache, together they would have pulled the same face. The twinsomeness of two monads finds here the limit of identity. Nevertheless there was otherness looking out of those eyes as we shall see.

It seems then that on the next day, the evil genius "going to and fro" in Tom's mind and "walking up and down in it," Tom once again, as his custom was, entered the room where the flowers stood on the table. He stopped, looked admiringly, and in a caressing voice said: "Flowers! Flowers!" And he lingered. The evil genius, more subtle "than all the beasts of the field," whispered "Flowers? Flowers?" For the first time Tom has an intimation of company, of some intimate partner in perception. Momentarily he is checked. He looks again at the flowers. "Flowers? Why, of course, flowers." Together they look out of the same eyes. Again the evil genius whispers, "Flowers?" The seed of suspicion is to be the question. But Tom now raises the flowers nearer to his eyes almost violently as though his eyes were not his own. He is, however, not perturbed. The evil genius only shakes their head. "Did you ever hear of illusions?" says he.

Tom, still surprisingly good-natured, responds: "But you saw them, didn't you? Surely you can see through my eyes. Come, let us bury my nose deep in these blossoms, and take one long breath together. Then tell whether you can recognize these as flowers."

So they dunked the one nose. But the evil genius said "Huh!" as much as to say: What has all this seeming and smelling to do with it? Still he explained nothing. And Tom remained as confident of the flowers as he had been at the first. The little seeds of doubt, "Flowers? Flowers?" and again "Flowers?" and "Illusions?" and now this stick in the spokes, "Huh!" made Tom uneasy. He went on: "Oh, so you are one of these seers that has to touch everything. You're a tangibilite. Very well, here's my hand, let's finger these flowers. Careful! They're tender."

The evil genius was amused. He smiled inwardly and rippled in a shallow humor. To be taken for a materialist! As though the grand illusionist was not a spirit! Nevertheless, he realized that though deception is easy where the lies are big enough (where had he heard that before?), a few scattered, questioning words are not enough to make guile grow. He was tempted to make a statement, and he did. He said, "Your flowers are nothing but illusions."

"My flowers illusions?" exclaimed Tom, and he took up the bowl and placed it before a mirror. "See," said he, "here are the flowers and here, in the mirror, is an illusion. There's a difference surely. And you with my eyes, my nose, and my fingers can tell what the difference is. Pollen on your fingers touching the illusion? send Milly the flowers in the mirror? Set a bee to suck honey out of this glass? You know all this as well as I do. I can tell flowers from illusions, and my flowers, as you now plainly see, are not illusions."

The evil genius was now sorely tried. He had his make-believe, but he also had his pride. Would he now risk the make-believe to save his pride? Would he explain? He explained.

"Tom," he said, "notice. The flowers in the mirror look like flowers, but they only look like flowers. We agree about that. The flowers before the mirror also look like flowers. But they, you say, are flowers because they also smell like flowers and they feel like flowers, as though they would be any more flowers because they also like flowers multiply. Imagine a mirror such that it reflected not only the looks of flowers, but also their fragrance and their petal surfaces, and then you smelled and touched, and the flowers before the mirror would be just like the flowers in the mirror. Then you could see immediately that the flowers before the mirror are illusions just as those in the mirror are illusions. As it is now, it is clear that the flowers in the mirror are thin illusions, and the flowers before the mirror are thick. Thick illusions are the best for deception. And they may be as thick as you like. From them you may gather pollen, send them to Milly, and foolish bees may sleep in them."

But Tom was not asleep. "I see that what you mean by thin illusions is what I mean by illusions, and what you mean by thick illusions is what I mean by flowers. So when you say that my flowers are your thick illusions this doesn't bother me. And as for your mirror that mirrors all layers of your thick illusions, I shouldn't call that a mirror at all. It's a duplicator, and much more useful than a mirror, provided you can control it. But I do suppose that when you speak of thick illusions you do mean that thick illusions are related to something you call flowers in much the same way that the thin illusions are related to the thick ones. Is that true?"

The evil genius was now diction-deep in explanations and went on. "In the first place let me assure you that these are not flowers. I destroyed all flowers. There are no flowers at all. There are only thin and thick illusions of flowers. I can see your flowers in the mirror, and I can smell and touch the flowers before the mirror. What I cannot smell and touch, having seen as in the mirror, is not even thick illusion. But if I cannot also *cerpicio* what I see, smell, touch, etc., what I have then seen is not anything real. *Esse est cerpici.* I just now tried to *cerpicio* your flowers, but there was nothing there. Man is after all a four- or five- or six-sense creature and you cannot expect much from so little."

Tom rubbed his eyes and his ears tingled with an eighteenth-century disturbance. Then he stared at the flowers. "I see," he said, "that this added sense of yours has done wickedly with our language. You do not mean by illusion what we mean, and neither do you mean by flowers what we mean. As for *cerpicio* I wouldn't be surprised if you'd made up that word just to puzzle us. In any case what you destroyed is what, according to you, you used to *cerpicio.* So there is nothing for you to *cerpicio* any more. But there still are what we mean by flowers. If your intention was to deceive, you must learn the language of those you are to deceive. I should say that you are like the doctor who prescribes for his patients what is so bad for himself and is then surprised at the health of his patients." And he pinned a flower near their nose.

The evil genius, discomfited, rode off on a corpuscle. He had failed. He took to an artery, made haste to the pineal exit, and was gone. Then "sun by sun" he fell. And he regretted his mischief.

I have tried in this essay to understand the boast of the evil genius. His boast was that he could deceive, deceive about "the heavens, the earth, the colors, figures, sound, and all other external things." In order to do this I have tried to bring clearly to mind what deception and such deceiving would be like. Such deception involves illusions and such deceiving involves the creation of illusions. Accordingly I have tried to imagine the evil genius engaged in the practice of deception, busy in the creation of illusions. In the first adventure everything is plain. The evil genius employs paper, paper making believe it's many other things. The effort to deceive, ingenuity in deception, being deceived by paper, detecting the illusion—all these are clearly understood. It is the second adventure, however, which is more crucial. For in this instance it is assumed that the illusion is of such a kind that no seeing, no touching, no smelling, are relevant to detecting the illusion. Nevertheless the evil genius sees, touches, smells, and does detect the illusion. He made the illusion; so, of course, he must know it. How then does he know it? The evil genius has a sense denied to men. He senses the flower-in-itself, Milly-in-her-self, etc. So he creates illusions made up of what can be seen, heard, smelled, etc., illusions all because when seeing, hearing, and smelling have seen, heard, and smelled all, the special sense senses nothing. So what poor human beings sense is the illusion of what only the evil genius can sense. This is formidable. Nevertheless, once again everything is clear. If we admit the special sense, then we can readily see how it is that the evil genius should have been so confident. He has certainly created his own illusions, though he has not himself been deceived. But neither has anyone else been deceived. For human beings do not use the word "illusion" by relation to a sense with which only the evil genius is blessed.

I said that the evil genius had not been deceived, and it is true that he has not been deceived by his own illusions. Nevertheless he was deceived in boasting that he could deceive, for his confidence in this is based upon an ignorance of the difference between our uses of the words, "heavens," "earth," "flowers," "Milly," and "illusions" of these things, and his own uses of these words. For though there certainly is an analogy between our own uses and his, the difference is quite sufficient to explain his failure at grand deception. We can also understand how easily Tom might have been taken in. The dog over the water dropped his meaty bone for a picture on the water. Tom, however, dropped nothing at all. But the word "illusion" is a trap.

I began this essay uneasily, looking at my hands and saying "no hands," blinking my eyes and saying "no eyes." Everything I saw seemed to me like something Cheshire, a piece of cheese, for instance, appearing and disappearing in the leaves of the tree. Poor kitty! And now? Well. . . .

The Argument from Illusion

A. J. AYER

IT DOES not normally occur to us that there is any need for us to justify our belief in the existence of material things. At the present moment, for example, I have no doubt whatsoever that I really am perceiving the familiar objects, the chairs and table, the pictures and books and flowers with which my room is furnished; and I am therefore satisfied that they exist. I recognize indeed that people are sometimes deceived by their senses, but this does not lead me to suspect that my own sense-perceptions cannot in general be trusted, or even that they may be deceiving me now. And this is not, I believe, an exceptional attitude. I believe that, in practice, most people agree with John Locke that "the certainty of things existing *in rerum natura*, when we have the testimony of our senses for it, is not only as great as our frame can attain to, but as our condition needs."[1]

When, however, one turns to the writings of those philosophers who have recently concerned themselves with the subject of perception, one may begin to wonder whether this matter is quite so simple. It is true that they do, in general, allow that our belief in the existence of material things is well founded; some of them, indeed, would say that there were occasions on which we knew for certain the truth of such propositions as "this is a cigarette" or "this is a pen." But even so they are not, for the most part, prepared to admit that such objects as pens or cigarettes are ever directly perceived. What, in their opinion, we directly perceive is always an object of a different kind from these; one to which it is now customary to give the name of "sense-datum." These sense-data are said to have the "presentative function"[2] of making us conscious of material things. But how they perform this function, and what is their relation to the material things which they present, are questions about which there is much dispute. There is dispute also about the properties of sense-data, apart from their relationship to material things: whether, for example, they are each of them private to a single observer; whether they can appear to have qualities that they

1 *An Essay concerning Human Understanding*, Book IV, ch. 2, section viii.

2 Cf. H. H. Price, *Perception*, p. 104.

Reprinted with permission of St. Martin's Press, Inc., Macmillan, London & Basingstoke from *The Foundations of Empirical Knowledge* by A. J. Ayer, 1955, pp. 1–11.

do not really have, or have qualities that they do not appear to have; whether they are in any sense "within" the percipient's mind or brain. I shall show later on that these are not empirical questions. They are to be settled by making it clear how the term "sense-datum" is intended to be used. But first I must explain why it is thought necessary to introduce such a term at all. Why may we not say that we are directly aware of material things?

The answer is provided by what is known as the argument from illusion. This argument, as it is ordinarily stated, is based on the fact that material things may present different appearances to different observers, or to the same observer in different conditions, and that the character of these appearances is to some extent causally determined by the state of the conditions and the observer. For instance, it is remarked that a coin which looks circular from one point of view may look elliptical from another; or that a stick which normally appears straight looks bent when it is seen in water; or that to people who take drugs such as mescal, things appear to change their colours. The familiar cases of mirror images, and double vision, and complete hallucinations, such as the mirage, provide further examples. Nor is this a peculiarity of visual appearances. The same thing occurs in the domains of the other senses, including the sense of touch. It may be pointed out, for example, that the taste that a thing appears to have may vary with the condition of the palate; or that a liquid will seem to have a different temperature according as the hand that is feeling it is itself hot or cold; or that a coin seems larger when it is placed on the tongue than when it is held in the palm of the hand; or, to take a case of complete hallucination, that people who have had limbs amputated may still continue to feel pain in them.

Let us now consider one of these examples, say that of the stick which is refracted in water, and see what is to be inferred. For the present it must be assumed that the stick does not really change its shape when it is placed in water. I shall discuss the meaning and validity of this assumption later on. Then it follows that at least one of the visual appearances of the stick is delusive; for it cannot be both crooked and straight. Nevertheless, even in the case where what we see is not the real quality of a material thing, it is supposed that we are still seeing something; and that it is convenient to give this a name. And it is for this purpose that philosophers have recourse to the term "sense-datum." By using it they are able to give what seems to them a satisfactory answer to the question: What is the object of which we are directly aware, in perception, if it is not part of any material thing? Thus, when a man sees a mirage in the desert, he is not thereby perceiving any material thing; for the oasis which he thinks he is perceiving does not exist. At the same time, it is argued, his experience is not an experience of nothing; it has a definite content. Accordingly, it is said that he is experiencing sense-data, which are similar in character to what he would be experiencing if he were seeing a real oasis, but are delusive in the sense that the material thing which they appear to present is not actually there. Or again, when I look at myself in the glass my body appears to be some distance behind the glass; but other observations indicate that it is in front of it. Since it is impossible for my body to be in both these places at once, these perceptions cannot all be veridical. I believe, in fact, that the ones that are delusive are those in which my body appears to be behind the glass. But can it be denied that when one looks at oneself in the glass one is seeing something? And if, in this case, there really is no such material thing as my body in the place where it appears to be, what is it that I am seeing? Once again the answer we are invited to give is that it is a sense-datum. And the same conclusion may be reached by taking any other of my examples.

If anything is established by this, it can be only that there are some cases in which the character of our perceptions makes it necessary for us to say that what we are directly experiencing is not a material thing but a sense-datum. It has not been shown that this is so in all cases. It has not been denied, but rather assumed, that there are some perceptions that do present material things to us as they really are; and in their case there seems at first sight to be no ground for saying that we directly experience sense-data rather than material things. But, as I have already remarked, there is general agreement among the philosophers who make use of the term "sense-datum," or some equivalent term, that what we immediately experience is always a sense-datum and never a material thing. And for this they give further arguments which I shall now examine.

In the first place it is pointed out that there is no intrinsic difference in kind between those of our perceptions that are veridical in their presentation of material things and those that are delusive.[3] When I look at a straight stick, which is refracted in water and so appears crooked, my experience is qualitatively the same as if I were looking at a stick that really was crooked. When, as the result of my putting on green spectacles, the white walls of my room appear to me to be green, my experience is qualitatively the same as if I were perceiving walls that really were green. When people whose legs have been amputated continue to feel pressure upon them, their experience is qualitatively the same as if pressure really were being exerted upon their legs. But, it is argued, if, when our perceptions were delusive, we were always perceiving something of a different kind from what we perceived when they were veridical, we should expect our experience to be qualitatively different in the two cases. We should expect to be able to tell from the intrinsic character of a perception whether it was a perception of a sense-datum or of a material thing. But this is not possible, as the examples that I have given have shown. In some cases there is indeed a distinction with respect to the beliefs to which the experiences give rise, as can be illustrated by my original example. For when, in normal conditions, we have the experience of seeing a straight stick, we believe that there really is a straight stick there; but when the stick appears crooked, through being refracted in water, we do not believe that it really is crooked; we do not regard the fact that it looks crooked in water as evidence against its being really straight. It must, however, be remarked that this difference in the beliefs which accompany our perceptions is not grounded in the nature of the perceptions themselves, but

[3] Cf. H. H. Price, *Perception*, p. 31.

depends upon our past experience. We do not believe that the stick which appears crooked when it stands in water really is crooked because we know from past experience that in normal conditions it looks straight. But a child who had not learned that refraction was a means of distortion would naturally believe that the stick really was crooked as he saw it. The fact, therefore, that there is this distinction between the beliefs that accompany veridical and delusive perceptions does not justify the view that these are perceptions of generically different objects, especially as the distinction by no means applies to all cases. For it sometimes happens that a delusive experience is not only qualitatively indistinguishable from one that is veridical but is also itself believed to be veridical, as in the example of the mirage; and, conversely, there are cases in which experiences that are actually veridical are believed to be delusive, as when we see something so strange or unexpected that we say to ourselves that we must be dreaming. The fact is that from the character of a perception considered by itself, that is, apart from its relation to further sense-experience, it is not possible to tell whether it is veridical or delusive. But whether we are entitled to infer from this that what we immediately experience is always a sense-datum remains still to be seen.

Another fact which is supposed to show that even in the case of veridical perceptions we are not directly aware of material things is that veridical and delusive perceptions may form a continuous series, both with respect to their qualities and with respect to the conditions in which they are obtained.[4] Thus, if I gradually approach an object from a distance I may begin by having a series of perceptions which are delusive in the sense that the object appears to be smaller than it really is. Let us assume that this series terminates in a veridical perception. Then the difference in quality between this perception and its immediate predecessor will be of the same order as the difference between any two delusive perceptions that are next to one another in the series; and, on the assumption that I am walking at a uniform pace, the same will be true of the difference in the conditions on which the generation of the series depends. A similar example would be that of the continuous alteration in the apparent colour of an object which was seen in a gradually changing light. Here again the relation between a veridical perception and the delusive perception that comes next to it in the series is the same as that which obtains between neighbouring delusive perceptions, both with respect to the difference in quality and with respect to the change in the conditions; and these are differences of degree and not of kind. But this, it is argued, is not what we should expect if the veridical perception were a perception of an object of a different sort, a material thing as opposed to a sense-datum. Does not the fact that veridical and delusive perceptions shade into one another in the way that is indicated by these examples show that the objects that are perceived in either case are generically the same? And from this it would follow, if it was acknowledged that the de-

[4] Cf. Price, *op. cit.*, p. 32.

lusive perceptions were perceptions of sense-data, that what we directly experienced was always a sense-datum and never a material thing.

The final argument that has to be considered in this context is based upon the fact that all our perceptions, whether veridical or delusive, are to some extent causally dependent both upon external conditions, such as the character of the light, and upon our own physiological and psychological states. In the case of perceptions that we take to be delusive this is a fact that we habitually recognize. We say, for example, that the stick looks crooked because it is seen in water; that the white walls appear green to me because I am wearing green spectacles; that the water feels cool because my hand is hot; that the murderer sees the ghost of his victim because of his bad conscience or because he has been taking drugs. In the case of perceptions that we take to be veridical we are apt not to notice such causal dependencies, since as a rule it is only the occurrence of the unexpected or the abnormal that induces us to look for a cause. But in this matter also there is no essential difference between veridical and delusive perceptions. When, for example, I look at the piece of paper on which I am writing, I may claim that I am seeing it as it really is. But I must admit that in order that I should have this experience it is not sufficient that there should actually be such a piece of paper there. Many other factors are necessary, such as the condition of the light, the distance at which I am from the paper, the nature of the background, the state of my nervous system and my eyes. A proof that they are necessary is that if I vary them I find that I have altered the character of my perception. Thus, if I screw up my eyes I see two pieces of paper instead of one; if I grow dizzy the appearance of the paper becomes blurred; if I alter my position sufficiently it appears to have a different shape and size; if the light is extinguished, or another object is interposed, I cease to see it altogether. On the other hand, the converse does not hold. If the paper is removed I shall cease to see it; but the state of the light or of my nervous system or any other of the factors that were relevant to the occurrence of my perception may still remain the same. From this it may be inferred that the relation between my perception and these accompanying conditions is such that, while they are not causally dependent upon it, it is causally dependent upon them. And the same would apply to any other instance of a veridical perception that one cared to choose.

This point being established, the argument proceeds as follows. It is held to be characteristic of material things that their existence and their essential properties are independent of any particular observer. For they are supposed to continue the same, whether they are observed by one person or another, or not observed at all. But this, it is argued, has been shown not to be true of the objects we immediately experience. And so the conclusion is reached that what we immediately experience is in no case a material thing. According to this way of reasoning, if some perceptions are rightly held to be veridical, and others delusive, it is because of the different relations in which their objects stand to material things, and it is a philosophical problem to discover what these relations are. We may be allowed to have indirect knowledge of the properties of material things. But this knowledge, it is held, must be obtained through the medium of sense-data, since they are the only objects of which, in sense-perception, we are immediately aware.

A Psychological Theory of Perception

M. D. VERNON

TO THE man in the street it may appear idle to discuss the manner in which he perceives the world around him. He is so familiar with this 'real world' and the objects it contains that it would not occur to him that there is any need to speculate as to how it is that the world appears as it does. The objects are out 'there' in space; they appear in their familiar aspects and therefore he knows what they are, what they do, and what he can do with them. Their identity is well known to him, and he does not expect them to change from moment to moment unless he can perceive something causing them to change—a wind to blow them away, a fire to burn them up. Moreover, even when they are hidden from view, he will expect them, or at least most of them, to be there when he again looks at them. Some of course may move away and disappear. But these fall into a particular category of movable objects. He would be greatly surprised if the buildings and the landscape changed while he was looking in another direction. Indeed, he *is* often surprised and even shocked if he returns after a few days to find that the houses which he knew have been pulled down for rebuilding. This change in the apparently stable features of his world may give him an uncomfortable feeling of mutability and insecurity.

Knowledge of the identity of objects and features in the environment is obviously valuable to us. Not only does the apparent stability and permanence of most of them create a feeling of security; it also enables us to react to them rapidly and appropriately. We learn by experience what are the uses of houses, shops, and other buildings. We also learn how to react to moving objects. There are appropriate forms of action with regard to vehicles, to animals of various kinds, to people. Once having learnt the most effective form of action—what we can do about these objects and what we can do with them—we can proceed without further thought to act in the same way whenever we encounter them. Again, if they do not behave in the expected way we are surprised and perhaps annoyed. But even then there are certain limitations on their activities which also come within our expectations. The train may fail to stop for us, the car travel much faster than we expected and we must hurry to avoid it; but neither is likely to soar up into the sky, nor vanish in smoke. So also with people: their appearance and their behaviour varies only to a limited extent. It is only in

---

dreams that 'your attorney . . . from Devon is a bit undersized and you don't feel surprised when he tells you he's only eleven!'

But how is it that we know what objects are, that we assume they will retain their identity unchanged, and that we expect them to behave in a characteristic way? Presumably the usual answer to the first question would be that we can see them with our eyes, and that they have always looked like that. But in fact the eyes play only a part in the identification of objects, in the perception of their appearance, their position in space, and so on, although of course it is an essential part. When we look at the world around us, those parts towards which our gaze is directed reflect light to the eyes which comes to them from the sun or from some source of artificial illumination. This light varies in wave-length, and the wave-length of the reflected light varies also, producing the variations in colour of the objects. The brightness of these objects also varies with the brightness of the light falling on them and the reflecting power of their surfaces. The light which reaches the eyes is focused by the lens on to the retina, the light-sensitive surface at the back of the eyeball. The cells of the retina react by initiating nerve impulses in the nerves of the eye, and these are conveyed by the optic nerve to an area at the back of the brain called the occipital area of the cortex.

We tend to think that a picture of the external world falls on the retina and is conveyed to the brain, and that this picture is similar to the picture formed on the film of a camera. But what in fact reaches the brain is a pattern of nerve impulses, the frequency of which corresponds more or less to the brightness of the light reaching the eye. And the particular point on the brain surface stimulated corresponds to the point excited in the retina, which in turn is related to the particular point in space from which the light comes. We know also that differences of wave-length in the light striking the eye are perceived as differences of colour, although the exact mechanisms by means of which this takes place are at present obscure. If therefore we could be directly conscious of the visual pattern created in the brain, we might see a flat pattern of light, shade, and colour. But it would be more like an 'abstract' picture, or a variegated piece of textile material, than the view of the world around us of which we are normally aware.* There would be nothing to tell us that this visual pattern represented solid objects with well-known identities, distributed about us in space. Therefore between the projection of this visual pattern on the brain, and our full consciousness of the world of objects, a series of elaborate mental processes takes place which converts the visual pattern into the perception of the world as we know it. Some of these processes occur spontaneously. Thus the child from early infancy has some awareness of the shapes and colours of things round him. But he knows little or nothing of their identity; nor has he any idea of what we

* In fact, the Impressionist painters apparently set out to represent nature in patches of light, shade, and colour as these appeared to them, irrespective of the objects which these patches formed. E. H. Gombrich, in *Art and Illusion* (Phaidon Press, London, 1960), has pointed out that these painters never were, or could be, completely successful in divorcing light and colour from their sources, the perceived objects.

conceive to be the nature of the physical environment and the objects it contains. This knowledge must be acquired, in a manner which will be described in the next chapter.

There is another point of importance. The visual pattern that impinges on the brain is not static; it continually moves and flickers. The light and shade and colour of the pattern alter as the light reaching the eyes changes in colour and brightness—as the sun rises and sets, or is covered by cloud. The patches of light and shade and colour shift their position whenever we move about; they flow backwards and forwards across the field of view as we look to and fro or move our heads. Again, if we were directly conscious of this pattern, we should see something like shimmering lights reflected from moving water. Yet the essential feature of the world as we perceive it is its constancy and stability. Thus the impression of the continuing identity of objects, the unalterability of their appearance, their steady and motionless position in space, is something which arises within the brain itself. We have to learn that when a visual impression passes across the moving eyes, it is the eyes or the body which are moving in relation to the environment and the objects in it, whereas these objects are motionless in space. We also learn that even the shape of a perceived object may vary when we see it in different positions in space; thus a dinner plate is circular when viewed directly from above, but elliptical when seen tilted or sideways—but it is still the same plate. Again, a pillar-box which appears scarlet in ordinary daylight may look purple in blueish artificial light. But we do not think that the pillar-box has changed; the alteration of colour is attributed to the change in colour of the illumination.

We shall consider later in more detail how it is that these changes in the visual pattern do not destroy our awareness of the identity of the objects, nor even greatly affect their appearance as we normally perceive them. But enough has been said to suggest that the perception of the world around us is by no means the simple affair that we may suppose; and that its appearance is not given us merely by the physical properties of the light falling on the eyes and the resulting physiological processes in the eyes and the optic nerves.

The Sense Datum Theory and Common Sense

J. L. AUSTIN

LET US have a look, then, at the very beginning of Ayer's *Foundations*—the bottom, one might perhaps call it, of the garden path. In these paragraphs[1] we already seem to see the plain man, here under the implausible aspect of Ayer

[1] Ayer, op. cit., pp. 1–2.

himself, dribbling briskly into position in front of his own goal, and squaring up to encompass his own destruction.

> It does not normally occur to us that there is any need for us to justify our belief in the existence of material things. At the present moment, for example, I have no doubt whatsoever that I really am perceiving the familiar objects, the chairs and table, the pictures and books and flowers with which my room is furnished; and I am therefore satisfied that they exist. I recognize indeed that people are sometimes deceived by their senses, but this does not lead me to suspect that my own sense-perceptions cannot in general be trusted, or even that they may be deceiving me now. And this is not, I believe, an exceptional attitude I believe that, in practice, most people agree with John Locke that 'the certainty of things existing *in rerum natura,* when we have the testimony of our senses for it, is not only as great as our frame can attain to, but as our condition needs.'
>
> When, however, one turns to the writings of those philosophers who have recently concerned themselves with the subject of perception, one may begin to wonder whether this matter is quite so simple. It is true that they do, in general, allow that our belief in the existence of material things is well founded; some of them, indeed, would say that there were occasions on which we knew for certain the truth of such propositions as 'this is a cigarette' or 'this is a pen.' But even so they are not, for the most part, prepared to admit that such objects as pens or cigarettes are ever directly perceived. What, in their opinion, we directly perceive is always an object of a different kind from these; one to which it is now customary to give the name of 'sense-datum.'

Now in this passage some sort of contrast is drawn between what we (or the ordinary man) believe (or believes), and what philosophers, at least 'for the most part,' believe or are 'prepared to admit.' We must look at both sides of this contrast, and with particular care at what is assumed in, and implied by, what is actually said. The ordinary man's side, then, first.

1. It is clearly implied, first of all, that the ordinary man believes that he perceives material things. Now this, at least if it is taken to mean that he would *say* that he perceives material things, is surely wrong straight off; for 'material thing' is not an expression which the ordinary man would use—nor, probably, is 'perceive.' Presumably, though, the expression 'material thing' is here put forward, not as what the ordinary man would *say*, but as designating in a general way the *class* of things of which the ordinary man both believes and from time to time says that he perceives particular instances. But then we have to ask, of course, what this class comprises. We are given, as examples, 'familiar objects' —chairs, tables, pictures, books, flowers, pens, cigarettes; the expression 'material thing' is not here (or anywhere else in Ayer's text) further defined.[2] But *does* the ordinary man believe that what he perceives is (always) something like furniture, or like these other 'familiar objects'—moderate-sized specimens of dry goods? We may think, for instance, of people, people's voices, rivers,

[2] Compare Price's list on p. 1 of *Perception*—'chairs and tables, cats and rocks'—though he complicates matters by adding 'water' and 'the earth.' See also p. 280, on 'physical objects,' 'visuo-tactual solids.'

mountains, flames, rainbows, shadows, pictures on the screen at the cinema, pictures in books or hung on walls, vapours, gases—all of which people say that they see or (in some cases) hear or smell, i.e. 'perceive.' Are these all 'material things?' If not, exactly which are not, and exactly why? No answer is vouchsafed. The trouble is that the expression 'material thing' is functioning *already*, from the very beginning, simply as a foil for 'sense-datum'; it is not here given, and is never given, any other role to play, and apart from this consideration it would surely never have occurred to anybody to try to represent as some single *kind of things* the things which the ordinary man says that he 'perceives.'

2. Further, it seems to be also implied (*a*) that when the ordinary man believes that he is not perceiving material things, he believes he is being deceived by his senses; and (*b*) that when he believes he is being deceived by his senses, he believes that he is not perceiving material things. But both of these are wrong. An ordinary man who saw, for example, a rainbow would not, if persuaded that a rainbow is not a material thing, at once conclude that his senses were deceiving him; nor, when for instance he knows that the ship at sea on a clear day is much farther away than it looks, does he conclude that he is not seeing a material thing (still less that he *is* seeing an immaterial ship). That is to say, there is no more a simple contrast between what the ordinary man believes when all is well (that he is 'perceiving material things') and when something is amiss (that his 'senses are deceiving him' and he is *not* 'perceiving material things') than there is between what he believes that he perceives ('material things') and what philosophers for their part are prepared to admit, whatever that may be. The ground is already being prepared for *two* bogus dichotomies.

3. Next, is it not rather delicately hinted in this passage that the plain man is really a bit naïve?[3] It 'does not normally occur' to him that his belief in 'the existence of material things' needs justifying—but perhaps it *ought* to occur to him. He has 'no doubt whatsoever' that he really perceives chairs and tables—but perhaps he ought to have a doubt or two and not be so easily 'satisfied.' That people are sometimes deceived by their senses 'does not lead him to suspect' that all may not be well—but perhaps a more reflective person *would* be led to suspect. Though ostensibly the plain man's position is here just being described, a little quiet undermining is already being effected by these turns of phrase.

4. But, perhaps more importantly, it is also implied, even taken for granted, that there is *room* for doubt and suspicion, whether or not the plain man feels any. The quotation from Locke, with which most people are said to agree, in fact contains a strong *suggestio falsi.* It suggests that when, for instance, I look at a chair a few yards in front of me in broad daylight, my view is that I have (*only*) as much certainty as I need and can get that there is a chair and that I see it. But in fact the plain man would regard doubt in such a case, not as farfetched or over-refined or somehow unpractical, but as plain *nonsense*; he would say, quite correctly, 'Well, if that's not seeing a real chair then *I don't know*

[3] Price, op. cit., p. 26, says that he *is* naïve, though it is not, it seems, certain that he is actually a Naïve Realist.

what is.' Moreover, though the plain man's alleged belief that his 'sense-perceptions' can 'in general' or 'now' be trusted is implicitly contrasted with the philosophers' view, it turns out that the philosophers' view is not just that his sense-perceptions *can't* be trusted 'now,' or 'in general,' or as often as he thinks; for apparently philosophers 'for the most part' really maintain that what the plain man believes to be the case is really *never* the case—'what, in their opinion, we directly perceive is *always* an object of a different kind.' The philosopher is not really going to argue that things go wrong more often than the unwary plain man supposes, but that in some sense or some way he is wrong all the time. So it is misleading to hint, not only that there is always room for doubt, but that the philosophers' dissent from the plain man is just a matter of degree; it is really not *that* kind of disagreement at all.

5. Consider next what is said here about deception. We recognize, it is said, that 'people are sometimes deceived by their senses,' though we think that, in general, our 'sense-perceptions' can 'be trusted.'

Now first, though the phrase 'deceived by our senses' is a common metaphor, it *is* a metaphor; and this is worth noting, for in what follows the same metaphor is frequently taken up by the expression 'veridical' and taken very seriously. In fact, of course, our senses are dumb—though Descartes and others speak of 'the testimony of the senses,' our senses do not *tell* us anything, true or false. The case is made much worse here by the unexplained introduction of a quite new creation, our 'sense-perceptions.' These entities, which of course don't really figure at all in the plain man's language or among his beliefs, are brought in with the implication that whenever we 'perceive' there is an *intermediate* entity *always* present and *informing* us about something *else*—the question is, can we or can't we trust what it says? Is it 'veridical?' But of course to state the case in this way is simply to soften up the plain man's alleged views for the subsequent treatment; it is preparing the way for, by practically attributing to *him*, the so-called philosophers' view.

Next, it is important to remember that talk of deception only *makes sense* against a background of general non-deception. (You can't fool all of the people all of the time.) It must be possible to *recognize* a case of deception by checking the odd case against more normal ones. If I say, 'Our petrol-gauge sometimes deceives us,' I am understood: though usually what it indicates squares with what we have in the tank, sometimes it doesn't—it sometimes points to two gallons when the tank turns out to be nearly empty. But suppose I say, 'Our crystal ball sometimes deceives us': this is puzzling, because really we haven't the least idea what the 'normal' case—*not* being deceived by our crystal ball—would actually be.

The cases, again, in which a plain man might say he was 'deceived by his senses' are not at all common. In particular, he would *not* say this when confronted with ordinary cases of perspective, with ordinary mirror-images, or with dreams; in fact, when he dreams, looks down the long straight road, or at his face in the mirror, he is not, or at least is hardly ever, *deceived* at all. This is worth remembering in view of another strong *suggestio falsi*—namely, that when the philosopher cites as cases of 'illusion' all these and many other very common phenomena, he is either simply mentioning cases which the plain man already concedes as cases of 'deception by the senses,' or at any rate is only extending a bit what he would readily concede. In fact this is very far indeed from being the case.

And even so—even though the plain man certainly does not accept anything like so *many* cases as cases of being 'deceived by his senses' as philosophers seem to—it would certainly be quite wrong to suggest that he regards all the cases he *does* accept as being of just the same kind. The battle is, in fact, half lost already if this suggestion is tolerated. Sometimes the plain man would prefer to say that his senses were deceived rather than that he was deceived by his senses—the quickness of the hand deceives the eye, &c. But there is actually a great multiplicity of cases here, at least at the edges of which it is no doubt uncertain (and it would be typically scholastic to try to decide) just which are and which are not cases where the metaphor of being 'deceived by the senses' would naturally be employed. But surely even the plainest of men would want to distinguish (*a*) cases where the *sense-organ* is deranged or abnormal or in some way or other not functioning properly; (*b*) cases where the *medium*—or more generally, the conditions—of perception are in some way abnormal or off-colour; and (*c*) cases where a wrong inference is made or a wrong construction is put on things, e.g. on some sound that he hears. (Of course these cases do not exclude each other.) And then again there are the quite common cases of misreadings, mishearings, Freudian over-sights, &c., which don't seem to belong properly under any of these headings. That is to say, once again there is no neat and simple dichotomy between things going right and things going wrong; things may go wrong, as we really all know quite well, in lots of *different* ways —which don't have to be, and must not be assumed to be, classifiable in any general fashion.

Finally, to repeat here a point we've already mentioned, of course the plain man does *not* suppose that all the cases in which he is 'deceived by his senses' are alike in the particular respect that, in those cases, he is not 'perceiving material things,' or *is* perceiving something not real or not material. Looking at the Müller-Lyer diagram (in which, of two lines of equal length, one looks longer than the other), or at a distant village on a very clear day across a valley, is a very different kettle of fish from seeing a ghost or from having D.T.s and seeing pink rats. And when the plain man sees on the stage the Headless Woman, what he sees (and this *is* what he sees, whether he knows it or not) is not something 'unreal' or 'immaterial,' but a woman against a dark background with her head in a black bag. If the trick is well done, he doesn't (because it's deliberately made very difficult for him) properly size up what he sees, or see *what* it is; but to say this is far from concluding that he sees something *else.*

In conclusion, then, there is less than no reason to swallow the suggestions *either* that what the plain man believes that he perceives most of the time constitutes a *kind* of things (*sc.* 'material objects'), *or* that he can be said to recognize any other single *kind* of cases in which he is 'deceived.'[4] Now let us consider what it is that is said about philosophers.

Philosophers, it is said, 'are not, for the most part, prepared to admit that such objects as pens or cigarettes are ever directly perceived.' Now of course what brings us up short here is the word 'directly'—a great favourite among philosophers, but actually one of the less conspicuous snakes in the linguistic grass. We have here, in fact, a typical case of a word, which already has a very special use, being gradually stretched, without caution or definition or any limit, until it becomes, first perhaps obscurely metaphorical, but ultimately meaningless. One can't abuse ordinary language without paying for it.[5]

1. First of all, it is essential to realize that here the notion of perceiving *in*directly wears the trousers—'directly' takes whatever sense it has from the contrast with its opposite:[6] while 'indirectly' itself (*a*) has a use only in special cases, and also (*b*) has *different* uses in different cases—though that doesn't mean, of course, that there is not a good reason why we should use the same word. We might, for example, contrast the man who saw the procession directly with the man who saw it *through a periscope*; or we might contrast the place from which you can watch the door directly with the place from which you can see it only *in the mirror. Perhaps* we might contrast seeing you directly with seeing, say, your shadow on the blind; and *perhaps* we might contrast hearing the music directly with hearing it relayed outside the concert-hall. However, these last two cases suggest two further points.

2. The first of these points is that the notion of not perceiving 'directly' seems most at home where, as with the periscope and the mirror, it retains its link with the notion of a kink in *direction.* It seems that we must not be looking *straight at* the object in question. For this reason seeing your shadow on the blind is a doubtful case; and seeing you, for instance, through binoculars or spectacles is certainly not a case of seeing you *indirectly* at all. For such cases as these last we have quite distinct contrasts and different expressions—'with the naked eye' as opposed to 'with a telescope,' 'with unaided vision' as opposed to 'with glasses on.' (These expressions, in fact, are much more firmly established in ordinary use than 'directly' is.)

[4] I am not denying that cases in which things go wrong *could* be lumped together under some single name. A single name might in itself be innocent enough, provided its use was not taken to imply either (*a*) that the cases were all alike, or (*b*) that they were all in certain ways alike. What matters is that the facts should not be pre-judged and (therefore) neglected.

[5] Especially if one abuses it without realizing what one is doing. Consider the trouble caused by unwitting stretching of the word 'sign', so as to yield—apparently—the conclusion that, when the cheese is in front of our noses, we see *signs* of cheese.

[6] Compare, in this respect, 'real', 'proper', 'free', and plenty of others. 'It's real'—what exactly are you saying it isn't? 'I wish we had a proper stair-carpet'—what are you complaining of in the one you've got? (That it's *im*proper?) 'Is he free?'—well, what have you in mind that he might be instead? In prison? Tied up in prison? Committed to a prior engagement?

3. And the other point is that, partly no doubt for the above reason, the notion of indirect perception is not naturally at home with senses other than sight. With the other senses there is nothing quite analogous with the 'line of vision.' The most natural sense of 'hearing indirectly,' of course, is that of being *told* something by an intermediary—a quite different matter. But do I hear a shout indirectly, when I hear the echo? If I touch you with a barge-pole, do I touch you indirectly? Or if you offer me a pig in a poke, might I feel the pig indirectly—*through* the poke? And what smelling indirectly might be I have simply no idea. For this reason alone there seems to be something badly wrong with the question, 'Do we perceive things directly or not?', where perceiving is evidently intended to cover the employment of *any* of the senses.

4. But it is, of course, for other reasons too extremely doubtful how far the notion of perceiving indirectly could or should be extended. Does it, or should it, cover the telephone, for instance? Or television? Or radar? Have we moved too far in these cases from the original metaphor? They at any rate satisfy what seems to be a necessary condition—namely, concurrent existence and concomitant variation as between what is perceived in the straightforward way (the sounds in the receiver, the picture and the blips on the screen) and the candidate for what we might be prepared to describe as being perceived indirectly. And this condition fairly clearly rules out as cases of indirect perception seeing photographs (which statically record scenes from the past) and seeing films (which, though not static, are not seen contemporaneously with the events thus recorded). Certainly, there *is* a line to be drawn somewhere. It is certain, for instance, that we should not be prepared to speak of indirect perception in *every* case in which we see something from which the existence (or occurrence) of something else can be inferred; we should *not* say we see the guns indirectly, if we see in the distance only the flashes of guns.

5. Rather differently, if we are to be seriously inclined to speak of something as being perceived indirectly, it seems that it has to be the kind of thing which we (sometimes at least) just perceive, or could perceive, or which—like the backs of our own heads—others could perceive. For otherwise we don't want to say that we perceive the thing *at all*, even indirectly. No doubt there are complications here (raised, perhaps, by the electron microscope, for example, about which I know little or nothing). But it seems clear that, in general, we should want to distinguish between seeing indirectly, e.g. in a mirror, what we might have just *seen*, and seeing signs (or effects), e.g. in a Wilson cloud-chamber, of something not itself perceptible at all. It would at least not come naturally to speak of the latter as a case of perceiving something indirectly.

6. And one final point. For reasons not very obscure, we always prefer in practice what might be called the *cash-value* expression to the 'indirect' metaphor. If I were to report that I see enemy ships indirectly, I should merely provoke the question what exactly I mean. 'I mean that I can see these blips on the radar screen'—'Well, why didn't you say so then?' (Compare 'I can see an unreal duck.'—'What on earth do you mean?' 'It's a decoy duck'—'Ah, I see. Why didn't you say so at once?') That is, there is seldom if ever any particular

point in actually saying 'indirectly' (or 'unreal'); the expression can cover too many rather different cases to be *just* what is wanted in any particular case.

Thus, it is quite plain that the philosophers' use of 'directly perceive,' whatever it may be, is not the ordinary, or any familiar use; for in *that* use it is not only false but simply absurd to say that such objects as pens or cigarettes are never perceived directly. But we are given no explanation or definition of this new use[7]—on the contrary, it is glibly trotted out as if we were all quite familiar with it already. It is clear, too, that the philosophers' use, whatever it may be, offends against several of the canons just mentioned above—no restrictions whatever seem to be envisaged to any special circumstances or to any of the senses in particular, and moreover it seems that what we are to be said to perceive indirectly is *never*—is not the kind of thing which ever *could* be—perceived directly.

All this lends poignancy to the question Ayer himself asks, a few lines below the passage we have been considering: 'Why may we not say that we are indirectly aware of material things?' The answer, he says, is provided 'by what is known as the argument from illusion'; and this is what we must next consider. Just possibly the answer may help us to understand the question.*

[7] Ayer takes note of this rather belatedly, on pp. 60–61.

* EDITOR'S NOTE: The reader is invited to look at Chapter III of *Sense and Sensibilia.*

INTRODUCTION TO EPISTEMOLOGY / Study Questions

SCEPTICISM AND PERCEPTION

Descartes

1. What is the importance of Descartes in intellectual history?
2. What is Descartes' stated aim in this selection?
3. How does he propose to carry out his aim?
4. Upon what principle does he think his former opinions rested?
5. State the three arguments that Descartes formulates to cast doubt on the validity of sense experience.
6. Why does Descartes believe the first argument is inadequate to do the job he wants done?
7. Suppose someone offers us a test to apply to determine whether we are at this moment dreaming or really awake. What objection ought Descartes, or any other proponent of the dream argument, raise against the validity of this test?
8. Why are the propositions of arithmetic and geometry immune to the doubt raised by the dream argument?
9. Apart from anything Descartes may have said, in what important ways are the statements of arithmetic and geometry different from statements about things in the world, for example, "I am wearing my dressing gown," "There is a fire in the fireplace," "The sun is shining," and so on?
10. Are there any statements immune to the doubts raised by the evil genius argument?
11. Would Descartes recognize a difference between saying "There is a round reddish area in my visual field" and saying "I see an apple?"

12. What is epistemological scepticism? Is Descartes' position at the end of this selection one of scepticism?

Bouwsma

1. What does Bouwsma intend to do in this paper?
2. Describe the evil genius' first attempt at deception. How was it carried out? How did Tom discover the deception?
3. According to Bouwsma, what is an illusion and what is presupposed in both the perpetration and detection of illusions?
4. Why is this first adventure not the kind of thing Descartes had in mind for the evil genius to be up to? What must the evil genius do in order to do his job properly?
5. Describe the circumstances of the second adventure in which the evil genius has been completely successful.
6. Can the evil genius convince Tom that the flowers are illusory?
7. What is the difference between "thick" and "thin" illusions? Can any sense be made of it?
8. Why must the evil genius be assumed to have an extra sense? Is this assumption of any help to *us* in understanding the possibility of total illusion?
9. In what way has the evil genius succeeded only in "bathing the word 'illusion' in a fog"?
10. Descartes entertains the possibility that the sentence "All experiences are illusory" may be true. Note that Bouwsma does not attack Descartes by making the counterclaim that the sentence is in fact false. Rather, Bouwsma wants to show that the sentence is unintelligible. What is the difference between a *false* sentence and one that is unintelligible?
11. What is the point of the allusion to the Cheshire cat in the last paragraph?

Ayer

1. According to Ayer do philosophers who have recently concerned themselves with perception believe that material objects are ever directly perceived? If not, what is said to be directly perceived?
2. What questions about sense data does Ayer say are in dispute?
3. What conclusion is the argument from illusion designed to support?
4. What examples of illusions does Ayer provide?
5. State the argument from illusion using the different examples of illusions Ayer provides. Is the argument valid?
6. Is the argument sufficient to establish that material objects are never directly perceived? What further arguments are required?
7. Is there any way to distinguish a veridical from a delusive experience by comparing the experiences themselves?
8. What are some of the causal factors upon which perception depends? Do veridical and delusive perceptions differ in their relation to these causal factors?
9. What is the difference between material objects and the objects of immediate perception? Is the recognition of this difference sufficient to establish the conclusion that material objects are never directly perceived?
10. If one holds a sense datum theory of perception and claims that material objects are never directly perceived, is one necessarily committed to scepticism? Can a sense know?
    datum theorist ever know that there are material objects and, if so, how would he

11. Would it be fair to describe Descartes' conclusion in the following way: I (Descartes) am aware of a large number of sense data, but I now have no way of knowing whether there are any material objects corresponding to and perhaps causing these sense data?
12. Do you think that Vernon is committed to a sense datum theory, or something very much like it?
13. A stick in water looks bent, but is it true to say that when I see the stick in water I am seeing something bent? Is there anything bent to be seen? Can I see something that isn't there? Do these considerations have any implications for the argument from illusion?

Vernon

1. According to Vernon what is the importance of our knowledge of objects in the world about us?
2. How does she suggest that the distinction between dreams and waking experience be drawn?
3. Describe briefly the physics and physiology of visual perception. Will a similar account hold for perception by means of the other senses as well?
4. According to Vernon what is the difference between the "visual pattern created in the brain" and "our full consciousness of the world of objects?"
5. What problem does the difference present to Vernon and how does she try to solve the problem?
6. Is the account of perception that Vernon gives in any way similar to that given by any psychology textbook with which you might be familiar?
7. Physiology is an empirical science. Our knowledge of what goes on in the eyes, nerves, and brain when we perceive is derived from observation and experiment. Could there be any observational or experimental evidence that would establish the existence and nature of the "elaborate mental processes" that are said to intervene between the "visual pattern" in the brain and our "perception of the world?"
8. Does Vernon suggest that "perceptions" are entities or things distinct from the objects perceived?
9. Given Vernon's theory of perception is there any way to know that our "perception of the world as we know it" gives us information about what the world is really like? Can we even know that the physiological descriptions the theory is based on are true? Is Vernon committed to scepticism?
10. Has Vernon confused the empirical question, "What goes on physiologically in the nervous system when we perceive something?" with the conceptual, that is, philosophical question, "What is perception?" Why cannot an answer to the one also be an answer to the other?

Austin

1. Austin thinks it is important to note Ayer's distinction between what ordinary people believe about perception and what philosophers believe. What is this distinction?
2. What does Austin find peculiar about the notion of "material things?" What role does he think the expression plays in philosophy?
3. What does Austin say is wrong about Ayer's account of the relation between the perception of material things and deception?
4. Is the plain man in fact naive about the existence of the things he perceives?
5. Why does Austin say it is nonsense to doubt the existence of the chair seen close to

in broad daylight? What is this kind of example supposed to show us about the philosopher's doubts?
6. Why is the expression "deceived by our senses" a metaphor?
7. What conditions must be realized for talk of deception to make sense?
8. In what different ways can people be deceived by their senses? Has a philosopher such as Ayer correctly described these circumstances?
9. What does a philosopher mean when he says that objects are never "directly perceived?" What *could* be meant by the claim that something is not directly perceived? What difficulties does Austin see in all this?
10. If Austin is correct, has Ayer succeeded in making an intelligible distinction between seeing objects and seeing sense data?

SUGGESTED FURTHER READINGS / Introduction to Epistemology

GENERAL

Ebersole, Frank. *Things We Know.* Eugene: University of Oregon, 1967.

Malcolm, Norman. *Knowledge and Certainty.* Englewood Cliffs, N.J.: Prentice-Hall, Inc., 1963.

Nagel, E., and R. B. Brandt, *Meaning and Knowledge.* New York: Harcourt Brace Jovanovich, Inc., 1965.

Wittgenstein, Ludwig. *On Certainty.* Oxford, England: Basil Blackwell, 1969.

LEARNING, KNOWLEDGE AND TRUTH

Armstrong, D. M. *Belief, Truth and Knowledge.* London: Cambridge University Press, 1973.

Griffiths, A. Phillips. *Knowledge and Belief.* London: Oxford University Press, 1967.

Peters, R. S., ed. *The Concept of Education.* London: Routledge & Kegan, Paul, 1967.

Pitcher, George, ed. *Truth.* Englewood Cliffs, N.J.: Prentice-Hall, Inc., 1964.

PERCEPTION AND SCEPTICISM

Bouwsma, O. K. *Philosophical Essays.* Lincoln: University of Nebraska Press, 1965.

Hamlyn, D. W. *Sensation and Perception.* London: Routledge & Kegan Paul, 1961.

Price, H. H. *Perception.* London: Methuen, 1932.

Ryle, G. *Dilemmas.* London: Cambridge University Press, 1954.

Warnock, G. J., ed. *The Philosophy of Perception.* London: Oxford University Press, 1967.

PART 4

Introduction to Social and Political Philosophy

Social and political philosophy is an extension of moral philosophy. In Part 1 on ethics, we were concerned primarily with evaluating the actions of individuals and with the metaethical questions that naturally arise in the course of such an evaluation. In this part we will be concerned with the extension of our evaluations to the actions of governments and to the moral relationships among groups of people rather than among individuals. The distinctions made in the introduction to Part 1, and many of the ideas developed in the readings therein, especially in the first section, are relevant to the concerns of political philosophers. We recommend that Part 1—or at least its introduction—be read in advance of this part.

We have made an effort throughout our introductions to point out the relevance of philosophy to other disciplines and to everyday life. Nowhere is this relevance more apparent than in social and political philosophy. A quick glance at some of the most prevalent and perennial issues in this area of philosophy should suffice to establish our point: What is the relationship between the state and the individual? To what extent is it legitimate for the state to coerce the individual or restrict his liberty? Do we have natural rights, or do all individual rights derive from the state? What is justice? Does justice require that goods be distributed equally or according to merit? What is equality and what does it mean with respect to such things as property rights, education, or suffrage?

Our concerns with these questions have their roots in Plato's dialogues. In the

---

We wish gratefully to acknowledge the assistance we received from our colleague, Professor John Exdell, in the preparation of this part, especially the second section on paternalism.

Crito, we find Socrates' friend Crito trying to convince Socrates that he ought to escape from Athens and from the unjust penalty of death imposed upon Socrates following his conviction on trumped-up charges. Socrates claims that, in the first place, escape would be morally wrong because it would wrong the state and we must not attempt to redress wrongs by wrongs. Secondly, Socrates claims that he has benefitted in many ways by living in Athens and so he has an obligation of fairness to stay and obey her laws. Finally, he claims that by living in Athens when he was free to emigrate was to make a tacit covenant of obedience to the government and its laws. In another dialogue, *The Republic*, Plato describes the just state, its laws, and those who would be its rulers. From Plato to the present day, almost every major philosopher has been concerned with the problems and questions of social and political philosophy.

These issues are also widely discussed by nonprofessional "philosophers" such as newspaper columnists, politicians, political scientists, sociologists, and many others. Thus it is important, we think, to remind the reader of the sorts of things philosophers would have to say about these questions. The first is that they are *normative*. They ask what *ought* to be done. They are not directly answered by a recital of the facts. Thus, a purely empirical study cannot tell us whether, for example, the government should prohibit the use of heroin, although any reasoned answer to this question must consider the facts about heroin and its users. Secondly, understanding the issues and evaluating proposed solutions will frequently hinge on *clarifying concepts*. Should it be argued, say in the case of heroin control, that it is proper for government to prevent persons from harming themselves, we may find that the whole issue hinges on the concept of *harm*, and that it will be necessary to clarify that concept and to determine the sorts of things that can count as proper instances of harm. Assuming that questions about the concept are satisfactorily resolved, we are nevertheless, still left with the normative question whether the government *ought* to prevent people from harming themselves.

As representative questions in social and political philosophy, we have chosen the issues of criminal punishment and paternalism. The first deals with the justification of punishment and its corollary, prison reform. This is a philosophical question that has received very wide attention from nonphilosophers. It also provides an excellent example of the contributions of philosophers, especially A. M. *Quinton* and Kurt *Baier*, to clarifying and helping resolve a complex issue of great popular concern. Additionally, it allows us to produce instances of nonphilosophers participating in philosophical discussion, some brilliantly like Dr. Thomas *Szasz* and others, perhaps, not so brilliantly.

The second section of this part deals with an important question about the alleged right of government to interfere with personal freedom in order to prevent persons from doing harm to themselves. This is the question of paternalism and as a preface to selections from four philosophers we have included the thinking of a trio of sociologists on the matter of heroin use and the problems of legislation and law enforcement it raises.

Sometimes it seems to those not very familiar with philosophy that we "make our own trouble" or that what concerns us are really rather esoteric questions of no practical moment. We have endeavored, however, even in our readings on epistemology and metaphysics—whose questions may seem, at first glance, most fitting of this description—to show the relevance of these philosophical questions to other disciplines. We believe that *this* part will go a long way toward proving that nonprofessional "philosophers" deal with philosophical questions and that what the philosopher has to say is relevant to nonphilosophers.

Punishment

We have chosen the topic of criminal punishment as one of our examples of social and political philosophy for the same reasons that have guided our choice of other representative philosophical questions: It is relevant to the concerns of nonphilosophers, it is widely discussed in nonphilosophical as well as philosophical circles, and it allows us to present philosophers at work on issues that are not so overly technical that they are beyond the grasp of the beginner.

The philosophical problem about punishment arises in this way. Punishment involves the infliction of suffering, pain, and deprivation. We would all agree that it is morally wrong to inflict pain and suffering upon others and that to do so requires a special justification. How, then, are we to justify this infliction of suffering, pain, or deprivation? We begin this section with a review of the theories of two competing groups of philosophers. One group, called retributivists, says that punishment is justified on grounds that the person being punished is guilty of some past criminal act. Punishment is thus to be justified by looking at past actions. Others, called utilitarians, claim that punishment is to be justified by its preventive, deterrent, or rehabilitory effects. Punishment, according to this group, is justified by probable future events. Each of these views claims the other to be seriously mistaken. The retributivists insist that utilitarianism leads to the abhorent conclusion that the punishing of an *innocent* person is "justified" so long as it has desired deterrent, preventive, or reformatory effects. On the other hand, the utilitarians counter with the objection that the retributivists have merely elevated the base and barbaric instinct for revenge to the status of moral principle. The typically philosophical aspect of the problem now comes into view. The two theories seem to exhaust the possible ways of answering the question about the justification of punishment, yet neither theory is satisfactory. How, then, can punishment be justified in the light of this *impasse*?

Our first selection is from Immanuel *Kant* who gives us a classical statement of the retributive position:

> Juridical punishment can never be administered merely as a means for promoting another good, either with regard to the criminal himself or to civil society, but must in all cases be imposed only because the individual on whom it is inflicted has committed a crime.

To punish someone who has not committed a crime on the grounds that it will deter others, or that punishment will prevent that person from committing a crime, is to treat the person as a means and not as an end in himself, something that Kant says is always wrong. Kant also adds the principle that the punishment should fit the crime, that there should be some proportion between the gravity of the crime and the severity of the punishment. (This is sometimes called the *lex talionis*.)

Our second selection is by the famous psychiatrist, Karl *Menninger*, who claims that our current penal system is outmoded and uncivilized, and that it fails either to deter or to rehabilitate. Citizens punish from a motive of vengeance and most of the time we punish criminals for doing what we want to do but dare not. Thus, criminals are made scapegoats and we vicariously participate in both their crime and their punishment. We maintain our current penal system not because it is called for by either the retributivist or the utilitarian justifications of punishment, but because "the public acts like a sick patient." That is, punishment of criminals satisfies psychological needs and our attempts at justification are really only rationalizations.

The second important claim made by Menninger is that crime is not a disease nor do we presently consider crime *per se* an illness. It is not a disease because,

> Diseases are undesired states of being which have been described and defined by doctors, usually given Greek or Latin appellations, and treated by long-established physical and pharmacological formulae. Illness is a state of impaired functioning of such a nature that the public expects the sufferer to repair to the physician for help.

Menninger says, however, that while we do not now look on crime as an illness, *we ought to*. He wants crime to be considered symptomatic of an illness treatable by psychiatry and its allied disciplines.

If Menninger's recommendations are to be accepted, then our problem of justifying punishment vanishes since crime becomes illness and punishment becomes treatment; and, of course, the practice of having doctors treat illnesses requires no justification.

Our third contribution is from another well-known psychiatrist, Thomas S. *Szasz*, who is diametrically opposed to Menninger's suggestion. Szasz claims that the legal and the medical professions have made a ludicrous "role-switch." Psychiatrists enter the courtroom and speak to the question of the defendant's responsibility or guilt, while at the same time judges arrogate to themselves the power to determine the length of stay in institutions of mental patients who have not been convicted of any crime. Szasz says that our current practice of "acquitting a person of a crime and then committing him" is highly dubious. "Once [a person] is acquitted, he must be considered (legally) innocent. If he is not so considered, the word 'acquittal' and the deed it designates will have lost their customary meanings." Judge David Bazelon of the District of Columbia Court of Appeals has said that persons acquitted on the grounds of insanity are "an exceptional class of persons" and that, while we are justified in punishing persons found guilty and awarding full liberty to those found innocent (on grounds other than insanity), nevertheless we *may* commit for an indefinite period of time persons found innocent by reason of insanity. Szasz objects that such a move is unconstitutional and that, if the person is committed for psychiatric treatment, his psychiatrist should be the sole determiner of the length of the commitment.

Szasz, in short, objects to imprisoning persons who have not been convicted on the grounds of protecting them, protecting society, or rehabilitating them. "It is a truism," he says, "that in a democracy, imprisonment (or loss of liberty) is justified only by conviction for a crime."

At this point, our problem appears to be still unsolved despite our being persuaded by the retributivist claims of Kant and Szasz, while also being sympathetic with the humanitarian values represented by Menninger. What is needed is a reexamination of the issue and a closer analysis of just what the dispute involves.

In his article, "On Punishment," A. M. *Quinton* claims to resolve the apparent dilemma of justifying punishment either by the retributivist claims or the utilitarian grounds by actually *dis*solving the dilemma. Quinton points out that what the retributivist is claiming is really a conceptual or logical truth, while the utilitarian is really making a moral claim. Thus, what is right about each does not lead to any conflict between them. "The infliction of suffering on a person is only properly described as punishment if that person is guilty. The retributivist thesis, therefore, is not a moral doctrine, but an account of the meaning of the word 'punishment.' " On the other hand, the moral question of when and how we should punish a guilty person is best answered by reference to utilitarian considerations.

Kurt *Baier*, in his article, "Is Punishment Retributive?" agrees with Quinton that the theory of retributivism is something other than a moral theory. He disagrees with him, however, on the reason why this is so. Baier says that punishment is a social activity, ritual, or "game" and that for some piece of behavior to count as a case of punishing, it must occur in the context of proscribing behavior, announcing penalties, and detecting offenses. Thus, while Quinton claims it is logically impossible to "punish" an innocent person, Baier claims that there is no logical impossibility in this as long as the punishment occurs in the required social context.

An important conclusion, whether one accepts Baier's analysis or Quinton's, is that retributivism is not a moral justification of punishment, but rather a clarification of the concept of *punishment.*

A Retributivist Justification of Punishment

IMMANUEL KANT

JUDICIAL or juridical punishment (*poena forensis*) is to be distinguished from natural punishment (*poena naturalis*), in which crime as vice punishes itself, and does not as such come within the cognizance of the legislator. Juridical punishment can never be administered merely as a means for promoting

---

Reprinted from *The Philosophy of Law*, part II by Immanuel Kant, W. Hastie, trans., Edinburgh: T. & T. Clark, 1887, pp. 194–198.

another good, either with regard to the criminal himself or to civil society, but must in all cases be imposed only because the individual on whom it is inflicted *has committed a crime*. For one man ought never to be dealt with merely as a means subservient to the purpose of another, nor be mixed up with the subjects of real right. Against such treatment his inborn personality has a right to protect him, even although he may be condemned to lose his civil personality. He must first be found guilty and *punishable*, before there can be any thought of drawing from his punishment any benefit for himself or his fellow-citizens. The penal law is a categorical imperative; and woe to him who creeps through the serpent-windings of utilitarianism to discover some advantage that may discharge him from the justice of punishment, or even from the due measure of it, according to the pharisaic maxim: 'It is better that *one* man should die than that the whole people should perish.' For if justice and righteousness perish, human life would no longer have any value in the world.—What, then, is to be said of such a proposal as to keep a criminal alive who has been condemned to death, on his being given to understand that if he agreed to certain dangerous experiments being performed upon him, he would be allowed to survive if he came happily through them? It is argued that physicians might thus obtain new information that would be of value to the commonweal. But a court of justice would repudiate with scorn any proposal of this kind if made to it by the medical faculty; for justice would cease to be justice, if it were bartered away for any consideration whatever.

But what is the mode and measure of punishment which public justice takes as its principle and standard? It is just the principle of equality, by which the pointer of the scale of justice is made to incline no more to the one side than the other. It may be rendered by saying that the undeserved evil which any one commits on another, is to be regarded as perpetrated on himself. Hence it may be said: 'If you slander another, you slander yourself; if you steal from another, you steal from yourself; if you strike another, you strike yourself; if you kill another, you kill yourself.' This is the right of retaliation (*jus talionis*); and properly understood, it is the only principle which in regulating a public court, as distinguished from mere private judgment, can definitely assign both the quality and the quantity of a just penalty. All other standards are wavering and uncertain; and on account of other considerations involved in them, they contain no principle conformable to the sentence of pure and strict justice. It may appear, however, that difference of social status would not admit the application of the principle of retaliation, which is that of 'like with like.' But although the application may not in all cases be possible according to the letter, yet as regards the effect it may always be attained in practice, by due regard being given to the disposition and sentiment of the parties in the higher social sphere. Thus a pecuniary penalty on account of a verbal injury, may have no direct proportion to the injustice of slander; for one who is wealthy may be able to indulge himself in this offence for his own gratification. Yet the attack committed on the honour of the party aggrieved may have its equivalent in the pain inflicted upon the pride of the aggressor, especially if he is condemned by the judgment of the court, not only to retract and apologize, but to submit to some meaner ordeal, as kissing the hand of the injured person. In like manner, if a man of the highest rank has violently assaulted an innocent citizen of the lower orders, he may be condemned not only to apologize but to undergo a solitary and painful imprisonment, whereby, in addition to the discomfort endured, the vanity of the offender would be painfully affected, and the very shame of his position would constitute an adequate retaliation after the principle of 'like with like.' But how then would we render the statement: 'If you *steal* from another, you steal from yourself'? In this way, that whoever steals anything makes the property of all insecure; he therefore robs himself of all security in property, according to the right of retaliation. Such a one has nothing, and can acquire nothing, but he has the will to live; and this is only possible by others supporting him. But as the state should not do this gratuitously, he must for this purpose yield his powers to the state to be used in penal labour; and thus he falls for a time, or it may be for life, into a condition of slavery.—But whoever has committed murder, must *die.* There is, in this case, no juridical substitute or surrogate, that can be given or taken for the satisfaction of justice. There is no likeness or proportion between life, however painful, and death; and therefore there is no equality between the crime of murder and the retaliation of it but what is judicially accomplished by the execution of the criminal. His death, however, must be kept free from all maltreatment that would make the humanity suffering in his person loathsome or abominable. Even if a civil society resolved to dissolve itself with the consent of all its members—as might be supposed in the case of a people inhabiting an island resolving to separate and scatter themselves throughout the whole world—the last murderer lying in the prison ought to be executed before the resolution was carried out. This ought to be done in order that every one may realize the desert of his deeds, and that bloodguiltiness may not remain upon the people; for otherwise they might all be regarded as participators in the murder as a public violation of justice.

The equalization of punishment with crime, is therefore only possible by the cognition of the judge extending even to the penalty of death, according to the right of retaliation . . .

Punishment Is a Crime

KARL MENNINGER

FEW WORDS in our language arrest our attention as do "crime," "violence," "revenge," and "injustice." We abhor crime; we adore justice; we boast that we live by the rule of law. Violence and vengefulness we repudiate as un-

---

Reprinted with permission of *Saturday Review* from "The Crime of Punishment," Sept. 7, 1968, 21–25, 55.

worthy of our civilization, and we assume this sentiment to be unanimous among all human beings.

Yet crime continues to be a national disgrace and a world-wide problem. It is threatening, alarming, wasteful, expensive, abundant, and apparently increasing! In actuality it is decreasing in frequency of occurrence, but it is certainly increasing in visibility and the reactions of the public to it.

Our system for controlling crime is ineffective, unjust, expensive. Prisons seem to operate with revolving doors—the same people going in and out and in and out. *Who cares?*

Our city jails and inhuman reformatories and wretched prisons are jammed. They are known to be unhealthy, dangerous, immoral, indecent, crime-breeding dens of iniquity. Not everyone has smelled them, as some of us have. Not many have heard the groans and the curses. Not everyone has seen the hate and despair in a thousand blank, hollow faces. But, in a way, we all know how miserable prisons are. *We want them to be that way.* And they are. *Who cares?*

Professional and big-time criminals prosper as never before. Gambling syndicates flourish. White-collar crime may even exceed all others, but goes undetected in the majority of cases. We are all being robbed and we know who the robbers are. They live nearby. *Who cares?*

The public filches millions of dollars worth of food and clothing from stores, towels and sheets from hotels, jewelry and knick-knacks from shops. The public steals, and the same public pays it back in higher prices. *Who cares?*

Time and time again somebody shouts about this state of affairs, just as I am shouting now. The magazines shout. The newspapers shout. The television and radio commentators shout (or at least they "deplore"). Psychologists, sociologists, leading jurists, wardens, and intelligent police chiefs join the chorus. Governors and mayors and Congressmen are sometimes heard. They shout that the situation is bad, bad, bad, and getting worse. Some suggested that we immediately replace obsolete procedures with scientific methods. A few shout contrary sentiments. Do the clear indications derived from scientific discovery for appropriate changes continue to fall on deaf ears? Why is the public so long-suffering, so apathetic and thereby so continuingly self-destructive? How many Presidents (and other citizens) do we have to lose before we do something?

The public behaves as a sick patient does when a dreaded treatment is proposed for his ailment. We all know how the aching tooth may suddenly quiet down in the dentist's office, or the abdominal pain disappear in the surgeon's examining room. Why should a sufferer seek relief and shun it? Is it merely the fear of pain of the treatment? Is it the fear of unknown complications? Is it distrust of the doctor's ability? All of these, no doubt.

But, as Freud made so incontestably clear, the sufferer is always somewhat deterred by a kind of subversive, internal opposition to the work of cure. He suffers on the one hand from the pains of his affliction and yearns to get well. But he suffers at the same time from traitorous impulses that fight against the accomplishment of any change in himself, even recovery! Like Hamlet, he wonders whether it may be better after all to suffer the familiar pains and aches associated with the old method than to face the complications of a new and strange, even though possibly better way of handling things.

The inescapable conclusion is that society secretly *wants* crime, *needs* crime, and gains definite satisfactions from the present mishandling of it! We condemn crime; we punish offenders for it; but we need it. The crime and punishment ritual is a part of our lives. We need crimes to wonder at, to enjoy vicariously, to discuss and speculate about, and to publicly deplore. We need criminals to identify ourselves with, to envy secretly, and to punish stoutly. They do for us the forbidden, illegal things we *wish* to do and, like scapegoats of old, they bear the burdens of our displaced guilt and punishment—"the iniquities of us all."

We have to confess that there is something fascinating for us all about violence. That most crime is not violent we know but we forget, because crime is a breaking, a rupturing, a tearing—even when it is quietly done. To all of us crime seems like violence.

The very word "violence" has a disturbing, menacing quality. . . . In meaning it implies something dreaded, powerful, destructive, or eruptive. It is something we abhor—or do we? Its first effect is to startle, frighten—even to horrify us. But we do not always run away from it. For violence also intrigues us. It is exciting. It is dramatic. Observing it and sometimes even participating in it gives us acute pleasure.

The newspapers constantly supply us with tidbits of violence going on in the world. They exploit its dramatic essence often to the neglect of conservative reporting of more extensive but less violent damage—the flood disaster in Florence, Italy, for example. Such words as crash, explosion, wreck, assault, raid, murder, avalanche, rape, and seizure evoke pictures of eruptive devastation from which we cannot turn away. The headlines often impute violence metaphorically even to peaceful activities. Relations are "ruptured," a tie is "broken," arbitration "collapses," a proposal is "killed."

Meanwhile on the television and movie screens there constantly appear for our amusement scenes of fighting, slugging, beating, torturing, clubbing, shooting, and the like which surpass in effect anything that the newspapers can describe. Much of this violence is portrayed dishonestly; the scenes are only semirealistic; they are "faked" and romanticized.

Pain cannot be photographed; grimaces indicate but do not convey its intensity. And wounds—unlike violence—are rarely shown. This phony quality of television violence in its mentally unhealthy aspect encourages irrationality by giving the impression to the observer that being beaten, kicked, cut, and stomped, while very unpleasant, are not very painful or serious. For after being slugged and beaten the hero rolls over, opens his eyes, hops up, rubs his cheek, grins, and staggers on. The *suffering* of violence is a part both the TV and movie producers *and* their audience tend to repress.

Although most of us *say* we deplore cruelty and destructiveness, we are partially deceiving ourselves. We disown violence, ascribing the love of it to other people. But the facts speak for themselves. We do love violence, all of us, and we all feel secretly guilty for it, which is another clue to public resistance to crime-control reform.

The great sin by which we all are tempted is the wish to hurt others, and this sin must be avoided if we are to live and let live. If our destructive energies can be mastered, directed, and sublimated, we can survive. If we can love, we can live. Our destructive energies, if they cannot be controlled, may destroy our best friends, as in the case of Alexander the Great, or they may destroy supposed "enemies" or innocent strangers. Worst of all—from the standpoint of the individual—they may destroy us.

Over the centuries of man's existence, many devices have been employed in the effort to control these innate suicidal and criminal propensities. The earliest of these undoubtedly depended upon fear—fear of the unknown, fear of magical retribution, fear of social retaliation. These external devices were replaced gradually with the law and all its machinery, religion and its rituals, and the conventions of the social order.

The routine of life formerly required every individual to direct much of his aggressive energy against the environment. There were trees to cut down, wild animals to fend off, heavy obstacles to remove, great burdens to lift. But the machine has gradually changed all of this. Today, the routine of life, for most people, requires no violence, no fighting, no killing, no life-risking, no sudden supreme exertion; occasionally, perhaps, a hard pull or a strong push, but no tearing, crushing, breaking, forcing.

And because violence no longer has legitimate and useful vents or purposes, it must *all* be controlled today. In earlier times its expression was often a virtue; today its control is the virtue. The control involves symbolic, vicarious expressions of our violence—violence modified; "sublimated," as Freud called it; "neutralized," as Hartmann described it. Civilized substitutes for direct violence are the objects of daily search by all of us. The common law and the Ten Commandments, traffic signals and property deeds, fences and front doors, sermons and concerts, Christmas trees and jazz bands—these and a thousand other things exist today to help in the control of violence.

My colleague, Bruno Bettelheim, thinks we do not properly educate our youth to deal with their violent urges. He reminds us that nothing fascinated our forefathers more. The *Iliad* is a poem of violence. Much of the Bible is a record of violence. One penal system and many methods of child-rearing express violence—"violence to suppress violence." And, he concludes [in the article "Violence: A Neglected Mode of Behavior"]: "We shall not be able to deal intelligently with violence unless we are first ready to see it as a part of human nature, and then we shall come to realize the chances of discharging violent tendencies are now so severely curtailed that their regular and safe draining-off is not possible anymore."

Why aren't we all criminals? We all have the impulses; we all have the provocations. But becoming civilized, which is repeated ontologically in the process of social education, teaches us what we may do with impunity. What then evokes or permits the breakthrough? Why is it necessary for some to bribe their consciences and do what they do not approve of doing? Why does all sublimation sometimes fail and overt breakdown occur in the controlling and managing machinery of the personality? Why do we sometimes lose self-control? Why do we "go to pieces"? Why do we explode?

These questions point up a central problem in psychiatry. Why do some people do things they do not want to do? Or things we do not want them to do? Sometimes crimes are motivated by a desperate need to act, to do *something* to break out of a state of passivity, frustration, and helplessness too long endured, like a child who shoots a parent or a teacher after some apparently reasonable act. Granting the universal presence of violence within us all, controlled by will power, conscience, fear of punishment, and other devices, granting the tensions and the temptations that are also common to us all, why do the mechanisms of self-control fail so completely in some individuals? Is there not some pre-existing defect, some moral or cerebral weakness, some gross deficiency of common sense that lets some people stumble or kick or strike or explode, while the rest of us just stagger or sway?

When a psychiatrist examines many prisoners, writes [Seymour] Halleck [in *Psychiatry and the Dilemmas of Crime*], he soon discovers how important in the genesis of the criminal outbreak is the offender's previous *sense of helplessness or hopelessness.* All of us suffer more or less from infringement of our personal freedom. We fuss about it all the time; we strive to correct it, extend it, and free ourselves from various oppressive or retentive forces. We do not want others to push us around, to control us, to dominate us. We realize this is bound to happen to some extent in an interlocking, interrelated society such as ours. No one truly has complete freedom. But restriction irks us.

The offender feels this way, too. He does not want to be pushed around, controlled, or dominated. And because he often feels that he is thus oppressed (and actually is) and because he does lack facility in improving his situation without violence, he suffers more intensely from feelings of helplessness.

Violence and crime are often attempts to escape from madness; and there can be no doubt that some mental illness is a flight from the wish to do the violence or commit the act. Is it hard for the reader to believe the suicides are sometimes committed to forestall the committing of murder? There is no doubt of it. Nor is there any doubt that murder is sometimes committed to avert suicide.

Strange as it may sound, many murderers do not realize whom they are killing, or, to put it another way, that they are killing the wrong people. To be sure, killing anybody is reprehensible enough, but the worst of it is that the person who the killer thinks should die (and he has reasons) is not the person he attacks. Sometimes the victim himself is partly responsible for the crime that is committed against him. It is this unconscious (perhaps sometimes conscious) participation in the crime by the victim that has long held up the very humanitarian and progressive-sounding program of giving compensation to victims. The public often judges the victim as well as the attacker.

Rape and other sexual offenses are acts of violence so repulsive to our sense of decency and order that it is easy to think of rapists in general as raging, oversexed, ruthless brutes (unless they are conquering heroes). Some rapists are. But most sex crimes are committed by undersexed rather than oversexed individuals, often undersized rather than oversized, and impelled less by lust than by a need for reassurance regarding an impaired masculinity. The unconscious fear of women goads some men with a compulsive urge to conquer, humiliate, hurt, or render powerless some available sample of womanhood. Men who are violently afraid of their repressed but nearly emergent homosexual desires, and men who are afraid of the humiliation of impotence, often try to overcome these fears by violent demonstrations.

The need to deny something in oneself is frequently an underlying motive for certain odd behavior—even up to and including crime. Bravado crimes, often done with particular brutality and ruthlessness, seem to prove *to the doer* that "I am no weakling! I am no sissy! I am no coward. I am no homosexual! I am a tough man who fears nothing." The Nazi storm troopers, many of them mere boys, were systematically trained to stifle all tender emotions and force themselves to be heartlessly brutal.

Man perennially seeks to recover the magic of his childhood days—the control of the mighty by the meek. The flick of an electric light switch, the response of an automobile throttle, the click of a camera, the touch of a match to a skyrocket—these are keys to a sudden and magical display of great power induced by the merest gesture. Is anyone already so blasé that he is no longer thrilled at the opening of a door specially for him by a magic-eye signal? Yet for a few pennies one can purchase a far more deadly piece of magic—a stored explosive and missile encased within a shell which can be ejected from a machine at the touch of a finger so swiftly that no eye can follow. A thousand yards away something falls dead—a rabbit, a deer, a beautiful mountain sheep, a sleeping child, or the President of the United States. Magic! Magnified, projected power. "Look what I can do. I am the greatest!"

It must have come to every thoughtful person, at one time or another, in looking at the revolvers on the policemen's hips, or the guns soldiers and hunters carry so proudly, that these are instruments made for the express purpose of delivering death to someone. The easy availability of these engines of destruction, even to children, mentally disturbed people, professional criminals, gangsters, and even high school girls is something to give one pause. The National Rifle Association and its allies have been able to kill scores of bills that have been introduced into Congress and state legislatures for corrective gun control since the death of President Kennedy. Americans still spend about $2 billion on guns each year.

Fifty years ago, Winston Churchill declared that the mood and temper of the public in regard to crime and criminals is one of the unfailing tests of the civilization of any country. Judged by this standard, how civilized are we?

The chairman of the President's National Crime Commission, Nicholas de B. Katzenbach, declared recently that organized crime flourishes in America because enough of the public wants its services, and most citizens are apathetic about its impact. It will continue uncurbed as long as Americans accept it as inevitable and, in some instances, desirable.

Are there steps that we can take which will reduce the aggressive stabs and self-destructive lurches of our less well-managing fellow men? Are there ways to prevent and control the grosser violations, other than the clumsy traditional maneuvers which we have inherited? These depend basically upon intimidation and slow-motion torture. We call it punishment, and justify it with our "feeling." We know it doesn't work.

Yes, there *are* better ways. There are steps that could be taken; some *are* taken. But we move too slowly. Much better use, it seems to me, could be made of the members of my profession and other behavioral scientists than having them deliver courtroom pronunciamentos. The consistent use of a diagnostic clinic would enable trained workers to lay what they can learn about an offender before the judge who would know best how to implement the recommendation.

This would no doubt lead to a transformation of prisons, if not to their total disappearance in their present form and function. Temporary and permanent detention will perhaps always be necessary for a few, especially the professionals, but this could be more effectively and economically performed with new types of "facility" (that strange, awkward word for institution).

I assume it to be a matter of common and general agreement that our object in all this is to protect the community from a repetition of the offense by the most economical method consonant with our other purposes. Our "other purposes" include the desire to prevent these offenses from occurring, to reclaim offenders for social usefulness, if possible, and to detain them in protective custody, if reclamation is *not* possible. But how?

The treatment of human failure or dereliction by the infliction of pain is still used and believed in by many non-medical people. "Spare the rod and spoil the child" is still considered wise counsel by many.

Whipping is still used by many secondary schoolmasters in England, I am informed, to stimulate study, attention, and the love of learning. Whipping was long a traditional treatment for the "crime" of disobedience on the part of children, pupils, servants, apprentices, employees. And slaves were treated for centuries by flogging for such offenses as weariness, confusion, stupidity, exhaustion, fear, grief, and even overcheerfulness. It was assumed and stoutly defended that these "treatments" cured conditions for which they were administered.

Meanwhile, scientific medicine was acquiring many new healing methods and devices. Doctors can now transplant organs and limbs; they can remove brain tumors and cure incipient cancers; they can halt pneumonia, meningitis, and other infections; they can correct deformities and repair breaks and tears and scars. But these wonderful achievements are accomplished on *willing* subjects, people who voluntarily ask for help by even heroic measures. And the reader will be wondering, no doubt, whether doctors can do anything with or for people who *do not want* to be treated at all, in any way! Can doctors cure willful aberrant behavior. Are we to believe that crime is a *disease* that can be reached by scientific measures? Isn't it merely "natural meanness" that makes all of us do wrong things at times even when we "know better"? And are not self-control, moral stamina, and will power the things needed? Surely there is no medical treatment for the lack of those!

Let me answer this carefully, for much misunderstanding accumulates here. I would say that according to the prevalent understanding of the words, crime is *not* a disease. Neither is it an illness, although I think it *should* be! It *should* be treated, and it could be; but it mostly isn't.

These enigmatic statements are simply explained. Diseases are undesired states of being which have been described and defined by doctors, usually given Greek or Latin appellations, and treated by long-established physical and pharmacological formulae. Illness, on the other hand, is best defined as a state of impaired functioning of such a nature that the public expects the sufferer to repair to the physician for help. The illness may prove to be a disease; more often it is only vague and nameless misery, but something which doctors, not lawyers, teachers, or preachers, are supposed to be able and willing to help.

When the community begins to look upon the expression of aggressive violence as the symptom of an illness or as indicative of illness, it will be because it believes doctors can do something to correct such a condition. At present, some better-informed individuals do believe and expect this. However angry at or sorry for the offender, they want him "treated" in an effective way so that he will cease to be a danger to them. And they know that the traditional punishment, "treatment-punishment," will not effect this.

What *will*? What effective treatment is there for such violence? It will surely have to begin with motivating or stimulating or arousing in a cornered individual the wish and hope and intention to change his methods of dealing with the realities of life. Can this be done by education, medication, counseling, training? I would answer *yes*. It can be done successfully in a majority of cases, if undertaken in time.

The present penal system and the existing legal philosophy do not stimulate or even expect such a change to take place in the criminal. Yet change is what medical science always aims for. The prisoner, like the doctor's other patients, should emerge from his treatment experience a different person, differently equipped, differently functioning, and headed in a different direction than when he began the treatment.

It is natural for the public to doubt that this can be accomplished with criminals. But remember that the public *used* to doubt that change could be effected in the mentally ill. No one a hundred years ago believed mental illness to be curable. Today *all* people know (or should know) that *mental illness is curable* in the great majority of instances and that the prospects and rapidity of cure are directly related to the availability and intensity of proper treatment.

The forms and techniques of psychiatric treatment used today number in the hundreds. No one patient requires or receives all forms, but each patient is studied with respect to his particular needs, his basic assets, his interests, and his special difficulties. A therapeutic team may embrace a dozen workers—as in a hospital setting—or it may narrow down to the doctor and the spouse. Clergymen, teachers, relatives, friends, and even fellow patients often participate informally but helpfully in the process of readaptation.

All of the participants in this effort to bring about a favorable change in the patient—i.e., in his vital balance and life program—are imbued with what we may call a *therapeutic attitude.* This is one in direct antithesis to attitudes of avoidance, ridicule, scorn, or punitiveness. Hostile feelings toward the subject, however justified by his unpleasant and even destructive behavior, are not in the curriculum of therapy or in the therapist. This does not mean that therapists approve of the offensive and obnoxious behavior of the patient; they distinctly disapprove of it. But they recognize it as symptomatic of continued imbalance and disorganization, which is what they are seeking to change. They distinguish between disapproval, penalty, price, and punishment.

Doctors charge fees; they impose certain "penalties" or prices, but they have long since put aside primitive attitudes of retaliation toward offensive patients. A patient may cough in the doctor's face or may vomit on the office rug; a patient may curse or scream or even struggle in the extremity of his pain. But these acts are not "punished." Doctors and nurses have no time or thought for inflicting unnecessary pain even upon patients who may be difficult, disagreeable, provocative, and even dangerous. It is their duty to care for them, to try to make them well, and to prevent them from doing themselves or others harm. This requires love, not hate. This is the deepest meaning of the therapeutic attitude. Every doctors knows this; every worker in a hospital or clinic knows it (or should).

There is another element in the therapeutic attitude. It is the quality of hopefulness. If no one believes that the patient can get well, if no one—not even the doctor—has any hope, there probably won't be any recovery. Hope is just as important as love in the therapeutic attitude.

"But you were talking about the mentally ill," readers may interject, "those poor, confused, bereft, frightened individuals who yearn for help from you doctors and nurses. Do you mean to imply that willfully perverse individuals, our criminals, can be similarly reached and rehabilitated? Do you really believe that effective treatment of the sort you visualize can be applied to people *who do not want any help*, who are so willfully vicious, so well aware of the wrongs they are doing, so lacking in penitence or even common decency that punishment seems to be the only thing left?"

Do I believe there is effective treatment for offenders, and that they *can* be changed? *Most certainly and definitely I do.* Not all cases, to be sure; there are also some physical afflictions which we cannot cure at the moment. Some provision has to be made for incurables—pending new knowledge—and these will include some offenders. But I believe the majority of them would prove to be curable. The willfulness and the viciousness of offenders are part of the thing for which they have to be treated. These must not thwart the therapeutic attitude.

It is simply not true that most of them are "fully aware" of what they are doing, nor is it true that they want no help from anyone, although some of them say so. Prisoners are individuals: some want treatment, some do not. Some don't know what treatment is. Many are utterly despairing and hopeless. Where treatment is made available in institutions, many prisoners seek it even with the full knowledge that doing so will not lessen their sentences. In some prisons, seeking treatment by prisoners is frowned upon by the officials.

Various forms of treatment are even now being tried in some progressive courts and prisons over the country—educational, social, industrial, religious, recreational, and psychological treatments. Socially acceptable behavior, new work-play opportunities, new identity and companion patterns all help toward community reacceptance. Some parole officers and some wardens have been extremely ingenious in developing these modalities of rehabilitation and reconstruction—more than I could list here even if I knew them all. But some are trying. The secret of success in all programs, however, is the replacement of the punitive attitude with a therapeutic attitude.

Offenders with propensities for impulsive and predatory aggression should not be permitted to live among us unrestrained by some kind of social control. *But the great majority of offenders, even "criminals," should never become prisoners if we want to "cure" them.*

There are now throughout the country many citizens' action groups and programs for the prevention and control of crime and delinquency. With such attitudes of inquiry and concern, the public could acquire information (and incentive) leading to a change of feeling about crime and criminals. It will discover how unjust is much so-called "justice," how baffled and frustrated many judges are by the ossified rigidity of old-fashioned, obsolete laws and state constitutions which effectively prevent the introduction of sensible procedures to replace useless, harmful ones.

I want to proclaim to the public that things are not what it wishes them to be, and will only become so if it will take an interest in the matter and assume some responsibility for its own self-protection.

Will the public listen?

If the public does become interested, it will realize that we must have more facts, more trial projects, more checked results. It will share the dismay of the President's Commission in finding that no one knows much about even the incidence of crime with any definiteness or statistical accuracy.

The average citizen finds it difficult to see how any research would in any way change his mind about a man who brutally murders his children. But just such inconceivably awful acts most dramatically point up the need for research. Why should—how can—a man become so dreadful as that in our culture? How is such a man made? Is it comprehensible that he can be born to become so depraved?

There are thousands of questions regarding crime and public protection which deserve scientific study. What makes some individuals maintain their interior equilibrium by one kind of disturbance of the social structure rather than by another kind, one that would have landed him in a hospital? Why do some individuals specialize in certain types of crime? Why do so many young people reared in areas of delinquency and poverty and bad example never become habitual delinquents? (Perhaps this is a more important question than why some of them do.)

The public has a fascination for violence, and clings tenaciously to its yen for vengeance, blind and deaf to the expense, futility, and dangerousness of the resulting penal system. But we are bound to hope that this will yield in time to the persistent, penetrating light of intelligence and accumulating scientific knowledge. The public will grow increasingly ashamed of its cry for retaliation, its persistent demand to punish. This is its crime, *our* crime against criminals—and, incidentally, our crime against ourselves. For before we can diminish our sufferings from the ill-controlled aggressive assaults of fellow citizens, we must renounce the philosophy of punishment, the obsolete, vengeful penal attitude. In its place we would seek a comprehensive constructive social attitude—therapeutic in some instances, restraining in some instances, but preventive in its total social impact.

In the last analysis this becomes a question of personal morals and values. No matter how glorified or how piously disguised, vengeance as a human motive must be personally repudiated by each and every one of us. This is the message of old religions and new psychiatries. Unless this message is heard, unless we, the people—the man on the street, the housewife in the home—can give up our delicious satisfactions in opportunities for vengeful retaliation on scapegoats, we cannot expect to preserve our peace, our public safety, or our mental health.

Psychiatry Does Not Belong in the Courtroom

THOMAS S. SZASZ

THE FOLLOWING brief comments are intended to call attention to what I believe are inroads of serious import which organized psychiatry is making into the area of civil liberties. The significance of this encroachment transcends the specialized interests of psychiatry and jurisprudence, for it involves the most basic value of Anglo-American democracy, namely, the worth of the individual's autonomy and dignity. Cast in the context of current political and social events, it would seem that what the Western democracies can put against the claims of opposing ideologies is not a high standard of living; nor is it the abstract notions of free enterprise, capitalism, or even the Christian ethic. What democracies, and *only* democracies, possess, and what can not be imitated by other ideologies —without themselves becoming democracies—is respect for the dignity and autonomy of the individual. Stripped of proud adjectives, this simply means that people must be taken seriously for what they do; and this implies holding them accountable for their actions.

Having argued elsewhere that psychiatric testimony concerning mental illness (as presently conceived) is distracting to judicial proceedings, and that acquittal from a criminal charge by reason of insanity followed by commitment to a mental hospital constitutes a serious infringement of a person's civil liberties, I shall turn, without further comment, to a recent case to illustrate and add to the points made previously.

The case is that of Miss Edith L. Hough. The following are the salient facts, as abstracted from the records of her appeal to the U.S. Court of Appeals for the District of Columbia Circuit. On May 30, 1957, Miss Hough shot and killed a male friend who came to call on her to express his sympathy over the recent death of her father. The next day she was ordered to St. Elizabeths Hospital for determination of her competency to stand trial. She was subsequently found incompetent to stand trial and was committed to the hospital until restoration of her competency. In May, 1958, she was declared competent. She was tried for her offense—first degree murder—on July 10, 1958, and was acquitted by reason of insanity. She was then committed to St. Elizabeths Hospital.

On October 20, 1958, the Superintendent of St. Elizabeths Hospital filed in the District Court a certificate stating in part:

> Miss Hough has now recovered sufficiently to be granted her conditional release from Saint Elizabeths Hospital pursuant to section 927 (e) of Public Law 313.

The District Court denied conditional release, whereupon the "patient" appealed to a higher court seeking reversal of this decision. The U.S. Court of Appeals for the District of Columbia Circuit heard the case and, on September 14, 1959, affirmed the decision of the lower court. In hearing the appeal, psychiatric testimony was obtained from Doctors Benjamin Karpman and Winfred Overholser, and judicial opinions were rendered by Judges David Bazelon and Wilbur K. Miller. In the context of decision-making in an actual, real-life situation, the opinions and actions of the various participants become clearer than any statement, concerning psychiatry and law, that could be made in the abstract. My comments will be based on testimony and opinion recorded in the transcript of the decision rendered by the Appellate Court.

The first point on which I shall comment is the problem of acquitting a person of a crime and then committing him. Once he is acquitted, he must be considered (legally) innocent. If he is not so considered, the word "acquittal" and the deed it designates will lose their customary meanings.

Commitment of the insane—a complex, and in my opinion, highly questionable procedure as presently practiced—must now be scrutinized. Courts are legally empowered to commit people to mental hospitals, provided that certain conditions obtain. Illustrative is the case of a person who manifests such behavior as is considered patently deranged in our culture. A young man, for example, may become increasingly withdrawn and uncommunicative; he may stop eating and start masturbating in the presence of others. Sooner or later in the course of these events, the patient's family would very likely seek the aid of a physician (who may or may not be a psychiatrist). The latter would then make out the necessary papers *certifying* that the patient is in need of involuntary hospitalization. Finally, the judge under whose jurisdiction this matter falls would, in the ordinary course of events, order the patient *committed.*

Another type of situation in which people might be committed as mentally ill has traditionally been associated with the general area of criminal behavior. Without entering into the complexities of this matter, I wish to note only that according to the Durham Rule and its implementations, persons charged with offenses but acquitted by reason of insanity are committed to St. Elizabeths Hospital. If this practice were to be carried out *seriously* such persons would have to be treated as if they were *bona fide innocent.* This is required by the fact that they have been tried and have been pronounced "*not guilty* (by reason of insanity)." While the court has the right to order commitment, once a patient has been committed he comes under the jurisdiction of the hospital authorities. Hospital psychiatrists should be able to release the patient should they wish to do so. In cases of ordinary civil commitment, the court has no jurisdiction over the actions of the hospital staff vis-à-vis patients. To be more exact, the courts do have a say concerning hospital-patient relationships even in such cases, but this is essentially limited to giving the patient freedom. In other words, if the patient wishes to be released from the hospital over the opposition of the psychiatrists, he can, by availing himself of the appropriate legal safeguards, *e.g., habeas corpus*, enlist the aid of the court to gain his freedom. The reverse of this does not obtain! Should the hospital wish to release the patient, the court cannot interfere and keep the patient confined. It can not do this simply because commitment is legally justified—and this shows how poor this justification really is —by the psychiatric testimony of the physician involved. Hence, if they (*i.e.*, the state hospital physicians) testify that the patient is sane, how can the court commit?

In the present case, it is to be noted that the court had the power not only to commit but also to regulate the patient's movements in and out of the hospital. This was in accord with a statute of the District of Columbia (D.C. Code #24.301 (e) Supp. VII, 1959). This meant, in effect, that the hospital functioned as an arm of the court. It had no real autonomy, but was merely a subordinate body to the superordinate power of the courts. If a hospital superintendent and his staff can not discharge a patient from their "hospital" when they wish, then, I submit, they are but the functionaries of those who do have the power to make this decision.

All this points to the fact that hospitals functioning in such a fashion are, in fact, jails. But we can go further than this, for jails have a high degree of regulatory autonomy over their inmates. Parole boards, for example, can decide—within certain legally set limits—when prisoners may be released. The courts, once having passed sentence, can not interfere in this process. The regulations governing the release of mental patients from St. Elizabeths Hospital thus give the staff of this institution less jurisdiction over (some of) its "patients" than have jails over their prisoners.

We must infer from this that the courts, after having relinquished their responsibility to the psychiatrists for judging and sentencing criminals, have turned around and have arrogated to themselves the responsibilities of physicians and psychiatrists. This conclusion must be drawn from the fact that the courts take it upon themselves to decide when a person is officially designated a "patient," and one who has been acquitted of a criminal charge in a duly conducted trial, and is therefore "innocent"—may or may not be released from a place called "hospital." As matters now stand, psychiatric testimony in criminal trials—to the effect that the accused is mentally ill—makes it virtually unnecessary to have juries and judges, for acquittal follows almost automatically. Similarly, judicial authority of the type considered makes it virtually unnecessary, for patients of *this type* at least, to have psychiatrists and psychotherapists in mental hospitals—for it is the court, in the last analysis, that will decide when the "patient" is well enough to be released. The tragi-comedy that has been called "psychiatric testimony" has traversed a full circle: The psychiatrists who displaced the legal authorities (the latter having abdicated their responsibilities for decision-making of this type) have, in their turn, been displaced by the legal authorities, who now function in the guise of psychiatrists and social therapists.

All this leads finally and inevitably to the psychiatrist's surrender of his professional responsibility. For, if a psychiatrist in charge of a patient—who is *not* a convicted criminal!—regards him, in his own best judgment, as ready to leave a hospital and assume the duties of a job, how can he, in his professional conscience, let a court tell him that this he can not do? What is the psychiatrist "treating" the patient for, anyway? To make him a good "prisoner"? The farcical, were it not tragic, character of the notion of mental illness is well illustrated by these impossible dilemmas into which psychiatrists and lawyers place themselves, each other, their patients, and their clients.

The peculiar legal condition of a person such as Miss Hough has not escaped the participants in this difficult affair. Judge Bazelon expressly affirmed that such a person is a "patient," not a "prisoner." The facts of the matter, however, vitiate the practical meaning of these terms. Judge Bazelon's words illustrate the crux of the problem:

> Nothing in the history of the statute—and nothing in its language—indicates that an individual committed to a mental hospital after acquittal of a crime by reason of insanity is other than a patient. The individual is confined in the hospital for the purpose of treatment, not punishment; and the length of confinement is governed solely by considerations of his condition *and* the public safety. Any preoccupation by the District Court with the need of punishment for crime is out of place in dealing with an individual who has been acquitted of the crime charged.
>
> It does not follow, however, that the hospital authorities are free to allow such a patient to leave the hospital without supervision. We readily grant that periodic freedom may be valuable therapy. So, we suppose, may outright release sometimes be. But the statute makes one in appellant's situation a member of "an exceptional class of people." It provides generally, that the District Court have a voice in any termination of her confinement, whether unconditional or conditional.

There is an attempt here to circumvent the problem by creating the somewhat mystical entity of "an exceptional class of people." What is meant by this? Are these people who are "legally innocent but really guilty"? Or are these people who, by virtue of their actions, shall henceforth and forever after be considered second-class citizens? Does this mean that we shall have two sets of laws, one for ordinary citizens and ordinary criminals, and another for the "mentally ill"? If these questions are answered in the affirmative—as they seem to be in this case—then surely we ought to ask: Is this in accord with the spirit and the letter of our Constitution, our Bill of Rights, and with the ethics of democracy?

Before bringing this discussion to an end, I wish to comment briefly on two other items found in this record. One is an opinion by Judge Wilbur K. Miller, stating:

> It is, of course, much easier to believe that a sane person will not in the reasonable future be dangerous to himself or others than to believe that an insane person will not be.

Here is an ancient view, equating violence and insanity, dressed in slightly more modern garb. What is being asserted here, if anything? Both "insanity" and "dangerousness" are such vague terms that it is impossible to know what is being asserted by such a statement. But not only is this statement vague, worse, it is tautologous, for we habitually infer a condition of "insanity" from acts of violence. This was precisely the case in the present instance, for Miss Hough was considered legally sane until after she committed a murder. But if we infer insanity from violence, naturally we shall always expect violence when we speak of insanity, even though, in everyday life, the latter term is often used quite independently of whether or not a person is considered "dangerous."

In this connection, we must also note that the common-sense formulation of "insanity" propounded by Judge Miller seems to serve the function of enabling the observer—and this means all of us, and especially juries and judges—to wrestle with the problem of a person's so-called possible future dangerousness. At the very least, by codifying acts of violence as expressions of "mental illness" and some sort of irrationality (which, according to *certain* criteria, they might well be), we neatly rid ourselves of the task of dealing with criminal offenses as rational, goal-directed acts in principle no different from other forms of conduct.

Finally, I wish to call attention to a portion of Doctor Overholser's testimony. Being challenged by the attorney for the appellee to show reason why the patient should be released from the hospital, he was asked this question:

> Now, if this woman, who has this major mental disease, were released conditionally into the community and met a great number of frustrations in adjusting herself in getting along, isn't there a probability or possibility that she might explode, so to speak, and even do harm to herself or to others?

His answer was:

> Well, there is that possibility with a great many people, some of whom have

never been in mental hospitals. I can't make any guarantee about permanence, or even about the conduct.

Here, it seems to me, Doctor Overholser spoke as a psychiatric scientist. As such, he could not predict with certainty, and surely could not guarantee, that this woman would not kill again. But if this is true, how can psychiatrists justify hospitalizing and "psychiatrically treating" someone whose "illness" appears to be mainly that she killed someone. Is being a murderer an illness? And if psychiatric treatment still leaves open the possibility of future crime, as obviously it must, then why use it as a *substitute* for legally codified imprisonment?

Does all this not mean that a logically simpler, and legally and psychiatrically clearer approach to a problem such as this might lie in treating persons in Miss Hough's predicament with the same dignity and firmness as we treat others confronted by serious problems? Why could she not be found guilty of a crime she obviously committed? Why could she not be imprisoned for a given term and, if necessary, given psychiatric help in jail? Is it not a truism that in a democracy, imprisonment (or loss of liberty) is justified only by conviction for a crime? But Miss Hough, and others in similar positions, were never convicted of a crime, but are, nevertheless, deprived of their liberty. This is clearly done as a *preventive measure!* Herein lies, I think, the worst and most dangerous feature of this procedure: it establishes legal precedent, and hence a measure of sanction, for prophylactic imprisonment! Let us not forget that this social act has, and with good reason, been regarded as the hallmark of the totalitarian state. The legal restraint of a person justified by *what he might do* (in the future) is there used with the explicit aim of social reform. Although not explicitly formulated, and perhaps only as an unwitting and undesired side-effect, this tactic of preventive restraint seems to be implicit in the operations of the Durham Rule and its subsequent modifications and applications.

The merits and risks of preventive imprisonment—even if some choose to call it "hospitalization"—are well worth the attention of every informed and intelligent person. This was my reason for stating at the outset that many problems of psychiatry and law transcend the boundaries of these disciplines and rightly concern all the people of the land. Let us at least entertain the possibility that by engaging in certain modifications of social living—for this is what we are doing—we run the risk of squandering the greatest asset of our Nation and its distinctive form of government, namely, the autonomy, integrity, responsibility, and freedom of the individual.

A recent decision rendered by the United States Court of Appeals for the District of Columbia Circuit was examined for the light it threw on some problems concerning crimes, psychiatry, and civil liberties. It was shown that acquittal by reason of insanity, followed by automatic commitment, seems to lead by easy steps to preventive jailing (hospitalization) of persons because of their alleged future dangerousness.

Increased psychiatric participation in the disposition of criminals seems to invite its corollary, namely, increased legal participation in psychiatric operations. We might raise the question: Do the questionable benefits of the Durham Rule (and its implementation) justify the risks of this "social therapy"? Could it be, perchance, that the cure, in this case, is worse than the disease? In other words, are the political and ethical risks of preventive jailing (preventive mental hospitalization) worth running, even if the psychiatric value of this measure were firmly established? (The psychiatric-scientific rationale of this procedure is hardly clear-cut or well established.) Personally, I hold that the value of formal psychiatric therapy for "criminals"—under present medico-legal conditions—is, at best, highly questionable. But beyond this, I believe that even if this psychiatric-legal procedure could be shown to be highly efficacious in restoring offenders of a certain type to useful social existence (which is the most that even its proponents claim for it), I would doubt that, *in a hierarchy of values*, such therapy of a small group could be justified *if* its results could be achieved *only* at the cost of a significant reduction in the autonomy and dignity of the majority of the people. In any case, the problem of crime and "mental illness" should be cast in a much broader context, and should be scrutinized by many more people, than it is at present.

Retributivism and Utilitarianism Are Not in Conflict

A. M. QUINTON

1. Introductory

THERE is a prevailing antinomy about the philosophical justification of punishment. The two great theories—retributive and utilitarian—seem, and at least are understood by their defenders, to stand in open and flagrant contradiction. Both sides have arguments at their disposal to demonstrate the atrocious consequences of the rival theory. Retributivists, who seem to hold that there are circumstances in which the infliction of suffering is a good thing in itself, are charged by their opponents with vindictive barbarousness. Utilitarians, who seem to hold that punishment is always and only justified by the good consequences it produces, are accused of vicious opportunism. Where the former insists on suffering for suffering's sake, the latter permits the punishment of the innocent. Yet, if the hope of justifying punishment is not to be abandoned altogether, one of these apparently unsavoury alternatives must be embraced. For they exhaust the possibilities. Either punishment must be self-justifying, as the retributivists claim, or it must depend for its justification on something other than itself, the general formula of "utilitarianism" in the wide sense appropriate here.

In this paper I shall argue that the antinomy can be resolved, since retributivism, properly understood, is not a moral but a logical doctrine, and that it does not provide a moral justification of the infliction of punishment but an elucida-

Reprinted with permission of Basil Blackwell & Mott Ltd. from "On Punishment" by A. M. Quinton in *Analysis*, XIV (1954), 133–142.

tion of the use of the word. Utilitarianism, on the other hand, embraces a number of possible moral attitudes towards punishment, none of which necessarily involves the objectionable consequences commonly adduced by retributivists, provided that the word "punishment" is understood in the way that the essential retributivist thesis lays down. The antimony arises from a confusion of modalities, of logical and moral necessity and possibility, of "must" and "can" with "ought" and "may." In brief, the two theories answer different questions: retributivism the question "when (logically) *can* we punish?", utilitarianism the question "when (morally) *may* we or *ought* we to punish?". I shall also describe circumstances in which there is an answer to the question "when (logically) *must* we punish?" Finally, I shall attempt to account for this difference in terms of a distinction between the establishment of rules whose infringement involves punishment from the application of these rules to particular cases.

2. The Retributive Theory

The essential contention of retributivism is that punishment is only justified by guilt. There is a certain compellingness about the repudiation of utilitarianism that this involves. We feel that whatever other considerations may be taken into account, the primary and indispensable matter is to establish the guilt of the person to be punished. I shall try to show that the peculiar outrageousness of the rejection of this principle is a consequence, not of the brutality that such rejection might seem to permit, but of the fact that it involves a kind of lying. At any rate the first principle of retributivism is that it is necessary that a man be guilty if he is to be punished.

But this doctrine is normally held in conjunction with some or all of three others which are logically, if not altogether psychologically, independent of it. These are that the function of punishment is the negation or annulment of evil or wrong-doing, that punishment must fit the crime (the *lex talionis*) and that offenders have a right to punishment, as moral agents they ought to be treated as ends not means.

The doctrine of "annulment," however carefully wrapped up in obscure phraseology, is clearly utilitarian in principle. For it holds that the function of punishment is to bring about a state of affairs in which it is as if the wrongful act had never happened. This is to justify punishment by its effects, by the desirable future consequences which it brings about. It certainly goes beyond the demand that only the guilty be punished. For, unlike this demand, it seeks to prescribe exactly what the punishment should be. Holding that whenever wrong has been done it must be annulled, it makes guilt—the state of one who has done wrong—the sufficient as well as the necessary condition of punishment. While the original thesis is essentially negative, ruling out the punishment of the innocent, the annulment doctrine is positive, insisting on the punishment and determining the degree of punishment of the guilty. But the doctrine is only applicable to a restricted class of cases, the order of nature is inhospitable to attempts to put the clock back. Theft and fraud can be compensated, but not murder, wounding, alienation of affection or the destruction of property or reputation.

Realising that things cannot always be made what they were, retributivists have extended the notion of annulment to cover the infliction on the offender of an injury equal to that which he has caused. This is sometimes argued for by reference to Moore's theory of organic wholes, the view that sometimes two blacks make a white. That this, the *lex talionis*, revered by Kant, does not follow from the original thesis is proved by the fact that we can always refrain from punishing the innocent but that we cannot always find a punishment to fit the crime. Some indeed would argue that we can never fit punishment to wrong-doing, for how are either, especially wrong-doing, to be measured? (Though, as Ross has pointed out, we can make ordinal judgments of more or less about both punishment and wrong-doing.)

Both of these views depend on a mysterious extension of the original thesis to mean that punishment and wrong-doing must necessarily be somehow equal and opposite. But this is to go even further than to regard guilt and punishment as necessitating one another. For this maintains that only the guilty are to be punished and that the guilty are always to be punished. The equal and opposite view maintains further that they are to be punished to just the extent that they have done wrong.

Finally retributivism has been associated with the view that if we are to treat offenders as moral agents, as ends and not as means, we must recognize their right to punishment. It is an odd sort of right whose holders would strenuously resist its recognition. Strictly interpreted, this view would entail that the sole relevant consideration in determining whether and how a man should be punished is his own moral regeneration. This is utilitarian and it is also immoral, since it neglects the rights of an offender's victims to compensation and of society in general to protection. A less extreme interpretation would be that we should never treat offenders merely as means in inflicting punishment but should take into account their right to treatment as moral agents. This is reasonable enough, most people would prefer a penal system which did not ignore the reformation of offenders. But it is not the most obvious correlate of the possible view that if a man is guilty he ought to be punished. We should more naturally allot the correlative right to have him punished to his victims or society in general and not to him himself.

3. The Retributivist Thesis

So far I have attempted to extricate the essentials of retributivism by excluding some traditional but logically irrelevant associates. A more direct approach consists in seeing what is the essential principle which retributivists hold utilitarians to deny. Their crucial charge is that utilitarians permit the punishment of the innocent. So their fundamental thesis must be that only the guilty are to be punished, that guilt is a necessary condition of punishment. This hardly lies open to the utilitarian counter-charge of pointless and vindicative barbarity, which could only find a foothold in the doctrine of annulment and in the *lex talionis.* (For that matter, it is by no means obvious that the charge can be sustained even against them, except in so far as the problems of estimating the measure of guilt lead to the adoption of a purely formal and external criterion which would not distinguish between the doing of deliberate and accidental injuries.)

Essentially, then, retributivism is the view that only the guilty are to be punished. Excluding the punishment of the innocent, it permits the other three possibilities: the punishment of the guilty, the non-punishment of the guilty and the non-punishment of the innocent. To add that guilt is also the sufficient condition of punishment, and thus to exclude the non-punishment of the guilty, is another matter altogether. It is not entailed by the retributivist attack on utilitarianism and has none of the immediate compulsiveness of the doctrine that guilt is the necessary condition of punishment.

There is a very good reason for this difference in force. For the necessity of not punishing the innocent is not moral but logical. It is not, as some retributivists think, that we *may* not punish the innocent and *ought* only to punish the guilty, but that we *cannot* punish the innocent and *must* only punish the guilty. Of course, the suffering or harm in which punishment consists can be and is inflicted on innocent people but this is not punishment, it is judicial error or terrorism or, in Bradley's characteristically repellent phrase, "social surgery." The infliction of suffering on a person is only properly described as punishment if that person is guilty. The retributivist thesis, therefore, is not a moral doctrine, but an account of the meaning of the word "punishment." Typhoid carriers and criminal lunatics are treated physically in much the same way as ordinary criminals, they are shut up in institutions. The essential difference is that no blame is implied by their imprisonment, for there is no guilt to which the blame can attach. "Punishment" resembles the word "murder," it is infliction of suffering on the guilty and not simply infliction of suffering, just as murder is wrongful killing and not simply killing. Typhoid carriers are no more (usually) criminals than surgeons are (usually) murderers. This accounts for the flavour of moral outrage attending the notion of punishment of the innocent. In a sense a contradiction in terms, it applies to the common enough practice of inflicting the suffering involved in punishment on innocent people and of sentencing them to punishment with a lying imputation of their responsibility and guilt. Punishment *cannot* be inflicted on the innocent, the suffering associated with punishment *may* not be inflicted on them, firstly, as brutal and secondly, if it is represented as punishment, as involving a lie.

This can be shown by the fact that punishment is always *for* something. If a man says to another "I am going to punish you" and is asked "what for," he cannot reply "nothing at all" or "something you have not done." At best, he is using "punish" here as a more or less elegant synonym for "cause to suffer." Either that or he does not understand the meaning of "punish." "I am going to punish you for something you have not done" is as absurd a statement as "I blame you for this event for which you were not responsible." "Punishment implies guilt" is the same sort of assertion as "ought implies can." It is not *pointless* to punish or blame the innocent, as some have argued, for it is often very useful. Rather the very conditions of punishment and blame do not obtain in these circumstances.

4. An Objection

But how can it be useful to do what is impossible? The innocent can be punished and scapegoats are not logical impossibilities. We do say "they punished him for something he did not do." For A to be said to have punished B it is surely enough that A thought or said he was punishing B and ensured that suffering was inflicted on B. However innocent B may be of the offence adduced by A, there is no question that, in these circumstances, he has been punished by A. So guilt cannot be more than a *moral* precondition of punishment.

The answer to this objection is that "punish" is a member of that now familiar class of verbs whose first-person-present use is significantly different from the rest. The absurdity of "I am punishing you for something you have not done" is analogous to that of "I promise to do something which is not in my power." Unless you are guilty I am no more in a position to punish you than I am in a position to promise what is not in my power. So it is improper to say "I am going to punish you" unless you are guilty, just as it is improper to say "I promise to do this" unless it is in my power to do it. But it is only *morally* improper if I do not *think* that you are guilty or that I can do the promised act. Yet, just as it is perfectly proper to say of another "he promised to do this," whether he thought he could do it or not, provided that he *said* "I promise to do this," so it is perfectly proper to say "they punished him," whether they thought him guilty or not, provided that they *said* "we are going to punish you" and inflicted suffering on him. By the first-person-present use of these verbs we *prescribe* punishment and *make* promises, these activities involve the satisfaction of conditions over and above what is required for *reports* or *descriptions* of what their prescribers or makers represent as punishments and promises.

Understandably "reward" and "forgive" closely resemble "punish." Guilt is a precondition of forgiveness, desert—its contrary—of reward. One cannot properly say "I am going to reward you" or "I forgive you" to a man who has done nothing. Reward and forgiveness are always *for* something. But, again, one can say "they rewarded (or forgave) him for something he had not done." There is an interesting difference here between "forgive" and "punish" or "reward." In this last kind of assertion "forgive" seems more peculiar, more inviting to inverted commas, than the other two. The three undertakings denoted by these verbs can be divided into the utterance of a more or less ritual formula and the consequences authorized by this utterance. With punishment and reward the consequences are more noticeable than the formula, so they come to be sufficient occasion for the use of the word even if the formula is inapplicable and so improperly used. But, since the consequences of forgiveness are negative, the absence of punishment, no such shift occurs. To reward involves giving a reward, to punish inflicting a punishment, but to forgive involves no palpable consequence, e.g. handing over a written certificate of pardon.

Within these limitations, then, guilt is a *logically* necessary condition of punishment and, with some exceptions, it might be held, a morally necessary condition of the infliction of suffering. Is it in either way a sufficient condition? As will be shown in the last section there are circumstances, though they do not obtain in our legal system, nor generally in extra-legal penal systems (e.g. parental), in which guilt is a logically sufficient condition of at least a sentence of punishment. The parallel moral doctrine would be that if anyone is guilty of wrong-doing he ought morally to be punished. This rather futile rigourism is not embodied in our legal system with its relaxations of penalties for first offenders. Since it entails that offenders should never be forgiven it is hardly likely to commend itself in the extra-legal sphere.

5. The Utilitarian Theory

Utilitarianism holds that punishment must always be justified by the value of its consequences. I shall refer to this as "utility" for convenience without any implication that utility must consist in pleasure. The view that punishment is justified by the value of its consequences is compatible with any ethical theory which allows meaning to be attached to moral judgments. It holds merely that the infliction of suffering is of no value or of negative value and that it must therefore be justified by further considerations. These will be such things as prevention of and deterrence from wrong-doing, compensation of victims, reformation of offenders and satisfaction of vindictive impulses. It is indifferent for our purposes whether these are valued as intuitively good, as productive of general happiness, as conducive to the survival of the human race or are just normatively laid down as valuable or derived from such a norm.

Clearly there is no *logical* relation between punishment and its actual or expected utility. Punishment *can* be inflicted when it is neither expected, nor turns out, to be of value and, on the other hand, it can be foregone when it is either expected, or would turn out, to be of value.

But that utility is the morally necessary or sufficient condition, or both, of punishment are perfectly reputable moral attitudes. The first would hold that no one should be punished unless the punishment would have valuable consequences, the second that if valuable consequences would result punishment ought to be inflicted (without excluding the moral permissibility of utility-less punishment). Most people would no doubt accept the first, apart from the rigourists who regard guilt as a morally sufficient condition of punishment. Few would maintain the second except in conjunction with the first. The first says when you may not but not when you ought to punish, the second when you ought to but not when you may not.

Neither permits or encourages the punishment of the innocent, for this is only logically possible if the word "punishment" is used in an unnatural way, for example as meaning any kind of deliberate infliction of suffering. But in that case they cease to be moral doctrines about punishment as we understand the word and become moral doctrines (respectively platitudinous and inhuman) about something else.

So the retributivist case against the utilitarians falls to the ground as soon as what is true and essential in retributivism is extracted from the rest. This may be unwelcome to retributivists since it leaves the moral field in the possession of the utilitarians. But there is a compensation in the fact that what is essential in retributivism can at least be definitely established.

6. Rules and Cases

So far what has been established is that guilt and the value or utility of consequences are relevant to punishment in different ways. A further understanding of this difference can be gained by making use of a distinction made by Sir David Ross in the appendix on punishment in *The Right and the Good.* This will also help to elucidate the notion of guilt which has hitherto been applied uncritically.

The distinction is between laying down a rule which attaches punishment to actions of a certain kind and the application of that rule to particular cases. It might be maintained that the utilitarian theory was an answer to the question "what kinds of action should be punished?" and the retributive theory an answer to the question "on what particular occasions should we punish?" On this view both punishment and guilt are defined by reference to these rules. Punishment is the infliction of suffering attached by these rules to certain kinds of action, guilt the condition of a person to whom such a rule applies. This accounts for the logically necessary relation holding between guilt and punishment. Only the guilty can be punished because unless a person is guilty, unless a rule applies to him, no infliction of suffering on him is properly called punishment, since punishment is infliction of suffering as laid down by such a rule. Considerations of utility, then, are alone relevant to the determination of what in general, what *kinds* of action, to punish. The outcome of this is a set of rules. Given these rules, the question of whom in particular to punish has a definite and necessary answer. Not only will guilt be the logically necessary but also the logically sufficient condition of punishment or, more exactly, of a sentence of punishment. For declaration of guilt will be a declaration that a rule applies and, if the rule applies, what the rule enjoins—a sentence of punishment—applies also.

The distinction between setting up and applying penal rules helps to explain the different parts played by utility and guilt in the justification of punishment, in particular the fact that where utility is a moral, guilt is a logical, justification. Guilt is irrelevant to the setting up of rules, for until they have been set up the notion of guilt is undefined and without application. Utility is irrelevant to the application of rules, for once the rules have been set up punishment is determined by guilt, once they are seen to apply the rule makes a sentence of punishment necessarily follow.

But this account is not an accurate description of the very complex penal systems actually employed by states, institutions and parents. It is, rather, a schema, a possible limiting case. For it ignores an almost universal feature of penal systems (and of games, for that matter, where penalties attend infractions of the rules)—discretion. For few offences against the law is one and only one fixed and definite punishment laid down. Normally only an upper limit is set. If guilt, the applicability of the rule, is established no fixed punishment is entailed but rather, for example, one not exceeding a fine of forty shillings or fourteen days' imprisonment. This is even more evident in the administration of such institutions as clubs or libraries and yet more again in the matter of parental discipline. The establishment of guilt does not close the matter, at best it entails some punishment or other. Precisely how much is appropriate must be determined by reference to considerations of utility. The variety of things is too great for any manageably concise penal code to dispense altogether with discretionary judgment in particular cases.

But this fact only shows that guilt is not a logically *sufficient* condition of punishment, it does not affect the thesis that punishment entails guilt. A man cannot be guilty unless his action falls under a penal rule and he can only be properly said to be punished if the rule in question prescribes or permits some punishment or other. So all applications of the notion of guilt necessarily contain or include all applications of the notion of punishment.

The Concept of Punishment and Its Social Context

KURT BAIER

IT WOULD seem that punishment must of its nature be retributive, and also that it cannot be. It must be, for the infliction of hardship on someone is not punishment, unless it is as retribution for something he has done. It cannot be, for it makes sense to say that someone was punished for something he did not do. This seemingly simple, but actually quite intricate problem, was recently discussed by Professor A. G. N. Flew in an article entitled "The Justification of Punishment.' and by Mr. A. M. Quinton in a paper entitled 'On Punishment.' Both appear to me to misrepresent the nature of punishment. I shall begin by stating briefly what I hold to be the correct solution, and then point out where exactly they went wrong.

1. To say that someone has punished someone else is to say that someone entitled to administer the penalty for a certain offense has administered this penalty to the person who has been found guilty of this offense by someone with the authority to do so. The question whether or not someone has punished someone else could not even arise unless he belonged to a group which had the practice of punishing people. We could not say of a group that it had the practice of punishing people unless all the following conditions were satisfied. There

---

Reprinted with permission of Basil Blackwell & Mott, Ltd. from "Is Punishment Retributive" by Kurt Baier in *Analysis*, XVI (1955), 25–27.

must be someone, such as a father or legislator, whose job it is to prescribe or prohibit the doing of certain things or types of thing by certain people, in the form of commands or regulations, someone whose task it is to decree how a person disobeying these commands or regulations shall be treated, someone, such as a father or policeman, entrusted with the task of detecting cases of disobedience, someone, such as a father or judge, charged with meeting out the penalty for such disobedience, and someone, such as a father or executioner, charged with administering it. Of course, all these different tasks may be entrusted to one and the same person, as in the case of punishment by a father or teacher.

It should be noticed that 'punishing' is the name of only a part-activity belonging to a complex procedure involving several stages. Giving orders or laying down laws, affixing penalties to them, ascertaining whether anyone has disobeyed the commands or laws, sentencing persons found guilty, are not themselves punishing or part of the activity of punishing. Yet these activities must be performed and must precede the infliction of hardship if we are to speak of punishment at all. Of course, these activities may take only rudimentary forms. A father does not legislate, but give orders; he does not necessarily affix penalties to breaches of these orders before the breaches occur, but determines the penalty after a breach or disobedience has occurred; he often does not take much trouble in finding out whether his child really is guilty, nor does he formally "find him guilty" or pronounce sentence. All this is merely tacitly implied, but it is quite definitely implied. It would be just as odd for a father to send his son to bed without supper for being late, if he had found the son not guilty of this—either because the son was not told to be home by a certain time or because he was home by the time mentioned—as it would be for a judge to pronounce sentence on the accused when he has just been acquitted by the jury.

It follows from the nature of this whole "game," consisting of rule-making, penalisation, finding guilty of a breach of a rule, pronouncing sentence, and finally administering punishment, that the last act cannot be performed unless things have gone according to the rules until then. It is one of the constitutive rules of this whole "game" that the activity called punishing, or administering punishment, cannot be performed if, at a previous stage of the "game," the person in question has been found 'not guilty.' The "game" has to proceed differently after the verdict 'not guilty,' from the way it must proceed after the verdict 'guilty.' It is only if the verdict is 'guilty' that there is any question of a sentence and its being carried out. And if, after the jury has found the accused 'not guilty,' the judge continues as if the jury had found him guilty, then his 'I sentence you to three years' hard labour' is not the pronouncement of the sentence, but mere words. If, for some reason, the administration acts on these words, then what they do to the accused is not the infliction of punishment, but something for which (since it never happens) we do not even have a word.

A method of inflicting hardship on someone cannot be called 'punishment' unless at least the following condition is satisfied. It must be the case that when someone is found "not guilty" it is not permissible to go on to pronounce sentence on him and carry it out. For 'punishment' is the name of a method, or system, inflicting hardship, *the aim of which* is to hurt all and only those who are guilty of an offence. For this reason, a system of punishment requires a more or less elaborate apparatus for detecting those who are guilty and for allotting to them the hardship prescribed by the system. To say that it is of the very nature of punishment to be retributive, is to say that a system of inflicting hardship on someone could not be properly called 'punishment,' unless it is the aim of this system to hurt all and only those guilty of an offence. Hence inflicting hardship on a person who has been found 'not guilty' (logically) cannot be punishing. This is a conceptual point about punishment.

The correct answer to our problem is that punishment is indeed of its very nature retributive, since the very aim of inflicting hardship *as punishment* would be destroyed, if it were inflicted on someone who had been found 'not guilty.' But at the same time, someone may be punished, i.e. have hardship inflicted on him *as punishment*, although he was guilty of no offence, since he may have been *found* guilty without *being* guilty. For all judges and jurymen are fallible and some are corrupt.

INTRODUCTION TO SOCIAL AND POLITICAL PHILOSOPHY / Study Questions

PUNISHMENT

Kant

1. What distinction does Kant draw between *judicial* and *natural* punishment?
2. What does Kant say is the only basis for the imposition of punishment?
3. How does he argue that the imposition (or withholding) of punishment should never be used for the promotion of some further purpose?
4. Explain Kant's "principle of equality" and give examples of how he suggests it can be put into practice.
5. Can the kind of claims that Kant makes about punishment be found stated explicitly in the U.S. Constitution? If so, where?

Menninger

1. Why does Menninger say that we need crime? Do you think he is right?
2. What special problem does he think violence creates in the modern world?
3. Explain Menninger's account of the causes of crime.
4. What, according to Menninger, is the purpose of the prison reform, and so on, of which he is in favor? Compare this position with that of Kant.
5. Explain the author's position of regarding crime as an illness.
6. How could one go about determining whether the contention "Crime is an illness" is true or false?
7. If we follow Menninger in considering crime an illness, can we distinguish between crimes that are manifestations of that illness and crimes that are the result of rational and deliberate choice?

Szasz

1. What danger does Szasz see in the intrusion of psychiatry into jurisprudence? How does the Hough case illustrate this?
2. Szasz says that once acquitted, a person must be considered legally innocent else the word *acquittal* loses its meaning. Why is this so and what does it show us about the nature of these questions concerning crime and punishment?
3. Explain what Szasz means when he says that judges and psychiatrists have changed roles.
4. Szasz says that the value of psychiatric therapy is questionable. Suppose it proved, on the contrary, very effective. Would this alter his position? If not, why not?
5. Write an imaginary dialogue between Szasz and Menninger on the question of what should be done with criminals.

Quinton

1. What is Quinton's purpose in this essay?
2. What is the thesis of retributivism? What theses with which it is sometimes conjoined are, in fact, irrelevant?
3. Why does Quinton say that one cannot punish an innocent person?
4. Explain the utilitarian theory of punishment. How does Quinton argue that the retributivist criticism of utilitarianism is unjustified?
5. How does Quinton think his account of rules illuminates the philosophical dispute about punishment?

Baier

1. What background conditions does Baier say must exist in order to be able to say that someone has punished someone else?
2. Explain the analogy that Baier sees between this background in which the concept of *punishment* functions and a game.
3. In what respects do Baier and Quinton agree?
4. Do you believe that Baier has resolved any difficulties about punishment?

Paternalism

It is generally agreed that a government not only has the right, but also is obliged, to protect its citizens against the harmful acts of fellow citizens. There is, however, a closely related issue about which there is no such general agreement: Does a government have rights and obligations with respect to the harm that a person may do to himself? In other words, ought a government intervene to protect someone from himself? If one answers this question affirmatively one is holding the view now commonly called paternalism. If one's answer is negative that view is called libertarianism or, sometimes, individualism. It is interesting to note that in the last century there has been virtually a complete role-switch by political "liberals" and "conservatives" on this issue. In the nineteenth century, political conservatives argued for paternalism while their liberal adversaries argued for a fairly extreme version of libertarianism. Anyone familiar with current American politics will quickly see that those whom we label "liberals" are responsible for such paternalistic social legislation as Social Security, governmental antismoking campaigns, seat-belt requirements, and so on. Those whom we label "conservatives" have fought such measures, usually unsuccessfully, often on what the student shall come to recognize as essentially libertarian grounds.

It is also worth noting that many of us have an almost instinctive general distrust of paternalism, even though we may readily agree with specific paternalistic practices of government in some areas. We may not be altogether certain about why we have that distrust; nor do many of us clearly understand what would prove our distrust is correct. Suffice it to say, however, that many of us believe that it is the burden of governments to give special justification for proposed paternalistic practices; whereas we do not feel that governmental restraint from paternalism needs any special justification. This raises the question, "Can a general case against paternalism actually be made?" That is, is there some general reason why paternalism is always wrong or is at least a *prima facie* wrong? (To say of some practice that it is a "*prima facie* wrong" is to say that it should always be regarded with suspicion, to be guarded against, and that it ought never to be allowed unless some special justification can be given for it in a particular case. To say of a practice that it is "always wrong" is, of course, to deny that any justification could *ever* be given for it.)

We do not believe that one can make a general case against paternalism, neither as always wrong nor even as a *prima facie* wrong. Instead, we suggest that the rights and wrongs of paternalism can only be settled in the context of specific kinds of cases (that may be rather diverse) where it might be offered as a solution to a social problem. There are, perhaps, some features in common among these cases; this suggests that there might be some sort of "test" we could apply to determine the moral appropriateness of a paternalistic proposal. That, however, would not be to set up a test to see whether a suspicious paternalism might still be justifiable for those cases. It would be, instead, a test to determine when paternalism is morally right (such that, for those cases, a government would be morally suspect if it did *not* engage in such practices).

In short, we believe that paternalistic practices, in and of themselves, are neither generally wrong, nor generally suspicious, nor generally right; they simply form one possible course governments might take in response to social problems. Whether such a course turns out to be a morally appropriate response or one that is morally outrageous depends on what factors are involved in the particular cases where it is suggested. This is the view, then, of the editors of this volume. It is not, as you will notice, agreed to explicitly by any of the authors whose writings appear in this section. However, we believe that the ultimate outcome of the arguments presented here, especially those by *Wolff*, *Exdell*, and *Feinberg*, should lead the student to the view just described.

We introduce the issue of paternalism by means of the article, "The Problem of Heroin," by James Q. *Wilson*, Mark H. *Moore*, and I. David *Wheat*, Jr. The facts of heroin traffic, use, and addiction present us with a set of important practical problems demanding some action. The problems are ones of law making and law enforcement respecting the sale and use of heroin. Wilson et al. argue that the sides that have been taken in the debate on heroin legislation, what they call the "punitive" versus the "medical" approach, have avoided the central question of whether the government has rights and obligations to protect a person from harming himself. They describe this question as a philosophical one and insist that it must be answered before the practical problems of law and its enforcement can be resolved satisfactorily.

Wilson et al. do believe that government not only has the right, but also the obligation, to protect a person from himself and thus is justified in taking legal action against heroin users as well as "pushers." They want to say that government has the positive obligation to improve the well-being of its citizens and that action against heroin helps contribute to this end. This is, of course, a paternalistic account of the relation between state and citizen.

They raise another question that we recognize as a typically conceptual one. Is the use of heroin in fact a case of harming oneself and is it something from which one must be saved? Although they have no doubt that it is, they do point out that there is simply a great deal that it not known about the effects of heroin upon the lives of its users. It will be useful for the student to speculate about how Wilson et al. understand this question. Do they understand it as a factual question to be settled definitively by the accumulation of more information, medical data, and so on? Is it indeed that sort of question? Once again we refer you to Part 1 on ethics, especially to discussions of facts and values. One point, however, must be made. This article makes abundantly clear that no rational moral or legal decisions can be made without taking into account all the facts—especially when the facts may be other than we have been led to believe they are. Nevertheless there remains the doubt whether this question can be settled entirely by an appeal to facts. Even were all the facts available we could still imagine disagreement over whether heroin use is a case of harming oneself. Here the student is invited to imagine the kind of case that might be made for this view and the kind of person that might make it.

As an alternative to their own position Wilson et al. mention the classical theory of utilitarianism. The central statement of the utilitarian stance on this issue is John Stuart *Mill*'s *On Liberty*. Mill seeks to draw a definite distinction between actions that impinge upon the interests of others and those that may be called altogether "self-regarding." Societies and governments, he concludes, are justified in intervening to protect and promote the general welfare; but there is no room for such intervention "when a person's conduct affects the interest of no persons besides himself. . . ." His arguments for this conclusion are the general utilitarian ones that each person is the best judge of his or her own interests and that interference in purely private matters would tend to do more harm than good, in the long run, to the general welfare.

Mill, of course, does not speak to the specific problem of heroin, but it is an interesting exercise to speculate what, given his position and the factual information provided by Wilson et al., he would have to say about it. Wilson et al. argue that policy toward heroin use worked out on utilitarian grounds need not differ from the policy they advocate on other philosophical grounds. The student may want to ask whether Mill would agree with that contention and, if so, just wherein does the difference lie between Mill's utilitarianism and the paternalistic theory of Wilson et al.

In the next selection, from the book, *The Poverty of Liberalism*, by Robert Paul *Wolff*, we encounter a sharp attack on purely utilitarian arguments against paternalism. Most critics of Mill have noticed that he does not actually limit himself to strictly utilitarian arguments in his defense of libertarianism. Wolff, however, sets that criticism aside and asks whether Mill could have done so. Wolff's conclusion is that a strictly utilitarian position would have to allow "that a bit of judicious meddling would considerably reduce the pain that imprudent persons inflict upon themselves; and of course (to the utilitarian) a pain avoided is as good as a pleasure engendered." The argument Wolff presents for this conclusion rests on a clarification of what Mill must mean if his claim that each man is the best judge of his own interests is to be more than the trivially true and quasi-psychological claim that each man is the only judge of what his interests are. Wolff shows that if we take the concept *interest* to refer not to one's purposes but to what will make one happy, Mill's claim of individual infallibility about one's interests is quite probably *false*. That being so, the utilitarian must see intervention as a legitimate maneuver in the promotion of general well-being. The only argument Mill is left with is the empirical prediction that governmental intervention will have worse effects, in the long run, than governmental constraint.

This is, of course, a debatable prediction. The upshot, then, of Wolff's argument is that a strictly utilitarian account cannot show that paternalism just *is* generally wrong; indeed it cannot even show that paternalism *might* be generally wrong. We believe that the correct conclusion to draw from Wolff's criticisms of Mill is that, at best, Mill can only argue that *if* we are able (in some specific kinds of cases) to show that paternalism would have long-run deleterious effects then (for just those cases) paternalism would be wrong. Wolff's countercases to Mill's thesis of infallibility may provide us with a starting point in delineating the sorts of cases in which an empirical prediction like Mill's might (or might not) be pertinent. Unfortunately, Wolff does not carry through on those cases to see if there might be some feature(s) of them that would help us make that delineation.

That, of course, could only work if we accept the basic normative claims of utilitarianism, namely, that if the adoption of some practice leads, in the long run, to some kind of pain then the practice is *therefore* wrong. One may, of course, object to this normative claim, quite apart from its outcome on the paternalism issue. This raises another possibility: Might we not argue against paternalism on general or altogether different grounds than those provided by the utilitarian? There are, it appears, two other lines of argument one might try out here. The first is that liberty, in and for itself, is valuable. Were that so, paternalistic interference would certainly be at least a *prima facie* wrong, and maybe even always wrong. Secondly, since persons must always be respected and, so, must be respected as free, paternalistic interference is to be regarded as a *prima facie* wrong. For, paternalistic interference, as its very name suggests, treats citizens as though they were children who are incapable of rational free action. Both of these lines of argument have occurred in contemporary political discussion. One needs only to read such newspaper columnists as William F. Buckley to find these arguments cropping up on issues like the controversy over seat-belt regulations and the welfare system. Since these lines of argument are so familiar we have chosen not to present any piece that argues them in any detail. Instead we present an article, written especially for this volume by John B. *Exdell*, that carefully and critically analyzes what is involved in the second of these arguments.

Exdell begins by distinguishing challenges that can be made against paternalism on utilitarian grounds from those that can be made on the grounds that paternalism violates basic human rights. Utilitarian considerations can at best lead to the contention that as a rule paternalism does not promote the general well-being; and we should expect the utilitarian to be forced to recognize numerous exceptions in which paternalism does promote general well-being. On the other hand, if objections to paternalism are made to rest on claims that it violates human rights, then these objections are much more strenuous and we should expect very few exceptions.

Exdell goes on to describe how a case against paternalism can be made on the grounds that it violates human rights. He takes as an example the traditional and most commonly advanced argument that paternalism violates respect for persons. He discusses two senses of the expression "respect for persons." He argues that in the first sense of that expression, not only is paternalism in itself unobjectionable, but also respect for persons does not seem to afford grounds for establishing any rights at all. Exdell argues, however, that in the second sense of the expression the appeal to respect for persons does establish important rights, but does not show that all forms of paternalism are violations of rights.

An important feature of this article is a brief methodological passage in which Exdell explains what criteria one needs to employ in deciding which principles demonstrate that a given practice violates rights and which principles do not. This passage is especially important for introductory students because it explicitly discusses the philosophical methods required to resolve such issues.

This section concludes with Joel *Feinberg*'s article, "Legal Paternalism." The problem that Feinberg sets for himself is to reconcile "our general repugnance" for paternalism with our commonsense realization that there are situations in which paternalistic interference seems appropriate in order to prevent persons from doing harm to themselves. Feinberg states that his approach is not "ideological," and we understand this to mean that he is going to appeal to our common moral understanding rather than to some normative or metaethical theory that would commit him in advance to a view about what lines of justification moral and political decision-making must involve. His strategy is first to make a number of distinctions between the various kind of cases in which a person could be said to harm himself or incur the risk of doing so, and then to focus on those cases where we usually believe that interference is warranted. By examining cases, he hopes to determine what the *grounds* are upon which to base a reasonable judgment about the warrant for paternalistic practices. He concludes that what seems common to those cases in which the state is justified in protecting a person against himself is the fact that, in each case, the actions involved are substantially "nonvoluntary" (in a sense that Feinberg explains). On the basis of this conclusion he goes on to distinguish a "strong" version of paternalism from a "weaker" one, and argues that the latter version is perfectly acceptable.

Feinberg, in his discussion of the weaker version of paternalism, admits that it is hardly a general or independent principle of governmental policy. This suggests that his view, in light of the many different kinds of considerations that he shows can count towards an action's being "nonvoluntary," is radically different in style from such traditional political theorizing as that which is exhibited by Mill (and criticized by Wolff) or that which is analyzed by Exdell. We find this article valuable, if for no other reason, because it clearly shows the many different kinds of cases and considerations that prove relevant to a careful resolution of a problem of this nature. This awareness of diversity, and hence of complexity, has not been characteristically a feature of traditional social and political philosophy.

The Problem of Heroin

JAMES Q. WILSON, MARK H. MOORE, and DAVID WHEAT, JR.

IT IS now widely believed that much of the recent increase in predatory crime is the result of heroin addicts supporting their habits; that heroin use has become a middle-class white as well as lower-class black phenomenon of alarming proportions; and that conventional law-enforcement efforts to reduce heroin use have not only failed but may in fact be contributing to the problem by increasing the cost of the drug for the user, leading thereby to the commission of even more crimes and the corruption of even more police officers. These generally held opinions have led to an intense debate over new policy initiatives to deal with heroin, an argument usually described as one between the advocates of a "*law-enforcement*" policy (which includes shutting off opium supplies in Turkey and heroin-manufacturing laboratories in France, arresting more heroin dealers in the United States, and the use of civil commitment procedures, detoxification centers, and methadone maintenance programs) and the partisans of a "*decriminalization*" policy (which includes legalization of the use or possession of heroin, at least for adults, and the distribution of heroin to addicts at low cost, or zero cost, through government-controlled clinics).

The intensity of the debate tends to obscure the fact that most of the widely accepted opinions on heroin use are not supported by much evidence; that the very concept of "addict" is ambiguous and somewhat misleading; and that many

Reprinted with permission of the authors from "The Problem of Heroin," *The Public Interest*, No. 29 (Fall 1972), pp. 3–12, 21–23, and 25–27.

of the apparently reasonable assumptions about heroin use and crime—such as the assumption that the legalization of heroin would dramatically reduce the rate of predatory crime, or that intensified law enforcement drives the price of heroin up, or that oral methadone is a universal substitute for heroin, or that heroin use spreads because of the activities of "pushers" who can be identified as such—turn out on closer inspection to be unreasonable, unwarranted, or at least open to more than one interpretation.

"Punitive" vs. "Medical" Approaches

Most important, the current debate has failed to make explicit, or at least to clarify, the philosophical principles underlying the competing positions. Those positions are sometimes described as the "*punitive*" versus the "*medical*" approach, but these labels are of little help. For one thing, they are far from precise: Putting an addict in jail is certainly "punitive," but putting him in a treatment program, however benevolent its intentions, may be seen by him as no less "punitive." Shifting an addict from heroin to methadone may be "medical" if he makes the choice voluntarily—but is it so if the alternative to methadone maintenance is a criminal conviction for heroin possession? And while maintaining an addict on heroin (as is done in Great Britain and as has been proposed for the United States) is not "punitive" in any legal sense, neither is it therapeutic in any medical sense. Indeed, there seem to be no forms of therapy that will "cure" addicts in any large numbers of their dependence on heroin. Various forms of intensive psychotherapy and group-based "personality restructuring" may be of great value to certain drug users, but by definition they can reach only very small numbers of persons and perhaps only for limited periods of time.

But the fundamental problem with these and other labels is that they avoid the central question: Does society have only the right to protect itself (or its members) from the harmful acts of heroin users, or does it have in addition the responsibility (and thus the right) to improve the well-being (somehow defined) of heroin users themselves? In one view, the purpose of the law is to insure the maximum amount of liberty for everyone, and an action of one person is properly constrained by society if—and only if—it has harmful consequences for another person. This is the utilitarian conception of the public interest and, when applied to heroin use, it leads such otherwise unlike men as Milton Friedman, Herbert Packer, and Thomas Szasz to oppose the use of criminal sanctions for heroin users. Professor Packer, for example, recently wrote that a desirable aspect of liberalism is that it allows people "to choose their own roads to hell if that is where they want to go."

In another view, however, society has an obligation to enhance the "well-being" of each of its citizens even with respect to those aspects of their lives that do not directly impinge on other people's lives. In this conception of the public good, all citizens of a society are bound to be affected—indirectly but perhaps profoundly and permanently—if a significant number are permitted to go to hell in their own way. A society is therefore unworthy if it permits, or is indifferent to, any activity that renders its members inhuman or deprives them of their essential (or "natural") capacities to judge, choose, and act. If heroin use is such an activity, then its use should be proscribed. Whether that proscription is enforced by mere punishment or by obligatory therapy is a separate question.

The alternative philosophical principles do not necessarily lead to diametrically opposed policies. A utilitarian might conclude, for example, that heroin use is so destructive of family life that society has an interest in proscribing it (though he is more likely, if experience is any guide, to allow the use of heroin and then deal with its effect on family life by advocating social services to "help problem families"). And a moralist might decide that although heroin should be illegal, any serious effort to enforce that law against users would be so costly in terms of other social values (privacy, freedom, the integrity of officialdom) as not to be worth it, and he thus might allow the level of enforcement to fall to a point just short of that at which the tutelary power of the law would be jeopardized. Still, even if principles do not uniquely determine policies, thinking clearly about the former is essential to making good judgments about the latter. And to think clearly about the former, it is as important to ascertain the effects of heroin on the user as it is to discover the behavior of a user toward society.

The User

There is no single kind of heroin user. Some persons may try it once, find it unpleasant, and never use it again; others may "dabble" with it on occasion but, though they find it pleasurable, will have no trouble stopping; still others may use it on a regular basis but in a way that does not interfere with their work. But some persons, who comprise a large (if unknown) percentage of all those who experiment with heroin, develop a relentless and unmanageable craving for the drug such that their life becomes organized around it: searching for it, using it, enjoying it, and searching for more. Authorities differ on whether all such persons—whom we shall call "addicts," though the term is not well-defined and its scientific status is questionable—are invariably physiologically dependent on the drug, as evidenced by painful "withdrawal" symptoms that occur whenever they cease using it. Some persons may crave the drug without being dependent, others may be dependent without craving it. We need not resolve these definitional and medical issues, however, to recognize that many (but not all) heroin users are addicts in the popular sense of the term.

No one knows how many users of various kinds there are, at what rate they have been increasing in number, or what happens to them at the end of their "run." That they *have* increased in number is revealed, not only by the testimony of police and narcotics officers, but by figures on deaths attributed to heroin. Between 1967 and 1971, the number of deaths in Los Angeles County attributed to heroin use more than tripled, and although improved diagnostic skills in the coroner's office may account for some of this increase, it does not (in the opinion of the University of Southern California student task force report) account for it all. A Harvard student task force has used several techniques to estimate the size of the heroin-user population in Boston, and concludes that there was a tenfold increase in the decade of the 1960's. Why that increase occurred, and whether it will continue, are matters about which one can only speculate. The USC group estimated that there are at least fifty thousand addicts in Los Angeles: the Harvard group estimated that there are six thousand in Boston; various sources conventionally refer (with what accuracy we do not know) to the "hundred thousand" addicts in New York.

No one has proposed a fully satisfactory theory to explain the apparent increase in addiction. There are at least four speculative possibilities, some or all of which may be correct. The rise in real incomes during the prosperity of the 1960's may simply have made possible the purchase of more heroin as it made possible the purchase of more automobiles or color television sets. The cult of personal liberation among the young may have led to greater experimentation with heroin as it led to greater freedom in dress and manners and the development of a rock music culture. The war in Vietnam may have both loosened social constraints and given large numbers of young soldiers easy access to heroin supplies and ample incentive (the boredom, fears, and demoralization caused by the war) to dabble in the drug. Finally, the continued disintegration of the lower-income, especially black, family living in the central city may have heightened the importance of street peer groups to the individual and thus (in ways to be discussed later in this essay) placed him in a social environment highly conducive to heroin experimentation. There are, in short, ample reasons to suppose (though few facts to show) that important changes in both the supply of and demand for heroin occurred during the last decade.

Heavy users of heroin, according to their own testimony, tend to be utterly preoccupied with finding and consuming the drug. Given an unlimited supply (that is, given heroin at zero cost), an addict will "shoot up" three to five times a day. Given the price of heroin on the black market—currently, about $10 a bag, with varying numbers of bags used in each fix—some addicts may be able to shoot up only once or twice a day. The sensations associated with heroin use by most novice addicts are generally the same: keen anticipation of the fix, the "rush" when the heroin begins to work in the bloodstream, the euphoric "high," the drowsy or "nodding" stage as the "high" wears off, and then the beginning of the discomfort caused by the absence of heroin. For the veteran addict, the "high" may no longer be attainable, except perhaps at the risk of a lethal overdose. For him, the sensations induced by heroin have mainly to do with anesthetizing himself against withdrawal pain—and perhaps against most other feelings as well—together with a ritualistic preoccupation with the needle and the act of injection.

The addict is intensely present-oriented. Though "dabblers" or other episodic users may save heroin for a weekend fix, the addict can rarely save any at all. Some, for example, report that they would like to arise in the morning with enough heroin for a "wake-up" fix, but almost none have the self-control to go to sleep at night leaving unused heroin behind. Others report getting enough heroin to last them for a week, only to shoot it all the first day. How many addicts living this way can manage a reasonably normal family and work life is not known, but clearly many cannot. Some become heroin dealers in order to earn money, but a regular heavy user seldom has the self-control to be successful at this enterprise for long. Addicts-turned-dealers frequently report a sharp increase in their heroin use as they consume much of their sales inventory.

It is this craving for the drug, and the psychological states induced by its use, that are the chief consequences of addiction; they are also the most important consequences about which, ultimately, one must have a moral or political view, whatever the secondary effects of addiction that are produced by current public policy. At the same time, one should not suppose that all of these secondary effects can be eliminated by changes in policy. For example, while there are apparently no specific pathologies—serious illnesses or physiological deterioration—that are known to result from heroin use *per se*, the addict does run the risk of infections caused by the use of unsterile needles, of poisoning as a result of shooting an overdose (or a manageable dose that has been cut with harmful products), and of thrombosed veins as a result of repeated injections. Some of these risks could be reduced if heroin were legally available in clinics operated by physicians, but they could not be eliminated unless literally everyone wishing heroin were given it in whatever dosage, short of a lethal one, he wished. In Great Britain, where pure heroin is legally available at low prices, addicts still have medical problems arising out of their use of the drug—principally, unsterile self-injections, involuntary overdoses, and voluntary overdoses (that is, willingly injecting more than they should in hopes of obtaining a new "high"). If, as will be discussed below, heroin were injected under a doctor's supervision (as it is not in England), the risk of sepsis and of overdoses would be sharply reduced—but at the cost of making the public heroin clinic less attractive to addicts who wish to consume not merely a maintenance dose but a euphoria-producing (and therefore risky) one.

Why Heroin?

No generally accepted theory supported by well-established facts exists to explain why some persons but not others become addicts. It is easy to make a list of factors that increase (statistically, at least) the risk of addiction: Black males living in low-income neighborhoods, coming from broken or rejecting families, and involved in "street life" have much higher chances of addiction than upper-middle-class whites in stable families and "normal" occupations. But some members of the latter category *do* become addicted and many members of the former category do not, why this should be the case, no one is sure. It is easy to argue that heroin use occurs only among people who have serious problems (and thus to argue that the way to end addiction is to solve the underlying problems), but in fact many heavy users seem to have no major problems at all. Isidor Chein and his co-workers in their leading study of addiction in New York (*The*

Road to H) found that between a quarter and a third of addicts seemed to have no problems for which heroin use was a compensation.

Though we cannot predict with much confidence who will and who will not become an addict, we can explain why heroin is used and how its use spreads. The simple fact is that heroin use is intensely pleasurable, for many people more pleasurable than anything else they might do. Heroin users will have experimented with many drugs, and when heroin is hard to find they may return to alcohol or other drugs, but for the vast majority of users heroin remains the drug of choice. The nature of the pleasure will vary from person to person—or, perhaps, the interpretive description of that pleasure will vary—but the desire for it remains the governing passion of the addicts' lives. All of us enjoy pleasure; an addict is a person who has found the supreme pleasure and the means to make that pleasure recur.

This fact helps explain why "curing" addiction is so difficult (for many addicts, virtually impossible) and how new addicts are recruited. Addicts sent to state or federal hospitals to be detoxified—i.e., to be withdrawn from heroin use—almost invariably return to such use after their release, simply because using it is so much more pleasurable than not using it, regardless of cost. Many addicts, probably a majority, resist and resent oral methadone maintenance because methadone, though it can prevent withdrawal pains, does not, when taken orally, supply them with the euphoric "high" they associate with heroin. (The intravenous use of methadone will produce a "high" comparable to that of heroin. The oral use of methadone is seen by addicts as a way to avoid the pain of heroin withdrawal but not as an alternative source of a "high.") Persons willingly on methadone tend to be older addicts who are "burned out," i.e., physically and mentally run down by the burdens of maintaining a heroin habit. A younger addict still enjoying his "run" (which may last 5 or 10 years) will be less inclined to shift to methadone.

The "Contagion" Model

When asked how they got started on heroin, addicts almost universally give the same answer: They were offered some by a friend. They tried it, often in a group setting, and found they liked it. Though not every person who tries it will like it, and not every person who likes it will become addicted to it, a substantial fraction (perhaps a quarter) of first users become regular and heavy users. Heroin use spreads through peer-group contacts, and those peer groups most vulnerable to experimenting with it are those that include a person who himself has recently tried it and whose enthusiasm for it is contagious. In fact, so common is this process that many observers use the word "contagious" or "contagion" deliberately—the spread of heroin use is in the nature of an epidemic in which a "carrier" (a recent and enthusiastic convert to heroin) "infects" a population with whom he is in close contact.

A recent study in Chicago has revealed in some detail how this process of infection occurs. Patrick H. Hughes and Gail A. Crawford found that a major heroin "epidemic" occurred in Chicago after World War II, reaching a peak in 1949, followed by a decline in the number of new cases of addiction during the 1950's, with signs of a new epidemic appearing in the early 1960's. They studied closely 11 neighborhood-sized epidemics that they were able to identify in the late 1960's, each producing 50 or more new addicts. In the great majority of cases, not only was the new user turned on by a friend, but the friend was himself a novice user still exhilarated by the thrill of a "high." Both recruit and initiator tended to be members of a small group that had already experimented heavily with many drugs and with alcohol. These original friendship groups broke up as the heavy users formed new associations in order to maintain their habits. Strikingly, the new user usually does not seek out heroin the first time he uses it, but rather begins to use it almost fortuitously, by the accident of personal contact in a polydrug subculture. In these groups, a *majority* of the members usually try heroin after it is introduced by one of them, though not all of these become addicted.

Such a theory explains the very rapid rates of increase that have occurred in a city such as Boston. The number of new users will be some exponential function of the number of initial users. Obviously, this geometric growth rate would soon, if not checked by other factors, make addicts of us all. Since we are not all going to become addicts, other factors must be at work, though their nature is not well understood. They may include "natural immunity" (some of us may find heroin unpleasant), breaks in the chain of contagion (caused by the absence of any personal linkages between peer groups that are using heroin and peer groups that are not), and the greater difficulty of finding a supply of heroin in some communities than others. *Perhaps most important, the analogy between heroin use and disease is imperfect: We do not choose to contract smallpox from a friend, but we do choose to use heroin offered by a friend.*

The Myth of the "Pusher"

If heroin use is something we choose, then the moral and empirical judgments one makes about heroin become important. If a person thinks heroin use wrong, or if he believes that heroin use can cause a serious pathology, then, other things being equal, he will be less likely to use it than if he made the opposite judgments. Chein found that the belief that heroin use was wrong was a major reason given by heroin "dabblers" for not continuing in its use. The extent to which the belief in the wrongness of heroin use depends on its being illegal is unknown—but it is interesting to note that many addicts tend to be strongly opposed to legalizing heroin.

The peer-group/contagion model also helps explain why the fastest increase in heroin use has been among young people, with the result that the average age of known addicts has fallen sharply in the last few years. In Boston, the Harvard student group found that one quarter of heroin users seeking help from a public agency were under the age of 18, and 80 per cent were under the age of 25. A study done at American University found that the average age at which identifiable addicts in Washington, D.C., began using heroin was under 19. Though stories of youngsters under 15 becoming addicts are commonplace, most studies place the beginning of heavy use between the ages of 17 and 19. It is persons in this age group, of course, who are most exposed to the contagion: They are intensely involved in peer groups; many have begun to become part of "street society," because they had either dropped out of or graduated from schools; and they are most likely to suffer from boredom and a desire "to prove themselves." It is claimed that many of those who become serious addicts "mature out" of their heroin use sometime in their thirties, in much the same way that many juvenile delinquents spontaneously cease committing criminal acts when they get older. Unfortunately, not much is known about "maturing out," and it is even possible that it is a less common cause of ending heroin use than death or imprisonment.

If this view of the spread of addiction is correct, then it is pointless to explain heroin use as something that "pushers" inflict on unsuspecting youth. The popular conception of a stranger in a dirty trench coat hanging around schoolyards and corrupting innocent children is largely myth—indeed, given what we know about addiction, it would almost have to be myth. No dealer in drugs is likely to risk doing business with strangers. The chances of apprehension are too great and the profits from dealing with friends too substantial to make missionary work among unknown "straights" worthwhile. And the novice user is far more likely to take the advice of a friend, or to respond to the blandishments of a peer group, than to take an unfamiliar product from an anonymous pusher.

An important implication of the peer-group/contagion model is that programs designed to treat or control established addicts may have little effect on the mechanism whereby heroin use spreads. Users tend to be "infectious" only early in their heroin careers (later, all their friends are addicts and the life-style seems less glamorous), and at this stage they are not likely to volunteer for treatment or to come to the attention of police authorities. In the Chicago study, for example, Hughes and Crawford found that police efforts directed at addiction were intensified only after the peak of the epidemic had passed, and though arrests increased sharply, they were principally of heavily addicted regular users, not of the infectious users. *No matter whether one favors a medical or a law-enforcement approach to heroin, the optimum strategy depends crucially on whether one's objective is to "treat" existing addicts or to prevent the recruitment of new ones.*

Containing the Contagion

The novice or would-be heroin user is quite vulnerable to changes, even small ones, in the availability of heroin. For one thing, a person who has not yet become a heavy user will not conduct an intensive search for a supply. Some studies have suggested that a "dabbler" may use heroin if it is immediately available but not use it if it requires two, three, or four hours of searching. Extending the search time for novices may discourage their use of heroin, or reduce the frequency of their use. In addition, a dealer in heroin is reluctant to sell to persons with whom he is not closely acquainted for fear of detection and apprehension by the police. When police surveillance is intensified, the dealer becomes more cautious about those with whom he does business. A casual user or distant acquaintance represents a threat to the dealer when police activity is high; when such activity is low, the casual or new customer is more attractive. Heroin customers can be thought of as a "queue" with the heaviest users at the head of the line and the casual ones at the end; how far down the queue the dealer will do business depends on the perceived level of risk associated with each additional customer, and that in turn depends on how strongly "the heat is on."

The price of heroin to the user will be affected by law enforcement in different ways, depending on the focus of the pressure. No one, of course, has the data with which to construct anything but a highly conjectural model of the heroin market; at the same time, we believe there is little reason for asserting that the *only* effect of law enforcement on the heroin market is to drive up the price of the product.

Enforcement aimed at the sources of supply may well drive up the price. The price of a "bag" on the street has risen steeply since the early 1950's and simultaneously the quality of the product has declined (which means that the real price increase is even higher than the nominal one). This was the result of a vast increase in demand (the heroin "epidemic" of the 1950's and 1960's) coupled with the increase in risks associated with dealing in the product. So the long-term effect of law-enforcement pressures on dealers is probably to force up the price of heroin by either increasing the cash price, decreasing the quality of the product, or requiring dealers to discriminate among their customers in order to avoid risky sales. But in the short term, anti-dealer law enforcement probably affects access (finding a "connection") more than price.

Suppose instead that law enforcement were directed at the *user* rather than the dealer. Taking users off the streets in large numbers would tend to reduce the demand for, and thus the price of, heroin. Furthermore, with many heavy customers gone, some dealers would have to accept the risks of doing business with novice users who, having smaller habits or indeed no real habits at all, would consume per capita fewer bags and pay lower prices. (Law enforcement aimed merely at known and regular users would not, however, result in the apprehension of many novice users and thus would not take off the streets a large fraction of the sources of heroin "infection.") Suppose, finally, that coupled with law enforcement aimed at known users there were a selective strategy of identifying and restraining the agents of contagion. This was tried in Chicago on an experimental basis by Hughes and Crawford, with promising though not conclusive results. On spotting a neighborhood epidemic, they intervened by seeking quickly to identify the friends and fellow users of an addict. They found in this case that one addict led them to 14 other addicts and, most important, to seven persons experimenting with heroin. The doctors were able to involve 11 of the 14 addicts and five of the seven experimenters in a treatment program; the remainder of the experimenters apparently discontinued heroin use, perhaps because the social structure in which their drug use took place was disrupted.

Possible Policy Directions

If nothing else, this discussion of the complexities of heroin use, marketing, and control should suggest the futility of arguments between the so-called "punitive" and "medical" approaches to addiction, the simplistic nature of unqualified recommendations that we adopt the "British system," and the imprecision of angry disputes between those who wish to "get tough" on "pushers" and those who wish to "decriminalize" heroin.

Beyond that, thinking about heroin requires one first of all to decide how one will handle the underlying philosophical issue—namely, whether the state is ever justified in protecting people from themselves, or whether it can only intervene to protect an innocent party from the actions of someone else. Put another way, the question is whether the state has any responsibility for the quality of human life in those cases where that quality (or lack of it) appears to be the result of freely exercised choice with no external effects on other parties. It is our view that the state does have such responsibilities, though its powers in this regard must be carefully exercised toward only the most important and reasonable goals. Even John Stuart Mill, whose defense of personal liberty is virtually absolute, argued against allowing a man to sell himself into slavery, "for by selling himself as a slave, he abdicates his liberty; he forgoes any future use of it beyond that simple act."

The next question is whether heroin addiction is such a form of "slavery" or is otherwise a state of being which should not be left to free choice. This is a more difficult question to answer in general terms, for somewhat surprisingly, we know rather little about what proportion of all heroin users are seriously incapacitated (or "captured") by it. Obviously, a large number are; but some might remain heavy users and yet hold jobs, lead responsible family lives, and retain other attributes of their humanity. Nobody knows what fraction are in this category, though we do know that the advocates of decriminalization tend to give (with little or no evidence) very generous estimates of it while proponents of "stamping out" heroin give very small ones. The lives of British addicts have not been carefully studied. But Griffith Edwards of the Addiction Research Institute reports "the impression of many of the clinic doctors" that "the majority of young heroin takers do not settle to a job, or otherwise manage their lives responsibly, do not keep to the prescribed dose, and tend to acquire drugs other than those prescribed." Furthermore, the mortality rate of British addicts, even without the need to steal to support a habit, is *28 times as large* as the death rate for the equivalent age group in the British population and *twice* that of American heroin addicts.

We think it clear that for a sufficiently large number of persons, heroin is so destructive of the human personality that it should not be made generally available. (Defending that view in the context of the current debate is not essential, however, because not even the most zealous advocate of decriminalization supports complete legalization.) We believe this to be the case, though we recognize the rejoinders that can be made. Alcohol, some will say, has consequences for many individuals and for society at least as destructive as those of heroin, yet no one would propose returning to a system of prohibition. Alcohol and heroin are different problems, however, both medically and legally. A far smaller proportion of alcohol users than of heroin users become addicted in any meaningful sense of that term; the risks to the average individual of experimentation are accordingly far less in the former than in the latter case. And of those "addicted" to alcohol, there have been a larger proportion of "cures," though not as many as one would wish. Finally, alcohol use is so widespread as to be nearly universal, while heroin use remains an exotic habit of relatively few, and thus presents easier problems of control. Perhaps because of this, while no advanced society has been able to eliminate alcohol use, *virtually every society but ours* has been able to eliminate, or keep to trifling proportions, heroin use.

If one accepts the view that it is desirable and possible, not only to provide better treatment for present addicts, but to reduce the rate of growth of the addict population, then one must also accept the need for some measure of compulsion; for nothing is clearer than the fact that most young addicts enjoying their "run" will not voluntarily choose a life without heroin in preference to a life with it. Such compulsion will be necessary whatever disposition is made of the constrained addict—whether he be put on probation or sent to prison, to a quarantine center, to a methadone program, or to a heroin maintenance program. The compulsion will be necessary to achieve two objectives: to insure that he remains in the appropriate treatment without "cheating" (i.e., simply using the treatment center as a cheap source of drugs to be sold on the street) and to insure that while treated he does not proselytize among non-addicts and spread the contagion. Furthermore, there is some evidence (inconclusive, to be sure) that the possibility of arrest followed by some penalty deters at least some potential users and makes access to heroin more difficult for others.

Finally, to the extent that people voluntarily elect not to use heroin, the fact of its illegality may contribute to the belief that such use is "wrong" and therefore enhance the probability that a non-user will remain a non-user. Or put another way, it is difficult to see how society can assert that heroin use is a grave evil if it also must admit that its use is perfectly legal.

Governments May Not Intervene

JOHN STUART MILL

IV. Of the Limits to the Authority of Society Over the Individual

WHAT, then, is the rightful limit to the sovereignty of the individual over himself? Where does the authority of society begin? How much of human life should be assigned to individuality, and how much to society?

Each will receive its proper share, if each has that which more particularly concerns it. To individuality should belong the part of life in which it is chiefly the individual that is interested; to society, the part which chiefly interests society.

Though society is not founded on a contract, and though no good purpose is answered by inventing a contract in order to deduce social obligations from it, every one who receives the protection of society owes a return for the benefit, and the fact of living in society renders it indispensible that each should be found to observe a certain line of conduct towards the rest. This conduct consists, first, in not injuring the interests of one another; or rather certain interests, which, either by express legal provision or by tacit understanding, ought to be considered as rights; and secondly, in each person's bearing his share (to be fixed on some equitable principle) of the labours and sacrifices incurred for defending the society or its members from injury and molestation. These conditions society is justified in enforcing, at all costs to those who endeavour to withhold fulfilment. Nor is this all that society may do. The acts of an individual may be hurtful to others, or wanting in due consideration for their welfare, without going the length of violating any of their constituted rights. The offender may then be justly punished by opinion, though not by law. As soon as any part of a person's conduct affects prejudicially the interests of others, society has jurisdiction over it, and the question whether the general welfare will or will not be promoted by interfering with it, becomes open to discussion. But there is no room for entertaining any such question when a person's conduct affects the interests of no persons besides himself, or needs not affect them unless they like (all the persons concerned being of full age, and the ordinary amount of understanding). In all such cases there should be perfect freedom, legal and social, to do the action and stand the consequences.

It would be a great misunderstanding of this doctrine, to suppose that it is one of selfish indifference, which pretends that human beings have no business with each other's conduct in life, and that they should not concern themselves about the well-doing or well-being of one another, unless their own interest is involved. Instead of any diminution, there is need of a great increase of disinterested exertion to promote the good of others. But disinterested benevolence can find other instruments to persuade people to their good, than whips and

---

Excerpted from *On Liberty* by John Stuart Mill, Chapter IV.

scourges, either of the literal or the metaphorical sort. I am the last person to undervalue the self-regarding virtues; they are only second in importance, if even second, to the social. It is equally the business of education to cultivate both. But even education works by conviction and persuasion as well as by compulsion, and it is by the former only that, when the period of education is past, the self-regarding virtues should be inculcated. Human beings owe to each other help to distinguish the better from the worse, and encouragement to choose the former and avoid the latter. They should be for ever stimulating each other to increased exercise of their higher faculties, and increased direction of their feelings and aims towards wise instead of foolish, elevating instead of degrading, objects and contemplations. But neither one person, nor any number of persons, is warranted in saying to another human creature of ripe years, that he shall not do with his life for his own benefit what he chooses to do with it. He is the person most interested in his own well-being: the interest which any other person, except in cases of strong personal attachment, can have in it, is trifling, compared with that which he himself has; the interest which society has in him individually (except as to his conduct to others) is fractional, and altogether indirect: while, with respect to his own feelings and circumstances, the most ordinary man or woman has means of knowledge immeasurably surpassing those that can be possessed by any one else. The interference of society to overrule his judgment and purposes in what only regards himself, must be grounded on general presumptions: which may be altogether wrong, and even if right, are as likely as not to be misapplied to individual cases, by persons no better acquainted with the circumstances of such cases than those are who look at them merely from without. In this department, therefore, of human affairs, individuality has its proper field of action. In the conduct of human beings towards one another, it is necessary that general rules should for the most part be observed, in order that people may know what they have to expect; but in each person's own concerns, his individual spontaneity is entitled to free exercise. Considerations to aid his judgment, exhortations to strengthen his will, may be offered to him, even obtruded on him, by others; but he himself is the final judge. All errors which he is likely to commit against advice and warning, are far outweighed by the evil of allowing others to constrain him to what they deem his good.

I do not mean that the feelings with which a person is regarded by others, ought not to be in any way affected by his self-regarding qualities or deficiencies. This is neither possible nor desirable. If he is eminent in any of the qualities which conduce to his own good, he is, so far, a proper object of admiration. He is so much the nearer to the ideal perfection of human nature. If he is grossly deficient in those qualities, a sentiment the opposite of admiration will follow. There is a degree of folly, and a degree of what may be called (though the phrase is not unobjectionable) lowness or depravation of taste, which, though it cannot justify doing harm to the person who manifests it, renders him necessarily and properly a subject of distaste, or, in extreme cases, even of contempt: a person could not have the opposite qualities in due strength without entertaining these feelings. Though doing no wrong to any one, a person may so act as to compel us to judge him, and feel to him, as a fool, or as a being of an inferior order: and since this judgment and feeling are a fact which he would prefer to avoid, it is doing him a service to warn him of it beforehand, as of any other disagreeable consequence to which he exposes himself. It would be well, indeed, if this good office were much more freely rendered than the common notions of politeness at present permit, and if one person could honestly point out to another that he thinks him in fault, without being considered unmannerly or presuming. We have a right, also, in various ways, to act upon our unfavourable opinion of any one, not to the oppression of his individuality, but in the exercise of ours. We are not bound, for example, to seek his society; we have a right to avoid it (though not to parade the avoidance), for we have a right to choose the society most acceptable to us. We have a right, and it may be our duty, to caution others against him, if we think his example or conversation likely to have a pernicious effect on those with whom he associates. We may give others a preference over him in optional good offices, except those which tend to his improvement. In these various modes a person may suffer very severe penalties at the hands of others, for faults which directly concern only himself; but he suffers these penalties only in so far as they are the natural and, as it were, the spontaneous consequences of the faults themselves, not because they are purposely inflicted on him for the sake of punishment. A person who shows rashness, obstinacy, self-conceit—who cannot live within moderate means—who cannot restrain himself from hurtful indulgences—who pursues animal pleasures at the expense of those of feeling and intellect—must expect to be lowered in the opinion of others, and to have a less share of their favourable sentiments; but of this he has no right to complain, unless he has merited their favour by special excellence in his social relations, and has thus established a title to their good offices, which is not affected by his demerits towards himself.

What I contend for is, that the inconveniences which are strictly inseparable from the unfavourable judgment of others, are the only ones to which a person should ever be subjected for that portion of his conduct and character which concerns his own good, but which does not affect the interests of others in their relations with him. Acts injurious to others require a totally different treatment. Encroachment on their rights; infliction on them of any loss or damage not justified by his own rights; falsehood or duplicity in dealing with them; unfair or ungenerous use of advantages over them; even selfish abstinence from defending them against injury—these are fit objects of moral reprobation, and, in grave cases, of moral retribution and punishment. And not only these acts, but the dispositions which lead to them, are properly immoral, and fit subjects of disapprobation which may rise to abhorrence. Cruelty of disposition; malice and ill-nature; that most anti-social and odious of all passions, envy; dissimulation and insincerity; irascibility on insufficient cause, and resentment disproportioned to the provocation; the love of domineering over others; the desire to engross more than one's share of advantages (the *πλεονεξια* of the Greeks); the pride which derives gratification from the abasement of others; the egotism which thinks self and its concerns more important than everything else, and decides all doubtful questions in its own favour—these are moral vices, and constitute a bad and odious moral character: unlike the self-regarding faults previously mentioned which are not properly immoralities, and to whatever pitch they may be carried, do not constitute wickedness. They may be proofs of any amount of folly, or want of personal dignity and self-respect; but they are only a subject of moral reprobation when they involve a breach of duty to others, for whose sake the individual is bound to have care for himself. What are called duties to ourselves are not socially obligatory, unless circumstances render them at the same time duties to others. The term duty to oneself, when it means anything more than prudence, means self-respect or self-development; and for none of these is any one accountable to his fellow creatures, because for none of them is it for the good of mankind that he be held accountable to them. . . .

The distinction here pointed out between the part of a person's life which concerns only himself, and that which concerns others, many persons will refuse to admit. How (it may be asked) can any part of the conduct of a member of society be a matter of indifference to the other members? No person is an entirely isolated being; it is impossible for a person to do anything seriously or permanently hurtful to himself, without mischief reaching at least to his near connexions, and often far beyond them. If he injures his property, he does harm to those who directly or indirectly derived support from it, and usually diminishes, by a greater or less amount, the general resources of the community. If he deteriorates his bodily or mental faculties, he not only brings evil upon all who depended on him for any portion of their happiness, but disqualifies himself for rendering the services which he owes to his fellow creatures generally; perhaps becomes a burthen on their affection or benevolence; and if such conduct were very frequent, hardly any offence that is committed would detract more from the general sum of good. Finally, if by his vices or follies a person does no direct harm to others, he is nevertheless (it may be said) injurious by his example; and ought to be compelled to control himself, for the sake of those whom the sight or knowledge of his conduct might corrupt or mislead.

And even (it will be added) if the consequences of misconduct could be confined to the vicious or thoughtless individual, ought society to abandon to their own guidance those who are manifestly unfit for it? If protection against themselves is confessedly due to children and persons under age, is not society equally bound to afford it to persons of mature years who are equally incapable of self-government? If gambling, or drunkenness, or incontinence, or idleness, or uncleanliness, are as injurious to happiness, and as great a hindrance to improvement, as many or most of the acts prohibited by law, why (it may be asked) should not law, so far as is consistent with practicability and social convenience, endeavour to repress these also? And as a supplement to the unavoidable imperfections of law, ought not opinion at least to organize a powerful police against these vices, and visit rigidly with social penalties those who are known to practise them? There is no question here (it may be said) about restricting individuality, or impeding the trial of new and original experiments in living. The only things it is sought to prevent are things which have been tried and condemned from the beginning of the world until now; things which experience has shown not to be useful or suitable to any person's individuality. There must be some length of time and amount of experience, after which a moral or prudential truth may be regarded as established: and it is merely desired to prevent generation after generation from falling over the same precipice which has been fatal to their predecessors.

I fully admit that the mischief which a person does to himself, may seriously affect, both through their sympathies and their interests, those nearly connected with him, and in a minor degree, society at large. When, by conduct of this sort, a person is led to violate a distinct and assignable obligation to any other person or persons, the case is taken out of the self-regarding class, and becomes amenable to moral disapprobation in the proper sense of the term. If, for example, a man, through intemperance or extravagance, becomes unable to pay his debts, or, having undertaken the moral responsibility of a family, becomes from the same cause incapable of supporting or educating them, he is deservedly reprobated, and might be justly punished; but it is for the breach of duty to his family or creditors, not for the extravagance. If the resources which ought to have been devoted to them, had been diverted from them for the most prudent investment, the moral culpability would have been the same. George Barnwell murdered his uncle to get money for his mistress, but if he had done it to set himself up in business, he would equally have been hanged. Again, in the frequent case of a man who causes grief to his family by addiction to bad habits, he deserves reproach for his unkindness or ingratitude; but so he may for cultivating habits not in themselves vicious, if they are painful to those with whom he passes his life, or who from personal ties are dependent on him for their comfort. Whoever fails in the consideration generally due to the interests and feelings of others, not being compelled by some more imperative duty, or justified by allowable self-preference, is a subject of moral disapprobation for that failure, but not for the cause of it, nor for the errors, merely personal to himself, which may have remotely led to it. In like manner, when a person disables himself, by conduct purely self-regarding, from the performance of some definite duty incumbent on him to the public, he is guilty of a social offence. No person ought to be punished simply for being drunk; but a soldier or a policeman should be punished for being drunk on duty. Whenever, in short, there is a definite damage, or a definite risk of damage, either to an individual or to the public, the case is taken out of the province of liberty, and placed in that of morality or law.

But with regard to the merely contingent, or, as it may be called, constructive injury which a person causes to society, by conduct which neither violates any specific duty to the public, nor occasions perceptible hurt to any assignable individual except himself; the inconvenience is one which society can afford to bear, for the sake of the greater good of human freedom. If grown persons are to be punished for not taking proper care of themselves, I would rather it were for their own sake, than under pretence of preventing them from impairing their capacity of rendering to society benefits which society does not pretend it has a right to exact. But I cannot consent to argue the point as if society had no means of bringing its weaker members up to its ordinary standard of rational conduct, except waiting till they do something irrational, and then punishing them, legally or morally, for it. Society has had absolute power over them during all the early portion of their existence: it has had the whole period of childhood and nonage in which to try whether it could make them capable of rational conduct in life. The existing generation is master both of the training and the entire circumstances of the generation to come; it cannot indeed make them perfectly wise and good, because it is itself so lamentably deficient in goodness and wisdom; and its best efforts are not always, in individual cases, its most successful ones; but it is perfectly well able to make the rising generation, as a whole, as good as, and a little better than, itself. If society lets any considerable number of its members grow up mere children, incapable of being acted on by rational consideration of distant motives, society has itself to blame for the consequences. Armed not only with all the powers of education, but with the ascendancy which the authority of a received opinion always exercises over the minds who are least fitted to judge for themselves; and aided by the *natural* penalties which cannot be prevented from falling on those who incur the distaste or the contempt of those who know them; let not society pretend that it needs, besides all this, the power to issue commands and enforce obedience in the personal concerns of individuals, in which, on all principles of justice and policy, the decision ought to rest with those who are to abide the consequences. Nor is there anything which tends more to discredit and frustrate the better means of influencing conduct, than a resort to the worse. If there be among those whom it is attempted to coerce into prudence or temperance, any of the material of which vigorous and independent characters are made, they will infallibly rebel against the yoke. No such person will ever feel that others have a right to control him in his concerns, such as they have to prevent him from injuring them in theirs; and it easily comes to be considered a mark of spirit and courage to fly in the face of such usurped authority, and do with ostentation the exact opposite of what it enjoins; as in the fashion of grossness which succeeded, in the time of Charles II, to the fanatical moral intolerance of the Puritans. With respect to what is said of the necessity of protecting society from the bad example set to others by the vicious or the self-indulgent; it is true that bad example may have a pernicious effect, especially the example of doing wrong to others with impunity to the wrong-doer. But we are now speaking of conduct which, while it does no wrong to others, is supposed to do great harm to the agent himself; and I do not see how those who believe this, can think otherwise than that the example, on the whole, must be more salutary than hurtful, since, if it displays the misconduct, it displays also the painful or degrading consequences which, if the conduct is justly censured, must be supposed to be in all or most cases attendant on it.

But the strongest of all the arguments against the interference of the public with purely personal conduct, is that when it does interfere, the odds are that it interferes wrongly, and in the wrong place. On questions of social morality, of duty to others, the opinion of the public, that is, of an overruling majority, though often wrong, is likely to be still oftener right; because on such questions they are only required to judge of their own interests; of the manner in which some mode of conduct, if allowed to be practised, would affect themselves. But the opinion of a similar majority, imposed as a law on the minority, on questions of self-regarding conduct, is quite as likely to be wrong as right; for in these cases public opinion means, at the best, some people's opinion of what is good or bad for other people; while very often it does not even mean that; the public, with the most perfect indifference, passing over the pleasure or convenience of those whose conduct they censure, and considering only their own preference. There are many who consider as an injury to themselves any conduct which they have a distaste for, and resent it as an outrage to their feelings; as a religious bigot, when charged with disregarding the religious feelings of others, has been known to retort that they disregard his feelings, by persisting in their abominable worship or creed. But there is no parity between the feeling of a person for his own opinion, and the feeling of another who is offended at his holding it; no more than between the desire of a thief to take a purse, and the desire of the right owner to keep it. And a person's taste is as much his own peculiar concern as his opinion or his purse. It is easy for any one to imagine an ideal public, which leaves the freedom and choice of individuals in all uncertain matters undisturbed, and only requires them to abstain from modes of conduct which universal experience has condemned. But where has there been seen a public which set any such limit to its censorship? or when does the public trouble itself about universal experience? In its interferences with personal conduct it is seldom thinking of anything but the enormity of acting or feeling differently from itself; and this standard of judgment, thinly disguised, is held up to mankind as the dictate of religion and philosophy, by nine-tenths of all moralists and speculative writers. These teach that things are right because they are right; because we feel them to be so. They tell us to search in our own minds and hearts for laws of conduct binding on ourselves and on all others. What can the poor public do but apply these instructions, and make their own personal feelings of good and evil, if they are tolerably unanimous in them, obligatory on all the world?

Utilitarian Arguments Against Paternalism Are Not Successful

ROBERT PAUL WOLFF

IF WE take Mill at his word, we will interpret the principle of individuality purely as a theorem of utilitarianism, for in addition to his initial rejection of any but utilitarian arguments, Mill offers estimates of future happiness—or at

---

Reprinted from *The Poverty of Liberalism* by Robert Paul Wolff, 1968, pp. 20–21 and 25–31.

least of "well-being"—in defense of the right of each individual to live as he wishes so long as he does not infringe upon the lives of others. On the other hand, the utilitarian defense of individuality is, as we shall see, even less convincing than the corresponding defense of free speech, and in the *Principles of Political Economy*, Mill acknowledges a series of exceptions to the principle so broad as to destroy its force entirely. It would seem that here, as elsewhere, charity dictates that we ignore Mill's professions and read him as a libertarian in the tradition of Locke rather than Bentham.

Nevertheless, I propose to hold Mill to his word, and take seriously his attempts to ground the liberty of the individual in a calculation of utility. My purpose in adopting this apparently unfriendly course is not polemic; more than one great philosopher has developed an insight or proved a principle despite himself, so to speak, and there is no wisdom to be gained from treating a philosophical text as though it were a legal brief, making much of each slight error or misplaced comma. Rather, I want to show that when we attempt a strictly utilitarian defense of extreme libertarianism, we very soon must acknowledge the weighty empirical evidence which can be brought against it. And when we then ask what new doctrine in place of libertarianism is called forth by the evidence, we find—or so I shall argue—that the natural answer is quite simply Welfare State Liberalism. . . .

Mill's argument requires that he prove three distinct propositions. First, he must show that there is a legitimate and reasonably sharp line to be drawn between self-regarding or private actions, belonging to the so-called inner sphere, and other-regarding or public actions, belonging to the outer or social sphere. Then, he must show that the cultivation and encouragement of individuality is, taking all in all, more conducive to human happiness than any set of legal and social constraints by which men's choices might be guided and their lives shaped. And finally, he must offer some evidence in support of the extreme dictum that absolute freedom from social interference is the best way of strengthening the growth of individuality and thereby of producing "the greatest happiness for the greatest number." . . .

The second of the three steps in Mill's argument is the claim that individuality is a significant element—indeed, possibly the most significant element—in happiness or well-being. Mill himself is unclear about the precise nature of his claim. On some occasions, he seems to say that the free development of individual tastes and inclinations is a valuable *means* to the end of happiness. So he writes:

> As it is useful that while mankind are imperfect there should be different opinions, so is it that there should be different experiments of living; that free scope should be given to varieties of character, short of injury to others; and that the worth of different modes of life should be proved practically, when any one thinks fit to try them.

At other times, his language suggests that individual expression is *itself* a satisfying experience and hence one of the ends of life, not merely a means to some end. The truth, most probably, is that Mill personally valued individuality for itself, but felt it necessary to defend it to the world by a utilitarian argument. Certainly some persons at least derive pleasure from the mere experience of self-expression, just as most of us like now and again to make our own decisions even if we make them badly. Certainly, too, the consequences of unfettered individuality are on at least some occasions beneficial to human happiness. The matter reduces, therefore, to the *third* of Mill's claims: Is the encouragement of individuality, and with it the expansion of human happiness, best accomplished by an absolute prohibition against *all* social interference in the inner sphere of each person's life? Even assuming that we can draw a sharp line between inner and outer, will we maximize happiness by resolutely refusing to place constraints upon the most destructive actions, so long as they are *self*-destructive, and hence harmful only to the agent himself? Indeed, we may wonder whether the absence of all constraint is conducive to the development of individuality itself, or whether perhaps judicious social limitations upon individual action might not actually be a better way of nurturing a truly autonomous person.

Despite the importance of the principle of nonintervention and the unconditionality with which he formulates it, Mill offers very little in the way of support for it. Here is his principal argument:

> Neither one person, nor any number of persons, is warranted in saying to another human creature of ripe years, that he shall not do with his life for his own benefit what he chooses to do with it. He is the person most interested in his own well-being; the interest which any other person, except in cases of strong personal attachment, can have in it, is trifling, compared with that which he himself has; the interest which society has in him individually (except as to his conduct to others) is fractional, and altogether indirect; while, with respect to his own feelings and circumstances, the most ordinary man or woman has means of knowledge immeasurably surpassing those that can be possessed by any one else. The interference of society to overrule his judgment and purposes in what only regards himself, must be grounded on general presumptions; which may be altogether wrong, and even if right, are as likely as not to be misapplied to individual cases, by persons no better acquainted with the circumstances of such cases than those are who look at them merely from without. In this department, therefore, of human affairs, Individuality has its proper field of action.

In other words, everybody is the best judge of his own interests.

There are two ways of interpreting this claim, one of which makes it trivially true, the other of which makes it significant and, so far as the evidence is concerned, probably false. Looking at the question in one way, we might choose to interpret the notion of an "interest" behaviorally and dispositionally. That is, when we said that a man had a certain interest, we might *mean* that he characteristically pursued the interest, committed resources to it, made sacrifices for it, and generally evinced the behavior associated with it. On this interpretation, when we said that a man liked opera, or took an interest in it, we would *mean* that he attended opera performances, bought records of operatic music, read opera reviews, and so forth. If he merely *said* that he liked opera but did none of these things even when the opportunity presented itself, then we would conclude that he was misrepresenting his own interests. A man's failure to act in pursuit of some interest would be taken not as evidence that he did not know his own interests, but rather as evidence that he did not *have* that interest. So when the alcoholic went off the wagon, instead of saying that he lacked the will power to stick to his own best interest, we would say that his taking a drink showed that he really had a stronger interest in drinking whiskey than in staying sober. On the behavioral interpretation of interests, it is logically impossible for someone to choose against his interest, for his choice is *definitive* of his interest. So Mill's claim that each man is the *best* judge of his own interests would become the claim that each man is the *only* judge of his own interests. Since interest is defined in terms of choice, this is equivalent to the tautology that each man makes his own choices. A good deal of the plausibility of Mill's argument derives from our tendency to interpret it in this tautological way.

The alternative is to define interest in terms of happiness. To say that a man has an interest in remaining sober, for example, would be to say that he will derive more satisfaction or happiness from sobriety than from drunkenness. Thus interpreted, assertions of interest are empirical judgments which bear a contingent relation to the facts of choice. A man can perfectly well choose in a way which will fail to maximize his happiness or satisfy his desires. So the question becomes this: Taking into consideration all the evidence of past social experiments in constraint and freedom, and weighing as accurately as possible the probable consequences of alternative courses of social action, is the totality of happiness in our society likely to be greater if society interferes with the private lives and personal choices of its members, or if it keeps hands off and allows each man to live his own life as he sees fit?

So long as we confine ourselves to a case-by-case consideration of individuals, it seems plain that a bit of judicious meddling would considerably reduce the pain which imprudent persons inflict upon themselves; and of course, in the felicific calculus, a pain avoided is as good as a pleasure engendered. A drug addict who has successfully kicked the habit is thoroughly justified on utilitarian grounds in stopping some incautious young experimenter from taking the first steps down a road which may prove to have no turning. He knows, as the uninitiated cannot, how great are the painful consequences of true addiction in comparison to its undoubted pleasures. And if a friend, momentarily blinded by grief, thinks to take his own life, I may be better able to see that his future promises satisfactions which will in time outweigh the pain he is now suffering. Can I possibly be wrong, *on grounds of utility*, if I prevent him from destroying himself?

When acts as serious as suicide or drug addiction are under consideration, there is another sort of argument which is sometimes used to salvage the libertarian position. Individuals who commit such acts, it is said, cannot possibly be in full possession of their rational faculties. Hence they may be assigned to the same residual category as children, idiots, and madmen, and treated as wards of the society rather than as mature adults capable of self-determination. This argument has much in common with the familiar doctrine, now much in vogue, that antisocial acts are evidences of psychological derangement and should be treated medically rather than legally. A serious discussion of this argument would take us too far afield of our subject, but it is worth pointing out that once we allow societal interference with individual choice in all the really important areas of personal life, very little is left of the doctrine of the liberty of the inner life. Mill's position will count for nothing unless he is prepared to insist that a man has a right to make his own decisions at the risk of ruining himself or losing his life.

Mill's answer to this argument, of course, is that governments are not at all like thoughtful friends. Governments interfere with the lives of their subjects by means of laws backed by a monopoly of physical force. We cannot therefore settle the question of the limits of social constraint merely by reflecting on the actions of friends and relations. We must ask whether the evil consequences of establishing legal mechanisms of constraint and interference may not be worse, taking all in all, than the particular good which here and there results.

Whatever the truth about this murky matter, modern welfare liberals have again and again come down against Mill's claim that government interference causes more unhappiness than a strict policy of noninterference in the private sphere. Consider, for example, the problem posed by those persons too old or infirm to work. A good nineteenth-century liberal would argue, first, that each individual should be left to make his own arrangements for old-age pensions through voluntary private savings; second, that collective pension schemes should be privately organized and run; and third, that government action, if indeed it can be justified at all, should be limited to the establishment of a purely voluntary pension scheme which workers could join or not as they wish. Instead, of course, American liberals instituted social security, a forced-savings pension plan designed to protect individuals against the consequences of their own imprudence. Liberals judged, correctly no doubt, that those who needed a pension plan most would be just the ones not to join a voluntary plan and stick to it. The less money one has, the less likely one is to set a bit of it aside each week against the day, twenty or thirty or forty years hence, when one no longer earns a wage. A benevolent, interfering government took into its own hands a task which, on Mill's principles, should have been left to private individuals. The same decision has been made with regard to medical insurance and a host of other dangers which threaten the imprudent individual. Even in so private an area as the decision to smoke cancer-producing cigarettes, liberals today incline toward protective government legislation.

What distinguishes the modern liberal from Mill is the belief that greater happiness will flow from government intervention than from government abstention. The modern conservative, on the other hand, clings to the factual estimates made by Mill. That is why the *Principles of Political Economy* so often read like a Republican handout. It is indicative of the consensual stability of American politics that the two major strains of political thought agree in their fundamental principles and differ principally on a question of sheer fact.

The absence of ideological rancor is traceable to this phenomenon, as is the superficiality of most political debates in contemporary America.

Legal Paternalism and Human Rights

JOHN B. EXDELL

> The only freedom which deserves the name is that of pursuing our own good in our own way, so long as we do not attempt to deprive others of theirs, or impede their efforts to obtain it. Each is the proper guardian of his own health, whether bodily or mental and spiritual.

SO WROTE John Stuart Mill in Chapter 1 of *On Liberty.* As is well known Mill's arguments for this doctrine were essentially utilitarian. If government is allowed to use force paternalistically, it will in the long run, he thought, do more harm than good.

Mill rested his case on several empirical claims. He argued that generally individuals were the best judges of their own interests. Each of us is the person best qualified to shape his life to suit his own special tastes and dispositions. The prescriptions of government, on the other hand, are clumsy, inept, and insensitive to individual differences. More often than not they express a moral prejudice rather than a disinterested concern for human well-being. Furthermore, freedom to choose and to make mistakes develops our mental and emotional faculties, making us better fit to pursue our own happiness and to contribute to the progress of society as well.

Mill developed these points persuasively and at great length. Philosophers generally agree, however, that he failed to establish the position that government should never coerce people for their own good. Mill's arguments may very well justify a healthy suspicion of too much paternalistic legislation. Perhaps it is true that as a general rule a policy of noninterference will bring about the greater balance of good over evil. Rules, however, admit of exceptions. It is just not *always* true that individuals will be better off if left to themselves. People are sometimes not the best judges of their own interests. Far too often they are weak-willed and careless. Government interference, on the other hand, is not inevitably inept. Nor will the adoption of some paternalistic legislation necessarily incline us to become habitual, uninhibited meddlers in the private lives of other people.

Utilitarian opposition to paternalism must therefore be far more qualified and tentative than Mill supposed. If we are exclusively concerned with human well-being, some paternalistic legislation must seem rational. If we insist, however, that coercing people for their own good is never legitimate, then appeal to an altogether different kind of moral consideration is necessary. The alterna-

---

This article was written especially for this volume. We are grateful to Prof. Exdell for providing us with a discussion of nonutilitarian objections to paternalism.

tive philosophers have most often advanced contends that laws which protect people from the harmful effects of their own conduct violate fundamental human rights.

It is important to understand the difference between this appeal to rights and the position taken by Mill. Mill urged us to establish a rule the would restrict government's authority to use force. Our only reason for founding this rule, and following it, would be the expectation that its general effect will be highly beneficial. A rule of this nature would not be iron-clad. We would be ready to depart from it whenever we could confidently predict that an exception would do some good, without at the same time tempting people to begin breaking the rule frivolously. Our sole concern, from this standpoint, would be to shape and preserve a policy that all in all would work for the greatest good for the greatest number.

If paternalistic coercion violates human rights, on the other hand, our opposition to it must be far more strict. A concern for promoting human well-being can no longer be paramount. For it is part of the very idea of a right that it places certain moral constraints on the pursuit of legitimate political ends. Our interest in the greater good must then give way to a concern that we not *wrong individuals.*

I

Does paternalistic legislation violate the rights of individuals?

The belief that it does is commonly reflected in the resentment some people feel when they are burdened by paternalistic restrictions on their liberty. We sometimes hear people angrily complain, for example, that they shouldn't be compelled to wear motorcycle helmets, pay extra for a car equipped with seat belts, or save a portion of their salary for security in their old age. "Why shouldn't it be my choice?" they protest. "As long as I'm not bothering anyone else, what right does the government have to tell me that I can't take these risks?" Statements such as these do not call into question the utilitarian value of paternalistic coercion. Rather they convey the belief that force used for this purpose wrongs individuals. It is felt as a trespass upon someone's right to liberty.

However, the fact that some people have these feelings, or even that a great many have them, does not establish that people do have a right not to be coerced for their own good. Rights are not defined by popular feeling. If it were the case, for example, that all imprisoned felons deeply resented their confinement, this would not demonstrate that imprisonment violated their rights. People often resent being forced to make sacrifices, even when the demands made upon them are morally justified. An emotional reaction to an imposition, therefore, cannot determine its moral legitimacy.

In order to show that legal paternalism violates rights, more is required than a survey of prevailing sentiment. We need to establish that a compelling moral principle renders paternalistic coercion a serious moral wrong. How can this be done? By finding a principle (1) which clearly condemns the use of force for the purpose of protecting people from the harmful consequences of their own actions and (2) which stands behind recognized moral rights that are fundamental and beyond question. This would be accomplished if we could show that legal paternalism offends the same principle that is violated, for example, by the institution of slavery or by acts of theft or murder.

Is there, then, a compelling moral principle that can serve to justify the claim that paternalism necessarily violates human rights? Some philosophers have held that one may be found in the requirement that we show "respect for persons." We have a duty, they argue, to respect human beings as persons—that is, as rational agents who are capable of freely choosing their own values and purposes. It is this duty which explains, among other things, why individuals have a right not to be enslaved and why they may not be discriminated against because of their race or sex. The very same obligation forbids us, they contend, to use force against individuals to prevent them from harming themselves.

The idea that paternalism fails to show respect for people has a certain plausibility. Consider again the resentment commonly felt by people who are being treated paternalistically. We may very well hear them protest, "You're treating me like a child!" This expresses their feeling that their supervisor, however well-intended, is not showing them sufficient respect. They feel belittled and perhaps humiliated. If a teenage girl is forbidden by her parents to date older boys, she might be justified in accusing her parents of not showing her sufficient respect. In that case they lack confidence in her character, or in her judgment, or simply in her ability to resist certain kinds of social pressure. The rule is set down to protect her against these weaknesses. Similarly, a wealthy man who thinks his son is stupid or immature may specify in his will that his fortune be placed in trust until his son reaches the age of thirty-five. Here too paternalistic action fails to show respect for people in the sense that it expresses a lack of confidence in their judgment, character, or competence.

Now this manner of showing disrespect for people does seem to explain much of the resentment felt by those who feel put upon and offended by paternalistic restrictions on their liberty. But does it show that legal paternalism violates their right? A little reflection shows that it does not.

First, the principle invoked here—"show respect for persons"—would not condemn all forms of legal paternalism. For the use of the law to protect people from themselves does not always imply a lack of confidence in their character or competence. Laws requiring that motorcycle riders wear helmets, for instance, do not imply that they are generally careless or inept. The law rests only on the observation that people who ride motorcycles have accidents, often through no fault of their own, and that the chances of serious injury are diminished by wearing helmets.

Second, the principle—if it is taken to mean that we ought to show respect for their ability or judgment—is not a principle which stands behind recognized, fundamental moral rights. Sometimes, in certain circumstances holding a low opinion of someone does do him an injustice. If it happens that we are wrong about his abilities, we could say that he is not getting the credit he deserves. But this is hardly reason for saying that his rights have been violated. On the other hand, when rights are violated, it is not because someone has failed to show sufficient respect for another person's abilities. We may have the highest regard for someone and still make him our slave. We may murder a person, even though we admire his talents and capacities. Thus, even if legal paternalism did always show a lack of respect for people's competence and character, and even if this disrespect were always unjustified, this would not be grounds for saying that people's rights were being violated—though it would properly be the cause of much resentment.

II

It seems that if paternalistic force violates rights because it shows disrespect for persons, then "respecting persons" cannot mean having confidence in their capacity to manage their affairs. In fact, philosophers who have relied upon this notion have had something quite different in mind. Persons are to be respected, they have held, not for their abilities or virtues, but because they are, in their very nature, beings able to choose their own values and purposes, and to govern their lives according to rational principles of morality. As such they all deserve a certain respect. We may not treat them as mere objects, as things which may be used to fulfill our own ends and desires. As Kant put it, "one man ought never to be dealt with merely as a means subservient to the purposes of another . . ."[1]

The duty to respect persons may be understood here as the injunction not to use people merely as a means. Perhaps the clearest violation of this principle occurs under the institution of slavery. If slavery is wrong, it is not because slaves are always tormented by their masters. Slaves were often treated quite well. Indeed some enjoyed a fair measure of security and comfort. Nevertheless, as slaves, they were victims of injustice. For even a well-treated slave is forced to serve his master. He is not free to act for his own ends. As an article of property, he is an instrument which his owner may put to use for his own purposes. The same principle explains why men have the right to the fruits of their labor. If someone steals the vegetables you have grown in your garden, he has acted on the maxim that your labor may be used, without your consent, to serve his ends. He has, in effect, treated you like a slave.

So understood, therefore, "respect for persons" does identify a principle that stands behind recognized and fundamental moral rights. Men are to be respected as beings who are free to pursue their own ends. As long as their actions affect only themselves, we may not force them to serve the purposes of other people.

Thus when the general intent and effect of legislation is not to give protection to those it compels, but to force some people to serve the interests of others,

[1] *The Philosophy of Law*, Part II, translated by W. Hastie, (Edinburgh: T. T. Clark, 1887), p. 194.

then the principle of respect for persons is violated. Laws prohibiting the sale and possession of heroin may very well fall into this category. Many support these laws because they are hostile to the life-style associated with heroin use which they deem to be too self-centered and insufficiently energetic. Now if in fact the main purpose served by heroin prohibition is to discourage people from such an unproductive manner of living, then the law is not designed to serve their interests at all. It shapes human lives according to someone's model of good citizenship by compelling people to maintain themselves as contributors to the social and economic life of their society. Here we may properly say that some people are being used by others merely as a means.

Suppose, however, that by coercing people we genuinely serve *their* interests and not the interests of others. Can we then fairly be charged with treating persons "merely as a means subservient to the purposes of another?" Have we not acted rather so that those coerced are better able to realize their own ends and aspirations?

We clearly do not treat someone as a means if, for example, we forcibly drag him from a damaged elevator that is about to plunge him ten stories to his death. Similarly, laws that require a license to engage in certain dangerous professions would not seem to render us mere tools for realizing the aims and interests of others. On the contrary, in that they protect us from the harmful effects of our own ignorance, they help us secure what we ourselves value dearly, our own health and well-being. It seems far-fetched to compare coercion of this kind with the force exerted on a slave by his master, where the evil lies in the fact that one individual is made to sacrifice his own interest for the benefit of another.

Doubts about this may arise, however, if we consider cases in which the law forbids people from taking risks which they really want to take. For example, some motorcycle riders would rather not have to wear helmets as the law requires. Hell's Angels and other motorcycle gangs regard this law as a serious disruption of their chosen style of life. These are people who are devoted to fearlessness, or at least to giving the appearance of it. Living dangerously is their creed. And a motorcycle gang cannot live dangerously enough, or appear to be truly fearless, if it wears helmets. The law, therefore, does not really serve the interests of these people. Given the nature of their commitments, it does them more harm than good.

Now motorcycle gangs and others who share this outlook are no doubt greatly outnumbered by people who are truly benefited by the law. The great majority of motorcyclists are simply prevented from taking foolish and unnecessary risks. But if we enforce the law against everyone, are we not sacrificing the interests of some for the benefit of others? And if so, are we not then violating the principle of respect for persons? The issue is important because probably all paternalistic legislation will affect some people adversely. If the Hell's Angels case counts as a violation of rights, then I think we should have to entertain the general presumption that paternalistic legislation is morally illegitimate.

However, I do not think we are driven to this conclusion. It is true that the helmet law disadvantages some people while benefiting others. But this is strictly coincidence. That is, the benefits enjoyed by some are not brought about *by way of* doing harm to others. Only if the sacrifice imposed on the minority were the *source* of these benefits could we say that people were being used "as a means." This is exactly what occurs when people are enslaved, robbed, or forced to be productive citizens. Some are made to serve the interests of others. The helmet law, and most other paternalistic legislation, does not require this of anyone.

III

In summary: The principle of respect for persons enjoins us not to treat people as mere means subordinate to the ends of others. It serves to explain why it is morally wrong to enslave people and to steal the fruits of their labor. But the duty to respect persons is not disregarded by laws which coerce people for their own good. As long as laws, in their general effect, truly serve the interests of others, then no such wrong is done. Paternalism does sometimes show a lack of respect for people's ability to manage their affairs. But even when this lack of confidence is unjustified, and produces understandable resentment, it cannot be said to violate anyone's rights. The view that legal paternalism violates rights is therefore not established by appeal to our duty to respect persons. Perhaps the claim that paternalism violates rights can be supported by some other principle. But if not, arguments for and against paternalistic legislation should appeal to utilitarian considerations. No general rejection of legal paternalism would then be warranted.

Criteria for Evaluating Paternalistic Proposals

JOEL FEINBERG

THE PRINCIPLE of legal paternalism justifies state coercion to protect individuals from self-inflicted harm, or in its extreme version, to guide them, whether they like it or not, toward their own good. Parents can be expected to justify their interference in the lives of their children (e.g. telling them what they must eat and when they must sleep) on the ground that "daddy knows best." Legal paternalism seems to imply that since the state often can know the interests of individual citizens better than the citizens know them themselves, it stands as a permanent guardian of those interests *in loco parentis.* Put in this blunt way, paternalism seems a preposterous doctrine. If adults are treated as children they will come in time to be like children. Deprived of the right to choose for themselves, they will soon lose the power of rational judg-

"Legal Paternalism" by Joel Feinberg. This material is here reprinted from Vol. 1, no. 1 of the *Canadian Journal of Philosophy*, by permission of the Canadian Association for Publishing in Philosophy.

ment and decision. Even children, after a certain point, had better not be "treated as children," else they will never acquire the outlook and capability of responsible adults.

Yet if we reject paternalism entirely, and deny that a person's own good is *ever* a valid ground for coercing him, we seem to fly in the face both of common sense and our long established customs and laws. In the criminal law, for example, a prospective victim's freely granted consent is no defense to the charge of mayhem or homicide. The state simply refuses to permit anyone to agree to his own disablement or killing. The law of contracts, similarly, refuses to recognize as valid, contracts to sell oneself into slavery, or to become a mistress, or a second wife. Any ordinary citizen is legally justified in using reasonable force to prevent another from mutilating himself or committing suicide. No one is allowed to purchase certain drugs even for therapeutic purposes without a physician's prescription (Doctor knows best). The use of other drugs, such as heroin, for pleasure merely, is permitted under no circumstances whatever. It is hard to find any plausible rationale for all such restrictions apart from the argument that beatings, mutilations, and death, concubinage, slavery, and bigamy are always bad for a person whether he or she knows it or not, and that antibiotics are too dangerous for any non-expert, and heroin for anyone at all, to take on his own initiative.

The trick is stopping short once we undertake this path, unless we wish to ban whiskey, cigarettes, and fried foods, which tend to be bad for people too, whether they know it or not. The problem is to reconcile somehow our general repugnance for paternalism with the apparent necessity, or at least reasonableness, of some paternalistic regulations. My method of dealing with this problem will not be particularly ideological. Rather, I shall try to organize our elementary intuitions by finding a principle that will render them consistent. Let us begin, then, by rejecting the views both that the protection of a person from himself is *always* a valid ground for interference in his affairs, and that it is *never* a valid ground. It follows that it is a valid ground only under certain conditions, and we must now try to state those conditions.[1]

I

It will be useful to make some preliminary distinctions. The first distinction is between harms or likely harms that are produced directly by a person upon himself and those produced by the actions of another person to which the first

[1] The discussion that follows has two important unstated and undefended presuppositions. The first is that in some societies, at least, and at some times, a line can be drawn (as Mill claimed it could in Victorian England) between other-regarding behavior and behaviour that is primarily and directly self-regarding and only indirectly and remotely, therefore trivially, other-regarding. If this assumption is false, there is no interesting problem concerning legal paternalism since all "paternalistic" restrictions, in that case, could be defended as necessary to protect persons other than those restricted, and hence would not be (wholly) paternalistic. The second presupposition is that the spontaneous repugnance toward parternalism (which I assume the reader shares with me) is well-grounded and supportable.

party has consented. Committing suicide would be an example of self-inflicted harm; arranging for a person to put one out of one's misery would be an example of a "harm" inflicted by the action of another to which one has consented. There is a venerable legal maxim traceable to the Roman Law that "*Volenti non fit inuria*," sometimes translated, misleadingly, as: "To one who consents no harm is done." Now, I suppose that the notion of consent applies, strictly speaking, only to the actions of another person that affect oneself. If so, then, consent to one's *own* actions is a kind of metaphor. Indeed, to say that I consented to my own actions, seems just a colorful way to saying that I acted voluntarily. My involuntary actions, after all, are, from the moral point of view, no different from the actions of someone else to which I have not had an opportunity to consent. In any case, it seems plainly false to say that a person cannot be *harmed* by actions, whether his own or those of another, to which he has consented. People who quite voluntarily eat an amount that is in fact too much cause themselves to suffer from indigestion; and girls who consent to advances sometimes become pregnant.

One way of interpreting the *Volenti* maxim is to take it as a kind of presumptive principle. A person does not generally consent to what he believes will be, on balance, harmful to himself, and by and large, an individual is in a better position to appraise risks to himself than are outsiders. Given these data, and considerations of convenience in the administration of the law, the *Volenti* maxim might be understood to say that for the purposes of the law (whatever the actual facts might be) nothing is to count as harm to a given person that he has freely consented to. If this presumption is held to be conclusive, then the *Volenti* maxim becomes a kind of "legal fiction" when applied to cases of undeniable harm resulting from behavior to which the harmed one freely consented. A much more likely interpretation, however, takes the *Volenti* maxim to say nothing at all, literal or fictional, about *harms*. Rather, it is about what used to be called "injuries," that is, injustices or wrongs. To one who freely consents to a thing no *wrong* is done, no matter how harmful to him the consequences may be. "He cannot waive his right," says Salmond, "and then complain of its infringement."[2] If the *Volenti* maxim is simply an expression of Salmond's insight, it is not a presumptive or fictional principle about harms, but rather an absolute principle about wrongs.

The *Volenti* maxim (or something very like it) plays a key role in the argument for John Stuart Mill's doctrine about liberty. Characteristically, Mill seems to employ the maxim in both of its interpretations, as it suits his purposes, without noticing the distinction between them. On the one hand, Mill's argument purports to be an elaborate application of the calculus of harms and benefits to the problem of political liberty. The state can rightly restrain a man to prevent harm to others. Why then can it not restrain a man to prevent him from harming himself? After all, a harm is a harm whatever its cause, and if our sole concern is to minimize harms all round, why should we distinguish be-

2 See Glanville Williams (ed.), *Salmond on Jurisprudence*, Eleventh Edition (London: Sweet & Maxwell, 1957), p. 531.

tween origins of harm? One way Mill answers this question is to employ the *Volenti* maxim in its first interpretation. For the purposes of his argument, he will presume conclusively that "to one who consents no *harm* is done." Self-inflicted or consented-to harm simply is not to count as harm at all; and the reasons for this are that the coercion required to prevent such harm is itself a harm of such gravity that it is likely in the overwhelming proportion of cases to outweigh any good it can produce for the one coerced; and moreover, individuals themselves, in the overwhelming proportion of cases, can know their own true interests better than any outsiders can, so that outside coercion is almost certain to be self-defeating.

But as Gerald Dworkin has pointed out,[3] arguments of this merely statistical kind at best create a strong but rebuttable presumption against coercion of a man in his own interest. Yet Mill purports to be arguing for an absolute prohibition. Absolute prohibitions are hard to defend on purely utilitarian grounds, so Mill, when his confidence wanes, tends to move to the second interpretation of the *Volenti* maxim. To what a man consents he may be harmed, but he cannot be wronged; and Mill's "harm principle," reinterpreted accordingly, is designed to protect him and others only from wrongful invasions of their interest. Moreover, when the state intervenes on any other ground, its *own* intervention is a wrongful invasion. What justifies the absolute prohibition of interference in primarily self-regarding affairs is *not* that such interference is self-defeating and likely (merely likely) to cause more harm than it prevents, but rather that it would itself be an injustice, a wrong, a violation of the private sanctuary which is every person's self; and this is so whatever the calculus of harms and benefits might show.[4]

The second distinction is between those cases where a person directly produces harm to himself, where the harm is the certain upshot of his conduct and its desired end, on the one hand, and those cases where a person simply creates a *risk* of harm to himself in the course of activities directed toward other ends.

[3] See his excellent article, "Paternalism" in *Morality and the Law*, ed. by R. A. Wasserstrom (Belmont, Calif.: Wadsworth Publishing Co., 1971).

[4] Mill's rhetoric often supports this second interpretation of his arguments. He is especially fond of such political metaphors as independence, legitimate rule, dominion, and sovereignty. The state must respect the status of the individual as an independent entity whose "*sovereignty* over himself" (in Mill's phrase), like Britain's over its territory, is absolute. In self-regarding affairs, a person's individuality ought to "*reign* uncontrolled from the outside" (another phrase of Mill's). Interference in those affairs, whether successful or self-defeating, is a violation of *legitimate boundaries*, like trespass in law, or aggression between states. Even self-mutilation and suicide are permissible if the individual truly chooses them, and other interests are not directly affected. The individual person has an absolute right to choose for himself, to be wrong, to go to hell on his own, and it is nobody else's proper *business* or *office* to interfere. The individual *owns* (not merely possesses) his life, he has *title* to it. He alone is arbiter of his own life and death. See how legalistic and un-utilitarian these terms are. The great wonder is that Mill could claim to have foregone any benefit in argument from the notion of an abstract right. Mill's intentions aside, however, I can not conceal my own preference for this second interpretation of his argument.

The man who knowingly swallows a lethal dose of arsenic will certainly die, and death must be imputed to him as his goal in acting. Another man is offended by the sight of his left hand, so he grasps an ax in his right hand and chops his left hand off. He does not thereby "endanger" his interest in the physical integrity of his limbs or "risk" the loss of his hand. He brings about the loss directly and deliberately. On the other hand, to smoke cigarettes or to drive at excessive speeds is not directly to harm oneself, but rather to increase beyond a normal level the probability that harm to oneself will result.

The third distinction is that between reasonable and unreasonable risks. There is no form of activity (or inactivity either for that matter) that does not involve some risks. On some occasions we have a choice between more and less risky actions and prudence dictates that we take the less dangerous course; but what is called "prudence" is not always reasonable. Sometimes it is more reasonable to assume a great risk for a great gain than to play it safe and forefeit a unique opportunity. Thus it is not necessarily more reasonable for a coronary patient to increase his life expectancy by living a life of quiet inactivity than to continue working hard at his career in the hope of achieving something important even at the risk of a sudden fatal heart attack at any moment. There is no simple mathematical formula to guide one in making such decisions or for judging them "reasonable" or "unreasonable." On the other hand, there are other decisions that are manifestly unreasonable. It is unreasonable to drive at sixty miles an hour through a twenty mile an hour zone in order to arrive at a party on time, but it may be reasonable to drive fifty miles an hour to get a pregnant wife to the maternity ward. It is foolish to resist an armed robber in an effort to protect one's wallet, but it may be worth a desperate lunge to protect one's very life, or the life of a loved one.

In all of these cases a number of distinct considerations are involved.[5] If there is time to deliberate one should consider: (1) the degree of probability that harm to oneself will result from a given course of action, (2) the seriousness of the harm being risked, i.e. "the value or importance of that which is exposed to the risk," (3) the degree of probability that the goal inclining one to shoulder the risk will in fact result from the course of action, (4) the value or importance of achieving that goal, that is, just how worthwhile it is to one (this is the intimately personal factor, requiring a decision about one's own preferences, that makes the reasonableness of a risk-assessment on the whole so difficult for the *outsider* to make), and (5) the necessity of the risk, that is, the availability or absence of alternative, less risky, means to the desired goal. Certain judgments about the reasonableness of risk-assumptions are quite uncontroversial. We can say, for example, that the greater are considerations (1)—the probability of harm to self, and (2)—the magnitude of the harm risked, the *less* reasonable the risk; and the greater considerations (3)—the probability the desired goal will result, (4)—the importance of that goal to the actor, and (5)—the neces-

[5] The distinctions in this paragraph are borrowed from: Henry T. Terry, "Negligence," *Harvard Law Review*, Vol. 29 (1915).

sity of the means, the *more* reasonable the risk. But in a given difficult case, even where questions of "probability" are meaningful and beyond dispute, and where all the relevant facts are known, the risk-decision may defy objective assessment because of its component personal value judgments. In any case, if the state is to be given the right to prevent a person from risking harm to himself (and only himself) this must not be on the ground that the prohibited action is risky, or even that it is extremely risky, but rather on the ground that the risk is extreme and, in respect to its objectively assessable components, manifestly *unreasonable.* There are very good reasons, sometimes, for regarding even a person's judgment of personal worthwhileness (consideration 4) to be "manifestly unreasonable," but it remains to be seen whether (or when) that kind of unreasonableness can be sufficient grounds for interference.

The fourth and final distinction is between fully voluntary and not fully voluntary assumptions of a risk. One assumes a risk in a fully voluntary way when one shoulders it while fully informed of all relevant facts and contingencies, with one's eyes wide open, so to speak, and in the absence of all coercive pressure of compulsion. There must be calmness and deliberateness, no distracting or unsettling emotions, no neurotic compulsion, no misunderstanding. To whatever extent there is compulsion, misinformation, excitement or impetuousness, clouded judgment (as e.g. from alcohol), or immature or defective faculties of reasoning, to that extent the choice falls short of perfect voluntariness. Voluntariness then is a matter of degree. One's "choice" is *completely involuntary* either when it is no choice at all, properly speaking—when one lacks all muscular control of one's movements, or when one is knocked down, or pushed, or sent reeling by a blow, or a wind, or an explosion—or when through ignorance one chooses something other than what one means to choose, as when one thinks the arsenic powder is table salt, and thus chooses to sprinkle it on one's scrambled eggs. Most harmful choices, as most choices generally, fall somewhere in between the extremes of perfect voluntariness and complete involuntariness.

Now, the terms "voluntary" and "involuntary" have a variety of disparate but overlapping uses in philosophy, law, and ordinary life, and some of them are not altogether clear. I should point out here that my usage does not correspond with that of Aristotle, who allowed that infants, animals, drunkards, and men in a towering rage might yet act voluntarily if only they are undeceived and not overwhelmed by external physical force. What I call a voluntary assumption of risk corresponds more closely to what Aristotle called "deliberate choice." Impulsive and emotional actions, and those of animals and infants are voluntary in Aristotle's sense, but they are not *chosen.* Chosen actions are those that are decided upon by *deliberation*, and that is a process that requires time, information, a clear head, and highly developed rational faculties. When I use such phrases then as "voluntary act," "free and genuine consent," and so on, I refer to acts that are more than "voluntary" in the Aristotelian sense, acts that Aristotle himself would call "deliberately chosen." Such acts not only have their origin "in the agent," they also represent him faithfully in some important way: they express his settled values and preferences. In the fullest sense, therefore, they are actions for which he can take responsibility.

II

The central thesis of John Stuart Mill and other individualists about paternalism is that the fully voluntary choice or consent of a mature and rational human being concerning matters that affect only his own interests is such a precious thing that no one else (and certainly not the state) has a right to interfere with it simply for the person's "own good." No doubt this thesis was also meant to apply to almost-but-not-quite fully voluntary choices as well, and probably also even to some substantially non-voluntary ones (e.g. a neurotic person's choice of a wife who will satisfy his neurotic needs but only at the price of great unhappiness, eventual divorce, and exacerbated guilt); but it is not probable that the individualist thesis was meant to apply to choices near the bottom of the scale of voluntariness, and Mill himself left no doubt that he did *not* intend it to apply to completely involuntary "choices." Nor should we *expect* anti-paternalistic individualism to deny protection to a person from his own nonvoluntary choices, for insofar as the choices are not voluntary they are just as alien to him as the choices of someone else.

Thus Mill would permit the state to protect a man from his own ignorance at least in circumstances that create a strong presumption that his uninformed or misinformed choice would not correspond to his eventual one.

> If either a public officer or anyone else saw a person attempting to cross a bridge which had been ascertained to be unsafe, and there were no time to warn him of his danger, they might seize him and turn him back, without any real infringement of his liberty; for liberty consists in doing what one desires, and he does not desire to fall into the river.[6]

Of course, for all the public officer may know, the man on the bridge does desire to fall into the river, or to take the risk of falling for other purposes. If the person is then fully warned of the danger and wishes to proceed anyway, then, Mill argues, that is his business alone; but because most people do *not* wish to run such risks, there was a solid presumption, in advance of checking, that this person did not wish to run the risk either. Hence the officer was justified, Mill would argue, in his original interference.

On other occasions a person may need to be protected not from his ignorance but from some other condition that may render his informed choice substantially less than voluntary. He may be "a child, or delirious, or in some state of excitement or absorption incompatible with the full use of the reflecting faculty."[7] Mill would not permit any such person to cross an objectively unsafe bridge. On the other hand, there is no reason why a child, or an excited person, or a drunkard, or a mentally ill person should not be allowed to proceed on his way

[6] J. S. Mill, *On Liberty* (New York: Liberal Arts Press, 1956), p. 117.

[7] *Op. cit.*

home across a perfectly safe thoroughfare. Even substantially nonvoluntary choices deserve protection unless there is good reason to judge them dangerous.

Now it may be the case, for all we can know, that the behaviour of a drunk or an emotionally upset person would be exactly the same even if he were sober and calm; but when the behaviour seems patently self-damaging and is of a sort that most calm and normal persons would not engage in, then there are strong grounds, if only a statistical sort, for inferring the opposite; and these grounds, on Mill's principle, would justify interference. It may be that there is no kind of action of which it can be said "No mentally competent adult in a calm, attentive mood, fully informed, etc. would *ever* choose (or consent to) *that.*" Nevertheless, there are actions of a kind that create a powerful *presumption* that any given actor, if he were in his right mind, would not choose them. The point of calling this hypothesis a "presumption" is to require that it be completely overridden before legal permission be given to a person, who has already been interfered with, to go on as before. So, for example, if a policeman (or anyone else) sees John Doe about to chop off his hand with an ax, he is perfectly justified in using force to prevent him, because of the presumption that no one could voluntarily choose to do such a thing. The presumption, however, should always be taken as rebuttable in principle; and now it will be up to Doe to prove before an official tribunal that he is calm, competent, and free, and that he still wishes to chop off his hand. Perhaps this is too great a burden to expect Doe himself to "prove," but the tribunal should require that the presumption against voluntariness be overturned by evidence from some source or other. The existence of the presumption should require that an objective determination be made, whether by the usual adversary procedures of law courts, or simply by a collective investigation by the tribunal into the available facts. The greater the presumption to be overridden, the more elaborate and fastidious should be the legal paraphernalia required, and the stricter the standards of evidence. (The law of wills might prove a model for this.) The point of the procedure would not be to evaluate the wisdom or worthiness of a person's choice, but rather to determine whether the choice really is his.

This seems to lead us to a form of paternalism that is so weak and innocuous that it could be accepted even by Mill, namely, that the state has the right to prevent self-regarding harmful conduct only when it is substantially nonvoluntary or when temporary intervention is necessary to establish whether it is voluntary or not. When there is a strong presumption that no normal person would voluntarily choose or consent to the kind of conduct in question, that should be a proper ground for detaining the person until the voluntary character of his choice can be established. We can use the phrase "the standard of voluntariness" as a label for the considerations that mediate the application of the principle that a person may properly be protected from his own folly. (Still another ground for forcible delay and inquiry that is perfectly compatible with Mill's individualism is the possibility that important third party interests might be involved. Perhaps a man's wife and family should have some say before he is permitted to commit suicide—or even to chop off his hand.)

III

Working out the details of the voluntariness standard is far too difficult to undertake here, but some of the complexities, at least, can be illustrated by a consideration of some typical hard cases. Consider first of all the problem of harmful drugs. Suppose Richard Roe requests a prescription of drug *X* from Dr. Doe, and the following discussion ensues:

Dr. Doe: I cannot prescribe drug *X* to you because it will do you physical harm.
Mr. Roe: But you are mistaken. It will not cause me physical harm.

In a case like this, the state, of course, backs the doctor. The state deems medical questions to be technical matters subject to expert opinions. This entails that a non-expert layman is not the best judge of his own medical interests. If a layman disagrees with a physician on a question of medical fact the layman can be presumed wrong, and if nevertheless he chooses to act on his factually mistaken belief, his action will be substantially less than fully voluntary in the sense explained above. That is to say that the action of *ingesting a substance which will in fact harm him* is not the action he voluntarily chooses to do. Hence the state intervenes to protect him not from his own free and voluntary choices, but from his own ignorance.

Suppose however that the exchange goes as follows:

Dr. Doe: I cannot prescribe drug *X* to you because it will do you physical harm.
Mr. Roe: Exactly. That's just what I want. I want to harm myself.

In this case Roe *is* properly apprised of the facts. He suffers from no delusions or misconceptions. Yet his choice is so odd that there exists a reasonable presumption that he has been deprived somehow of the "full use of his reflecting faculty." It is because we know that the overwhelming majority of choices to inflict injury for its own sake on oneself are not fully voluntary that we are entitled to presume that the present choice too is not fully voluntary. If no further evidence of derangement, or illness, or severe depression, or unsettling excitation can be discovered, however, and the patient can convince an objective panel that his choice is voluntary (unlikely event!) and further if there are no third party interests, for example those of wife or family, that require protection, then our "voluntariness standard" would permit nc further state constraint.

Now consider the third possibility:

Dr. Doe: I cannot prescribe drug *X* to you because it is very likely to do you physical harm.
Mr. Roe: I don't care if it causes me physical harm. I'll get a lot of pleasure first, so much pleasure in fact, that it is well worth running the risk of physical harm. If I must pay a price for my pleasure I am willing to do so.

This is perhaps the most troublesome case. Roe's choice is not patently irrational on its face. He may have a well thought-out philosophical hedonism as one of his profoundest convictions. He may have made a fundamental decision of principle committing himself to the intensely pleasurable, even if brief life. If no third party interests are directly involved, the state can hardly be permitted to declare his philosophical convictions unsound or "sick" and prevent him from practicing them, without assuming powers that it will inevitably misuse disastrously.

On the other hand, this case may be very little different from the preceding one, depending of course on what the exact facts are. If the drug is known to give only an hour's mild euphoria and then cause an immediate violently painful death, then the risks incurred appear so unreasonable as to create a powerful presumption of nonvoluntariness. The desire to commit suicide must always be presumed to be both nonvoluntary and harmful to others until shown otherwise. (Of course in some cases it *can* be shown otherwise.) On the other hand, drug *X* may be harmful in the way nicotine is now known to be harmful; twenty or thirty years of heavy use may create a grave risk of lung cancer or heart disease. Using the drug for pleasure merely, when the risks are of this kind, may be to run unreasonable risks, but that is no strong evidence of nonvoluntariness. Many perfectly normal, rational persons voluntarily choose to run precisely these risks for whatever pleasures they find in smoking.[8] The way for the state to assure itself that such practices are truly voluntary is continually to confront smokers with the ugly medical facts so that there is no escaping the knowledge of what the medical risks to health exactly are. Constant reminders of the hazards should be at every hand and with no softening of the gory details. The state might even be justified in using its taxing, regulatory, and persuasive powers to make smoking (and similar drug usage) more difficult or less attractive; but to prohibit it outright for everyone would be to tell the voluntary risk-taker that even his informed judgments of what is worthwhile are less reasonable than those of the state, and that therefore, he may not act on them. This is paternalism of the strong kind, unmediated by the voluntariness standard. As a principle of public policy, it has an acrid moral flavour, and creates serious risks of governmental tyranny.

IV

Another class of hard cases are those involving contracts in which one party agrees to restrict his own liberty in some respect. The most extreme case is that in which one party freely sells himself into slavery to another, perhaps in exchange for some benefit that is to be consumed before the period of slavery begins, perhaps for some reward to be bestowed upon some third party. Our point of departure will be Mill's classic treatment of the subject:

> In this and most other civilized countries . . . an engagement by which a person should sell himself, or allow himself to be sold, as a slave would be null and void, neither enforced by law nor by opinion. The ground for *thus limiting his*

[8] Perfectly rational men can have "unreasonable desires" as judged by other perfectly rational men, just as perfectly rational men (e.g. great philosophers) can hold "unreasonable beliefs" or doctrines as judged by other perfectly rational men. Particular unreasonableness, then, can hardly be strong evidence of general irrationality.

> *power of voluntarily disposing of his own lot in life* is apparent, and is very clearly seen in this extreme case. The reason for not interfering, unless for the sake of others, with a person's voluntary acts is consideration for his liberty. His voluntary choice is evidence that what he so chooses is desirable, or at least endurable to him, and his good is on the whole best provided for by allowing him to take his own means of pursuing it. But by selling himself for a slave, he abdicates his liberty; he foregoes any future use of it beyond that single act. He therefore defeats, in his own case, the very purpose which is the justification of allowing him to dispose of himself. He is no longer free, but is thenceforth in a position which has no longer the presumption in its favour that would be afforded by his voluntarily remaining in it. The principle of freedom cannot require that he should be free not to be free.[9] [my italics]

It seems plain to me that Mill, in this one extreme case, has been driven to embrace the principle of paternalism. The "harm-to-others principle," as mediated by the *Volenti* maxim[10] would permit a competent, fully informed adult, who is capable of rational reflection and free of undue pressure, to be himself the judge of his own interests, no matter how queer or perverse his judgment may seem to others. There is, of course, always the presumption, and a very strong one indeed, that a person who elects to "sell" himself into slavery is either incompetent, unfree, or misinformed. Hence the state should require very strong evidence of voluntariness—elaborate tests, swearings, psychiatric testifying, waiting periods, public witnessing, and the like—before validating such contracts. Similar forms of official "making sure" are involved in marriages and wills, and slavery is even more serious a thing, not to be rashly undertaken. Undoubtedly, very few slavery contracts would survive such procedures, perhaps even none at all. It may be literally true that "no one in his right mind would sell himself into slavery," but if this is a truth it is not an *a priori* one but rather one that must be tested anew in each case by the application of independent, non-circular criteria of mental illness.

The supposition is at least intelligible, therefore, that every now and then a normal person in full possession of his faculties would voluntarily consent to permanent slavery. We can imagine any number of intelligible (if not attractive) motives for doing such a thing. A person might agree to become a slave in exchange for a million dollars to be delivered in advance to a loved one or to a worthy cause, or out of a religious conviction requiring a life of humility or penitence, or in payment for the prior enjoyment of some supreme benefit, as in the *Faust* legend. Mill, in the passage quoted above, would disallow such a contract no matter how certain it is that the agreement is fully voluntary, apparently on the ground that the permanent and irrevocable loss of freedom is such a great evil, and slavery so harmful a condition, that no one ought ever to be allowed to choose it, even voluntarily. Any person who thinks that he can be a gainer,

[9] Mill, *op. cit.*, p. 125.

[10] That is, the principle that prevention of harm to others is the sole ground for legal coercion, *and* that what is freely consented to is not to count as harm. These are Mill's primary normative principles in *On Liberty.*

in the end, from such an agreement, Mill implies, is simply wrong whatever his reasons, and can be known *a priori* to be wrong. Mill's earlier argument, if I understand it correctly, implies that a man should be permitted to mutilate his body, take harmful drugs, or commit suicide, provided only that his decision to do these things is voluntary and no other person will be directly and seriously harmed. But voluntarily acceding to slavery is too much for Mill to stomach. Here is an evil of another order, he seems to say; so the "harm to others" principle and the *Volenti* maxim come to their limiting point here, and paternalism in the strong sense (unmediated by the voluntariness test) must be invoked, if only for this one kind of case.

There are, of course, other ways of justifying the refusal to enforce slavery contracts. Some of these are derived from principles not acknowledged in Mill's moral philosophy but which at least have the merit of being non-paternalistic. One might argue that what is odious in "harsh and unconscionable" contracts, even when they are voluntary on both sides, is not that a man should suffer the harm he freely risked, but rather that another party should "exploit" or take advantage of him. What is to be prevented, according to this line of argument, is one man exploiting the weakness, or foolishness, or recklessness of another. If a weak, foolish, or reckless man freely chooses to harm or risk harm to himself, that is all right, but that is no reason why another should be a party to it, or be permitted to benefit himself at the other's expense. (This principle, however, can only apply to extreme cases, else it will ban all competition.) Applied to voluntary slavery, the principle of non-exploitation might say that it isn't aimed at preventing one man from being a slave so much as preventing the other from being a slave-owner. The basic principle of argument here is a form of legal moralism. To own another human being, as one might own a table or a horse, is to be in a relation to him that is inherently immoral, and therefore properly forbidden by law. That, of course, is a line of argument that would be uncongenial to Mill, as would also be the Kantian argument that there is something in every man that is not his to alienate or dispose of, *viz.*, the "humanity" that we are enjoined to "respect, whether in our own person or that of another." (It is worth noting, in passing, that Kant was an uncompromising foe of legal paternalism.)

There are still other ways of arguing against the recognition of slavery contracts, however, that are neither paternalistic (in the strong sense) nor inconsistent with Mill's primary principles. One might argue, for example, that weakening respect for human dignity (which is weak enough to begin with) can lead in the long run to harm of the most serious kind to non-consenting parties. Or one might use a variant of the "public charge" argument commonly used in the nineteenth century against permitting even those without dependents to assume the risk of penury, illness, and starvation. We could let men gamble recklessly with their own lives, and then adopt inflexibly unsympathetic attitudes toward the losers. "They made their beds," we might say in the manner of some proper Victorians, "now let them sleep in them." But this would be to render the whole national character cold and hard. It would encourage insensitivity generally and impose an unfair economic penalty on those who possess the socially useful virtue of benevolence. Realistically, we just can't let men wither and die right in front of our eyes; and if we intervene to help, as we inevitably must, it will cost us a lot of money. There are certain risks then of an *apparently* self-regarding kind that men cannot be permitted to run, if only for the sake of others who must either pay the bill or turn their backs on intolerable misery. This kind of argument, which can be applied equally well to the slavery case, is at least not *very* paternalistic.

Finally, a non-paternalistic opponent of voluntary slavery might argue (and this the argument to which I wish to give the most emphasis) that while exclusively self-regarding and fully voluntary "slavery contracts" are unobjectionable in principle, the legal machinery for testing voluntariness would be so cumbersome and expensive as to be impractical. Such procedures, after all, would have to be paid for out of tax revenues, the payment of which is mandatory for taxpayers. (And psychiatric consultant fees, among other things, are very high.) Even expensive legal machinery might be so highly fallible that there could be no sure way of determining voluntariness, so that some mentally ill people, for example, might become enslaved. Given the uncertain quality of evidence on these matters, and the enormous general presumption of nonvoluntariness, the state might be justified simply in *presuming nonvoluntariness conclusively in every case as the least risky course.* Some rational bargain-makers might be unfairly restrained under this policy, but on the alternative policy, even more people, perhaps, would become unjustly (mistakenly) enslaved, so that the evil prevented by the absolute prohibition would be greater than the occasional evil permitted. The principles involved in this argument are of the following two kinds: (1) It is better (say) that one hundred people be wrongly denied permission to be enslaved than that one be wrongly permitted, and (2) If we allow the institution of "voluntary slavery" at all, then no matter how stringent our tests of voluntariness are, it is likely that a good many persons *will* be wrongly permitted.

V

Mill's argument that leads to a (strong) paternalistic conclusion in this one case (slavery) employs only calculations of harms and benefits and the presumptive interpretation of *Volenti non fit inuria.* The notion of the inviolable sovereignty of the individual person over his own life does not appear in the argument. Liberty, he seems to tell us, is one good or benefit (though an extremely important one) among many, and its loss, one evil or harm (though an extremely serious one) among many types of harm. The aim of the law being to prevent harms of all kinds and from all sources, the law must take a very negative attitude toward forfeitures of liberty. Still, by and large, legal paternalism is an unacceptable policy because in attempting to impose upon a man an external conception of his own good, it is very likely to be self-defeating. "His voluntary choice is *evidence* (emphasis added) that what he so chooses is desirable, or at least endurable to him, and his good is *on the whole* (more emphasis added) best provided for by allowing him to take his own means of pursuing it." On the whole, then, the harm of coercion will outweigh any good it can produce for the person coerced. But when the person chooses slavery, the scales are clearly and necessarily tipped the other way, and the normal case against intervention is defeated. The ultimate appeal in this argument of Mill's is to the prevention of personal harms, so that permitting a person voluntarily to sell all his freedom would be to permit him to be "free not to be free," that is, free to inflict an *undeniable* harm upon himself, and this (Mill would say) is as paradoxical as permitting a legislature to vote by a majority to abolish majority rule. If, on the other hand, our ultimate principle expresses respect for a person's voluntary choice *as such*, even when it is the choice of a loss of freedom, we can remain adamantly opposed to paternalism even in the most extreme cases of self-harm, for we shall be committed to the view that there is something more important (even) than the avoidance of harm. The principle that shuts and locks the door leading to strong paternalism is that every man has a human right to "voluntarily dispose of his own lot in life" whatever the effect on his own net balance of benefits (including "freedom") and harms.

What does Mill say about less extreme cases of contracting away liberty? His next sentence (but one) is revealing: "These reasons, the force of which is so conspicuous in this particular case [slavery], are evidently of far wider application, yet a limit is everywhere set to them by the necessities of life, which continually require, not indeed that we should resign our freedom, but that we should consent to this and the other limitation of it."[11] Mill seems to say here that the same reasons that justify preventing the total and irrevocable relinquishment of freedom also militate against agreements to relinquish lesser amounts for lesser periods, but that unfortunately such agreements are sometimes rendered necessary by practical considerations. I would prefer to argue in the very opposite way, from the obvious permissibility of limited resignations of freedom to the permissibility in principle even of extreme forfeitures, except that in the latter case (slavery) the "necessities of life"—administrative complications in determining voluntariness, high expenses, and so on—forbid it.

Many perfectly reasonable employment contracts involve an agreement by the employee virtually to abandon his liberty to do as he pleases for a daily period, and even to do (within obvious limits) whatever his boss tells him, in exchange for a salary that the employer, in turn, is not at liberty to withhold. Sometimes, of course, the terms of such agreements are quite unfavourable to one of the parties, but when the agreements have been fairly bargained, with no undue pressure or deception (i.e. when they are fully voluntary) the courts enforce them even though lopsided in their distribution of benefits. Employment contracts, of course, are relatively easily broken; so in that respect they are altogether different from "slavery contracts." Perhaps better examples for our purposes, therefore, are contractual forfeitures of some extensive liberty for long

[11] *Loc. cit.*

periods of time or even forever. Certain contracts "in restraint of trade" are good examples. Consider contracts for the sale of the "good will" of a business:

> Manifestly, the buyer of a shop or of a practice will not be satisfied with what he buys unless he can persuade the seller to contract that he will not immediately set up a competing business next door and draw back most of his old clients or customers. Hence the buyer will usually request the seller to agree not to enter into competition with him. . . . Clauses of this kind are [also] often found in written contracts of employment, the employer requiring his employee to agree that he will not work for a competing employer after he leaves his present work.[12]

There are limits, both spatial and temporal, to the amount of liberty the courts will permit to be relinquished in such contracts. In general, it is considered reasonable for a seller to agree not to reopen a business in the same neighborhood or even the same city for several years, but not reasonable to agree not to re-enter the trade in a distant city, or for a period (say) of fifty years. The courts insist that the agreed-to-self-restraint be no wider "than is reasonably necessary to protect the buyer's purchase;"[13] but where the buyer's interests are very large the restraints may cover a great deal of space and time:

> For instance, in the leading case on the subject, a company which bought an armaments business for the colossal sum of £287,000 was held justified in taking a contract from the seller that he would not enter into competition with this business anywhere in the world for a period of twenty-five years. In view of the fact that the business was world-wide in its operations, and that its customers were mainly governments, any attempt by the seller to re-enter the armament business anywhere in the world might easily have affected the value of the buyer's purchase.[14]

The courts then do permit people to contract away extensive liberties for extensive periods of time in exchange for other benefits in reasonable bargains. Persons are even permitted to forfeit their future liberties in exchange for cash. Sometimes such transactions are perfectly reasonable, promoting the interests of both parties. Hence there would appear to be no good reason why they should be prohibited. Selling oneself into slavery is forfeiting *all* one's liberty for the rest of one's life in exchange for some prized benefit, and thus is only the extreme limiting case of contracting away liberty, but not altogether different in principle. Mill's argument that liberty is not the sort of good that by its very nature can properly be traded, then, does not seem a convincing way of arguing against voluntary slavery.

On the other hand, a court does not permit the seller of a business freely to forfeit any more liberty than is reasonable or necessary, and reserves to *itself* the right to determine the question of reasonableness. This restrictive policy *could* be an expression of paternalism designed to protect contracters from their own foolishness; but in fact it is based on an entirely different ground—the

12 P. S. Atiyah, *An Introduction to the Law of Contracts* (Oxford: Clarendon Press, 1961), p. 176.

13 *Ibid.*, pp. 176–77.

14 *Ibid.*, p. 177.

public interest in maintaining a competitive system of free trade. The consumer's interests in having prices determined by a competitive marketplace rather than by uncontrolled monopolies requires that the state make it difficult for wealthy businessmen to buy off their competitors. Reasonable contracts "in restraint of trade" are a limited class of exceptions to a general policy designed to protect the economic interests of third parties (consumers) rather than the expression of an independent paternalistic policy of protecting free bargainers from their own mistakes.

There is still a final class of cases that deserve mention. These too are instances of persons voluntarily relinquishing liberties for other benefits; but they occur under such circumstances that prohibitions against them could not plausibly be justified except on paternalistic grounds, and usually not even on those grounds. I have in mind examples of persons who voluntarily "put themselves under the protection of rules" that deprive them and others too of liberties, when those liberties are unrewarding and burdensome. Suppose all upperclass undergraduates are given the option by their college to live either in private apartment buildings entirely unrestricted or else in college dormitories subject to the usual curfew and parietal rules. If one chooses the latter, he or she must be in after a certain hour, be quiet after a certain time, and so on, subject to certain sanctions. In "exchange" for these forfeitures, of course, one is assured that the other students too must be predictable in their habits, orderly, and quiet. The net gain for one's interests as a student over the "freer" private life could be considerable. Moreover, the curfew rule can be a great convenience for a girl who wishes to "date" boys very often, but who also wishes: (a) to get enough sleep for good health, (b) to remain efficient in her work, and (c) to be free of tension and quarrels when on dates over the question of when it is time to return home. If the rule requires a return at a certain time then neither the girl nor the boy has any choice in the matter, and what a boon that can be! To invoke these considerations is *not* to resort to paternalism unless they are employed in support of a prohibition. It is paternalism to *forbid* a student to live in a private apartment "for his own good" or "his own safety." It is not paternalism to *permit* him to live under the governance of coercive rules when he freely chooses to do so, and the other alternative is kept open to him. In fact it would be paternalism to deny a person the liberty of trading liberties for other benefits when he voluntarily chooses to do so.

VI

In summary: There are weak and strong versions of legal paternalism. The weak version is hardly an independent principle and can be entirely acceptable to the philosopher who, like Mill, is committed only to the "harm to others" principle as mediated by the *Volenti* maxim, where the latter is more than a mere presumption derived from generalizations about the causes of harm. According to the strong version of legal paternalism, the state is justified in protecting a person, against his will, from the harmful consequences even of his fully voluntary choices and undertakings. Strong paternalism is a departure from the "harm to others" principle and the strictly interpreted *Volenti* maxim that Mill should not, or need not, have taken in his discussion of contractual forfeitures of liberty. According to the weaker version of legal paternalism, a man can rightly be prevented from harming himself (when other interests are not directly involved) only if his intended action is substantially nonvoluntary or can be presumed to be so in the absence of evidence to the contrary. The "harm to others" principle, after all, permits us to protect a man from the choices of other people; weak paternalism would permit us to protect him from "nonvoluntary choices," which, being the choices of no one at all, are no less foreign to him.

INTRODUCTION TO SOCIAL AND POLITICAL PHILOSOPHY / Study Questions

PATERNALISM

Wilson et al.

1. What positions have been taken in the debate on the heroin problem?
2. What do Wilson et al. see as the "central question" that must be answered before the debate can be resolved?
3. What is the authors' description of the utilitarian position? What position do they oppose to it?
4. In what way are the facts about heroin and its use important in this debate? Specifically, given the facts laid out in the article, can one meaningfully say that heroin addicts are harming themselves? What *would* have to happen to addicts in order to use the concept of *harm* here? How does this affect the "punitive" and "medical" approaches to the problem of heroin?
5. What "philosophical" position is taken by Wilson et al. in the heroin debate?
6. What problem do they see about whether heroin addiction is a state of being that should not be left to free choice? Do they offer a way of definitively settling that issue?

Mill

1. What is the question that Mill sets out to answer?
2. Over what aspects of a person's conduct does he say that society has jurisdiction?
3. What is Mill's position on a person's being the final judge of his own interests? Does Mill agree with Wilson et al. about this?
4. According to Mill, what is the strongest argument against public interference in purely personal conduct? Can this argument show that there is anything wrong *in principle* with the doctrine of paternalism?
5. Mill, of course, does not discuss the heroin problem. What do you think his utilitarian theory would demand that he say about it? Does the representation of utilitarian theory given by Wilson et al. agree with your extrapolation of Mill?
6. Wilson et al. say that policies advocated on utilitarian grounds need not differ from those advocated on paternalistic grounds. If this is so, then is there really any difference between the two theories? If there is, what is it?

Wolff

1. What is Wolff's purpose in this article with respect to Mill's theory?
2. What are the three distinct propositions that Wolff says Mill's argument must prove?

3. What ambiguity does Wolff find in Mill's account of the value of individuality? How does he think the matter reduces to the third of Mill's claims?
4. In what two ways can Mill's claim that everybody is the best judge of his own interests be interpreted? What makes one of these *trivial*? What makes the other *empirical*?
5. Is it a weakness in Mill's defense of libertarianism that it rests upon empirical grounds?
6. How does Wolff say that Mill would have to answer these objections?
7. What is the position of modern liberalism with respect to Mill's views?

Exdell

1. Why, according to Exdell, do utilitarian arguments fail to show that paternalism is always wrong?
2. If utilitarian objections fail, what other kind of objection to paternalism can be entertained?
3. In what ways is the belief that paternalistic legislation violates human rights frequently manifested? Do these manifestations establish the case against paternalism?
4. According to Exdell, what must be done in order to show that paternalism violates human rights?
5. What can be meant by the expression "respect for persons"? Can the principle "show respect for persons," in either of its senses, underwrite a general objection to paternalism?
6. Explain the difference that Exdell sees in the cases of heroin legislation and motorcycle helmet legislation. What is the role of the notions of *coercion, rights,* and *interests* in these two cases.
7. Is there any inconsistency between Exdell's concluding remarks about paternalism and utilitarian considerations and his earlier criticism of utilitarian arguments?

Feinberg

1. What is the problem about paternalism that Feinberg wishes to solve in this paper?
2. What is meant by the principle of "*Volenti non fit inuria*"? Of what two interpretations is it capable? Which interpretation does Feinberg favor?
3. How does Feinberg claim that Mill's use of the principle is inconsistent? Why must Mill be inconsistent?
4. How does Feinberg discuss the question—raised by Wilson et al.—whether drug taking is actually a case of harm?
5. What problems does Feinberg say Mill meets in his treatment of selling oneself into slavery?
6. What are some ways, other than Mill's, that the refusal to enforce slavery contracts could be justified?
7. Explain the distinctions between the strong and the weak versions of paternalism that Feinberg describes. What are his conclusions about paternalism?

SUGGESTED FURTHER READINGS / Introduction to Social and Political Philosophy

GENERAL

Diggs, B. J. *The State, Justice, and the Common Good.* Glenview, Ill.: Scott Foresman and Company, 1974.

Feinberg, Joel, *Social Philosophy.* Englewood Cliffs, N.J.: Prentice-Hall, Inc., 1973.

Flathman, Richard E. *Concepts in Social and Political Philosophy*. New York: Macmillan Publishing Co., Inc., 1973.

Krimmerman, Leonard I., and Lewis Perry. *Patterns of Anarchy*. Garden City, N.Y.: Doubleday & Company, Inc., 1966.

Taylor, Richard. *Freedom, Anarchy, and the Law*. Prentice-Hall Englewood Cliffs, N.J.: Prentice-Hall, Inc., 1973.

PUNISHMENT

Acton, H. B., ed. *The Philosophy of Punishment*. London: Macmillan & Company, Ltd., 1969. (with bibliography)

A. F. S. C. (American Friends Service Committee). *Struggle for Justice*. New York: Hill & Wang, 1971.

Hart, H. L. A. *Punishment and Responsibility: Essays in the Philosophy of Law*. Oxford, England: Oxford University Press 1968.

Murphy, Jeffry G. *Punishment and Rehabilitation*. Belmont, Calif.: Wadsworth Publishing Co., Inc., 1973.

Szasz, Thomas. *Psychiatric Justice*. New York: Macmillan Publishing Co., Inc., 1965.

———, *Law. Liberty and Psychiatry: An Inquiry into the Social Uses of Mental Health Practices*. New York: Macmillan Publishing Co., Inc., 1963.

PATERNALISM

Devlin, Patrick. *The Enforcement of Morals*. London: Oxford University Press, 1965.

Hart, H. L. A. *Law, Liberty, and Morality*. Oxford, England: Oxford University Press, 1963.

Leiser, Burton M. *Liberty, Justice, and Morals*. New York: Macmillan Publishing Co., Inc., 1973.

Stephen, James Fitzjames. *Liberty, Equality, Fraternity*. Cambridge, England: Cambridge University Press, 1967.

Wasserstrom, Richard A. *Morality and the Law*. Belmont, Calif., Wadsworth Publishing Co., Inc., 1971.

PART 5

Introduction to Philosophy of Religion

What we now call philosophy of religion had its historical roots (in our culture) in the clash of Semitic cultures with that of the Greco-Roman world, beginning with the Hellenization of ancient Semitic and Aryan lands (roughly from what we know as Turkey through the Middle East and on into India). Under Alexander the Great and his generals the Greeks conquered, colonized, and opened up new economic relations and trade routes, bringing with them the distinctively Greek way of asking questions and reasoning about the world, man, and gods. The conquered peoples in all of these regions separated into factions over how to deal with this new attitude towards what in retrospect they must have regarded as distinctively religious issues. Some opted for the new way altogether—possibly persuaded by the visible might-of-arms of the Greeks and, later, the Romans. Others, jealous of their heritage and believing in a jealous god, resisted this influence fiercely. The majority of Jews, especially, saw the physical might of the Greeks and Romans as, alternatively, a blight on the land that God would not allow to continue forever or as the hand of God punishing Jews for swerving from His chosen way. In neither case did they believe the phenomenon was anything permanent; nor did they think the might of the conquerors showed them that their faith in the power of the Almighty was mistaken.

But it is with a third attitude that we are interested; for in it are found the beginnings of philosophy of religion as we know it. Some, rather than either capitulating to the Greco-Roman patterns of philosophical speculation or resisting it, sought instead to retain and protect their faith by explaining it to the Greco-Roman mind. And the vehicle they chose for this task was the philosophy of the conquerors!

That is, they *appropriated* Greco-Roman philosophy and sought to use *it* to explain their religion. What makes this important to us is that it introduces, for the first time, the idea that religion, any religion, can and ought to be *explained* in addition to being preached, taught, believed in, practiced, and lived. This new element—the attempt to explain religion—is philosophy of religion.

Now, of course, this is a little too easy. There are many motives one might have for seeking to explain religion, for example, to preserve the faith when it is under attack, to convert those to whom you are explaining the faith, or to satisfy purely intellectual interests. Each motive will to some degree affect what one takes to be the crucial problems in explaining religion (or a religion). Each motive will also affect what one looks to as the intellectual background against which to argue for one's explanation. For example, if one is primarily interested in gaining respect for the faith from those who are attacking it, one might most naturally see questions of a general metaphysical sort to be most crucial and to seek to explain the faith in the terms of current metaphysical speculation. The great Jewish philosopher Philo gives us an example of such a project. We find Philo addressing essentially the same problems and dealing with them in the same way as the Greek philosopher Plotinus. Not incidentally, the most heavily Hellenized gospel in the Christian scriptures, the *Gospel of John*, has as its historical setting the attempt to gain respect for Christian teaching from predominantly Greek (non-Jewish) antagonists—and the *Gospel of John* begins with a prologue that is deeply influenced by the writings of Philo! For a second example, if one's interests are with conversion and evangelism, one might find philosophies that place importance on "live problems" for people in their everyday lives—such as ethics and legal philosophy—the most appropriate background against which to explain the faith. In the writings of the Apostle Paul, especially his *Letter to the Romans* in the Christian scriptures, one finds just such a maneuver. Paul, a Jewish Christian, sought to explain to his non-Jewish readers the Christian perspective on salvation and the need for salvation by a series of analogies from Roman law and legal theory with which his readers were quite familiar.

So far we have been concerned with just the beginnings of the development, in our culture, of philosophy of religion. The crucial point is that philosophy of religion is concerned with *explanations* of religion. And this is true whether philosophy of religion arises historically as the result of clashes of cultures (as in Western civilization) or as the result of internal movements within a culture and religion (as, for example, in Hindu philosophies). But beyond this central focus on explanation we need to notice that philosophy of religion is a quite diverse discipline. That is, there are *many different* things that philosophers have been interested in explaining about religion. This, of course, should come as no surprise; for religion is a *very* complex phenomenon. It encompasses, in varying degrees of importance, prescriptions for behavior (both ritual behavior and actions of a moral nature), exhortations to adopt and achieve desired attitudes and states of mind, commitments to certain beliefs and concepts, and commitments to certain forms of group life (including commitments having to do with the role of the religious group with respect to society-at-large). So, for example, the relation between religions as distinct social groups and the societies in which they live is one thing that philosophers have had an interest in explaining. The criticisms of religion by Karl Marx arise out of philosophical concerns in this area. Or, for another example, one might look with philosophical interest at the attitudes and states of mind desired by religion, or a religion, and seek to explain what is going on here. The philosophical defense of religion by the psychologist Dewey and the equally philosophical attack on religion by Freud are cases of this sort of interest. Or, for a final example, one might wish to determine the consequences for morality of adhering to strictly religious prescriptions on matters of morals. The famous attack on religion by the philosopher Nietzsche, on the grounds that religious morality (especially that of Christianity) subverts both the autonomy of individuals and respect for the virtue of self-reliance, stems from these sorts of concerns.

But the mainstream of philosophical interest in explaining religion has focused on matters of *belief*. And, in keeping with that, our two issues here will be within that focus. But before we go on to introduce those issues, a little more background will be helpful. To begin with, these issues arise because human beings, in most of their religions, express what appear to be straightforward beliefs about the world, its origins, and the existence of a being or force that created, governs, and/or controls the universe. It is important to notice that almost no one who comes to hold these beliefs does so out of a conviction that some *evidence*, of one sort or another, shows the beliefs are true. They arrive at these beliefs as the result either of belief in a revelation, of training, of personal psychological experiences that are deeply profound, and/or of life-long desires and needs for a sense of the fitness or purposefulness of things. But when one tries to explain religious beliefs one realizes that citing such motives for coming to believe are not explanations of the beliefs themselves but of the *behavior of the believers*! So, quite naturally, one has to look elsewhere to try to find a way to explain religious beliefs.

The most likely prospect, it has seemed, is to treat religious belief as a perfectly ordinary sort of thing that happens to be about extraordinary phenomena. So one begins to look for evidence. But to do this is to treat religious beliefs as metaphysical claims of the traditional type; and, as such, they are subject to the same kinds of criticisms that the positivists levelled at traditional metaphysical claims and questions (see the introduction to Part 2 on metaphysics). That is, it can be argued that religious belief-claims are essentially *meaningless*! This, of course, seems wrong; if only on the grounds that the human race is not so stupid that most of its members most of the time would go around babbling incoherently while thinking they were making perfect sense. So, perhaps, we got off on the wrong foot by regarding religious belief as ordinary belief (albeit about extraordinary phenomena). This, in turn, leads us to ask what *sort* of discourse we *are* engaged in when we express some religious belief or other. What happens here is that, in trying to explain the what and why of religious beliefs, the usual route one wants to follow leads us into a situation where the very meaningfulness of religious belief itself is called into question. And we end up trying to explain not the *truth* of religious claims but their *meaning*. We shall see this pattern hovering over the two issues we present in this part.

The Justification of Religious Belief

Far and away the most important religious belief to be explained is the belief in a god or gods. At the outset you must remember that it just will not do to try to explain and justify such a belief by appeal to a special revelation. First, this is likely to tell us more about the believer than the belief—that is, what sort of things persuade the believer. Secondly, it is precisely that revelation, the *content* of that revelation, which wants explanation—so to appeal to it is to reason in a vicious circle. We must go outside that circle to explain such beliefs. It is the attempt to go outside of revelation to prove the existence of a deity that is characteristic of what, among Western philosophers, is called Natural Theology. And it is the proofs of Natural Theology—their statement, their failure, and the consequences of that failure—with which we are concerned in this section.

There are three such arguments, or *forms* of arguments, that have gotten most attention from philosophers. The first of these, called the Cosmological Argument, reasons that the facts of causality and motion require—in order for them to be intelligible to us—that there be a *first* (or, uncaused) cause and a *first* (or unmoved) mover. The second, called the Ontological Argument, does not appeal to facts at all; rather it appeals to the very *idea* of a Deity. According to this argument, to have an idea of a Deity one must be conceiving of a perfect being; but if one conceives of a being as not existing, one is not conceiving of a perfect being (surely the real dollar in my pocket is better than the imaginary dollar in my pocket)! So, with this argument, the claim that a Deity exists is true in virtue of the meaning of the word *Deity*; just as the claim that a triangle has three sides is true in virtue of the meaning of the word *triangle*. The third argument, called the Teleological Argument, again appeals to very general facts. According to this argument, it is a fact of nature that nature, in all of its parts, is orderly and regular, thereby exhibiting all the "earmarks" of design. But to say nature is designed implies that someone or something designed it. Therefore a Deity must exist.

These arguments are not the only ones that have cropped up over the centuries; but they are the ones most people (at least those who have been inclined to be persuaded by arguments) have found worthy of attention. And, too, they seem on the whole to be *logically* better than most others—at least their flaws are less easy to expose. So these are the ones on which we shall concentrate.

We are first presented with some of these arguments in a selection from a work that was, for several centuries, *the* central theological text in the Roman rite—namely, the *Summa Theologica* by St. Thomas *Aquinas*. In this selection we are given five arguments. According to Aquinas, they all are arguments that appeal to evidence (in some broad sense). The first four are clearly different versions of the Cosmological Argument. Each is concerned to show that some very general facts about the world require the hypothesis of the existence of God. Without such an hypothesis those same facts would elude our understanding. The first two arguments are, you will notice, concerned with general facts about causal chains and series of movements. They are, then, fairly standard versions of the Cosmological Argument. The next two vary the general theme of this argument in interesting ways. In the third, Aquinas attempts to argue that factual claims about what is necessary and what is possible apply naturally to what is necessarily *existent* and what is only possibly *existent*. This could, he argues, make sense only if there were something that does exist necessarily: namely, God. In the fourth, Aquinas attempts to show that factual claims of a comparative nature (for example, "X is cooler than Y") also have a natural application to what is more or less existent. Yet, just as ordinary comparative statements entail a maximum state (for example, "X is cooler than Y" entails that something, Z, is coldest), so also statements comparing items relative to their existence presuppose that something (namely, God) has perfection in being. The final argument Aquinas presents is a fairly standard version of the Teleological Argument. In it, Aquinas argues that the universe exhibits evidence of being governed. To explain these facts we must hypothesize the existence of some being that governs the universe.

So far, you will notice, we have not given an example of the Ontological Argument. We turn to that now. Actually, the Ontological Argument has had a long and varied history. It was first given a clear statement by St. Anselm about 1070. Shortly after St. Anselm formulated the argument, it was strongly attacked by a monk named Gaunilo. Gaunilo's central criticisms of the argument have been widely discussed and are generally agreed to be valid criticisms against at least parts of St. Anselm's version of the argument. (Aquinas, whose *Summa Theologica* was written almost two hundred years later, appears not to have thought much of it.) Yet it was not without its supporters. And what we present here is a reformulation of the argument, by *Descartes*. (Descartes himself actually presents *two* versions of the argument, but we have not presented the version in his "Third Meditation" because it is too involved with Descartes' own rather unique epistemological views about "ideas" and "what may be doubted.") Since that time the Ontological Argument has occurred in philosophy on an off and on basis. Some ten years ago it began to excite some interest again, this time in connection with developments in a new branch of logic, called modal logic. We have not included any piece representing this revived interest, basically because the discussion has become so technical that most beginning students in philosophy would be at a loss to comprehend it. We have, however, cited several good sources on the current discussion in the list of suggested readings at the end of Part 5.

But aside from its place in this history, Descartes' version of the argument has a very interesting feature of which students should be aware. Much of the burden of proof in this argument is carried by seeing the question of God's existence as analogous with questions and propositions in mathematics. Specifically, the analogy is drawn with questions and propositions that "describe" such mathematical objects as triangles. Certain properties of triangles can be deduced from the very concept of a triangle. Just so, according to this argument, certain attributes may be deduced from the very concept of a divine being. Among those, according to Descartes, is the property of existence. So, on his view, it would be as senseless to conceive of a nonexistent God as it is to conceive of a triangle without three sides. Thus, since we can conceive of God, God must exist.

The next selection, "The Existence of God," by J. J. C. *Smart*, is an attempt to refute each of the three major arguments we have presented in the Aquinas and Descartes readings. A good many philosophers, in our opinion, have offered convincing refutations of these arguments; so our choice of this piece by Smart deserves some explaining. We think that despite some defects on details, this article by Smart has two very valuable features. First, unlike some others, Smart is careful and attentive in drawing out the questionable analogies on which these arguments rest. And it is our experience that students frequently have been led into finding the arguments persuasive by an uncritical acceptance of those analogies. Secondly, Smart takes pains to instruct the reader on the issues concerning the nature of empirical and analytic claims over which each of these arguments stumbles. Thus, he tends to exhibit already the point that the difficulty with these arguments is not with evidence or proof, or truth or falsity; rather the difficulty with these arguments is in *understanding* what they purport to prove and how we are supposed to follow the proofs.

But what if the proofs do fail, as Smart argues they do? Is that the end of the world for a believer? Of course not. But it is the end of *something*; and what that might be is the subject of the last two articles in this section. Up to now we have assumed that religious beliefs are perfectly ordinary beliefs about some extraordinary things. One might now suspect that, since neither proofs nor evidence shows they are true *or* false, they are not ordinary beliefs at all. But that judgment may be too hasty.

In the excerpt we present here from his essay, "The Will to Believe," William *James* argues that certain hypotheses, even though no evidence could determine their truth or falsity, are still genuine hypotheses and are crucial ones as well. In such a case we are involved in making choices on which we are "betting our lives." Here, he argues, we may have *good reason* for believing in the truth of these claims *despite* the lack of evidence. And what counts as a good reason here is whether the results of choosing (willing) to believe is an outcome that in some sense "works" for us. Indeed, James argues, this is not only true of religious beliefs but also of some very significant scientific beliefs as well. Behind all this is James' own theory of truth, called the Pragmatist Theory, in which it is held that what is true for anyone *is* just what has pragmatic value, what "works." (See the introduction to "Learning, Knowledge, and Truth" in

Part 3.) But that general theory is not at issue here; it could be false without necessarily invalidating this justification of having some religious beliefs. But, in that case, James' explanation of religious belief would have a deep flaw. It would end up telling us more about the *believer*—that is why a believer believes—than it would about *what* he or she believes and *whether* that belief is, in fact, true or false.

The point at which we leave James must cause us to wonder just exactly what sort of claims religious claims are. In the next selection, a passage from his book, *Language, Truth and Logic,* A. J. *Ayer* argues the positivist line that religious claims are meaningless. Two points are important here. First, Ayer is treating religious beliefs as traditional metaphysical claims. So he argues that, since their truth or falsity is neither provable by logic alone nor demonstrable by appeals to facts, they are perforce nonsensical. In the introduction on metaphysics in Part 2 we suggested that the positivist dogmas of the analytic/synthetic distinction and the reliance on the verifiability criterion of meaning were inadequate for a proper understanding of metaphysical claims. However, the religious believer cannot escape Ayer's arguments here by the route we suggested there; for we claimed that metaphysical claims, when correct, might be rendered into "harmless" remarks about our *conceptual schemes.* Yet no amount of twisting will allow religious beliefs to be rendered into such innocuous claims—they just refuse to be anything other than squarely straightforward beliefs *about the world.* Secondly, Ayer is neither an atheist nor an agnostic. This is a point beginning students find difficult; so let us explain it. An atheist believes that there is good evidence for believing there is no God or that the lack of evidence for God's existence renders it improbable that God exists. An agnostic believes that since there is no good evidence one way or the other we ought simply to take a we-just-do-not-know attitude here. But Ayer argues that nothing *could* count as evidence for or against God's existence or for or against any other religious claims. Thus, he argues, we don't even know what these claims *mean.* Nor can we know; for since we do not know what would count as evidence we do not know how to find out what they mean. So, according to Ayer, they are all—the claims of the theist, the atheist, and the agnostic—equally nonsensical!

Five Proofs of God's Existence

ST. THOMAS AQUINAS

OBJECTION 1. It seems that God does not exist; because if one of two contraries be infinite, the other would be altogether destroyed. But the name *God* means that He is infinite goodness. If, therefore, God existed, there would be

---

no evil discoverable; but there is evil in the world. Therefore God does not exist.

OBJ. 2. Further, it is superfluous to suppose that what can be accounted for by a few principles has been produced by many. But it seems that everything we see in the world can be accounted for by other principles, supposing God did not exist. For all natural things can be reduced to one principle, which is nature; and all voluntary things can be reduced to one principle, which is human reason, or will. Therefore there is no need to suppose God's existence.

On the contrary, It is said in the person of God: *I am Who am* (Exod. iii. 14).

I answer that, The existence of God can be proved in five ways.

The first and more manifest way is the argument from motion. It is certain, and evident to our senses, that in the world some things are in motion. Now whatever is moved is moved by another, for nothing can be moved except it is in potentiality to that towards which it is moved; whereas a thing moves inasmuch as it is in act. For motion is nothing else than the reduction of something from potentiality to actuality. But nothing can be reduced from potentiality to actuality, except by something in a state of actuality. Thus that which is actually hot, as fire, makes wood, which is potentially hot, to be actually hot, and thereby moves and changes it. Now it is not possible that the same thing should be at once in actuality and potentiality in the same respect, but only in different respects. For what is actually hot cannot simultaneously be potentially hot; but it is simultaneously potentially cold. It is therefore impossible that in the same respect and in the same way a thing should be both mover and moved, *i.e.*, that it should move itself. Therefore, whatever is moved must be moved by another. If that by which it is moved be itself moved, then this also must needs be moved by another, and that by another again. But this cannot go on to infinity, because then there would be no first mover, and, consequently, no other mover, seeing that subsequent movers move only inasmuch as they are moved by the first mover; as the staff moves only because it is moved by the hand. Therefore it is necessary to arrive at a first mover, moved by no other; and this everyone understands to be God.

The second way is from the nature of efficient cause. In the world of sensible things we find there is an order of efficient causes. There is no case known (neither is it, indeed, possible) in which a thing is found to be the efficient cause of itself; for so it would be prior to itself, which is impossible. Now in efficient causes it is not possible to go on to infinity, because in all efficient causes following in order, the first is the cause of the intermediate cause, and the intermediate is the cause of the ultimate cause, whether the intermediate cause be several, or one only. Now to take away the cause is to take away the effect. Therefore, if there be no first cause among efficient causes, there will be no ultimate, nor any intermediate, cause. But if in efficient causes it is possible to go on to infinity, there will be no first efficient cause, neither will there be an ultimate effect, nor any intermediate efficient causes; all of which is plainly false. Therefore it is necessary to admit a first efficient cause, to which everyone gives the name of God.

The third way is taken from possibility and necessity, and runs thus. We find in nature things that are possible to be and not to be, since they are found to be generated, and to be corrupted, and consequently, it is possible for them to be and not to be. But it is impossible for these always to exist, for that which can not-be at some time is not. Therefore, if everything can not-be, then at one time there was nothing in existence. Now if this were true, even now there would be nothing in existence, because that which does not exist begins to exist only through something already existing. Therefore, if at one time nothing was in existence, it would have been impossible for anything to have begun to exist; and thus even now nothing would be in existence—which is absurd. Therefore, not all beings are merely possible, but there must exist something the existence of which is necessary. But every necessary thing either has its necessity caused by another, or not. Now it is impossible to go on to infinity in necessary things which have their necessity caused by another, as has been already proved in regard to efficient causes. Therefore we cannot but admit the existence of some being having of itself its own necessity, and not receiving it from another, but rather causing in others their necessity. This all men speak of as God.

The fourth way is taken from the gradation to be found in things. Among beings there are some more and some less good, true, noble, and the like. But *more* and *less* are predicated of different things according as they resemble in their different ways something which is the maximum, as a thing is said to be hotter according as it more nearly resembles that which is hottest; so that there is something which is truest, something best, something noblest, and, consequently, something which is most being, for those things that are greatest in truth are greatest in being, as it is written in [Aristotle's] *Metaphysics* ii. Now the maximum in any genus is the cause of all in that genus, as fire, which is the maximum of heat, is the cause of all hot things, as is said in the same book. Therefore there must also be something which is to all beings the cause of their being, goodness, and every other perfection, and this we call God.

The fifth way is taken from the governance of the world. We see that things which lack knowledge, such as natural bodies, act for an end, and this is evident from their acting always, or nearly always, in the same way, so as to obtain the best result. Hence it is plain that they achieve their end, not fortuitously, but designedly. Now whatever lacks knowledge cannot move towards an end, unless it be directed by some being endowed with knowledge and intelligence; as the arrow is directed by the archer. Therefore some intelligent being exists by whom all natural things are directed to their end: and this being we call God.

REPLY OBJ. 1. As Augustine says: *Since God is the highest good, He would not allow any evil to exist in His works; unless His omnipotence and goodness were such as to bring good even out of evil.* This is part of the infinite goodness of God, that He should allow evil to exist, and out of it produce good.

REPLY OBJ. 2. Since nature works for a determinate end under the direction of a higher agent, whatever is done by nature must be traced back to God as to its first cause. So likewise whatever is done voluntarily must be traced back to some higher cause other than human reason and will, since these can change and fail; for all things that are changeable and capable of defect must be traced back to an immovable and self-necessary first principle, as has been shown.

The Ontological Argument

RENÉ DESCARTES

AND WHAT I here find to be most important is that I discover in myself an infinitude of ideas of certain things which cannot be esteemed as pure negations, although they may possibly have no existence outside of my thought, and which are not framed by me, although it is within my power either to think or not to think them, but which possess natures which are true and immutable. For example, when I imagine a triangle, although there may nowhere in the world be such a figure outside my thought, or ever have been, there is nevertheless in this figure a certain determinate nature, form, or essence, which is immutable and eternal, which I have not invented, and which in no wise depends on my mind, as appears from the fact that diverse properties of that triangle can be demonstrated, viz. that its three angles are equal to two right angles, that the greatest side is subtended by the greatest angle, and the like, which now, whether I wish it or do not wish it, I recognise very clearly as pertaining to it, although I never thought of the matter at all when I imagined a triangle for the first time, and which therefore cannot be said to have been invented by me.

Nor does the objection hold good that possibly this idea of a triangle has reached my mind through the medium of my senses, since I have sometimes seen bodies triangular in shape; because I can form in my mind an infinitude of other figures regarding which we cannot have the least conception of their ever having been objects of sense, and I can nevertheless demonstrate various properties pertaining to their nature as well as to that of the triangle, and these must certainly all be true since I conceive them clearly. Hence they are something, and not pure negation; for it is perfectly clear that all that is true is something, and I have already fully demonstrated that all that I know clearly is true. And even although I had not demonstrated this, the nature of my mind is such that I could not prevent myself from holding them to be true so long as I conceive them clearly; and I recollect that even when I was still strongly attached to the objects of sense, I counted as the most certain those truths which I conceived clearly as regards figures, numbers, and the other matters which pertain to arithmetic and geometry, and, in general, to pure and abstract mathematics.

But now, if just because I can draw the idea of something from my thought, it follows that all which I know clearly and distinctly as pertaining to this object does really belong to it, may I not derive from this an argument demonstrating the existence of God? It is certain that I no less find the idea of God, that is to say, the idea of a supremely perfect Being, in me, than that of any figure or

---

Excerpted from *Meditations on First Philosophy* by René Descartes, Meditation V.

number whatever it is; and I do not know any less clearly and distinctly that an [actual and] eternal existence pertains to this nature than I know that all that which I am able to demonstrate of some figure or number truly pertains to the nature of this figure or number, and therefore, although all that I concluded in the preceding Meditations were found to be false, the existence of God would pass with me as at least as certain as I have ever held the truths of mathematics (which concern only numbers and figures) to be.

This indeed is not at first manifest, since it would seem to present some appearance of being a sophism. For being accustomed in all other things to make a distinction between existence and essence, I easily persuade myself that the existence can be separated from the essence of God, and that we can thus conceive God as not actually existing. But, nevertheless, when I think of it with more attention, I clearly see that existence can no more be separated from the essence of God than can its having its three angles equal to two right angles be separated from the essence of a [rectilinear] triangle, or the idea of a mountain from the idea of a valley; and so there is not any less repugnance to our conceiving a God (that is, a Being supremely perfect) to whom existence is lacking (that is to say, to whom a certain perfection is lacking), than to conceive of a mountain which has no valley.

But although I cannot really conceive of a God without existence any more than a mountain without a valley, still from the fact that I conceive of a mountain with a valley, it does not follow that there is such a mountain in the world; similarly although I conceive of God as possessing existence, it would seem that it does not follow that there is a God which exists; for my thought does not impose any necessity upon things, and just as I may imagine a winged horse, although no horse with wings exists, so I could perhaps attribute existence to God, although no God existed.

But a sophism is concealed in this objection; for from the fact that I cannot conceive a mountain without a valley, it does not follow that there is any mountain or any valley in existence, but only that the mountain and the valley, whether they exist or do not exist, cannot in any way be separated one from the other. While from the fact that I cannot conceive God without existence, it follows that existence is inseparable from Him, and hence that He really exists; not that my thought can bring this to pass, or impose any necessity on things, but, on the contrary, because the necessity which lies in the thing itself, i.e. the necessity of the existence of God determines me to think in this way. For it is not within my power to think of God without existence (that is of a supremely perfect Being devoid of a supreme perfection) though it is in my power to imagine a horse either with wings or without wings.

And we must not here object that it is in truth necessary for me to assert that God exists after having presupposed that He possesses every sort of perfection, since existence is one of these, but that as a matter of fact my original supposition was not necessary, just as it is not necessary to consider that all quadrilateral figures can be inscribed in the circle; for supposing I thought of this, I should be constrained to admit that the rhombus might be inscribed in the circle since it is a quadrilateral figure, which, however, is manifestly false. [We must not, I say, make any such allegations because] although it is not necessary that I should at any time entertain the notion of God, nevertheless whenever it happens that I think of a first and a sovereign Being, and, so to speak, derive the idea of Him from the storehouse of my mind, it is necessary that I should attribute to Him every sort of perfection, although I do not get so far as to enumerate them all, or to apply my mind to each one in particular. And this necessity suffices to make me conclude (after having recognised that existence is a perfection) that this first and sovereign Being really exists; just as though it is not necessary for me ever to imagine any triangle, yet, whenever I wish to consider a rectilinear figure composed only of three angles, it is absolutely essential that I should attribute to it all those properties which serve to bring about the conclusion that its three angles are not greater than two right angles, even although I may not then be considering this point in particular. But when I consider which figures are capable of being inscribed in the circle, it is in no wise necessary that I should think that all quadrilateral figures are of this number; on the contrary, I cannot even pretend that this is the case, so long as I do not desire to accept anything which I cannot conceive clearly and distinctly. And in consequence there is a great difference between the false suppositions such as this, and the true ideas born within me, the first and principal of which is that of God. For really I discern in many ways that this idea is not something factitious, and depending solely on my thought, but that it is the image of a true and immutable nature; first of all, because I cannot conceive anything but God himself to whose essence existence [necessarily] pertains; in the second place because it is not possible for me to conceive two or more Gods in this same position; and, granted that there is one such God who now exists, I see clearly that it is necessary that He should have existed from all eternity, and that He must exist eternally; and finally, because I know an infinitude of other properties in God, none of which I can either diminish or change.

Why the Proofs Do Not Work

J. J. C. SMART

THIS lecture is not to discuss whether God exists. It is to discuss reasons which philosophers have given for saying that God exists. That is, to discuss certain arguments.

First of all it may be as well to say what we may hope to get out of this. Of course, if we found that any of the traditional arguments for the existence of God were sound, we should get out of our one hour this Sunday afternoon some-

This is a very slightly revised version of "The Existence of God" by J. J. C. Smart, a public lecture at the University of Adelaide in 1951, reprinted in *Church Quarterly Review*, 1955. Reprinted by permission of the author.

thing of inestimable value, such as one never got out of any hour's work in our lives before. For we should have got out of one hour's work the answer to that question about which, above all, we want to know the answer. (This is assuming for the moment that the question 'Does God exist?' is a proper question. The fact that a question is all right as far as the rules of ordinary grammar are concerned does not ensure that it has a sense. For example, 'Does virtue run faster than length?' is certainly all right as far as ordinary grammar is concerned, but it is obviously not a meaningful question. Again, 'How fast does time flow?' is all right as far as ordinary grammar is concerned, but it has no clear meaning. Now some philosophers would ask whether the question 'Does God exist?' is a proper question. The greatest danger to theism at the present moment does not come from people who deny the validity of the arguments for the existence of God, for many Christian theologians do not believe that the existence of God can be proved, and certainly nowhere in the Old or New Testaments do we find any evidence of people's religion having a metaphysical basis. The main danger to theism today comes from people who want to say that 'God exists' and 'God does not exist' are equally absurd. The concept of God, they would say, is a nonsensical one. Now I myself shall later give grounds for thinking that the question 'Does God exist?' is not, in the full sense, a proper question, but I shall also give grounds for believing that to admit this is not necessarily to endanger theology.)

However, let us assume for the moment that the question 'Does God exist?' is a proper question. We now ask: Can a study of the traditional proofs of the existence of God enable us to give an affirmative answer to this question? I contend that it can not. I shall point out what seem to me to be fallacies in the main traditional arguments for the existence of God. Does proving that the arguments are invalid prove that God does not exist? Not at all. For to say that an argument is invalid is by no means the same thing as to say that its conclusion is false. Still, if we do find that the arguments we consider are all fallacious, what do we *gain* out of our investigation? Well, one thing we gain is a juster (if more austere) view of what philosophical argument can do for us. But, more important, we get a deeper insight into the logical nature of certain concepts, in particular, of course, the concepts of deity and existence. Furthermore we shall get some hints as to whether philosophy can be of any service to theologians, and if it can be of service, some hints as to how it can be of service. I think that it can be, but I must warn you that many, indeed perhaps the majority, of philosophers today would not entirely agree with me here.

One very noteworthy feature which must strike anyone who first looks at the usual arguments for the existence of God is the extreme brevity of these arguments. They range from a few lines to a few pages. St. Thomas Aquinas presents five arguments in three pages! Would it not be rather extraordinary if such a great conclusion should be got so easily? Before going on to discuss any of the traditional arguments in detail I want to give general grounds for suspecting anyone who claims to settle a controversial question by means of a short snappy argument.

My reason for doubting whether a short snappy argument can ever settle any controversial question is as follows: *any argument can be reversed.* Let me explain this. A question of elementary logic is involved. Let us consider an argument from two premisses, p, q, to a conclusion r:

$$\begin{array}{c} p \\ q \\ \hline r \end{array}$$

If the argument is valid, that is, if r really does follow from p and q, the argument will lead to agreement about r provided that there already is agreement about p and q. For example, if we have the premisses

p All A, B and C grade cricketers are entitled to a free pass to the Adelaide Oval for Test matches, Sheffield Shield matches, etc. (quite uncontroversial, it can be got from the rules of the South Australian Cricket Association).

q John Wilkin is an A, B or C grade cricketer. (Quite uncontroversial, everyone knows it.)

we may conclude

r John Wilkin is entitled to a free pass to the Adelaide Oval for Test matches, Sheffield Shield matches, etc.

But we now consider this argument[1]:

p Nothing can come into existence except through the activity of some previously existing thing or being.

q The world had a beginning in time.

therefore

r The world came into existence through the activity of some previously existing thing or being.

If this argument is valid (as it certainly is) then it is equally the case that

(not-r) The world did not come into existence through the activity of some previously existing thing or being

implies that either

(not-p) Something *can* come into existence otherwise than through the activity of a previously existing thing or being

or

(not-q) The world had no beginning in time.

That is, if $\begin{array}{c} p \\ q \\ \hline r \end{array}$ is valid $\begin{array}{c} \text{not-}r \\ q \\ \hline \text{not-}p \end{array}$ and $\begin{array}{c} \text{not-}r \\ p \\ \hline \text{not-}q \end{array}$ must be equally valid.

Now it is possible that a person might think that we have *fewer* reasons for believing r than we have for believing (not-p) or (not-q). In which case the argument $\begin{array}{c} p \\ q \\ \hline r \end{array}$ though perfectly valid will not convince him. For he will be in-

[1] I owe this illustration, and the whole application to the idea of 'reversing the argument,' to Prof. D. A. T. Gasking of Melbourne.

clined to argue in the opposite direction, that is, from the falsity of *r* to the falsity of either *p* or *q*.

This last example is perhaps itself a—not very good—argument for the existence of God, but I have given it purely as an example to show *one* of the things to look out for when criticizing more serious arguments. The other thing to look out for, of course, is whether the argument is *valid.* It is my belief that in the case of any metaphysical argument it will be found that if the premisses are uncontroversial the argument is unfortunately not valid, and that if the argument is valid the premisses will unfortunately be just as doubtful as the conclusion they are meant to support.

With these warnings in mind let us proceed to the discussion of the three most famous arguments for the existence of God. These are:

1. The Ontological Argument.
2. The Cosmological Argument.
3. The Teleological Argument.

The first argument—the ontological argument—really has no premisses at all. It tries to show that there would be a contradiction in denying that God exists. It was first formulated by St. Anselm and was later used by Descartes. It is not a convincing argument to modern ears, and St. Thomas Aquinas gave essentially the right reasons for rejecting it. However, it is important to discuss it, as an understanding of what is wrong with it is necessary for evaluating the second argument, that is, the cosmological argument. This argument does have a premiss, but not at all a controversial one. It is that something exists. We should all, I think, agree to that. The teleological argument is less austere in manner than the other two. It tries to argue to the existence of God not purely *a priori* and not from the mere fact of *something* existing, but from the actual features we observe in nature, namely those which seem to be evidence of design or purpose.

We shall discuss these three arguments in order. I do not say that they are the only arguments which have been propounded for the existence of God, but they are, I think, the most important ones. For example, of St. Thomas Aquinas' celebrated 'Five Ways' the first three are variants of the cosmological argument, and the fifth is a form of the teleological argument.

The Ontological Argument. This as I remarked, contains no factual premiss. It is a *reductio-ad-absurdum* of the supposition that God does not exist. Now *reductio-ad-absurdum* proofs are to be suspected whenever there is doubt as to whether the statement to be proved is *significant.* For example, it is quite easy, as anyone who is familiar with the so-called Logical Paradoxes will know, to produce a not *obviously* nonsensical statement, such that both it *and* its denial imply a contradiction. So unless we are sure of the significance of a statement we cannot regard a *reductio-ad-absurdum* of its contradictory as proving its truth. This point of view is well known to those versed in the philosophy of mathematics; there is a well-known school of mathematicians, led by Brouwer, who refuse in certain circumstances to employ *reductio-ad-absurdum* proofs. However, I shall not press this criticism of the ontological argument, for this criticism is somewhat abstruse (though it has been foreshadowed by Catholic philosophers, who object to the ontological argument by saying that it does not first show that the concept of an infinitely perfect being is a *possible* one). We are at present assuming that 'Does God exist?' is a proper question, and if it is a proper question there is no objection so far to answering it by means of a *reductio-ad-absurdum* proof. We shall content ourselves with the more usual criticisms of the ontological argument.

The ontological argument was made famous by Descartes. It is to be found at the beginning of his Fifth Meditation. As I remarked earlier it was originally put forward by Anselm, though I am sorry to say that to read Descartes you would never suspect that fact! Descartes points out that in mathematics we can deduce various things purely *a priori*, 'as for example,' he says, 'when I imagine a triangle, although there is not and perhaps never was in any place . . . one such figure, it remains true nevertheless that this figure possesses a certain determinate nature, form, or essence, which is . . . not framed by me, nor in any degree dependent on my thought; as appears from the circumstance, that diverse properties of the triangle may be demonstrated, for example that its three angles are equal to two right, that its greatest side is subtended by its greatest angle, and the like.' Descartes now goes on to suggest that just as having the sum of its angles equal to two right angles is involved in the idea of a triangle, so *existence* is involved in the very idea of an infinitely perfect being, and that it would therefore be as much of a contradiction to assert that an infinitely perfect being does not exist as it is to assert that the three angles of a triangle do not add up to two right angles or that two of its sides are not together greater than the third side. We may then, says Descartes, assert that an infinitely perfect being *necessarily* exists, just as we may say that two sides of a triangle are together *necessarily* greater than the third side.

This argument is highly fallacious. To say that a so-and-so exists is not in the least like saying that a so-and-so has such-and-such a property. It is not to amplify a concept but to say that a concept applies to something, and whether or not a concept applies to something can not be seen from an examination of the concept itself. Existence is not a property. 'Growling' is a property of tigers, and to say that 'tame tigers growl' is to say something about tame tigers, but to say 'tame tigers exist' is not to say something about tame tigers but to say that there are tame tigers. Prof. G. E. Moore once brought out the difference between existence and a property such as that of being tame, or being a tiger, or being a growler, by reminding us that though the sentence 'some tame tigers do not *growl*' makes perfect sense, the sentence 'some tame tigers do not *exist*' has no clear meaning. The fundamental mistake in the ontological argument, then, is that it treats 'exists' in 'an infinitely perfect being exists' as if it ascribed a property existence to an infinitely perfect being, just as 'is loving' in 'an infinitely perfect being is loving' ascribes a property, or as 'growl' in 'tame tigers growl' ascribes a property: the verb 'to exist' in 'an infinitely perfect being exists' does not ascribe a property to something already conceived of as existing but says that the concept of an infinitely perfect being applies to something. The verb 'to exist' here takes us right out of the purely conceptual world. This being so, there can never be any *logical contradiction* in denying that God exists. It is worth mentioning that we are less likely to make the sort of mistake that the ontological argument makes if we use the expression 'there is a so-and-so' instead of the more misleading form of words 'a so-and-so exists.'

I should like to mention another interesting, though less crucial, objection to Descartes' argument. He talks as though you can deduce further properties of, say, a triangle, by considering its definition. It is worth pointing out that from the definition of a triangle as a figure bounded by three straight lines you can only deduce trivialities, such as that it is bounded by more than one straight line, for example. It is not at all a contradiction to say that the two sides of a triangle are together not greater than the third side, or that its angles do not add up to two right angles. To get a contradiction you have to bring in the specific axioms of Euclidean geometry. (Remember school geometry, how you used to prove that the angles of a triangle add up to two right angles. Through the vertex *C* of the triangle *ABC* you drew a line parallel to *BA*, and so you assumed the axiom of parallels for a start. Definitions, by themselves, are not deductively potent. Descartes, though a very great mathematician himself, was profoundly mistaken as to the nature of mathematics. However, we can interpret him as saying that from the definition of a triangle, *together with the axioms of Euclidean geometry*, you can deduce various things, such as that the angles of a triangle add up to two right angles. But this just shows how pure mathematics is a sort of game with symbols; you start with a set of axioms, and operate on them in accordance with certain rules of inference. All the mathematician requires is that the axiom set should be *consistent.* Whether or not it has application to reality lies outside pure mathematics. Geometry is no fit model for a proof of real existence.

We now turn to the *Cosmological Argument.* This argument does at least seem more promising than the ontological argument. It does start with a factual premiss, namely that something exists. The premiss that something exists is indeed a very abstract one, but nevertheless it *is* factual, it does give us a foothold in the real world of things, it does go beyond the consideration of mere concepts. The argument has been put forward in various forms, but for present purposes it may be put as follows:

Everything in the world around us is *contingent.* That is, with regard to any particular thing, it is quite conceivable that it might not have existed. For example, if you were asked why you existed, you could say that it was because of your parents, and if asked why they existed you could go still further back, but however far you go back you have not, so it is argued, made the fact of your existence really intelligible. For however far back you go in such a series you only get back to something which itself might not have existed. For a really satisfying explanation of why anything contingent (such as you or me or this table) exists you must eventually begin with something which is not itself contingent, that is, with something of which we cannot say that it might not have existed, that is, we must begin with a necessary being. So the first part of the argument boils down to this. *If anything exists an absolutely necessary being must exist. Something exists. Therefore an absolutely necessary being must exist.*

The second part of the argument is to prove that a necessarily existing being must be an infinitely perfect being, that is, God. Kant[2] contended that this second stage of the argument is just the ontological argument over again, and of course if this were so the cosmological argument would plainly be a fraud; it begins happily enough with an existential premiss ('something exists') but this would only be a cover for the subsequent employment of the ontological argument. This criticism of Kant's has been generally accepted but I think that certain Thomist philosophers have been right in attributing to Kant's own criticism a mistake in elementary logic. Let us look at Kant's criticism. Kant says, correctly enough, that the conclusion of the second stage of the cosmological argument is 'All necessarily existing beings are infinitely perfect beings.' This, he says, implies that 'Some infinitely perfect beings are necessarily existing beings.' Since, however, there could be only one infinitely perfect, unlimited, being, we may replace the proposition 'Some infinitely perfect beings are necessarily existing beings' by the proposition 'All infinitely perfect beings are necessarily existing beings.' (To make this last point clearer let me take an analogous example. If it is true that some men who are Prime Minister of Australia are Liberals and if it is also true that there is only one Prime Minister of Australia, then we can equally well say that all men who are Prime Minister of Australia are Liberals. For 'some' means 'at least one,' and if there is only one Prime Minister, then 'at least one' is equivalent to 'one,' which in this case is 'all.') So the conclusion of the second stage of the cosmological argument is that "all infinitely perfect beings are necessarily existing beings.' This, however, is the principle of the ontological argument, which we have already criticized, and which, for that matter, proponents of the cosmological argument like Thomas Aquinas themselves reject.

Kant has, however, made a very simple mistake. He has forgotten that the existence of a necessary being has already been proved (or thought to have been proved) in the first part of the argument. He changes 'All necessary beings are infinitely perfect beings' round to 'Some infinitely perfect beings are necessary beings.' If this change round is to be valid the existence of a necessary being is already presupposed. Kant has been misled by an ambiguity in 'all.' 'All X's are Y's' may take it for granted that there are some X's or it may not. For example if I say, 'All the people in this room are interested in Philosophy,' it is already agreed that there are some people in this room. So we can infer that 'Some of the people interested in Philosophy are people in this room.' So 'All the people in this room are interested in Philosophy' says more than 'If anyone were in this room he would be interested in Philosophy,' for this would be true even if there were in fact no people in this room. (As I wrote this lecture I was quite sure that *if* anyone came he would be interested in Philosophy, and I could

[2] *Critique of Pure Reason*, A 603.

have been quite sure of this even if I had doubted whether anyone would come.) Now sometimes 'All X's are Y's does mean only 'If anything is an X it is a Y.' Take the sentence 'All trespassers will be prosecuted.' This does not imply that some prosecuted people will be trespassers, for it does not imply that there are or will be any trespassers. Indeed the object of putting it on a notice is to make it more likely that there won't be any trespassers. All that 'All trespassers will be prosecuted' says is, 'If anyone is a trespasser then he will be prosecuted.' So Kant's criticism won't do. He has taken himself and other people in by using 'all' sometimes in the one way and sometimes in the other.

While agreeing thus far with Thomist critics of Kant[3] I still want to assert that the cosmological argument is radically unsound. The trouble comes much earlier than where Kant locates it. The trouble comes in the *first* stage of the argument. For the first stage of the argument purports to argue to the existence of a necessary being. And by 'a necessary being' the cosmological argument means 'a *logically* necessary being,' i.e. 'a being whose non-existence is inconceivable in the sort of way that a triangle's having four sides is inconceivable.' The trouble is, however, that the concept of a logically necessary being is a self-contradictory concept, like the concept of a round square. For in the first place 'necessary' is a predicate of *propositions*, not of things. That is, we can contrast *necessary* propositions such as '$3 + 2 = 5$,' 'a thing cannot be red and green all over,' 'either it is raining or it is not raining,' with *contingent* propositions, such as 'Mr. Menzies is Prime Minister of Australia,' 'the earth is slightly flattened at the poles,' and 'sugar is soluble in water.' The propositions in the first class are guaranteed solely by the rules for the use of the symbols they contain. In the case of the propositions of the second class a genuine possibility of agreeing or not agreeing with reality is left open; whether they are true or false depends not on the conventions of our language but on reality. (Compare the contrast between 'the equator is 90 degrees from the pole,' which tells us nothing about geography but only about our map-making conventions, and 'Adelaide is 55 degrees from the pole,' which does tell us a geographical fact.) So no informative proposition can be logically necessary. Now since 'necessary' is a word which applies primarily to propositions, we shall have to interpret 'God is a necessary being' as 'The proposition "God exists" is logically necessary.' But this *is* the principle of the ontological argument, and there is no way of getting round it this time in the way that we got out of Kant's criticism. No existential proposition can be logically necessary, for we saw that the truth of a logically necessary proposition depends only on our symbolism, or to put the same thing in another way, on the relationship of concepts. We saw, however, in discussing the ontological argument, that an existential proposition does not say that one concept is involved in another, but that a concept applies to something. An existential proposition must be very different from any logically necessary one, such as a

[3] See, for example, Fr. T. A. Johnston, *Australasian Journal of Philosophy*, Vol. XXI, pp. 14–15, or D. J. B. Hawkins, *Essentials of Theism*, pp. 67–70, and the review of Fr. Hawkins' book by A. Donagan, *Australasian Journal of Philosophy*, Vol. XXVIII, especially p. 129.

mathematical one, for example, for the conventions of our symbolism clearly leave it open for us either to affirm or deny an existential proposition; it is not our symbolism but reality which decides whether or not we must affirm it or deny it.

The demand that the existence of God should be *logically* necessary is thus a self-contradictory one. When we see this and go back to look at the first stage of the cosmological argument it no longer seems compelling, indeed it now seems to contain an absurdity. If we cast our minds back, we recall that the argument was as follows: that if we explain why something exists and is what it is, we must explain it by reference to something else, and we must explain that thing's being what it is by reference to yet another thing, and so on, back and back. It is then suggested that unless we can go back to a logically necessary first cause we shall remain intellectually unsatisfied. We should otherwise only get back to something which might have been otherwise, and with reference to which the same questions can again be asked. This is the argument, but we now see that in asking for a logically necessary first cause we are doing something worse than asking for the moon. It is only *physically* impossible for us to get the moon; if I were a few million times bigger I could reach out for it and give it to you. That is, I know what it would be *like* to give you the moon, though I cannot in *fact* do it. A logically necessary first cause, however, is not impossible in the way that giving you the moon is impossible; no, it is *logically* impossible. 'Logically necessary being' is a self-contradictory expression like 'round square.' It is not any good saying that we would only be intellectually satisfied with a logically necessary cause, that nothing else would do. We can easily have an absurd wish. We should all like to be able to eat our cake and have it, but that does not alter the fact that our wish is an absurd and self-contradictory one. We reject the cosmological argument, then, because it rests on a thorough absurdity.

Having reached this conclusion I should like to make one or two remarks about the necessity of God. First of all, I think that it is undeniable that if worship is to be what religion takes it to be, then God must be a necessary being in some sense or other of 'necessary.' He must not be just one of the things in the world, however big. To concede that he was just one of the things in the world, even a big one, would reduce religion to something near idolatry. All I wish to point out is that God can not be a *logically* necessary being, for the very supposition that he is is self-contradictory. (Hence, of course, to say that God is not logically necessary is not to place any limitations on him. It is not a limitation on your walking ability that you cannot go out of the room and not go out. To say that someone cannot do something self-contradictory is not to say that he is in any way impotent, it is to say that the sentence 'he did such and such and did not do it' is not a possible description of anything.) Theological necessity cannot be logical necessity. In the second place, I think I can see roughly what sort of necessity theological necessity might be. Let me give an analogy from physics. It is not a *logical* necessity that the velocity of light in a vacuum should be constant. It would, however, upset physical theory considerably if we denied it. Similarly it is not a logical necessity that God exists. But it would clearly upset the structure of our religious attitudes in the most violent way if we denied it or even entertained the possibility of its falsehood. So if we say that it is a *physical* necessity that the velocity of light *in vacuo* should be constant—(deny it and prevailing physical theory would have to be scrapped or at any rate drastically modified)—similarly we can say that it is a *religious* necessity that God exists. That is, we believe in the necessity of God's existence because we are Christians; we are not Christians because we believe in the necessity of God's existence. There are no short cuts to God. I draw your attention to the language of religion itself, where we talk of *conversion*, not of *proof*. In my opinion religion can stand on its own feet, but to found it on a metaphysical argument *a priori* is to found it on absurdity born of ignorance of the logic of our language. I am reminded of what was said about the Boyle lectures in the eighteenth century: that no one doubted that God existed until the Boyle lectures started to prove it.

Perhaps now is the time to say why I suggested at the beginning of the lecture that 'Does God exist?' is not a proper question. Once again I make use of an analogy from science. 'Do electrons exist?' (asked just like that) is not a proper question. In order to acquire the concept of an electron we must find out about experiments with cathode-ray tubes, the Wilson cloud chamber, about spectra and so on. We then find the concept of the electron a useful one, one which plays a part in a mass of physical theory. When we reach this stage the question 'Do electrons exist?' no longer arises. Before we reached this stage the question 'Do electrons exist?' had no clear meaning. Similarly, I suggest, the question 'Does God exist?' has no clear meaning for the unconverted. But for the converted the question no longer arises. The word 'God' gets its meaning from the part it plays in religious speech and literature, and in religious speech and literature the question of existence does not arise. A theological professor at Glasgow once said to me: 'Religion is "O God, if you exist, save my soul if it exists!"' This of course was a joke. It clearly is just *not* what religion is. So within religion the question 'Does God exist?' does not arise, any more than the question 'Do electrons exist?' arises within physics. Outside religion the question 'Does God exist?' has as little meaning as the question 'Do electrons exist?' as asked by the scientifically ignorant. Thus I suggest that it is possible to hold that the question 'Does God exist?' is not a proper question without necessarily also holding that religion and theology are nonsensical.

The cosmological argument, we saw, failed because it made use of the absurd conception of a *logically* necessary being. We now pass to the third argument which I propose to consider. This is the *Teleological Argument.* It is also called 'the Argument from Design.' It would be better called the argument *to* design, as Kemp Smith does call it, for clearly that the universe has been designed by a great architect is to assume a great part of the conclusion to be proved. Or we could call it 'the argument from apparent design.' The argument is very fully discussed in Hume's *Dialogues concerning Natural Religion*, to which I should like to draw your attention. In these dialogues the argument is presented as follows: 'Look round the world: Contemplate the whole and every part of it:

You will find it to be nothing but one great machine, subdivided into an infinite number of lesser machines. . . . The curious adapting of means to ends, throughout all nature, resembles exactly, though it much exceeds, the productions of human contrivance. . . . Since therefore the effects resemble each other, we are led to infer, by all the rules of analogy, that the causes also resemble; and that the Author of nature is somewhat similar to the mind of man; though possessed of much larger faculties, proportioned to the grandeur of the work which he has executed.'

This argument may at once be criticized in two ways: (1) We may question whether the analogy between the universe and artificial things like houses, ships, furniture, and machines (which admittedly are designed) is very close. Now in any ordinary sense of language, it is true to say that plants and animals have *not* been designed. If we press the analogy of the universe to a plant, instead of to a machine, we get to a very different conclusion. And why should the one analogy be regarded as any better or worse than the other? (2) Even if the analogy were close, it would only go to suggest that the universe was designed by a *very great* (not infinite) architect, and note, an *architect*, not a *creator*. For if we take the analogy seriously we must notice that we do not create the materials from which we make houses, machines and so on, but only *arrange* the materials.

This, in bare outline, is the general objection to the argument from design, and will apply to any form of it. In the form in which the argument was put forward by such theologians as Paley, the argument is, of course, still more open to objection. For Paley laid special stress on such things as the eye of an animal, which he thought must have been contrived by a wise Creator for the special benefit of the animal. It seemed to him inconceivable how otherwise such a complex organ, so well suited to the needs of the animal, should have arisen. Or listen to Henry More: 'For why have we three joints in our legs and arms, as also in our fingers, but that it was much better than having two or four? And why are our fore-teeth sharp like chisels to cut, but our inward teeth broad to grind, [instead of] the fore-teeth broad and the other sharp? But we might have made a hard shift to have lived through in that worser condition. Again, why are the teeth so luckily placed, or rather, why are there not teeth in other bones as well as in the jaw-bones? for they might have been as capable as these. But the reason is, nothing is done foolishly or in vain; that is, there is a divine Providence that orders all things.' This type of argument has lost its persuasiveness, for the theory of Evolution explains why our teeth are so luckily placed in our jaw-bones, why we have the most convenient number of joints in our fingers, and so on. Species which did not possess advantageous features would not survive in competition with those which did.

The sort of argument Paley and Henry More used is thus quite unconvincing. Let us return to the broader conception, that of the universe as a whole, which seems to show the mark of a benevolent and intelligent Designer. Bacon expressed this belief forcibly: 'I had rather beleave all the Fables in the Legend and the Talmud and the Alcoran than that this Universal Frame is without a Minde.' So, in some moods, does the universe strike us. But sometimes, when we are in other moods, we see it very differently. To quote Hume's dialogues again: 'Look around this Universe. What an immense profusion of beings, animated and organized, sensible and active! You admire this prodigous variety and fecundity. But inspect a little more narrowly these living existences, the only beings worth regarding. How hostile and destructive to each other! How insufficient all of them for their own happiness! . . . the whole presents nothing but the idea of a blind Nature, impregnated by a great vivifying principle, and pouring forth from her lap, without discernment or parental care, her maimed and abortive children!' There is indeed a great deal of suffering, some part of which is no doubt attributable to the moral choices of men, and to save us from which would conflict with what many people would regard as the greater good of moral freedom, but there is still an immense residue of apparently needless suffering, that is, needless in the sense that it could be prevented by an omnipotent being. The difficulty is that of reconciling the presence of evil and suffering with the assertion that God is both omnipotent and benevolent. If we *already* believe in an omnipotent and benevolent God, then some attempt may be made to solve the problem of evil by arguing that the values in the world form a sort of organic unity, and that making any *part* of the world better would perhaps nevertheless reduce the value of the whole. Paradoxical though this thesis may appear at first sight, it is perhaps not theoretically absurd. If, however, evil presents a *difficulty* to the believing mind, it presents an *insuperable* difficulty to one who wishes to argue rationally from the world as we find it to the existence of an omnipotent and benevolent God. As Hume puts it: 'Is the world considered in general, and as it appears to us in this life, different from what a man . . . would *beforehand* expect from a very powerful, wise and benevolent Deity? It must be a strange prejudice to assert the contrary. And from thence I conclude, that, however consistent the world may be, allowing certain suppositions and conjectures, with the idea of such a Deity, it can never afford us an inference concerning his existence.'

The teleological argument is thus extremely shaky, and in any case, even if it were sound, it would only go to prove the existence of a very great architect, not of an omnipotent and benevolent Creator.

Nevertheless, the argument has a fascination for us that reason can not easily dispel. Hume, in his twelfth dialogue, and after pulling the argument from design to pieces in the previous eleven dialogues, nevertheless speaks as follows: 'A purpose, an intention, a design strikes everywhere the most careless, the most stupid thinker; and no man can be so hardened in absurd systems as at all times to reject it . . . all the sciences almost lead us insensibly to acknowledge a first Author.' Similarly Kant, before going on to exhibit the fallaciousness of the argument, nevertheless says of it: 'This proof always deserves to be mentioned with respect. It is the oldest, the clearest and the most accordant with the common reason of mankind. It enlivens the study of nature, just as it itself derives its existence and gains ever new vigour from that source. It suggests ends and purposes, where our observation would not have detected them by itself, and extends our knowledge of nature by means of the guiding-concept of a special unity, the principle of which is outside nature. This knowledge . . . so strengthens the belief in a supreme Author of nature that the belief acquires the force of an irresistable conviction.' It is somewhat of a paradox that an invalid argument should command so much respect even from those who have demonstrated its invalidity. The solution of the paradox is perhaps somewhat as follows[4]: The argument from design is no good as an argument. But in those who have the seeds of a genuinely religious attitude already within them the facts to which the argument from design draws attention, facts showing the grandeur and majesty of the universe, facts that are evident to anyone who looks upwards on a starry night, and which are enormously multiplied for us by the advance of theoretical science, these facts have a powerful effect. But they only have this effect on the already religious mind, on the mind which has the capability of feeling the religious type of awe. That is, the argument from design is in reality no argument, or if it is regarded as an argument it is feeble, but it is a potent instrument in heightening religious emotions.

Something similar might even be said of the cosmological argument. As an argument it cannot pass muster at all; indeed it is completely absurd, as employing the notion of a logically necessary being. Nevertheless it does appeal to something deep seated in our natures. It takes its stand on the fact that the existence of you or me or this table is not logically necessary. Logic tells us that this fact is not a fact at all, but is a truism, like the 'fact' that a circle is not a square. Again, the cosmological argument tries to base the existence of you or me or this table on the existence of a logically necessary being, and hence commits a rank absurdity, the notion of a logically necessary being being self-contradictory. So the only rational thing to say if someone asks 'Why does this table exist?' is some such thing as that such and such a carpenter made it. We can go back and back in such a series, but we must not entertain the absurd idea of getting back to something logically necessary. However, now let us ask, 'Why should anything exist at all?' Logic seems to tell us that the only answer which is not absurd is to say, 'Why shouldn't it?' Nevertheless, though I know how any answer on the lines of the cosmological argument can be pulled to pieces by a correct logic, I still feel I want to go on asking the question. Indeed, though logic has taught me to look at such a question with the gravest suspicion, my mind often seems to reel under the immense significance it seems to have for me. That anything should exist at all does seem to me a matter for the deepest awe. But whether other people feel this sort of awe, and whether they or I ought to is another question. I think we ought to. If so, the question arises: If 'Why should anything exist at all?' cannot be interpreted after the manner of the cosmological argument, that is, as an absurd request for the nonsensical postulation of a logically necessary being, what sort of question is it? What sort of question is this question 'Why should anything exist at all?' All I can say is, that I do not yet know.

[4] See also N. Kemp Smith's Henrietta Hertz Lecture, 'Is Divine Existence Credible?', *Proceedings of the British Academy*, 1931.

The Will to Believe

WILLIAM JAMES

IN THE recently published Life by Leslie Stephen of his brother, Fitz-James, there is an account of a school to which the latter went when he was a boy. The teacher, a certain Mr. Guest, used to converse with his pupils in this wise: "Gurney, what is the difference between justification and sanctification?—Stephen, prove the omnipotence of God!" etc. In the midst of our Harvard free-thinking and indifference we are prone to imagine that here at your good old orthodox College conversation continues to be somewhat upon this order; and to show you that we at Harvard have not lost all interest in these vital subjects, I have brought with me to-night something like a sermon on justification by faith to read to you,—I mean an essay in justification *of* faith, a defence of our right to adopt a believing attitude in religious matters, in spite of the fact that our merely logical intellect may not have been coerced. 'The Will to Believe,' accordingly, is the title of my paper.

I have long defended to my own students the lawfulness of voluntarily adopted faith; but as soon as they have got well imbued with the logical spirit, they have as a rule refused to admit my contention to be lawful philosophically, even though in point of fact they were personally all the time chock-full of some faith or other themselves. I am all the while, however, so profoundly convinced that my own position is correct, that your invitation has seemed to me a good occasion to make my statements more clear. Perhaps your minds will be more open than those with which I have hitherto had to deal. I will be as little technical as I can, though I must begin by setting up some technical distinctions that will help us in the end.

I

Let us give the name of *hypothesis* to anything that may be proposed to our belief; and just as the electricians speak of live and dead wires, let us speak of any hypothesis as either *live* or *dead.* A live hypothesis is one which appeals as a real possibility to him to whom it is proposed. If I ask you to believe in the Mahdi, the notion makes no electric connection with your nature,—it refuses to scintillate with any credibility at all. As an hypothesis it is completely dead. To an Arab, however (even if he be not one of the Mahdi's followers), the hypothesis is among the mind's possibilities: it is alive. This shows that deadness and liveness in an hypothesis are not intrinsic properties, but relations to the individual thinker. They are measured by his willingness to act. The maximum of liveness in an hypothesis means willingness to act irrevocably. Practically,

---

Reprinted from "The Will to Believe" by Williams James in *The New World*, June, 1896.

that means belief; but there is some believing tendency wherever there is willingness to act at all.

Next, let us call the decision between two hypotheses an *option*. Options may be of several kinds. They may be—1, *living* or *dead*; 2, *forced* or *avoidable*; 3, *momentous* or *trivial*; and for our purposes we may call an option a *genuine* option when it is of the forced, living, and momentous kind.

1. A living option is one in which both hypotheses are live ones. If I say to you: "Be a theosophist or be a Mohammedan," it is probably a dead option, because for you neither hypothesis is likely to be alive. But if I say: "Be an agnostic or be a Christian," it is otherwise: trained as you are, each hypothesis makes some appeal, however small, to your belief.

2. Next, if I say to you: "Choose between going out with your umbrella or without it," I do not offer you a genuine option, for it is not forced. You can easily avoid it by not going out at all. Similarly, if I say, "Either love me or hate me," "Either call my theory true or call it false," your option is avoidable. You may remain indifferent to me, neither loving nor hating, and you may decline to offer any judgment as to my theory. But if I say, "Either accept this truth or go without it," I put on you a forced option, for there is no standing place outside of the alternative. Every dilemma based on a complete logical disjunction, with no possibility of not choosing, is an option of this forced kind.

3. Finally, if I were Dr. Nansen and proposed to you to join my North Pole expedition, your option would be momentous; for this would probably be your only similar opportunity, and your choice now would either exclude you from the North Pole sort of immortality altogether or put at least the chance of it into your hands. He who refuses to embrace a unique opportunity loses the prize as surely as if he tried and failed. *Per contra*, the option is trivial when the opportunity is not unique, when the stake is insignificant, or when the decision is reversible if it later prove unwise. Such trivial options abound in the scientific life. A chemist finds an hypothesis live enough to spend a year in its verification: he believes in it to that extent. But if his experiments prove inconclusive either way, he is quit for his loss of time, no vital harm being done.

It will facilitate our discussion if we keep all these distinctions well in mind.

II

The next matter to consider is the actual psychology of human opinion. When we look at certain facts, it seems as if our passional and volitional nature lay at the root of all our convictions. When we look at others, it seems as if they could do nothing when the intellect had once said its say. Let us take the latter facts up first.

Does it not seem preposterous on the very face of it to talk of our opinions being modifiable at will? Can our will either help or hinder our intellect in its perceptions of truth? Can we, by just willing it, believe that Abraham Lincoln's existence is a myth, and that the portraits of him in McClure's Magazine are all of some one else? Can we, by any effort of our will, or by any strength of wish that it were true, believe ourselves well and about when we are roaring with rheumatism in bed, or feel certain that the sum of the two one-dollar bills in our pocket must be a hundred dollars? We can *say* any of these things, but we are absolutely impotent to believe them; and of just such things is the whole fabric of the truths that we do believe in made up,—matters of fact, immediate or remote, as Hume said, and relations between ideas, which are either there or not there for us if we see them so, and which if not there cannot be put there by any action of our own.

In Pascal's Thoughts there is a celebrated passage known in literature as Pascal's wager. In it he tries to force us into Christianity by reasoning as if our concern with truth resembled our concern with the stakes in a game of chance. Translated freely his words are these: You must either believe or not believe that God is—which will you do? Your human reason cannot say. A game is going on between you and the nature of things which at the day of judgment will bring out either heads or tails. Weigh what your gains and your losses would be if you should stake all you have on heads, or God's existence: if you win in such case, you gain eternal beatitude; if you lose, you lose nothing at all. If there were an infinity of chances, and only one for God in this wager, still you ought to stake your all on God; for though you surely risk a finite loss by this procedure, any finite loss is reasonable, even a certain one is reasonable, if there is but the possibility of infinite gain. Go, then, and take holy water, and have masses said; belief will come and stupefy your scruples,—*Cela vous fera croire et vous abêtira.* Why should you not? At bottom, what have you to lose?

You probably feel that when religious faith expresses itself thus, in the language of the gaming-table, it is put to its last trumps. Surely Pascal's own personal belief in masses and holy water had far other springs; and this celebrated page of his is but an argument for others, a last desperate snatch at a weapon against the hardness of the unbelieving heart. We feel that a faith in masses and holy water adopted wilfully after such a mechanical calculation would lack the inner soul of faith's reality; and if we were ourselves in the place of the Deity, we should probably take particular pleasure in cutting off believers of this pattern from their infinite reward. It is evident that unless there be some pre-existing tendency to believe in masses and holy water, the option offered to the will by Pascal is not a living option. Certainly no Turk ever took to masses and holy water on its account; and even to us Protestants these means of salvation seem such foregone impossibilities that Pascal's logic, invoked for them specifically, leaves us unmoved. As well might the Mahdi write to us, saying, "I am the Expected One whom God has created in his effulgence. You shall be infinitely happy if you confess me; otherwise you shall be cut off from the light of the sun. Weigh, then, your infinite gain if I am genuine against your finite sacrifice if I am not!" His logic would be that of Pascal; but he would vainly use it on us, for the hypothesis he offers us is dead. No tendency to act on it exists in us to any degree.

The talk of believing by our volition seems, then, from one point of view, simply silly. From another point of view it is worse than silly, it is vile. When one turns to the magnificent edifice of the physical sciences, and sees how it was reared; what thousands of disinterested moral lives of men lie buried in its mere foundations; what patience and postponement, what choking down of preference, what submission to the icy laws of outer fact are wrought into its very stones and mortar; how absolutely impersonal it stands in its vast augustness,—then how besotted and contemptible seems every little sentimentalist who comes blowing his voluntary smoke-wreaths, and pretending to decide things from out of his private dream! Can we wonder if those bred in the rugged and manly school of science should feel like spewing such subjectivism out of their mouths? The whole system of loyalties which grow up in the schools of science go dead against its toleration; so that it is only natural that those who have caught the scientific fever should pass over to the opposite extreme, and write sometimes as if the incorruptibly truthful intellect ought positively to prefer bitterness and unacceptableness to the heart in its cup.

> It fortifies my soul to know
> That, though I perish, Truth is so—

sings Clough, while Huxley exclaims: "My only consolation lies in the reflection that, however bad our posterity may become, so far as they hold by the plain rule of not pretending to believe what they have no reason to believe, because it may be to their advantage so to pretend [the word 'pretend' is surely here redundant], they will not have reached the lowest depth of immorality." And that delicious *enfant terrible* Clifford writes: "Belief is desecrated when given to unproved and unquestioned statements for the solace and private pleasure of the believer. . . . Whoso would deserve well of his fellows in this matter will guard the purity of his belief with a very fanaticism of jealous care, lest at any time it should rest on an unworthy object, and catch a stain which can never be wiped away. . . . If [a] belief has been accepted on insufficient evidence [even though the belief be true, as Clifford on the same page explains] the pleasure is a stolen one. . . . It is sinful because it is stolen in defiance of our duty to mankind. That duty is to guard ourselves from such beliefs as from a pestilence which may shortly master our own body and then spread to the rest of the town. . . . It is wrong always, everywhere, and for every one, to believe anything upon insufficient evidence."

III

All this strikes one as healthy, even when expressed, as by Clifford, with somewhat too much of robustious pathos in the voice. Free-will and simple wishing do seem, in the matter of our credences, to be only fifth wheels to the coach. Yet if any one should thereupon assume that intellectual insight is what remains after wish and will and sentimental preference have taken wing, or that pure reason is what then settles our opinions, he would fly quite as directly in the teeth of the facts.

It is only our already dead hypotheses that our willing nature is unable to bring to life again. But what has made them dead for us is for the most part a previous action of our willing nature of an antagonistic kind. When I say 'willing nature,' I do not mean only such deliberate volitions as may have set up habits of belief that we cannot now escape from,—I meant all such factors of belief as fear and hope, prejudice and passion, imitation and partisanship, the circumpressure of our caste and set. As a matter of fact we find ourselves believing, we hardly know how or why. Mr. Balfour gives the name of 'authority' to all those influences, born of the intellectual climate, that make hypotheses possible or impossible for us, alive or dead. Here in this room, we all of us believe in molecules and the conservation of energy, in democracy and necessary progress, in Protestant Christianity and the duty of fighting for 'the doctrine of the immortal Monroe,' all for no reasons worthy of the name. We see into these matters with no more inner clearness, and probably with much less, than any disbeliever in them might possess. His unconventionality would probably have some grounds to show for its conclusions; but for us, not insight, but the *prestige* of the opinions, is what makes the spark shoot from them and light up our sleeping magazines of faith. Our reason is quite satisfied, in nine hundred and ninety-nine cases out of every thousand of us, if it can find a few arguments that will do to recite in case our credulity is criticised by someone else. Our faith is faith in some one else's faith, and in the greatest matters this is most the case. Our belief in truth itself, for instance, that there is a truth, and that our minds and it are made for each other,—what is it but a passionate affirmation of desire, in which our social system backs us up? We want to have a truth; we want to believe that our experiments and studies and discussions must put us in a continually better and better position towards it; and on this line we agree to fight out our thinking lives. But if a pyrrhonistic sceptic asks us *how we know* all this, can our logic find a reply? No! certainly it cannot. It is just one volition against another,—we willing to go in for life upon a trust or assumption which he, for his part, does not care to make.[1]

As a rule we disbelieve all facts and theories for which we have no use. Clifford's cosmic emotions find no use for Christian feelings. Huxley belabors the bishops because there is no use for sacerdotalism in his scheme of life. Newman, on the contrary, goes over to Romanism, and finds all sorts of reasons good for staying there, because a priestly system is for him an organic need and delight. Why do so few 'scientists' even look at the evidence for telepathy, so called? Because they think, as a leading biologist, now dead, once said to me, that even if such a thing were true, scientists ought to band together to keep it suppressed and concealed. It would undo the uniformity of Nature and all sorts of other things without which scientists cannot carry on their pursuits. But if this very man had been shown something which as a scientist he might *do* with telepathy, he might not only have examined the evidence, but even have found it good enough. This very law which the logicians would impose upon us—if I

[1] Compare the admirable page 310 in S. H. Hodgson's *Time and Space*, London, 1865.

may give the name of logicians to those who would rule out our willing nature here—is based on nothing but their own natural wish to exclude all elements for which they, in their professional quality of logicians, can find no use.

Evidently, then, our non-intellectual nature does influence our convictions. There are passional tendencies and volitions which run before and others which come after belief, and it is only the latter that are too late for the fair; and they are not too late when the previous passional work has been already in their own direction. Pascal's argument, instead of being powerless, then seems a regular clincher, and is the last stroke needed to make our faith in masses and holy water complete. The state of things is evidently far from simple; and pure insight and logic, whatever they might do ideally, are not the only things that really do produce our creeds.

IV

Our next duty, having recognized this mixed-up state of affairs, is to ask whether it be simply reprehensible and pathological, or whether, on the contrary, we must treat it as a normal element in making up our minds. The thesis I defend is, briefly stated, this: *Our passional nature not only lawfully may, but must, decide an option between propositions, whenever it is a genuine option that cannot by its nature be decided on intellectual grounds; for to say, under such circumstances, "Do not decide, but leave the question open," is itself a passional decision,—just like deciding yes or no,—and is attended with the same risk of losing the truth.* The thesis thus abstractly expressed will, I trust, soon become quite clear. But I must first indulge in a bit more of preliminary work.

Religious Claims Are Meaningless

A. J. AYER

It is now generally admitted, at any rate by philosophers, that the existence of a being having the attributes which define the god of any non-animistic religion cannot be demonstratively proved. To see that this is so, we have only to ask ourselves what are the premises from which the existence of such a god could be deduced. If the conclusion that a god exists is to be demonstratively certain, then these premises must be certain; for, as the conclusion of a deductive argument is already contained in the premises, any uncertainty there may be about the truth of the premises is necessarily shared by it. But we know that no empirical proposition can ever be anything more than probable. It is only *a priori* propositions that are logically certain. But we cannot deduce the existence of a god from an *a priori* proposition. For we know that the reason why *a priori*

Reprinted with permission of Victor Gollancz Ltd. from *Language, Truth and Logic* by A. J. Ayer, 1936, pp. 114–120.

propositions are certain is that they are tautologies. And from a set of tautologies nothing but a further tautology can be validly deduced. It follows that there is no possibility of demonstrating the existence of a god.

What is not so generally recognised is that there can be no way of proving that the existence of a god, such as the God of Christianity, is even probable. Yet this also is easily shown. For if the existence of such a god were probable, then the proposition that he existed would be an empirical hypothesis. And in that case it would be possible to deduce from it, and other empirical hypotheses, certain experiential propositions which were not deducible from those other hypotheses alone. But in fact this is not possible. It is sometimes claimed, indeed, that the existence of a certain sort of regularity in nature constitutes sufficient evidence for the existence of a god. But if the sentence "God exists" entails no more than that certain types of phenomena occur in certain sequences, then to assert the existence of a god will be simply equivalent to asserting that there is the requisite regularity in nature; and no religious man would admit that this was all he intended to assert in asserting the existence of a god. He would say that in talking about God, he was talking about a transcendent being who might be known through certain empirical manifestations, but certainly could not be defined in terms of those manifestations. But in that case the term "god" is a metaphysical term. And if "god" is a metaphysical term, then it cannot be even probable that a god exists. For to say that "God exists" is to make a metaphysical utterance which cannot be either true or false. And by the same criterion, no sentence which purports to describe the nature of a transcendent god can possess any literal significance.

It is important not to confuse this view of religious assertions with the view that is adopted by atheists, or agnostics.[1] For it is characteristic of an agnostic to hold that the existence of a god is a possibility in which there is no good reason either to believe or disbelieve; and it is characteristic of an atheist to hold that it is at least probable that no god exists. And our view that all utterances about the nature of God are nonsensical, so far from being identical with, or even lending any support to, either of these familiar contentions, is actually incompatible with them. For if the assertion that there is a god is nonsensical, then the atheist's assertion that there is no god is equally nonsensical, since it is only a significant proposition that can be significantly contradicted. As for the agnostic, although he refrains from saying either that there is or that there is not a god, he does not deny that the question whether a transcendent god exists is a genuine question. He does not deny that the two sentences "There is a transcendent god" and "There is no transcendent god" express propositions one of which is actually true and the other false. All he says is that we have no means of telling which of them is true, and therefore ought not to commit ourselves to either. But we have seen that the sentences in question do not express propositions at all. And this means that agnosticism is also ruled out.

Thus we offer the theist the same comfort as we gave to the moralist. His

[1] This point was suggested to me by Professor H. H. Price.

assertions cannot possibly be valid, but they cannot be invalid either. As he says nothing at all about the world, he cannot justly be accused of saying anything false, or anything for which he has insufficient grounds. It is only when the theist claims that in asserting the existence of a transcendent god he is expressing a genuine proposition that we are entitled to disagree with him.

It is to be remarked that in cases where deities are identified with natural objects, assertions concerning them may be allowed to be significant. If, for example, a man tells me that the occurrence of thunder is alone both necessary and sufficient to establish the truth of the proposition that Jehovah is angry, I may conclude that, in his usage of words, the sentence "Jehovah is angry" is equivalent to "It is thundering." But in sophisticated religions, though they may be to some extent based on men's awe of natural processes which they cannot sufficiently understand, the "person" who is supposed to control the empirical world is not himself located in it; he is held to be superior to the empirical world, and so outside it; and he is endowed with super-empirical attributes. But the notion of a person whose essential attributes are non-empirical is not an intelligible notion at all. We may have a word which is used as if it named this "person," but, unless the sentences in which it occurs express propositions which are empirically verifiable, it cannot be said to symbolise anything. And this is the case with regard to the word "god," in the usage in which it is intended to refer to a transcendent object. The mere existence of the noun is enough to foster the illusion that there is a real, or at any rate a possible entity corresponding to it. It is only when we enquire what God's attributes are that we discover that "God," in this usage, is not a genuine name.

It is common to find belief in a transcendent god conjoined with belief in an after-life. But, in the form which it usually takes, the content of this belief is not a genuine hypothesis. To say that men do not ever die, or that the state of death is merely a state of prolonged insensibility, is indeed to express a significant proposition, though all the available evidence goes to show that it is false. But to say that there is something imperceptible inside a man, which is his soul or his real self, and that it goes on living after he is dead, is to make a metaphysical assertion which has no more factual content than the assertion that there is a transcendent god.

It is worth mentioning that, according to the account which we have given of religious assertions, there is no logical ground for antagonism between religion and natural science. As far as the question of truth or falsehood is concerned, there is no opposition between the natural scientist and the theist who believes in a transcendent god. For since the religious utterances of the theist are not genuine propositions at all, they cannot stand in any logical relation to the propositions of science. Such antagonism as there is between religion and science appears to consist in the fact that science takes away one of the motives which make men religious. For it is acknowledged that one of the ultimate sources of religious feeling lies in the inability of men to determine their own destiny; and science tends to destroy the feeling of awe with which men regard an alien world, by making them believe that they can understand and anticipate the course of natural phenomena, and even to some extent control it. The fact that it has recently become fashionable for physicists themselves to be sympathetic towards religion is a point in favour of this hypothesis. For this sympathy towards religion marks the physicists' own lack of confidence in the validity of their hypotheses, which is a reaction on their part from the anti-religious dogmatism of nineteenth-century scientists, and a natural outcome of the crisis through which physics has just passed.

It is not within the scope of this enquiry to enter more deeply into the causes of religious feeling, or to discuss the probability of the continuance of religious belief. We are concerned only to answer those questions which arise out of our discussion of the possibility of religious knowledge. The point which we wish to establish is that there cannot be any transcendent truths of religion. For the sentences which the theist uses to express such "truths" are not literally significant.

An interesting feature of this conclusion is that it accords with what many theists are accustomed to say themselves. For we are often told that the nature of God is a mystery which transcends the human understanding. But to say that something transcends the human understanding is to say that it is unintelligible. And what is unintelligible cannot significantly be described. Again, we are told that God is not an object of reason but an object of faith. This may be nothing more than an admission that the existence of God must be taken on trust, since it cannot be proved. But it may also be an assertion that God is the object of a purely mystical intuition, and cannot therefore be defined in terms which are intelligible to the reason. And I think there are many theists who would assert this. But if one allows that it is impossible to define God in intelligible terms, then one is allowing that it is impossible for a sentence both to be significant and to be about God. If a mystic admits that the object of his vision is something which cannot be described, then he must also admit that he is bound to talk nonsense when he describes it.

For his part, the mystic may protest that his intuition does reveal truths to him, even though he cannot explain to others what these truths are; and that we who do not possess this faculty of intuition can have no ground for denying that it is a cognitive faculty. For we can hardly maintain *a priori* that there are no ways of discovering true propositions except those which we ourselves employ. The answer is that we set no limit to the number of ways in which one may come to formulate a true proposition. We do not in any way deny that a synthetic truth may be discovered by purely intuitive methods as well as by the rational method of induction. But we do say that every synthetic proposition, however it may have been arrived at, must be subject to the test of actual experience. We do not deny *a priori* that the mystic is able to discover truths by his own special methods. We wait to hear what are the propositions which embody his discoveries, in order to see whether they are verified or confuted by our empirical observations. But the mystic, so far from producing propositions which are empirically verified, is unable to produce any intelligible propositions at all. And therefore we say that his intuition has not revealed to him any facts.

It is no use his saying that he has apprehended facts but is unable to express them. For we know that if he really had acquired any information, he would be able to express it. He would be able to indicate in some way or other how the genuineness of his discovery might be empirically determined. The fact that he cannot reveal what he "knows," or even himself devise an empirical test to validate his "knowledge," shows that his state of mystical intuition is not a genuinely cognitive state. So that in describing his vision the mystic does not give us any information about the external world; he merely gives us indirect information about the condition of his own mind.

These considerations dispose of the argument from religious experience, which many philosophers still regard as a valid argument in favour of the existence of a god. They say that it is logically possible for men to be immediately acquainted with God, as they are immediately acquainted with a sense-content, and that there is no reason why one should be prepared to believe a man when he says that he is seeing a yellow patch, and refuse to believe him when he says that he is seeing God. The answer to this is that if the man who asserts that he is seeing God is merely asserting that he is experiencing a peculiar kind of sense-content, then we do not for a moment deny that his assertion may be true. But, ordinarily, the man who says that he is seeing God is saying not merely that he is experiencing a religious emotion, but also that there exists a transcendent being who is the object of this emotion; just as the man who says that he sees a yellow patch is ordinarily saying not merely that his visual sense-field contains a yellow sense-content, but also that there exists a yellow object to which the sense-content belongs. And it is not irrational to be prepared to believe a man when he asserts the existence of a yellow object, and to refuse to believe him when he asserts the existence of a transcendent god. For whereas the sentence "There exists here a yellow-coloured material thing" expresses a genuine synthetic proposition which could be empirically verified, the sentence "There exists a transcendent god" has, as we have seen, no literal significance.

We conclude, therefore, that the argument from religious experience is altogether fallacious. The fact that people have religious experiences is interesting from the psychological point of view, but it does not in any way imply that there is such a thing as religious knowledge, any more than our having moral experiences implies that there is such a thing as moral knowledge. The theist, like the moralist may believe that his experiences are cognitive experiences, but, unless he can formulate his "knowledge" in propositions that are empirically verifiable, we may be sure that he is deceiving himself. It follows that those philosophers who fill their books with assertions that they intuitively "know" this or that moral or religious "truth" are merely providing material for the psycho-analyst. For no act of intuition can be said to reveal a truth about any matter of fact unless it issues in verifiable propositions. And all such propositions are to be incorporated in the system of empirical propositions which constitutes science.

INTRODUCTION TO PHILOSOPHY OF RELIGION / Study Questions

THE JUSTIFICATION OF RELIGIOUS BELIEF

Aquinas

1. Aquinas raises two objections to the claim that God exists. What are they? Which of these are Aquinas' arguments supposed to answer *directly*?
2. State the arguments of Aquinas as clearly as you can, using terminology that is more familiar to you wherever possible. Which of these seems to you to be the strongest argument? Which the weakest? Why? (This should have something to do with the arguments, not with *your* preferences.)
3. How do these arguments give direct support to Aquinas' reply to Objection 2? Do they give any support (direct or indirect) to his reply to Objection 1; or is that reply simply *ad hoc*?

Descartes

1. Descartes argues that certain things, that may not exist outside of thought, still "cannot be said to be in themselves nothing." What does this mean? How does the example of imagining a triangle help reveal his meaning here?
2. How does Descartes' version of the Ontological Argument go?
3. How does Descartes respond to the "mountain/valley" objection? How does he respond to the objection that the premise ("God exists necessarily") is not necessary; and what exactly is that objection all about?
4. What does it mean, if anything, to say that existence is a "perfection?"
5. How does Descartes reason that his proof is a proof of the existence of *God*, and, furthermore of just *one* God?

Smart

1. Smart presents three criticisms of the Ontological Argument. Which does he think is the crucial one, and how does it go? What is the relevance of G. E. Moore's example to Smart's argument? Is Moore's example a good one?
2. According to Smart, how does the first part of the Cosmological Argument go? What else is required (the second part) to prove the existence of *God?*
3. What is Kant's objection to the second part of the argument; and what is wrong with Kant's objection? Where, according to Smart, is the real fallacy in the Cosmological Argument? Is it statements or *things,* according to Smart, that can be said to be necessary? What makes a statement necessarily true, according to Smart? Can the statement, "God exists" be necessarily true; and why not? What does Smart mean when he says that "the demand that the existence of God should be *logically* necessary is . . . a self-contradictory one?"
4. Why does Smart claim that "theological necessity cannot be logical necessity?" Why is this important?
5. Why does Smart believe that the question, "Does God exist?" is "not a proper question?" Does it follow that religion is nonsensical, according to Smart? Explain.
6. What is the Teleological Argument? Look up the word *teleology* or *teleological* in a good dictionary. Why is this called the Teleological Argument?
7. What are the two lines we may take in criticising the Teleological Argument? How does Smart's discussion of the "problem of evil" lend support to his attack on the analogy

appealed to in the Teleological Argument? Why does Smart believe that this argument, even though "feeble," still has a "fascination for us that reason can not easily dispel?"

James

1. Briefly outline the explanation James gives of such things as an hypothesis, an option, and the differences between "live" and "dead" options, between "forced" and "avoidable" options, and "momentous" or "trivial" options. What is a "genuine" option?
2. James argues that it seems absurd to say that a decision between two hypotheses is largely a matter of what one is willing to believe. How does the Lincoln example support this? What is Pascal's wager; and why does it fail to show that "believing by our volition" is not silly?
3. How does James use the distinction between "live" and "dead" options to show that "believing by our volition" is not, in fact, silly? What are his examples of things we believe in "for no reasons worthy of the name?" According to James, can we ever *know* those beliefs are true? How is his case of "telepathy" supposed to support these arguments?
4. What is James' thesis? In his statement of the thesis, what is the final argument for it? Given his view of "genuine" options, is it conceivable that the only choices are to believe, disbelieve, or merely *refuse* to make a choice?
5. Does James see any difference in the logical/conceptual status of propositions expressing scientific theories, political doctrines, foreign policies, and religious faith?
6. Does his concern with *justifying* the having of religious faith suggest that he thinks of religious beliefs as on a logical par with scientific theories?
7. Would you agree with the following as an adequate characterization of James' position? "There is no agreed upon test of truth in science, everyday life, or religion. Most of our decisions, even about the truth of scientfic theories, are made on passionate (emotional) grounds, therefore there is no reason not to make religious decisions on emotional grounds." Putting aside the question of whether this is an adequate account of what James said, is it an adequate account of science and religion?

Ayer

1. What is Ayer's argument to show that the existence of God cannot be demonstratively proved? What does it mean to say something can be proved in this way? What is an *a priori* statement, a tautology, and an empirical proposition?
2. What is Ayer's argument to show that the existence of God is not an empirical issue? What is another term for an "experiential proposition?" How does the proposition that nature has a "certain sort of regularity" fail to be an experiential proposition of the kind required to test the hypothesis that God exists?
3. Is Ayer's view compatible with either atheism or agnosticism? Why not?
4. How do the claims that gods exist, where the gods in question "are identified with natural objects," remain significant despite Ayer's argument?
5. What is Ayer's diagnosis of the tendency to suppose that there must be a "person" answering to the descriptions of God found in "sophisticated religions?" What does it mean to say that " 'God' . . . is not a genuine name?"
6. Is there, according to Ayer, any grounds for "antagonism between religion and natural science?" Explain.
7. How does Ayer respond to the objection that "intuition" may reveal truths and, so, that

people who don't have the ability to intuit those truths cannot lightly dismiss that ability in others? How does his answer constitute a refutation of the argument from religious experience?

The Meaning of Religious Language

Ayer's argument in the previous section sets the stage for the selections we present here; for there are at least two ways one might dissent from that view. On the one hand, one could try to argue that religious beliefs are not ordinary beliefs about extraordinary things but are in fact a special *kind* of belief. In such a case one might reason that the special nature of that evidence can reveal what the logical status of these belief-claims is. Such is the view—in different forms—of the theologians, Paul *Tillich* and Rudolf *Bultmann*, and the philosopher, Raphael *Demos*, from whose writings we have selected passages for this section. Secondly, however, one might *agree* that there could be no evidence—not even of a special kind—for or against religious belief, yet argue that this does not mean such claims are nonsensical. Rather, it shows that so-called religious beliefs are not "beliefs" in the ordinary sense at all. This is the view argued for here by Paul *Schmidt*. We do not include, in this selection, the passages in which he attempts to show what type of claims religious claims are, if not belief-claims (after all, he has written a whole book to do that job.) But we do include a piece by another philosopher that shows one sort of direction one might want to take in dealing with this problem.

Each of the three views that argue for the first alternative takes up a different manner in which one might try to explain religious beliefs as a special sort of belief supported by special kinds of "evidence." Tillich, in a selection from his book, *The Dynamics of Faith*, argues that religious claims are metaphorical in nature. He gives an analysis of the concept of *metaphor* that, he suggests, sheds light on the manner in which one must speak of certain realities about the world. He then presents a series of arguments to the effect that *God*, as Tillich explains the term, refers to such a "reality." So according to Tillich, whatever facts we can know about God can only be expressed metaphorically.

Raphael Demos takes another tack in a selection from his paper, "Are Religious Dogmas Cognitive and Meaningful?" Demos begins with an argument that beliefs based on faith, rather than evidence, are not peculiar to religion. Indeed, he argues, they underlie everyday beliefs and the beliefs of science as well. They do so in the following way: Granted that most people's everyday and scientific beliefs rest on evidence, the question still remains *why* they count as evidence the sort of things they do. Demos' answer is that they believe that certain things count as evidence—and this belief is *based* on *faith*. Why then should religious belief be regarded as unusual? Can we not determine in a reasonable way what this religious person counts, on faith, as evidence for his or her beliefs? Demos thinks we can; and he argues that religious claims are fundamentally analogical. He then gives an account of the notion of an analogy that, he believes, can explain the sense of religious beliefs and the exact nature of the special, that is, analogical, evidence to be appealed to in determining the truth or falsity of religious beliefs.

The third of these views is presented in the article by Rudolf Bultmann, "What Sense is There to Speak of God?" Bultmann, like Demos, resists the distinction between scientific statements as statements of fact and religious claims as pure speculation. His objection, as we see it, is that this *way* of drawing the distinction misses what is really different about such claims. Bultmann argues that it is characteristic of scientific claims that they "talk *about*" their subject matter and that this entails "a standpoint apart from that which is being talked *about*." Yet, he argues, if we were to think of God as a thing to be talked about this would be as senseseless as thinking of oneself as such a thing. One may, of course, talk about oneself in this way—as an animal of the human species, exhibiting such-and-such behavior—but in an important sense one is no longer actually speaking of *oneself*. Such talk misses the sense one has of his own reality, motives, and so on. Just so, reasons Bultmann, to speak of God in this object-oriented way is senseless. It *is* unintelligible, according to his view, to "talk *about*" God. But it is no more unintelligible to speak of God than it is to speak of oneself.

This, of course, needs explanation. And Bultmann does attempt to explain it. There are two leading features to his proferred explanation: (a) to talk meaningfully of God is to speak of *the* basic "condition of our existence" and (b) to speak of this condition is to confront something that is and must remain baffling to us. One may attempt to describe one's relationship with his or her father as a relationship "between individuals of a species"; yet, as this sort of object-oriented description goes it cannot get at the reality—the felt reality—of, for example, a father/son relationship. For, described in this way, no one would see the relationship as binding or occasioning responsibilities *for oneself*. On the other hand, as soon as one sees the relationship (from the "inside") as being the condition *within which* obligations are incurred, one is no longer seeing the relationship as an object of scientific study. Instead one sees the relationship as a condition of one's life. Similarly, Bultmann argues, to take seriously the claims of God's omnipotence and God's attempts to address Himself to the human situation, one is forced to speak of God from the "inside" of a binding and obligatory relationship that derives from God's being *the* supreme condition of our existence. To speak of God in any other way, however well meant, is both unintelligible and *sinful*! This leads to Bultmann's second point, which is that in speaking of God intelligibly one is speaking about the very condition of one's existence and that condition is and always must be baffling to us. What is "known" of our existence, in Bultmann's sense, is that it is given to us to care for, but also that there is nothing we can do to preserve it. This, Bultmann argues, is the source of our perpetual perplexity. The perplexity can never be overcome; but by faith one may make his peace with it.

The three views we have so far encountered are not without their difficulties. In the case of Tillich there are several problems. One can argue that his analysis of metaphors is more problematic than clarifying. One can also point out, as several philosophers have, that Tillich's view of God requires the use of "irreducible" metaphors; yet any ordinary metaphors can always be reduced to literal talk. So, this criticism continues, to say that religious language is metaphorical (in Tillich's sense), is to do no more than to admit that its sense cannot be explained. This, of course, was precisely where we came in. Thirdly, we can argue that Tillich's implicit suggestion that there are "metaphorical facts" is obscure to the point of being unintelligible.

Similar problems beset the view of Demos. First of all, we can explain ordinary analogies—that is, we can point out what objects, events and so on are said to be analogous and describe the respect in which they are said to be analogous. But, when it comes to God, this is precisely what Demos thinks we cannot do, so we are left with "analogies" that are not at all like ordinary analogies. One can also ask what sense it might make to speak of "analogical facts." Is it a *fact* about some objects, events, and so on that they are analogous? Or is it a fact about us (an important fact, to be sure) that we see likenesses between things? What is it to "see a likeness"? These are troublesome questions that have bothered the greatest philosophical minds; yet Demos offers us no clear explanation why he adopts the view he takes on these questions. But most importantly, Demos' claim that we are free (within a "system of thought") to adopt any canons of evidence whatever is surely absurd. When a scientist accepts the occurrence of certain events as evidence for a given claim he is not, as Demos wishes us to believe, expressing an *article of faith* about what counts as evidence. What Demos fails to see is that any of those things that might be called "systems of thought" are just so many claims that can be expressed in a language. The limits on what can count as evidence are not imposed by, decided upon in, nor articles of faith in, the systems of thought. *Those* limits are instead built into the language. One cannot, upon pain of unintelligibility, call just anything at all "evidence" for the truth of some belief. The scientist does not *decide* or *believe* that such-and-such is evidence—he calls it evidence because he knows the meaning of the word *evidence*.

These are not the only problems in these views. But we believe they are difficulties which are close to the heart of the issue in this group of selections. We have dwelt on them here because we do not present any readings that deal with such views directly. The remaining articles lead us in a different direction altogether. Instead of trying to make a case for saying religious claims are factual beliefs of an extraordinary sort, the remaining articles begin by assuming there really is a problem here. Paul Schmidt devotes his efforts to showing that the problem is genuine and that if we try to force religious language into the model of fact-claims we *shall* be speaking nonsense. However, he argues, it is only the superficial "grammar" of these sentences that could lead us to try forcing religious language into that model. Actually, he argues, religious claims are not very much like ordinary fact-claims at all. He presents us with six or seven criteria of a fact-claim and discusses religious claims in the light of that list. His conclusion is that religious language must be explicated on some other model.

We do not go on to present the model(s) Schmidt thinks are appropriate—for the reasons just cited. But some of the alternatives are as follows. One may try to think of religious claims as expressions of basic attitudes of (for example) hope and purposefulness, expressions of emotional exuberance, expressions of a felt communal fellowship, disguised expressions of psychological distress and/or adjustment, and so on. The crucial difficulties with attempts like these are first, few believers would be willing to reduce the *meaning* of their claims to any one (or even all) of these sorts of expressions. Secondly, none of these forms of discourse seems close enough to factual discourse to explain why believers are inclined to think of their claims as factual.

In the concluding selection we encounter one representative attempt to explicate the sense of religious claims. This attempt appears to avoid the difficulties just mentioned; but it also has other difficulties, as you will discover. This final piece is a selection from R. B. *Braithwaite's* book, *An Empiricist's View of the Nature of Religious Belief*. Briefly, Braithwaite's view is that religious claims are expressions of intention to behave in ways that adhere to certain moral teachings. The content of those teachings is given in what he calls "stories." It is the fact that the moral policy in religion is given in *stories*—stories that exemplify not only outward behavior of the desired sort but requisite "inner" attitudes as well—that characterizes the difference between religious claims and purely moral claims. What makes the different faiths distinctive, in turn, is not that they assert different fact-claims about the world but that the moral teachings (that *may* be essentially the same) are given in different stories.

Of course the mention of "stories" here may strike us as question-begging. For, was it not the intelligibility of just those stories (elevated, perhaps, to creedal formulae) that was at issue here? Braithwaite's response to this is interesting. It is his view that, inasmuch as the crucial question of meaning is settled by seeing religious claims as a type of moral claim, it is clear that the stories alluded to in religious claims need not be taken as true historical narratives. For it is only the moral significance of the stories that is important. Thus, in the final analysis, Braithwaite would say that when a religious individual says "God is love" it may look like he is making an assertion. But in fact he is signalling his intention to behave in a certain way. If we want to determine just what policy he is adopting we can look at his subsequent behavior *and* listen to the stories he is inclined to tell in connection with his original utterance.

Braithwaite's view, in the end, may not be satisfactory. But we present it here because it is a good example of the healthy new directions that can be taken in our philosophical understanding of the nature of religious language. After all religious language is not esoteric code—it is English, German, or Greek. So, if it can be understood at all—and the presumption must be that it can—our account of it will show it to be very like some perfectly ordinary use(s) of language. That religious language is not empirical discourse, that is, used to make fact-claims about the world, should now be obvious. What other uses of language are present here is not so obvious; but, in turning away from fruitless defences of its supposed empirical nature, we are surely on the right track.

Religious Utterances Are Symbolic (Metaphorical)

PAUL TILLICH

1. The Meaning of Symbol

MAN'S ultimate concern must be expressed symbolically, because symbolic language alone is able to express the ultimate. This statement demands explanation in several respects. In spite of the manifold research about the meaning and function of symbols which is going on in contemporary philosophy, every writer who uses the term "symbol" must explain his understanding of it.

Symbols have one characteristic in common with signs; they point beyond themselves to something else. The red sign at the street corner points to the order to stop the movements of cars at certain intervals. A red light and the stopping of cars have essentially no relation to each other, but conventionally they are united as long as the convention lasts. The same is true of letters and numbers and partly even words. They point beyond themselves to sounds and meanings. They are given this special function by convention within a nation or by international conventions, as the mathematical signs. Sometimes such signs are called symbols; but this is unfortunate because it makes the distinction between signs and symbols more difficult. Decisive is the fact that signs do not participate in the reality of that to which they point, while symbols do. Therefore, signs can be replaced for reasons of expediency or convention, while symbols cannot.

This leads to the second characteristic of the symbol: It participates in that to which it points: the flag participates in the power and dignity of the nation for which it stands. Therefore, it cannot be replaced except after an historic catastrophe that changes the reality of the nation which it symbolizes. An attack on the flag is felt as an attack on the majesty of the group in which it is acknowledged. Such an attack is considered blasphemy.

The third characteristic of a symbol is that it opens up levels of reality which otherwise are closed for us. All arts create symbols for a level of reality which cannot be reached in any other way. A picture and a poem reveal elements of reality which cannot be approached scientifically. In the creative work of art we encounter reality in a dimension which is closed for us without such works.

The symbol's fourth characteristic not only opens up dimensions and elements of reality which otherwise would remain unapproachable but also unlocks dimensions and elements of our soul which correspond to the dimensions and elements of reality. A great play gives us not only a new vision of the human scene, but it opens up hidden depths of our own being. Thus we are able to receive what the play reveals to us in reality. There are within us dimensions of which we cannot become aware except through symbols, as melodies and rhythms in music.

Symbols cannot be produced intentionally—this is the fifth characteristic. They grow out of the individual or collective unconscious and cannot function without being accepted by the unconscious dimension of our being. Symbols which have an especially social function, as political and religious symbols, are created or at least accepted by the collective unconscious of the group in which they appear.

The sixth and last characteristic of the symbol is a consequence of the fact that symbols cannot be invented. Like living beings, they grow and they die. They grow when the situation is ripe for them, and they die when the situation changes. The symbol of the "king" grew in a special period of history, and it died in most parts of the world in our period. Symbols do not grow because people are longing for them, and they do not die because of scientific or practical criticism. They die because they can no longer produce response in the group where they originally found expression.

These are the main characteristics of every symbol. Genuine symbols are created in several spheres of man's cultural creativity. We have mentioned already the political and the artistic realm. We could add history and, above all, religion, whose symbols will be our particular concern.

2. *Religious Symbols*

We have discussed the meaning of symbols generally because, as we said, man's ultimate concern must be expressed symbolically! One may ask: Why can it not be expressed directly and properly? If money, success, or the nation is someone's ultimate concern, can this not be said in a direct way without symbolic language? Is it not only in those cases in which the content of the ultimate concern is called "God" that we are in the realm of symbols? The answer is that everything which is a matter of unconditional concern is made into a god. If the nation is someone's ultimate concern, the name of the nation becomes a sacred name and the nation receives divine qualities which far surpass the reality of the being and functioning of the nation. The nation then stands for and symbolizes the true ultimate, but in an idolatrous way. Success as ultimate concern is not the natural desire of actualizing potentialities, but is readiness to sacrifice all other values of life for the sake of a position of power and social predominance. The anxiety about not being a success is an idolatrous form of the anxiety about divine condemnation. Success is grace; lack of success, ultimate judgment. In this way concepts designating ordinary realities become idolatrous symbols of ultimate concern.

The reason for this transformation of concepts into symbols is the character of ultimacy and the nature of faith. That which is the true ultimate transcends the realm of finite reality infinitely. Therefore, no finite reality can express it directly and properly. Religiously speaking, God transcends his own name. This is why the use of his name easily becomes an abuse or a blasphemy. Whatever we say about that which concerns us ultimately, whether or not we call it God, has a symbolic meaning. It points beyond itself while participating in that to which it points. In no other way can faith express itself adequately. The language of faith is the language of symbols. If faith were what we have shown that it is not, such an assertion could not be made. But faith, understood as the state of being ultimately concerned, has no language other than symbols. When saying this I always expect the question: Only a symbol? He who asks this question shows that he has not understood the difference between signs and symbols nor the power of symbolic language, which surpasses in quality and strength the power of any nonsymbolic language. One should never say "only a symbol," but one should say "not less than a symbol." With this in mind we can now describe the different kinds of symbols of faith.

The fundamental symbol of our ultimate concern is God. It is always present in any act of faith, even if the act of faith includes the denial of God. Where there is ultimate concern, God can be denied only in the name of God. One God can deny the other one. Ultimate concern cannot deny its own character as ultimate. Therefore, it affirms what is meant by the word "God." Atheism, consequently, can only mean the attempt to remove any ultimate concern—to remain unconcerned about the meaning of one's existence. Indifference toward the ultimate question is the only imaginable form of atheism. Whether it is possible is a problem which must remain unsolved at this point. In any case, he who denies God as a matter of ultimate concern affirms God, because he affirms ultimacy in his concern. God is the fundamental symbol for what concerns us ultimately. Again it would be completely wrong to ask: So God is nothing but a symbol? Because the next question has to be: A symbol for what? And then the answer would be: For God! God is symbol for God. This means that in the notion of God we must distinguish two elements: the element of ultimacy, which is a matter of immediate experience and not symbolic in itself, and the element of concreteness, which is taken from our ordinary experience and symbolically applied to God. The man whose ultimate concern is a sacred tree has both the ultimacy of concern and the concreteness of the tree which symbolizes his relation to the ultimate. The man who adores Apollo is ultimately concerned, but not in an abstract way. His ultimate concern is symbolized in the divine figure of Apollo. The man who glorifies Jahweh, the God of the Old Testament, has both an ultimate concern and a concrete image of what concerns him ultimately. This is the meaning of the seemingly cryptic statement that God is the symbol of God. In this qualified sense God is the fundamental and universal content of faith.

It is obvious that such an understanding of the meaning of God makes the discussions about the existence or nonexistence of God meaningless. It is meaningless to question the ultimacy of an ultimate concern. This element in the idea of God is in itself certain. The symbolic expression of this element varies endlessly through the whole history of mankind. Here again it would be meaningless to ask whether one or another of the figures in which an ultimate concern is symbolized does "exist." If "existence" refers to something which can be found within the whole of reality, no divine being exists. The question is not this, but: which of the innumerable symbols of faith is most adequate to the meaning of faith? In other words, which symbol of ultimacy expresses the ultimate without idolatrous elements? This is the problem, and not the so-called "existence of God"—which is in itself an impossible combination of words. God as the ultimate in man's ultimate concern is more certain than any other certainty, even that of oneself. God as symbolized in a divine figure is a matter of daring faith, of courage and risk.

God is the basic symbol of faith, but not the only one. All the qualities we attribute to him, power, love, justice, are taken from finite experiences and applied symbolically to that which is beyond finitude and infinity. If faith calls God "almighty," it uses the human experience of power in order to symbolize the content of its infinite concern, but it does not describe a highest being who can do as he pleases. So it is with all the other qualities and with all the actions, past, present and future, which men attribute to God. They are symbols taken from our daily experience, and not information about what God did once upon a time or will do sometime in the future. Faith is not the belief in such stories, but it is the acceptance of symbols that express our ultimate concern in terms of divine actions.

Another group of symbols of faith are manifestations of the divine in things and events, in persons and communities, in words and documents. This whole realm of sacred objects is a treasure of symbols. Holy things are not holy in themselves, but they point beyond themselves to the source of all holiness, that which is of ultimate concern.

3. Symbols and Myths

The symbols of faith do not appear in isolation. They are united in "stories of the gods," which is the meaning of the Greek word "mythos"—myth. The gods are individualized figures, analogous to human personalities, sexually differentiated, descending from each other, related to each other in love and struggle, producing world and man, acting in time and space. They participate in human greatness and misery, in creative and destructive works. They give to man cultural and religious traditions, and defend these sacred rites. They help and threaten the human race, especially some families, tribes or nations. They appear in epiphanies and incarnations, establish sacred places, rites and persons, and thus create a cult. But they themselves are under the command and threat of a fate which is beyond everything that is. This is mythology as developed most impressively in ancient Greece. But many of these characteristics can be found in every mythology. Usually the mythological gods are not equals.

There is a hierarchy, at the top of which is a ruling god, as in Greece; or a trinity of them, as in India; or a duality of them, as in Persia. There are savior-gods who mediate between the highest gods and man, sometimes sharing the suffering and death of man in spite of their essential immortality. This is the world of the myth, great and strange, always changing but fundamentally the same: man's ultimate concern symbolized in divine figures and actions. Myths are symbols of faith combined in stories about divine-human encounters.

Myths are always present in every act of faith, because the language of faith is the symbol. They are also attacked, criticized and transcended in each of the great religions of mankind. The reason for this criticism is the very nature of the myth. It uses material from our ordinary experience. It puts the stories of the gods into the framework of time and space although it belongs to the nature of the ultimate to be beyond time and space. Above all, it divides the divine into several figures, removing ultimacy from each of them without removing their claim to ultimacy. This inescapably leads to conflicts of ultimate claims, able to destroy life, society, and consciousness.

The criticism of the myth first rejects the division of the divine and goes beyond it to one God, although in different ways according to the different types of religion. Even one God is an object of mythological language, and if spoken about is drawn into the framework of time and space. Even he loses his ultimacy if made to be the content of concrete concern. Consequently, the criticism of the myth does not end with the rejection of the polytheistic mythology.

Monotheism also falls under the criticism of the myth. It needs, as one says today, "demythologization." This word has been used in connection with the elaboration of the mythical elements in stories and symbols of the Bible, both of the Old and the New Testaments—stories like those of the Paradise, of the fall of Adam, of the great Flood, of the Exodus from Egypt, of the virgin birth of the Messiah, of many of his miracles, of his resurrection and ascension, of his expected return as the judge of the universe. In short, all the stories in which divine-human interactions are told are considered as mythological in character, and objects of demythologization. What does this negative and artificial term mean? It must be accepted and supported if it points to the necessity of recognizing a symbol as a symbol and a myth as a myth. It must be attacked and rejected if it means the removal of symbols and myths altogether. Such an attempt is the third step in the criticism of the myth. It is an attempt which never can be successful, because symbol and myth are forms of the human consciousness which are always present. One can replace myth by another, but one cannot remove the myth from man's spiritual life. For the myth is the combination of symbols of our ultimate concern.

A myth which is understood as a myth, but not removed or replaced, can be called a "broken myth." Christianity denies by its very nature any unbroken myth, because its presupposition is the first commandment: the affirmation of the ultimate as ultimate and the rejection of any kind of idolatry. All mythological elements in the Bible, and doctrine and liturgy should be recognized as mythological, but they should be maintained in their symbolic form and not be replaced by scientific substitutes. For there is no substitute for the use of symbols and myths: they are the language of faith.

The radical criticism of the myth is due to the fact that the primitive mythological consciousness resists the attempt to interpret the myth of myth. It is afraid of every act of demythologization. It believes that the broken myth is deprived of its truth and of its convincing power. Those who live in an unbroken mythological world feel safe and certain. They resist, often fanatically, any attempt to introduce an element of uncertainty by "breaking the myth," namely, by making conscious its symbolic character. Such resistance is supported by authoritarian systems, religious or political, in order to give security to the people under their control and unchallenged power to those who exercise the control. The resistance against demythologization expresses itself in "literalism." The symbols and myths are understood in their immediate meaning. The material, taken from nature and history, is used in its proper sense. The character of the symbol to point beyond itself to something else is disregarded. Creation is taken as a magic act which happened once upon a time. The fall of Adam is localized on a special geographical point and attributed to a human individual. The virgin birth of the Messiah is understood in biological terms, resurrection and ascension as physical events, the second coming of the Christ as a telluric, or cosmic, catastrophe. The presupposition of such literalism is that God is a being, acting in time and space, dwelling in a special place, affecting the course of events and being affected by them like any other being in the universe. Literalism deprives God of his ultimacy and, religiously speaking, of his majesty. It draws him down to the level of that which is not ultimate, the finite and conditional. In the last analysis it is not rational criticism of the myth which is decisive but the inner religious criticism. Faith, if it takes its symbols literally, becomes idolatrous! It calls something ultimate which is less than ultimate. Faith, conscious of the symbolic character of its symbols, gives God the honor which is due him.

One should distinguish two stages of literalism, the natural and the reactive. The natural stage of literalism is that in which the mythical and the literal are indistinguishable. The primitive period of individuals and groups consists in the inability to separate the creations of symbolic imagination from the facts which can be verified through observation and experiment. This stage has a full right of its own and should not be disturbed, either in individuals or in groups, up to the moment when man's questioning mind breaks the natural acceptance of the mythological visions as literal. If, however, this moment has come, two ways are possible. The one is to replace the unbroken by the broken myth. It is the objectively demanded way, although it is impossible for many people who prefer the repression of their questions to the uncertainty which appears with the breaking of the myth. They are forced into the second stage of literalism, the conscious one, which is aware of the questions but represses them, half consciously, half unconsciously. The tool of repression is usually an acknowledged authority with sacred qualities like the Church or the Bible, to which one owes unconditional surrender. This stage is still justifiable, if the questioning power is very weak and can easily be answered. It is unjustifiable if a mature mind is broken in its personal center by political or psychological methods, split in his unity, and hurt in his integrity. The enemy of a critical theology is not natural literalism but conscious literalism with repression of and aggression toward autonomous thought.

Symbols of faith cannot be replaced by other symbols, such as artistic ones, and they cannot be removed by scientific criticism. They have a genuine standing in the human mind, just as science and art have. Their symbolic character is their truth and their power. Nothing less than symbols and myths can express our ultimate concern.

One more question arises, namely, whether myths are able to express every kind of ultimate concern. For example, Christian theologians argue that the word "myth" should be reserved for natural myths in which repetitive natural processes, such as the seasons, are understood in their ultimate meaning. They believe that if the world is seen as a historical process with beginning, end and center, as in Christianity and Judaism, the term "myth" should not be used. This would radically reduce the realm in which the term would be applicable. Myth could not be understood as the language of our ultimate concern, but only as a discarded idiom of this language. Yet history proves that there are not only natural myths but also historical myths. If the earth is seen as the battleground of two divine powers, as in ancient Persia, this is an historical myth. If the God of creation selects and guides a nation through history toward an end which transcends all history, this is an historical myth. If the Christ—a transcendent, divine being—appears in the fullness of time, lives, dies and is resurrected, this is an historical myth. Christianity is superior to those religions which are bound to a natural myth. But Christianity speaks the mythological language like every other religion. It is a broken myth, but it is a myth; otherwise Christianity would not be an expression of ultimate concern.

Religious Utterances Are Analogical

RAPHAEL DEMOS

ALTHOUGH in this paper I am solely concerned with the cognitive elements of religion, I do not of course assume that cognition is all that is important in religion. In this paper, by religion I will mean chiefly the Christian religion; this is the one I know best by far and it is the one in whose truth I believe. I will first discuss religious belief and then I will explore religious meaning. My study of religious cognition will also involve extended digressions into general epistemology.

Reprinted with permission of University of Pennsylvania Press from "Are Religious Dogmas Cognitve and Meaningful?" by Raphael Demos in *Academic Freedom, Logic, and Religion*, 1953.

We may tentatively distinguish the following systems of belief: common sense, science, animism, religion and philosophy. In this scheme common sense stands to science as animism to religion, the first member of the pair representing a relatively undeveloped version of the second. Later on, I will make a similar distinction of philosophical levels.*

It is generally taken for granted that the appeal to faith is a uniquely distinguishing feature of religious belief. Certainly religious thinkers do not hesitate to declare that faith is a valid source of belief in religion; thus, the author of the Epistle to the Hebrews speaks of faith as the 'evidence' of things unseen. In this passage faith means belief not resting on the evidence of the senses; but the word has for me a wider meaning; namely, as belief which rests on no evidence whatever, whether empirical or a priori. Of the other systems of belief it is popularly assumed that scientific beliefs rest on empirical evidence exclusively; and that so do those of common sense, although with a lesser degree of firmness. It is also believed that philosophers at any rate *intend* to ground their doctrines rationally, by appealing to experience or to self-evidence, and more vaguely, to intelligent speculation.

Religion seems to stand, then, apart from these other systems, by unashamedly resting its beliefs on faith—standing not only apart from, but behind these systems so to speak; and thus remaining in the rear of the progress of the human mind. Now I will try to show that religion is not alone, but that all the systems of belief I have cited are in the same boat, all floating on the infirm waters of faith. Putting the matter more cautiously, I will say that all the above-mentioned systems of belief rest on ultimate commitments. For instance, why do I, as a man of common sense, believe in the existence of independent physical objects? Because I believe it. Why do I believe that other people exist? Because I believe it. Perhaps for both cases I should add that I believe as I do because other people believe likewise; because these beliefs are part of common sense. (The circle in this 'argument' should be noted). And this is what I call faith.

One reason why in the case of both science and philosophy the element of faith is unnoticed is because the commitments are unconscious. These are, to a considerable extent, commitments as to what is a valid way of knowing. The air of important demonstration in science and philosophy is dissipated as soon as we notice that both make basic assumptions as to what constitutes evidence; for instance as to the meaning and validity of 'experience,' as to the validity of memory, as to the criteria of valid theory—and so forth.

Let me dwell on memory for a moment. Memory, it is agreed, is of the past which, because it is past cannot be given to the mind; thus memory is contrasted with experience—and in a wider sense of 'experience,' with rational intuition in Descartes' sense of the word, when he opposed it to deduction. That science must rely on memory is obvious; we are obliged to remember the evidence of the senses obtained in the past, on which we base our present the-

* EDITOR'S NOTE: We have not included the later portion of this article where this distinction is made.

ories. It is true that most scientific observations are preserved in records; but in order that such records be authentic and not fairy tales, they must at some point be connected with memory. Possibly even so-called report-sentences or protocols depend on a memory of the sensory given; for the latter has a very brief duration and it takes time to write, utter, or even think the protocol sentences.

I submit that reliance on memory is a sheer trust or faith. For, let us agree that there are many good reasons—proofs, if you like—for believing that memory is veridical. I will not go into these reasons, since it does not matter here what they are. But these reasons are not now present in my mind; I only remember them, and in so doing, I am using memory to support memory.

Of course, I may once more and now go through these reasons. So now I know that memory is trustworthy. But so long as I have these reasons present to my mind I cannot engage in remembering. The business of justifying memory is self-defeating. While actually involved in memory, I cannot be also intuiting the reasons which justify it; and, as we have just noted, so long as I am contemplating the reasons, I am to engage in remembering. It is as though an instrument invariably disintegrated in the very process of performing its function.

So far as I know, Descartes was the first philosopher to point up the relevance of memory not only for science but for mathematics. He showed that trust in memory was involved in the carrying out of any extended mathematical proof. Descartes realized that the reliance of mathematicians on memory is a matter of sheer trust or faith; he therefore tried to correct the situation by proving the existence of God who, being perfect, will not deceive man in the various faculties with which he endows men—faculties inclusive of memory and our disposition to believe in the existence of physical objects. Nevertheless Descartes, too, is obliged to remember the proofs of God and so must trust the memory which justifies the trust. As distinct from mathematics, science relies on sense-experience. But for science too memory is more important than sense-experience. Immediacy functions in science in a Pickwickian sense; it is remembered immediacy. Both immediacy and inference function as materials for memory. As scientists and as plain men we live in the past.

What of the assumed relevance of sense-data for the purpose of confirming predictions in science? Here we are forced to distinguish between sense-data and images, for images have no confirmatory value. But how distinguish the one from the other? Not surely by the criterion of voluntary control, for there are compulsive images, not subject to the conscious will. Berkeley suggested that sense-data are regular, obeying laws. But surely images obey laws too? Surely a scientist would not deny that there are causes even for images, physiological or both, even when he cannot point to these causes. Berkeley only evaded the issue when he asserted that sense-data, as distinct from images, obey 'natural' laws; natural laws are simply those laws which sense-data obey and images do not. Thus science is able to verify generalizations by rigorously selecting as data just those elements in experience which do, in principle, verify generalizations in science.

It is said that religious belief in the existence of God rests on faith. But natural science too entails an undemonstrated belief in something like the uniformity of nature—a belief, that is to say, that nature has the kind of structure which justifies our taking its behavior in the past as a clue to its behavior in the future. Thus, not only in their source, but in their content too, the two systems of belief seem to me to be analogous, in that both seem to be beliefs in the existence of something like an order of nature. To be more specific, the belief in God is equivalent to the view that things make 'moral' sense in the universe; that, although there is evil in nature, this evil will somehow be overcome by good. The natural scientist has *his* evil too, which is chance; yet he too believes that somehow there is an explanation for everything that happens.

But to return to the question of justification—I would say that the religious belief is no more of a faith than is the belief that nature is uniform. They are both acts of faith, not only in that they go *beyond* the evidence but in that, at least up to a point, they go *against* the evidence. Job said: "Though he slay me, yet will I trust in him." And the scientists' position may be caricatured by putting these words in his mouth: "I will find an explanation even if it kills me;" more accurately; "I will go on believing that there is an explanation, even though I cannot find one." It may be urged that modern science, in recognizing the so-called Heisenberg principle of uncertainty has correspondingly *limited* the range of the principle of explanation. To this I might answer that there is an analogous phenomenon in modern doctrines of religion in so far as they recognize a limited God. But I prefer to dispute the truth of the above interpretation of the impact of the principle of uncertainty on the principle of explanation. Heisenberg himself views his principle merely as an extension of the doctrine of secondary qualities. He writes:

> According to Democritus, atoms have lost the qualities like colors, taste, etc., they only occupied space, but geometrical assertions about atoms were admissible and required no further analysis. In modern physics, atoms lose this last property, they possess geometrical qualities in no higher degree than color, taste, etc. . . . Only the experiment of an observer forces the atom to indicate *a position*, (italics mine) a color and a quantity of heat. (*Philosophic Problems of Nuclear Physics*, p. 38; see also pp. 105–6.)

I have referred earlier to the religious belief that events in nature make "moral" sense. There is here a notion of meaningfulness which requires elucidation. For the scientist, too, as was noted, the universe is meaningful, though in a different sense of the term. Meaningfulness as a religious notion may be approached by its application to conduct. Echoing Kant, we speak today of action being rational (or reasonable) in the sense that it is not self-inconsistent, or not self-defeating. What I have in mind, however, is something different, although it too has connections with Kant, namely with what he was reaching out for when arguing for his postulates. The notion of meaningfulness in religious language is essentially a common sense one and untechnical. We say that life is meaningful when it achieves values in some stable fashion. Mere action and change are meaningless, we say; they must aim at something; and at something worthwhile. But striving without a chance of accomplishment is also deemed meaningless. And ends, once accomplished, must be capable of preservation, for the activity to be meaningful.

This is meaningfulness in living. Now, we say, derivatively, that the real world is meaningful in so far as it makes such accomplishment possible, probable, nay perhaps certain. Religion is the belief that the world is meaningful in this fashion. For such a belief the senses provide no evidence—certainly not any conclusive evidence; and the scientifically-minded see no reason for adopting this belief. Certainly such a belief is founded on faith, but no more so than the scientist's own belief that nature is meaningful in his sense, namely that nature is such that it enables us to make successful predictions and generalizations.

The reader will recall Spinoza's doctrine that God's attributes are infinite. By this Spinoza meant that each attribute is self-contained and complete, never intersecting with another attribute. I wish to say that in some sense both the scientific and the religious accounts are, like Spinoza's attributes, infinite, that is to say, autonomous. Or, to use Prof. Tillich's phrase for theology (*Systematic Theology, I*, p. 8), each system is a circle, in other words a closed system.

Let us, for instance, compare the scientific account of thunder with the magical account. The scientist will of course reject the latter; but he cannot refute it. The animist will introduce, let us say, evidence from a dream; but dream images are irrelevant for the scientist. Each system has its own definition of fact. Each system carries a lantern by which to illuminate the darkness. While what is thereby seen is seen indeed, the lantern itself is not illuminated, or rather the lantern shines both on itself and other things. The lanterns are different, and each is checked by its own light.

It may be thought that science is able to crash into the animistic circle by an appeal to pragmatic considerations. Science 'works.' Our own kind of medical men can cure diseases which the witch-doctors cannot; also we can produce crops as the magician cannot. But the fact is that pragmatism is an appeal to values, and that the values, too, are part of the system. The religious believer, for instance, may say that his values are not material primarily, that what he is concerned with is the salvation of his soul and with blessedness. There are also differences involving factual matters. Where the scientist may claim that his system provides greater satisfaction for life on this earth, the religious believer might retort that he is concerned with what happens to him in the life after death. And for the scientist to say that there is no life after death is to beg the (factual) question. . . .

I come now to the problem of religious meaning.

Take such apparently descriptive phrases as the following: God is a Spirit; God is a Person; God is Eternal Life; God is Love; the Lord God Almighty; the Lord Most High; Our Father in Heaven. What is the way to view such representations of God?

(a) It is possible to think of them as literal descriptions of God; this is the position of fundamentalist Christianity. It is not satisfactory because it leads to idolatry: identifying God with what is at best an image of God.

(b) At an other extreme is the view that these are not descriptions at all, but purely mythical or symbolic. By 'symbol' I mean a word whose meaning is exclusively emotive. A symbol does not refer to anything in the object; its function is to arouse appropriate attitudes, feelings and responses.

(c) This view in turn leads to a still more extreme doctrine—that we can know nothing of God's attributes. This is the alternative of nescience. I am rejecting both *b* and *c*. Against the latter, I maintain that we can know God; against the former, that in using attribute-words for God we are referring to properties in the object. Nevertheless I deny the first alternative; I do not think that the descriptions of God are literal.

(d) But if attribute-words in religion are neither literal nor emotive, might they be metaphors? I use this word in the sense of allegory; although a metaphor has emotive overtones like a symbol, I distinguish it from the latter because a metaphor is descriptive. A metaphor may be defined as condensed literal meaning, and when the meaning is spread out, the metaphor evaporates.

Adopting then the view that a metaphor is *potentially* descriptive (literally) as distinguished from what might be called ordinary prose (which is an actual literal description) I would deny that religious attribute-words like 'person' 'love' 'spirit' are metaphors; I take this position because I do not think that the descriptions into which a metaphor could be translated apply to God literally. Religious attribute-words, while descriptive, are not literal; they are, in fact, *analogical.*

To sum up the above diversities of meaning and arranging them in an ascending order:

1. Words with zero meaning, as in nescience.
2. Symbols—terms with emotive meaning only.
3. Metaphors—literal, quasi-descriptive.
4. Analogical terms—descriptive but not literal.
5. 'Prose' terms—both descriptive and literal.

Before defining what I mean by analogical terms, I will explain why I believe that the descriptive terms in religious discourse are not literal. This is not at all because of any assumption on my part that God has no essence, or that, if he has an essence such an essence is intrinsically un-intelligible. God can certainly comprehend his own nature. It is only that man, because of the finite nature of his mind, cannot comprehend God's nature in terms of his (God's) intrinsic properties. Hence man must have recourse to terms of comparison; he can understand God's nature by comparing it with properties which he knows literally. Take the familiar statement that man is (created as) an image of God. Therefore, God can be thought of in the image of man. Moreover, this relation of analogy between God and man is known literally. While, if I say that God is a person in an analogical sense, I am not ascribing the attribute of personality to God in a literal sense, yet I am ascribing literally a certain analogical relation between personality in man and personality in God.

It is sometimes said that although we cannot literally know *what* God is we can literally know *that* God is. The similarity to Kant's doctrine of things-in-themselves is obvious here; there are things in themselves but we cannot literally know what they are. Against Kant's view, the valid question has been raised: "If you cannot know what the noumena are, how can you even know that they are? Surely the reasons preventing you from knowing their essence would operate equally to prevent you from knowing their existence." So with God. The statement that while we can know that God exists, we cannot know what he is, is facile. In fact, just as we can ascribe personality to God analogically only, so do we ascribe existence to God in an analogical—and in no other—sense. In this connection I would like to quote from Prof. Stace's recent and important work *Time and Eternity.* "Religion is the desire to break away from being and existence altogether. . . ." (p. 5). "The nothingness of God finds expression in other phrases having the same sense. God is Non-Being, Nothing, Emptiness, the Void, the Abyss. Silence and darkness, used as privative terms importing the absence of sound, the absence of light, are also used as metaphors of his Non-Being." (p. 8). Nevertheless Mr. Stace denies that the statement that God is Nothing is equivalent to the statement that there is no God. For the proposition "God does not exist" is false too. (pp. 7, 61). Thus in some sense of existence it is false that God exists, but in another sense it is true that God exists; the former is the literal, the latter the analogical sense. (I am not in any way suggesting that Mr. Stace would accept the interpretation I put on his statements. Nevertheless, as the reader will gather from my later remarks, my debt to his book in this essay is considerable.)

Now for the reasons why an appeal to analogy is necessary. In attempting to describe God, theologians seem compelled to make contradictory statements. Thus God is said to be transcendent, yet also immanent; eternal yet also temporal; personal, yet also impersonal. The Kingdom of Heaven is within us; yet also forever beyond us. Such assertion of contradictory statements superficially suggests that God is intrinsically unintelligible and that theological truth is irrationalistic. Of course, Hegel has made a logic out of anti-logic through his formulation of the dialectic. But Christian theology need not be Hegelian. The descriptions of God cited above are not in fact inconsistent because, to take one example, the sense in which time is denied of God and that in which time is ascribed to God are not the same senses; yet they are not different either; the senses are analogical.

As we know, the mystics have proclaimed that God is ineffable. St. Chrysostom wrote five sermons on the incomprehensibility of God, in which he rises to flights of sublime eloquence. St. Chrysostom quotes St. Paul to show that God is unapproachable as well as inconceivable. Yet St. Paul also writes: "The invisible things of him (of God) from the creation of the world are *clearly seen*, being understood by the things that are made, even his eternal power and Godhead." (*Romans I*, 2). What is the answer to the paradox? The nature of God cannot be known intrinsically; it can be known by comparison with other things. Now, anyone would be rash to contradict the mystics; but in fact, the mystics are inconsistent, like St. Paul. Of course when the mystics assert that God is incomprehensible they do not mean that God is uncognizable. What they mean is that God is cognizable by a mode of cognition which is unique—different from sense-perception and from conception. The real question is whether what is cognized in the mystical mode can be translated into the language of some other mode. And here mystics divide themselves into two groups: those who maintain that the language of the mystic is not translatable into any other, and those who assert that it is. Of the second group are those mystics who regard nature as the manifestation of God ("the heavens declare the glory of God") and who regard natural events as 'symbolic' of divine meanings.

When I say that both Smith and Jones are men, the sense in which I use the term man in the two cases is exactly the same. Thus, as the schoolmen would say, the sense of man in this example is univocal. When I use the word post for the mail and also to designate a pillar I am using the word in two different senses. This is what the schoolmen called the equivocal use of a term. Now I submit that identity of sense and difference of sense do not exhaust the meaning of sense; there is a third alternative, namely that the sense of a term is analogical—neither the same nor different. Some scholastic philosophers have tried to define analogy as part-identity and part-difference. I regard this view as wrong; analogy is an irreducible relation, other than both identify and difference. When religious analogy is misconstrued as difference, we are liable to get the extreme forms of mysticism, merging with the doctrine of nescience. When analogy is misconstrued as identity (that is to say, taken as literally descriptive) we find anthropomorphism. Of course, the doctrine of analogy is taken from Aristotle, although in a modified version.

Compare analogy with likeness. In its ordinary sense (which I will call conceptual likeness) this relation is always reducible, and reducible to identity and difference together. Thus when I say that Smith is like Jones, you can always ask me: in what respect? and I can answer: in intelligence or in height; both Smith and Jones are smart or they are both tall. Here, likeness between two things means that A and B have a common property. Thus conceptual likeness is reducible to identity in a certain respect, and is the same as Aristotle's generic identity—for instance, that men and dogs are both animals. Now analogy is not, at all, that kind of likeness (if likeness it be). It is likeness perhaps in that we are comparing two things; but it is not a likeness which is reducible to the possession of a common property; it is not likeness in this or that 'respect'; it is just likeness. It is reported that Wittgenstein said something as follows: "To propose to think in violation of the law of contradiction is like proposing to play chess without the queen; and that is all one can say about the comparison." Now this would be an instance of analogical likeness: A is to B, as C is to D.

To return to theology: God exists; God has or is a mind; God is a living God; God is love; God has designs and purposes—in all these sentences the attributions must be taken analogically. Thus God loves, but his love is not the sort of thing we mean when we say, man loves; when we ascribe purposiveness to God, we must not be taken to mean that he proceeds by the route of means and ends, as when man acts purposively. Now, these are negative statements; and there have been mystics according to whom the only statements we can make about God are negations. Yet this is half the story; the senses of 'love' and 'design' are analogical. Thus affirmative statements about God are available.

How We Speak of God

RUDOLF BULTMANN

I

IF BY speaking "of God" one understands to *talk "about God,"* then such style of speaking has no sense at all; for in the moment when it happens the subject (*Gegenstand*), God, has been lost. For when the thought "God" is thought at all, the implication is that God is the Almighty, i.e., the reality controlling everything. But this thought is not thought at all when I *talk about* God—that is, when I regard God as an object of thought toward which I can take a position; when I adopt a point of view from which I stand indifferent to the problem of God; when I suggest propositions concerning God's way and reality which I can reject or, if they are illuminating, accept. Anyone who is moved by proofs to have faith in God's *reality* can be certain that he has comprehended nothing of the reality *of God*; and whoever thinks to proclaim something of God's reality by means of evidences of God is debating about a mirage. For every "talking *about*" presupposes a standpoint apart from that which is being talked *about*. But there can be no standpoint apart from God, and for that reason God does not permit himself to be spoken of in general propositions, universal truths which are true without reference to the concrete existential situation of the one who is talking.

It makes just as little sense to talk about God as it does to talk about *love*. In fact it is impossible to talk *about* love unless the talking about love be itself an act of love. All other talking about love is no speech of love, for it takes a position outside love. In short a psychology of love would be something quite different from speaking about love. Love is no given situation (*Gegebenheit*) *for the sake of which* (*woraufhin*) something done or something spoken, something not done or not spoken, is possible. It comes into being only as a condition of life itself; it only *is* in that I love or am loved, not as something secondary or derivative (*daneben oder dahinter*). The same is true of the relationship of fatherhood and childhood. Viewed as a natural circumstance—so that one can talk about it—it does not reveal its unique nature at all, but is simply a single

Reprinted from "What Sense Is There to Speak of God?" by Rudolf Bultmann in *The Christian Scholar,* **43** (1960), 213–222.

incident in a certain natural event which takes place between individuals of a species. Where the relationship really comes into being it cannot be seen from the outside, i.e., it isn't something *for the sake of which* for example a son accepts or even allows this or that, feels himself obligated to this or that. The moment the reflection "for the sake of which" enters the relationship, it is ruined. It only *is* at the point where the father actually lives as father, the son as son.

If this be true, then the possible *atheism* of a science could not assert itself for example in denying the reality of God: it would be just as atheistic if it asserted itself to be a science. For to speak in scientific propositions, i.e., in universal truths, about God means nothing else than to speak in propositions which have their precise meaning in that they are generally applicable, that they are detached from the concrete situation of the speaker. But exactly because the speaker does that, he puts himself outside the actual reality of his existence, therefore apart from God; and he speaks of something quite different from God.

To talk about God in this sense is however not only error and foolishness: it is *sin.* In his *Commentary on Genesis* Luther made the point very clearly that Adam's sin was not the deed itself with which he, eating of the forbidden fruit, broke the commandment. Rather it was that he entertained the question: Should God have spoken?—the "disputare de deo" that sets itself apart from God and makes of God's claim on men a disputable issue. For if we want to avoid this conclusion and say, this dispute isn't necessarily so badly purposed after all; on the contrary it can be well meant; indeed it can arise from the quest for the true (*Wahrhaftigkeit*), the longing for God—then we show again that we have not comprehended the thought of God. This would be to fall into the old error and put forward the omnipotence of God and our being conditioned by it as a fact which is comprehended as a universal truth, something like the fact that every earthly object is determined by the law of causation. But it is precisely this that would not encompass what the determining of our existence by God means: for it means at the same time the *claim* of God upon us. Thus every standing apart from God is a denial of the claim of God upon us, that is, godlessness, sin. It could be otherwise only if a position of neutrality in relation to God were possible. But in this the thought of God would be sacrificed. Adam thought he could flee from God; but God's claims are not met by flight. Thus talking about God becomes sin.

And the fact remains: it is *sin* even when it comes from an honest search for God. And from this it is only too clear that when we are in such a situation in which we honestly must debate about God, then we are sinners and cannot do anything to get out of sin through our own power. For it wouldn't do us any good at all if, because of a right understanding of the thought of God, we should cease to argue about God (*disputare de deo*). For to speak otherwise of God, namely in God, is something we obviously cannot presume for ourselves. For as *our* effort it would again be sin, precisely because it would be *our* effort in which the thought of God's almighty sway would be sacrificed. To speak of God as being *in* God is obviously something which can only be given by God.

II

It is therefore evident that if one wishes to speak of God he must certainly *speak of himself.* But how? For if I speak of myself am I not speaking of a human being? And is there not likewise in the thought of God most assuredly the thought that *God is the "wholly other,"* over and beyond the human (*Aufhebung des Menschen*)? Then do we not stand between two negative commandments, as a result of which only the condition of resignation, of silence is possible? On the one hand there is the definite insight: that every speech in which we stand apart from our own specific existence is no speaking of God; that it can only be a statement about our own existence? On the other hand the equally definite insight: all speaking of ourselves can never be a speaking of God because the speaking is only of men?

For in fact every confession of faith, every speaking of experience and inner life, would be to speak of the human. And however enthusiastic the confessions of another might be, these would not help me with my doubt unless I wish to deceive myself. Yes, even my own experiences, if I would comfort myself with them or depend upon them in the situation of doubt, would slip through my fingers. For who assures me that each personal experience was not an illusion? that I should not move beyond it? that I do not now see reality more clearly?

Or must we claim that we speak indeed *in* God when we bear witness, when our inner life speaks, when our experience expresses itself? Without doubt that can be the case. But in *that* very moment when we set up our confession of faith, our inner life, our experiences, as that which brings us to trust God; or which we recommend to others as that whereby they shall be certain of God—in *that* very moment we are *talking about* our existence and have by that fact separated ourselves from it. And that is also the case when we consciously seek after experiences for ourselves: we are then concerned about ourselves rather than questing for God. When I seek after myself—looking backwards or forwards—then I have at the same time split my ego; and the ego which seeks after itself is my existential ego; the other ego after which I seek, which I assume as a fact, is a mirage without existential reality. And the existential ego which is concerned about itself, which quests, shows itself in this very questioning, in this self-concern to be godless. If we wish to speak of God, we obviously cannot begin as though we would speak of our experiences and our inner life, which as soon as we objectify them, have lost their existential character. And over against this human being, seen as a condition, stands the word that *God is the wholly other.*

But this word has its meaning only in its strong dependence upon the first word—that God is the reality which determines our existence. Cut loose from that, the phrase can only mean that God is some*thing* quite different from man, a metaphysical being, some kind of an ethereal world, some combination of secret powers, a creative original force (whereby the possible claim that this is meant only figuratively contradicts itself, because in this context God is in fact thought about quite naturalistically), or finally the *irrational.* A piety which wished to base itself on this idea of God would be flight from God, because in it man wishes in fact to escape from the reality in which he stands; he wishes indeed to run away from his concrete existence in which alone he can comprehend the reality of God. In this modern piety it becomes very clear how right Luther was in saying that the natural man flees from God and hates God. He seeks indeed, in wishing to escape from the reality of his concrete existence, to escape that in which alone he can find God. It is of course very understandable that the Pseudo-God of the creative or the irrational can bewitch the human yearning for God; for it promises man that he can get away from himself. But this promise is a misconception and a deception; for because a man wishes *thus* to get away from himself, he runs away from God—provided that God is the power shaping his concrete existence—and runs into his own arms, provided the thoughts of a creative original force and of the irrational are human abstractions and the experiences—in which a man puts his trust in such circumstances—are all too human events. The thought of the "wholly other" cannot be pursued in this way at all. Moreover of course that man does not in truth escape God at all; but while his attitude toward God is that of aversion, his existence is—insofar as it is determined by God—that of the sinner.

The thought of *God as the wholly other* cannot mean therefore, if the talk is to be of God the Almighty, that God were something apart from me which I must first seek, and that I must first flee from myself in order to find. That God, who determines my existence, at the same time is the wholly other, can only mean that he confronts me, the sinner, as *the* wholly other; that, insofar as I am *world*, he confronts me as *the* wholly other. To speak of God as the wholly other only makes sense when I have seen that the actual situation of man is that of the sinner—who wants to speak of God and cannot; who wants to speak of his existence and cannot do that either. He would have to speak of his existence as one determined by God and he can only speak of it as such as a sinner: i.e., as of being in an existence in which *he* cannot see God, in which God is confronted as the wholly other.

III

The circumstances of our existence are indeed as startling in their own way as the Divine; we cannot really talk about either and we have control of neither. What does that mean?

The *reality* about which we usually speak is the world-image which has dominated our thinking since the Renaissance and Enlightenment—under the influence of the world-view of Greek science. We accept something as real when we can comprehend it in the total unity of this world, whether this relationship is conceived in terms of causal or teleological destiny, whether its elements and powers are conceived as material or spiritual; for the contrast of materialistic and idealistic ideology is, in terms of the issue here at stake, irrelevant.

For this view of the world is conceived without consideration of our own existence; we ourselves are treated rather as an object among other objects and placed in the context of this world-view which is posited quite apart from the question of our own existence. It is customary to call the perfection of such a world-view through the inclusion of the human element, an ideology (*Weltanschauung*), and we are usually longing for it, and if we assume that we have it, we propagate it. That such ideologies are very popular, even if they do not speak of mankind in flattering terms—perhaps as the accidental result of a combination of atoms, as the highest of the vertebrates and cousin of the apes, or as an interesting example of psychic complexes—is easily understood. For they perform for man again the great service that they release him from himself, that they lift from him the problem-complex of his concrete existence, the anxiety about it and the responsibility for it. That is indeed the foundation of the longing of man for such a so-called ideology, that in the face of the enigma of fate and death he can withdraw to it, that precisely in the moment when his existence is shaken and problematical he declines to take this moment seriously, in order to understand it rather as one case among others, to organize it in a relationship, to objectify it—and so to free himself from his own existence. And precisely this is the arch-deception (*πρῶτον ψεῦδος*), and it leads necessarily to the erroneous comprehension of our existence, in that we see ourselves from the outside as the object of self-orienting thinking. And that is not improved when, in contrast with the other objects with which we see ourselves in relationship, we put ourselves forward as protagonists. For man seen by himself as a protagonist is still viewed from the outside. In the question of our existence therefore the distinction between subject and object has to be dropped completely. And the case is not improved at all by having a theistic or a Christian ideology, based on the view that our existence is grounded in God—as though an ideology which includes this proposition satisfies the demands and comprehends our existence. For in this too God is viewed as an outside object just as man. Whoever has a modern world-view which is constituted by the concept of law has a godless world-view—even when he thinks of universal laws as a result of the powers and forms of divine action or when he looks at God as the source of this law. For the acts of God cannot be viewed as general events, at which we could look, as in the contemplation of laws, disregarding our own existence, and which we could later incorporate into our own existence—in order to make it intelligible. For thereby we would sacrifice the primary thought of God as the reality which determines our existence. And we concede this unwillingly or unknowingly, in distinguishing ourselves in our individual being quite clearly from the universal laws. For nobody will conceive the life relationships of love, thankfulness, and reverence in which he is tied to others as law; in any event not when he actually lives in these relationships. It is clearly impossible therefore to conceive God as the foundation (*Prinzip*) of the world by which the world and thereby our own existence becomes intelligible. For in this God would be viewed from the outside, and the proposition of his existence would be a universal truth, a truth which would more or less have its proper place in a system of knowledge (of universal truths), in short in a system which sustains itself and our existence too, instead of being an expression of our existence itself. God would then be a given factor, to which a relationship of perception would be possible, a relationship which could be realized according to wish. God, that is, his existence, would then be a Thing, *toward which* (*woraufhin*) an attitude—this or that—would be possible for us. And just this is again the arch-deception (πρῶτον ψεῦδος): if the thought of God is taken seriously, then God is nothing *toward which* something or other can be undertaken. He would then be seen from the outside, and just so we would have seen ourselves from the outside. For example we cannot say: because God rules reality he is also my master. Only when man knows himself to be addressed (*angesprochen*) by God in his own life does it make sense to speak of God as the lord of reality. For every talking about reality which ignores the sole moment in which we can have reality, that is, the moment of our own existence, is self deception. God is never something seen from the outside, something over which we have disposition, something "toward which . . ." or "for the sake of which. . . ."

If it be true that the world seen from the outside is godless and that we, in so far as we see ourselves as a part of the world, are godless, then it is again clear that God is not the wholly other in that he is somewhere outside the world but in that this world, being godless, is also sinful. This world seen from the outside, in which we move about as protagonists, is exactly our world—which we take seriously and thereby denote as sinful.

There are in fact only two things clear to us about our existence: (1) that we have the care and responsibility for it; for it signifies indeed, "necessity compels thee" (*tua res agitur*); (2) that it is absolutely uncertain and we can not make it secure; for to do so we should have to stand outside it and be God himself. We can not talk about our existence because we can not talk about God; and we can not talk about God because we can not talk about our existence. We could only do one if we could do the other. If we could talk of God *in* God, then we could also talk of our existence, and vice versa. In any case a talking about God, *if* it were possible, would have to be at the same time a talking about us. Thus it remains true: if it be asked how it is possible to speak of God, then it must be answered, only by speaking of us.

IV

But doesn't perhaps something quite different follow from the situation described, that as we are sinners, we shouldn't speak at all? That would naturally mean at the same time that we should not act at all! Does not the point of view that God is the wholly other to men, that he is over and beyond the human, lead to *Quietism*? Whoever thought thus would be making the old mistake. He would, that is, be seeing the thought of God as something *toward which* a certain relationship would be possible or proper; the mistake that the thought of God could be calculated at all as a thing given for our relationship over which we have control. If the thoughts of God as the Almighty and the Wholly Other are taken seriously in their close dependence upon each other, then they clearly mean that we are not given authority for such a self-determining question and self-decision based upon reflection, whether we speak or are quiet, act or relax; that the decision in the matter is God's and that for us there is only a *necessity* (*Müssen*) of speaking or silence, a necessity of acting or not acting. And in fact this is the only answer to the question if and when we can speak of God: when we *must.*

It has meaning for us however to reflect on what this *necessity* actually means. For according to our traditional way of thinking we immediately see this "necessity" as something from the outside again; that is, we see ourselves, the compelled (*Müssenden*), as object which stands under the causal compulsion of a subject; and in this case we see God, the commander, as the subject. That means: we see this situation of man as conditioned by God—which is implied in the "necessity" mentioned as a natural process—from the outside. But here only a necessity can be intended which is a *free act*; for such only derives from our existential being, *in* such alone *are* we ourselves and are we whole. Such act is obedience; for obedience means: to respond to necessity by a free act. It signifies no work which we had to decide on because of the will of God; for then God would be seen from the outside, and in work which we accomplish and present to God we are not ourselves; rather we stand outside it. Such an act means utter dependence, not as pious feeling but rather precisely as a free act, for only in the act are we ourselves. This necessity signifies therefore obedience.

This means that one can never turn to generalities when this necessity is put to us. One cannot know about this necessity in advance, for then a position outside of the necessity would be required, a position that is outside of our being as those who must, and one would not understand at all the meaning of this existential necessity. The action cannot be taken as something freely intended because a necessity lies at hand but only as something free and *at the same time* as that made necessary. It hardly needs mentioning that this does not mean that the act breaks forth from a necessity of enthusiasm or passion, out of a secret depth of our inner being. For that would be to talk of natural necessity. The much or little of enthusiasm is as unimportant as the much or little of resistance or self-conquest or that the deed can seem to the human eye as a greater or smaller sacrifice. It is not a question of a psychological necessity. The "thou shalt" is spoken by God and is entirely outside our control. Ours is the free act alone. We can only say hypothetically that we have the possibility to speak and act in God *if* it is given us as necessity. But whether such a necessity will become reality for us, we cannot know in advance. We can only make clear to ourselves what this necessity means, namely that it can signify a free act on our part only because otherwise it would not include our existential being. On the question whether this necessity is reality, we can only *have faith.*

V

Now just this and nothing else is the meaning of *faith.* But of course this is not the total of all that it means. For when we said ours was only the free act, then this proposition too, or rather the conviction that something determined is our free act, is only faith. For free act, being the expression of our existence, precisely because only in it and nowhere else do we exist, cannot be known in the sense of something objectively established. It cannot be put forward as an hypothesis supported by evidence. For thereby we would objectify it and put ourselves outside it. Rather it can only be done (and so far as we *speak* of this action its possibility can only be held) by faith.

At last we see ourselves led to the point that even our existence—for it is based indeed in our act—can never be known by us. Is it illusion? Unreality? Certainly it is nothing of which we know, about which we can talk, and yet it is that alone—when it is real in our speaking and acting—which can give reality to speaking and acting. We can only have it by faith. And does this faith lie in our hand, so that we can decide for it? Obviously this faith must also be free act, the original act (*Urtat*), in which we become certain of our existence—and yet it should definitely not be an arbitrary assumption, which we make, but obedience, necessity, precisely *faith.*

The question how such a faith is arrived at is insoluble when it is intended as a search for the process which runs its course when we see ourselves from the outside; it makes no difference whether we define the process rationalistically or psychologically, dogmatically or pietistically. The quest only has meaning—and in this sense it is in fact unavoidable—when it asks about the meaning of faith. This faith can only be the affirmation of God's acting upon us, the answer to his word directed to us. For if faith refers to the comprehension of our existence and if our existence is grounded in God—that is, not comprehensible apart from God—then to comprehend our existence is to comprehend God. But if God is not a general law, a foundation, a given factor, then we can comprehend him only in that which he speaks to us, in that he acts upon us. We can only speak of him in so far as we speak of his word directed to us, his acting upon us. "Of God we can only tell what he does to us."[1]

The meaning of this word of God, this acting of God upon us, would obviously be this, that God, in giving us our existence, changes us from sinners to righteous men, in that he forgives the sins, justifies us. This would not mean that he forgives us this or that, light or serious mistake (*Missgriff*); rather he gives us the freedom to speak and to act in God. For only in acting as the free expression of a person—nay, rather in that relationship wherein a person exists at all—can a person enter into a relationship with another person; and everything is spoiled right away of course when the acting is determined from the standpoint of a legal event (*gesetzlichen Geschehens*).

That cannot mean that he inspires us, makes of us ecstatics and doers of wonders, but that he accepts us as justified while we are separated from him and can only talk *about* him, quest for him. It is therefore not as though something extraordinary, recognizable had happened in our life, that extraordinary qualities were channeled into us and we did extraordinary things or spoke extraordinary words which were not human. Think of all that we could do and say

[1] W. Hermann, *Die Wirklichkeit Gottes* (1914), p. 42.

that would *not* be human! But *this* has happened—that all of our doing and speaking has been released by the curse—to separate us from God. It always remains sinful so long as it is something undertaken by us. But precisely as something *sinful* it is justified, that is, it is justified by *grace.* We *know* nothing of God; we *know* nothing of our own reality; we have both only in faith in God's grace.

Does this mean that faith is the Archimedean point by which the world is lifted from the corners and changed from a world of sin to the world of God? Yes, that is the message of the faith. But whoever would ask further about the necessity and about the lawfulness, about the ground of faith—he would receive only one answer, in that he would be referred to the message of faith which comes to him with the claim to be believed. He would receive no answer which would give the validation of faith by some final authority (*Instanz*) or other. If this were not so the word would not be *God's* word; but rather God would be called to account; faith would not be obedience. The word enters our world entirely fortuitously, entirely contingently, entirely as an event. No guarantee is there by means of which faith can be held. No one's summons has a claim (*Platz*) in the faith of others whether it be Paul or Luther. Indeed faith can never be for us a standpoint toward which we take a position but always and ever a new act, new obedience. Always uncertain, as soon as we look about ourselves as men and question; ever uncertain, as soon as we reflect on it, as soon as we talk about it; only certain as deed. Only certain as faith in the grace of God unto the forgiveness of sins which justifies me—when it pleases him—although I have not the capacity to speak in God but can only talk about God. All of our doing and speaking has meaning only by grace of the forgiveness of sins, and over that we do not dispose; we can only have faith in it.

This address also is a talking about God and as such, if God is, it is sinful; and if God is not, it is senseless. Whether it is meaningful and whether it is justified rests with no one of us.

Religious Utterances Are Not Empirical Claims

PAUL F. SCHMIDT

THE SECOND type of knowledge by description that might include religious claims concerns matters of fact. Such factual knowledge, or empirical knowledge as it is also called, is exemplified by the natural, social, and historical sciences as well as by the enormous amount of everyday information. The distinction between formal and empirical knowledge goes back a long way in the history of thought to the Greek philosophers, but it was not until the present century that each was sufficiently well understood for the essential differences between them to be clearly presented. Credit for this clear separation goes to the Logical Positivists. In their early exhuberance they propounded some rash analyses of religion and ethics,[1] but these were the signs of fresh insight and novelty, and they cleared the ground for our own analysis. Unknowingly, they pointed a way for us, and their doctrine is a fire of purification.

Our first task is to delineate the subject matter of empirical knowledge and the types of statements found therein. Its subject matter has been variously described as nature, the external world, the space-time order, the phenomenal realm, and sense-datum experience. All of these are dangerous and misleading in different ways. They suggest a dualism of knower and known, a subjectivism of experience, a dematerialization of the world, and a gap between nature and reality. But we can avoid all this by setting down the general procedures that investigators agree upon in these areas. Empirical knowledge deals with events and objects for which operational definitions could be given and, in some cases, with unobservable events and objects that are linked by logical-mathematical relations to operationally defined objects and events. Such operational definitions tell us what investigators do to identify and describe, in terms of observable behavior, some event or object. Is this copper? What is its atomic weight? Is this society polygamous? Did Plato visit Egypt? We answer such questions more or less firmly, without making use of the puzzling metaphysical terms like nature, external world, phenomena, or sense data.

For our purposes, we shall approach the types of statements involved in a system of empirical knowledge with an eye on their relevance to the question of religious knowledge. First, there are the many particular statements about matters of fact, usually the result of observations or some refinements thereof. Second, we find general statements summarizing matters of fact, and abstract statements belonging to hypotheses and theories sometimes involving mention of objects and events that are not observable. Third, there are procedural statements about methods of empirical research, specific and general. And fourth, we have logical and mathematical statements serving as tools for organization and prediction within the sciences.

The structure of systems of empirical knowledge varies somewhat, depending on the degree of development of theories. In history, theory development is at a minimum; in physics it is at a maximum. But we do not find generically different kinds of structures. We find that a theory is made up of general laws specifying the characteristics and relationships of some objects and events in such a manner that when we add some particular statements of matters of fact and some procedural statements, this combined whole yields, by logical or mathematical rules of derivation, other particular statements of matters of fact that can then be put to an observational or experimental test.

The question often arises: from whence the theory? An answer cannot, at the present time, be formulated that sets down a series of steps an investigator

[1] A. J. Ayer, *Language, Truth and Logic* (London: Victor Gollanz, Ltd., 1948).

can proceed to perform in order to lead to a new theory. Scientific discovery of new theories depends upon the creative imagination of the scientist. On the other hand, the question of when we should accept a theory has quite a definite answer. Scientific justification can be specified in a series of steps giving the experimental procedures for the verification or falsification of a theory. There has been much technical analysis of the procedures of justification (verification, confirmation, hypothetical-deduction, and induction), but the differences of interpretation do not affect our argument.

When are statements accepted or rejected in empirical knowledge? A particular statement is accepted if (1) it follows as a consequence from an accepted theory or if (2) it can be observed directly or by some experimental instruments. It is rejected if its denial is acceptable. It may be neither acceptable nor rejectable. A theory is accepted when a sufficient number of consequences that follow from it can be positively observed, directly or experimentally. It is rejected if some of its consequences are rejected. It is common to say that accepted statements and theories are true or empirically true or factual truths and that rejected statements and theories are false.

True and false are most commonly used in this manner, and no end of confusion has arisen in the history of thought from taking this use as the only use of these terms. Worse yet, this use was incorrectly combined with the uses appropriate to formal knowledge, with the consequence that both types of knowledge failed to receive a proper analysis until this century. This confusion of uses still exists with respect to ethical statements and also for religious claims. When people say ethical or religious claims are true, they simply carry over the use from empirical knowledge, with little understanding of its inappropriateness. The search for a single use of true and false is another of the great ghosts of thought never to be caught, for there is nothing to catch. It would not be possible to take up this search if one understood the proper use of these terms. It is absolutely essential to use these terms with their proper qualifiers, that is, to see them in their relationship to some type of knowledge.

So far, we have dealt with the subject matter of empirical knowledge, namely, with matters of fact and the theories explaining them; with the structure of such systems; and with the procedures of justification for different types of statements in the structures. Thus, we have met the two conditions for a type of knowledge by description: what it is about and how claims are tested. What are the characteristics of empirical knowledge?

Empirical knowledge gives us *concrete information about, or causal explanations of, matters of fact.* The warrant for this characteristic consists of the enormous body of scientific knowledge and everyday information: physics, chemistry, biology, psychology, sociology, history, and all the many crafts practiced by man. In contrast to formal knowledge, which makes no reference beyond its own symbolic expression, empirical knowledge has reference to matters of fact; it tells us something about the environment we live in. I suppose this is why it has become the model of knowledge for most people.

Second, this information can be *tested.* It is being continually revised by the elimination of some claims, the more precise statement of other claims, and the addition of new information. The possibility of putting such claims to a test distinguishes them from apparently factual claims that cannot be put to such a test. Such apparent factual claims can be found in metaphysics and in most religious systems, and we shall have more to say about this later.

Third, these testing procedures are *public*; they are not restricted to any particular class of persons, seers, medicine men, witch doctors, or enlightened individuals. Anyone can carry out these tests to satisfy himself if he can undergo a period of appropriate training. Such publicity of testing leads to common information for all. Hence, it is not arbitrary. We cannot invent whatever systems of empirical knowledge we like, as we can in formal knowledge.

As a consequence of testability and publicity, the information is *objective.* By objective I do not mean finding out what nature really is. This notion of objectivity is connected with the idea of an omniscient observer, like a deity, but scientists are not omniscient observers. According to our analysis of empirical knowledge, objectivity means that, relative to some chosen frame of reference, the carrying out of appropriate testing procedures by any trained investigator will yield identical empirical descriptions.

The logical character of the testing procedure for accepting theories leads to a very important characteristic of empirical knowledge. Such theories are at best *probable* or *tentative*, never certain or final. Consider their general form: if a theory is given, along with some initial conditions, then certain observable consequences will follow. The consequences are tested by observation or experiment. Is that theory the only possibility? No. Others might entail the same consequences. At best, in empirical knowledge we have a theory, but we never know if it is the only theory. Scientists have sometimes talked and acted otherwise, but in so doing they were turning to other than empirical knowledge. Historically, this logical point was overlooked in the enormous success of modern science, especially that of physics in the eighteenth and nineteenth centuries. Physics was so highly successful that few doubted its certainty. Then came the shocks of the twentieth-century revolutions in physics.

The last characteristic I want to notice is the *changing conception of the world* given to us by scientific information as empirical investigations proceed. We do not arrive at the one conception of the world, whatever that means. Nor can we say that each conception comes closer to this one correct conception, approaching it like an asymptote. For what could be the criterion for such an approach? Wouldn't any criterion assume some way of getting a "sneak peek" at reality in order to measure how close we are getting? But if such a peek is possible, why bother with the inferior kind of knowledge that only approaches it? All we can say is that conception change according to their degree of adequacy for dealing with the known data. Each is better than the previous one in its adequacy.

This is, perhaps, a good place to make some remarks about the term "reality" in relation to this analysis. It is commonplace to suppose that the philosopher is concerned with reality, and as regards knowledge, with knowing that reality.

Yet if one studies the work of mathematicians and scientists in formal and factual knowledge, respectively, one will find no need to mention "knowing reality." Nor did I need to mention it in my description of these two types of knowledge. Reality was a conception introduced into Western philosophy by the Greeks, a conception which played an important role but which is now no longer a useful term. Its use now generates philosophical problems instead of clarifying them, as it may have done in the past. Because I make no use of the term "reality," you are not to assume that I deny it, hold it unknowable, or any other such doctrine. We are quite beyond such doctrines in the mid-twentieth century so far as a description of knowledge goes. Religions seem to want to continue using this term, and this suggests that religious language is not to be assimilated to either formal or factual knowledge.

With our list of characteristics of factual knowledge, we are ready to raise the question whether religious claims belong to empirical knowledge. There is no doubt that, traditionally, most religious persons intended some of their religious statements to be factual, to state historical, cosmological, and theological facts about the world. Even today, a large number of people continue to believe that some of their religious statements are factual. To see that this is not the case constitutes a difficult but all-important step forward. Our point-by-point procedure hopes to make this clear. The classic examples of such factual claims in Christianity are the cosmological picture in Genesis, the biological claims about the origin and nature of man, and the astronomical and physical views. Each of these has come into sharp conflict with the development of modern science. Galileo, Darwin, and Copernicus were among the iconoclasts who precipitated these conflicts between science and religion. I shall discuss some features of this conflict in a later chapter. I mention them here as examples of the factual claims of religion.

Factual knowledge is at best probable; religious claims in the factual area have been presented as certain. Such dogmas are to be believed without question; they are often said to be the very center of a faith; to have that faith is to hold those beliefs without question. In science, in contrast, every belief can be questioned and should be held only tentatively. It will be pointed out that religious dogmas have changed in the course of history. Doesn't this show that someone held them open to doubt and question? Isn't this just like our doubt and questioning of scientific statements? I don't think so. There has been change from one dogma to another in religion, but it is a change from one certainty to another, neither of which is held with the tentativeness of factual knowledge. Against this difference, others will point to the many doctrinal interpretations of a given dogma as evidence for the revision and alteration of views parallel to that of scientific knowledge.[2] For example, there are the different doctrinal interpretations of the dogma "that in Jesus Christ God became incarnate."[3] Although these different doctrinal interpretations are open to doubt and, in this

[2] I use this distinction between dogma and doctrine as given by John Hick in *Faith and Knowledge* (Ithaca, N.Y.: Cornell University Press, 1957), pp. 198–99.

[3] *Ibid.*, p. 198.

way, parallel science in their tentativeness, they fail to parallel science with respect to the characteristics of objectivity and testability. This point we shall treat shortly. Finally, it is said that any really devout person has periods of questioning and doubt in his religious life. Doesn't this parallel the questioning attitude of the scientist? No. The differences are in the psychological attitudes of the persons and in the way the questioning is carried on. For the scientist, the questioning is genuinely open to the possibility of the answer being true or false, and either alternative is a worthwhile result. Furthermore, the questioning is submitted to public, objective tests. For the religious person it is doubtful whether a negative answer would be adopted or welcomed. In addition, his questioning involves private and subjective methods.

Now let us look more closely at these differences in testing procedures. Empirical knowlege uses testing procedures in which experimentation plays a major role leading to public information. In contrast, religions use testing procedures that make little use of experimentation. It is simply a matter of history that religions have not used experimentation to provide the warrant for their claims. But, someone will say, have they not used observation and experience, and aren't these the forerunners of experimentation? To suppose so is to exploit an ambiguity. There is all the difference in the world between an observation or experience restricted to a limited group of people or to an individual, and an observation or experience that could be had by anyone under conditions that could be fulfilled by anyone.

This ambiguity leads straight to the difference between public and private, objective and subjective. The traditional testing procedures used by religions are revelation, authority of person or text, intuitive insight, mystical insight, and personal consequences ("By their fruits, ye shall know them"). It is clear, to begin with, that none of these test procedures is used by empirical knowledge in the experimental testing of the consequences of a theory. Hence, religious claims are not tested by the procedures of empirical knowledge. These religious procedures have a common difficulty in that two different persons using them often arrive at contradictory or contrary results. Therefore, it is not the case that anyone can employ the procedures to confirm a common result. This is what we mean by public, and the common result achieved is what we call an objective piece of information. It is all too notorious that one religion holds one claim while another holds the opposite, that one mystic apprehends the universe this way and another flatly denies it. Further, it is well known that some people who seriously try to use these methods to gain religious knowledge fail to do so. When the sort of result obtained depends upon who the subjects are that use the procedures, we call the procedures subjective. We see that the religious procedures are of this sort.

A word of warning is perhaps in order now. The fact that we find that religious claims fail to have the characteristics of formal or factual knowledge is no reason to disapprove of religion. This feeling is likely to arise, and care must be taken to point out that this feeling is not justified by the analysis. Actually, our aim is to show that a serious intellectual confusion will occur if religious statements are thought to belong to formal or factual knowledge. We are aiming at a clarification of religious statements. By clearly distinguishing such statements, we can better appreciate just what their function is, and from this we may be able to understand their meaning.

A special word is also in order about the testing procedure of personal consequences. No one can deny that the lives of some persons have been radically and permanently altered as a result of religious experience, and it is supposed that the consequences in human deeds of that altered life attest to the genuineness of the religious experience. It is then claimed that this is parallel to testing the consequences of a theory. Much confusion has come from this gambit. The key difference is that the consequences of a scientific theory follow regardless of whether I believe the theory to be true or commit myself to it, while for the religious view we are required to commit ourselves firmly to it. But how can we critically and dispassionately appraise a view when the first condition for testing it is a commitment which forces us to relinquish our impartial position? Once again, let us refrain from attaching pro-and-con value judgments to these points. Commitment is an important feature of religious language, to be dealt with later. The point here is that the method of consequences in science does not involve commitment, while the method of consequences in religion does depend on commitment.

The last characteristic of empirical knowledge I want to discuss in relation to religion is that it gives us concrete information or causal explanations of matters of fact. Religious claims seem to have this characteristic. God is often conceived as the ultimate explanation, and in a first-cause argument he is conceived as the ultimate cause. Furthermore, there is no end of concrete information presented in sacred texts. We seem to have found a common feature.

But this difficulty emerges: if the religious claim is about a matter of fact that belongs within the area of one of the recognized sciences, then it will have to abide by the tests appropriate to that science; it cannot be accepted on any other basis, lest it forfeit its claim to give empirical knowledge. On the other hand, if it is said that the claim does not belong to any one of the recognized sciences, then we cannot accept it until criteria are presented that delineate the new area of empirical facts to which it belongs and that indicate how it is to be tested publicly. I do not think that this second alternative has been eliminated, nor has it been presented so as to convince anyone. On the former alternative, there remains nothing distinctively religious about the claim, and it is handed over to the appropriate science. These two difficulties show that religious claims do not provide us with concrete information in the same manner as empirical knowledge.

We have now answered, point by point, our question whether religious claims belong to empirical knowledge. The answer is that they do not, although on superficial analysis one might say that they do. Certainly many people have thought and still do think that they do. The major reason for the confusion stems from an older and inadequate understanding of empirical knowledge. Only in the last half century have we come to an adequate understanding of such knowledge. In answering the question, I have had in mind those religious claims which I called cosmological, theological, and historical. I have not dealt with the other sorts because I do not think people generally suppose them to be making empirical claims; I, at least, do not interpret them as doing so.

Religious Utterances Express Moral Intentions

R. B. BRAITHWAITE

THE MEANING of any statement, then, will be taken as being given by the way it is used. The kernel for an empiricist of the problem of the nature of religious belief is to explain, in empirical terms, how a religious statement is used by a man who asserts it in order to express his religious conviction.

Since I shall argue that the primary element in this use is that the religious assertion is used as a moral assertion, I must consider how moral assertions are used. According to the view developed by various moral philosophers since the impossibility of regarding moral statements as verifiable propositions was recognized, a moral assertion is used to express an *attitude* of the man making the assertion. It is not used to assert the proposition that he has the attitude—a verifiable psychological proposition; it is used to show forth or evince his attitude. The attitude is concerned with the action which he asserts to be right or to be his duty, or the state of affairs which he asserts to be good; it is a highly complex state, and contains elements to which various degrees of importance have been attached by moral philosophers who have tried to work out an 'ethics without propositions.' One element in the attitude is a feeling of approval towards the action; this element was taken as the fundamental one in the first attempts, and views of ethics without propositions are frequently lumped together as 'emotive' theories of ethics. But discussion of the subject during the last twenty years has made it clear, I think, that no emotion or feeling of approval is fundamental to the use of moral assertions; it may be the case that the moral asserter has some specific feeling directed on to the course of action said to be right, but this is not the most important element in his 'pro-attitude' towards the course of action: what is primary is his intention to perform the action when the occasion for it arises.

The form of ethics without propositions which I shall adopt is therefore a conative rather than an emotive theory: it makes the primary use of a moral assertion that of expressing the intention of the asserter to act in a particular sort of way specified in the assertion. A utilitarian, for example, in asserting that he ought to act so as to maximize happiness, is thereby declaring his intention to act, to the best of his ability, in accordance with the policy of utilitarianism: he is not asserting any proposition, or necessarily evincing any feeling of approval; he is subscribing to a policy of action. There will doubtless be empirical proposi-

Reprinted from *An Empiricist's View of the Nature of Religious Beliefs* by R. B. Braithwaite, New York: Cambridge University Press, 1955, pp. 11–28 and 29–35.

tions which he may give as reasons for his adherence to the policy (e.g. that happiness is what all, or what most people, desire), and his having the intention will include his understanding what is meant by pursuing the policy, another empirically verifiable proposition. But there will be no specifically moral proposition which he will be asserting when he declares his intention to pursue the policy. This account is fully in accord with the spirit of empiricism, for whether or not a man has the intention of pursuing a particular behaviour policy can be empirically tested, both by observing what he does and by hearing what he replies when he is questioned about his intentions.

Not all expressions of intentions will be moral assertions: for the notion of morality to be applicable it is necessary either that the policy of action intended by the asserter should be a general policy (e.g. the policy of utilitarianism) or that it should be subsumable under a general policy which the asserter intends to follow and which he would give as the reason for his more specific intention. There are difficulties and vaguenesses in the notion of a general policy of action, but these need not concern us here. All that we require is that, when a man asserts that he ought to do so-and-so, he is using the assertion to declare that he resolves, to the best of his ability, to do so-and-so. And he will not necessarily be insincere in his assertion if he suspects, at the time of making it, that he will not have the strength of character to carry out his resolution.

The advantage this account of moral assertions has over all others, emotive non-propositional ones as well as cognitive propositional ones, is that it alone enables a satisfactory answer to be given to the question: What is the reason for my doing what I think I ought to do? The answer it gives is that, since my thinking that I ought to do the action is my intention to do it if possible, the reason why I do the action is simply that I intend to do it, if possible. On every other ethical view there will be a mysterious gap to be filled somehow between the moral judgment and the intention to act in accordance with it: there is no such gap if the primary use of a moral assertion is to declare such an intention.

Let us now consider what light this way of regarding moral assertions throws upon assertions of religious conviction. The idealist philosopher McTaggart described religion as 'an emotion resting on a conviction of a harmony between ourselves and the universe at large,'[1] and many educated people at the present time would agree with him. If religion is essentially concerned with emotion, it is natural to explain the use of religious assertions on the lines of the original emotive theory of ethics and to regard them as primarily evincing religious feelings or emotions. The assertion, for example, that God is our Heavenly Father will be taken to express the asserter's feeling secure in the same way as he would feel secure in his father's presence. But explanations of religion in terms of feeling, and of religious assertions as expressions of such feelings, are usually propounded by people who stand outside any religious system; they rarely satisfy those who speak from inside. Few religious men would be prepared to admit that their religion was a matter merely of feeling: feelings—of joy, of consola-

[1] J. M. E. McTaggart, *Some Dogmas of Religion* (1906), p. 3.

tion, of being at one with the universe—may enter into their religion, but to evince such feelings is certainly not the primary use of their religious assertions.

This objection, however, does not seem to me to apply to treating religious assertions in the conative way in which recent moral philosophers have treated moral statements—as being primarily declarations of adherence to a policy of action, declarations of commitment to a way of life. That the way of life led by the believer is highly relevant to the sincerity of his religious conviction has been insisted upon by all the moral religions, above all, perhaps, by Christianity. 'By their fruits ye shall know them.' The view which I put forward for your consideration is that the intention of a Christian to follow a Christian way of life is not only the criterion for the sincerity of his belief in the assertions of Christianity; it is the criterion for the meaningfulness of his assertions. Just as the meaning of a moral assertion is given by its use in expressing the asserter's intention to act, so far as in him lies, in accordance with the moral principle involved, so the meaning of a religious assertion is given by its use in expressing the asserter's intention to follow a specified policy of behaviour. To say that it is belief in the dogmas of religion which is the cause of the believer's intending to behave as he does is to put the cart before the horse: it is the intention to behave which constitutes what is known as religious conviction.

But this assimilation of religious to moral assertions lays itself open to an immediate objection. When a moral assertion is taken as declaring the intention of following a policy, the form of the assertion itself makes it clear what the policy is with which the assertion is concerned. For a man to assert that a certain policy ought to be pursued, which on this view is for him to declare his intention of pursuing the policy, presupposes his understanding what it would be like for him to pursue the policy in question. I cannot resolve not to tell a lie without knowing what a lie is. But if a religious assertion is the declaration of an intention to carry out a certain policy, what policy does it specify? The religious statement itself will not explicitly refer to a policy, as does a moral statement; how then can the asserter of the statement know what is the policy concerned, and how can he intend to carry out a policy if he does not know what the policy is? I cannot intend to do something I know not what.

The reply to this criticism is that, if a religious assertion is regarded as representative of a large number of assertions of the same religious system, the body of assertions of which the particular one is a representative specimen is taken by the asserter as implicitly specifying a particular way of life. It is no more necessary for an empiricist philosopher to explain the use of a religious statement taken in isolation from other religious statements than it is for him to give a meaning to a scientific hypothesis in isolation from other scientific hypotheses. We understand scientific hypotheses, and the terms that occur in them, by virtue of the relation of the whole system of hypotheses to empirically observable facts; and it is the whole system of hypotheses, not one hypothesis in isolation, that is tested for its truth-value against experience. So there are good precedents, in the empiricist way of thinking, for considering a system of religious assertions as a whole, and for examining the way in which the whole system is used.

If we do this the fact that a system of religious assertions has a moral function can hardly be denied. For to deny it would require any passage from the assertion of a religious system to a policy of action to be mediated by a moral assertion. I cannot pass from asserting a fact, of whatever sort, to intending to perform an action, without having the hypothetical intention to intend to do the action if I assert the fact. This holds however widely fact is understood—whether as an empirical fact or as a non-empirical fact about goodness or reality. Just as the intention-to-act view of moral assertions is the only view that requires no reason for my doing what I assert to be my duty, so the similar view of religious assertions is the only one which connects them to ways of life without requiring an additional premiss. Unless a Christian's assertion that God is love (*agape*) —which I take to epitomize the assertions of the Christian religion—be taken to declare his intention to follow an agapeistic way of life, he could be asked what is the connexion between the assertion and the intention, between Christian belief and Christian practice. And this question can always be asked if religious assertions are separated from conduct. Unless religious principles are moral principles, it makes no sense to speak of putting them into practice.

The way to find out what are the intentions embodied in a set of religious assertions, and hence what is the meaning of the assertions, is by discovering what principles of conduct the asserter takes the assertions to involve. These may be ascertained both by asking him questions and by seeing how he behaves, each test being supplemental to the other. If what is wanted is not the meaning of the religious assertions made by a particular man but what the set of assertions would mean were they to be made by anyone of the same religion (which I will call their *typical* meaning), all that can be done is to specify the form of behaviour which is in accordance with what one takes to be the fundamental moral principles of the religion in question. Since different people will take different views as to what these fundamental moral principles are, the typical meaning of religious assertions will be different for different people. I myself take the typical meaning of the body of Christian assertions as being given by their proclaiming intentions to follow an agapeistic way of life, and for a description of this way of life—a description in general and metaphorical terms, but an empirical description nevertheless—I should quote most of the Thirteenth Chapter of I Corinthians. Others may think that the Christian way of life should be described somewhat differently, and will therefore take the typical meaning of the assertions of Christianity to correspond to their different view of its fundamental moral teaching.

My contention then is that the primary use of religious assertions is to announce allegiance to a set of moral principles: without such allegiance there is no 'true religion.' This is borne out by all the accounts of what happens when an unbeliever becomes converted to a religion. The conversion is not only a change in the propositions believed—indeed there may be no specifically intellectual change at all; it is a change in the state of will. An excellent instance is C. S. Lewis's recently published account of his conversion from an idealist metaphysic—'a religion [as he says] that cost nothing'—to a theism where he faced (and he quotes George MacDonald's phrase) 'something to be neither more nor less nor other than *done*.' There was no intellectual change, for (as he says) 'there had long been an ethic (theoretically) attached to my Idealism': it was the recognition that he had to do something about it, that 'an attempt at complete virtue must be made.'[2] His conversion was a re-orientation of the will.

In assimilating religious assertions to moral assertions I do not wish to deny that there are any important differences. One is the fact already noticed that usually the behaviour policy intended is not specified by one religious assertion in isolation. Another difference is that the fundamental moral teaching of the religion is frequently given, not in abstract terms, but by means of concrete examples—of how to behave, for instance, if one meets a man set upon by thieves on the road to Jericho. A resolution to behave like the good Samaritan does not, in itself, specify the behaviour to be resolved upon in quite different circumstances. However, absence of explicitly recognized general principles does not prevent a man from acting in accordance with such principles; it only makes it more difficult for a questioner to discover upon what principles he is acting. And the difficulty is not only one way round. If moral principles are stated in the most general form, as most moral philosophers have wished to state them, they tend to become so far removed from particular courses of conduct that it is difficult, if not impossible, to give them any precise content. It may be hard to find out what exactly is involved in the imitation of Christ; but it is not very easy to discover what exactly is meant by the pursuit of Aristotle's *eudaemonia* or of Mill's *happiness*. The tests for what it is to live agapeistically are as empirical as are those for living in quest of happiness; but in each case the tests can best be expounded in terms of examples of particular situations.

A more important difference between religious and purely moral principles is that, in the higher religions at least, the conduct preached by the religion concerns not only external but also internal behaviour. The conversion involved in accepting a religion is a conversion, not only of the will, but of the heart. Christianity requires not only that you should behave towards your neighbour as if you loved him as yourself: it requires that you should love him as yourself. And though I have no doubt that the Christian concept of *agape* refers partly to external behaviour—the agapeistic behaviour for which there are external criteria—yet being filled with *agape* includes more than behaving agapeistically externally: it also includes an agapeistic frame of mind. I have said that I cannot regard the expression of a feeling of any sort as the primary element in religious assertion; but this does not imply that intention to feel in a certain way is not a primary element, nor that it cannot be used to discriminate religious declarations of policy from declarations which are merely moral. Those who say that Confucianism is a code of morals and not, properly speaking, a religion are, I think, making this discrimination.

The resolution proclaimed by a religious assertion may then be taken as referring to inner life as well as to outward conduct. And the superiority of re-

[2] C. S. Lewis, *Surprised by Joy* (1955), pp. 198, 212–13.

ligious conviction over the mere adoption of a moral code in securing conformity to the code arises from a religious conviction changing what the religious man wants. It may be hard enough to love your enemy, but once you have succeeded in doing so it is easy to behave lovingly towards him. But if you continue to hate him, it requires a heroic perseverence continually to behave as if you loved him. Resolutions to feel, even if they are only partly fulfilled, are powerful reinforcements of resolutions to act.

But though these qualifications may be adequate for distinguishing religious assertions from purely moral ones, they are not sufficient to discriminate between assertions belonging to one religious system and those belonging to another system in the case in which the behaviour policies, both of inner life and of outward conduct, inculcated by the two systems are identical. For instance, I have said that I take the fundamental moral teaching of Christianity to be the preaching of an agapeistic way of life. But a Jew or a Buddhist may, with considerable plausibility, maintain that the fundamental moral teaching of his religion is to recommend exactly the same way of life. How then can religious assertions be distinguished into those which are Christian, those which are Jewish, those which are Buddhist, by the policies of life which they respectively recommend if, on examination, these policies turn out to be the same?

Many Christians will, no doubt, behave in a specifically Christian manner in that they will follow ritual practices which are Christian and neither Jewish nor Buddhist. But though following certain practices may well be the proper test for membership of a particular religious society, a church, not even the most ecclesiastically-minded Christian will regard participation in a ritual as the fundamental characteristic of a Christian way of life. There must be some more important difference between an agapeistically policied Christian and an agapeistically policied Jew than that the former attends a church and the latter a synagogue.

The really important difference, I think, is to be found in the fact that the intentions to pursue the behaviour policies, which may be the same for different religions, are associated with thinking of different *stories* (or sets of stories). By a story I shall here mean a proposition or set of propositions which are straightforwardly empirical propositions capable of empirical test and which are thought of by the religious man in connexion with his resolution to follow the way of life advocated by his religion. On the assumption that the ways of life advocated by Christianity and by Buddhism are essentially the same, it will be the fact that the intention to follow this way of life is associated in the mind of a Christian with thinking of one set of stories (the Christian stories) while it is associated in the mind of a Buddhist with thinking of another set of stories (the Buddhist stories) which enables a Christian assertion to be distinguished from a Buddhist one.

A religious assertion will, therefore, have a propositional element which is lacking in a purely moral assertion, in that it will refer to a story as well as to an intention. The reference to the story is not an assertion of the story taken as a matter of empirical fact: it is a telling of the story, or an alluding to the story, in the way in which one can tell, or allude to, the story of a novel with which one is acquainted. To assert the whole set of assertions of the Christian religion is both to tell the Christian doctrinal story and to confess allegiance to the Christian way of life.

The story, I have said, is a set of empirical propositions, and the language expressing the story is given a meaning by the standard method of understanding how the story-statements can be verified. The empirical story-statements will vary from Christian to Christian; the doctrines of Christianity are capable of different empirical interpretations, and Christians will differ in the interpretations they put upon the doctrines. But the interpretations will all be in terms of empirical propositions. Take, for example, the doctrine of Justification by means of the Atonement. Matthew Arnold imagined it in terms of

> . . . a sort of infinitely magnified and improved Lord Shaftesbury, with a race of vile offenders to deal with, whom his natural goodness would incline him to let off only his sense of justice will not allow it; then a younger Lord Shaftesbury, on the scale of his father and very dear to him, who might live in grandeur and splendour if he liked, but who prefers to leave his home, to go and live among the race of offenders, and to be put to an ignominious death, on condition that his merits shall be counted against their demerits, and that his father's goodness shall be restrained no longer from taking effect, but any offender shall be admitted to the benefit of it on simply pleading the satisfaction made by the son;—and then, finally, a third Lord Shaftesbury, still on the same high scale, who keeps very much in the background, and works in a very occult manner, but very efficaciously nevertheless, and who is busy in applying everywhere the benefits of the son's satisfaction and the father's goodness.[3]

Arnold's 'parable of the three Lord Shaftesburys' got him into a lot of trouble: he was 'indignantly censured' (as he says) for wounding 'the feelings of the religious community by turning into ridicule an august doctrine, the object of their solemn faith.'[4] But there is no other account of the Anselmian doctrine of the Atonement that I have read which puts it in so morally favourable a light. Be that as it may, the only way in which the doctrine can be understood verificationally is in terms of human beings—mythological beings, it may be, who never existed, but who nevertheless would have been empirically observable had they existed.

For it is not necessary, on my view, for the asserter of a religious assertion to believe in the truth of the story involved in the assertions: what is necessary is that the story should be entertained in thought, i.e. that the statement of the story should be understood as having a meaning. I have secured this by requiring that the story should consist of empirical propositions. Educated Christians of the present day who attach importance to the doctrine of the Atonement certainly do not believe an empirically testable story in Matthew Arnold's or any other form. But it is the fact that entertainment in thought of this and other

[3] Matthew Arnold, *Literature and Dogma* (1873), pp. 306–7.

[4] Matthew Arnold, *God and the Bible* (1875), pp. 18–19.

Christian stories forms the context in which Christian resolutions are made which serves to distinguish Christian assertions from those made by adherents of another religion, or of no religion.

What I am calling a *story* Matthew Arnold called a *parable* and a *fairy-tale.* Other terms which might be used are *allegory, fable, tale, myth.* I have chosen the word 'story' as being the most neutral term, implying neither that the story is believed nor that it is disbelieved. The Christian stories include straightforward historical statements about the life and death of Jesus of Nazareth; a Christian (unless he accepts the unplausible Christ-myth theory) will naturally believe some or all of these. Stories about the beginning of the world and of the Last Judgment as facts of past or of future history are believed by many unsophisticated Christians. But my contention is that belief in the truth of the Christian stories is not the proper criterion for deciding whether or not an assertion is a Christian one. A man is not, I think, a professing Christian unless he both proposes to live according to Christian moral principles and associates his intention with thinking of Christian stories; but he need not believe that the empirical propositions presented by the stories correspond to empirical fact.

But if the religious stories need not be believed, what function do they fulfil in the complex state of mind and behaviour known as having a religious belief? How is entertaining the story related to resolving to pursue a certain way of life? My answer is that the relation is a psychological and causal one. It is an empirical psychological fact that many people find it easier to resolve upon and to carry through a course of action which is contrary to their natural inclinations if this policy is associated in their minds with certain stories. And in many people the psychological link is not appreciably weakened by the fact that the story associated with the behaviour policy is not believed. Next to the Bible and the Prayer Book the most influential work in English Christian religious life has been a book whose stories are frankly recognized as fictitious—Bunyan's *Pilgrim's Progress*; and some of the most influential works in setting the moral tone of my generation were the novels of Dostoevsky. It is completely untrue, as a matter of psychological fact, to think that the only intellectual considerations which affect action are beliefs; it is *all* the thoughts of a man that determine his behaviour; and these include his phantasies, imaginations, ideas of what he would wish to be and do, as well as the propositions which he believes to be true. . . .

. . . My contention that the propositional element in religious assertions consists of stories interpreted as straightforwardly empirical propositions which are not, generally speaking, believed to be true has the great advantage of imposing no restriction whatever upon the empirical interpretation which can be put upon the stories. The religious man may interpret the stories in the way which assists him best in carrying out the behaviour policies of his religion. He can, for example, think of the three persons of the Trinity in visual terms, as did the great Christian painters, or as talking to one another, as in the poems of St. John of the Cross. And since he need not believe the stories he can interpret them in ways which are not consistent with one another. It is disastrous for anyone to try to believe empirical propositions which are mutually inconsistent, for the courses of action appropriate to inconsistent beliefs are not compatible. The needs of practical life require that the body of believed propositions should be purged of inconsistency. But there is no action which is appropriate to thinking of a proposition without believing it; thinking of it may, as I have said, produce a state of mind in which it is easier to carry out a particular course of action, but the connexion is causal: there is no intrinsic connexion between the thought and the action. Indeed a story may provide better support for a long range policy of action if it contains inconsistencies. The Christian set of stories, for example, contains both a pantheistic sub-set of stories in which everything is a part of God and a dualistic Manichaean sub-set of stories well represented by St. Ignatius Loyola's allegory of a conflict between the forces of righteousness under the banner of Christ and the forces of darkness under Lucifer's banner. And the Marxist religion's set of stories contains both stories about an inevitable perfect society and stories about a class war. In the case of both religions the first sub-set of stories provides confidence, the second spurs to action.

There is one story common to all the moral theistic religions which has proved of great psychological value in enabling religious men to persevere in carrying out their religious behaviour policies—the story that in so doing they are doing the will of God. And here it may look as if there is an intrinsic connexion between the story and the policy of conduct. But even when the story is literally believed, when it is believed that there is a magnified Lord Shaftesbury who commands or desires the carrying out of the behaviour policy, that in itself is no reason for carrying out the policy: it is necessary also to have the intention of doing what the magnified Lord Shaftesbury commands or desires. But the intention to do what a person commands or desires, irrespective of what this command or desire may be, is no part of a higher religion; it is when the religious man finds that what the magnified Lord Shaftesbury commands or desires accords with his own moral judgement that he decides to obey or to accede to it. But this is no new decision, for his own moral judgement is a decision to carry out a behaviour policy; all that is happening is that he is describing his old decision in a new way. In religious conviction the resolution to follow a way of life is primary; it is not derived from believing, still less from thinking of, any empirical story. The story may psychologically support the resolution, but it does not logically justify it.

In this lecture I have been sparing in my use of the term 'religious belief' (although it occurs in the title), preferring instead to speak of religious assertions and of religious conviction. This was because for me the fundamental problem is that of the meaning of statements used to make religious assertions, and I have accordingly taken my task to be that of explaining the use of such assertions, in accordance with the principle that meaning is to be found by ascertaining use. In disentangling the elements of this use I have discovered nothing which can be called 'belief' in the senses of this word applicable either to an empirical or to a logically necessary proposition. A religious assertion, for me, is the assertion of an intention to carry out a certain behaviour policy, subsumable under a sufficiently general principle to be a moral one, together with the implicit or explicit statement, but not the assertion, of certain stories. Neither the assertion of the intention nor the reference to the stories includes belief in its ordinary senses. But in avoiding the term 'belief' I have had to widen the term 'assertion,' since I do not pretend that either the behaviour policy intended or the stories entertained are adequately specified by the sentences used in making isolated religious assertions. So assertion has been extended to include elements not explicitly expressed in the verbal form of the assertion. If we drop the linguistic expression of the assertion altogether the remainder is what may be called religious belief. Like moral belief, it is not a species of ordinary belief, of belief in a proposition. A moral belief is an intention to behave in a certain way: a religious belief is an intention to behave in a certain way (a moral belief) together with the entertainment of certain stories associated with the intention in the mind of the believer. This solution of the problem of religious belief seems to me to do justice both to the empiricist's demand that meaning must be tied to empirical use and to the religious man's claim for his religious beliefs to be taken seriously.

Seriously, it will be retorted, but not objectively. If a man's religion is all a matter of following the way of life he sets before himself and of strengthening his determination to follow it by imagining exemplary fairy-tales, it is purely subjective: his religion is all in terms of his own private ideals and of his own private imaginations. How can he even try to convert others to his religion if there is nothing objective to convert them to? How can he argue in its defence if there is no religious proposition which he believes, nothing which he takes to be the fundamental truth about the universe? And is it of any public interest what mental techniques he uses to bolster up his will? Discussion about religion must be more than the exchange of autobiographies.

But we are all social animals; we are all members one of another. What is profitable to one man in helping him to persevere in the way of life he has decided upon may well be profitable to another man who is trying to follow a similar way of life; and to pass on information that might prove useful would be approved by almost every morality. The autobiography of one man may well have an influence upon the life of another, if their basic wants are similar.

But suppose that these are dissimiliar, and that the two men propose to conduct their lives on quite different fundamental principles. Can there be any reasonable discussion between them? This is the problem that has faced the many moral philosophers recently who have been forced, by their examination of the nature of thinking, into holding non-propositional theories of ethics. All I will here say is that to hold that the adoption of a set of moral principles is a matter of the personal decision to live according to these principles does not imply that beliefs as to what are the practical consequences of following such principles are not relevant to the decision. An intention, it is true, cannot be logically based upon anything except another intention. But in considering what conduct to intend to practise, it is highly relevant whether or not the consequences of practising that conduct are such as one would intend to secure. As

R. M. Hare has well said, an ultimate decision to accept a way of life, 'far from being arbitrary, . . . would be the most well-founded of decisions, because it would be based upon a consideration of everything upon which it could possibly be founded.'[5] And in this consideration there is a place for every kind of rational argument.

Whatever may be the case with other religions Christianity has always been a personal religion demanding personal commitment to a personal way of life. In the words of another Oxford philosopher, 'the questions "What shall I do?" and "What moral principles should I adopt?" must be answered by each man for himself.'[6] Nowell-Smith takes this as part of the meaning of morality: whether or not this is so, I am certain that it is of the very essence of the Christion religion.

5 R. M. Hare, *The Language of Morals* (1952), p. 69.
6 P. H. Nowell-Smith, *Ethics* (1954), p. 320.

INTRODUCTION TO PHILOSOPHY OF RELIGION / Study Questions

THE MEANING OF RELIGIOUS LANGUAGE

Tillich

1. What are the similarities and differences between symbols and signs, according to Tillich? What does it mean to say that a stop sign "points to the order to stop?" What is the difference between an "essential" relation and a "conventional" relation? How does Tillich use this discussion to introduce what he calls the first and second "characteristics" of symbols? What are these characteristics?
2. What are the remaining four characteristics? Can you give concrete examples of some things we usually take to be symbols that illustrate these characteristics?
3. Are the six characteristics listed by Tillich an exhaustive list? Is each and every one essential to a thing's being viewed as a symbol?
4. What do you think Tillich has in mind by the expressions "ultimate concern" and "matters of unconditional concern?" What is his argument to show that someone's ultimate concern may only be expressed symbolically? What does he have in mind when he says that "God transcends his own name?"
5. What according to Tillich are the two elements in the "notion of God" and how is this distinction supposed to explain Tillich's cryptic assertion that "God is the symbol of God?"
6. What is the context in which symbols appear? What does Tillich mean by *myth*? What are the stages in "the criticism of the myth?" Can a religious myth be completely replaced by "scientific substitutes" (and what is this replacement supposed to be like)?
7. When Tillich says, at the beginning, that a symbol "opens up levels of reality which are otherwise closed to us" does he mean that we would never appreciate the *significance* of, for example, some historical events unless we described them symbolically; or does he mean we could never otherwise know what events actually went on? What is the difference?
8. Consider any symbol with which you are familiar. How is it that you understand what

it is a symbol for? Try this out by seeing how you would explain, to someone unfamiliar with it, both that it is a symbol and what it symbolizes.

9. When Tillich asserts that ultimate concern "can only be expressed symbolically" and that in religion "there is no substitute for the use of symbols and myths," he appears to be saying that some symbolic utterances can never be explained in nonsymbolic language. If this were so, could we ever *understand* what they are symbols for? What conclusion about the meaningfulness of religious language can be drawn from this?

Demos

1. What does Demos have in mind by the expression, a "system of belief?" Give some examples not listed by Demos.
2. How does Demos propose to show that all systems of belief, including scientific theories, are "floating on the infirm waters of faith?" Why does he think that this "element of faith" is unnoticed in science and philosophy?
3. How does Demos argue that reliance on memory is a matter of faith? What is the importance of that, according to Demos?
4. What is the "undemonstrated belief" that lies at the heart of natural science? What is the religious parallel with this belief?
5. Demos proposes to compare the scientific and the religious belief systems. What are the points of comparison and what does Demos have to say about each?
6. What are the four ways in which one may construe the descriptive phrases that occur in religious discourse? What are the differences among symbols, metaphors, analogical terms, and "prose" terms? Which of these does Demos believe religious descriptive phrases are most like? Explain.
7. Explain Demos' discussion of "analogy," "identity," and "likeness." What are the two kinds of "likeness?" Which of these is involved in drawing analogies?
8. Demos claims that descriptive phrases in religion seem of necessity to be contradictory. This, he suggests, *requires* that we regard them as analogical. Why does it *require* "an appeal to analogy?" That is, why couldn't someone just say they *are* self-contradictory and, so, dismiss them?
9. Assuming that Demos would answer the previous question in terms of different "senses" of descriptive phrases, would he not be forced to explain (in particular cases) what those senses are? That being the case, what can be made of his later claim that the analogies involved in religious descriptive phrases are analogical likenesses that admit of no explanation?
10. In cases of drawing ordinary analogies one needs to be familiar with both of the things between which one comes to see a likeness (this would be true even for cases like Demos' "analogical likeness"). Since Demos thinks that the sentence "God exists" is *also* analogical, could one *ever* get into a position to see a likeness between one thing, man, and another thing, God?

Bultmann

1. Why, according to Bultmann, can there be no intelligible "talking *about*" God? How is the example of "love" supposed to be analogous here? What is the difference between a "situation . . . *for the sake of which* . . . something [is] done . . ." and a "condition of life?" Could this difference be illustrated by (a) a legal marriage arranged for political reasons and (b) a marriage for love? How is the parent/child example an illustration of this?
2. Why does Bultman believe that to "speak of God" is to "speak of" oneself? What does

this mean? How is this to be contrasted with a confession of faith or exhortations to others about one's faith? How does this discussion lead into Bultmann's characterization of God as "the wholly other?" What is that supposed to mean; and what is it *not* supposed to mean?

3. In what ways are the "circumstances of our existence . . . startling?" What things are "clear to us about our existence?" What consequences follow about our "talk about our existence?"
4. According to Bultmann, why does his view not lead into "Quietism?" What is "Quietism?"
5. Explain Bultmann's discussion of the concept of *faith*. What is the meaning of Bultmann's last paragraph?
6. Bultman seems to say that one can "speak of" the relationship one has with a parent or child but one cannot "talk about" it. The reason is that, if one talks about it, one takes it as an object of study and, so, a situation for the sake of which something might be done; yet, he says, it is not like that—it is a condition of life. Does Bultmann really mean that it is unintelligible to "talk about" the relationship; or does he mean that "talk about" it misses something that is crucial to being able to understand why parents and children act towards each other in certain ways?
7. If he means the first, would it not follow that an orphan would not be able to understand such a relationship? How can this be, in view of the fact that orphans (who are, admittedly, sometimes puzzled by the actions of others) can still use the words *parent, child,* and so on, as well as anyone else?
8. If he means the second thing, this seems to entail that "talk about" the relationship is intelligible, but merely deficient. Yet he denies that "talk about" God is intelligible. How are we to square this? (It might be that we shall be even more puzzled when we look at Bultmann's last paragraph, in which he seems to suggest the question of God's existence *is* intelligible.)

Schmidt

1. What, according to Schmidt, are the types of statements involved in a "system of empirical knowledge?" Schmidt claims that, while our understanding of theory-*formation* in such systems is sketchy, we can outline what is involved in theory-*justification*. What is involved in this? Explain Schmidt's discussion of the concepts *true* and *false* in this connection.
2. What, in detail, are the six "characteristics" of empirical knowledge, according to Schmidt? Explain, in particular, what Schmidt means by the terms *public* and *objective*.
3. How does Schmidt argue that religious claims are not and cannot be taken as "probable?" What are the differences between the "tests" of empirical systems and those of religion?
4. In what ways are religious "tests" private and subjective? What consequences does this have?
5. How does Schmidt argue that religious claims do not give us "concrete information or causal explanations of matters of fact?"
6. Does Schmidt believe that religious claims are nonsense? Explain.

Braithwaite

1. How, according to Braithwaite, are we to determine the meaning of any statement? What does he believe is the primary use of religious assertions?
2. How does Braithwaite criticize emotive theories in ethics; and what is an emotive

theory? What sort of theory does Braithwaite propose? What is the relation between moral assertions and (the larger class of) expressions of intention?

3. How does the conative theory of moral assertions help explain religious claims? What advantage does it have over emotive theories? In what ways are religious claims and *ordinary* moral assertions different?
4. What, in Braithwaite's terminology, are we to understand by the word *story*? Must a believer take the stories as true historical narratives? What role do stories play in the making of religious assertions, according to Braithwaite?
5. What is the point and the significance of Braithwaite's example of "the magnified Lord Shaftesbury?" (Who was Lord Shaftesbury?)
6. What is Braithwaite's solution to the problem of religious belief; and what, exactly, is that problem?
7. How does Braithwaite respond to the charge that, in making religious assertions out to be expressions of intention, he has turned them into autobiographical reports that can be dismissed as "purely subjective?"
8. Given, what seems to be the case, that most believers think of their assertions as claims of objective fact, how can Braithwaite justify claiming that they are actually *used* as expressions of intention?
9. Evaluate Braithwaite's conative theory of moral assertions. See if you can construct plausible cases in which someone believes an action is wrong yet intends to do it. How might Braithwaite analyze such a case? If we could never show that a person knew some action was wrong and that he also intended to do it, could we ever hold him fully responsible for doing it?

SUGGESTED FURTHER READINGS / Introduction to Philosophy of Religion

GENERAL

Hick, John, ed. *Classical and Contemporary Readings in the Philosophy of Religion*, 2nd ed. Englewood Cliffs, N.J.: Prentice-Hall, Inc., 1970.

Hook, Sidney, ed. *Religious Experience and Truth*. New York: New York University Press, 1961.

THE JUSTIFICATION OF RELIGIOUS BELIEF

Hick, John, and Arthur McGill, eds. *The Many-Faced Argument*. New York: Macmillan Publishing Co., Inc., 1967.

Matson, Wallace I. *The Existence of God*. Ithaca, N.Y.: Cornell University Press, 1965.

Paton, H. J. *The Modern Predicament*. New York: Macmillan Publishing Co., Inc., 1955.

Plantinga, Alvin, ed. *The Ontological Argument, from St. Anselm to Contemporary Philosophers*. Garden City, N.Y.: Doubleday & Company, Inc., 1965.

Taylor, Richard. *Metaphysics*. Englewood Cliffs, N.J.: Prentice-Hall, Inc., 1963.

THE MEANING OF RELIGIOUS LANGUAGE

Blackstone, William T. *The Problem of Religious Language*. Englewood Cliffs, N.J.: Prentice-Hall, Inc., 1963.

Flew, A. N., and Alastair Macintyre, eds. *New Essays in Philosophical Theology*. London: Student Christian Movement Press, 1955.

Mitchell, Basil, ed. *Faith and Logic*. London: George Allen and Unwin Ltd., 1957.

Ramsey, Ian T. *Religious Language*. London: Student Christian Movement Press, 1957.

PART 6

Introduction to Philosophy of Language

It would not be an exaggeration to say that the major preoccupation of twentieth-century philosophy has been with language. This preoccupation was to a large extent the result of turn-of-the-century investigations into the foundations of logic and mathematics undertaken by philosophers such as Gottlob Frege and Bertrand Russell. In these investigations certain technical problems were encountered with the special symbolisms required by mathematics and modern logic. These problems demanded a careful examination of this symbolism, of how the symbols themselves have meaning, and of how they combine with other symbols to form meaningful formulae. Results obtained in these specialized investigations were almost immediately generalized into theories about language as a whole.

One of the first tasks of modern philosophy of language was to inquire into the nature of meaning with the aim of arriving at a criterion for distinguishing sense from nonsense. It was suspected by some, for example, Bertrand Russell and the philosophers known as logical positivists, that many of the theories and claims of past philosophers were dictated by certain unacknowledged and uncritical assumptions about the nature of language and meaning. Because these assumptions were mistaken, such philosophical theories were therefore devoid of meaning. All of this produced quite a novel challenge to the philosopher. In the past a philosopher always had to be prepared to defend his theories against the charge that they were false; now he also had to be prepared to defend them against the charge that they are senseless. (The student is referred to Part 2 on metaphysics for some specific examples of this sort of thing.)

A proper philosophical theory of

language was thought to hold the key to philosophy generally. Traditional philosophical problems were thought to arise out of an inadequate understanding of language and meaning and it was believed that a correct philosophy of language would have far reaching beneficial effects in such disparate areas as theory construction in physics on the one hand and literary criticism on the other.

We agree with the broad contention that in one way or another problems about language and meaning are the very essence of philosophy; the whole of this volume is a witness to that. We would question, however, that a *theory* of meaning is possible or that we shall ever have a neat set of criteria whereby infallibly to distinguish sense from nonsense. There is no royal road to unraveling the conceptual snarls that generate philosophical problems.

We have not chosen to lead students through a review of the principal theories of meaning that have dominated twentieth-century philosophy and the various objections that can be brought against each of them nor has it been our intention to introduce them to some sampling of the other highly technical problems in contemporary philosophy of language. Rather, we have chosen to begin with a nontechnical look at some questions about meaning and what it means for a word to have a meaning. These are questions that students may have already met outside the philosophy classroom and have sufficient intrinsic importance to interest those for whom the details of the development of modern philosophy of language are of no great concern.

Another kind of twentieth-century interest in language is exhibited by the science of linguistics. In the past linguistics has been largely an empirical study of languages. The linguist has been interested in studying such things as the grammatical structure of various natural languages, how a language changes with time, how one language may borrow words from another, and the regularities shown in how the borrowed words are modified. In recent years, however, linguistics has come to have more and more a theoretical orientation. Theoretical linguists are now asking questions about meaning and understanding and the psychological processes that may underlie and make possible the speaking of a language. Some of these questions are considered in the second section of this part under "Thinking and Speaking." We would suggest that these questions are not empirical questions to be answered by scientific observation and experiment, but are really philosophical, that is, conceptual, questions about the nature of language and its speakers. In fact, some of these questions involving the relation between thought and speech belong as much to the philosophy of mind as they do to the philosophy of language. It is always in order to remind our students that there is something a bit artificial about any division of philosophical issues into *nice* categories.

The Meaning of a Word

Students are likely to have encountered the questions about words and meaning discussed in this section in situations like the following. In the debate of recent years about abortion, questions are sometimes raised whether abortion is murder or whether a fetus is a human being. Sometimes people have tried to resolve such questions by describing them as "merely questions of semantics". (The word *semantics* is from the Greek and means roughly "meaning.") They will go on to say that the answer you give to the questions will depend upon what you mean by the key words *murder* and *human being*. They will point out that when one person claims that abortion *is* murder and another makes the counterclaim that it *is not* murder, the dispute can frequently be settled by showing that the two parties each meant something different by the word *murder*. How, then, are we to go about resolving disputes in this way? How do we determine what someone means by a word? Some further questions are immediately suggested. What is it for a word to *have* a meaning? What *is* the meaning of a word? What is it to *understand* the meaning of a word?

There are no doubt some disputes that can be settled by the "merely a question of semantics" move. Suppose two men have come to blows because they both claim to be in love with Cynthia when in fact they are in love with different girls who just happen to share the same name. The quarrel is easily extinguished by showing that when Tom speaks of Cynthia he means *this* girl and when Dick speaks of Cynthia he means *that* girl. Now the word *Cynthia* is a name and it is by their names that we *call* people and *refer* to them. Thus, to describe the quarrel between Tom and Dick as a matter of semantics is just to say that the two were using the same word to name or refer to different girls. Perhaps what is true of Tom's and Dick's case is also true of the abortion disputes and suggests that to talk about what is meant by *murder* or *human being* is really to talk about what these words *name* or *refer to*.

The thesis can appear very plausible that words are essentially the names of things and that the meaning of a word is what it names. It is easy to suppose that the difference between meaningful words such as *red* or *chair* and nonsense "words" such as Lewis *Carroll's brillig* and *tove* lies in the fact that *red* and *chair* name or stand for things in the world while *brillig* and *tove* do not. St. *Augustine*, in a brief chapter from his justly famous *Confessions*, gives a very clear and straightforward statement of this thesis that words are names in his account of how he supposedly learned language as a child. A somewhat similar account of meaning is given by John *Locke* although with certain important differences. Locke agrees with Augustine that words are names, but he thinks that instead of things in the world, they name what he calls "ideas in the mind." Locke's use of the word *idea* is a remarkably broad one and is not without its ambiguities. In Locke's theory, ideas include such things as perceptions, sensations and feelings, and thoughts and theories. As Locke did hold that all ideas are derived from experience it can possibly be inferred that words, in naming ideas, are in fact indirectly naming the things in the world that our ideas are derived from by way of experience.

Locke, however, is concerned not only with meaning, but also with understanding. A parrot can speak words as well as a man, but a parrot has no understanding of the words he mouths. What is the difference, then, between the speech of a parrot and that of a man? Locke's answer is that a man can "use these sounds as signs of internal conceptions . . . and make them stand as marks for the ideas within his own mind." The parrot has no ideas attached to his words and so there is no understanding or meaning behind the noises he makes. This theory of meaning and understanding produces an interesting account of communication. Suppose I have certain thoughts or ideas in my mind that I wish to share with you. According to Locke we cannot be aware of the ideas in another's mind, therefore I must employ words to be the outward and visible signs of the inward and invisible ideas. When you hear or read my words certain ideas are aroused in your mind and you will have understood what I say if you attach the same ideas (meanings) to the words that I do. A problem, however, immediately arises that Locke does not consider. Locke has made meaning and understanding a matter of the occurrence of certain psychological events; the meaning of a word is identified with a mental process, an idea occurring in the mind. But Locke has a picture of mental events as invisible happenings known only to the person who has them and to no other. It has to follow, then, that one person can never know what another person means by the words he utters since he can never know what ideas his words stand for. This, it will be recognized, is another instance of the "other minds" problem.

The chapter from S. I. *Hayakawa's Language in Thought and Action* has been included for two reasons: First, because the kind of semantic theory it represents has had considerable influence in many colleges and universities (students may well have met it in one or another of their courses) and secondly, because it is a good example of how a certain kind of philosophical theory can influence thinking about other things. Hayakawa's theory of meaning is essentially that of St. Augustine and Locke; words are names, they symbolize or stand for things. An interesting feature of Hayakawa's chapter is the use he makes of this theory of meaning to provide a diagnosis of social and political problems. He places great emphasis on the point already suggested by Locke that there is no necessary connection between the words of language and the things for which they stand. We tend, he thinks, to be very naive about language and suppose, mistakenly, that the presence of the symbol guarantees the existence of the thing symbolized. Thus we tend to believe anything we are told by deceitful politicians and other shapers of opinion. And this, he concludes, is the cause of the social and political conflicts that are at the basis of the world's problems. The solution, he argues, is in a better understanding of the "symbolic process," that is, in a theory about the meaning of words.

We see Hayakawa's theory as embodying a series of mistakes. In the first place, the theory of meaning that he shares with Augustine and Locke is a very questionable one and is duly criticized later in this section. In the second place, Hayakawa seems to suppose that a sentence is a symbol in the same way that an individual word is a symbol. In other words, he thinks that sentences have meaning in the same way that individual words have meaning. There is, however, a simple consideration that shows this to be wrong. When you encounter a word that you have not heard before, one that is not in your vocabulary, you cannot understand it until its meaning is explained to you, but, curiously enough, this is not true of a sentence you have not heard before. So long as the words in the new sentence are all familiar you understand it immediately without an explanation. Note that the force of this argument is independent of any particular theory of meaning. Whatever kind of philosophical theory is to be given for the meaning of sentences it must be different from the explanation given for the meaning of words.

In the third place, it is by no means certain that social and political conflicts are the result of a naive failure to be critical about what we accept as true. This is not to deny the obvious fact that some conflicts have resulted from misinformation, but is rather to point out that it can also be the case that to know the truth about another party and his intentions is to despise him all the more. The danger in what Hayakawa is saying is that it invites us to concentrate our attention on a very questionable, and in this context possibly irrelevant, philosophical theory of meaning rather than on the nature of the moral, social, and political issues themselves that underlie those conflicts.

The selection from *Swift*'s *Gulliver's Travels* is a marvelously enlightening parody of the philosophical theory of meaning we have been discussing. It is as if the professors from the royal academy have taken Hayakawa's warnings about naive attitudes toward symbols to heart and have done away with the symbols in favor of the things they symbolize. In one stroke they have gotten rid of what Hayakawa claims is a major source of difficulty. We invite the student to conduct his affairs in the new way. We believe this kind of parody can be a very useful philosophical tool; it invites us to treat a theory seriously and to take a philosopher at his word. Sometimes in this way the absurdity of a theory that was disguised in its original statement can be made manifest. Swift shows us that something in the theory has gone very wrong, but not how it has gone wrong or what improved account should take its place. Nevertheless, the reader is warned away from one mistaken conclusion. One might think that the value of words over things is merely one of convenience, that one can carry a great many more words about with one than things.

With the chapter from William *James' Pragmatism*, we return to the question about settling disputes by deciding what a word is to mean. James' trivial example of the man and the squirrel is intended to illustrate an important point about his "pragmatic method" for settling philosophical disputes. There are two questions that must be raised about this. Has James in fact given us two equally correct meanings for the expression "going round" and can any substantive questions in philosophy, or anywhere else, be settled so easily? To answer the second of these questions the student must look carefully at the philosophical problems treated in any of the parts of this book and we shall not lay out for him here the conclusion he is to draw.

As for the first question, might it not be the case that the connection between words and their meanings really is arbitrary and that we are free to use words as we see fit? After all, if a father chooses to name his daughter Cynthia he could just as easily have chosen to name her Matilda and if someone chooses to call *these* things "going round" or "murder" or "human being" then another is free to call *those other* things by these names. The identification of meaning with naming does seem to suggest such possibilities.

The classical exposition of the folly of this way of thinking about words and their meanings is found in Lewis Carroll's wonderful description of the encounter between Alice and Humpty Dumpty. It would be a profanation to attempt to summarize Humpty Dumpty's insolent confidence and Alice's modest reservations; it is enough to say that we come away from it wiser in the ways of language, and in *that* there is a measure of glory for you.

We have chosen as a final reading a chapter from Friedrich *Waismann's Principles of Linguistic Philosophy*. Waismann's account of language and meaning is largely an exposition of the views of Ludwig Wittgenstein in his *Philosophical Investigations*; and we have included it because of its concise summary of a position that seriously undercuts the kind of theory held by Augustine, Locke, and Hayakawa. Waismann begins by taking issue specifically with Augustine's theory of meaning. He argues against the identification of meaning with naming and also against the Lockean theory that understanding is a mental process. He points out that the word *meaning* itself has a number of meanings and suggests that when we do philosophy we are better off examining the *use* of words rather than looking for something called "the meaning." Words have many uses and naming things is only one of them. In this, words are like the pieces on a chessboard. Chessmen do not all move in the same way and have different roles to play in the game. This allows us to see what is wrong in supposing that the questions, whether abortion is murder or a fetus a human being, can be settled by deciding what a word is to mean. Words such as *murder* and *human being* are not arbitrary labels to be hung, Humpty Dumpty fashion, on anything we choose; for these words aren't names at all, but instead play very complex roles in moral and legal situations. Think of the consequences that follow, in the law courts if nowhere else, from describing a deed as one of *murder*.

One last question. If understanding is not something mental, then is it not conceivable that someone—or a parrot or a machine—could use words correctly in the absence of any understanding of them at all? Waismann's—and it is also Wittgenstein's—answer to this is that what distinguishes a mere game with words from actual language is the fact that in language the words are integrated into life and a man's understanding of words is shown in how he uses them in everyday situations. The student, however, may well wonder how this constitutes an answer to the question about language and meaning; and although we believe it is in this direction that the answer does in fact lie, we must also admit that it is going to take much more showing than Waismann's exposition of Wittgenstein supplies.

Words Are Names

ST. AUGUSTINE

FROM infancy I came to boyhood, or rather it came to me, taking the place of infancy. Yet infancy did not go: for where was it to go? Simply it was no longer there. For now I was not an infant, without speech, but a boy, speaking. This I remember; and I have since discovered by observation how I learned to speak. I did not learn by elders teaching me words in any systematic way, as I was soon after taught to read and write. But of my own motion, using the mind which You, my God, gave me, I strove with cries and various sounds and much moving of my limbs to utter the feelings of my heart—all this in order to get my own way. Now I did not always manage to express the right meanings to the right people. So I began to reflect. [I observed that] my elders would make some particular sound, and as they made it would point at or move towards some particular thing: and from this I came to realize that the thing was called by the sound they made when they wished to draw my attention to it. That they intended this was clear from the motions of their body, by a kind of natural language common to all races which consists in facial expressions, glances of the eye, gestures, and the tones by which the voice expresses the mind's state—for example whether things are to be sought, kept, thrown away, or avoided. So, as I heard the same words again and again properly used in different phrases, I came gradually to grasp what things they signified; and forcing my mouth to the same sounds, I began to use them to express my own wishes. Thus I learnt to convey what I meant to those about me; and so took another long step along the stormy way of human life in society, while I was still subject to the authority of my parents and at the beck and call of my elders.

Reprinted from *The Confessions of St. Augustine*, trans. by F. J. Sheed, Copyright 1954, Sheed & Ward, Inc., New York. The excerpt is from Book I, Chapter VIII.

Words Name Ideas in the Mind

JOHN LOCKE

Of Words or Language in General

Man Fitted to Form Articulate Sounds

§ 1. GOD having designed man for a sociable creature, made him not only with an inclination, and under a necessity to have fellowship with those of his own kind, but furnished him also with language, which was to be the great instru-

---

Reprinted from *An Essay Concerning Human Understanding*, Book III, Chapters I and II, by John Locke.

ment and common tie of society. Man therefore had by nature his organs so fashioned as to be fit to frame articulate sounds, which we call words. But this was not enough to produce language; for parrots and several other birds will be taught to make articulate sounds distinct enough, which yet, by no means, are capable of language.

To Make Them Signs of Ideas

§ 2. Besides articulate sounds, therefore, it was farther necessary that he should be able to use these sounds as signs of internal conceptions; and to make them stand as marks for the ideas within his own mind, whereby they might be made known to others, and the thoughts of men's minds be conveyed from one to another.

To Make General Signs

§ 3. But neither was this sufficient to make words so useful as they ought to be. It is not enough for the perfection of language, that sounds can be made signs of ideas, unless those signs can be so made use of as to comprehend several particular things: for the multiplication of words would have perplexed their use, had every particular thing need of a distinct name to be signified by. To remedy this inconvenience, language had yet a farther improvement in the use of general terms, whereby one word was made to mark a multitude of particular existences: which advantageous use of sounds was obtained only by the difference of the ideas they were made signs of: those names becoming general, which are made to stand for general ideas, and those remaining particular, where the ideas they are used for are particular.

§ 4. Besides these names which stand for ideas, there be other words which men make use of, not to signify any idea, but the want or absence of some ideas simple or complex, or all ideas together; such as are *nihil* in Latin, and in English, ignorance and barrenness. All which negative or privative words cannot be said properly to belong to, or signify no ideas: for then they would be perfectly insignificant sounds; but they relate to positive ideas, and signify their absence.

Words Ultimately Derived From Such As Signify Sensible Ideas

§ 5. It may also lead us a little towards the original of all our notions and knowledge, if we remark how great a dependence our words have on common sensible ideas; and how those, which are made use of to stand for actions and notions quite removed from sense, have their rise from thence, and from obvious sensible ideas are transferred to more abstruse significations, and made to stand for ideas that come not under the cognizance of our senses: *v.g.* to imagine, apprehend, comprehend, adhere, conceive, instil, disgust, disturbance, tranquility, &c. are all words taken from the operations of sensible things, and applied to certain modes of thinking. Spirit, in its primary signification, is breath: angel, a messenger: and I doubt not, but if we could trace them to their sources, we should find, in all languages, the names, which stand for things that fall not under our senses, to have had their first rise from sensible ideas. By which we may give some kind of guess what kind of notions they were, and whence derived, which filled their minds who were the first beginners of languages; and how nature, even in the naming of things, unawares suggested to men the originals and principles of all their knowledge: whilst, to give names that might make known to others any operations they felt in themselves, or any other ideas that came not under their senses, they were fain to borrow words from ordinary known ideas of sensation, by that means to make others the more easily to conceive those operations they experimented in themselves, which made no outward sensible appearances: and then when they had got known and agreed names, to signify those internal operations of their own minds, they were sufficiently furnished to make known by words all their other ideas; since they could consist of nothing, but either of outward sensible perceptions, or of the inward operations of their minds about them: we having, as has been proved, no ideas at all, but what originally come either from sensible objects without, or what we feel within ourselves, from the inward workings of our own spirits, of which we are conscious to ourselves within.

Distribution

§ 6. But to understand better the use and force of language, as subservient to instruction and knowledge, it will be convenient to consider,

First, To what it is that names, in the use of language, are immediately applied.

Secondly, Since all (except proper) names are general, and so stand not particularly for this or that single thing, but for sorts and ranks of things; it will be necessary to consider, in the next place, what the sorts and kinds, or, if you rather like the Latin names, what the species and genera of things are; wherein they consist, and how they come to be made. These being (as they ought) well looked into, we shall the better come to find the right use of words, the natural advantages and defects of language, and the remedies that ought to be used, to avoid the inconveniences of obscurity or uncertainty in the signification of words, without which it is impossible to discourse with any clearness or order concerning knowledge: which being conversant about propositions, and those most commonly universal ones, has greater connexion with words than perhaps is suspected.

These considerations therefore shall be the matter of the following chapters.

Of the Significance of Words

Words Are Sensible Signs Necessary for Communication

§ 1. MAN, though he has great variety of thoughts, and such from which others, as well as himself, might receive profit and delight; yet they are all within his own breast, invisible and hidden from others, nor can of themselves be made appear. The comfort and advantage of society not being to be had without communication of thoughts, it was necessary that man should find out some external sensible signs, whereof those invisible ideas, which his thoughts are made up of, might be made known to others. For this purpose nothing was so fit, either for plenty or quickness, as those articulate sounds, which with so much case and variety he found himself able to make. Thus we may conceive how words, which were by nature so well adapted to that purpose, come to be made use of by men, as the signs of their ideas; not by any natural connexion that there is between particular articulate sounds and certain ideas, for then there would be but one language amongst all men; but by a voluntary imposition, whereby such a word is made arbitrarily the mark of such an idea. The use then of words is to be sensible marks of ideas; and the ideas they stand for are their proper and immediate signification.

Words Are the Sensible Signs of His Ideas Who Uses Them

§ 2. The use men have of these marks being either to record their own thoughts for the assistance of their own memory, or as it were to bring out their ideas, and lay them before the view of others; words in their primary or immediate signification stand for nothing but the ideas in the mind of him that uses them, how imperfectly soever or carelessly those ideas are collected from the things which they are supposed to represent. When a man speaks to another, it is that he may be understood; and the end of speech is, that those sounds, as marks, may make known his ideas to the hearer. That then which words are the marks of are the ideas of the speaker: nor can any one apply them, as marks, immediately to any thing else but the ideas that he himself hath. For this would be to make them signs of his own conceptions, and yet apply them to other ideas; which would be to make them signs, and not signs of his ideas at the same time; and so in effect to have no signification at all. Words being voluntary signs, they cannot be voluntary signs imposed by him on things he knows not. That would be to make them signs of nothing, sounds without signification. A man cannot make his words the signs either of qualities in things, or of conceptions in the mind of another, whereof he has none in his own. Till he has some ideas of his own, he cannot suppose them to correspond with the conceptions of another man; nor can he use any signs for them: for thus they would be the signs of he knows not what, which is in truth to be the signs of nothing. But when he represents to himself other men's ideas by some of his own, if he consent to give them the same names that other men do, it is still to his own ideas; to ideas that he has, and not to ideas that he has not.

§ 3. This is so necessary in the use of language, that in this respect the knowing and the ignorant, the learned and unlearned, use the words they speak (with any meaning) all alike. They, in every man's mouth, stand for the ideas he has, and which he would express by them. A child having taken notice of nothing in the metal he hears called gold, but the bright shining yellow colour, he applies the word gold only to his own idea of that colour, and nothing else; and therefore calls the same colour in a peacock's tail gold. Another that hath better observed, adds to shining yellow great weight: and then the sound gold, when he uses it, stands for a complex idea of a shining yellow and very weighty substance. Another adds to those qualities fusibility: and then the word gold signifies to him a body, bright, yellow, fusible, and very heavy. Another adds malleability. Each of these uses equally the word gold, when they have occasion to express the idea which they have applied it to: but it is evident, that each can apply it only to his own idea; nor can he make it stand as a sign of such a complex idea as he has not.

Words Often Secretly Referred, First to the Ideas in Other Men's Minds

§ 4. But though words, as they are used by men, can properly and immediately signify nothing but the ideas that are in the mind of the speaker; yet they in their thoughts give them a secret reference to two other things.

First, they suppose their words to be marks of the ideas in the minds also of other men, with whom they communicate: for else they should talk in vain, and could not be understood, if the sounds they applied to one idea were such as by the hearer were applied to another; which is to speak two languages. But in this, men stand not usually to examine whether the idea they and those they discourse with have in their minds be the same: but think it enough that they use the word, as they imagine, in the common acceptation of that language; in which they suppose, that the idea they make it a sign of is precisely the same, to which the understanding men of that country apply that name.

Secondly, to the Reality of Things

§ 5. Secondly, Because men would not be thought to talk barely of their own imaginations, but of things as really they are; therefore they often suppose the words to stand also for the reality of things. But this relating more particularly to substances, and their names, as perhaps the former does to simple ideas and modes, we shall speak of these two different ways of applying words more at large, when we come to treat of the names of fixed modes, and substances in particular: though give me leave here to say, that it is a perverting the use of words, and brings unavoidable obscurity and confusion into their signification, whenever we make them stand for any thing but those ideas we have in our own minds.

Words by Use Readily Excite Ideas

§ 6. Concerning words also it is farther to be considered: first, that they being immediately the signs of men's ideas, and by that means the instruments whereby men communicate their conceptions, and express to one another those thoughts and imaginations they have within their own breasts; there comes by constant use to be such a connexion between certain sounds and the ideas they stand for, that the names heard almost as readily excite certain ideas, as if the objects themselves, which are apt to produce them, did actually affect the senses. Which is manifestly so in all obvious sensible qualities; and in all substances that frequently and familiarly occur to us.

Words Often Used Without Signification

§ 7. Secondly, That though the proper and immediate signification of words are ideas in the mind of the speaker, yet because by familiar use from our cradles we come to learn certain articulate sounds very perfectly, and have them readily on our tongues, and always at hand in our memories, but yet are not always careful to examine or settle their significations perfectly; it often happens that men, even when they would apply themselves to an attentive consideration, do set their thoughts more on words than things. Nay, because words are many of them learned before the ideas are known for which they stand; therefore some, not only children, but men, speak several words no otherwise than parrots do, only because they have learned them, and have been accustomed to those sounds. But so far as words are of use and signification, so far is there a constant connexion between the sound and the idea, and a designation that the one stands for the other; without which application of them, they are nothing but so much insignificant noise.

Their Signification Perfectly Arbitrary

§ 8. Words by long and familiar use, as has been said, come to excite in men certain ideas so constantly and readily, that they are apt to suppose a natural connexion between them. But that they signify only men's peculiar ideas, and that by a perfect arbitrary imposition, is evident, in that they often fail to excite in others (even that use the same language) the same ideas we take them to be the signs of: and every man has so inviolable a liberty to make words stand for what ideas he pleases, that no one hath the power to make others have the same ideas in their minds that he has, when they use the same words that he does. And therefore the great Augustus himself, in the possession of that power which ruled the world, acknowledged he could not make a new Latin word: which was as much as to say, that he could not arbitrarily appoint what idea any sound should be a sign of, in the mouths and common language of his subjects. It is true, common use by a tacit consent appropriates certain sounds to certain ideas in all languages, which so far limits the signification of that sound, that unless a man applies it to the same idea, he does not speak properly: and let me add, that unless a man's words excite the same ideas in the hearer, which he makes them stand for in speaking, he does not speak intelligibly. But whatever be the consequence of any man's using of words differently, either from their general meaning, or the particular sense of the person to whom he addresses them, this is certain, their signification, in his use of them, is limited to his ideas, and they can be signs of nothing else.

The Symbolic Process and Social Problems

S. I. HAYAKAWA

> I find it difficult to believe that words have no meaning in themselves, hard as I try. Habits of a lifetime are not lightly thrown aside.
>
> STUART CHASE

Signal and Symbol Reaction

ANIMALS struggle with each other for food or for leadership, but they do not, like human beings, struggle with each other for things that *stand for* food or leadership: such things as our paper symbols of wealth (money, bonds, titles), badges of rank to wear on our clothes, or low-number license-plates, supposed by some people to stand for social precedence. For animals the relationship in which one thing *stands for* something else does not appear to exist except in very rudimentary form. For example, a chimpanzee can be taught to drive a car, but there is one thing wrong with its driving: its reactions are such that if a red light shows when it is halfway across a street, it will stop in the middle of the crossing, while if a green light shows while another car is stalled in its path, it will go ahead regardless of consequences. In other words, so far as a chimpanzee is concerned, the red light can hardly be said to *stand for* stop; it *is* stop.

Let us then introduce two terms to represent this distinction between the "red light *is* stop" relationship, which the chimpanzee understands, and the "red light *stands for* stop" relationship, which the human being understands. To the chimpanzee, the red light is, we shall say, a *signal*, and we shall term its reaction a *signal reaction; that is, a complete and invariable reaction which occurs whether or not the conditions warrant such a reaction.* To the human being, on the other hand, the red light is, in our terminology, a *symbol*, and we shall term his reaction a *symbol reaction; that is, a delayed reaction, conditioned upon the circumstances.* In other words, the nervous system capable only of signal reactions *identifies the signal with the thing for which the signal stands*; the human nervous system, however, working under normal conditions, understands *no necessary connection* between the symbol and the thing for which the symbol stands. Human beings do not automatically jump up in the expectation of being fed whenever they hear an ice-box door slam.

The Symbolic Process

Human beings, because they can understand certain things to *stand for* other things, have been able to develop what we shall term the *symbolic process.* Whenever two or more human beings can communicate with each other, they can, by agreement, make anything stand for anything. Feathers worn on the

---

head can be made to stand for tribal chieftanship; cowrie shells or rings of brass or pieces of paper can stand for wealth; crossed sticks can stand for a set of religious beliefs; buttons, elks' teeth, ribbons, special styles of ornamental hair-cutting or tattooing, can stand for social affiliations. The symbolic process permeates human life at the most savage as well as at the most civilized levels. Warriors, medicine men, policemen, doormen, telegraph boys, cardinals, and kings wear costumes that symbolize their occupations. Savages collect scalps, college students collect dance programs and membership keys in honorary societies, to symbolize victories in their respective fields. There are very few things that men do or want to do, possess or want to possess, that have not, in addition to their mechanical or biological value, a symbolic value.

All fashionable clothes, as Thorstein Veblen has point out in his *Theory of the Leisure Class*, are highly symbolic: materials, cut, and ornament are dictated only to a slight degree by considerations of warmth, comfort, or practicability. The more we dress up in fine clothes, the more do we restrict our freedom of action. But by means of delicate embroideries, easily soiled fabrics, starched shirts, high heels, long and pointed fingernails, and other such sacrifices of comfort, the wealthy classes manage to symbolize the fact that they don't have to work for a living. The not so wealthy, on the other hand, by imitating these symbols of wealth, symbolize their conviction that, even if they do work for a living, they are just as good as anybody else. Again, we select our furniture to serve as visible symbols of our taste, wealth, and social position; we trade in perfectly good cars for later models, not always to get better transportation, but to give evidence to the community that we can afford such luxuries; we often choose our residential localities on the basis of a feeling that it "looks well" to have a "good address"; we like to put expensive food on our tables, not always because it tastes better than cheap food, but because it tells our guests that we like them, or, just as often, because it tells them that we are well fixed financially.

Such complicated and apparently unnecessary behavior leads philosophers, both amateur and professional, to ask over and over again, "Why can't human beings live simply and naturally?" Perhaps, unconsciously, they would like to escape the complexity of human life for the relative simplicity of such lives as dogs and cats lead. But the symbolic process, which makes possible the absurdities of human conduct, also makes possible language and therefore all the human achievements dependent upon language. The fact that more things can go wrong with motorcars than with wheelbarrows is no reason for going back to wheelbarrows. Similarly, the fact that the symbolic process makes complicated follies possible is no reason for wanting to return to a cat-and-dog existence.

Language as Symbolism

Of all forms of symbolism, language is the most highly developed, most subtle, and most complicated. It has been pointed out that human beings, by agreement, can make anything stand for anything. Now, human beings have agreed, in the course of centuries of mutual dependency, to let the various noises that they can produce with their lungs, throats, tongues, teeth, and lips systematically stand for specified happenings in their nervous systems. We call that system of agreements *language.* For example, we who speak English have been so trained that when our nervous systems register the presence of a certain kind of animal, we may make the following noise: "There's a cat." Anyone hearing us would expect to find that by looking in the same direction, he would experience a similar event in his nervous system—one that would have led him to make an almost identical noise. Again, we have been so trained that when we are conscious of wanting food, we make the noise, "I'm hungry."

There is, as has been said, *no necessary connection between the symbol and that which is symbolized.* Just as men can wear yachting costumes without ever having been near a yacht, so they can make the noise, "I'm hungry," without being hungry. Furthermore, just as social rank can be symbolized by feathers in the hair, by tattooing on the breast, by gold ornaments on the watch chain, by a thousand different devices according to the culture we live in, so the fact of being hungry can be symbolized by a thousand different noises according to the culture we live in: "J'ai faim," or "Es hungert mich," or "Ho appetito," or "Hara ga hetta," and so on.

Linguistic Naïveté

However obvious these facts may appear at first glance, they are actually not so obvious as they seem except when we take special pains to think about the subject. Symbols and things symbolized are independent of each other; nevertheless, all of us have a way of feeling as if, and sometimes acting as if, there were necessary connections. For example, there is the vague sense that we all have that foreign languages are inherently absurd. Foreigners have "funny names" for things: why can't they call things by their "right names?" This feeling exhibits itself most strongly in those American and English tourists who seem to believe that they can make the natives of any country understand English if they shout it at them loud enough. They feel, that is, that the symbol *must necessarily* call to mind the thing symbolized.

Anthropologists report similar attitudes among primitive peoples. In talking with natives, they frequently come across unfamiliar words in the native language. When they interrupt the conversation to ask, "*Guglu*? What is a *guglu?*" the natives laugh, as if to say, "Imagine not knowing what a *guglu* is! What amazingly silly people!" When an answer is insisted upon, they explain, when they can get over laughing, "Why, a *guglu* is a GUGLU, of course!" Very small children think in this respect the way primitive people do; often when policemen say to a whimpering lost child, "All right, little girl, we'll find your mother for you. Who is your mother? What's your mother's name?" the little child can only bawl, "My muvver is *mummy.* I want *mummy*!" This leaves the police, as they say in murder mysteries, baffled. Again, there is the little boy who is reported to have said, "Pigs are called pigs because they are such *dirty* animals."

Similar naïveté regarding the symbolic process is illustrated by an incident in the adventures of a theatrical troupe playing melodramas to audiences in the western ranching country. One night, at a particularly tense moment in the play, when the villain seemed to have the hero and the heroine in his power, an overexcited cowpuncher in the audience suddenly rose from his seat and shot the villain. The cowpuncher of this story, however, is no more ridiculous than those thousands of people today, many of them adults, who write fan letters to a ventriloquist's dummy, or those goodhearted but impressionable people who send presents to the broadcasting station when two characters in a radio serial get married, or those astonishing patriots who rushed to recruiting offices to help defend the nation when the United States was "invaded" by an "army from Mars."

These, however, are only the more striking examples of primitive and infantile attitudes towards symbols. There would be little point in mentioning them if we were uniformly and permanently aware of the independence of symbols from things symbolized. But we are not. Most of us retain many habits of evaluation ("thinking habits") more appropriate to life in the jungle than to life in modern civilization. Moreover, all of us are capable of reverting to them, especially when we are overexcited or when subjects about which we have special prejudices are mentioned. Worst of all, various people who have easy access to such instruments of public communication as the press, the radio, the lecture platform, and the pulpit actively encourage primitive and infantile attitudes towards symbols. Political and journalistic charlatans, advertisers of worthless or overpriced goods, and promoters of religious bigotry stand to profit either in the terms of money or power or both, if the majority of people can be kept thinking like savages or children.

The Word-Deluge We Live In

The interpretation of words is a never-ending task for any citizen in modern society. We now have, as the result of modern means of communication, hundreds of thousands of words flung at us daily. We are constantly being talked at, by teachers, preachers, salesmen, public officials, and moving-picture sound tracks. The cries of the hawkers of soft drinks, soap chips, and laxatives pursue us into our very homes, thanks to the radio—and in some houses the radio is never turned off from morning to night. Daily the newsboy brings us, in large cities, from thirty to fifty enormous pages of print, and almost three times that amount on Sundays. The mailman brings magazines and direct-mail advertising. We go out and get more words at bookstores and libraries. Billboards confront us on the highways, and we even take portable radios with us to the seashore. Words fill our lives.

This word-deluge in which we live is by no means entirely to be regretted. It is to be expected that we should become more dependent on mutual intercommunications as civilization advances. But, with words being flung about as heedlessly of social consequences as they now are, it is obvious that if we approach them with primitive habits of evaluation, or even with a tendency to revert occasionally to primitive habits of evaluation, we cannot do otherwise than run into error, confusion, and tragedy.

Why Is the World a Mess? One Theory

But, the reader may say, surely educated people don't think like savages! Unfortunately they do—some about one subject, some about another. The educated are frequently quite as naïve about language as the uneducated, although the ways in which they exhibit their naïveté may be less easily discernible. Indeed, many are worse off than the uneducated, because while the uneducated often realize their own limitations, the educated are in a position to refuse to admit their ignorance and conceal their limitations from themselves by their skill at word-juggling. After all, education as it is still understood in many circles is principally a matter of learning facility in the manipulation of words.

Such training in word-manipulation cannot but lead to an unconscious assumption that if any statement *sounds* true, it must be true—or, if not true, at least passable. This assumption (always unconscious) leads even learned men to make beautiful "maps" of "territories" that do not exist—without ever suspecting their nonexistence. Indeed, it can safely be said that whenever people are more attached to their verbal "maps" than to the factual "territories" (that is, whenever they are so attached to pet theories that they cannot give them up in the face of facts to the contrary), they are exhibiting serious linguistic naïveté. Some educated and extremely intelligent people are so attached to the verbal "maps" they have created that, when they can find no territories in the known world to correspond to them, they create "supersensory" realms of "transcendental reality," so that they will not have to admit the uselessness of their maps.[1] Such people are often in a position to impose their notions on others, in beautifully written books and in eloquent lectures, and they thus spread the results of linguistic naïveté wherever their influence can reach.

As this is being written, the world is becoming daily a worse madhouse of murder, hatred, and destruction. It would seem that the almost miraculous efficiency achieved by modern instruments of communication should enable nations to understand each other better and co-operate more fully. But, as we know too well, the opposite has been the case; the better the communications, the bloodier the quarrels.

Linguistic naïveté—our tendency to think like savages about practically all subjects other than the purely technological—is not a factor to be ignored in trying to account for the mess civilization is in. By using the radio and the newspaper as instruments for the promotion of political, commercial, and sectarian balderdash, rather than as instruments of public enlightenment, we seem to have increased the infectiousness of savagery of thought. Men react to meaningless noises, maps of nonexistent territories, as if they stood for actualities, and

[1] See Eric Temple Bell, *The Search for Truth*; also Thurman W. Arnold, *The Folklore of Capitalism.*

never suspect that there is anything wrong with the process. Political leaders hypnotize themselves with the babble of their own voices and use words in a way that shows not the slightest concern with the fact that if language, the basic instrument of man's humanity, finally becomes as meaningless as they would make it, co-operation will not be able to continue, and society itself will fall apart.

But to the extent that we too think like savages and babble like idiots, we all share the guilt for the mess in which human society finds itself. To cure these evils, we must first go to work on ourselves. An important beginning step is to understand how language works, what we are doing when we open these irresponsible mouths of ours, and what it is that happens, or should happen, when we listen or read.

Applications

The following hobby is suggested for those who wish to follow the argument of this book. In a scrapbook or, perhaps better, on 5 × 7 filing cards, start a collection of quotations, newspaper clippings, editorials, anecdotes, bits of overheard conversation, advertising slogans, etc., that illustrate in one way or another linguistic naïveté. The ensuing chapters of this book will suggest many different kinds of linguistic naïveté and confusion to look for, and the methods for classifying the examples found will also be suggested. The simplest way to start will be to look for those instances in which people seem to think that there are *necessary* connections between symbols and things symbolized—between words and what words stand for. Innumerable examples can be found in books on cultural anthropology, especially in those sections dealing with word-magic. After a few such examples are chosen and studied, the reader will be able to recognize readily similar patterns of thought in his contemporaries and friends. Here are a few items with which such a collection might be begun:

1. "The Malagasy soldier must eschew kidneys, because in the Malagasy language the word for kidney is the same as that for 'shot'; so shot he would certainly be if he ate a kidney."—J. G. FRAZER, *The Golden Bough* (one-volume abridged edition), p. 22.

2. [A child is being questioned.] "Could the sun have been called 'moon' and the moon 'sun'?—*No.*—Why not?—*Because the sun shines brighter than the moon.* . . . But if everyone had called the sun 'moon,' and the moon 'sun,' would we have known it was wrong?—*Yes, because the sun is always bigger, it always stays like it is and so does the moon.*—Yes, but the sun isn't changed, only its name. Could it have been called . . . etc.?—*No. . . . Because the moon rises in the evening, and the sun in the day.*" —PIAGET, *The Child's Conception of the World*, pp. 81–82.

3. The City Council of Cambridge, Massachusetts, unanimously passed a resolution (December, 1939) making it illegal "to possess, harbor, sequester, introduce or transport, within the city limits, any book, map, magazine, newspaper, pamphlet, handbill or circular containing the words Lenin or Leningrad."

4. The gates of the 1933 Century of Progress Exposition at Chicago were opened, through the use of the photoelectric cell, by the light of the star Arcturus. It is reported that a woman, on being told of this, remarked, *"Isn't it wonderful how those scientists know the names of all those stars!"*

5. "State Senator John McNaboe of New York bitterly opposed the bill for the control of syphilis in May, 1937, because 'the innocence of children might be corrupted by a widespread use of the term. . . . This particular word creates a shudder in every decent woman and decent man.' "—STUART CHASE, *The Tyranny of Words,* p. 63.

6. A picture in the magazine *Life* (October 28, 1940) shows the backs of a sailor's hands, with the letters "H-O-L-D F-A-S-T" tattooed on the fingers. The captain explains, "This tattoo was supposed to keep sailors from falling off yardarm."

How to Get Rid of Words

JONATHAN SWIFT

WE NEXT went to the School of Languages, where three professors sat in consultation upon improving that of their own country.

The first project was to shorten discourse by cutting polysyllables into one, and leaving out verbs and participles, because in reality all things imaginable are but nouns.

The other was a scheme for entirely abolishing all words whatsoever; and this was urged as a great advantage in point of health as well as brevity. For it is plain that every word we speak is in some degree a diminution of our lungs by corrosion and consequently contributes to the shortening of our lives. An expedient was therefore offered that, since words are only names for *things*, it would be more convenient for all men to carry about them such *things* as were necessary to express the particular business they are to discourse on. And this invention would certainly have taken place, to the great ease as well as health of the subject, if the women, in conjunction with the vulgar and illiterate, had not threatened to raise a rebellion unless they might be allowed the liberty to speak with their tongues, after the manner of their forefathers; such constant irreconcilable enemies to science are the common people. However, many of the most learned and wise adhere to the new scheme of expressing themselves by *things*, which hath only this inconvenience attending it, that if a man's business be very great and of various kinds, he must be obliged in proportion to carry a greater bundle of *things* upon his back, unless he can afford one or two strong servants to attend him. I have often beheld two of those sages almost sinking under the weight of their packs, like pedlars among us; who when they met in the street would lay down their loads, open their sacks, and

---

Reprinted from *Gulliver's Travels* by Jonathan Swift, London: Oxford University Press, 1947, pp. 212–213.

hold conversation for an hour together; then put up their implements, help each other to resume their burthens, and take their leave.

But for short conversations a man may carry implements in his pockets and under his arms, enough to supply him, and in his house he cannot be at a loss; therefore the room where company meet who practise this art is full of all *things* ready at hand, requisite to furnish matter for this kind of artificial converse.

Another great advantage proposed by this invention was that it would serve as an universal language to be understood in all civilised nations, whose goods and utensils are generally of the same kind or nearly resembling, so that their uses might easily be comprehended. And thus ambassadors would be qualified to treat with foreign princes or ministers of state to whose tongues they were utter strangers.

Solving Problems by Deciding What a Word Is to Mean

WILLIAM JAMES

SOME years ago, being with a camping party in the mountains, I returned from a solitary ramble to find every one engaged in a ferocious metaphysical dispute. The *corpus* of the dispute was a squirrel—a live squirrel supposed to be clinging to one side of a tree-trunk; while over against the tree's opposite side a human being was imagined to stand. This human witness tries to get sight of the squirrel by moving rapidly round the tree, but no matter how fast he goes, the squirrel moves as fast in the opposite direction, and always keeps the tree between himself and the man, so that never a glimpse of him is caught. The resultant metaphysical problem now is this: *Does the man go round the squirrel or not*? He goes round the tree, sure enough, and the squirrel is on the tree; but does he go round the squirrel? In the unlimited leisure of the wilderness, discussion had been worn threadbare. Every one had taken sides, and was obstinate; and the numbers on both sides were even. Each side, when I appeared therefore appealed to me to make it a majority. Mindful of the scholastic adage that whenever you meet a contradiction you must make a distinction, I immediately sought and found one, as follows: "Which party is right," I said, "depends on what you *practically mean* by 'going round' the squirrel. If you mean passing from the north of him to the east, then to the south, then to the west, and then to the north of him again, obviously the man does go round him, for he occupies these successive positions. But if on the contrary you mean being first in front of him, then on the right of him, then behind him, then on his left, and finally in front again, it is quite as obvious that the man fails to go round him, for by the compensating movements the squirrel makes, he keeps his belly

---

Reprinted from "What Pragmatism Means" in *Pragmatism* by William James, New York: David McKay, 1909, pp. 43–45.

turned towards the man all the time, and his back turned away. Make the distinction, and there is no occasion for any farther dispute. You are both right and both wrong according as you conceive the verb 'to go round' in one practical fashion or the other."

Although one or two of the hotter disputants called my speech a shuffling evasion, saying they wanted no quibbling or scholastic hair-splitting, but meant just plain honest English 'round,' the majority seemed to think that the distinction had assuaged the dispute.

Humpty Dumpty's Theory of Meaning

LEWIS CARROLL

HOWEVER, the egg only got larger and larger, and more and more human: when she had come within a few yards of it, she saw that it had eyes and a nose and mouth; and, when she had come close to it, she saw clearly that it was HUMPTY DUMPTY himself. "It ca'n't be anybody else!" she said to herself. "I'm as certain of it, as if his name were written all over his face!"

It might have been written a hundred times, easily, on that enormous face. Humpty Dumpty was sitting, with his legs crossed like a Turk, on the top of a high wall—such a narrow one that Alice quite wondered how he could keep his balance—and, as his eyes were steadily fixed in the opposite direction, and he didn't take the least notice of her, she thought he must be a stuffed figure, after all.

"And how exactly like an egg he is!" she said aloud, standing with her hands ready to catch him, for she was every moment expecting him to fall.

"It's *very* provoking," Humpty Dumpty said after a long silence, looking away from Alice as he spoke, "to be called an egg—*very!*"

"I said you *looked* like an egg, Sir," Alice gently explained. "And some eggs are very pretty, you know," she added, hoping to turn her remark into a sort of compliment.

"Some people," said Humpty Dumpty, looking away from her as usual, "have no more sense than a baby!"

Alice didn't know what to say to this: it wasn't at all like conversation, she thought, as he never said anything to *her*: in fact, his last remark was evidently addressed to a tree—so she stood and softly repeated to herself:—

> Humpty Dumpty sat on a wall:
> Humpty Dumpty had a great fall.
> All the King's horses and all the King's men
> Couldn't put Humpty Dumpty in his place again.

"That last line is much too long for the poetry," she added, almost out loud, forgetting that Humpty Dumpty would hear her.

Reprinted from *Through the Looking Glass* by Lewis Carroll, New York: Random House, Inc., pp. 118–126.

"Don't stand chattering to yourself like that," Humpty Dumpty said, looking at her for the first time, "but tell me your name and your business."

"My *name* is Alice, but——"

"It's a stupid name enough!" Humpty Dumpty interrupted impatiently. "What does it mean?"

"*Must* a name mean something?" Alice asked doubtfully.

"Of course it must," Humpty Dumpty said with a short laugh: *my* name means the shape I am—and a good handsome shape it is, too. With a name like yours, you might be any shape, almost."

"Why do you sit out here all alone?" said Alice, not wishing to begin an argument.

"Why, because there's nobody with me!" cried Humpty Dumpty. "Did you think I didn't know the answer to *that*? Ask another."

"Don't you think you'd be safer down on the ground?" Alice went on, not with any idea of making another riddle, but simply in her good-natured anxiety for the queer creature. "That wall is so *very* narrow!"

"What tremendously easy riddles you ask!" Humpty Dumpty growled out. "Of course I don't think so! Why, if ever I *did* fall off—which there's no chance of—but *if* I did——" Here he pursed up his lips, and looked so solemn and grand that Alice could hardly help laughing. "*If* I *did* fall," he went on, "*the King has promised me*—ah, you may turn pale, if you like! You didn't think I was going to say that, did you? *The King has promised me—with his very own mouth*—to—to——"

"To send all his horses and all his men," Alice interrupted, rather unwisely.

"Now I declare that's too bad!" Humpty Dumpty cried, breaking into a sudden passion. "You've been listening at doors—and behind trees—and down chimneys—or you couldn't have known it!"

"I haven't, indeed!" Alice said very gently. "It's in a book."

"Ah, well! They may write such things in a *book*," Humpty Dumpty said in a calmer tone. "That's what you call a History of England, that is. Now, take a good look at me! I'm one that has spoken to a King, *I* am: mayhap you'll never see such another: and, to show you I'm not proud, you may shake hands with me!" And he grinned almost from ear to ear, as he leant forwards (and as nearly as possible fell off the wall in doing so) and offered Alice his hand. She watched him a little anxiously as she took it. "If he smiled much more the ends of his mouth might meet behind," she thought: "And then I don't know *what* would happen to his head! I'm afraid it would come off!"

"Yes, all his horses and all his men," Humpty Dumpty went on. "They'd pick me up again in a minute, *they* would! However, this conversation is going on a little too fast: let's go back to the last remark but one."

"I'm afraid I ca'n't quite remember it," Alice said, very politely.

"In that case we start afresh," said Humpty Dumpty, "and it's my turn to choose a subject——" ("He talks about it just as if it was a game!" thought Alice.) "So here's a question for you. How old did you say you were?"

Alice made a short calculation, and said "Seven years and six months."

"Wrong!" Humpty Dumpty exclaimed triumphantly. "You never said a word like it!"

"I thought you meant 'How old *are* you?' " Alice explained.

"If I'd meant that, I'd have said it," said Humpty Dumpty.

Alice didn't want to begin another argument, so she said nothing.

"Seven years and six months!" Humpty Dumpty repeated thoughtfully. "An uncomfortable sort of age. Now if you'd asked *my* advice, I'd have said 'Leave off at seven'——but it's too late now."

"I never ask advice about growing," Alice said indignantly.

"Too proud?" the other enquired.

Alice felt even more indignant at this suggestion. "I mean," she said, "that one ca'n't help growing older."

"*One* ca'n't, perhaps," said Humpty Dumpty; "but *two* can. With proper assistance, you might have left off at seven."

"What a beautiful belt you've got on!" Alice suddenly remarked. (They had had quite enough of the subject of age, she thought: and, if they really were to take turns in choosing subjects, it was *her* turn now.) "At least," she corrected herself on second thoughts, "a beautiful cravat, I should have said—no, a belt, I meant—I beg your pardon!" she added in dismay, for Humpty Dumpty looked thoroughly offended, and she began to wish she hadn't chosen that subject. "If only I knew," she thought to herself, "which was neck and which was waist!"

Evidently Humpty Dumpty was very angry, though he said nothing for a minute or two. When he *did* speak again, it was in a deep growl.

"It is a—*most*—*provoking*—thing," he said at last, "when a person doesn't know a cravat from a belt!"

"I know it's very ignorant of me," Alice said, in so humble a tone that Humpty Dumpty relented.

"It's a cravat, child, and a beautiful one, as you say. It's a present from the White King and Queen. There now!"

"Is it really?" said Alice, quite pleased to find that she *had* chosen a good subject after all.

"They gave it me," Humpty Dumpty continued thoughtfully as he crossed one knee over the other and clasped his hands round it, "they gave it me—for an un-birthday present."

"I beg your pardon?" Alice said with a puzzled air.

"I'm not offended," said Humpty Dumpty.

"I mean, what *is* an un-birthday present?"

"A present given when it isn't your birthday, of course."

Alice considered a little. "I like birthday presents best," she said at last.

"You don't know what you're talking about!" cried Humpty Dumpty. "How many days are there in a year?"

"Three hundred and sixty-five," said Alice.

"And how many birthdays have you?"

"One."

"And if you take one from three hundred and sixty-five what remains?"

"Three hundred and sixty-four, of course."

Humpty Dumpty looked doubtful. "I'd rather see that done on paper," he said.

Alice couldn't help smiling as she took out her memorandum-book, and worked the sum for him:

$$\begin{array}{r} 365 \\ 1 \\ \hline 364 \end{array}$$

Humpty Dumpty took the book and looked at it carefully. "That seems to be done right——" he began.

"You're holding it upside down!" Alice interrupted.

"To be sure I was!" Humpty Dumpty said gaily as she turned it round for him. "I thought it looked a little queer. As I was saying, that *seems* to be done right—though I haven't time to look it over thoroughly just now—and that shows that there are three hundred and sixty-four days when you might get un-birthday presents——"

"Certainly," said Alice.

"And only *one* for birthday presents, you know. There's glory for you!"

"I don't know what you mean by 'glory,'" Alice said.

Humpty Dumpty smiled contemptuously. "Of course you don't—till I tell you. I meant 'there's a nice knock-down argument for you!'"

"But 'glory' doesn't mean 'a nice knock-down argument,'" Alice objected.

"When *I* use a word," Humpty Dumpty said, in rather a scornful tone, "it means just what I choose it to mean—neither more nor less."

"The question is," said Alice, "whether you *can* make words mean so many different things."

"The question is," said Humpty Dumpty, "which is to be master——that's all."

Alice was too much puzzled to say anything; so after a minute Humpty Dumpty began again. "They've a temper, some of them—particularly verbs: they're the proudest—adjectives you can do anything with, but not verbs—however, *I* can manage the whole lot of them! Impenetrability! That's what *I* say!"

"Would you tell me please," said Alice, "what that means?"

"Now you talk like a reasonable child," said Humpty Dumpty, looking very much pleased. "I meant by 'impenetrability' that we've had enough of that subject, and it would be just as well if you'd mention what you mean to do next, as I suppose you don't mean to stop here all the rest of your life."

"That's a great deal to make one word mean," Alice said in a thoughtful tone.

"When I make a word do a lot of work like that," said Humpty Dumpty, "I always pay it extra."

"Oh!" said Alice. She was too much puzzled to make any other remark.

"Ah, you should see 'em come round me of a Saturday night," Humpty Dumpty went on, wagging his head gravely from side to side, "for to get their wages, you know."

(Alice didn't venture to ask what he paid them with; and so you see I ca'n't tell *you.*)

Meaning As Use

FRIEDRICH WAISMANN

1. SUBSTANTIVE AND SUBSTANCE. Remember the account which St. Augustine gives of the learning of language. In his words we are presented with a certain picture of the nature of human speech, namely this: the words of language name objects; sentences are combinations of such names.

In this picture of language we find the root of the idea: every word has a meaning. This meaning is co-ordinated with the word. It is the object for which the word stands.

This philosophic conception of meaning is indwelling in the primitive notion of the ways in which language works. In Chapter V we described various games that we play when learning language. In these games there occurs something which may be called a 'convention' or 'rule.' We say that the words have been given a meaning by virtue of these rules, or that they 'mean something.' We say, also, 'Before we learned the game, the words had no meaning; but now, as a result of these rules, they have "acquired a meaning."' Again, it may be said, "Teaching the rules of the game is tantamount to explaining the meaning of the words.' It should be noticed that, in saying this, we introduce the word 'meaning' (and 'mean') *in certain contexts* only. As long as we consider this 'natural usage,' we never meet the idea of meaning in its enigmatic and almost mystifying aspect.

In considering such a game as that with the five cubes,* one may divine how far the universal idea of meaning enshrouds language in mists which makes it impossible to see its features clearly. When we are asked, 'How is it that the builder's man is able to carry out the command "Five cubes!"?', we are inclined to reply, 'Because he just understands what the words mean, because he has grasped their meaning.' And in saying that we seem to refer to a definite mental process going on in his mind. This mental process seems to be what is really important, whereas the words are mere means to induce such processes in the

* EDITOR'S NOTE: Waismann imagines a situation in which a builder is erecting a building and an assistant has to hand him appropriate stones upon command. There are different kinds of stones, cubes, columns, slabs. The assistant is trained to respond to a command like "Five cubes" by repeating the numerals from one to five and handing over a cube as he says each one.

Reprinted with permission of St. Martin's Press, Inc., Macmillan, London & Basingstoke from *Principles of Linguistic Philosophy* by F. Waismann, 1965, pp. 153–162.

mind. Without these processes the words seem dead. We picture to ourselves the relation between a word and what it means as if it were a psychological one; then we puzzle ourselves how it is that the mind has the miraculous capacity to perform things which no dead mechanism could perform, namely to *mean* something.

Now, one of the dangers of such a view is this: it makes us look for something which is the meaning. (This is particularly striking in the case that we mean something which does not exist.) This in itself is part of a general tendency which leads us, in the case of every substantive, to seek for an object which is designated by it. Here we are up against one of the sources of philosophical confusion. The strength of this propensity to hypostatization can still be studied in certain modes of thought that appeared in former stages of physics. Thus a force may readily be pictured as an unseen entity lurking in space and pulling like a stretched spring. In antiquity fire was conceived as an element. Likewise the features of substance were lent to energy, and the principle of conservation of energy interpreted as if there were in nature a subtle fluid that kept its identity through every change, and merely altered its form. And was it not ideas such as these which, partly masked by others, played a part in the hypothesis of a caloric fluid? Lord Salisbury once defined the ether as the nominative of the verb 'to undulate,' thus expressing with the greatest terseness the conflict between thought and the spirit of language.

Is it really of so little consequence whether one philosopher finds in his language substantives like 'soul,' 'ego,' 'being,' etc.? Would philosophers who grow up in a quite different domain of language, in which the function of nouns were very much less developed, be found on the same paths of thought? A question such as 'What is the number five?' cannot even be raised in Chinese, because 'five' can only occur in phrases such as 'five men,' 'five houses,' but never as subject in this language. Here we begin to see how deep an influence language can exercise on thought.

'Sleep is the gentler brother of Death.' Such a saying instances the mythological use of nouns. And there is much in philosophy that suggests a pale reflection of mythology. 'What is Time? What is this Being, made up of movement alone, without anything that moves?' (Schopenhauer).

One might compare our word-language with a script in which the letters are used for several purposes: sometimes for signifying sounds, sometimes for signifying accentuation, and sometimes as punctuation marks. Anyone regarding these characters as a notation of sounds might misinterpret them to mean that a single sound corresponded to every letter, as if the letters had not also quite different functions.

2. MEANINGS OF THE WORD 'MEANING.' Sometimes two words mean the same thing, e.g. 'riches' and 'wealth'; they are then used in the same way. The opposite of this case is that of a word with two different meanings. Let us take as an example of this, 'Black is Black,' when the one word refers to a person, the other to a colour. What is it that draws attention to the difference of meaning between the two? Obviously, it might be said, the fact that the two words obey

different sets of grammatical rules. But this needs qualification, for there is really only one word there. Shall we then say that this one word obeys two different sets of rules? What could be meant by this? Let us consider an analogous case in chess. Can I lay down two different sets of rules for moving the queen? Surely only in the sense that I wish to describe two different sorts of games of chess and set down the descriptions side by side for comparison. But in a single game I cannot move this piece according to two different sets of instructions. The difficulty is resolved, however, when we see that we can simply introduce different words. If we express the proposition in question by the words 'Mr Black is black,' we could well regard 'Mr Black' as one word and 'black' as another one, or 'Black' as one and 'is black' as another. And this *is*, more or less, how we proceed when we want to explain to a child how one word can have many meanings (often by no means an easy task). We may say to him 'Look here, Mr. Black strides up and down the room; the colour black cannot stride up and down.' In this way we should have substituted for the one word two new expressions.

Let us recall for a moment the way we became clear as to the different meanings of the word 'is.'

Now we can say: a word '*a*' means different things in different contexts, if in the one case it can be replaced by '*b*' and in the other by '*c*' but not by '*b*.' Let us apply this generalization to the words 'meaning' and 'mean' themselves, by setting the following examples next one another:

i. His expression on Friday was full of meaning.
ii. He meant well.
iii. There is much meaningless formality in everyday life.
iv. These clouds mean rain.
v. Your friendship means much to me.
vi. I meant him to go.
vii. The superstitious ascribe a meaning to the purest accident.
viii. In the light of this information the incident acquires a fresh meaning.
ix. These two words have the same meaning.

If the reader considers what other expressions are substitutable for the two words in the above sentences, he will gain some idea of the many senses in which they are used.

It is 'meaning' only in the sense of the last example which interests us here.

3. MEANING AS USE. We said that a word acquires meaning by the conventions of the game in which it occurs. But then we do not ask *what the meaning is*. The question in itself is, indeed, the expression of a misunderstanding of the substantive 'meaning.' It is already influenced by a misleading grammatical background; for in answer to a question 'What is *x*?' we expect a sentence of the form '*x* is . . .,' supposed in some way to be equivalent to an ostensive definition ('*x* is *this*'). And now we are tempted to be on the lookout for some thing which is the meaning. This conception is strengthened by certain modes of expression in our language. When we say that two words have the same meaning,

we may be inclined to think 'So there is something owned by both,' in the same way that we say 'This house is owned by Smith and Jones.' Speaking of meaning being *attached* to words is also misleading, because it sounds as if the meaning were a sort of magical entity, united to the word very much as the soul is to the body. But the meaning is not a soul in the body of the word, but what we call the 'meaning' manifests itself in the use of the word. The whole point of our explication could be summed up by saying 'If you want to know what a word means, look and see how it is used.' [1]

How should we, for example, explain to anyone what the word 'naïve' means? We should, perhaps, first circumscribe the meaning with words which come fairly near to meaning the same as 'naïve.' We should say naïve means something like 'inexperienced, uncritical, unsuspicious, natural, not blasé, not over-worried with doubts,' and so on. But then we should say 'That does not exactly hit off what the word means,' and should give an example of its use. We might tell an anecdote, describe a characteristic situation, and say 'There, do you see, that man was naïve.' What exactly does the word 'exactly' mean? Is there a definition for it? No; but in the very words of my question I have provided an instance of its use.

The reader can consider for himself examples such as 'perhaps,' 'indeed,' 'even,' 'good gracious,' 'bother,' 'by dint of,' etc.

If the usage of a word alters in the course of time its meaning alters also, e.g. 'villain' (originally = serf), 'awful,' 'nice' (precise), 'simple,' 'silly' (in Anglo-Saxon = blessed), 'lust' (innocent delight, as in Chaucer), 'luxury' (lasciviousness), 'naughty, (in Middle English = poor, needy; sixteenth–seventeenth centuries = wicked). In what else could a change of meaning consist, if not in a change of usage? Consider this moreover: a word is untranslatable if in the language into which it is to be translated there is no word used in exactly the same way. There are no English equivalents of, e.g., 'Gestalt,' 'Weltanschauung' 'esprit,' 'élan.' Life requires the continual birth of words of novel use, and so of new meanings, e.g. 'wireless,' 'autarky,' 'ironclad,' 'expressionist,' 'pointillistes,' 'surrealist,' 'Oblomovism,' 'Pasteurization.'

It sounds so natural to say 'every sign must signify something.' Yet this idea will not survive serious examination. What does 'Oh dear!' signify? Say we say 'it does not mean anything?' If we want to explain it to anyone, we say, for instance, 'Oh dear, it is raining again' in an appropriate tone of voice, and our hearer understands what it means. Some words might be designated as just 'vocal vents.' What does a full stop mean? It divides sentences. Here the meaning is the function performed. In the word 'meaning' we sum up the whole, often vastly complicated, mode of use of a sign.

Objection. But the use is surely only the outward form; the meaning is the inner reality that can only be understood from within.

Reply. Have we any means of describing the meaning of a sign without going into its use? Is giving the use only, so to speak, a roundabout way whereby to

[1] Here again we develop an idea of Wittgenstein; cf. *Philosophical Investigations,* § 43.

reach the meaning? If so, what is the other direct way? If the meaning is more than the use, in what does the difference consist? If I have taught someone how a word is used in different connections, different situations, and have taught the appropriate expression with which to speak it in each case, does he still not know its meaning? And what more should I do to enable him to perceive this meaning?

'But could I not know the use of a word and nevertheless follow it mechanically without understanding it, as in a certain sense I do the singing of a bird? Could not the use for me always remain something outward, so that I can describe it without understanding?' It seems here as if the rules describe only in a purely external manner a use that must first be given meaning from within. Cases where this is so do sometimes occur. Consider the following example. A certain community agree to use the words of their language in a peculiar way, e.g. to put only words of the same number of syllables next one another; this might be a game. If someone came into the society who knew nothing of this arrangement, he would not understand what was going on. He might, in time, if he were a good observer, make out for himself the rules according to which the words were used and yet the sense of the whole arrangement might remain entirely obscure to him. But in this case what he does not understand is the *point* of the whole affair; which might lead him to suspect that he has only been watching a game. Hence we could put the question like this: 'What distinguishes a game, as we have just described it, from actual language?' The answer may be put in a word: its integration into life. The words in a verbal game bear a far less close relation to life than words used in earnest. What is the difference, if the teacher on the one hand says (meaning it) 'Stand up,' and on the other, in the English lesson says the same sentence as an example of a command? What distinguishes a chess game from an example of such a game, fencing from a duel?

If I see language against the background of life, if I follow exactly the parts played therein by the single words, does the kernel of the matter, the meaning, still escape me, leaving me only the outer shell of usage?

4. MEANING AND MENTAL IMAGE. The sentence 'The meaning of a word is the inner reality' might be interpreted thus: 'The meaning is the mental image.' We do, in fact, often test our understanding of the meaning of a word by conjuring up an image of what it means. Most people if asked 'Do you know what a merry-go-round is?' may well form a mental picture of a merry-go-round. But let us consider other cases before accepting this view. What do people think of when they hear the word 'Naples?' One may see a picture of the gulf with Vesuvius in front of him, another the map of Italy with Naples marked on it, a third only an image of the printed word. Those who know Naples picture it differently from those who do not, those who were there but a little time ago differently from those whose memories are faded. If all had the right to consider their own ideas of the city as constituting the meaning of the word 'Naples,' it would mean something different for everyone and it would be impossible for any sentence in which it occurred to have a public meaning. Do only those who

can picture to themselves such a figure understand the word 'icosahedron?' Is there anyone who can picture a chiliagon? What comes to the reader's mind on reading the expression 'lien,' 'conduct of civil suits?' It may be that these words give rise to certain definite images, but do such images constitute the meaning of the words? And how about words like 'electron,' 'photon,' 'quantum' that allow of no visual interpretation, nay even preclude it? Can it be maintained that there are special images for 'if,' 'because,' 'although' and 'so?'

At this point we might admit that in general the meaning of a word is nothing pictureable, and content ourselves with the narrower assertion that when a word stands for something pictureable its meaning is represented by the picture. Thus the meaning of the word 'red' would be the red colour of which I have an image. But, first of all, each person has a different image, while the meaning is the same for all. Moreover, the image that one associates with the word 'red' is not the meaning of the word, but an example of its use. (We may here think of Berkeley's question, whether it is possible to have a general image of a triangle—which is neither oblique, nor right-angled, equilateral, nor scalene, but all and none of these at once.) Finally, is it always true that whenever we hear the word 'red' we have a red image? Do we really represent to ourselves red and white when we say, for instance, 'The War of the Red and White Roses?' Let the reader observe what goes on in him while he reads a book: does every colour word that he reads really call up a colour image? And if not, would he say that he has not understood what he read?

Why then are we tempted to say that the meaning is the image? I think for two reasons. In the first place, it is often the case that the occurrence of an image is the proof of understanding. Not being able to understand a word comes in a large number of cases simply to failing to have any idea that corresponds to it. (But is this so in all cases? Is it true of the concepts of physics?) The second reason is that images seem sometimes to guide us when we apply language; for instance, when we act on a command. Let us suppose someone has been told to fetch a gilly-flower out of the garden, and fulfils this order. We might ask 'How could he know what to do if all that has happened is that he has heard certain words?' Here it is natural to answer that when he heard the words, he had an image of the flower which enabled him to look for it. Surely, we might say, it is the image which in this case fills the gap between word and action. In many cases this is so, but is it so in all? Suppose the injunction is to have an image of a certain shade of green, say emerald green. Is there here an image which acts as intermediary between the word and the required performance? But if so, having this image *is* the performance. Indeed, we might imagine that on hearing the words 'emerald green' someone would first look up a colour pattern-book, look at the colour, and only then know what sort of image he has to conjure up. Could we not say in such a case that the pattern-book was what filled the gap between word and image?

Let us now consider what in fact happens when I send someone into the garden to pick a gilly-flower. There are various possibilities:

(i) I may give him a gilly-flower to make it clear what sort of flower it is I wish him to pick. He takes this pattern into the garden and compares flowers in the garden with it until he finds one of the same sort.

(ii) Instead of a real flower, I give him a picture of one, or a description in words (e.g. out of a gardener's handbook).

(iii) I show him a gilly-flower, and he goes to look for another by remembering what I showed him.

(iv) He has entirely forgotten in what circumstances he learned what a gilly-flower was, but he can evoke an image of one at will, by means of which he can fetch me one.

(v) He goes into the garden, looks around, and as soon as his glance lights on a gilly-flower he picks it. *Must* he at that moment have a picture of a gilly-flower in his memory or in his imagination and compared it with what he was looking at? No, he may or may not have had one. It may be that he could not have imagined the flower beforehand, but nevertheless recognized it is soon as he saw it.

Let the reader make the attempt to visualize the letter G in Gothic script; if he is not trained, he will hardly succeed in doing so; but nevertheless he does recognize the letter at first sight when he sees it.

In daily life we often use words in this way. If someone says 'Turn off the light,' I do it. Must I really have pictured to myself the whole process of turning off the light before I do it? Such a view would impose on us far too strenuous a mental exertion. It is, in fact, the case that a considerable part of communication is free from images.

Suppose that people could not hold an image in mind for longer than five minutes (that this were a psychological law), and that after this time the image was invariably forgotten. Would communication in these circumstances be impossible? And what would a language be like in these conditions? The words would practically never be accompanied by images. Would it, on this account, be correct to say they were devoid of meaning?

Such examples throw light on the view that a word has meaning only when it evokes some image in us. Imagination and memory images are characteristic of only one sort of use of words: in another use we may only be concerned with illustrations, samples, tables, etc. There is even a point in saying 'Everything inside our minds can, for certain purposes, be replaced by something outside.' Images can be replaced by pictures, calculations in our heads by calculations on paper, thinking by speaking, and conviction by a tone of conviction.

Compare now the following suggestions:

(i) The meaning of a word is the object to which it refers.

(ii) The meaning of a word is the image which we have when we speak, or hear the word.

(iii) The meaning of a word is the effects it has on a hearer. It is clear that none of these reaches the heart of the matter. And yet they force themselves upon the mind ever and again in philosophic literature. Let us, then, dwell for a moment on the question why one is tempted to reach after such an explanation. In the first place, because one wishes to embody in the definition what is important. The object referred to by a word and the image which accompanies it undoubtedly play a certain part in the use of the word. Secondly, we instinctively seek for what may be called a substantival definition of meaning: we want to find amongst the already existing substantives of language one that is synonymous with the word 'meaning'; that is to say, is used as the word 'meaning' is used; so we say either 'The object referred to is the meaning' or 'The idea is the meaning' or 'The effects of a word are its meaning.' If we *had* to give a substantival explanation of meaning the best we could do is to say, following Wittgenstein, 'The meaning of a word is its use.'

5. AN OBJECTION. The suggestion, that the explanation of a word consists in describing its use, might give rise to the following objection: If we answer the questions 'What is style?,' 'What is culture?,' 'What is humour?' in the manner suggested, that is to say by displaying the use of these words through examples, are we not answering them in a merely superficial way? A good explanation gives us the feeling 'Yes, that is right, here we have the essentials.' The reply to our question may show profundity or shallowness. How is this compatible with our view? Should the explanation not disclose the deeper meaning which we dimly perceive behind those words?

But what is it that is sought by him who seeks the essence of culture? Does he want a definition? Or is he already familiar with the use of the word, and desirous of insight into the thing it denotes? If we gave a man who had just heard the word 'culture' for the first time Weininger's explanation, 'Culture is a feeling for problems,' would he then understand what the word means? And would he be in a position to use it correctly? Obviously not. Such explanations are flashes of light which, as it were, reveal for a moment an unsuspected connection, intelligible only to those who are already familiar with the meaning of the word.

The question 'What is culture?' is in some respects similar to 'What is heat?' This question can be understood in two ways. If it is about the meaning of the word 'heat,' it is answered by a description of the use of this word. But it can also mean 'What is the physical nature of heat?' To this question the answer would be 'Irregular molecular movement.' This is not a definition but a piece of scientific information.

INTRODUCTION TO PHILOSOPHY OF LANGUAGE / Study Questions

THE MEANING OF A WORD

St. Augustine

1. Describe St. Augustine's account of how a child learns language.
2. What theory about the meaning of words seems to be embodied in this account?
3. Is this theory a plausible account of the meaning of *all* the words in our language? What sorts of words might it not fit?
4. Has St. Augustine correctly described the way in which children learn to speak?

5. Is there a problem about St. Augustine's description of a small child, who is only beginning to talk, understanding intentions, facial expressions, and the like?
6. Compare the case of a child learning to talk with that of a foreigner learning the names of everyday objects in a new language. Which case does St. Augustine's description seem best to fit?

Locke

1. According to Locke, what distinguishes a man's use of language from a parrot's saying words? Does Locke argue for the distinction being what he says it is? How might it be argued for?
2. What does Locke say that words signify?
3. What, according to Locke, is the purpose of language? Is he right about this?
4. What does Locke mean when he says there is no natural connection between words and ideas?
5. What account must Locke give of the distinction between meaningful words and words (sounds) that have no meaning?
6. In terms of Locke's theory what must be the case if communication is to take place between two people?
7. Can a man choose to mean anything he pleases by a word?
8. In the light of everything that Locke says about both words and ideas can we ever know what another man means when he speaks?

Hayakawa

1. What distinction does Hayakawa draw between *signs* and *symbols*? What examples are given us?
2. In what way is language supposed to be a system of symbols? What are the noises (words) of language said to symbolize?
3. If one were to substitute Locke's talk about *ideas* for Hayakawa's talk about *happenings in the nervous system*, would the two theories be roughly equivalent? Are there any other similarities between Locke and Hayakawa?
4. Hayakawa says that words stand for happenings in the nervous system and at other places says that words are the names of things. Is this consistent?
5. Is it plausible to suppose that words "stand for" things in the same way that badges and uniforms "stand for" offices and authority?
6. Hayakawa seems to assume that sentences have meaning, stand for things, in the same way that individual words have meaning, stand for things. Thus the word *chair* stands for, means, the chair in the same way that "The martians are invading" stands for, means, presumably the fact that the martians are invading. Are there any problems in this assimilation of sentence meaning to word-meaning?
7. Given Hayakawa's theory of meaning, is a word to which there corresponds no object for it to be the name of, for example, *unicorn*, necessarily without meaning? Is a statement corresponding to no fact, for example, a false statement such as "The martians are invading," necessarily without meaning?
8. In what way does Hayakawa believe that a primitive or naive attitude to language might be responsible for the world's troubles? Is there any reason to believe that a proper understanding of the "symbolic process" will contribute to men living in peace and harmony? Might one argue plausibly that it may rather contribute only to a sharper articulation of what divides men? If this is true, would it tend to show that the world's troubles actually have very little to do with language as Hayakawa understands it?

9. It is undeniable that many people are far too credulous and will believe anything they are told. Can this shortcoming be plausibly attributed to *linguistic* naivety, to ignorance of the nature of the "symbolic process?" Are any of Hayakawa's examples of foolish behavior genuinely the result of linguistic naivety?
10. Semanticists such as Hayakawa are fond of saying that many difficulties arise from confusing symbols with what they symbolize. Can you think of a genuine example of such a mistake? Could you imagine someone trying to sit on the word *chair*?

Swift

1. According to the professors of Lagado, what is the relation between words and things?
2. What is the connection between this view and those of St. Augustine, Locke, and Hayakawa?
3. Would the Lagadian method of communication avoid the problems of word misuse and deception that Hayakawa deplores?
4. Try the experiment of carrying on a conversation after the fashion of Lagado. What are the results?
5. What sorts of misunderstandings are liable to arise in this kind of "conversation?" During the course of your "conversation" suppose one of the participants picks up a pencil. How are you to decide whether this means the statement, "This is a pencil"; the question, "Is this a pencil?"; the request, "Write with this pencil"; or something else altogether?
6. Is the kind of parody that Swift gives us here of any use in achieving philosophical understanding?

James

1. Describe the problem about the man and the squirrel.
2. What does James say can be "practically meant" by "going around the squirrel?" Are these two descriptions equally good instances of "going around?"
3. Suppose the man were to remain in one place and the squirrel spun around. Would this case fit one of the meanings James offers for "going around?"
4. What is the *pragmatic method*?
5. Can any of the philosophical problems discussed in this book be solved by deciding between different meanings of a word? Are there any problems that can be solved in this way?

Carroll

1. What is glory for you?
2. What is Humpty Dumpty's theory of meaning? Is it consistent with that of other philosophers in this section: St. Augustine, Locke, Hayakawa, James?
3. Humpty Dumpty says that you don't know what he means till he tells you. Will his explanation be of any help?
4. Is there any limit to how much a word can mean?
5. Is it important to be master of one's words? Is Humpty Dumpty's account of this mastery correct? If not, what is involved in being master of one's words?

Waismann

1. In what way does Waismann suggest that it is natural to think of understanding as a mental process?

2. How does that view of understanding lead us to look for something called the meaning of a word?
3. What are some of the different meanings of the word *meaning*?
4. Explain the analogy between the use of words in language and the use of the various pieces in a game such as chess.
5. How does this analogy suggest that the search for "the meaning" as something independent of words is a confusion?
6. Give various examples of how the meanings of words are explained. Is it always done in the same way?
7. How is Waismann's account of language and meaning so far open to the charge that someone might learn to use language, say in a mechanical or parrot-like fashion, while having no understanding of what he is doing and the words he is using? How does Waismann deal with this objection?
8. How does Waismann argue against the identification of meaning with having mental images? Are these considerations damaging to Locke's theory of meaning?
9. How would Waismann argue against the theory that all words are names and that the meaning of a word is what it names? Would these considerations also tell against Hayakawa's claim that words are symbols?
10. Can the point that words play different roles, have different uses, in language, just as pieces in chess have different roles, uses, in the game, shed any light on why the "language" of Lagado is bound to fail?

Thinking and Speaking

We noted in the previous section that if we accept *Locke*'s account of the meaning of words as names of "ideas," a rather remarkable theory of communication seems to follow. Essentially it is the theory that words in speech are a kind of code by which we refer to our "ideas." We believe that the selections by *Swift, Carroll,* and *Waismann* show that there is certainly something wrong with saying that we *refer to* our "ideas" in speech. But this leaves untouched another and yet more puzzling question, namely, "What *is* the relation between speech and thought?" This question is the subject of the next set of articles.

Probably the most natural answer to the question is that in speech we *express* our thoughts. But this "answer" is as unclear as it is natural. For the issue here really is about how we are to suppose that the expression of ideas in speech takes place. Philosophers and linguists have, generally, fallen into two camps over the question. There are those who hold that the explanation is still to be given by the code-model; though most of them have given up the idea that the signs in the code *refer to* our ideas. On the other side are those who believe that thinking just is a species of *speaking*, in this case speaking-to-oneself. These are the extreme views. And there is no dearth of philosophers and linguists who would like somehow to articulate and defend a position on the middle ground between the extremes. For some of the difficulties of the extreme views should be obvious immediately. If one believes that thinking is speaking-to-oneself, it follows that knowing a language is required in order to think. For mere sounds are not speech; it is language that is spoken. Yet this requirement is thought by some to contradict our experience. Specifically it may be argued that young infants (and even cats, dogs, and so on) engage in what can be described as thoughtful behavior.

Interestingly enough it is these same facts which poses one of the difficulties for those who believe that speech is an outward code for our ideas. For to say that someone does something thoughtfully does not require that we say he has thought some particular thought. Yet if the code-model of the relation between speaking and thinking were correct one should be able to give a clear sense to the expression "a wordless thought"; and cases of thoughtful nonverbal behavior do not *necessarily* provide the sort of cases one needs to give that expression a sense.

We will say more on these points as we go along. But now it will be useful to focus on two questions that the student has probably already been asking about this issue. First, isn't this really a matter of fact, a matter for study by scientists and not by philosophers? Secondly, who cares anyway; what's the importance, *if any*, of settling this issue? In answer to the first question we should begin by noting that some philosophers and linguists have believed that the issue *is* empirical—that one can simply settle the matter by examining the facts about the verbal and nonverbal behavior of human beings. This, however, will not do.

We have already noticed that there are cases in which we might say that someone's nonverbal behavior was done thoughtfully. (We describe the behavior this way because we have observed, for example, an expression on the face, a tone of voice, someone's lack of surprise at the consequences of his or her actions, and so on.) But when we first mentioned such cases we pointed out that they do not establish any answer at all to our question. For we are not required to say of such cases that the persons involved were thinking some particular thoughts. Furthermore, even if we did claim that some silent thinker was thinking a particular thought (even if *he* claimed such a thing) we still would not be required to say anything at all about *how* he did it—that is, whether he did it with *or* without some words going through his mind. Of course if we or he were to try to explain what he was thinking on that occasion this *would* require language. But that fact does not settle the matter either. In explaining *what* he was thinking we are not forced to say that he did his thinking of the thought either with *or* without words. So the facts about thoughtful nonverbal behavior and about our explanation of the content of silent thinking do not settle the matter. The issue is clearly not an empirical issue. If there is a genuine problem here at all, and not a mere puzzle, it will be a conceptual matter that lies at the very foundations of theories of language.

But why is it important? The best way to see why many people think the issue is important is to set it in the context of a more general debate over the nature and subject matter of the emerging science called linguistics. It seems endemic to such "new sciences" as psychology, sociology, and anthropology that in their early stages they go through a phase in which there is a debate concerning what exactly it is that they are studying and what methods of investigation are the proper methods for the science. The same is true for linguistics just now. The questions here may be put as follows: (a) Is language, the object of study for linguistics, a set of behavior that is governed by a system or systems of abstract rules; or is language a set of behavior that is essentially arbitrary but regular and predictable, having regular and predictable connections with other human behavior? And (b) does the science of linguistics have as its primary task the elucidation and logical investigation of the rules of language that render sentences "grammatical" (in some broad sense) and that a speaker of a language learns and follows; or is the primary task the empirical study of an arbitrarily but regularly structured set of behavior that is "learned" by some sort of *conditioning*? If we see these questions as the larger issue within which our question stands, it should be easy now to see its importance.

Those who opt for the second alternatives in the questions—the "behaviorists" —are likely to argue that thinking is a species of speaking. If they could make good on that claim they would lend support to their view that language is essentially arbitrary (but regular) behavior. For then they would not have to go on to say that any distinctively mental phenomena occur that give linguistic behavior meaning. According to their view there are no pieces of mental phenomena—there is only linguistic *behavior.* Thinking *is* speaking; and speaking is, on principle, public behavior. (The student is invited to look further at philosophical behaviorism in some of its other aspects in Part 2 on Freedom or Determinism and the Mind-Body Problem.)

Those who hold for the first alternatives to the aforementioned questions—the new "rationalists" in linguistics—are likely to argue that speaking is an encoding of thoughts. If they could make good on that claim they would lend support to their view that speech is behavior that is governed by rules. For to see language in this way seems to require that speakers of the language are *following rules*—that is, that they *intend* to say certain things and are, though perhaps not consciously, *constructing* the sentences they utter *in order to* say those things. All of this talk of "following rules," "intending," "constructing," and so on is precisely that sort of "mental talk" to which the behaviorists object so strenuously. So our issue here is generally thought to be a crucial one for the larger debate about linguistics.

A nice example of how exactly our question fits into that larger debate can be gained from the first selection, "Mentalism in Linguistics" by Jerrold *Katz.* Katz' main argument is directed at the behaviorists. However, he prefers to use the expression "taxonomic linguistics" to refer to that form of behaviorism that has been characteristic in linguistics from its inception right up the the so-called "Chomskyan revolution." Chomsky, whose views Katz is defending, is what we have called a "rationalist"—though Katz prefers to speak of him as a "mentalistic linguist." As such, in any case, Chomsky is inclined to use the code-model in explaining how communication of ideas takes place. In reading Katz' article, the student should look for the occurrence of this view.

It will also help students to understand this piece if they notice that Katz' strategy here is to show, by both argument and the citing of instances, that mentalistic theories in linguistics are better able to account for the facts of linguistic behavior than are "taxonomic" theories. Taxonomic theories in linguistics are ones that take utterances in language to be no more than publicly observable stretches of physical sound. (The student should notice that this is essentially the view of behaviorism.) Yet, Katz argues, such theories cannot adequately *explain* what is known by speakers of a language, how that knowledge is used in communication, nor how that knowledge is acquired. Katz' point is not that the behaviorist cannot offer some plausible account of these things; rather his point is that such accounts, in the final analysis, are not *adequate*. It is in connection with making these points that Katz articulates an "explanatory model" of communication that is essentially the code-model.

Incidentally it will also be noticed that, to avoid "countenancing such occult mental entities as a 'spirit' and 'soul,'" Katz also holds to a version of the mind-brain identity theory. The reader is invited to compare Katz' version of this theory with that offered by Smart (and criticized by Malcolm) in Part 2. The student might also ask whether Katz' acceptance of the theory is required by mentalistic linguistics or is merely an *ad hoc* maneuver to avoid the manifest problems of Cartesian dualism. In working on this question the student should evaluate the plausibility of the claim that when the mentalistic linguist speaks of mental mechanisms underlying the speaking of language, he is doing nothing more than what the physicist does when he speaks of photons, neutrinos, and so on.

The classic statement of contemporary behaviorism on the relation between speaking and thinking is to be found in our next selection, the final chapter of *Verbal Behavior* by B. F. *Skinner*, presented almost in its entirety. Skinner is at pains to deny any need to say that there is "something going on" in our "minds" that we call thinking, that is encoded in speech, and that gives meaning to our verbal utterances. However, the reader will notice that Skinner does not actually take the extreme view, so often associated with behaviorism, that thinking just is subaudible speaking. Instead he argues that only *some* thinking may be identified as covert verbal behavior. Other cases of thinking, Skinner says, will not fit into this mold. Nevertheless, thinking is still *behavior*; and, although it is frequently covert behavior (though not necessarily verbal behavior), it is still observable.

Of course such an account requires some explanation both of "covert" and "overt" behavior and of the manner in which the behavior called thinking is related to overt verbal behavior (that is, speaking). Skinner provides an account of this, as follows. Since thinking "is not some mysterious process responsible for behavior but the very behavior itself in all the complexity of its controlling relations," the relation between thinking and speaking is no more problematic than the relation between any other two forms of behavioral responses the human organism makes towards its environment. The trick is, according to Skinner, simply to see what controlling variables dictate whether the response the organism makes is to be that of thinking or of speaking. Knowing these factors will enable us clearly to describe, predict, and explain such phenomena as silent soliloquy, problem-solving, thinking aloud, the so-called "effects of language on thought," and the so-called difficulties with "expressing an idea" or expressing "the same idea in two languages." The student will notice that none of these phenomena, according to Skinner's view, involves us in having some ineffable things called "ideas" that we subsequently attempt to express. So, of course, his *general* view of the relation between thinking and speaking is diametrically opposed to that offered by Katz. The student, however, is encouraged to notice that in some *particular* cases Skinner seems to think that what is called thinking may be a neurological event. Yet this should not obscure the fundamental differences between Katz and Skinner.

The next selection is from Maurice *Merleau-Ponty*'s most important book, *Phenomenology of Perception*, and is entitled "The Body as Expression, and Speech." As the title suggests, Merleau-Ponty holds that we can best understand the phenomena of speech and language by seeing them as analogous to bodily expressions of emotions, attitudes, "thought": indeed Merleau-Ponty suggests that we think of speech as a "linguistic gesture." He claims that we "come to understand the meanings of words through their place in a context of action and by taking part in a communal life . . ." Thus words, like gestures, carrying their meaning with them, as it were. "Faced with an angry or threatening gesture, I have no need, in order to understand it, to recall the feelings which I myself experienced when I used these gestures on my own account. . . . The gesture *does not make me think of anger . . .*"

It is obvious, from the foregoing, that Merleau-Ponty is in deep disagreement with the rationalists—he calls them "intellectualists"—who regard thinking as independent of language, and words as but conventional codes for communicating already-completed thought. In fact he presents several arguments against such theories in linguistics. For example he argues that we do not, upon hearing some words, give them meaning; yet this would be entailed by a view such as Katz'. He also argues that there are many occasions (he sometimes suggests implausibly that this is always the case) wherein we actually do not know what we are thinking until we formulate our thoughts in speech. Speech, says Merleau-Ponty, "accomplishes" thought.

Is Merleau-Ponty a behaviorist then? His view certainly retains the emphasis placed by Skinner on context and community. Yet it would be superficial to make Merleau-Ponty out to be a behaviorist. For he does not picture speech or language as mere physical phenomena as does the behaviorist. Nor does he view thinking as some physical behavior (including sometimes, verbal behavior) of an organism. To argue for the first claim, according to Merleau-Ponty, is to remove any possibility of understanding a *speaker* as *doing* something or *saying* something. Yet of course, he contends, in order to understand the sense of what someone utters we must understand the utterance as something some particular *person* has uttered, for a particular point, in a particular context. On the subject of thinking, Merleau-Ponty does share with the behaviorist—he calls such views "empiricist" or "mechanist"—the suspicion of mysterious mental events that are somehow to cause and accompany our speaking. Yet he does not argue that thinking is therefore just behavior.

The crucial flaw with both theoretical tendencies, according to Merleau-Ponty, is that they neglect the meaning of words. Words, he says, have meaning. Yet the rationalist must argue that they do not—nothing we say has meaning until and unless it is given meaning by a speaker or listener. The empiricist or mechanist must also argue that words do not have meaning—for they are mere responses to the environment and their significance (this must not be taken to say "meaning") is derived solely from the consequences of their utterance. So, according to Merleau-Ponty, "we refute both intellectualism and empiricism by simply saying that *the word has a meaning*." Unfortunately, simply *saying* this is not a refutation until it is clear what exactly is meant by saying it. And Merleau-Ponty does not help us very much to understand how he intends us to take the "having" of meaning by a word.

What then is Merleau-Ponty's final word on the relationship between thinking and speaking? Here again, unfortunately, Merleau-Ponty is not very helpful. He focuses his discussion on what might be called "thoughtful speech" and only obliquely touches on "thoughtless speech" and the question whether knowing a language is necessary to doing any thinking. Scattered throughout his piece are the suggestions that speech "accomplishes" thought, that thought and speech are "internally related," that the "inner life" of thinking "is an inner language," and so on. But couched as they are these suggestions are altogether too cryptic. They, as it turns out, need clarification—so we can hardly rely on them to settle this issue.

The final selection we present is from Gilbert *Ryle's* article ,"A Puzzling Element in the Notion of Thinking." Ryle, unlike Merleau-Ponty, does not concern himself directly with the larger debate about the direction of linguistics. This has, as it happens, certain advantages for us. So far the question of the relation between thinking and speaking has itself been uncritically accepted as having a clear sense. This has been dictated by our concern with the larger debate which, because *it* is important, has seemed to lend a clear sense and significance to the question. Furthermore, the content of that debate has also dictated the manner in which the question is phrased: namely, "Whether thinking presupposes knowing a language." In virtually ignoring the larger debate, Ryle enables us to look afresh at this phrasing of the question without prejudice in favor of any particular answer *and* without presupposing that the question itself, so phrased, really *has* a clear sense.

What Ryle seems to be asking us then is just this: Can we give a sense to asking whether thinking is or presupposes any behavior, ability, or whatever, at all? Of course, if a clear examination of the use of the word *thinking* reveals that thinking requires no "proprietary" actions or goings on, then, specifically, it cannot be said to require knowing a language. However, it is important to notice that the cases Ryle presents in support of this view *do* show that there are "certain special thinking-activities which certainly do seem to require our saying things in our heads or *sotto voce* or aloud." Yet this is a far cry from saying that in those cases we are thinking *in* words, *by means of* words, or that our thinking in those cases *consists* in saying things. What Ryle finds puzzling in the notion of thinking is our persistent temptation to ask what thinking consists in, by what mechanism thinking takes place, or what it is that we think *in* (words, images, or what-have-you).

It is a temptation that he resists, convincingly, we believe. The upshot of this for behaviorism will of course be obvious. When Skinner identifies thinking as behavior he accepts the sense of questions like, "In what does thinking consist?" And he attempts to give the answer: behavior. According to Ryle's view what would be wrong with this "answer" is that there is no intelligible question to which this could *count* as an answer. So the claim, "Thinking is behavior," is also unintelligible.

The results of Ryle's examination of the concept of *thinking* for the rationalists program in linguistics will not be so obvious. Yet, we believe, they are equally damaging. For, as Ryle shows, related to the unintelligibility of asking for the "stuff" thinking consists in is the equal nonsensicality of arguing that an expression of thought in speech is a chronicle of "items of a procession of quick fading internal phenomena." When we explain what we or someone else was thinking on a particular occasion we may say much more in expressing the thought than what could be *reported* about what words or images flitted through one's head (or about what behavior one engaged in) on that occasion. Expressions of thought, as Ryle thus shows, are not chronicles of items, they are not *reports* of anything. The reason for this is that there is no stuff, no mechanism, nothing which the thought can be said to consist in, to make reports about! So, of course, if expressions of thought are not reports, we cannot make sense of Katz' view that speech is an encoding of our thoughts. This is because to see speech as a coded message communicating our thoughts is precisely to view speech as *reporting*, albeit in code, some "thoughts" or goings-on in our heads. And the difficulty, again, with this is that there is nothing going on there that can *also* intelligibly be described as what the thought consists in.

Speech Is An Encoding of Thoughts

JERROLD J. KATZ

LINGUISTS who conceive of their science as a discipline which collects utterances and classifies their parts often pride themselves on their freedom from mentalism. But freedom from mentalism is an inherent feature of the taxonomic conception of linguistics, for, according to this conception, a linguist

---

Reprinted with permission of the author and publisher from "Mentalism in Linguistics" by Jerrold J. Katz in *Language*, Vol. 40, No. 2 (April–June, 1964), 124, 126–134 and 135–137. Published by the Linguistic Society of America.

starts his investigation with observable physical events and at no stage imports anything else.

We may expand on this inherent freedom from mentalistic commitment as follows. Utterances are stretches of physical sound. Since the primary data for a taxonomic linguistic investigation is a set of utterances elicited from informants or obtained from texts, the linguist begins with observable physical events, sounds or inscriptions. At the first stage of classification—the cataloguing of phonemes on the basis of these stretches of sound or some grouping of them—the linguist erects classes of significant sounds. At the next stage he forms classes of sequences of phonemes, thus producing a catalog of the morphemes of the language. Finally he classifies sequences of morphemes as sentential constituents of various types. Even if at some point the linguist should also consider an aspect of the speaker himself (such as his intuitive judgments about well-formedness) or an aspect of the speaker's environment (such as what he is referring to), such consideration is restricted to just those aspects that are capable of being observed by anyone who cares to carry out the same investigation. Therefore, on the taxonomic conception of linguistics, there is nowhere from the beginning to the end of a linguistic investigation, any appeal to mental capacities or mental processes. Alternatively, the taxonomic conception is a very narrow form of reductionism, which holds that every linguistic construction, at any level, reduces ultimately, by purely classificational procedures, to physical segments of utterances. . . .

One may formulate the controversy between taxonomic linguistics and mentalistic linguistics in terms of the following opposition. The linguist who adopts a causal conception of mentalism is contending that purely linguistic theories cannot succeed in predicting and explaining the facts of linguistic performance without making reference to the mental events, capacities, and processes of speakers, i.e. that linguistic theories must contain concepts which enable linguists to formulate the principles of mental operation that underlie speech. On the other hand, the linguist who adopts the taxonomic conception of linguistics is contending that purely linguistic theories can succeed in predicting and explaining the facts of linguistic performance.

It might appear that there is no way to settle this controversy short of some abstruse examination of the philosophical principles underlying the taxonomic and mentalistic positions, but this is false. The dispute can be settled simply by determining whether a taxonomic or a mentalistic theory is, in principle, better able to account for what is known about the general facts of linguistic phenomena. This determination can be made by showing that a mentalistic theory accounts for everything that a taxonomic theory accounts for, and, in addition and with no extension of the theory, for many things that the taxonomic theory must fail to account for. This is the spirit of Chomsky's criticisms of theories of grammar constructed within the taxonomic framework.[1] Unfortunately, Chom-

[1] Cf. N. Chomsky, 'A transformational approach to syntax' and 'Current issues in linguistic theory', *The structure of language: Readings in the philosophy of language*, ed. by J. Fodor and J. J. Katz (Englewood Cliffs, N.J., 1964).

sky's arguments are often not taken in this way but are taken rather as trying to establish a new kind of taxonomic system.

The basic point of Chomsky's criticisms is that the failure of a taxonomic theory to handle the full range of facts about linguistic structure is due to the failure of such theories to concern themselves with mental capacities, events, and processes. The point which has been missed by those who interpret his arguments as trying to establish a new kind of taxonomic system is that only by introducing mentalistic concepts into our theories do we provide ourselves with the conceptual machinery which makes it possible to account for the full range of linguistic facts.

The general form of Chomsky's criticism of taxonomic linguistics is summarized as follows. The best kind of theory is one which systematizes the widest range of facts; hence a mentalistic theory is better than a taxonomic one because the former can handle any fact that the latter can handle, whereas the latter is unable to handle many kinds of facts that the former handles easily and naturally. The difference in the facts that these theories can handle is a direct function of the difference in the conceptual machinery they contain.

If it is to be shown that mentalism thus succeeds where taxonomic linguistics fails, it will be necessary to clarify certain features of the mentalist conception of linguistic theories. In particular, it must be made clear just what a mentalist means when he says that reference to mental states is a necessary aspect of any adequate linguistic theory, and just what status he intends mentalistic concepts to have. Unless his meaning is clarified, it will remain unclear whether it is the reference to mental states that is responsible for the margin of explanatory power by which mentalistic theories excel taxonomic theories. Unless the status of his concepts is clarified, it will remain open for the taxonomic linguist to claim that, although the mentalist says that his reference to mental states is a reference to things or events within the causal realm, the actual way in which this reference is made gives no clue how mental states might stand as causal antecedents of physical events like vocalization and speech sounds. These matters must be clarified in such a way that those who construe Chomsky's arguments as seeking to establish a new kind of taxonomic system cannot claim that the machinery in Chomsky's theories which produce the margin of explanatory power by which they are more empirically successful have no psychological reality but are merely new kinds of data-cataloguing devices.

First, how can mental events like those referred to in mentalistic linguistic theories be links in the causal chain that contains also vocalizations and sound waves? To explain how speakers are able to communicate in their language, the mentalist hypothesizes that, underlying a speaker's ability to communicate, there is a highly complex mechanism which is essentially the same as that underlying the linguistic ability of other speakers. He thus views the process of linguistic communication as one in which such mechanisms operate to encode and decode verbal messages. The aim of theory construction in linguistics is taken to be the formulation of a theory that reveals the structure of this mechanism and explains the facts of linguistic communication by showing them to be behavioral consequences of the operation of a mechanism with just the structure that the formulated theory attributes to it.

The step of hypothesizing such a mechanism in the process of theory construction in linguistics is no different from hypothetical postulation in theory construction in any other branch of science where some component of the system about which we wish to gain understanding is inaccessible to observation. The linguist can no more look into the head of a fluent speaker than a physicist can directly observe photons or a biologist directly inspect the evolutionary events that produced the human species. The linguist, like the physicist and biologist, can only achieve scientific understanding by constructing a model of the system which contains a hypothesis about the structure of the components of the system that are not observable. If the logical consequences of the model match the observable behavior of the system and would not do so without the hypothesis, the scientist may say that this hypothesis accounts for the behavior of the system in terms of the behavior of the unobservable but causally efficient component. If the model is the simplest one which enables the scientist to derive all the known facts and predict previously unknown ones as effects of the hypothesized component, he can assert that his model correctly pictures the structure of the system and its unobservable components. In this way, a linguist can assert that his theory correctly represents the structure of the mechanism underlying the speaker's ability to communicate with other speakers.

This mechanism is, according to the mentalist linguist, a brain mechanism, a component of a neural system. It is inaccessible to observation in the sense that, even if the linguist could look inside a speaker's head, he would be unable to figure out the structure of the mechanism from the electrochemical events going on there. But, as I have just pointed out, this limitation does not doom the linguist's program of discovering the nature of the speaker's ability to communicate in language. Hence it cannot be taken as grounds for supposing that a linguistic theory is not about a brain mechanism and its concepts are not about mental states. It is perhaps because, from the behaviorist viewpoint, this observational inaccessibility of the neural mechanism represents the boundary of the subject matter of linguistics, that taxonomic linguists have denied that theoretical concepts in a linguistic theory can have psychological reality. It would certainly explain why they have confined themselves to the corpus of elicitable utterances, behavioral responses to such utterances, and observable features of the context in which utterances occur, and why they have refused to regard the internal psychological properties of speakers as part of the subject matter of a linguistic theory.

Of course, the view that the reality of theoretical concepts in linguistics is mentalistic yet (in principle) irreducible to brain states, is a form of psychophysical dualism that a linguist should be reluctant to accept. But holding that brain states are observationally inaccessible and, at the same time, that linguistic constructions have an underlying phychological reality does not commit one to accepting such a dualism.

Let us suppose that the linguist constructs a theory by inferring hypothetically the characteristics of the mechanism underlying linguistic communication. His inference begins by positing a mechanism of which the observable events of linguistic communication are causal consequences. He invents a theory about the structure of this mechanism and the causal chain connecting the mechanism to observable events, to explain how these internal causes produce linguistic communication as their effect. Now it is clear that the linguist, though he claims that his theory describes a neurological mechanism, cannot immediately translate the theory into neurological terms, i.e. into talk about synapses, nerve fibers, and such. But—and this is the crucial point in showing that the mentalist is not a psychophysical dualist—this failure to have a ready neurological translation means only that he cannot yet specify what kind of physical realization of his theoretical description is inside the speaker's head. Since linguistics and neurophysiology are independent fields, it does not matter for the linguist what kind of physical realization is there. For the purpose of linguistic investigation, it is immaterial whether the mechanism inside the speaker's head is in reality a network of electronic relays, a mechanical system of cardboard flip-flops and rubber bands, or, for that matter, a group of homunculi industriously at work in a tiny office. All of these possibilities, and others, are on a par for the linguist as physical realizations of this mechanism, so long as each is isomorphic to the representation of linguistic structure given by the theory of the language. The critical distinction is, then, between an abstract, formal characterization of linguistic structure—the theory itself—and a physical system of some kind which instances this structure.[2] Discovering what kind of a physical system in the human brain instantiates the representation of structure given by a linguistic theory is the task of the neurophysiologist. The linguist's task is to provide a theory which represents the structure that any physical system must possess if it is to be capable of linguistic communication as we know it.

The theoretical constructions used by a mentalist linguist in building his theories are intended by him to have psychological reality. They do not, for the linguist, require translation into neurophysiological terms, even though reference to mental states is construed as reference to brain states. This is why the events to which the mentalist's constructions refer can stand as links in the causal chain that contains vocalizations and sound waves as other links.

Why, now, do mentalistic linguistic theories excel taxonomic linguistic theories in descriptive and explanatory power, and why must mentalistic concepts be given credit for this excellence?

The three fundamental questions with which a synchronic description of a particular language deals are these:

(1) What is known by a speaker who is fluent in a natural language? That is, what facts about his language underlie his ability to communicate with others in that language?

(2) How is such linguistic knowledge put into operation to achieve communication? That is, how does a speaker use such linguistic knowledge to con-

2 Cf. H. Putnam, 'Minds and machines', *Dimensions of mind*, ed. by S. Hook (New York, 1960).

vey his thoughts, opinions, wishes, demands, questions, emotions, and so on to other speakers?

(3) How do speakers come to acquire this ability? That is, what innate dispositions and developmental processes are responsible for transforming a nonverbal infant into a fluent speaker?

An answer to (1) may be referred to as a 'linguistic description.'[3] A linguistic description has three components: syntactic, phonological, and semantic. If the linguistic description is a mentalistic theory, the syntactic component is a generative system which enumerates strings of minimally syntactically functioning units (which may be called formatives), together with a description of their syntactic structure. These structural descriptions, the output of the syntactic component in a linguistic description, are the input to both the phonological component and the semantic component. These two components are interpretative systems: the former interprets the abstract, formal descriptions of the syntactic structure of sentences as representations of vocal sound by assigning them a phonetic shape; the latter interprets them as meaningful messages. That is, the semantic component converts the outputs of the syntactic component into the messages that the sentences communicate to those who understand the language. The phonological and semantic components have no systematic connection with each other: one is concerned with pronunciation and the other with conceptualization.

An answer to (2) consists of at least two procedures. One is a 'sentence recognition procedure,' whose function is to assign to any given perceived utterance a phonetic representation, a syntactic description, and a semantic interpretation. The function of the other procedure is to choose an appropriate syntactic structure for any message that the speaker wishes to communicate and to provide a phonetic representation for that structure; it is a 'sentence production procedure.' Together, the two procedures determine how the knowledge of the language embodied in the linguistic description is used by a speaker to understand and produce sentences.

An answer to (3) is a theory of language acquisition. Such a theory explains how a nonverbal infant who is exposed in the normal way to a sample of sentences and nonsentences, and perhaps other data as well, comes to possess a linguistic description and procedures of sentence recognition and sentence production.

The first of the three questions is logically prior to the others. We must know what linguistic facts a speaker knows before we can say how those facts enable him to communicate and before we can say how he acquired them: linguistic description must precede inquiry into the nature of language use and acquisition. But this logical priority does not mean that the attempt to answer (2) and (3) must wait for a full answer to (1); rather, it means that substantive contributions toward an answer to (1) must be available in order that attempts to answer (2) and (3) can begin. Furthermore, it means—and this is critical—that

[3] For further discussion on this concept cf. J. J. Katz and P. Postal, *An integrated theory of linguistic descriptions* (Cambridge, Mass., 1964).

the kind of answer that will be given, or sought, for (2) and (3) is determined by the kind of answer which is given or sought for (1). Since (2) is, in the same sense, logically prior to (3), the same applies to these two.

The basic fact about languages that a full answer to (1) must account for is that speakers can understand indefinitely many sentences never before encountered by them. So ubiquitous and commonplace is this fact that its theoretical significance is often missed: the very fact that almost every sentence we encounter is heard for the first time keeps us from fully appreciating how amazing it is that a fluent speaker is able to understand new sentences. But if we think about learning a foreign language, the theoretical significance of this feat becomes apparent immediately. We do not credit a person with mastery of a foreign language if he is only able to understand those sentences which he has been previously taught. The test of fluency is whether he can understand sentences that he has not been taught. The theoretical significance of understanding new sentences is that this ability is the test of whether one has mastery of a natural language.

To account for this feat in answering (1), the grammar must take the form of a system of rules which describe the structure of every sentence that a speaker would (in the absence of linguistically irrelevant psychological limitations) understand if he were to encounter it. Such rules must describe an infinite set of sentences because in a natural language there is no longest sentence. Given a sentence composed of n formatives, there is always another composed of $n + r$ formatives, formed from the first by various syntactic procedures, for instance by replacing a noun by a noun and a modifier which contains another noun, itself replaceable by a noun and a modifier, and so on. There will, of course, be a point at which still longer sentences cannot be either produced or understood by normal speakers in normal situations; but this limitation has to do with perceptual limits, the finite bound on memory storage, human mortality, and other linguistically inessential considerations. If we mistakenly identify these speech limitations with a finite-length limitation on what qualifies as a grammatical sentence of the language, we are forced to the absurd conclusion that, as such limitations are weakened (say, by the use of paper and pencil), either a new language is being used or the old one has undergone radical change.

This shows that a taxonomic grammar which describes only the sentences in a corpus fails to be empirically adequate: infinitely many grammatical sentences are left undescribed. Some taxonomic grammars are intended to describe the full set of sentences—that is, to segment and classify not only the sentences in a corpus but also of those that might be elicited and those that are of the same syntactic form as the elicited and elicitable sentences. But this should not obscure the theoretically more significant fact that such grammars are nonetheless put forth as data-cataloguing systems, the data being strings of syntactically well-formed formatives. Accordingly, their rules have no psychological reality, and cannot be construed as accounting for the knowledge that a speaker has which enables him to understand new sentences of his language. Furthermore, such rules cannot be the basis for an answer to (2), since an answer to (2) must relate the speaker's knowledge of the structure of sentences to procedures for applying this knowledge. For the same reason, such rules cannot be the basis for an answer to (3), since an answer to (3) is an input-output device which explains how a sample of sentences and nonsentences as input gives as output a linguistic description and procedures of sentence production and sentence recognition.

To show that a mentalistic theory of linguistic communication can succeed in answering (1), (2), and (3), and why mentalistic concepts are essential in giving it that power, we require an overall model which shows how the mechanism of linguistic communication operates in an actual situation. Such a model represents the most rudimentary form of the theory of linguistic communication which mentalists seek to construct, and is thus a first approximation toward an exact formulation of that theory in its fully sophisticated form. It should be stressed, however, that even as a first approximation such a model shares with the fully elaborated and precise theory the character and status of a hypothetically inferred theoretical construction.

Given that both speaker and hearer are equipped with a linguistic description and procedures for sentence production and recognition, we can reconstruct the communication situation in these terms. The speaker, for reasons that are biographically but not linguistically relevant, chooses some message he wants to convey to the hearer. He selects some thought he wishes to express to him, some command he wants to give him, or some question he needs to ask him. This message is, we may assume, in whatever form the semantic component of his linguistic description uses to represent the meaning content of thoughts, commands, questions, or the like. The speaker then uses the sentence production procedure to obtain an abstract syntactic structure having the proper conceptualization of his thought, command, or question as its semantic interpretation. This procedure helps him find a sentence that is suitable to the circumstances by rejecting all syntactic structures which, though they bear the proper semantic interpretation, are for sentences that are too long, syntactically too complicated, too pedantic, etc. After he has a suitable syntactic structure, the speaker utilizes the phonological component of his linguistic description to produce a phonetic shape for it. This phonetic shape is encoded into a signal that causes the speaker's articulatory system to vocalize an utterance of the sentence. The sound waves of which these utterances consist are transmitted through the air and, after they reach the hearer's auditory system, are converted into a signal which is decoded into a phonetic shape. On the basis of that shape the hearer's sentence recognition procedure then provides a syntactic structure. That is, the procedure converts the signal produced by hearing the utterance into a phonetic shape whose physical realization is what reached the ear, and recovers the syntactic structure that the speaker originally chose as a formalization of his message. Once the hearer is in possession of this syntactic structure, he employs the semantic component of his linguistic description to obtain its semantic interpretation. He thus represents to himself the same message that the speaker wished to convey to him, and communication has taken place.

Although this model is phrased as if the process described were conscious, no such assumption is involved. It is not an essential feature of mentalism that the processes postulated by the mentalist as going on inside a speaker's head should be open to the speaker's conscious awareness. This point alone ought to remove one source of opposition to mentalism in modern linguistics.

Within the framework of the above model of linguistic communication, every aspect of the mentalistic theory involves psychological reality. The linguistic description and the procedures of sentence production and recognition must correspond to independent mechanisms in the brain. Componential distinctions between the syntactic, phonological, and semantic components must rest on relevant differences between three neural submechanisms of the mechanism which stores the linguistic description. The rules of each component must have their psychological reality in the input-output operations of the computing machinery of this mechanism. The ordering of rules within a component must, contrary to the claims of Bloomfield and many others,[4] have its psychological reality in those features of this computing machinery which group such input-output operations and make the performance of operations in one group a precondition for those in another to be performed.

There are two further points concerning the superiority of a mentalistic theory. First, since the psychologist and the mentalistic linguist are constructing theories of the same kind, i.e. theories with the same kind of relation to the neurophysiology of the human brain, it follows that the linguist's theory is subject to the requirement that it harmonize with the psychologist's theories dealing with other human abilities and that it be consistent with the neurophysiologist's theories concerning the type of existing brain mechanisms. A linguistic theory that meets this requirement will have a wider range of facts into whose explanation it can enter and so will be a better theory than one which is otherwise equivalent to it in explanatory power. Such a theory enters into the explanation of many of those psychological theories with which it harmonizes. Theories of perception, theories of memory, of thinking, of learning, and other psychological theories leave open various questions about the effect of language on these processes and the effect of these processes on language; only a mentalistic theory of linguistic structure can hope to answer them. Further, by subjecting a linguistic theory to this requirement we make it more easily testable. For the requirement enables us to refute a linguistic theory if we can find psychological theories or facts that are inconsistent with it or neurophysiological accounts which describe brain structure in a way that precludes the linguistic theory from being isomorphic to any of the structures in the human brain. Again, a fruitful requirement like this can only be imposed on a mentalistic theory.

Second, a mentalistic theory also can provide a psychological reality for lin-

[4] This, then, is the answer to Hockett's question about how to construe ordering otherwise than historically; cf. 'Two models of linguistic description', *Word* 10.233 (1964): . . . if it is said that the English past tense form *baked* is "formed" from *bake* by a "process" of "suffixation", then no matter what disclaimer of historicity is made, it is impossible not to conclude that some kind of priority is being assigned to *bake* as against *baked* or the suffix. And if this priority is not historical, what is it?

guistic universals. Instead of linguistic universals being treated simply as common features of the linguistic description of every language, as they are in the taxonomic view, the fact that such common features are universal, i.e. are necessary features of natural languages, is explained in terms of the psychology of human language learners, the one constant feature among all the individual differences between speakers of different natural languages, and all the differences between the situations in which they learn to speak. One clear-cut sense of psychological reality for linguistic universals is that proposed by Chomsky.[5] According to Chomsky's account, there are two kinds of linguistic universals, substantive and formal. The formal universals are specifications of the form of the rules that appear in each of the components of any empirically successful linguistic description of a natural language; the substantive universals are theoretical terms which enter into the formulation of the rules of particular linguistic descriptions. Chomsky's hypothesis is that the child is innately equipped with a language-learning device that contains such linguistic universals and a simplicity principle; the latter enables him to acquire the simplest linguistic description of the form determined by the linguistic universals which accords with the sample of utterances he is exposed to. Linguistic universals thus have psychological reality as part of the internal structure of the innate mechanism responsible for a child's acquisition of a language. Such a hypothesis, if true, explains why there should be a certain structure and content found in every language: they are found in every language because they are implanted by the innately given language-learning device that makes the acquisition of a natural language possible for normal humans. . . .

As described above, the mentalist explains the facts about a speaker's and hearer's linguistic performance in terms of a model that reconstructs the process by which a message is transmitted from the speaker to the hearer through the speaker's encoding the message in the form of an utterance and the hearer's decoding that utterance back to the speaker's original message. Such a model explains why an utterance has a certain linguistic property, and what function that property has in the process of communication, by locating the property in the causal chain which links the utterance on one side to the neurophysiological mechanisms that perform the encoding and articulation, on the other side to those that accomplish the perception and decoding. But if, with the taxonomic viewpoint, we interpret any of the elements of the mentalist's description of the process of communication as merely fictions, rather than references to neurophysiological links in such a causal chain, the whole explanation collapses. For that interpretation would amount to the claim that there are gaps in the causal chain. If there are gaps, we cannot account for the causal antecedents of a linguistic property and of its effects. The Bloomfieldian mode of interpreting features of a linguistic description is like contending that the pressure of a gas on the walls of its container is the effect of molecules striking the walls, and at the

[5] Chomsky, "Review of *Verbal Behavior* by B. F. Skinner," *Language* Vol. 35, 26–58 (1959).

same time denying that a molecule is a real physical object. The hypothesis of a mechanism of linguistic communication, with the kind of structure attributed to it by an optimal linguistic description, can explain how linguistic communication takes place only if the mechanism and all its features have the same ontological status as the utterance itself. The hypothesized mechanism must be capable of affecting the articulatory system of a speaker so as to produce an utterance, and capable of being affected by the output of his receptor system when stimulated by an utterance. This implies, however (to stress it again), no commitment for the mentalist to any particular kind of physical realization for the linguistic description, except that whatever is inside the speaker's head must be capable of causal connection with the physical sounds that serve as the vehicle of linguistic communication.[6]

The taxonomic linguist assumes that only his conception and treatment of linguistics saves the linguist from countenancing such occult mental entities as a 'spirit' and 'soul.' The truth is, rather, that mentalism also—in the only sense of 'mentalism' for which any serious claim to validity is made—avoids those occult entities. Both taxonomic and mentalist linguists deal exclusively with physically real events and structures. Both leave it to other sciences to determine the exact nature of the physical reality of the phenomena they theorize about. Just as the taxonomic linguist must leave it to the physicist to tell him about the physical reality of sound waves, and (if he is behavioristically inclined) to the physiologist to tell him about the physical reality of muscular contractions and glandular secretions, so the mentalist linguist must leave it to the neurophysiologist to tell him about the neurophysiological realization of his abstract linguistic description.

The actual difference between the taxonomic and the mentalistic conceptions of linguistics lies in what linguistic theories built on each of these conceptions can accomplish by way of answering questions (1), (2), and (3). We have found that the taxonomic linguist confines linguistic investigation to stating those facts about the structure of a natural language which can be formulated within the framework of a classificational system, while the mentalist goes far beyond this in seeking a full answer to all three questions. This difference is important: it justifies us in rejecting the taxonomic conception in favor of the mentalistic one. Taxonomic linguistics can only describe the utterances of a language; mentalistic linguistics not only can do this but can also explain how speakers communicate by using the utterances, and how the ability to communicate is acquired. Instead of the taxonomic linguist having a just complaint against the mentalist for appealing to occult entities, the mentalist has a just complaint against the taxonomic linguist for excluding from linguistics, a priori and arbitrarily, just what it is most important for this science to do. The freedom from mentalism inherent in the taxonomic conception of linguistics is its inherent weakness.

6 For a general discussion of the fictionalist view of scientific theories cf. Katz. 'On the existence of theoretical entities', in preparation.

Thinking Is Behavior

B. F. SKINNER

AN ACCOUNT of verbal behavior is not complete until its relation to the rest of the behavior of the organism has been made clear. This can be done conveniently by discussing the problem of thinking.

Covert Verbal Behavior

If someone who is sitting quite still is asked *What are you doing?*, he may reply *Nothing, I'm just thinking.* In the terminology of the layman (and of many specialists) thinking is often simply opposed to doing. But as a living organism a man is behaving in some sense while "doing nothing," even though his behavior may not be easily observed by others or possibly even by himself. We do not discuss these activities effectively because they are almost always accessible only to the "thinker" and useful verbal responses to them cannot easily be developed. Some progress has been made in improving public observation through the instrumental amplification of small-scale behavior, but the problem of explaining the normal occurrence of such behavior remains.

In a sense verbal behavior which cannot be observed by others is not properly part of our field. It is tempting to avoid the problems it raises by confining ourselves to observable events, letting anyone extend the analysis to his own covert behavior who wishes to do so. But there would then be certain embarrassing gaps in our account. In intraverbal chaining, for example, necessary links are sometimes missing from the observable data. When someone solves a problem in "mental arithmetic," the initial statement of the problem and the final overt answer can often be related only by inferring covert events. We also have to account for verbal behavior which is under the control of covert speech—

EDITORS' NOTE: Throughout this selection Skinner uses certain technical terms that are discussed thoroughly in earlier chapters of his book. We will give rough definitions of these for the reader here. A "mand" is a piece of verbal behavior reinforced by a *characteristic consequence* and has no specific relation to a *prior* stimulus. It includes questions, demands, commands, reprimands, and so on. A "tact" is a piece of verbal behavior evoked by a particular prior stimulus that is a particular *object* or *event* or a particular *property* of an object or event. Pieces of verbal behavior that are responses to *verbal* stimuli are not called "tacts" by Skinner. Instead they are treated in a more complex way. A piece of verbal behavior is said to be an "echoic" response if it "generates a sound pattern similar to that of the stimulus" (*Verbal Behavior*, p. 55). If it is a response to a written stimulus, it is called a "textual" response. If a piece of verbal behavior is a natural link in an ongoing verbal chain (as "four" is in the chain that begins "two plus two equals . . ."), it is said to be an "intraverbal" response. Skinner includes under this last class such things as puns, translations, paraphrase, mathematical problem-solving, answers to questions, and a great deal more. An "autoclitic" response is a piece of verbal behavior that either is evoked by or modifies other behavior of the speaker himself. Within this class are included such utterances as "I remember . . .," "I imagine . . .," "let x equal . . .," "for example . . .," and so on. More importantly, perhaps, this class of responses includes all those having to do with organizing other verbal responses into grammatical sentences.

---

which reports it . . . or qualifies it with autoclitics, . . . Covert behavior has also had to be considered in discussing grammar, . . . sentence composition, . . . editing, . . . and other topics. Some discussion of its dimensions is therefore required.

Covert behavior often seems to be like overt except that it occurs on a smaller scale. If we recite the alphabet while speaking and whispering alternate letters, it is easy to observe the voicing which makes the difference: *A-b-C-d-E-f-G-h.* . . . If we whisper every other letter while saying the rest silently, we observe what appears to be a comparable difference between overt and covert forms: *a*-( )-*c*-( )-*e*-( )-*g*-( ). . . . But the silent response may recede to very subtle dimensions. The muscular involvement demonstrated by mechanical or electrical amplification can often be detected by trying to "think" such a response as *bubble, bubble* while holding the mouth as wide open as possible. But this can often be done, especially after a little practice, and there are other difficulties in assuming that covert behavior is always executed by the muscular apparatus responsible for the overt form. Experienced public speakers, especially those who say the same thing many times, appear to "think" one verbal response while saying another aloud, and one sometimes appears to read aloud mechanically while carrying on, say, a "fantasied" conversation. Small-scale muscular activity is also not very plausible in representing incipient verbal behavior. *I was going to say* . . . may be followed by a response which has not been previously emitted, even subaudibly. A rapid speaker may compose a sentence to provide for a response which has yet to be executed, and it is difficult to explain this by assuming rapid silent rehearsal. We break off an unhappy remark before damage is done and, though we may complete it subaudibly, evidently before it has actually occurred.

We do not need to make guesses about the muscular or neural substratum of verbal events. We account for the probability or strength of a suppressed or manipulated response as we account for the probability of any behavior. In an instance of editing, for example, we observe that behavior which is ordinarily followed by a given response is suddenly interrupted. The fact that it is "ordinarily" so followed is a behavioral fact concerning past occurrences of the response under given circumstances. Physiological processes mediate the probability of covert and overt responses alike, as they undoubtedly mediate all the relations disclosed in a functional analysis of behavior, but we can talk about both forms of response "when they are not being emitted" without identifying physiological mediators. The data which give rise to the notion of covert speech can be dealt with as such with the degree of rigor prevailing elsewhere in a science of verbal behavior at the present time.

Other questions, however, remain to be answered. Why should a response become covert at all? Operant behavior almost always begins in a form which affects the external environment, for it would not otherwise be reinforced. (Exceptions are certain responses which are automatically reinforced by the organism itself.) Why does it not remain overt?

Behavior becomes covert when, in the first place, its strength drops below the value needed for overt emission. It may be weak because the controlling variables are deficient. When we say *I thought that was Jones* (*but I see it is not*), we actually emit the response *Jones*; but we are describing a previous covert instance which was weak because the stimulus was inadequate. If the response *Jones* had been weak because it was poorly conditioned or partially forgotten, the report might have taken the form *I thought his name was Jones.*

Covert behavior may be strong, however, as shown by the fact that it will appear at the overt level under other circumstances. The covert response is simply the easiest or, for any reason, the likeliest at the moment. The energy level of nonverbal behavior usually declines so long as the reinforcing contingencies are maintained. When Thorndike reinforced a cat for licking its paw, the movement grew slighter and slighter until it could scarcely be detected.[1] The reinforcing contingencies could not be maintained beyond that point. (We might say that the cat could not be reinforced for "thinking" about licking its paw.) But a considerable reinforcement survives in covert *verbal* behavior when the speaker is his own listener. One important consequence of our definition is that, when talking to oneself, it is unnecessary to speak aloud and easier not to. A response which is subaudible for reasons of convenience will become audible if an advantage is to be gained. We speak aloud to ourselves upon occasion—for example, when the audible response improves intraverbal chaining. In the solution of a difficult problem, mathematical or otherwise, we resort to overt responses, vocal or written. For the same reason such covert behavior as counting money or adding figures is likely to become overt in the presence of distracting stimuli.

Covert speech is not, however, wholly or perhaps even primarily a labor-saving practice. As we have seen, verbal behavior is frequently punished. Audible behavior in the child is reinforced and tolerated up to a point; then it becomes annoying, and the child is punished for speaking. Comparable aversive consequences continue into the adult years. Punishment is not always in the nature of reproof, for speech which is overheard may have other kinds of undesirable effects, such as giving away a secret. The privacy of covert behavior has a practical value. So long as a verbal response is emitted primarily for its effect upon the speaker himself, it is best confined to that audience. (The content of autistic verbal behavior is often significant to the therapist just because it is relatively free of the control exercised by a punishing audience.)

That avoidance of punishment is a more likely explanation than convenience is shown by the fact that covert behavior returns to the overt level when a punishing audience is no longer in control though convenience has not been altered. Many people who live alone gradually come to talk to themselves aloud. In the presence of other people the return to the overt level may take time, for the nonpunishing character of an audience cannot be established in a moment. It is usually hard to induce people to "think aloud"—that is, to emit in the presence of an external audience behavior which is primarily controlled by the

[1] Thorndike, E. L., *Animal Intelligence* (New York, 1898).

speaker himself. The extent of the special control exerted by the private audience is seen in the fact that overt behavior in the absence of an external listener frequently generates anxiety or other emotional effects. Many people are embarrassed when using a dictating machine for the first time, or when rehearsing a speech aloud in an empty room. A full release of previously covert behavior at the audible level may come very slowly. The noncensuring audience provided by the psychoanalyst is not immediately effective, though overt speech of otherwise punishable form may eventually appear.

There are, then, important variables which determine whether a response will be overt or covert. But they do not greatly affect its other properties. They do not suggest that there is any important distinction between the two levels or forms. Nothing is gained, therefore, by identifying thinking with subaudible talking. This was done in certain early behavioristic analyses, apparently in an effort to find replacements for the so-called mental processes. The traditional view that an idea occurs first and that the speaker then expresses in words had to be discarded. The actual precursors of speech are, as we have seen, the independent variables of which it is a function, but these are for the most part outside the organism and hence not very plausible replacements for ideas as inner causes. It was tempting to suppose that the speaker "thought about what he was going to say" in the simple sense of saying it first to himself. But the covert response, if it occurs, is in no sense the cause of the overt. The full force of the expression of ideas cannot be carried by a mere sequence of covert and overt responses.

Other "mental processes" rejected in a behavioristic analysis are not easily replaced by covert verbal behavior, but their traditional prestige no doubt contributed to the need to find inner replacements. Some of these are exemplified when a speaker acquires or retains a response (the mental processes of "learning" and "memory"), responds differently to different stimuli ("discrimination"), reacts with one response-form rather than another ("differentiation"), responds in a given way to a new stimulus bearing some resemblance to the old ("generalization," "metaphor," or "analogical thinking"), responds under the control of a single property or a special set of properties of a stimulus ("abstraction"), arrives at a constructed response through a controlled intraverbal chain ("reasoning"), and so on. These are not *behaviors*, covert or overt. They are controlling relations or the changes in probability which result from changes in such relations.

The theory that thinking was merely subaudible speech had at least the favorable effect of identifying thinking with behaving. But speech is only a special case of behavior and subaudible speech a further subdivision. The range of verbal behavior is roughly suggested, in descending order of energy, by shouting, loud talking, quiet talking, whispering, muttering "under one's breath," subaudible speech with detectable muscular action, subaudible speech of unclear dimensions, and perhaps even the "unconscious thinking" sometimes inferred in instances of problem solving. There is no point at which it is profitable to draw a line distinguishing thinking from acting on this continuum. So far as we know, the events at the covert end have no special properties, observe no special laws, and can be credited with no special achievements.

The Speaker as His Own Listener

A better case can be made for identifying thinking with behaving which automatically affects the behavior and is reinforcing because it does so. This can be either covert or overt. We can explain the tendency to identify thinking with covert behavior by pointing out that the reinforcing effects of covert behavior *must* arise from self-stimulation. But self-stimulation is possible, and indeed more effective, at the overt level.

When a man talks to himself, aloud or silently, he is an excellent listener. He speaks the same language or languages and has had the same verbal and nonverbal experience as his listener. He is subject to the same deprivations and aversive stimulations, and these vary from day to day or from moment to moment in the same way. As listener he is ready for his own behavior as speaker at just the right time and is optimally prepared to "understand" what he has said. Very little time is lost in transmission and the behavior may acquire subtle dimensions. It is not surprising, then, that verbal self-stimulation has been regarded as possessing special properties and has been identified with thinking.

Simple Soliloquy

The speaker's own verbal behavior automatically supplies stimuli for echoic, textual, or intraverbal behavior, and these in turn generate stimuli for further responses. The result is the "soliloquy"—as exemplified in its dramatic use and in some stream-of-consciousness writing. It is not essentially productive thinking. Unexpected twists may turn up, but subsequent soliloquizing is modified only slightly, if at all, as a result. Dashiell[2] has analyzed Hamlet's *To be or not to be* in this spirit. An intraverbal connection between *die* and *sleep* leads to another between *sleep* and *dream*, and *dream* then strengthens an incipient response which is broken off with *Aye, there's the rub.* Regardless of the respectability of the connections, such a "train of thought" is a mere intraverbal or self-echoic linkage and scarcely to be distinguished from a "flight of ideas."

Thinking is more productive when verbal responses lead to specific consequences *and are reinforced because they do so.* Autistic behavior is a step in this direction. The verbal fantasy, whether overt or covert, is automatically reinforcing to the speaker as listener. Just as the musician plays or composes what he is reinforced by hearing, or as the artist paints what reinforces him visually, so the speaker engaged in verbal fantasy says what he is reinforced by hearing or writes what he is reinforced by reading. This is the realm of the verbal daydream and of much poetry, fiction, and other forms of literature. The writer composes

[2] Dashiell, J. F., *Fundamentals of Objective Psychology* (Boston, 1928).

verbal stimuli which arouse (in himself and, incidentally, in others) emotional or other kinds of responses, or serve as prompts or probes to permit him to behave verbally when he would otherwise remain silent for lack of energy or wit or because of punishing circumstances. The writer constitutes within himself an adequate community for the sustained production of literary behavior, and he may continue to write for a long time with no further contribution from the external community. The practices of the inner community often drift toward disturbing idiosyncrasies, however, as the work of such a poet as Emily Dickinson suggests.

Verbal Behavior Having Practical Effects Upon the Speaker As Listener

Aside from autistic or artistic behavior, verbal responses may be automatically reinforced by practical consequences. These may follow even when the speaker is his own listener. Although he cannot extend his own sensory or motor powers, many of the substantial mediating contingencies which generate and maintain verbal behavior continue in force.

A self-mand is not as useless as it may at first appear. A man may enjoin himself to get out of bed on a cold morning, to stop when he has made a mistake, or to be sure to remember an errand. These are not wholly magical mands. The verbal response comes first because it has less aversive consequences than the behavior manded. *Get up!*, for example, is easier to execute than getting out of bed and less likely to be followed by a cold shock. It may be strong by induction from instances in which we have induced other people to get up, and it may be effective if it increases the likelihood of our getting out of bed by induction from behavior with respect to other speakers. It might be supposed that self-mands supported only by induction would eventually suffer extinction as the two audiences are more sharply discriminated, but there are continuing sources of reinforcement. Let us suppose that a man is learning to hunt under circumstances in which it is advantageous to stand quite still (in order to let the quarry approach) in spite of a strong inclination to reduce the distance more quickly by advancing. An instructor generates the correct behavior by saying *Stand still!*, and the would-be hunter may achieve the same effect by manding his own behavior. He may have acquired the verbal response at an earlier date—perhaps from a book—or it may have been more readily learned on the spot as a briefer and more sharply defined response than "standing still." In any case the hunter who can tell himself *Stand still!* is probably at an advantage in controlling himself effectively in the field. The result may continue to reinforce verbal behavior in the form of self-mands.

The possibility that the speaker may respond to his own *verbal* stimuli in echoing himself or reading notes he has written has already been pointed out. He may also respond to his own intraverbal stimuli, as in opening a combination lock by following the directions he gives himself by reciting the combination as an intraverbal chain.

A man may usefully "speak to himself" or "write to himself" in the form of tacts. Thus, from some momentary point of vantage he may compose a text which he then responds to as a reader at a later date. Daybooks, diaries, memoranda, and similar devices bridge the temporal gap between behavior and controlling variables. The ultimate behavior may be verbal or nonverbal. The self-tact has an immediate effect in helping the speaker identify or clarify the situation to which it is a response. A confusing international situation falls into a standard pattern with the official declaration *This is war.* One's behavior with respect to a vaguely familiar person changes when his name can at least be recalled. Faced with an unfamiliar object in a hardware store, one can marshal appropriate behavior (and dismiss a possibly aversive state of puzzlement) if one can say, even tentatively, *It's a can-opener.* Categorizing responses are especially effective in this way. The zoologist hitting upon the proper classification of an unfamiliar insect, the young mother identifying the behavior of her child as an example of a pattern described by a psychologist, or the business man deciding that a chart shows that the time has come to buy a particular stock, all show substantial changes in behavior as a result of categorizing responses. *Nomina si nescis, perit et cognitio rerum.*

The automatic clarification produced by the tact is no doubt supported by self-instruction. The speaker's future behavior will be different, although the response is not necessarily emitted again. In thinking out a difficult problem, we may reaffirm certain key relationships or re-identify relevant facts, especially when these tend to be forgotten or obscured by other matters, even though the categorizing effect has already been felt. Thus, in solving a detective-story crime we may find ourselves insisting that a character is guilty in spite of a small but conclusive bit of evidence to the contrary. As we drift again and again toward the wrong conclusion, we may re-instruct ourselves: *No! No! It CAN'T be Billingsly. Billingsly was in the conservatory talking to the gardener.* We are not telling ourselves anything we did not know, but we are altering the *extent* to which we know it, and we make it less likely that we shall emit other responses placing Billingsly at the scene of the crime.

Although the speaker may find his own responses useful when they have the form of tacts, the special consequences which destroy the purity of the relation . . . are likely to be operative. Since automatic reinforcement need not respect the contingencies which prevail in the external verbal environment, controlling relations can be "stretched" at will, beginning perhaps with a slight exaggeration but leading eventually to fiction and lying. The verbal behavior of people who live alone and talk mostly to themselves often seems "queer" to the occasional external listener. The speaker, as his own audience, has come to control a special subdivision of his verbal repertoire, distorted by special effects. The public contingencies may need replenishment, although some automatic correction will occur if the intrusion of irrelevant consequences destroys eventual practical advantages.

The special characteristics of verbal behavior having multiple sources of strength prevail when the speaker is his own listener and provide other reasons for talking to oneself. Indeed, they may be especially marked because of the optimal correspondence in verbal strength between the speaker and listener in the same skin. The auto-clitics and the grammatical and syntactical ordering of verbal behavior in composition are imposed upon verbal behavior primarily for their effects upon the speaker himself, and the principal activity in editing may be specifically attributed to such efforts, particularly when they result from earlier punishment. The special conditions under which editing is at a minimum and verbal behavior therefore "released" may be ultimately reinforcing to the speaker and lead him to arrange or induce such conditions.

Another source of automatic reinforcement is seen in "problem solving," where the speaker generates stimuli to *supplement* other behavior already in his repertoire. He prompts and probes his own behavior, as in recalling a half-forgotten name or teasing out an effective classifying response. He may do this because he has been reinforced for similar behavior by other listeners, but automatic practical consequences may supply the necessary contingencies. Scientific behavior "pays off" even when the scientist is talking to himself. Thus, it is often automatically reinforcing to calculate the odds at poker rather than to play according to accidental reinforcements. It is often automatically reinforcing to count a number of objects rather than estimate them. It is automatically reinforcing to use a watch (a special kind of text) rather than trust to one's own "sense of time." It is automatically reinforcing to use special mnemonics or algorithms in the construction of new verbal behavior rather than trust to the miscellaneous intraverbals of the moment.

Verbal self-supplementation plays an important role in decision making. A man escapes from an aversive indecision by tossing a coin. Having set up the substitutability of *Go!* for *Heads* and *Stay!* for *Tails*, he constructs one or the other of these texts (by tossing the coin), reads it, makes the appropriate substitution, and responds to the resulting mand.

The Freudian dynamisms describe activities which are automatically reinforcing, usually because they permit one to avoid or escape from aversive consequences due to previous punishment. Many are verbal, and some almost necessarily so. "Rationalizing" is an example. Men are generally punished for hurting others but are permitted to hurt in special cases—for example, in punishing undesirable behavior or bringing bad news which cannot be concealed. The community distinguishes between two classes of rather similar behavior, punishing only one of them. As a result, when an emotional situation disposes a man to hurt someone, a member of the unpunished class of injurious responses is most likely to emerge. That is to say, men are more likely to punish or carry bad news to those whom they do not like. When the two classes of behavior are not easily distinguished, as is often the case, a man is less likely to be punished by the external community or to suffer the conditioned aversive stimulation of "guilt" if he can characterize his behavior as belonging in the unpunished class: *I spanked him "for his own good."*

Another sort of rationalization consists of characterizing an event as positively reinforcing when it is more likely to be aversive. We may suffer less from an unfortunate event by calling it a blessing in disguise. Boswell reports that Dr. Johnson was aware of the process:

> Sir, all the arguments which are brought to represent poverty as no evil, show it to be evidently a great evil. You never find people laboring to convince you that you may live very happily upon a plentiful fortune.

As these examples suggest, verbal behavior which is reinforced because it alters subsequent behavior in the speaker is often of ethical significance. The troublesome expressions *ought* and *should* can be interpreted as describing contingencies of reinforcement. When we say *The young man ought to have said "No,"* we assert that there were consequences of saying *No*, not further identified, which were reinforcing. Perhaps *No* would have saved him from aversive labor or injury. In the ethical case, where saying *No* is the "right" thing to do, the response might have prevented group censure or brought praise. When, then, a man tells himself *I ought to say "No,"* he is asserting that *No* would have certain reinforcing consequences (not further specified). His response differs from the self-mand *Say "No"* in the source of its power. The mand exploits an old paradigm of controlling relations which may ultimately lose its effectiveness, but the response containing *ought* identifies or clarifies a more lasting reinforcing contingency and may successfully increase its effect on the speaker. The vicar of society within the individual, the Freudian superego or the Judaeo-Christian conscience, is essentially verbal. It is the "still small *voice."*

A "resolution" is a sort of mand upon oneself which masquerades as a tact. *I am not going to smoke for the next three months* is not a response to a future event. Its value in self-control lies in the fact that it can be made now when appropriate contingencies, possibly involving aversive events, are powerful, whereas "not smoking for three months" requires three months for its execution, during which time the underlying deprivation or aversive stimulation may change. The resolution creates a set of conditions under which smoking is particularly punished (as "breaking a promise") either by the speaker himself or by others. The effect is greater if the resolution is publicly announced or, better, conspicuously posted during the period in which it is in force.

The following example of sustained self-stimulating verbal behavior exemplifies many of these points. It is a direct transcription of the responses a nine-year-old girl made to herself while practicing the piano. The behavior was overt, but of the sort which would have receded to the covert level with a little more punishment. The transcription begins after several minutes at the piano. A mistake is made. *No, wait!* (Plays correctly and reaches end of piece.) *Hah!* (Plays a few bars of a new piece.) *Let's see. Is that right? I'll do it once more.* (Finishes the piece.) *Ah, now I can study on something else.* (Looks at new piece.) *That's written in the key of G.* (Plays and sings words at same time. Finishes and looks at clock.) *That takes one minute. One minute to play that whole song.* (Starts another piece, and makes mistake.) *All right, now I'll start the whole thing over.* (Makes another mistake.) *I'll have to start all over again.* (Difficult piece. Emits a few *Gosh's.* Works on difficult passage. Presses finger on correct key.) *Oh, my finger, it hurts so much! But I'm going to MAKE it work!* (Forces finger against key again. Looks at finger.) *Hah! Makes beautiful designs on it.*

(Notices clock.) *Wowee! I've taken some of my other things' time.* (Looks at another piece.) *Aw, I can't do that!* (Notices clock.) *Just a minute.* (Takes up clock.) *I'm putting it back five minutes. There! Got a lot more time to practice.* (Plays, notices clock again.) *Hey! Don't! Don't do that. You're going too fast.* (Adjusts clock.) *Better. Five minutes.* (Plays and makes mistake.) *Aw*! (Looks at clock.) *Come ON!* (Adjusts clock. Calls out to father in next room.) *Daddy, I'm making this clock go slowly—I don't have time to practice. I turned it around an hour. I've got so much time to practice.*

In this example of "thinking aloud" mands like *No, wait, Just a minute*, and *Is that right?* accompany behavior of stopping and looking, which they may have some effect in strengthening. The resolutions *I'll do it once more* and *I'll have to start all over again* precede the behavior which they appear to describe. They may or may not strengthen it, but they clarify each act as an instance of "starting all over because of a mistake." The tact *That's written in the key of G* is probably helpful in strengthening appropriate nonverbal behavior. *My finger, it hurts so much* can scarcely be useful in the same way and seems to be a mere comment—emitted because of the special strength of the stimulus. The juxtaposition of *I'm putting it back five minutes* and *Got a lot more time to practice* may strengthen further behavior toward the clock. A similar pair of responses occur later, and turning the clock back an hour may be the result of the clarification of the connection between moving the clock and having more time to practice. The magical mand addressed to the clock *Don't do that! You're going too fast!* may also contribute to the behavior of turning the clock back. There is very little intraverbal chaining in the sample because it is intimately connected with concurrent nonverbal behavior. The chaining is from verbal to nonverbal and back again. The example is closer to productive verbal thinking for this reason.

There are good reasons, then, why a speaker also conditioned by the verbal community as a listener should turn his verbal behavior upon himself. The result is close to "thinking" in many traditional senses of the term. Such behavior can, of course, be subtle and swift, especially because the speaker is optimally prepared for his own speech as listener. But all the important properties of the behavior are to be found in verbal systems composed of separate speakers and listeners. A necessary connection between verbal thinking and self-stimulation might be said to arise from the fact that, in the strictest sense of our definition, any behavior which is reinforced because it modifies subsequent behavior in the same individual is necessarily verbal regardless of its dimensions. The reinforcement is "mediated by an organism," if not strictly another organism, and responses which do not have the usual dimensions of vocal, written, or gestured behavior may acquire some of the characteristics of verbal behavior. The refinement of the definition, however, permits us to maintain such a distinction as that between visual and verbal fantasy, for example, by excluding the former from the verbal category. In any case, although self-stimulating behavior may be in some sense necessarily verbal, verbal behavior need not be self-stimulating. When Plato asks, then, "Is not thought the same as speech with this exception: thought is the unuttered conversation of the soul with herself?", we must decline to allow the exception.

Thought as Verbal Behavior

Are we to be content with the rest of Plato's phrase: "thought is the same as speech?" Disregarding the distinction between overt and covert and the possibility that verbal behavior may be especially effective upon the speaker himself, are we to conclude that thinking is simply verbal behavior? Admittedly, this has been an appealing notion. "He gave man speech, and speech created thought, which is the measure of the Universe." [3] Some version of the doctrine has been actively propounded by behaviorists as a solution to the psychological problem of knowledge, and by logical positivists for their own epistemological purposes. Much earlier, in *The Diversions of Purley*,[4] John Horne Tooke attacked British empiricism in the same spirit:

> Perhaps it was for mankind a lucky mistake, for it was a mistake, which Mr. Locke made, when he called his book "An Essay on Human Understanding," for some part of the inestimable benefit of that book has, merely on account of its title, reached to many thousands more than, I fear, it would have done, had he called it (what it is merely) a *Grammatical* Essay, or a Treatise on *Words*, or on *Language*. . . .
>
> . . . . I only desire you to read the Essay over again with attention, and see whether all that its immortal author has justly concluded will not hold equally true and clear, if you substitute the composition [association]. &c. of terms, wherever he has supposed a composition [association], &c. of ideas.[5]

Tooke and others who have advocated this solution have been preoccupied with a kind of human behavior which, because it is verbal, possesses certain properties relevant to the problem of thinking. It is tempting to suppose that other peculiarly verbal properties will solve the problem as a whole. But this is evidently not the case. The results of thinking are often quite surprising and apparently impossible to explain. We can sympathize with the urge to find an explanation at the earliest possible moment and with the belief that the process will be found to have a touch of the mysterious or even miraculous. Covert behavior is an appealing modern substitute for thought processes because of its

[3] Shelley, Percy Bysshe, *Prometheus Unbound.*

[4] Tooke, John Horne, *The Diversions of Purley* (London, 1857).

[5] Compare also the following passage (written, as is most of the book, in the form of a dialogue):

"B—What difference then do you imagine it would have made in Mr. Locke's Essay, if he had sooner been aware of the inseparable connexion between words and knowledge; or, in the language of Sir Hugh, in Shakespear, that the lips is parcel of the *mind?*'

H—Much. And amongst many other things, I think he would not have talked of the *composition of ideas*; but would have seen that it was merely a contrivance of Language: and that the only composition was in *terms*; and consequently that it was as improper to speak of a *complex* idea, as it would be to call a constellation a complex star: And that they are not ideas, but merely terms, which are general and *abstract*. . . ."

difficult dimensions, and verbal behavior which is self-stimulating is also a promising candidate because of the fact that it *can* be private and that after a long period of working alone the thinker may emit astonishingly effective behavior. (It has always been easy for "thinkers" to claim special powers.)

Verbal behavior, quite apart from its covert or overt form or from the identity of the listener upon whom it is effective, also has some of the magic we expect to find in a thought process. It is relatively free of environmental conditions and temporal restrictions. Faced with a piece of music at the piano, we can react nonverbally to its being in the key of G (for example, by playing it correctly) but we cannot do this all at once. The verbal response *That's in the key of G* is quick and clear-cut, and it achieves an immediate result by clarifying the situation and heightening the probable effectiveness of the nonverbal behavior to follow. A unitary response to something which takes place over a period of time or in more than one place is almost necessarily verbal, and it seems to transcend great obstacles in achieving this result. When we solve a practical problem verbally, we construct a guide to a nonverbal solution; but before we have made use of it, we have found the *whole* solution at once in verbal form. Responses which are concerned with number illustrate the same point. If there is an act which is equivalent to, or identical with, "thinking of one hundred," it is the verbal response *one hundred.* Whether it is constructed by counting a hundred objects or in some other way (when it is under the control of other variables), it seems to transcend the awkward numerosity of one hundred things.

A verbal response makes it possible to "think about" *one* property of nature at a time. Since there is no practical response appropriate to all instances of red, the abstract tact *red* is an evidently unique verbal accomplishment. The response *fox* is abstract in this sense, in spite of the fact that it refers to an object which is usually called concrete, and our reaction to the fact that one has said *fox* may be nothing more than our own verbal response *fox*, particularly if we possess no useful practical behavior with respect to foxes. A piece of music may lead us to say *I think that's Mozart*, and there is little more to be done to the music of Mozart *as such.* Locke[6] himself was aware of this function of terms. "In mixed moods," he says, "it is the name that ties the combination together and makes it a species." Thus, without the term *triumphus* we might have had descriptions of what "passed in that solemnity: but yet, I think, that which holds those different parts together, in the unity of one complex idea, is that very word annexed to it; without which the several parts of that would no more be thought to make one thing, than any other show. . . ." For Locke, however, the term merely supported the idea for which it stood.

These are important and distinctive functions of verbal behavior, but they are nevertheless not relevant to a definition of thinking. Nor are certain other accidental reasons why this solution has been so often reached. Those who have looked at themselves thinking have frequently seen *verbal* behavior. Led by prevailing philosophies to search for inner thought processes, they have naturally

[6] Locke, John, *Essay on Human Understanding.*

been impressed by the convenience of execution of covert verbal behavior—as contrasted, say, with nonverbal parallels such as turning a cartwheel or driving a car "silently," which the coordination of movement normally involves the physical environment. Verbal behavior is also easy to see because it is relatively easy to describe. We can report *I said to myself "That's ridiculous"* much more readily than we can describe covert nonverbal behavior evoked under the same circumstances. A verbal conclusion "comes to one," or "is reached," in a relatively conspicuous way.

But not all covert behavior is verbal. Most people can turn some sort of elliptical cartwheel privately, and we discover that we are driving from the back seat when, in an emergency, we break into overt behavior and press our feet against the floor to stop the car. The layman's use of *I think* covers nonverbal behavior. *I think I shall be going* can be translated *I find myself going, I seem to be going*, or *I am on the point of going.* It would be awkward to interpret this by saying that the behavior of going gives rise to the verbal response *I am going* and that this is qualified by the response *I think.* Covert nonverbal behavior is described, as it is in the less committal *It occurs to me to go.* Nonverbal "ideas" and "thoughts" are common in descriptions of problem solving. In *The thought (or idea) occurred to me to try the door* the speaker is reporting the appearance of a nonverbal act.

Thought as Behavior

The simplest and most satisfactory view is that thought is simply *behavior*—verbal or nonverbal, covert or overt. It is not some mysterious process responsible for behavior but the very behavior itself in all the complexity of its controlling relations, with respect to both man the behaver and the environment in which he lives. The concepts and methods which have emerged from the analysis of behavior, verbal or otherwise, are most appropriate to the study of what has traditionally been called the human mind.

The field of human behavior can be conveniently subdivided with respect to the problems it presents and the corresponding terms and methods to be used. A useful distinction may be made between reflexes, conditioned or otherwise, and the operant behavior generated and maintained by the contingencies of reinforcement in a given environment. Tradition and expedience seem to agree in confining the analysis of human thought to operant behavior. So conceived, thought is not a mystical cause or precursor of action, or an inaccessible ritual, but action itself, subject to analysis with the concepts and techniques of the natural sciences, and ultimately to be accounted for in terms of controlling variables.

The emphasis upon controlling variables is important. A practical consequence is that such a scientific account implies a technology. There is no reason why methods of thinking and of the teaching of thinking cannot be analyzed and made more effective. But there is a more immediate theoretical issue. Nothing is gained by regarding thought as behavior in the sense of a mere *form* of action. We cannot move very far in the study of behavior apart from the circumstances under which it occurs. Bertrand Russell has tried to improve upon a merely formal analysis, but he has never been fully successful because the methods available to the logician are not appropriate to the study of behavior. Consider, for example, the following passage from *An Inquiry into Meaning and Truth:*[7]

> Thought, in so far as it is communicable, cannot have any greater complexity than is possessed by the various possible kinds of series to be made out of twenty-six kinds of shapes. Shakespeare's mind may have been very wonderful, but our evidence of its merits is wholly derived from black shapes on a white ground.

Russell might have gone a step further and reduced all of Shakespeare's "mind" to a series of dots and dashes, since the plays and poems could be sent or received in that form by a skilled telegraphist. It is true that evidence of the "merits of Shakespeare's mind" is derived from black shapes on a white ground, but it does not follow that thought, communicable or not, has no greater "complexity." Shakespeare's thought was his behavior *with respect to his extremely complex environment.* We do not, of course, have an adequate record of it in that sense. We have almost no independent information about the environment and cannot infer much about it from the works themselves. In discussing Shakespeare's thought, then, we merely guess at a plausible set of circumstances or deal with our own behavior in responding to the works. This is not very satisfactory, but we cannot improve the situation by identifying thought with mere form of behavior.[8]

An emphasis upon form obscures the significance of behavior in relation to controlling variables. It is obvious that two forms of response constitute very different "thoughts" if they are emitted under different circumstances. Moreover, some apparent instances of verbal behavior, satisfying all the formal criteria, may not be "thoughts" at all. Thus, accidental arrangements of anagrams or sentences constructed by the random manipulation of printed words are not records of verbal behavior, although they may be read as texts. It may serve some purpose in logic to say that "For any sentence, however long, we can construct a longer sentence by adding 'and the moon is round,' " but the resulting sentences could be accounted for in relation to trivial variables which do not warrant our calling them verbal. A similar neglect of the controlling relation is seen in Russell's remark "It is difficult to describe a statement without making it." Emitting a response having the form of a statement as an echoic response or hypostatical tact is not to be confused with emitting the same form of response under the kinds of circumstances which permit us to call it a statement.

This concern with form has left the study of the content of thought in an unsatisfactory state, but the "facts," "propositions," and other "referents of

[7] Russell, Bertrand, *An Inquiry into Meaning and Truth* (New York, 1940), p. 413.

[8] Molière carried the formalistic argument one step nearer the ridiculous. All that is most beautiful in literature, one of his characters argues, is to be found in the dictionaries. "It is only the words which are transposed."

statements" find an adequate representation among our controlling variables. The functional relations between behavior and the environment are usually complex and very often confusing, but we are not in doubt as to their dimensions or the techniques with which they may be studied. We can disregard the troublesome dissection of human thought into the familiar pattern of (1) a *man* possessing (2) *knowledge* of (3) a *world.* Men are part of the world, and they interact with other parts of it, including other men. As their behavior changes, they may interact more effectively, gaining control and power. Their "knowledge" is their behavior with respect to themselves and the rest of the world and can be studied as such.

The "effects of language on thought" must, of course, be restated. If it is "impossible to express a given idea" in a given language because a necessary term is lacking, we have only to say that the contingencies arranged by a given verbal community fail to respect a possible variable. If it is difficult "to express the same idea in two languages," we have merely to say that the reinforcing practices of two verbal communities differ. Any sort of behavior may be confusing and ineffective. The subtle contingencies of reinforcement arranged by a verbal community easily miscarry: a tact may be extended beyond warrant, an important autoclitic may be omitted, incompatible responses may result from faulty constructions. From the point of view of the listener, verbal behavior may fall far short of the nonverbal circumstances under which it arose; the thing itself may seem very different from the description of the thing. There is *indescribable* beauty in the sense in which there are colors which cannot be named in a given language. There are *ineffable* thoughts in the sense that contingencies in a nonverbal environment generate behavior which has no parallel among verbal responses. All behavior, verbal or otherwise, is subject to Kantian a priori's in the sense that man as a behaving system has inescapable characteristics and limitations.

When we study human thought, we study behavior. In the broadest possible sense, the thought of Julius Caesar was simply the sum total of his responses to the complex world in which he lived. We can study only those of which we have records. For obvious reasons, it is primarily his verbal behavior which has survived in recorded form, but from this and other records we know something about his nonverbal behavior. When we say that he "thought Brutus could be trusted," we do not necessarily mean that he ever said as much. He behaved, verbally and otherwise, as if Brutus could be trusted. The rest of his behavior, his plans and achievements, are also part of his thought in this sense.

It is a salutary consequence of this point of view to accept the fact that the thoughts of great men are inaccessible to us today. When we study great works, we study the effect *upon us* of surviving records of the behavior of men. It is *our* behavior with respect to such records which we observe; we study *our* thought, not theirs. Fortunately, the contemporary thinker can be subjected to a different kind of analysis. So far as a science of behavior is concerned, Man Thinking is simply Man Behaving.

There is nothing exclusively or essentially verbal in the material analyzed in this book. It is all part of a broader field—of the behavior of a most complex creature in contact with a world of endless variety. For practical purposes a special field has been set apart in terms of characteristics imparted to it by special controlling variables. It is in terms of these variables—of the contingencies arranged by the verbal community—that verbal behavior can be defined and analyzed.

The Body As Expression, and Speech

MAURICE MERLEAU-PONTY

WE HAVE seen in the body a unity distinct from that of the scientific object. We have just discovered, even in its 'sexual function,' intentionality and sense-giving powers. In trying to describe the phenomenon of speech and the specific act of meaning, we shall have the opportunity to leave behind us, once and for all, the traditional subject—object dichotomy.

The realization that speech is an originating realm naturally comes late. Here as everywhere, the relation of *having*, which can be seen in the very etymology of the word habit, is at first concealed by relations belonging to the domain of *being*, or, as we may equally say, by ontic relations obtaining within the world.[1] The possession of language is in the first place understood as no more than the actual existence of 'verbal images,' or traces left in us by words spoken or heard. Whether these traces are physical, or whether they are imprinted on an 'unconscious psychic life,' is of little importance, and in both cases the conception of language is the same in that there is no 'speaking subject.' Whether the stimuli, in accordance with the laws of neurological mechanics, touch off excitations capable of bringing about the articulation of the word, or whether the states of consciousness cause, by virtue of acquired associations, the appearance of the appropriate verbal image, in both cases speech occurs, in a circuit of third person phenomena. There is no speaker, there is a flow of words set in motion independently of any intention to speak. The meaning of words is considered to be given with the stimuli or with the states of consciousness

[1] This distinction of having and being does not coincide with M. G. Marcel's (*Être et Avoir*), although not incompatible with it. M. Marcel takes having in the weak sense which the word has when it designates a proprietary relationship (I have a house, I have a hat) and immediately takes being in the existential sense of belonging to . . ., or taking up (I am my body, I am my life). We prefer to take account of the usage which gives to the term 'being' the weak sense of existence as a thing, or that of predication (the table is, or is big), and which reserves 'having' for the relation which the subject bears to the term into which it projects itself (I have an idea, I have a desire, I have fears). Hence our 'having' corresponds roughly to M. Marcel's being, and our being to his 'having'.

Reprinted with permission of Humanities Press, Inc., New Jersey and Routledge and Kegan Paul Ltd. from "The Body as Expression, and Speech" by Maurice Merleau-Ponty in *Phenomenology of Perception,* Colin Smith, trans., 1962, pp. 174–190.

which it is simply a matter of naming; the shape of the word, as heard or phonetically formed, is given with the cerebral or mental tracks; speech is not an action and does not show up the internal possibilities of the subject: man can speak as the electric lamp can become incandescent. Since there are electric disturbances which attack the spoken language to the exclusion of the written one, or *vice versa*, and since language can disintegrate into fragments, we have to conclude that it is built up by a set of independent contributions, and that speech in the general sense is an entity of rational origin.

The theory of aphasia and of language seemed to be undergoing complete transformation when it became necessary to distinguish from anarthria,* which affects the articulation of the word, true aphasia which is inseparable from disturbances affecting intelligence—and from automatic language, which is in effect a third person motor phenomenon, an intentional language which is alone relevant to the majority of cases of aphasia. The individuality of the 'verbal image' was, indeed, dissociated: what the patient has lost, and what the normal person possesses, is not a certain stock of words, but a certain way of using them. The same word which remains at the disposal of the patient in the context of automatic languages escapes him in that of language unrelated to a purpose—the patient who has no difficulty in finding the word 'no' in answer to the doctor's questions, that is when he intends to furnish a denial arising from his present experience, cannot do so when it is a question of an exercise having no emotional and vital bearing. There is thus revealed, underlying the word, an attitude, a function of speech which condition it. The word could be identified as an instrument of action and as a means of disinterested designation. Though 'concrete' language remained a third person process, gratuitous language, or authentic denomination, became a phenomenon of thought, and it is in some disturbance of thinking that the origin of certain forms of aphasia must be sought. For example, amnesia concerning names of colours, when related to the general behaviour of the patient, appeared as a special manifestation of a more general trouble. The same patients who cannot name colours set before them, are equally incapable of classifying them in the performance of a set task. If, for example, they are asked to sort out samples according to basic colour, it is immediately noticed that they do it more slowly and painstakingly than a normal subject: they slowly place together the samples to be compared and fail to see at a glance which ones 'go together.' Moreover, having correctly assembled several blue ribbons, they make unaccountable mistakes: if for example the last blue ribbon was of a pale shade, they carry on by adding to the collection of 'blues' a pale green or pale pink—as if it were beyond them to stick to the proposed principle of classification, and to consider the samples from the point of view of basic colour from start to finish of the operation. They have thus become unable to subsume sense-data under a category, to see immediately the samples as representatives of the *eidos* blue. Even when, at the beginning of the test, they proceed correctly, it is not the conformity of the samples to an

* *Anarthria:* loss of power of articulate speech (Translator's note).

idea which guides them, but the experience of an immediate resemblance, and hence it comes about that they can classify the samples only when they have placed them side by side. The sorting test brings to light in these subjects a fundamental disorder, of which forgetting names of colours is simply another manifestation. For to name a thing is to tear oneself away from its individual and unique characteristics to see it as representative of an essence or a category, and the fact that the patient cannot identify the samples is a sign, not that he has lost the verbal image of the words red or blue, but that he has lost the general ability to subsume a sense-datum under a category, that he has lapsed back from the categorical to the concrete attitude.[2] These analyses and other similar ones lead us, it would seem, to the antithesis of the theory of the verbal image, since language now appears as conditioned by thought.

In fact we shall once again see that there is a kinship between the empiricist or mechanistic psychologies and the intellectualist ones, and the problem of language is not solved by going from one extreme to the other. A short time ago the reproduction of the word, the revival of the verbal image, was the essential thing. Now it is no more than what envelops true denomination and authentic speech, which is an inner process. And yet these two conceptions are at one in holding that the word *has* no significance. In the first case this is obvious since the word is not summoned up through the medium of any concept, and since the given stimuli or 'states of mind' call it up in accordance with the laws of neurological mechanics of those of association, and that thus the word is not the bearer of its own meaning, has no inner power, and is merely a psychic, physiological or even physical phenomenon set alongside others, and thrown up by the working of an objective causality. It is just the same when we duplicate denomination with a categorial operation. The word is still bereft of any effectiveness of its own, this time because it is only the external sign of an internal recognition, which could take place without it, and to which it makes no contribution. It is not without meaning, since behind it there is a categorial operation, but this meaning is something which it does not *have*, does not possess, since it is thought which has a meaning, the word remaining an empty container. It is merely a phenomenon of articulation, of sound, or the consciousness of such a phenomenon, but in any case language is but an external accompaniment of thought. In the first case, we are on this side of the word as meaningful; in the second we are beyond it. In the first there is nobody to speak; in the second, there is certainly a subject, but a thinking one, not a speaking one. As far as speech itself is concerned, intellectualism is hardly any different from empiricism, and is no better able than the latter to dispense with an explanation in terms of involuntary action. Once the categorial operation is performed, the appearance of the word which completes the process still has to be explained, and this will still be done by recourse to a physiological or psychic mechanism, since the word is a passive shell. Thus we refute both intellectualism and empiricism by simply saying that *the word has a meaning.*

2 Gelb and Goldstein, *Über Farbennamenamnesie.*

If speech presupposed thought, if talking were primarily a matter of meeting the object through a cognitive intention or through a representation, we could not understand why thought tends towards expression as towards its completion, why the most familiar thing appears indeterminate as long as we have not recalled its name, why the thinking subject himself is in a kind of ignorance of his thoughts so long as he has not formulated them for himself, or even spoken and written them, as is shown by the example of so many writers who begin a book without knowing exactly what they are going to put into it. A thought limited to existing for itself, independently of the constraints of speech and communication, would no sooner appear than it would sink into the unconscious, which means that it would not exist even for itself. To Kant's celebrated question, we can reply that it is indeed part of the experience of thinking, in the sense that we present our thought to ourselves through internal or external speech. It does indeed move forward with the instant and, as it were, in flashes, but we are then left to lay hands on it, and it is through expression that we make it our own. The denomination of objects does not follow upon recognition; it is itself recognition. When I fix my eyes on an object in the half-light, and say: 'It is a brush,' there is not in my mind the concept of a brush, under which I subsume the object, and which moreover is linked by frequent association with the word 'brush,' but the word bears the meaning, and, by imposing it on the object, I am conscious of reaching that object. As has often been said,[3] for the child the thing is not known until it is named, the name is the essence of the thing and resides in it on the same footing as its colour and its form. For pre-scientific thinking, naming an object is causing it to exist or changing it: God creates beings by naming them and magic operates upon them by speaking of them. These 'mistakes' would be unexplainable if speech rested on the concept, for the latter ought always to know itself as distinct from the former, and to know the former as an external accompaniment. If it is pointed out in reply that the child learns to know objects through the designations of language, that thus, given in the first place as linguistic entities, objects receive only secondarily their natural existence, and that finally the actual existence of a linguistic community accounts for childish beliefs, this explanation leaves the problem untouched, since, if the child can know himself as a member of a linguistic community before knowing himself as thinking about some Nature, it is conditional upon the subject's being able to overlook himself as universal thought and apprehend himself as speech, and on the fact that the word, far from being the mere sign of objects and meanings, inhabits things and is the vehicle of meanings. Thus speech, in the speaker, does not translate ready-made thought, but accomplishes it.[4] *A fortiori* must it be recognized that the listener receives thought from speech itself. At first sight, it might appear that speech heard can bring him nothing: it is he who gives to words and sentences their meaning, and the very

[3] E.g. Piaget, *La Représentation du Monde chez l'Enfant*, pp. 60 and ff.

[4] There is, of course, every reason to distinguish between an authentic speech, which formulates for the first time, and second-order expression, speech about speech, which makes up the general run of empirical language. Only the first is identical with thought.

combination of words and sentences is not an alien import, since it would not be understood if it did not encounter in the listener the ability spontaneously to effect it. Here, as everywhere, it seems at first sight true that consciousness can find in its experience only what it has itself put there. Thus the experience of communication would appear to be an illusion. A consciousness constructs—for *x*—that linguistic mechanism which will provide another consciousness with the chance of having the same thoughts, but nothing really passes between them. Yet, the problem being how, to all appearances, consciousness learns something, the solution cannot consist in saying that it knows everything in advance. The fact is that we have the power to understand over and above what we may have spontaneously thought. People can speak to us only a language which we already understand, each word of a difficult text awakens in us thoughts which were ours beforehand, but these meanings sometimes combine to form new thought which recasts them all, and we are transported to the heart of the matter, we find the source. Here there is nothing comparable to the solution of a problem, where we discover an unknown quantity through its relationship with known ones. For the problem can be solved only if it is determinate, that is, if the cross-checking of the data provides the unknown quantity with one or more definite values. In understanding others, the problem is always indeterminate[5] because only the solution will bring the data retrospectively to light as convergent, only the central theme of a philosophy, once understood, endows the philosopher's writings with the value of adequate signs. There is, then, a taking up of others' thought through speech, a reflection in others, an ability to think *according to others*[6] which enriches our own thoughts. Here the meaning of words must be finally induced by the words themselves, or more exactly, their conceptual meaning must be formed by a kind of deduction from a *gestural meaning*, which is immanent in speech. And as, in a foreign country, I begin to understand the meaning of words through their place in a context of action, and by taking part in a communal life—in the same way an as yet imperfectly understood piece of philosophical writing discloses to me at least a certain 'style'—either a Spinozist, criticist or phenomenological one—which is the first draft of its meaning. I begin to understand a philosophy by feeling my way into its existential manner, by reproducing the tone and accent of the philosopher. In fact, every language conveys its own teaching and carries its meaning into the listener's mind. A school of music or painting which is at first not understood, eventually, by its own action, creates its own public, if it really *says* something; that is, it does so by secreting its own meaning. In the case of prose or poetry, the power of the spoken word is less obvious, because we have the illusion of already possessing within ourselves, in the shape of the common property meaning of words, what is required for the understanding of any text whatsoever. The obvious fact is, however, that the colours of the palette or the

5 Again, what we say here applies only to first-hand speech—that of the child uttering its first word, of the lover revealing his feelings, of the 'first man who spoke', or of the writer and philosopher who reawaken primordial experience anterior to all traditions.

6 *Nachdenken, nachvollziehen* of Husserl, *Ursprung der Geometrie*, pp. 212 and ff.

crude sounds of instruments, as presented to us in natural perception, are insufficient to provide the musical sense of music, or the pictorial sense of a painting. But, in fact, it is less the case that the sense of a literary work is provided by the common property meaning of words, than that it contributes to changing that accepted meaning. There is thus, either in the man who listens or reads, or in the one who speaks or writes, a *thought in speech* the existence of which is unsuspected by intellectualism.

To realize this, we must turn back to the phenomenon of speech and reconsider ordinary descriptions which immobilize thought and speech, and make anything other than external relations between them inconceivable. We must recognize first of all that thought, in the speaking subject, is not a representation, that is, that it does not expressly posit objects or relations. The orator does not think before speaking, nor even while speaking; his speech is his thought. In the same way the listener does not form concepts on the basis of signs. The orator's 'thought' is empty while he is speaking and, when a text is read to us, provided that it is read with expression, we have no thought marginal to the text itself, for the words fully occupy our mind and exactly fulfil our expectations, and we feel the necessity of the speech. Although we are unable to predict its course, we are possessed by it. The end of the speech or text will be the lifting of a spell. It is at this stage that thoughts on the speech or text will be able to arise. Previously the speech was improvised and the text understood without the intervention of a single thought; the sense was everywhere present, and nowhere posited for its own sake. The speaking subject does not think of the sense of what he is saying, nor does he visualize the words which he is using. To know a word or a language is, as we have said, not to be able to bring into play any pre-established nervous network. But neither is it to retain some 'pure recollection' of the word, some faded perception. The Bergsonian dualism of habit-memory and pure recollection does not account for the near-presence of the words I know: they are behind me, like things behind my back, or like the city's horizon round my house, I reckon with them or rely on them, but without having any 'verbal image.' In so far as they persist within me, it is rather as does the Freudian Imago which is much less the representation of a former perception than a highly specific emotional essence, which is yet generalized, and detached from its empirical origins. What remains to me of the word once learnt is its style as constituted by its formation and sound. What we have said earlier about the 'representation of movement' must be repeated concerning the verbal image: I do not need to visualize external space and my own body in order to move one within the other. It is enough that they exist for me, and that they form a certain field of action spread around me. In the same way I do not need to visualize the word in order to know and pronounce it. It is enough that I possess its articulatory and acoustic style as one of the modulations, one of the possible uses of my body. I reach back for the word as my hand reaches towards the part of my body which is being pricked; the word has a certain location in my linguistic world, and is part of my equipment. I have only one means of representing it, which is uttering it, just as the artist has only one means of representing the work on which he is engaged: by doing it. When I imagine Peter absent, I am not aware of contemplating an image of Peter numerically distinct from Peter himself. However far away he is, I visualize him in the world, and my power of imagining is nothing but the persistence of my world around me.[7] To say that I imagine Peter is to say that I bring about the pseudo-presence of Peter by putting into operation the 'Peter-behaviour-pattern.' Just as Peter in imagination is only one of the modalities of my being in the world, so the verbal image is only one of the modalities of my phonetic gesticulation, presented with many others in the all-embracing consciousness of my body. This is obviously what Bergson means when he talks about a 'motor framework' of recollection, but if pure representations of the past take their place in this framework, it is not clear why they should need it to become actual once more. The part played by the body in memory is comprehensible only if memory is, not only the constituting consciousness of the past, but an effort to reopen time on the basis of the implications contained in the present, and if the body, as our permanent means of 'taking up attitudes' and thus constructing pseudo-presents, is the medium of our communication with time as well as with space.[8] The body's function in remembering is that same function of projection which we have already met in starting to move: the body converts a certain motor essence into vocal form, spreads out the articulatory style of a word into audible phenomena, and arrays the former attitude, which is resumed, into the panorama of the past, projecting an intention to move into actual movement, because the body is a power of natural expression.

These considerations enable us to restore to the act of speaking its true physiognomy. In the first place speech is not the 'sign' of thought, if by this we understand a phenomenon which heralds another as smoke betrays fire. Speech and thought would admit of this external relation only if they were both thematically given, whereas in fact they are intervolved, the sense being held within the word, and the word being the external existence of the sense. Nor can we con-

7 Sartre, *L'Imagination*, p. 148.

8 '. . . when I awoke like this, and my mind struggled in an unsuccessful attempt to discover where I was, everything would be moving round me through the darkness, things, places, years. My body, still too heavy with sleep to move, would make an effort to construe the form which its tiredness took as an orientation of its various members, so as to induce from that where the wall lay and the furniture stood, to piece together and to give a name to the house in which it must be living. Its memory, the composite memory of its ribs, knees, and shoulder-blades offered it a whole series of rooms in which it had at one time or another slept; while the unseen walls kept changing, adapting themselves to the shape of each successive room that it remembered, whirling madly through the darkness. . . . My body, the side upon which I was lying, loyally preserving from the past an impression which my mind should never have forgotten, brought back before my eyes the glimmering flame of the night-light in its bowl of Bohemian glass, shaped like an urn and hung by chains from the ceiling, and the chimney-piece of Sienna marble in my bedroom at Combray, in my great-aunt's house, in those far-distant days which, at the moment of waking, seemed present without being clearly defined.' (Proust, *Swann's Way*, I, trans. C. K. Scott Moncrieff, Chatto and Windus, pp. 5–6.)

cede, as is commonly done, that speech is a mere means of fixation, nor yet that it is the envelope and clothing of thought. Why should it be easier to recall words or phrases than thoughts, if the alleged verbal images need to be reconstructed on every occasion? And why should thought seek to duplicate itself or clothe itself in a succession of utterances, if the latter do not carry and contain within themselves their own meaning? Words cannot be 'strongholds of thought,' nor can thought seek expression, unless words are in themselves a comprehensible text, and unless speech possesses a power of significance entirely its own. The word and speech must somehow cease to be a way of designating things or thoughts, and become the presence of that thought in the phenomenal world, and, moreover, not its clothing but its token or its body. There must be, as psychologists say, a 'linguistic concept' (*Sprachbegriff*)[9] or a word concept (*Wortbegriff*), a 'central inner experience, specifically verbal, thanks to which the sound, heard, uttered, read or written, becomes a linguistic fact.'[10] Certain patients can read a text, 'putting expression into it,' without, however, understanding it. This is because the spoken or written words carry a top coating of meaning which sticks to them and which presents the thought as a style, an affective value, a piece of existential mimicry, rather than as a conceptual statement. We find here, beneath the conceptual meaning of the words, an existential meaning which is not only rendered by them, but which inhabits them, and is inseparable from them. The greatest service done by expression is not to commit to writing ideas which might be lost. A writer hardly ever re-reads his own works, and great works leave in us at a first reading all that we shall ever subsequently get out of them. The process of expression, when it is successful, does not merely leave for the reader and the writer himself a kind of reminder, it brings the meaning into existence as a thing at the very heart of the text, it brings it to life in an organism of words, establishing it in the writer or the reader as a new sense organ, opening a new field or a new dimension to our experience. This power of expression is well known in the arts, for example in music. The musical meaning of a sonata is inseparable from the sounds which are its vehicle: before we have heard it no analysis enables us to anticipate it; once the performance is over, we shall, in our intellectual analyses of the music, be unable to do anything but carry ourselves back to the moment of experiencing it. During the performance, the notes are not only the 'signs' of the sonata, but it is there through them, it enters into them.[11] In the same way the actress becomes invisible, and it is Phaedra who appears. The meaning swallows up the signs, and Phaedra has so completely taken possession of Berma that her passion as Phaedra appears the apotheosis of ease and naturalness.[12] Aesthetic expression confers on what it expresses an existence in itself, installs it in nature as a thing

[9] Cassirer, *Philosophie der symbolischen Formen*, III, p. 383.

[10] Goldstein, *L'Analyse de l'aphasie et l'essence du language*, p. 459.

[11] Proust, *Swann's Way*, II, trans. C. K. Scott Moncrieff, p. 185.

[12] Proust, *The Guermantes Way*, I, pp. 55 and ff.

perceived and accessible to all, or conversely plucks the signs themselves—the person of the actor, or the colours and canvas of the painter—from their empirical existence and bears them off into another world. No one will deny that here the process of expression brings the meaning into being or makes it effective, and does not merely translate it. It is no different, despite what may appear to be the case, with the expression of thoughts in speech. Thought is no 'internal' thing, and does not exist independently of the world and of words. What misleads us in this connection, and causes us to believe in a thought which exists for itself prior to expression, is thought already constituted and expressed, which we can silently recall to ourselves, and through which we acquire the illusion of an inner life. But in reality this supposed silence is alive with words, this inner life is an inner language. 'Pure' thought reduces itself to a certain void of consciousness, to a momentary desire. The new sense-giving intention knows itself only by donning already available meanings, the outcome of previous acts of expression. The available meanings suddenly link up in accordance with an unknown law, and once and for all a fresh cultural entity has taken on an existence. Thought and expression, then, are simultaneously constituted, when our cultural store is put at the service of this unknown law, as our body suddenly lends itself to some new gesture in the formation of habit. The spoken word is a genuine gesture, and it contains its meaning in the same way as the gesture contains its. This is what makes communication possible. In order that I may understand the words of another person, it is clear that his vocabulary and syntax must be 'already known' to me. But that does not mean that words do their work by arousing in me 'representations' associated with them, and which in aggregate eventually reproduce in me the original 'representation' of the speaker. What I communicate with primarily is not 'representations' or thought, but a speaking subject, with a certain style of being and with the 'world' at which he directs his aim. Just as the sense-giving intention which has set in motion the other person's speech is not an explicit thought, but a certain lack which is asking to be made good, so my taking up of this intention is not a process of thinking on my part, but a synchronizing change of my own existence, a transformation of my being. We live in a world where speech is an *institution.* For all these many commonplace utterances, we possess within ourselves ready-made meanings. They arouse in us only second order thoughts; these in turn are translated into other words which demand from us no real effort or expression and will demand from our hearers no effort of comprehension. Thus language and the understanding of language apparently raise no problems. The linguistic and intersubjective world no longer surprises us, we no longer distinguish it from the world itself, and it is within a world already spoken and speaking that we think. We become unaware of the contingent element in expression and communication, whether it be in the child learning to speak, or in the writer saying and thinking something for the first time, in short, in all who transform a certain kind of silence into speech. It is, however, quite clear that constituted speech, as it operates in daily life, assumes that the decisive step of expression has been taken. Our view of man will remain superficial so long as we fail to go back to that origin, so long as we fail to find, beneath the chatter of words, the primordial silence, and as long as we do not describe the action which breaks this silence. The spoken word is a gesture, and its meaning, a world.

Modern psychology[13] has demonstrated that the spectator does not look within himself into his personal experience for the meaning of the gestures which he is witnessing. Faced with an angry or threatening gesture, I have no need, in order to understand it, to recall the feelings which I myself experienced when I used these gestures on my own account. I am not well able to visualize, in my mind's eye, the outward signs of anger, so that a decisive factor is missing for any association by resemblance or reasoning by analogy, and what is more, I do not see anger or a threatening attitude as a psychic fact hidden behind the gesture, I read anger into it. The gesture *does not make me think* of anger, it is anger itself. However, the meaning of the gesture is not perceived as the colour of the carpet, for example, is perceived. If it were given to me as a thing, it is not clear why my understanding of gestures should for the most part be confined to human ones. I do not 'understand' the sexual pantomime of the dog, still less of the cockchafer or the praying mantis. I do not even understand the expression of the emotions in primitive people or in circles too unlike the ones in which I move. If a child happens to witness sexual intercourse, it may understand it although it has no experience of desire and of the bodily attitudes which translate it. The sexual scene will be merely an unfamiliar and disturbing spectacle, without meaning unless the child has reached the stage of sexual maturity at which this behaviour becomes possible for it. It is true that often knowledge of other people lights up the way to self-knowledge: the spectacle outside him reveals to the child the meaning of its own impulses, by providing them with an aim. The example would pass unnoticed if it did not coincide with the inner possibilities of the child. The sense of the gestures is not given, but understood, that is, seized upon by an act on the spectator's part. The whole difficulty is to conceive this act clearly without confusing it with a cognitive operation. The communication or comprehension of gestures comes about through the reciprocity of my intentions and the gestures of others, of my gestures and intentions discernible in the conduct of other people. It is as if the other person's intention inhabited my body and mine his. The gesture which I witness outlines an intentional object. This object is genuinely present and fully comprehended when the powers of my body adjust themselves to it and overlap it. The gesture presents itself to me as a question, bringing certain perceptible bits of the world to my notice, and inviting my concurrence in them. Communication is achieved when my conduct identifies this path with its own. There is mutual confirmation between myself and others. Here we must rehabilitate the experience of others which has been distorted by intellectualist analyses, as we shall have to re-

[13] For example, M. Scheler, *Nature et Formes de la Sympathie*, pp. 347 and ff.

habilitate the perceptual experience of the thing. When I perceive a thing, a fireplace for example, it is not the concordance of its various aspects which leads me to believe in the existence of the fireplace as the flat projection and collective significance of all these perspectives. On the contrary I perceive the thing in its own self-evident completeness and this is what gives me the assurance that, in the course of perceptual experience, I shall be presented with an indefinite set of concordant views. The identity of the thing through perceptual experience is only another aspect of the identity of one's own body throughout exploratory movements; thus they are the same kind as each other. Like the body image, the fireplace is a system of equivalents not founded on the recognition of some law, but on the experience of a bodily presence. I become involved in things with my body, they co-exist with me as an incarnate subject, and this life among things has nothing in common with the elaboration of scientifically conceived objects. In the same way, I do not understand the gestures of others by some act of intellectual interpretation; communication between consciousnesses is not based on the common meaning of their respective experiences, for it is equally the basis of that meaning. The act by which I lend myself to the spectacle must be recognized as irreducible to anything else. I join it in a kind of blind recognition which precedes the intellectual working out and clarification of the meaning. Successive generations 'understand' and perform sexual gestures, such as the caress, before the philosopher[14] makes its intellectual significance clear, which is that we lock within itself a passive body, enwrap it in a pleasurable lethargy, thus imposing a temporary respite upon the continual drive which projects it into things and towards others. It is through my body that I understand other people, just as it is through my body that I perceive 'things.' The meaning of a gesture thus 'understood' is not behind it, it is intermingled with the structure of the world outlined by the gesture, and which I take up on my own account. It is arrayed all over the gesture itself—as, in perceptual experience, the significance of the fireplace does not lie beyond the perceptible spectacle, namely the fireplace itself as my eyes and movements discover it in the world.

The linguistic gesture, like all the rest, delineates its own meaning. This idea seems surprising at first, yet one is forced to accept it if one wishes to understand the origin of language, always an insistent problem, although psychologists and linguistics both question its validity in the name of positive knowledge. It seems in the first place impossible to concede to either words or gestures an immanent meaning, because the gesture is limited to showing a certain relationship between man and the perceptible world, because this world is presented to the spectator by natural perception, and because in this way the intentional object is offered to the spectator at the same time as the gesture itself. Verbal 'gesticulation,' on the other hand, aims at a mental setting which is not given to everybody, and which it is its task to communicate. But here what nature does not provide, cultural background does. Available meanings, in other words former

[14] Here J. P. Sartre, *L'Être et le Néant*, pp. 453, and ff.

acts of expression, establish between speaking subjects a common world, to which the words being actually uttered in their novelty refer as does the gesture to the perceptible world. And the meaning of speech is nothing other than the way in which it handles this linguistic world or in which it plays modulations on the keyboard of acquired meanings. I seize it in an undivided act which is as short as a cry. It is true that the problem has been merely shifted one stage further back: how did the available meanings themselves come to be constituted? Once language is formed, it is conceivable that speech may have meaning, like the gesture, against the mental background held in common. But do syntactical forms and vocabulary, which are here presupposed, carry their meaning within themselves? One can see what there is in common between the gesture and its meaning, for example in the case of emotional expression and the emotions themselves: the smile, the relaxed face, gaiety of gesture really have in them the rhythm of action, the mode of being in the world which are joy itself. On the other hand, is not the link between the word sign and its meaning quite accidental, a fact demonstrated by the existence of a number of languages? And was not the communication of the elements of language between the 'first man to speak' and the second necessarily of an entirely different kind from communication through gesture? This is what is commonly expressed by saying that gesture or emotional pantomime are 'natural signs,' and the word a 'natural convention.' But conventions are a late form of relationship between men; they presuppose an earlier means of communication, and language must be put back into this current of intercourse. If we consider only the conceptual and delimiting meaning of words, it is true that the verbal form—with the exception of endings—appears arbitrary. But it would no longer appear so if we took into account the emotional content of the word, which we have called above its 'gestural' sense, which is all-important in poetry, for example. It would then be found that the words, vowels and phonemes are so many ways of 'singing' the world, and that their function is to represent things not, as the naïve onomatopoeic theory had it, by reason of an objective resemblance, but because they extract, and literally express, their emotional essence. If it were possible, in any vocabulary, to disregard what is attributable to the mechanical laws of phonetics, to the influences of other languages, the rationalization of grammarians, and assimilatory processes, we should probably discover in the original form of each language a somewhat restricted system of expression, but such as would make it not entirely arbitrary, if we designate night by the word 'nuit,' to use 'lumière' for light. The predominance of vowels in one language, or of consonants in another, and constructional and syntactical systems, do not represent so many arbitrary conventions for the expression of one and the same idea, but several ways for the human body to sing the world's praises and in the last resort to live it. Hence the *full* meaning of a language is never translatable into another. We may speak several languages, but one of them always remains the one in which we live. In order completely to assimilate a language, it would be necessary to make the world which it expresses one's own, and one never does belong to two worlds at once.[15] If there is such a thing as universal thought, it is achieved by taking up the effort towards expression and communication in *one* single language, and accepting all its ambiguities, all the suggestions and overtones of meaning of which a linguistic tradition is made up, and which are the exact measure of its power of expression. A conventional algorism—which moreover is meaningful only in relation to language—will never express anything but nature without man. Strictly speaking, therefore, there are no conventional signs, standing as the simple notation of a thought pure and clear in itself, there are only words into which the history of a whole language is compressed, and which effect communication with no absolute guarantee, dogged as they are by incredible linguistic hazards. We think that language is more transparent than music because most of the time we remain within the bounds of constituted language, we provide ourselves with available meanings, and in our definitions we are content, like the dictionary, to explain meanings in terms of each other. The meaning of a sentence appears intelligible throughout, detachable from the sentence and finitely self-subsistent in an intelligible world, because we presuppose as given all those exchanges, owed to the history of the language, which contribute to determining its sense. In music, on the other hand, no vocabulary is presupposed, the meaning appears as linked to the empirical presence of the sounds, and that is why music strikes us as dumb. But in fact, as we have said, the clearness of language stands out from an obscure background, and if we carry our research far enough we shall eventually find that language is equally uncommunicative of anything other than itself, that its meaning is inseparable from it. We need, then, to seek the first attempts at language in the emotional gesticulation whereby man superimposes on the given world the world according to man. There is here nothing resembling the famous naturalistic conceptions which equate the artificial sign with the natural one, and try to reduce language to emotional expression. The artificial sign is not reducible to the natural one, because in man there is no natural sign, and in assimilating language to emotional expressions, we leave untouched its specific quality, if it is true that emotion, viewed as a variation of our being in the world, is contingent in relation to the mechanical resources contained in our body, and shows the same power of giving shape to stimuli and situations which is at its most striking

15 'In my case, the effort for these years to live in the dress of Arabs, and to imitate their mental foundation, quitted me of my English self, and let me look at the West and its conventions with new eyes: they destroyed it all for me. At the same time I could not sincerely take on the Arab skin: it was an affectation only. Easily was a man made an infidel, but hardly might he be converted to another faith. I had dropped one form and not taken on the other, and was become like Mohammed's coffin in our legend. . . . Such detachment came at times to a man exhausted by prolonged physical effort and isolation. His body plodded on mechanically, while his reasonable mind left him, and from without looked down critically on him, wondering what futile lumber did and why. Sometimes these selves would converse in the void; and then madness was very near, as I believe it would be near the man who could see things through the veils at once of two customs, two educations, two environments.' T. E. Lawrence, *The Seven Pillars of Wisdom*, Jonathan Cape, pp. 31–2.

at the level of language. It would be legitimate to speak of 'natural signs' only if the anatomical organization of our body produced a correspondence between specific gestures and given 'states of mind.' The fact is that the behaviour associated with anger or love is not the same in a Japanese and an Occidental. Or, to be more precise, the difference of behaviour corresponds to a difference in the emotions themselves. It is not only the gesture which is contingent in relation to the body's organization, it is the manner itself in which we meet the situation and live it. The angry Japanese smiles, the westerner goes red and stamps his foot or else goes pale and hisses his words. It is not enough for two conscious subjects to have the same organs and nervous system for the same emotions to produce in both the same signs. What is important is how they use their bodies, the simultaneous patterning of body and world in emotion. The psychophysiological equipment leaves a great variety of possibilities open, and there is no more here than in the realm of instinct a human nature finally and immutably given. The use a man is to make of his body is transcendent in relation to that body as a mere biological entity. It is no more natural, and no less conventional, to shout in anger or to kiss in love[16] than to call a table 'a table.' Feelings and passional conduct are invented like words. Even those which, like paternity, seem to be part and parcel of the human make-up are in reality institutions.[17] It is impossible to superimpose on man a lower layer of behaviour which one chooses to call 'natural,' followed by a manufactured cultural or spiritual world. Everything is both manufactured and natural in man, as it were, in the sense that there is not a word, not a form of behaviour which does not owe something to purely biological being—and which at the same time does not elude the simplicity of animal life, and cause forms of vital behaviour to deviate from their pre-ordained direction, through a sort of *leakage* and through a genius for ambiguity which might serve to define man. Already the mere presence of a living being transforms the physical world, bringing to view here 'food,' there a 'hiding place,' and giving to 'stimuli' a sense which they have not hitherto possessed. *A fortiori* does this apply to the presence of a man in the animal world. Behaviour creates meanings which are transcendent in relation to the anatomical apparatus, and yet immanent to the behaviour as such, since it communicates itself and is understood. It is impossible to draw up an inventory of this irrational power which creates meanings and conveys them. Speech is merely one particular case of it.

What is true, however—and justifies the view that we ordinarily take of language, as being in a peculiar category—is that, alone of all expressive processes, speech is able to settle into a sediment and constitute an acquisition for use in human relationships. This fact cannot be explained by pointing out that speech

16 It is well known that the kiss is not one of the traditional customs of Japan.

17 Paternity is unknown to the Trobriand Islanders. Children are brought up under the authority of the maternal uncle. A husband, on his return from a long journey, is delighted to find new children in his home. He looks after them, watches over them and cherishes them as if they were his own children. Malinowski, *The Father in Primitive Psychology*, quoted by Bertrand Russell, *Marriage and Morals*, Allen and Unwin, pp. 20 and ff.

can be recorded on paper, whereas gestures or forms of behaviour are transmitted only by direct imitation. For music too can be written down, and, although there is in music something in the nature of an initiation into the tradition, although, that is, it would probably be impossible to graduate to atonal music without passing through classical music, yet every composer starts his task at the beginning, having a new world to deliver, whereas in the realm of speech, each writer is conscious of taking as his objective the same world as has already been dealt with by other writers. The worlds of Balzac and Stendhal are not like planets without communication with each other, for speech implants the idea of truth in us as the presumptive limit of its effort. It loses sight of itself as a contingent fact, and takes to resting upon itself; this is, as we have seen, what provides us with the ideal of thought without words, whereas the idea of music without sounds is ridiculous. Even if this is pushing the principle beyond its limits and reducing things to the absurd, even if a linguistic meaning can never be delivered of its inherence in some word or other, the fact remains that the expressive process in the case of speech can be indefinitely reiterated, that it is possible to speak about speech whereas it is impossible to paint about painting, and finally that every philosopher has dreamed of a form of discourse which would supersede all others, whereas the painter or the musician does not hope to exhaust all possible painting or music. Thus there is a privileged position accorded to Reason. But if we want to understand it clearly, we must begin by putting thought back among the phenomena of expression.

A Puzzling Element in the Notion of Thinking

GILBERT RYLE

USUALLY when we philosophers discuss questions about thinking, we concentrate, for very good reasons, upon what people do or might think; that is, on the opinions that they form, the beliefs that they have, the theories that they construct, the conclusions that they reach and the premisses from which they reach them. In a word, our usual questions are questions about the truths or falsehoods that people do or might accept. Their thoughts, of which we discuss the structures, the implications and the evidential backings, are the results in which their former ponderings and calculations have terminated. For when a person knows or believes that something is the case, his knowledge or belief is something that he now has or possesses, and the pondering which got him there is now over. While he is still wondering and pondering, he is still short of his destination. When he has settled his problem, his task of trying to settle it is finished.

It should not be forgotten that some of the problems that we have to try to

Reprinted by permission of the author and publisher from "A Puzzling Element in the Notion of Thinking," *Proceedings of the British Academy*, vol. XLIV, 1958.

settle are not theoretical problems but practical problems. We have to try to decide what to do, as well as try to decide what is the case. The solution of a problem is not always a truth or a falsehood.

We should not assume, either, that all thinking is trying to settle problems, whether theoretical or practical. This would be too restrictive. A person is certainly thinking when he is going over a poem that he knows perfectly, or dwelling on the incidents of yesterday's football match. He has, or need have, no problems to solve or results to aim at. Not all of our walks are journeys.

Lastly, we should not assume that all or even most of the truths or falsehoods that are ours are the fruits of our own ponderings. Fortunately and unfortunately, a great part of what we believe and know we have taken over from other people. Most of the things that we know we have not discovered for ourselves, but have been taught. Most of the things that we believe we believe simply because we have been told them. As with worldly goods, so with truths and falsehoods, much of what we possess is inherited or donated.

It is a vexatious fact about the English language that we use the verb 'to think' both for the beliefs or opinions that a man has, and for the pondering and reflecting that a man does; and that we use the noun 'thought' both for the truth or falsehood that he accepts, and for the activity of reflecting which, perhaps, preceded his acceptance of it. To think, in the sense of 'believe,' is not to think, in the sense of 'ponder.' There is only the verbal appearance of a contradiction in saying that while a person is still thinking, he does not yet know what to think; and that when he does know what to think, he has no more thinking to do.

The problems which I wish to discuss are questions not about the propositions that a person does or might believe, but about his activities of pondering, perpending, musing, reflecting, calculating, meditating, and so on. I shall be talking about the thinking which is the travelling and not the being at one's destination; the winnowing and not the grain; the bargaining and not the goods; the work and not the repose.

A person does not have to be advanced in age or highly schooled in order to be able to give satisfactory answers to ordinary interrogations about his thinking. A child who has never heard a word of psychological or philosophical discourse is not in the least embarrassed at being asked what he had been thinking about while sitting in the swing. Indeed, if asked not very long afterwards, he is likely to be quite ready to give a moderately detailed account of the thoughts that he had had, and even perhaps of the rough sequence in which he had had them. The task does not feel to him hugely different from the task of recounting what he had been doing so quietly or so noisily in the nursery or what he had seen and whom he had met during his afternoon walk.

Nonetheless, familiar though we are with the task of recounting our thoughts, we are embarrassed by a quite different task, set to us by the psychologist or the philosopher, the task, namely, of saying what the having of these thoughts had consisted in. I mean this. If during a certain period I had been, say, singing or mending a gate or writing a testimonial, then when recounting afterwards what I had been doing, I could, if required, mention the concrete ingredients of my activity, namely the noises that I had uttered, the hammer-blows that I had struck, and the ink-marks that I had made on the paper. Of course, a mere catalogue of these concrete happenings would not yet amount to an account of what I had been doing. Singing a song is not just uttering one noise after another; the sequence of noises must be a directed sequence. Still, if no noises are made, no song is sung; and if no ink-marks are produced, no testimonial is written. If I recollect singing or writing a testimonial, then I recollect that I made some noises or some ink-marks.

But when I recollect, however clearly, a stretch, however recent, of my musing or pondering, I do not seem to be, in the same way, automatically primed with answers to questions about the concrete ingredients of the thoughts the having of which I have no difficulty in recounting. I tell you, for example, '. . . and then the idea occurred to me that, since it was Sunday, I might not be able to get petrol at the next village.' If now you ask me to say what concrete shape the occurring of this slightly complex idea had taken, I may well be stumped for an answer, so stumped, even, as half to resent the putting of the question.

You might press your irksome question in this way. You say, 'Well, you have just recounted to us in a dozen or more English words the idea that had occurred to you. Did the idea itself occur to you in English words? Does your recollection of the idea occurring to you incorporate the recollection of your saying something to yourself in a dozen or more English words, whether in your head or *sotto voce*? Or, having recently returned from France, did you perhaps say something to the same effect to yourself in a dozen or more French words? 'To this very specific question my answer might be, 'Yes; I do now recall saying something to myself in my head, in English words, to the effect that as it was Sunday there might be no petrol available in the next village.' But my answer might be, 'No; I don't recall saying anything to myself at all.' Or my answer might me, 'Well, I'm not absolutely sure that I did not just say "Sunday" in my head, but I'm sure that I did not say anything more.'

Your pertinacity is irritating, since I want to say that it does not really matter whether I said anything to myself or not. Having the idea in question did not require my saying anything to myself, in the way in which singing does require uttering noises and repairing a gate does require *either* hammering *or* wire-tying *or* bolt-tightening *or* something of the same concrete sort.

Ignoring my irritation you now press me with another batch of specific queries. You say, 'If when you had that idea you did not say anything to yourself in your head or *sotto voce*, then was it that instead you saw some things in your mind's eye? Was it that you had mental pictures blurred or sharp, well coloured or ill coloured, maybe of villagers entering a village church, and of a garage with its doors closed; so that it was in this concrete shape, or something like it, that the idea came to you that since it was Sunday you might not be able to get petrol?' Again I might answer, 'Yes, I did visualize scenes like this.' But I might answer, 'No, I am sure that I did not visualize anything.' Or I might answer, 'Well, I do remember seeing in my mind's eye the duck-pond of the village in question: I usually do when I think of that village. But this had nothing to do with the special idea that the garage there might be closed for Sunday.' Once again I might be irked at the question being pressed at all. Why should my thinking the thought have gone with either the saying of something to myself or with the seeing of something in my mind's eye or with any other proprietary happenings?

There are, however, certain special thinking-activities which certainly do seem to require our saying things in our heads or *sotto voce* or aloud, and we need to examine what there is about these special activities which requires the inward or outward production of words and phrases.

(*a*) If I have been trying to compose a poem or an after-dinner speech, then I must indeed have been producing to myself words and phrases, examining them, cancelling or improving them, assembling them and rehearsing assemblages of them. That is, if my thinking happens to be a piece of thinking what to say and how to say it, then it must incorporate the tentative, exploratory, and critical saying of things to myself; and then, if asked to recount in retrospect whether I had been saying things to myself in English or in French, I should answer without hesitation. There is here no question of my first thinking out my poem or my speech, and only then, in reply to posthumous interrogations, putting my composition into words. The thinking was itself a piece of word-hunting, phrase-concocting, and sentence-mending. It was thinking *up* words, phrases and sentences.

(*b*) If I have been doing a slightly complex piece of computation, whether in my head or on paper, like multiplying £13 12*s.* 4*d.* by 7, then not only must my answer, if I obtain one, be a numerical or worded formula, £95 6*s.* 4*d.*, perhaps, but also the results of the interim multiplying-operations, dividing-operations, and adding-operations will be numbers. What I say to myself in my head, if I do the sum in my head, will parallel the things that I should write down one after another if I worked the sum out on paper, and these will be numbers of pounds, shillings, or pence. If asked afterwards whether I had, at a certain stage, said to myself 'Seven twelves are eighty-four, plus two, makes eighty-six' or whether I had in my mind's eye seen the corresponding numerals, or both together, I might recollect just which I had done; and I should not feel irked at the suggestion that I must have done one or the other. Certainly, multiplying does not consist merely in saying numbers aloud or in our heads; but we are ready to allow that it requires this, or some alternative, in the same sort of way as singing a song requires, though it does not reduce to, the uttering of noises. Trying to get the correct answer, unlike just making a guess at it, involves trying to establish checkable intermediate steps, in order to make the correct moves from those steps to the right answer; and these steps, to be checkable, must be formulated.

(*c*) Some kinds of problems, like those of advocates, debaters, and philosophers, have something in common with the task of composition and something in common with the task of computation. The thinker has, all the time, both to be trying to find out what to say and how to say it, and also to be trying to establish as true what he says. He wants his hearers—including himself—not only to understand what he says but also to accept it, and to accept it perforce. As his task is, in two dimensions, a forensic task, his thinking involves him in producing and canvassing, in however sketchy a manner, words, phrases, and sentences, conclusions, reasons, and rebuttals of objections.

Now if, improvidently, we pick on one of these three special varieties of thinking as our universal model, we shall be tempted to say, as Plato said, that 'in thinking the soul is conversing [or perhaps 'debating'] with herself,' and so postulate that any piece of meditating or pondering whatsoever has got, so to speak, to run on the wheels of words, phrases, and sentences.

Or, if forced by our own reminiscences to allow that sometimes we have thoughts when no wording of these thoughts takes place, we may then be tempted simply to give to the model one extension and postulate that in thinking the soul is *either* conversing with itself *or else* performing some one specific alternative to conversing, such as visualizing things. In either case we are presupposing that thinking, of whatever sort, must, so to speak, employ a concrete apparatus or some specifiable kind or other, linguistic or pictorial or something else. This general presupposition is sometimes formulated in the following way. Just as an Englishman who has become perfectly familiar with the French language may say that he can now think in French, so, and in the same sense of 'in,' he must always think either 'in' his native English or else 'in' some alternative apparatus, like French or visual imagery or algebraical symbols or gestures or something else that he can produce, on demand, from his own resources. The generic term 'symbol' is sometimes used to cover all the postulated vehicles of thinking. It is a psychological necessity, or perhaps even a part of the very concept of thinking, that when thinking occurs, there occur, internally or externally, things or symbols that the thinker thinks in.

It is if we make this presupposition that we are especially embarrassed at being required to tell in retrospect in what symbols (in this awkwardly distended use of the word) we had, for example, the idea that as it was Sunday there might be no petrol available at the next village. For often we cannot recollect any such vehicles being present on the occasion when, as we clearly do recollect, we had that thought.

I want to attack this presupposition. I want to deny that it even makes sense to ask, in the general case, what special sort or sorts of things we think *in.* The very collocation of 'think' with 'in so and so' seems to me factitious, save in our very special case of the Englishman who describes himself as now being able to think in French. So let us clear his case out of the way.

The primary thing that he means when he says that he now thinks in French is that when he has to talk to Frenchmen, he does not any longer have to think out how to say in French what he wants to say. He no longer, for example, has first to say to himself in English what he wants to say, and then to struggle to translate from English into French for the benefit of his French audience. The composition of French remarks is no longer any more difficult for him than the composition of English remarks, that is, it is not difficult at all. But to say that he no longer has to think out how to say things in French has not the slightest tendency to show that all or most of the thoughts that he thinks are now accompanied or 'carried' by the production of French words. It is only to say that *when he is conversing with Frenchmen* he does not have to think about the vehicles of this conversing. When he does have to compose in French he does not have to think *up* French words. But most of the things he thinks about are not matters of French composition, just as most of the things we think about are not matters of English composition. Roughly, he thinks in French when he says what he wants to say in French without any groping or fumbling.

Secondarily, when he says that he now thinks in French, he may also mean that *when* he debates matters with himself he conducts these debates in French without wondering how to put his points in French; and, more generally, that *when* he converses with himself in internal monologue he does this in French without having to consider how to say in French what he wants to say. Even so, to describe him as thinking in French, because what he says to himself he says effortlessly in French, is to put a new strain on the phrase 'thinking in,' under which it did not labour in our primary use of the phrase 'to think in French.' One never does ask it, but *could* one ask a friend who has been deliberating what to do whether he had been deliberating in English? If we did ask him this, I suspect that he would reply that while he had said or half-said a lot of things to himself in English, this had not been any part of his deliberating. He had not deliberated *by means* of saying things to himself, any more than the proof-corrector searches for misprints *by means of* putting marks in the margins of the galley-proof.

But anyhow, what is true of his debatings and conversings, whether with Frenchmen or with himself, need not be true of his thinkings which are done when no debating or conversing is done. The phrases 'in French' and 'in English' do attach natively to verbs of saying; it does not follow that they attach to verbs of thinking, unless the thinking happens to be thinking what to say or how to say it.

Strained though it may be, save in the one special context, to speak of a person thinking in French or in English, it is worse than strained to speak of him as thinking in, say, mental pictures. Certainly it is true, not of all people, but of many, when thinking about certain sorts of matters, though not of all, that they see things in their mind's eyes, and even that their ability to solve some of their problems is tied up, somehow, with their ability to visualize clearly. Doubtless, some chess-players can think out chess problems in their heads, if and only if they can visualize chess situations clearly and steadily.

Consider this case of the would-be solver of a chess problem. First let us provide him with a chess-board and the requisite chessmen. He disposes the pieces in their proper places and then, with his eyes fixed on the board and his fingers moving piece after piece, he tries to think out the solution to his problem. Are we to say that the thinking that he is doing is done 'in' pieces of ivory or 'in' the experimental moves that he makes with these pieces of ivory? Clearly, there is no place for the word 'in' here. He is thinking *about* the pieces; he is thinking out what they could and could not do or suffer if he moved elsewhere or if kept where they are.

But now suppose that we refuse to provide him with a chessboard, so that he has to tackle his task entirely in his head. The chess problem itself that he has to solve is exactly the same as before; but he is now confronted with an extra set of tasks which he had not had to cope with before. He has, among other things, to remember, at each given moment, exactly where each of the pieces is, whereas previously he just looked and saw where it was. He is like the hostess who can see which of her guests is sitting next to which until the light fails; then she has to remember their positions. This remembering may be preceded by the labour of trying to remember; or she may not have to try. She may just remember. Now if the chess-player has to struggle to remember the positions of his pieces, this struggling could obviously not be described as involving the employment of mental pictures of their positions. He struggles because he cannot yet remember and therefore cannot yet see in his mind's eye how the pieces had been disposed. If in the course of this struggling alternative possible dispositions are pictured, still these, if wrong, have to be scrapped. They are not the vehicles but the boss-shots of the thinking. Conversely, when, after struggling to remember the positions of the pieces, the chess-player does remember, then his seeing them in his mind's eye, if he does do this, is not something by means of which he gets himself to remember. It is the goal, not a vehicle of his struggle to remember. *A fortiori*, if he remembers without having to try to remember, then his mental picture of the positions of the pieces is not something that he thought *in* or *with* or *on*, since he did not have to think at all.

Certainly this chess-player has to *use his memory* in trying to solve the chess problem in his head, where he had not had to use his memory when he had had the board in front of him. But this is not at all the same thing as to say that he *uses his memory images* in trying to solve the problem in his head. If we hanker still to reserve some special sense for the phrase 'using images,' this will be very different from the sense of the verb in which we speak of someone using such and such French words when speaking to Frenchmen. That we cannot talk French without using French words is a dull truism; that some people cannot solve chess problems in their heads without, in some sense, using mental pictures may be true, but it is not a logicians' truism.

So now we seem to be farther off than ever from achieving what we thought that we wanted, namely to nominate some reasonably concrete stuff to be the peculiar apparatus of all of our thinkings.

No singing without noises, no testimonial-writing without ink-marks, no thinking without . . ., but we can nominate no proprietary things or sets of things to fill this gap. Indeed, we have, I hope, become suspicious of the very attempt to assimilate in this way thinking with these other special activities, which do possess their own proprietary implements or materials.

We may be tempted to postpone the evil day by suggesting that thinking differs from singing and testimonial-writing just because its proprietary stuff is a very peculiar stuff, more transparent and more shapeless than jelly-fishes, more scentless than the most scentless gases, and more uncapturable than rainbows. Perhaps its stuff is the stuff that dreams are made of, mental or spiritual stuff, and that is why it slips through our retrospective sieves. But we are soon brought to our senses if we remind ourselves that our own neighbours' very ordinary children, Tommy and Clara, make no more bones about recounting the thoughts that they have had than in recounting the games that they have played or the incidents that they have witnessed. They seem to need no esoteric instructions in order to be able to tell us of the ideas that have come to them or the thinking that they have done. In a way these are the most domestic and everyday sorts of things that there could be. The seeming mysteriousness of thinking derives from some sophisticated theoretical presuppositions, presuppositions which induce us, though only when theorizing, to try to squeeze out of our reminiscences or our introspections some evasive but pervasive drop of something, some psychic trace-element the presence of which, in bafflingly minute doses, is required if thinking is to occur. Yet Tommy and Clara, who were never told of any such psychic trace-element, describe their thinkings in ways which we understand perfectly; nor, when we tell them of the thoughts that crossed Cinderella's mind as she sat among the ashes, do we employ a strange para-chemical vocabulary.

Now let us drop, for the time being, the attempt to find a filling or a set of alternative fillings for the gap in the slogan 'No thinking without such and such' and consider a different, though connected, problem.

When a person who has been for a short or a long time musing or pondering is asked what he had been thinking about, he can usually, though not quite always, give a seemingly complete and definite answer. All sorts of answers are allowable; for example, that he had been thinking about his father, or about the next General Election, or about the possibility of getting his annual holiday early, or about yesterday's football match, or how to answer a letter. What he has been thinking about may or may not be, or contain, a problem. We can ask him whether he had decided how to answer the letter and if so what his decision was. But his thoughts about yesterday's football match may have been entirely uninterrogative. He was thinking it over, but not trying to think anything out. His thinking terminated in no results; it aimed at none. Now though, normally, the thinker can give a seemingly complete and definite answer to the question What had he been thinking about?, he can very often be brought to acknowledge that he had had in mind things which, at the start, it had not occurred to him to mention. To take a simple instance. A rowing enthusiast says that he had been thinking about the Oxford University crew; and if asked bluntly, would deny that he had at that moment been thinking about the Cambridge crew. Yet it might transpire that his thought about the Oxford crew was, or included, the thought that, though it was progressing, it was not progressing fast enough. 'Not fast enough for what?' we ask. 'Not fast enough to beat Cambridge next Saturday.' So he had been thinking about the Cambridge crew, only thinking about it in a sort of threshold way. Or I ask a tired visitor from London what he had been thinking about. He says, 'Just about the extraordinary peacefulness of your garden.' If asked, 'Than what do you find it so much more peaceful?' he replies, 'Oh, London, of course.' So in a way he was thinking not only of my garden but of London, though he would not, without special prompting, have said for himself that he had had London in mind at all. Or my visitors says, 'How lovely your roses are,' and then sighs. Why does he sigh? May he not, in a marginal way, be thinking of his dead wife who had been particularly fond of roses?—though he himself would have said, if asked, that he was only thinking about my roses. He does not say to me or to himself, 'Roses—her favourite flowers.' But roses are, for him, her favourite flower. The thought of them is an incipient thought of her.

Take one more case. I ask the schoolboy what he is thinking about, and he says that he had been trying to think what 8 × 17 makes. On further questioning it turns out that his total task is to multiply £9 17*s.* 4*d.* by 8, and that at that particular moment he had got to the 17*s.* So I ask him whether he had forgotten the 2*s.* 8*d.* that he had got when multiplying the 4*d.* by 8; and now he says that he had not forgotten this; indeed he was keeping the 2*s.* in mind ready to add to his shillings column. So, in a way, his thought was not totally filled by the problem of multiplying 17 × 8. The thought of the total multiplication task was, in a controlling though background way, built into his interim but foreground task of multiplying 17 × 8. For it was not just 17, but the seventeen shillings of the £9 17*s.* 4*d.* that he was then engaged in multiplying by 8. He would have gone on from the shillings to the pounds if I had not interrupted.

It was not that my widowed visitor just *forgot* and had to be reminded that he had been thinking about his wife as well as about the roses, but that his task of telling just what he had had in mind was in some important ways totally unlike the task of trying to recall, say, just how many telephone calls he had made during the morning. The difference between merely thinking how fine these roses are and thinking how she would have admired them is not like the difference between having made eleven and having made twelve telephone calls, namely a difference in the number of happenings to be recorded. Recounting one's thoughts is not like turning back to an earlier page and trying to give an exhaustive inventory of the items one rediscovers there. The question whether or not the Cambridge crew had been in the rowing-enthusiast's mind was not one that he could settle by racking his brains to recollect a bygone fleeting something. In our example it was settled in quite a different way, namely by asking him what the rate of progress of the Oxford crew had seemed to him inadequate for. When he acknowledges that he had been, in a threshold way, thinking of the Cambridge crew, one thing that he does not say is, 'Ah yes, your question *reminds* me that the Cambridge crew was in my thoughts after all.' He had not been reminded of a forgotten item but shown how his account of his thought had been an incomplete account. He had failed to indicate part of its internal tenor.

Reporting one's thoughts is not a matter of merely chronicling the items of a procession of quick-fading internal phenomena. If we can pick out any such phenomena and record them, our record of them is not yet a statement of the drift or content of a piece of thinking. The way in which the widower's thinking of the roses was, in a way, thinking about his wife is not that during the time that he was thinking about the roses there occurred one or two very fleeting wafts of recollections of his wife. Such wafts do occur, but it was not them that he was acknowledging when he acknowledged that in thinking of the roses he had been incipiently thinking of his wife. Rather, he had thought of the roses *as* her favourite flower; in the way in which the rowing-enthusiast had thought of the progress of the Oxford crew *as* insufficient to beat Cambridge; or in the way in which the schoolboy had thought of the 17 that he was multiplying by 8 *as* the 17*s.* to be dealt with after the 4*d.* and before the £9.

What, then, is the virtue of this 'as,' which makes a young man's thought of next Thursday *as* his 21st birthday different from his mother's thought of next Thursday *as* early-closing day for Oxford shops?

We can approach at least a part of the answer in this way. Sometimes we deliberately advise people to think of something *as* so and so. For instance, when giving a child his very first explanation of what a map is, we might tell him to think of the map of Berkshire *as* a photograph taken from an aeroplane very high up over the middle of Berkshire. This may already lead him to expect to find big things showing up on the map, like towns, rivers, highroads, and railways, but not very small things like people, motor-cars, or bushes. A little later he enquires, in perplexity, what the contour-lines are which wriggle so conspicuously along and around the Berkshire Downs. We tell him to think of them *as* high-water marks left by the sea, which had risen to drown even the highest parts of the county. This flood, he is to suppose, subsided exactly fifty feet every night, leaving a high-water mark each time. So a person walking along one high-water mark would remain all the time at the same height above the normal level of the sea; and he would all the time be 100 feet higher than someone else who was following the next high-water mark but one below him. Quite likely the child could now work out for himself why the contour-lines are closely packed on the side of a steep hill and widely separated on a gradual incline.

Getting him to think of the map as a photograph taken from very high up, and of the contour-lines as high-water marks makes it natural or at least quite easy for him to think further thoughts for himself. It is to implant the germs of these further thoughts into his initially sterile thoughts about the map. If there was no follow-up, however embryonic and whether in the desired direction or any other, then he had not thought of the map as a photograph or of the contours as high-water marks. To describe someone as thinking of something as so and so is to say of him, at least *inter alia*, that it would be natural or easy for him to follow up this thought in some particular direction. His thinking had those prospects, that trend in it. It should be noticed that what thinking of something as so and so leads naturally or easily into may be subsequent thinkings, but it may equally well be subsequent doings. The golf professional who tells me to think of my driver not as a sledge-hammer but as a rope with a weight on the end expects me to cease to bang at the ball and to begin to sweep smoothly through the ball. The parent who gets his child to think of policemen not as enemies but as friends gets him not only to think certain consequential thoughts but also to go to policemen for help when lost.

A person who thinks of something as something is, *ipso facto*, primed to think and do some particular further things; and this particular possible future that his thinking paves the way for needs to be mentioned in the description of the particular content of that thinking—somewhat as the mention of where the canal goes to has to be incorporated in our account of what this adjacent canal-stretch is. Roughly, a thought comprises what it is incipiently, namely what it is the natural vanguard of. Its burthen embodies its natural or easy sequel.

There are other things as well which are, in partly similar ways, constitutionally inceptive. To lather one's chin is to prepare to wield one's razor. Here the vanguard act is an intentional or even deliberate preparation for the future act. We had to learn thus to pave the way for shaving. To brace onself is to get ready to jump or resist at the next moment; but this inceptive movement is not normally intentional or the result of training; it is instinctive. The tenors that our thoughts possess are similarly sometimes the products of training; but often not. In all cases alike, however, the description of an inceptive act requires the prospective specification of its due or natural sequel. Notice that its due or natural sequel may not actually come about. Having lathered my chin, I may be called to the telephone; and the dog, having braced himself, may be reassured or shot. We must employ the future tense in our description of the inceptive act, but we must hedge this future tense with some 'unlesses.'

At first sight we may suspect the presence of a circularity in the description of something as essentially the foreshadowing of its own succession. But this feature, without any air of circularity, belongs also to our descriptions of promises, precautions, threats and betrothals, and even of nightfalls, thaws and germinations. There could be no complete description of such things which was not proleptic. However, our special case seems to be in a worse plight since I am saying that a piece of thinking of something as something is natively inceptive of, *inter alia*, subsequent thinkings in a way in which a thaw is not the inception of another thaw, or a nightfall the beginning of another nightfall.

So here we are reminded, if not of circles, at least of the verse:

> Big fleas have little fleas upon their backs to bite 'em,
> Little fleas have lesser fleas and so *ad infinitum.*

But is this reminder disconcerting? Were we not already aware in our bones of just such a feature of thinking, namely that any attempt to catch a particular thought tends to develop into an attempt to catch up with something further? Our story of a particular piece of thinking seems in the nature of the case to terminate in nothing stronger than a semi-colon. It is not incidental to thoughts that they belong to trains of thought.

Now maybe we can begin to see the shape of the answers to both of our two dominant questions. We can begin to see why it is that the narrative of a piece of my thinking cannot be merely the chronicling of actual, monitored happenings 'in my head.' For the content of the thinking comprised its tenor and to describe its particular tenor is prospectively to mention its natural or easy sequels.

But also we can begin to see why we cannot, and do not in our heart of hearts wish to reserve for our thinkings any peculiar concrete stuff, apparatus, or medium, *X*, such that we can say, 'As no singing without noises, so no thinking without *X*.' For adverting to anything whatsoever can be what puts a person, at a particular moment, in mind of something or other. The motorist in the last village but one before home may think of the petrol-station alongside of him *as* being possibly the last place for buying petrol on a Sunday. The widower thinks of my roses that he is gazing at as being of the sort of which she was so fond. The schoolboy thinks of the number 17 that his eye is on as the 17*s.* in the total of £9 17*s.* 4*d.* that he has to multiply by eight. The poet thinks of the word 'annihilating' that crops up in a conversation as a candidate for the gap in his half-composed couplet. The housewife thinks of next Thursday as the day when she will not be able to shop in Oxford after lunch, while her son thinks of it as the day when he comes of age. We could stretch our slogan, if we hanker for a slogan, to read 'No thinking without adverting to something or other, no matter what,' but then it would be as empty as the slogans 'no eating without food,' 'no building without materials' and 'no purchases without commodities.'

However, the very vacuousness of our new slogan 'no thinking without adverting to something or other, no matter what' has a certain tension-relieving effect. From the start we felt, I hope, a gnawing uneasiness at the very programme of treating thinking as a special, indeed a very special activity, special in the way in which singing is one special activity and gardening is a battery of other special activities. For while there certainly are lots of special kinds of brands of thinking, such as computing, sonnet-composing, anagram-solving, philosophizing, and translating, still thinking is not an activity in which we are engaged only when we are *not* singing, writing testimonials, gardening, and so on. Thinking is not a rival occupation to these special occupations, in the sense that our time has to be parcelled out between them and thinking, in the way in which our time does have to be parcelled out between golf and gardening, between testimonial-writing and lecturing, between anagram-solving and chess-playing, and so on. For we have to be thinking if we are to be singing well, writing a just testimonial, or gardening efficiently. Certainly, we had better not be doing sums or anagrams in our heads while singing or lecturing; but this is because we had better be thinking how to perform our present task of singing or lecturing. We had unwittingly sold the central fort from the start, when we asked ourselves, in effect, 'Given that noise-making, of a certain sort, is what goes to make singing the proprietary occupation that it is, what is it that, analogously, makes thinking the proprietary occupation that it is?' The verbal noun 'thinking' does not, as we knew in our bones all along, denote a special or proprietary activity in the way in which 'singing' does. Thinking is not one department in a departmentstore, such that we can ask What line of goods does it provide, and what lines of goods does it, *ex officio, not* provide? Its proper place is in all the departments—that is, there is no particular place which is its proper place, and there are no particular places which are not its proper place.

If we had worded our original programme by asking 'What department and what proprietary apparatus are reserved for *the using of our wits*?' we should have seen through this question straightaway. We do not, notoriously, use our wits wherever and whenever we should use them, but there is no field or department of human activity or experience of which we can say, 'Here people can use their fingers, their noses, their vocal chords or their golf-clubs, but not their wits.' Or if we had worded our early question by asking 'In what special medium or with what special instruments is our use of our wits conducted?,' we should have seen through this question too. We swim in water, we sing in noises, we hammer with hammers, but using our wits is not a co-ordinate special operation with its own counterpart medium, material, or implements. For one can use one's wits in swimming, singing, hammering, or in anything else whatsoever. I do not suggest that the idiom of *using one's wits* is a pure substitute for the idiom of *thinking*. There is an element of congratulation in our description of someone as having used his wits, an element which would be out of place, for example, in talking of my widower's thinking of roses as his wife's favourite flower. None the less, if we realize why it would be absurd to try to isolate out a proprietary activity of using one's wits and a reserved field for it, we realize why it actually was absurd to try to isolate out a proprietary activity of thinking and a reserved field for it.

Why do we not require our schools to give separate lessons in thinking, as they do give separate lessons in computing, translating, swimming, and cricket? The answer is obvious. It is because all the lessons that they give are lessons in thinking. Yet they are not lessons in two subjects at the same time.

INTRODUCTION TO PHILOSOPHY OF LANGUAGE / Study Questions

THINKING AND SPEAKING

Katz

1. What is the taxonomic conception of linguistics and how, in detail, is it "inherently" free from mentalistic commitment?
2. What is the controversy about between taxonomic linguistics and mentalistic linguistics? What is Katz' strategy for settling the controversy? What, according to Katz, is Chomsky's criticism of taxonomic linguistics?
3. In explicating the mentalist position, Katz attempts to show that reference to mental states is both necessary and is "reference to things or events within the causal realm." How does he establish the first point? How does his identification of the mental mechanism with the brain establish the second point?
4. How does Katz argue that the mentalist avoids psychophysical dualism?
5. In terms of what three questions, that a linguist must ask of any particular language,

does Katz attempt to show the advantages of mentalistic linguistics? What factors are involved in these questions and what is their interrelationship?

6. Why is it that taxonomic theories are inadequate for answering the first question? How does the concept of a *rule* enter into this discussion? What is Katz' suggested model of linguistic communication; and how does Katz' development of this model enter into this discussion?
7. What are the two final advantages to a mentalistic conception of linguistics, according to Katz?
8. Katz' model of communication could be called the code-model. Imagine true-to-life cases of someone using a code. What sorts of things are involved in encoding and decoding a message? Does following a rule, as in translating a code, actually appear in Katz' model? What is the importance, for this issue, of Katz' discussion of "unconscious" processes?
9. Does having a code presuppose already knowing a language, into and out of which the code may be translated? What significance does this have for Katz' view?
10. Is there a difference between describing a practice in terms of rules and discovering the rules followed in a practice? Which of these is involved in Katz' picture (or, conception) of linguistics? What would be the results of thinking of linguistic rules in the other way?

Skinner

1. What is the relation between covert verbal behavior and overt verbal behavior? How does his account of that relation succeed, according to Skinner, while avoiding the apparent need "to make guesses about the muscular or neural substratum of verbal events"?
2. Why, according to Skinner's view, does covert speech take place at all? How do these same variables control whether covert behavior becomes overt?
3. What is wrong, according to Skinner, with identifying thinking with subaudible talking? What was that identification's "favorable effect"?
4. Need thinking be identified with only covert behavior? Explain.
5. What are the patterns of reinforcement involved in soliloquy, artistic behavior, self-mands, tacts uttered to oneself, and problem-solving? How does Skinner's discussion of these patterns of reinforcement support his contention that thinking cannot be simply identified with speaking to oneself (either covertly or overtly, or both)?
6. Why can we not identify thinking with verbal behavior in general? What are the initial strengths of such a move? Why, however, are such considerations not really "relevant to a definition of thinking"?
7. How, finally, does Skinner define thinking? Why is the "emphasis on controlling variables" in this definition important? How does this definition help us explain such phenomena as having difficulty expressing an idea and having difficulty expressing the same idea in two languages? Why are the thoughts of others inaccessible to us?
8. What sort of definition of thinking does Skinner offer: that is, has he given a definition that reports our ordinary usage of *thinking* or is this a definition that stipulates how *thinking* is to be used in behaviorist psychology? If it seems unclear which sort of definition Skinner is giving, what remarks in his piece can be assembled as "evidence" for each, and what remarks seem ambiguous on this point?
9. If thinking is behavior, as Skinner argues, might it not be possible that one might be mistaken about what one is thinking? Try to imagine ordinary cases where one might be so mistaken. (Be careful not to confuse this with describing situations in which we

say "I don't know [or, remember] what I was thinking" or "I don't know what to think of this. . ." You are to try to describe a situation in which you say "I don't know what I am now thinking".)

10. Imagine a case in which you might try to guess what someone was thinking by looking at his behavior; imagine this as a game, perhaps. How would you be able to determine who had got it right? (Bear in mind that, in Skinner's view, a verbal utterance by the person whose behavior we are looking at is merely another item in "his responses to the complex world" in which he lives.) What does this suggest to you about the adequacy of Skinner's account of the relation between thinking and speaking?

Merleau-Ponty

1. How does Merleau-Ponty criticize the view that the possession of language is "no more than the actual existence of 'verbal images,' or traces left in us by words spoken or heard"? What is the significance of his "electric lamp" analogy?
2. In his criticism of the view that language is "conditioned by thought," Merleau-Ponty claims there is a kinship between this (the intellectualist) view and the empiricist theories (the "verbal image" theories). At what point does that kinship appear? What does Merleau-Ponty have in mind when he asserts that "the word has a meaning"?
3. In continuing his criticism of the intellectualist view, Merleau-Ponty suggests that instead of speech "presupposing" thought, thought "tends towards expression as its completion." What is the difference? In support of this suggestion Merleau-Ponty claims that "for the child the thing is not known until it is named." If this is not to be the trivially true claim that a child cannot *say* what a thing is until he or she knows its name, what does it mean? (How would anyone discover that what Merleau-Ponty claims is true?)
4. What does Merleau-Ponty have in mind, then, when he says that "speech, in the speaker, does not translate ready-made thought, but accomplishes it"? How does he go on to criticize the code-model of communication?
5. What is the "*gestural meaning*, which is immanent in speech" of which Merleau-Ponty speaks? How does Merleau-Ponty's notion of "gestural meaning" help illumine what he has in mind when he says "there is. . . an ability to think *according to others*"? How is this supposed to be illustrated by music, paintings, poems, and literary works?
6. Explain Merleau-Ponty's discussion of the "orator's" thinking and speaking with reference to the question: "What is the relation between thought and speech?" With reference to the same question, discuss his example of "imagining Peter absent."
7. What is the "true physiognomy" of the "act of speaking," according to Merleau-Ponty? Is there an "external relation" between thought and speech? What consequences does Merleau-Ponty's answer to that question have for theories about the meaning of a word? How is the "musical meaning of a sonata" illustrative of the meaning of a word?
8. Compare Merleau-Ponty's analysis of the inability to express the same idea in two languages with that provided by Skinner. Are they substantively different analyses?
9. Merleau-Ponty claims that we "begin to understand the meanings of words (in a foreign language) through their place in a context of action, and by taking part in a communal life." Under what circumstances would this be an accurate account of how a person having one language begins to learn another? Would it be a good account of how one learns a first language?
10. In the claim just referred to, Merleau-Ponty implies that this is only the way one *begins* to understand those words. What more *is* there to understanding words? Does Merleau-Ponty attempt to suggest what "more" there might be?

11. Merleau-Ponty claims that "the thinking subject himself is in a kind of ignorance of his thoughts so long as he has not formulated them (in words) for himself." What *kind* of ignorance is this supposed to be? Imagine a case of which this claim might be an accurate description (bearing in mind that Merleau-Ponty wants to deny that we have thoughts in advance of formulating them).
12. Imagine a case in which someone says "Yesterday I thought I would be going to Chicago, but now I realize that I cannot." Supposing that the person in question did not, on yesterday, formulate the thought in words (as, for example, "I will be going to Chicago"), how would Merleau-Ponty handle such a case? Would he have to say that the person did not have the thought yesterday? Suppose the person insists that he did —can we accuse him of being mistaken?

Ryle

1. What are the ordinary questions about our thinking that we know how to answer, according to Ryle? How is the question, "What do your thoughts consists in?" different from these others? Might we not be able to give any number of different answers to this question? What is the significance of that?
2. What are the "special thinking-activities which. . . do seem to require our saying things in our heads or *sotto voce* or aloud"? Is it correct, according to Ryle, to pick one of these as "our universal model" of thinking? If not in saying words, in what other things might we be tempted to say our thought consists?
3. What is it that Ryle wants to deny in this piece? What does someone mean when he says "I can now think in French"? How does Ryle's account of this illumine his general claim?
4. Explain Ryle's discussion of the chess player solving a problem in his head. How does that discussion support his general claim?
5. Why won't it do to say that the "stuff" in which thinking consists is "the stuff that dreams are made of"?
6. What exactly is the "different, but connected problem" of which Ryle speaks? How do the cases Ryle presents suggest that telling your thoughts is unlike telling what you had done sometime before? What are the differences?
7. How does the idea of "thinking of something *as* so-and-so" help to explain the relation between what we think and what we say when we say what we think? How does Ryle's characterization of some cases of thinking as "constitutionally inceptive" differ from Merleau-Ponty's view that speech "accomplishes" thought (in the thinking subject)?
8. If Ryle is right that saying what we are thinking is not a report or chronicle of goings-on in our heads, what can be made of Katz' model of communication? If he is right that it is senseless to ask what our thinking consists in, what are we to make of Skinner's identification of thinking with behavior?
9. What does Ryle conclude about the concept of *thinking* and its grammatical analogies with such concepts as *singing, gardening,* and so on? How does substituting the phrase "using of our wits" for the word *thinking* enable us to see that thinking is not an *activity*?

SUGGESTED FURTHER READINGS / Introduction to Philosophy of Language

GENERAL

Alston, William P. *Philosophy of Language*. Englewood Cliffs, N.J.: Prentice-Hall, Inc., 1964.
Ayer, A. J., ed. *Logical Positivism*. New York: The Free Press 1959.

Black, Max, ed. *The Importance of Language*. Prentice-Hall (Englewood Cliffs, N.J.: Prentice-Hall, Inc., 1962.
Olshewsky, Thomas M., ed. *Problems in the Philosophy of Language*. New York: Holt, Rinehart & Winston, Inc., 1969.
Urmson, J. O. *Philosophical Analysis*. London: Oxford University Press, 1956.

THE MEANING OF A WORD

Austin, J. L. *How to do Things with Words*. London: Oxford University Press, 1962.
Drury, M. O'C. *The Danger of Words*. London: Routledge & Kegan Paul, 1973.
Parkinson, G. H. R., ed. *The Theory of Meaning*. London: Oxford University Press, 1968.
Wittgenstein, Ludwig. *The Blue and Brown Books*. Oxford, England: Basil Blackwell and Mott, Ltd., 1958.

THINKING AND SPEAKING

Chomsky, Noam. "Current Issues in Linguistic Theory," *The Structure of Language: Readings in the Philosophy of Language*, ed. by J. Fodor and J. J. Katz. Englewood Cliffs, N.J.: Prentice-Hall, Inc., 1964.
Chomsky, Noam. "Review of Skinner's *Verbal Behavior*," *Language*, 35, No. 1 (1959), 26–58.
Ryle, Gilbert. *The Concept of Mind*. New York: Barnes & Noble, Inc., 1949. (Also in paperback: Baltimore: Penguin Books.)
Thomson, Robert. *The Psychology of Thinking*. Baltimore: Penguin Books, 1959.
White, Alan R. *Attention*. Oxford, England: Basil Blackwell and Mott, Ltd., 1965.
Wittgenstein, Ludwig. *Philosophical Investigations*, trans. G. E. Anscombe. New York: Macmillan Publishing Co., Inc., 1958.